ON OUR OWN

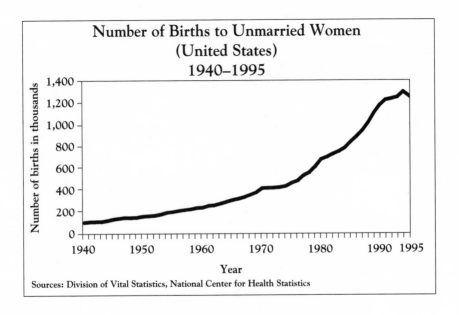

Number of Births to Unmarried Women
(United States)
1940–1995

Number of births in thousands

Year

Sources: Division of Vital Statistics, National Center for Health Statistics

ON OUR OWN

Unmarried Motherhood
in America

MELISSA LUDTKE

Random House New York

Copyright © 1997 by Melissa Ludtke
All rights reserved under International and Pan-American
Copyright Conventions. Published in the United States
by Random House, Inc., New York, and
simultaneously in Canada by Random House
of Canada Limited, Toronto.

Grateful acknowledgment is made to Alfred A. Knopf, Inc., for
permission to reprint "Dream Deferred" from Collected Poems by
Langston Hughes. Copyright © 1994 by the Estate of Langston
Hughes. Reprinted by permission of Alfred A. Knopf, Inc.

Library of Congress Cataloging-in-Publication Data
Ludtke, Melissa.
On our own : unmarried motherhood in America / by Melissa Ludtke.
p.   cm.
Includes bibliographical references and index.
ISBN 0-679-42414-8
1. Unmarried mothers—United States.
2. Unmarried mothers—United States—Biography.
3. Single mothers—United States.
4. Ludtke, Melissa.
I. Title.
HQ759.45.G55   1997
306.85'6—dc21   96-52233

Random House website address: http://www.randomhouse.com

Printed in the United States of America on acid-free paper
98765432
First Edition
Book design by Tanya M. Pérez-Rock

For my mother, Jean

Contents

Prologue   ix

1. My Story: Decision-making About Unmarried Motherhood   3

2. Unmarried Motherhood: A Half-Century of Change   20

3. Having a Baby: Unmarried Adolescent Mothers   34

4. Having a Baby: Unmarried Older Mothers   102

5. Raising Children: Unmarried Adolescent Mothers   162

6. Raising Children: Unmarried Older Mothers   236

7. Where's Daddy? Unmarried Adolescent Mothers   284

8. Where's Daddy? Unmarried Older Mothers   339

9. Unmarried Mothers: Who We Are and Where We're Headed   409

Acknowledgments   435

Bibliography   439

Index   453

Prologue

Women who become mothers without becoming wives are in the view of some a curiosity, to others a monstrosity. As we head into the twenty-first century these women, hundreds of thousands of whom are beginning families each year, some by intent, others by accident, are at the hub of national debates about "family values," the reform of welfare, and the well-being of children. In the eyes of some onlookers, these women are the destroyers of what family ought to be. Others see them as creating, for a multitude of social, economic, and cultural reasons, alternative forms of what American families can be and are becoming.

What cannot be disputed is that unmarried mothers are people about whom much is said and concluded, but from whom very little is heard. Too often, amid the din of public ridicule and rage, these women's voices are lost, pushed so deep into the background of discussions as to fade away. In the following pages, the voices of unmarried mothers, young and older, will be heard as they describe decisions they've made, situations they confront, and views they hold about the family lives they and their children experience. Their words, intimate, powerful, and unpredictable, will guide us along a journey of discovery about why they are having and raising children outside of marriage and what their daily lives are like.

For me, this voyage of discovery had two starting points, one personal, the other professional. In this book the two paths converge. In my personal life, I pursued unmarried motherhood as I approached my fortieth year. Divorced, childless, and on my own, I wanted more than anything to become a mother. In thinking about this new way of creating a family I sought out other women to talk with whose life circumstances had brought them to similar junctures of contemplation and action. Why were they and I willing to set out along this path to unmarried motherhood, a path that generations of women before us rarely headed down? And where was this path leading us and the children we might have?

Personal concerns such as these crisscrossed with my professional life. I was then a correspondent for *Time* magazine and spent much of my time writing about children and family issues. Again and again, as I spoke with policymakers and researchers about social issues such as child care, welfare, poverty, and education, many of them raised questions about unmarried motherhood similar to the ones I was asking myself. However, their inquiries focused primarily on younger women, whose lives were very different from my own. Most of those unwed mothers were growing up poor and ill-educated, having children when they were still children themselves; their sons' and daughters' lives were often beset by problems.

Questions about unmarried motherhood among women of my age and those much younger fascinated me. I read what I could about these women's lives, but I wanted to know much more. My personal exploration of this territory introduced me to emotional layers of decision-making illuminated by no book or article I read. I now knew what it felt like to be obsessed with wanting to be a mother and to be internally driven toward that end, while at the same time feeling great discomfort about how my motherhood might be achieved and what my life as a single parent might be like for me and my child. In trying to resolve my conflicted feelings, I became more curious about how other women see themselves as unwed mothers and what they think about the family lives their circumstances and decisions are creating. The desire to know more about the personal dimensions of these women's lives impelled me to write this book.

Several years ago I set out to listen to unmarried mothers of various ages and backgrounds. Instead of surveying hundreds of women with detailed questionnaires, I devoted a lot of time to getting to know several dozen unmarried mothers. Our conversations evolved out of the decisions and events their individual lives presented and not out of formulaic queries I brought with me. It was, after all, the dailiness of their single-parenting lives and the ways in which women responded to challenges they confronted that interested me most.

The women I visited with each lived within a few hours' drive of my home in Cambridge, Massachusetts. It was in their homes and communities that I came to know them and where we visited and talked while their daily routines unfolded. I decided to interview women who lived relatively close to me so that I could visit them often, establish long-term, trusting relationships, and watch as their parenting lives evolved. What I saw and what they shared with me are, I believe, essentially the same as the personal experiences of unmarried mothers elsewhere in this country.

The mothers I met come from disparate backgrounds. Some are extremely well-off, while others survive month to month on public assistance. Some have legal or medical degrees, while others don't have a high school diploma. Some mothers were as old when they had children as some of the grandmothers who were helping to care for children of the unwed teenage mothers I came to know. Whether the women were fortysomething or in their teens when they became mothers, whether they were economically secure or struggling, I discovered that the stories about their experiences, decision-making, and emotional reactions were woven with common threads. They spoke about fathers being separated from their children's lives and about how adequate financial resources were hard to come by. Many told of how emotional support was often hard to find and of how judgments others made about them from afar could hurt so much. They also told me how motherhood, complicated, exhausting, and demanding as it was, gave their lives a sense of purpose and meaning they'd never found in anything else.

This book travels through that common ground. The stories in this book alternate between two sets of unmarried mothers about whom there is much public discussion: teenagers, among whom the incidence of non-marital births is extremely high, as are the resulting costs of public assistance; and older women, unwed mothers whom people often refer to as Murphy Browns, women who don't rely on public assistance but receive the currency of public opinion about their choice of unwed motherhood.

Often, our public discourse about unmarried motherhood categorizes and stereotypes these women and their children by race, age, and their family's anticipated problems. From these data, generalizations are often inferred about the history and future prospects of individual lives. Rarely do participants in discussions about these women look very far beyond these demographic and statistical markers. In this book, we will.

To encourage these women to speak freely about their private lives, I agreed to change their names and a few identifying facts. But the personal moments described are as the women told them to me or as I observed them. Their words are taken from transcripts of tape-recorded conversations. That these unmarried mothers speak as forthrightly as they do about their lives and their children's is testimony to a strong desire I sensed in each of them to finally be heard, to be better understood, and to have their lives be respected.

These mothers' individual experiences are also embedded in many of the pivotal changes taking place in the economic, social, and cultural progress of our nation. It is necessary, therefore, to place what we learn about the individual lives within a broader context. To do this, I have relied on the research of those who study this kind of family formation and include the voices of some who comment on it. Through the intermingling of observations from the private voices of unmarried mothers and the public pronouncements of researchers and commentators, all of us may come to understand in a richer way our own reactions to the extraordinary change we are witnessing in American family life.

The first story in this book is my own, told with all the candor I can call forth. It is about my own struggle over whether I should become an unmarried mother. By committing my innermost thoughts to the pages of this book, I hope to offer a deeper appreciation of the personal dimension of this decision and the action it can entail. Though it is impossible for me to describe other women's lives with this same depth of insight and understanding, the mothers who entrusted me with their stories gave me astonishing gifts: they shared some of their most private moments and feelings so that others can learn from them. I now pass on their gifts to you.

ON OUR OWN

1

My Story: Decision-making About Unmarried Motherhood

Nothing my mother has ever said to me surprises me as much as what I hear her saying right now. "I've been thinking a lot about you recently and wondering whether you might want to consider having a child on your own." Her voice is brisk and encouraging. Her words pierce the silence that has blanketed the kitchen since I settled into my seat at the table ten minutes ago.

It is a Saturday morning and I'm visiting my parents at their house on Cape Cod. My unusual quiet on this morning reflects the subdued mood I've been in during the past few weeks. Sullen and detached, I've not been much fun to be around. Even my usually quite tolerant family is having a hard time figuring out how to treat me. As I drifted around the house on Friday evening, I delivered hints of my anger and sadness but refused to talk with anyone. This morning, undaunted by my moodiness—or perhaps because of it—my mother is trying to penetrate my discontent. She is standing barely a dozen feet from me, rinsing some plates in the sink as she speaks to me.

Before I can respond to what she's already said, my mother moves on, eager to complete her thoughts. Her tone is utterly matter-of-fact, not revealing a hint of awareness of the shock I feel at what she's said. "You could consider using a sperm bank," she says.

Fortunately, I am shielded from eye contact with her by the newspaper

I have unfolded in front of my face. Of course, this is not the first time I have thought about having a child on my own. But it is the first time anyone else, especially my mother, has voiced this option aloud—and the first time sperm banks have been mentioned.

My mother's aim this morning is perfect. Tossed like darts in a splendid arc, her words land in the innermost circle of my emotional core. This moment engraves itself in my memory. Our exchange alters forever the way I will think about my life.

There is nothing I want more right now than to become a mother, to create a family of my own. After thirty-seven years of seeing myself as my parents' oldest child, I ache for a new alignment: me as a parent, my mother and father as grandparents, my sisters as aunts, my brother as an uncle, my niece as a cousin. I want to add layers of caring and connection and responsibility to my life, a rich and satisfying life that seems suddenly to have sprung a gaping hole.

Until recently, my life seemed quite full. Though I'd experienced my share of sad moments and painful times, day-to-day I'd found pleasure and a sense of accomplishment in my job as a correspondent with *Time* magazine. And when I'm not at work, I am fortunate to bask in the close-knit company of caring friends and the enduring love of my family. I know how lucky I am to have all this, as well as good health. Now, however, I want more. I want to be a mother. What I want is to look across my breakfast table—as my parents have looked across theirs—and see my child's eyes staring back at me. I want that sense of deep connection with a son or daughter, a person who will trust in and depend on me just as during my childhood I depended on my mother and father. Even though I haven't articulated these desires to my mother, in things I've said and done it must be obvious. How else could she know so well what is weighing on my mind?

Now these thoughts, given voice by my mother, inhabit the space between us. To raise a child on my own? To have a child using sperm donated by a man neither I nor my child would ever know? As I think of creating my child in this way, my head spins at how unnatural it seems, how distancing and impersonal it feels. It has no sense of the closeness, warmth, or comfort I associate with creating a child with a husband. Now, as I hear my mother say, "You could consider using a sperm bank," I suddenly feel utterly detached from the image of motherhood I'd been holding on to, in which I am sharing the experience with a man. And the detachment also triggers my anger at how unfair this all seems: "Why," I ask myself, "can't this happen with someone I love? Why do I have to do this by myself?"

Self-pity is not my style. Instead of feeling sorry for myself, I switch gears to wonder how my child might one day think about ⎯sion to be a parent by myself. What if she can never identify her biological father? Or what if this child of mine might never have a daddy in his life at all? Do I really have the energy, patience, and resources to raise a child on my own? Would I be able to supply the necessary discipline for a child who would have me as her only parent—and, at that, only during hours when I wasn't at my job, earning money to pay our bills? During my childhood my mother and father each played a big role; each stirred ingredients into the mix that created who I have become. Which, if any, of these ingredients would my child miss out on if I did this alone? On my own, would I be able to compensate for them?

"You don't think it's a good idea, do you?"

"We'd be there to help if you needed us," my mother says. It's been several minutes since anything has been said. Now her voice is softer and more gentle.

Because I know pretty well my mother's perspective on such things, I interpret what she means by this offer to "help." She does not mean daily assistance of the kind I might like to rely on if I were a single mother. After devoting a good many of her sixty-four years to raising me and my four siblings, my mother has made it abundantly clear to all of us that she has little interest in assuming day-to-day care of grandchildren. She deeply enjoys the different and special kind of love a grandparent has earned, but she is not willing to trade her long-awaited freedom—to pursue her own anthropological research and to write—to repeat the tough work of child-rearing. What my mother is saying to me is that in an emergency, as always, she and my father would be there to help.

In my mother's kind offer, the words that leap out at me are "we" and "us," as in "your father and I." Hearing them reminds me anew of what would be the solitary nature of my parenting experience. It also makes me wonder, for the first time since our conversation began, where my father is. I twist around in my chair to scan the living room. There he is, seated in a high-backed armchair, hidden behind yesterday's *Wall Street Journal*. A few minutes later, I hear the sound of his newspaper being folded and the squeak of his leather chair as he gets up and walks toward the kitchen.

Still rattled by my mother's suggestion, I am relieved when my father saunters by the table. I feel myself revving up inside to fend off my mother's scary yet intriguing idea, while another part of me wonders if maybe it isn't so scary after all. Maybe it's what I really want to do. I figure my father's involvement in this will at least give me more time to compose my thoughts, so as he walks by I invite him to join our conversation. I know he's heard what my mother has said to me this morning. I am guessing, too, that she probably talked with him about it before she mentioned her idea to me.

"Did you hear what Mother said about me having a baby using a sperm bank?" I ask him. Without giving my father even a moment to respond, I toss out an answer. "I mean, you don't think it's a good idea, do you?"

My father doesn't reply. As he does in many of our family's forays into territory of any emotional consequence, he keeps a bit of distance. His custom is to stay along the sidelines until my mother signals him into action. He musters just a few words about how he doesn't know much about any of this. In my apparent eagerness to shove my mother's idea away, I assume this means he agrees with me that this isn't a good idea. Before I can engage him more in this conversation, he wanders off and leaves me and my mother and this idea together again.

"My friend told me I'd never be able to explain to a woman who wants to have a child why I don't want to."

While my mother's idea whirls around in my mind, it collides with the anger and melancholy that have been consuming me. I'm trying very hard but not very successfully to regain my equilibrium after a sad and prolonged ending to a three-year relationship with a man with whom I thought I wanted to have children. Tears still come quickly when I find myself remembering our time together.

This man and I shared so much so easily. Our love of the sea near where we both grew up wove our lives together. When we were with each other my mind occasionally drifted into an imagined future in which our children would play on the same beaches we did as children. Their childhood would be like ours—at least, I hoped a child of mine would be as lucky. I knew a child of ours would one day marvel at the ocean's beauty and sail upon her waves as her father and I so enjoyed doing.

But each time these visions came to me, I shook them away. I had to. My partner let me know he didn't share my dream. He didn't want to have a child. It wasn't that he didn't want to have a child with me, he told me; he wasn't ever going to have one with anyone. At first I refused to believe him, choosing to believe instead that, as our relationship grew, so would his comfort with this idea of our having a family. But over the years it became clearer that despite our feelings for each other we weren't going to make it over this hurdle together. In trying to drag him over it—by trying to make him understand why he should want to have children with me—I hastened the end of our relationship.

During what turned out to be our last conversation about this topic, my partner leaned on the railing of his living room deck, a good distance from where I sat, and nervously smoked several cigarettes while he shared with me the advice a friend had given him. "He said I'd never be able to explain to a woman who wants to have a child why I don't want to," he said to me, and told me that he'd decided to heed this guidance. He was not going to try again to tell me why he felt the way he did. That afternoon I finally realized there was no ground left upon which we could compromise. I spent the next weekend packing while he went away to visit friends. His home, which for a long time I had shared, and where I'd hoped our family would live, no longer seemed able to contain these differing visions of where we were headed. I left the house key he'd given me years before on the kitchen counter, the first thing he'd see when he returned home on Sunday evening.

Now, a few weeks later, I know that in suggesting that I have a baby using a sperm bank my mother is trying to snap me out of my funk by getting me to think about my future. But her words are spinning me around, catapulting me even further back into my past, to memories I thought I'd successfully packed away.

"What I really wanted to do was have a child with someone I love, a person who wants to have a child with me."

In my mind's eye, I am thirty-two years old again, newly divorced and wondering then, as I am wondering now, if I will ever have a family of my own. I remember how I gave some thought then to whether I might try to become a single parent. But, in those days, I'd never reached the point of confronting the questions my mother is thrusting at me today. When I was in my early thirties, the idea of intentionally becoming an unwed mother seemed daunting, even selfish. My marriage wasn't working out, and one reason I left it when I did was the hope that I could make a fresh beginning. I saw the years ahead churning with possibility, and with the probability that I'd find a new marriage partner and start a family.

"You know, I thought of having a child on my own after I was divorced," I tell my mother, revealing something I'd never discussed with her before. "But it wasn't something I wanted to do. What I really wanted was to have a child with someone I love, a person who wants to have a child with me. I don't want to have one with some anonymous donor at a sperm bank."

There it is. A response to her idea spills out, almost involuntarily. I am surprised, as I hear myself speaking, at how definite and negative I sound. Not all of me, or even the bigger part of me, really wants to dismiss my mother's idea so quickly. Only the part of me that is frightened by the magnitude of this solitary action wants to toss it aside.

"I simply know how much you want to have a child," my mother replies, directly, quietly. "This might be a way for you to do it. We will be there for you. It is just an idea for you to think about."

"I am certain he sensed my 'baby panic' and backed away; how could he not?"

That afternoon I go sailing. It is a perfect escape. On the boat I am able to laugh and enjoy the exhilaration of being in an old wooden schooner at sea, among good friends. During the rest of this weekend, not another word is exchanged about the baby-making idea.

No one needs to say more about it. The idea is firmly planted in my mind. I know, and my mother senses, that she's tapped a part of me I have been afraid to touch. I'm grateful my mother did this for me. By saying what she did, she has pulled off a bandage and revealed a wound. It hurts to have my wound opened to the air but, as with most cuts, it will speed the healing.

During the next few weeks, whether I'm at home or in the office or out with friends, my mother's idea—which has by now transformed itself into my own—won't leave me alone. It keeps rattling around inside me. Battle lines form. Her words pop into view, and then a garrison of logic springs up to fight against them. But an equally well-equipped and competing emotional force stubbornly adheres to the possibility, holding its ground, as well.

In time I come to accept that the notion of having a baby on my own has a compelling power stronger than my ability to simply cast it away. Only by fully exploring the idea will I be able to let go of it. Or embrace it. For now I can rule out neither option. Daily there begins anew a spirited encounter between what I know about myself so far and what I'm in the process of finding out. Whether I decide to move ahead and try to have a baby on my own will depend in large measure on how confident I am of my ability to handle motherhood without a partner and how fair I believe my decision will be to my child.

As the weeks go by, I am more and more aware of how different this exploration feels to me than it did five years before. The years which then seemed to stretch so far out ahead of me now feel compressed, like an accordion after its final note. Soon I will be thirty-eight years old. Suppose I meet a man tomorrow, one who wants to have a child, and we fall in love, and we give ourselves time to make certain our relationship is solid before we decide to get married. Even if I get pregnant right away—which is hardly likely, given my age—I am likely to be in my early forties by the time my child is born. I might even be in my mid-forties if these steps take longer than my most optimistic calculations. I begin to wonder whether I'm willing to wait for these possibilities to occur to lead me to what I want most of all—a child.

Each of the steps—meeting this man, falling in love, making certain our relationship is a solid one, deciding to get married, becoming pregnant—carries with it unlikely odds. Just meeting someone who would be compatible as a life partner and who'd want to settle down with me and start a family is not likely to be easy. To begin with, it's hard for me to imagine how I'd go about it. I am uncomfortable circulating at parties, dreadfully awkward at the kind of introductory small talk that leaves lasting first impressions. I am an abysmal failure when it comes to flirting. I simply don't know how to do it, nor have I felt comfortable with it the few times I've tried. Every so often I find myself scanning the personal ads, but I've never placed or responded to one. As far back as I can remember, I met the men with whom I've had long-lasting relationships by going about the day-to-day business of living my life. They happened to walk into it. But will this strategy work again? From listening to my single friends and reading about the lonesome plight of unmarried women who are in their late thirties, I at least have to recognize that the odds of meeting the "right man" and getting married do not seem promising.

The falling-in-love part seems easier, if and when "he" walks through my life. But I worry a lot about whether my yearning for motherhood might push me into the wrong marriage. I've already made one mistake, choosing a wholly inappropriate marital partner for reasons I now understand. He proposed marriage at a time of great vulnerability for me, and I said yes right away. Though I kept my word to him, as I walked down the aisle on my father's arm I knew the marriage was not going to work. Yet I was afraid to admit that to anyone, most of all to myself, and stubbornly refused to back away despite plenty of advice from family and friends to do so. Would my resolve be strong enough now to prevent me from making a mistake like that again? The more I think about this, the more I realize that what I fear most isn't that I won't get married but that I might marry the wrong man out of desperation to beat my biological clock.

Awareness of this invites me to question for the first time if perhaps this sense of desperation was a silent player in my recent relationship. Did my partner's awareness of my "baby panic" contribute to our losing the physical intimacy we once shared? As I think about what happened, I am certain he sensed this "baby panic" and backed away; how could he not? It is now becoming clear to me how connected these things were in our relationship. When he talked of getting married, the idea of having a child was never part of his equation. My response was always no. I could not make a commitment to a life together unless I knew we would be parents. Now, with hindsight, I am better able to appreciate what he was probably hearing in my words: "I don't want to be with you as much as I want your sperm." To hear that from someone he loved must have hurt.

"A writer calls these men 'sperm banks on legs.'"

As I contemplate the difficulties of finding a partner, I find some comfort in knowing how common my situation is. Like other women of my generation, born in the early 1950s, I had been greeted during my teenage years by reverberations of Betty Friedan's book *The Feminine Mystique*. A boisterous, important revival of the women's movement was taking place. After graduating from Wellesley College in 1973, I'd set out with great confidence—some might say cockiness—into territory where before my time mostly men had journeyed. Art history was my college major, but my first full-time job was as a researcher with *Sports Illustrated*. I was assigned to the baseball beat, so I began to spend a lot of time at stadiums interviewing ballplayers. By 1978 I was the plaintiff in a highly publicized lawsuit in which a federal court judge ruled that women reporters should be given equal access to interview athletes, even if it meant entering their locker rooms. By the 1980s my attention switched to news reporting for *Time* magazine. There I pursued what has become a passionate interest of mine, reporting on the lives of children and families.

Like many of my peers I reaped extraordinary rewards—not of wealth but of personal contentment—from my professional accomplishments. Also, like many of my contemporaries, I didn't think a lot during my twenties about finding a permanent partner with whom to share this exhilarating journey. There'd be plenty of time for that once our careers were under way. Now, in our late thirties, many of my unmarried women friends share stories with each other about how difficult it now seems to meet "eligible" men who want marriage, fatherhood, and will accept the egalitarian relationship that we've come to believe is possible and that we expect for our family lives.

As my friends and I compare notes on our failures to construct such partnerships, we discover that single men our age and older fall roughly into three categories. Some are natural-born bachelors who intend to keep things that way; my former boyfriend seemed to be one of these. I didn't need to fall in love with another man like him. Others are divorced and have children; they are, perhaps, more eager to find a partner but unwilling to have more children. Or they're homosexual. Several of my friends observed that the few eligible men who seemed relatively open to the idea of marriage and fatherhood tended to fix their sights on younger women who might not have such sharp expectations about the need for a truly egalitarian marriage.

After surveying my not-so-promising prospects for gluing this marriage-and-family package together, I start to think more seriously about my options for becoming a single parent. As soon as I open myself up to learning more, I am surprised to discover from several articles that many women like me are pursuing this route. This reminds me that when you open your eyes to something, you often start to see it. Or is it, perhaps, that just as I'm contemplating this, the media are also discovering that many among my generation of financially secure women appear willing to travel along this new route to motherhood?

A few women whom I read about describe canvassing male friends to see if they'd be willing to donate sperm—either with a doctor's assistance or in person—to help them create a baby. The women promise friends who are willing to help that their sperm donation will entail no financial obligation once a child is born. Some of these women and men sign agreements prior to the child's birth, setting out their views on custody, visitation, and support. The writer of one story called such donors "sperm banks on legs." It is, I think, an apt description, and about as far away as words can take me from the image of shared parenting that I find myself still holding on to.

At a meeting where women whose lives have reached a point similar to mine gather to talk about how we might have babies on our own, a lawyer explains that such agreements reached before a baby is born don't mean much if a father decides he wants to be involved in his child's life. In imagining all sorts of potential complications, including an inharmonious relationship with a donor—a relationship like the one I'd experienced during my marriage—I decide right then to put this approach to baby-making aside.

Other women explain how they plan to get pregnant by letting an "accident" happen. They never mention marriage as part of the plan. This has the feel of an old-fashioned strategy with a modern twist: bed a man for his sperm and then send him on his way once the baby is conceived. For me, this approach is also out of the question. What if the man does not want to father a child? Is it right to trick him? What if my child wants to know her father, but he pushes her away? Even during the difficult waning months of my recent relationship, I never considered tricking my partner into fatherhood. I didn't feel I had the right to do that to a man who told me he didn't want to be a father. Nor would I want my child to face the circumstance of having a father who didn't want her.

"Why have I been wrestling so hard with this if everyone agrees it's right for me?"

A few months have now passed since my mother's words took root. Her idea of using an anonymous donor is starting to make a lot more sense to me. One night I dream that it has happened: I have a baby on my own. I am a parent. I am scared and overwhelmed but also extraordinarily happy. After I awaken the next morning, I discover for the first time that I can say out loud, "I want to have a baby and I will do it by myself."

"I have decided to have a baby!" I announce to my tennis partner that morning. She is an older woman, long ago separated and the mother of two children whom she raised all but on her own. She responds quickly and crisply: "I think it's a good idea." This reply gives me a big boost of confidence. "You've got a lot of friends and family who will give you support. If you have to travel, I could help out," she tells me, walking close to me as she picks up a ball.

Her reaction turns out to be typical of what friends say to me as I start to share my plan with them. I'm a bit surprised when they aren't more shocked by my news. Why have I been wrestling so hard with this, if everyone thinks it's so right for me to do?

A man I worked with a few years ago invites me to lunch that week. I tell him about what I intend to do. "If there is anyone who can do this, it's you," he tells me. I gratefully acknowledge what I assume is a compliment, even if I'm not certain why he's giving me such a vote of confidence for a job I have never done. He is worried, he says, not about my competence as a parent but because I may be lonely—and at times maybe resentful— as I assume the full weight of parental responsibility with no backup in sight. I share his concerns, particularly when I think about how I'll pay for the help I'll need. But I am trying to be upbeat.

"I already have many moments when I feel very much alone," I say to him, responding to his concern about loneliness. Having a child, I know, will at least make these feelings of aloneness go away.

Later that day I try this idea out on my cousin, who is nearly forty; she is stepmother to two grown boys and the mother of a three-year-old daughter. "Wow. What? I mean, are you sure? Great." My cousin's words tumble out faster than she can coordinate her thoughts. She and I have been as close as sisters since childhood, when we spent summers together at my grandparents' Cape Cod house. Now we live near each other in Cambridge. Laughter comes easily to us when we spend time together, but we are also good at listening to each other's problems.

That afternoon we talk about mothering and our own mothers and then about how I might manage on my own. She makes me laugh by recalling moments when married friends of ours who are mothers complain about how much easier it might be to raise children by themselves. Being with a man can be like having another child to take care of—or at least, that's often what these women say. Sharing such stories offers my cousin a chance to grow accustomed to this idea I've sprung on her. It also gives me a chance, for the first time in a long while, to simply sit with her and giggle as we used to in girlhood. There is no doubt that my melancholy is finally lifting.

But even as my cousin and I chuckle about these married mothers' stories, I know these women didn't—and most wouldn't—choose to be parents on their own. I wouldn't choose this path either if it didn't seem the only way I could now become a mother. But what I also hear my cousin saying, as the two of us continue to talk, is that I should not let my opportunity for motherhood slip by only because there isn't a man in my life who wants to father a child with me. "I don't think it's impossible at all," my cousin says. "You could do it."

In a phone conversation with a close friend in California, I hear a similar message. "I couldn't do it," my friend tells me, "because I don't have my life pulled together yet. But I think you could do it." Another friend, a woman who relishes her life as a grandmother to her stepdaughter's child, tells me, "That's exactly what I would do if I were your age. You have my full support."

That's what I hear from everyone: "You can do it." But how is it that they know this about me, and I don't? What do they see in me that gives them confidence I could make this work? How do they know I would be happy raising a child alone? Why do they seem so confident, when I'm not, that my child would turn out okay?

A few days later I am sitting again with my cousin in her living room. She's been at home all day with her three-year-old, who refused to take her afternoon nap. Now it's early evening. Her daughter's crankiness is straining her patience, so she summons her husband, who is exercising upstairs. "I'd go crazy if he wasn't here right now to take care of her," she says once her daughter is out of the room. Her thoughts turn to me and what it would be like not to have someone else to help. "At the end of the day the two of us talk about things with each other," she says. "These are the kind of things you wouldn't have."

How well aware I am becoming of the trade-offs involved in this decision. On the one hand there is the intense emptiness I feel in my present life, an emptiness I think is there because I don't have a child. On the other hand, in parenting by myself I may feel a different kind of loneliness when I don't have my child's father to share in the joys and responsibilities that come with being a parent. But if it comes down to not having a child, or to having one on my own—as it seems to do—then I am comfortable with choosing the latter. After all, having a child by myself at this age doesn't mean we'll always be alone. Plenty of single parents find new partners when their marriages have failed. And even though my baby-making years will soon be over, I suspect that my desire for a loving relationship with a man won't vanish when I am a mother.

At times I even imagine my prospects for finding a partner might be brighter then. Instead of the incredible awkwardness involved in discovering how a man feels about "having" a child, being a mother would establish my position about this right from the start and I could judge how any relationship with a man would fit in with my life and my child's. In fact, friends tell me that men seem more comfortable fitting themselves into a ready-made family, rather than feeling pressured to start one of their own. This clearly shouldn't be the reason to have a child on my own, but at the same time it's reassuring to know this decision might not diminish the probability of my finding a relationship as well.

"You might as well get accustomed to the criticism right now and build yourself up to ignore it."

It is time for me to seek medical advice: I need to learn whether what I want to do can be done. It is Christmas season, almost the New Year, and it seems propitious that the only appointment my gynecologist has available is late on the afternoon of December 31. "Perfect," I tell myself. "I'll take it." There could not be a better way for me to welcome in the New Year than with an actual plan in place for having a baby. I'm excited to have turned this corner and to finally be doing something instead of just thinking about it. I jot down the time in my appointment book: it's the final entry of that year.

Perhaps because my friends are so supportive, I expect to hear similar encouragement from my doctor. I am wrong. Grudgingly, and with a shame-on-you tone in his voice, he offers me a few names of physicians who do donor inseminations. But he wonders aloud if they will agree to take me. I am, after all, unmarried. He says that no single woman has ever asked him this before. "You know there's a sperm bank out in California with all those Nobel Prize winners' sperm," he says. "I'm not sure they'd do it out there either." His implication isn't lost on me: outlandish ideas like this one belong on the Other Coast. Only his New Englander's reserve prevents him from coming right out and stating his personal disapproval, though his tone conveys plenty.

This is the first time anyone has been so negative about my plan. During my hour-and-a-half drive to my parents' house, where I'm to spend New Year's Eve celebrating the launch of my baby-making plans, I'm reduced to feeling only anger at how my life has turned out. When I arrive at the house, my sister greets me. She is a year younger than I, married, the mother of an eight-year-old daughter, and a practicing attorney. She's able to quiet my distress. "All sorts of people are going to have opinions and make judgments about your decision to have a child on your own," she tells me. "Many of them are going to disapprove, so you might as well get accustomed to the criticism right now. You'd better build yourself up to ignore it. You're the only one who must be certain. When you are, it will be the right thing for you to do."

Her reassuring words comfort me that evening.

"Just as my parents raised me and my siblings together, I want that kind of parenting for my child."

More months pass, and my mind zigzags like a billiard ball. I seem driven by alternating forces: one is a pulsating desire for a child; the other, my still inescapable fears and uncertainty about parenting alone. One night I write a letter to my former boyfriend, asking him if we can try to start again. I tell him my decision about a baby can wait until our relationship grows stronger. But it takes only a few days of being together again for us to realize my promise isn't possible for me to keep. I cannot put the baby issue aside so easily. Neither can he. Again I am tossed into sadness and confusion. Tearfully, we say good-bye.

I decide to seek professional counseling to help me cope with this rejuvenated sadness and with the pull I still feel to be a mother. During our weekly sessions the therapist and I focus on what appear to be major stumbling blocks preventing me from moving ahead. After all the time I've been thinking about this, it seems strange to me that I haven't resolved the very questions I posed to myself on that morning when my mother spoke of my having a child on my own: Am I really comfortable having a child who will never know her father? Can I be the kind of parent I want to be, if I do this on my own? Will my child be angry at me?

Conceiving a child by using an anonymous donor still cuts deeply against my long-held expectation of what becoming a mother would be like. I can't seem to let go of wanting a man to be a parent with me. It seems too lonely not to have someone with whom I'll be able to share my child's moments of discovery, someone who will help me to raise this child, someone whom my child will know as her daddy. How do I discard these images of motherhood, which I've carried with me for a lifetime? My parents raised me and my siblings *together;* I always wanted that kind of family life for my child.

During these therapy sessions I realize how much of me remains captive to these images. The 1950s were the era when the new creature called television beamed portrayals of motherhood into millions of America's homes, mine included. I grew up seeing these television moms—Donna Reed, Harriet Nelson, June Cleaver—and also watching my own mother's life, which did not look so different from theirs. Despite the many changes in women's lives, those images of motherhood seem hard to erase. I tell myself that what I need to remember now, as I think about being a mother, is that those TV moms and my own lived in vastly different times than I do. Their lives cannot be models for my own. Yet inside me a tug-of-war rages. Part of me longs for the simplicity of these TV moms' lives, even though I know from my mother's experience that for many women the veneer of contentedness was just that. Another part of me knows that whatever family arrangement I one day have—whether I marry and then have a child, or vice versa—my daily life will be very different from these mothers'. But is what I'm considering—intentionally becoming a mother on my own—*too* different? And where do I look to find workable models for my version of motherhood?

One of the most difficult things for me to figure out is how my decision to have a baby on my own will work out for my child. How can I know? Yet I need to try as hard as I can to envision this and understand how my child might one day feel. I need to think about how I'll respond to questions my child will inevitably ask: "Who is my daddy?" "Where is my daddy?" "Why didn't you give me a daddy?" I can't know exactly what my child will want to know about her father, but I know with certainty that she will be curious. If I use an anonymous donor, I will need to tell my child the truth about her conception when she is able to understand. Will

I find words to soothe whatever anger she might have because of this empty spot I've handed her? Are there any words that can adequately explain this?

In thinking about this, I examine with my therapist how it is that children and adolescents explore their identity, especially when they don't know one half of their parentage. She suggests that I look back in my own life to examine where I found a sense of who I am and how I developed my self-esteem. My parents spring immediately to mind. The older I become the more I recognize how much of what I am each of them gave to me. From my mother, I absorbed a daredevilish, world-be-damned attitude. She is there to give me a reach-for-the-stars affirmation for even my wackiest ideas. Though she and I often view the world through very different lenses, I know she will be there for me whenever I stumble or falter. To my father, who is a fanciful storyteller and my sporting companion, I trace an unflappable steadiness that underpins my approach to life. "Don't act in haste!" I hear him advise me, before I've even asked. He conveys an inner calm quite unlike my mother's up-and-down emotions and constant swirl of energy.

It is difficult for me to imagine how different my life would be if my parents were not there, in the tag-team alignment that is their enduring marriage. Perhaps I would have done fine, as many children do, seeking out these missing ingredients from other people in my life. But in thinking about my child, I can't stop myself from wanting her to experience the daily consistency of my parents' yin-and-yang parenting style. Can I supply this on my own? It's hard for me to imagine how I can.

My therapist urges me to think of people outside my family who also contributed to making me who I am. I can remember special teachers and close friends and friends' parents and coaches and other adults who came in and out of my life. Each has contributed to shaping my life. In focusing on these forces, I gradually become more comfortable with the idea that I could serve as a kind of hub for my child. I'd be like an air traffic controller, constantly communicating with other people and routing an abundance of loving support into my child's life. My child would also have a built-in network of aunts and uncles, grandparents and cousins. The friends who are so enthusiastic about my having a child would also be an important and enriching part of her or his life. And I would become involved with a whole new set of friends I'd meet at my child's day care, at school, and through weekend activities.

The more I dwell on all this, the clearer it is becoming to me that no one can be certain how being a parent will work out. So many impossible-to-predict circumstances will be swept into the mix. In this respect, it doesn't matter whether I am married or not. I cannot possibly know now whether my best efforts to compensate for the absence of my child's other parent will be enough. All I can do is what I am trying to do: ask what I hope are the right questions and allow myself the chance to thoroughly think about those aspects of the situation that I can, to a degree, predict.

These months of contemplation are accomplishing something very important, shifting my thinking away from myself and onto my child. This feels like progress. And though I haven't found all the answers I am looking for, I find that by addressing these issues I am moving closer to deciding to go ahead.

"I think there is a high probability these mothers may be better parents than many married couples who have children."

One afternoon I have news I want to share with my mother. I dial my parents' number and wait for her to answer. She does. But before I can start to tell her my news, she says my father wants to talk to me. This seems odd. Usually I talk with him only at the end of a conversation with my mother, and then only long enough to hear a brief description of his most recent golf game.

"Melissa," he says as he gets on the line.

"Yeah," I respond. "It's me."

"Well, this morning I went over to town to have my car serviced and there I was, sitting in the waiting room while the car was being fixed. Just a tune-up, but it was taking a while. And on the television set in the waiting room there were women talking about why they'd had children by themselves."

Now I am beginning to understand why my mother insisted that my father talk with me. As it turns out, one of the morning talk-show hosts was interviewing unmarried women about my age who had become parents on their own. But my father's story has less to do with that than with what happened in this waiting room. An older, heavyset man who was sitting near my father started talking to the television set, ridiculing these women as they spoke about how and why they'd done this. According to my father, this man believed the women were engaged in sinful activity: at one point he said that if any more proof was needed of the decline of moral standards in our country, these women offered it. His rantings became impossible for my father to ignore.

"I don't think this has anything to do with sin," my dad said to this man as the other customers listened in. "It's got more to do with the right of free choice. I can't speak about *these* women, but I think there is a high probability these mothers may be better parents than many married couples who have children."

By now I am listening to my father's story with rapt attention. Even if I wanted to interrupt, I know from my years of being his daughter that until he has finished, my words won't be heard. He goes on to explain how he'd told this man that he was impressed by the women's commitment and sincerity. Upon hearing this, the stranger walked out, flashing my father a dismissive grin. Everyone else in the small waiting room focused on my father. No one uttered a word. Everyone sat silently as the interviews went on, listening as the studio audience aired its own divided feelings.

"I didn't personalize it," my father assures me. "I didn't say, 'My daughter is doing this.' "

What he's just said astonishes me: "My daughter is doing this." How could he know I am no longer only thinking about trying to become a mother on my own? In fact, that is the news I have called to share with my mother and, in turn, to share with him. To hear my father telling me this story makes this seem like a serendipitous moment. As he hands the telephone over to my mother, I feel a surge of strength rising inside me. It is a warm feeling, as though my parents' arms are wrapped lovingly around my shoulders. It is comforting to know that my entire family understands.

2

Unmarried Motherhood: A Half-Century of Change

The landscape of family life is so vastly different today than it was when I was growing up that it almost defies comparison. New family configurations, the hectic pace of contemporary lives, changed expectations men and women have about one another and themselves, economic demands on families, and the vast array of external influences to which children are exposed—all these create new, often frightening challenges for parents. The road maps for family life many of us carried out of childhood no longer seem adequate to guide our travels today, even when two parents are in the home. For mothers who don't have partners, scarcely a day passes when something doesn't happen to remind them of how challenging and difficult it is to be parents on their own.

As I contemplated what my family life might be like if I became a mother on my own, my mind's eye transported me back to my own childhood. The clash between the images I recollected and what I saw happening around me reflected the profound social, cultural, and economic changes that have taken place during my lifetime. This juxtaposition of past and present also made me realize in very personal terms just how profound some of these changes have been and how they have influenced family life since I was a child.

In the summer of 1951 my mother and father packed our belongings in cardboard boxes and suitcases and loaded them into the first car either of them had ever owned, a baby-blue Plymouth sedan. It was time for our family to move. For three years my parents had lived in Iowa City, long enough for my father to earn his Ph.D. in economics and for my mother to complete her master's degree in geology and geography. Now my father, at the age of twenty-seven, had been hired as a professor at the University of Massachusetts, and we were moving there. In September he would teach finance to college students while my mother, who was also twenty-seven, would stay at home to take care of me. Born in May of that year, I was their first child.

My father drove; my mother navigated and kept a watchful eye on me. Much of the time I slept as I rode in my baby carriage's cloth basket, which my parents set down on the backseat. Infant car seats didn't exist. We stopped to say a long good-bye to my grandparents before leaving behind my father's childhood home in Waterloo, Iowa, and heading across the Mississippi River. Our hot midsummer journey east took us along a circuitous and scenic route, past places such as Niagara Falls. My parents tell me that toward the end of our trip I cried a lot. When we arrived at my mother's childhood home near Boston, my father deposited us with her parents. Then he left for Amherst, a small, rural college town about ninety miles away. His job was to hunt for a place for us to live and settle into his new job before we joined him.

By mid-October my father, my mother, and I were together again as a family. We lived in a third-floor, two-bedroom apartment in a low-lying brick complex of university-owned housing. There was a large, grassy playground next to our building, with swing sets and slides. During the day it was filled with lots of professors' wives and their children. Ours was a self-contained community. No one we knew had to drive on a highway to get to work. The campus was across the street from where we lived, so my dad and my playmates' fathers walked to work. In the afternoon my mother took me for a walk and we'd stop by my father's office just to say hello. As I became older, visiting my father at his office became a habit. There seemed something magical to me about being where my father worked: students stopped in to ask him questions, and secretaries sat in an adjoining office to answer phones and type letters. To look at him in his office was to see a person who seemed more important than when he was just being my dad at home. Perhaps in being there I felt I was important, too.

Within a year of our arrival in Amherst, my sister Leslie was born. Many of my parents' apartment-dwelling friends were also expanding their families and, like them, my parents were starting to think about moving into a house of our own. Within another year or so my father was granted tenure, and with that news the future became something my parents could predict with a measure of accuracy. They purchased an acre of woodsy land and had built on it a spacious three-bedroom house. They relied on my father's income to pay the mortgage. A twenty-year Veterans Administration loan at an interest rate of 4 percent meant that the $87 monthly mortgage equaled about a fifth of my father's salary. My mother never had to think about finding a job to bring in a second income. While our house was being built, my brother, Mark, was conceived. He was born just after we moved in. Within five years, my parents nearly doubled the size of our house to accommodate the arrival of my sisters Betty and Rebecca.

My family looked like my friends'. Perhaps our family, with its five children, had grown a bit larger than many of my friends', but the at-home patterns of our childhood lives were pretty much the same. My father went to work, just as my friends' fathers did. My mother stayed at home, just as their mothers did. My mother took us with her when she did the household shopping. She also did the laundry, cleaned up after all of us, prepared the meals, and chaperoned the five of us to every imaginable kind of lesson—piano, tap dancing, ballet, horseback riding, gymnastics, skating, swimming, and tennis. She was always on call to shuttle us back and forth to our friends' homes.

In those days I simply assumed my parents would be together forever. There was no reason to think otherwise. No one I knew had only one parent. I remember how shocked I and my friends were when we found out that the parents of another friend were getting divorced. I was in the eighth grade and this was the first time I remember hearing of such a thing happening.

As soon as Leslie and I learned to ride bicycles, to cross a busy street, and to navigate our town, my mother sent us off on our own, relieved that we didn't need to rely on her for our transportation. She had plenty to keep her busy with our siblings. We were no older than six or seven, yet we'd ride a mile or so to the community swimming pool or to a friend's house. My mother had the usual worries about whether we'd get into an accident, but she'd never heard of a child being kidnapped or hurt by a stranger. Our community was regarded as safe for children. My parents never warned us that strangers were people to be frightened of. To us, the world seemed a trustworthy place.

My parents bought their first television set when I was six years old. We could watch programs on only a few channels, and those could be seen clearly only if we patiently adjusted the wires of our tiny antenna. To switch stations we had to get up, rotate the knob, and then play with the antenna again. Often, the picture remained fuzzy. At times black-and-white images scrolled across the screen like film that had jumped its sprockets. However, the shows we did see—*Leave It to Beaver, Ozzie and Harriet, Father Knows Best*—re-created for us the placid, predictable image of my family's daily life.

In the tiny world that my childhood eyes could see, I knew that a family was what we had.

Four decades of tumultuous change have altered the way families look and act and the ways and environments in which children are raised. Nowadays most families of all economic circumstances send fathers *and* mothers into the labor market before the children are even one year old. During the 1990s, many two-income couples meet their family's economic needs by transforming themselves into what the U.S. Labor Department has referred to as the "three-job marriage." In these families, nearly as many mothers as fathers hold more than one wage-earning job. Parental time gets swallowed up in the complex logistics of just keeping a family financially afloat.

In the 1990s more women are parenting alone than ever before, except during times of war. It's predicted that more than half the babies born this year will live with only one parent during some of their childhood—the vast majority with their mothers. With the energy, time, and diminished financial resources of one, a mother must figure out how to perform parental tasks usually accomplished by two. This is particularly difficult when the father does not share even the financial responsibility of supporting his children.

Parents, whether married or single, worry with good reason about their children's well-being. Instead of designing itself in ways that would welcome and embrace its youngest members, American society sings lullabies about its concern for children without actually investing enough resources in family-focused supports. Parents and children bemoan the sense of abandonment evoked by the lack of buttressing and encouragement from the larger society. Only in recent years, and often grudgingly, have employers begun to accommodate themselves to the pull-and-tug of family obligations. Yet a parent who works full-time cannot be at home after school; consequently, many children, even those who are quite young, go home alone and take care of themselves. Whether married or single, a parent may not be able to be at home to help a child with homework or to tell a bedtime story because of obligations at work. A lot of parents can't find those special moments to listen with undivided attention to a child's rambling report on the progress of a day, something my parents always did. Household tasks and leftover work from the office often occupy the time parents have at home. Or exhaustion takes over. Family gatherings around the dinner table, of the kind my family had every night, become another casualty of an overstretched, demanding life.

The world outside the home is portrayed to youngsters, often by necessity, as hostile and frightening. Knives, drugs, and anger travel with kids to school the way hula hoops, comic books, and curiosity used to accompany us. Many children grow up fearing violence in their communities and their homes. In neighborhoods considered dangerous, parents convey suspicion of people who live nearby, and children often remain secluded in their homes—safer, perhaps, but also isolated and alone.

Television can become a child's secure companion. Dependable and always ready to play, it consumes vast amounts of children's time. Now, with the click of a remote control button, a TV screen delivers to children a confusing collage of images. *Click!* A child can see the brutality of the streets brought into her living room. *Click!* A studio audience laughs and then applauds as men and women weave tales of betrayal out of the unhappy circumstances of their lives. *Click!* A news report shows piles of bodies being bulldozed into shallow graves in a country far away. Could it happen here? No one is present to offer reassurance that it can't. *Click!* A situation comedy finds parents and kids trying to be a family while the strains of daily life seem to be ripping them apart. Is a child meant to cry or laugh?

In this gigantic world that children's eyes now take in, the images of family are not as monochromatic as they once appeared to me.

From Divorce to Unmarried Motherhood

The American family no longer comes in any predictable size or shape, though families these days are generally smaller than those my parents' generation created. Today a larger proportion of people than ever before don't even live in a household that the Census Bureau describes as a family, because they live alone; in the early 1990s, one-quarter of all American households contained one person. The mom-and-pop-and-kids family now accounts for a bit more than one-fourth of our household arrangements. Just two decades ago, closer to half of all households were made up of such families. And today many fewer of the mom-pop-kids families resemble—in roles their parents play—the kind of household arrangement I lived in as a child. Only when my youngest sibling entered first grade did my mother resume her studies: for her, being at home with her children was a full-time occupation for sixteen years. Today, full-time motherhood usually lasts for only a matter of months after each child is born.

Except for the massive influx of mothers of young children into the workforce, the most visible and consequential change in family life during the past four decades involves the dramatic increase in families headed by single parents. By the mid-1990s, three of every ten families with young children had only one parent (usually their mother) living with them. In 1970, family arrangements of this kind were found in about one in eight homes where children lived.

Divorce has been a major contributor to this increase in single-parent families. The rate of divorce began to escalate steadily by the late 1950s; during the 1970s the annual growth in divorce accelerated rapidly. Not surprisingly, during those same years the increase in the number of single-parent families also became very high, averaging 6 percent each year. In the 1970s, the growth in single-parent families was largely attributed to marital breakups, especially among white families. But another factor—out-of-wedlock births—was also contributing significantly to the formation of one-parent families, particularly in African-American communities. By the mid-1990s, slightly more children lived with never-married mothers than with moms who were divorced.

Since 1940, when 89,500 out-of-wedlock births were recorded in this country, childbearing among unmarried women of all ages and socioeconomic backgrounds has been rising steadily. In 1940, out-of-wedlock births accounted for 4 percent of all the babies born that year. By 1970, that figure had grown to 10 percent. Now, a quarter of a century later, more than a million such births occur every year; nearly a third of all babies are born to unmarried mothers. Whereas in the past, many children born to unwed mothers, especially white ones, were adopted by two-parent families, today only a very small percentage of these infants are placed for adoption. In January 1994, an analysis of nonmarital births by the Children's Defense Fund concluded that "if the proportion of births to unmarried women continues to climb over the next seven years as it has in the past seven years, more than 40 percent of all babies born in 2001 will go home from the hospital to a single parent family."

As we approach the twenty-first century, unmarried mothers are the fastest-growing segment of the single-mother population. Roughly a quarter of the million-plus babies born out of wedlock go home with their two unmarried parents, but the majority begin their childhood with single mothers. However, nonmarital relationships dissolve faster than marriages do, so even the babies who start off living with two parents have a higher probability of spending some of their childhood with only one.

Contrary to popular belief, most women who give birth to children out of wedlock are not teenagers. Mothers who are between the ages of twenty and twenty-four account for 35 percent of these births, and women twenty-five and older account for another 35 percent. This means that teenagers give birth to a bit fewer than a third of out-of-wedlock babies. However, many of the births to unmarried women in their early twenties are to mothers who had their first child as a teenager, so adolescence is indeed the prime time when many single-parent families are formed. In fact, teen moms account for more than half of all *first* births to unmarried women.

On the older end of the spectrum, the number and rate of out-of-wedlock births to women in their late thirties is comparatively small. But during the past decade, women who are thirty-five and older have experienced a more rapid increase in the rate of out-of-wedlock births than have women in younger age groups. In 1994, 6 percent of women who had graduated from college and were not married gave birth; a decade earlier, the comparable figure was 2.7 percent. During that decade, while the birthrate among young, unwed black women was declining, the percentage of women who gave birth out of wedlock and work in managerial and professional jobs more than doubled, increasing from 3.1 percent to 8.3 percent.

However, one similarity between these older mothers and teenagers is that many of the older women are also having their first child out of wedlock—starting a family in the absence of a marriage. And as births to older unmarried women become more common, the proportion of out-of-wedlock births among teen mothers declines. Twenty-five years ago half of such births were to teenagers; in the 1990s, as we've learned, that proportion has fallen to less than one-third.

Most women who have babies out of wedlock grew up in families with very limited resources. Indeed, 87 percent of teen mothers—the vast majority of whom are not married—are poor or near poor. And a woman who belongs to a minority population is likelier to become an unwed mother than a white woman is. But these characteristics by no means account for all unmarried moms. More and more often today, out-of-wedlock births occur among young white women. This is especially apparent in blue-collar communities which only a few decades ago were thriving factory towns. Today, industries that once produced plentiful, lifelong jobs with wages high enough to enable one worker to support a family either have shut down or have fewer secure, well-paid jobs to offer the community's younger, less-educated members.

Even if the decades-long increase in out-of-wedlock births reverses itself in 1996—as it did slightly in 1995—millions of children will still be born to unwed women and will be raised in families from which their fathers are largely absent. Family formation has changed in the last half of the twentieth century, and the consequences associated with this change cannot be wished away.

Unmarried Motherhood: The Increasing Convergence of Black and White

Because the majority of Americans are white, it is not surprising that the majority of out-of-wedlock births are to white parents. What is less well understood—or accepted—by many people is that in recent years the rate of unwed motherhood has been rising more rapidly among white women than among their black peers. Perhaps this fact does not surface often in discussions about single motherhood because the nonmarital birthrate, although rising faster among whites, remains, as it always has been, much higher among nonwhite American women.

It was Daniel Patrick Moynihan's report "The Negro Family: The Case for National Action" that first drew national attention to the high rate of nonmarital births among black women. That happened thirty years ago. At the time, one in every five black children was being born to an unmarried mother; the comparable figure among whites was one in forty. In his report to President Lyndon B. Johnson, Moynihan, who was then an assistant secretary of labor and is now a U.S. senator, analyzed economic and demographic data and issued a warning: unless this direction of family formation was reversed, the black community was in grave danger of losing whatever gains it was then making in its struggle for civil rights.

> From the wild Irish slums of the 19th century Eastern seaboard to the riot-torn suburbs of Los Angeles, there is one unmistakable lesson in American history: A community that allows a large number of young men to grow up in broken families, dominated by women, never acquiring any stable relationship to male authority, never acquiring any rational expectations about the future—that community asks for and gets chaos. . . . [In such a society] crime, violence, unrest, unrestrained lashing out at the whole social structure—these are not only to be expected, they are virtually inevitable.

In his report's most widely quoted phrase, Moynihan borrowed from black historian E. Franklin Frazier's earlier analysis of the Negro poor and referred to matriarchal black families as being engulfed in a "tangle of pathology" at the center of which "is the weakness of the family structure." Moynihan cited two other factors he said played a central role in moving

black families toward unmarried motherhood: rising black male unemployment and economic inequality. But these other factors were all but
forgotten amid the backlash that greeted his report.

Moynihan's behavioral thesis (epitomized by his use of the phrase
"tangle of pathology") led him to be accused of racial insensitivity. The
Reverend Martin Luther King, Jr., reacted by saying that "the danger will
be that problems will be attributed to innate Negro weaknesses and used
to justify neglect and rationalize oppression." King's sentiments were
echoed by many other leaders, black and white, and soon, despite
Moynihan's desire to make these findings a "case for national action," the
topic instead turned into a forbidden realm for either discussion or
research. Until the late 1980s, the subject of out-of-wedlock births in the
black community was considered still too controversial to discuss.

The racial disparity in the rate of out-of-wedlock births is attributed to
a variety of causes; some scholars regard blacks' greater propensity to form
families without marriage as an enduring legacy of slavery. Slaves could
not be legally married, and the stability of families depended on whether
family members were sold to other slave owners. Other researchers
attribute the decrease in the marriage rate during the 1960s and 1970s to
the increasing economic displacement black families encountered after
many moved from the agrarian economy of the South to join the urban
labor force of the North. Whatever the mix of reasons for this change,
marriage and birth records tell us that from 1890 until 1940, the pattern
of family formation exhibited by whites and blacks was essentially the
same. It was during the 1950s—a time many whites nostalgically recall as
an era of contented nuclear families—that more and more black children
began to be born out of wedlock and raised by women alone.

At the time Moynihan released his report, more than half of all black
women were in the workforce, compared with 42 percent of white women.
Thanks to the civil rights movement, black women were beginning to be
hired for jobs other than domestic help. Their wages were rising, as was an
accompanying sense of independence. At the same time, the manufacturing jobs that had drawn black men to seek employment in northern
cities were becoming scarcer. Without work, or with jobs that paid lower
wages and offered less security, men were less able to be the family breadwinners. The wage disparity between black men and women began to be
significantly reduced, and as it did men became less attractive, from an
economic perspective, as mates. With less economic security to lose,
women became less willing to rely on marriage as a prerequisite for having
children.

Now, thirty years later, similar economic displacement, a shrinking of the wage disparity between the sexes, and a lessening of the stigma attached to out-of-wedlock childbirth are affecting family formation among younger whites, especially those who have the least education and have been raised in poverty. A 1994 study by the Family Research Council found that among those between the ages of fifteen and twenty-four, 70 percent believe an unwed teenager who has a child should feel no negative judgment. Today, babies are being born to unwed white women at the same rate as they were born to unwed black women in 1960: one out of every five white children is now born to an unwed woman. Some analysts point to the fact that young white males are now less able than their fathers' generation was to support a family on the wages they're able to earn. And like the many black women who several decades ago eschewed marriage when it didn't offer economic security, today young white women are unwilling to enter or remain in bad marriages for the sake of having or rearing children.

In his book *Two Nations: Black and White, Separate, Hostile, Unequal*, political scientist Andrew Hacker unfolds a historical, comparative look at rates of out-of-wedlock births among whites and blacks. He finds that in 1950, nearly 17 percent of black babies were born to unmarried mothers; the figure for white infants was 1.7 percent. This means that at the midpoint of the twentieth century the proportion of nonwhite babies being born out of wedlock was nearly ten times that of whites. By 1994, however, the racial disparity in births to unmarried women had been reduced to a multiple of 2.8: 70 percent of black babies were born to unwed mothers; among whites, the figure was 25 percent.* As Hacker writes: "Even though the number of births to unwed black women has ascended to an all-time high, white births outside of marriage have been climbing at an even faster rate."

Unmarried Motherhood and Money

The best-documented consequence of this movement toward single-parent families—no matter which ethnic or racial group is involved—is disparities in family incomes. In 1993, the U.S. Census Bureau reported that among families in which a child's two parents remain together, the median income was $43,500. When two members of a household are available to move into the labor force, the family has a greater earning

---

*Hacker ends his racial comparison in 1989. Stephanie J. Ventura, a research statistician at the National Center for Health Statistics, updated his figures to 1994.

capacity. (Nevertheless, in 1994 more than 2 million young children who were poor lived with married parents.) Single-parent families, with only one wage-earning adult—usually a woman, which means that her wages will often be low—will usually have a relatively small income. Not surprisingly, the lowest incomes are those of families headed by mothers who have never been married; their annual median income in 1993 was slightly above $9,000. Not surprisingly, 60 percent of children living with unmarried mothers are poor.

The primary reason never-married mothers' income is often so low is that nonmarital births occur most frequently among women who are poor before they become pregnant and don't have the skills or education they need to secure well-paid jobs. Some 42 percent of unmarried mothers do not have even a high school education. Beginning their families when they are themselves at such severe economic disadvantage means they have little chance of altering their poor economic circumstances or their children's. Many young, never-married mothers rely on public assistance during at least some of their children's early years. Recent statistics tell us that nearly three out of every five children who receive welfare live in families with mothers who never married.

Welfare payments do not lift children out of poverty, nor do many of the low-wage jobs that poorly educated, never-married mothers are able to find. Even during booming economic cycles, the well-being of these families improves very little. In a report on single-parent families in Massachusetts, two University of Massachusetts economists found that even during the state's economic good times in the mid-1980s, female-headed families fell further and further behind financially. These mothers worked, on average, as many hours each year as wives in two-parent families, but neither their hourly wages nor their job advancement kept pace with their married peers'.

The study's authors, Randy Albelda and Chris Tilly, bundled reasons for this disparity into what they called the triple whammy, a combination punch that hits single mothers whenever they try to enter the labor market: their children need child care (and high-quality reliable care is costly and can be hard to find); their family has only one income; and the wage earner is female. These intertwined factors help explain why two-thirds of unmarried mothers are living in poverty while raising children. When these never-married mothers do move out of poverty, it isn't usually because of what they earn but because they get married.

Within the past decade there has been a large increase in the number of older and more economically secure unmarried women bearing or adopting children. Their financial circumstances present a contrast to the usual notions about such families. A study involving more than 150 older, well-educated unmarried mothers in the New York City area found that their median income ranged from $55,800 (among women using anonymous sperm donors to become pregnant) to $42,600 (among those who intended to have a baby with but not marry a sexual partner). A majority of these women had graduate degrees and worked in professional jobs. Most of them said they'd waited to take on unmarried parenthood until they were convinced it was their only route to motherhood and knew they were financially prepared to handle it. Yet, even with their relatively high salaries, these unmarried mothers were discovering that raising and supporting a child on their own is extremely taxing on their wallets and on their energy for parenting.

Unmarried Motherhood: The Consequences

American children who grow up with only one parent face a myriad of predicted circumstances, many of which are disadvantageous to their healthy development. More of these children than of those born to married women arrive premature and underweight, because unmarried mothers, as a group, obtain less prenatal care than married mothers do. During their preschool years, many of these children don't receive the devoted caretaking and appropriate stimulation essential to healthy development; this is usually because their mothers don't have the necessary know-how or resources. By the elementary grades, children who live with single mothers tend to do less well on standard tests of verbal and math ability than do peers who live with two parents. When they're in middle school, these children, on average, earn lower grades and display more behavior problems and higher rates of chronic health disorders, physical and mental. For teenagers, being raised by a single mother is associated with greater risk of having a child themselves, dropping out of high school, ending up in jail, and being unemployed.

It's difficult for researchers to disentangle the causes of these various consequences. Do they result from the poverty in which so many of the children are raised? Or from the single-parent structure of the family? Or does the combination of these factors create the greater risk that poor outcomes will occur? To these fundamental questions, there are no simple answers. For example, family income has been found to be more powerfully related than family structure to five-year-old children's IQ, although family structure clearly corresponds to income. Studies also suggest that a mother's level of education is the most significant variable in predicting her child's academic success. However, in other studies, children's behavior problems appear to depend less on family income than on having a single parent as head of the family.

One researcher whose scholarly work is dedicated to trying to unravel these threads of causality is Sara S. McLanahan, a professor of sociology and public affairs at Princeton University. Her research is highly regarded even by those who might not want to agree with the conclusions she draws from it. In 1994 she and sociologist Gary Sandefur wrote the book *Growing Up with a Single Parent: What Hurts, What Helps,* which presents the most up-to-date evidence. On the book's very first page, McLanahan and Sandefur state that "children who grow up in a household with only one biological parent are worse off, on average, than children who grow up in a household with both of their biological parents, regardless of the parents' race or educational background." However, within a few paragraphs the fundamental question of establishing causality is addressed. This is an important topic at a time when the list of social ills being blamed on out-of-wedlock births is growing quite lengthy.

"Are single motherhood and father absence therefore the root cause of child poverty, school failure, and juvenile delinquency?" the authors ask. And they respond: "Our findings lead us to say no. While living with just one parent increases the risk of each of these negative outcomes, it is not the only, or even the major, cause of them. Growing up with a single parent is just one among many factors that put children at risk of failure."

Social scientists such as McLanahan know that establishing a relationship between two circumstances is not the same as proving causation. Research can, however, illuminate the relative risks that various factors pose. In their careful examination of data from four national studies of children and families, various risk factors are evaluated. These analyses lead to some provocative discoveries. For example, McLanahan and Sandefur write that "the average young woman from a white one-parent family has about the same risk of becoming a teen mother as the average black or Hispanic young woman from a two-parent family." Of children whose parents don't have high school educations, the authors report that they have "a bleak future, regardless of whether they live with one or both parents." Similar findings across many other dimensions of child well-being lead McLanahan and Sandefur to conclude that family structure is one among several related factors—including race and parental education levels—affecting the risks that American children encounter.

When children of never-married mothers are studied, their experiences are often lumped together with those of divorced, separated, or widowed mothers. This makes it difficult to separate out some of the more distinct factors that arise from their different situations. And the bulk of what we know about the impact of having and raising children outside of marriage emerges out of research involving poorly educated young mothers who have few resources and many of whom are members of racial or ethnic minorities. Because out-of-wedlock birth has become as likely a route to single motherhood as divorce only within the past decade, there remains much to be learned about the specific risk factors facing children whose lives begin in this way. This is especially true when it comes to finding out more about the family lives of never-married women who are older, better educated, and more financially secure when they have children on their own. If the children are not raised in poverty, will the consequences of unmarried motherhood be different?

Unmarried Motherhood as We Greet the Twenty-first Century

Statistical portraits inform us of similarities and differences among large groups of people. What they cannot do is elucidate the day-to-day circumstances or personal decisions of the individuals who make up the groups. Individuals' voices become mute. Their motivations remain mysterious. Only by listening to the voices of unmarried mothers will we be able to learn why their lives headed them down this path and what they worry about now that they are parents. Yet few of those who speak out vehemently about the social consequences these families' lives present spend much time listening to what these mothers have to say. That seems an important thing to do, regardless of what one thinks from afar about these women and the families they've created.

3

Having a Baby: Unmarried Adolescent Mothers

"Anna. You busy?"

Hearing Debbie's familiar voice startles Anna. They spoke only a month or so ago. At the time Debbie was recovering from an early miscarriage. Anna remembers how she tried to appear sympathetic, even though she actually felt relieved that Debbie wouldn't be having another baby right then. At seventeen, Debbie is already caring for her two-year-old daughter, a beautiful child with unforgettable brown eyes. They live in an apartment in a house specially designed for teenage mothers and children. They depend on welfare. When she was fourteen and pregnant, Debbie left school. Despite coaxing from Anna and others, she has not returned, at least not on any consistent basis. She always has some excuse, usually related to the chaos of her single-parenting life.

"Come on in," Anna says, gesturing Debbie toward a molded plastic chair across from her desk.

At twenty-four, Anna is several years older than the teenage girls she counsels on family planning at this Boston hospital clinic. Anna's reassuring manner conveys the maturity she's grown into after a difficult adolescence. In her stylish sweater-and-pants outfits, with her lips brightened by deep shades of red or pink, and gold sparkling bracelets dangling against her dark skin, Anna looks to those she counsels like a model of sophistication.

Debbie fidgets in her chair, sweeping her long, brown, curly hair behind her, as Anna searches for clues as to what this unscheduled visit might be about. She knows Debbie well enough not to read too much into her sad and withdrawn expression. Debbie rarely smiles—even, Anna has noticed, when her words reveal she is happy.

"Can I close the door?" Debbie asks, her voice soft and hesitant. Anna nods, and Debbie extends her right arm to nudge the office door shut.

Anna met Debbie several years ago, a few months before she got pregnant with her daughter. She was barely a teenager, but she hinted to Anna how much she wanted to be a mother. Her friends were having babies. She wanted to dress a baby of her own in frilly, doll-like outfits. Most of all, she wanted to push her around the neighborhood in a stroller and show her off as her friends did their babies. "She hated that they had babies and she didn't," Anna explains. When she was pregnant, all Debbie thought about was how much she wanted her baby to be a girl.

Anna hears this refrain about wanting to have a baby so often that she can finish a girl's sentence once she utters the first words. Desire for a little someone to hold and to love, for a baby who will love her, who will belong to her, who will stay with her, is strong. It is difficult for Anna to find words powerful enough to convince girls to act against this urge. That doesn't mean she stops trying. Again and again Anna tries to find ways to deliver the message that girls would do better to put off motherhood until they are further along in their own lives, when they are married and can better handle the responsibilities of being a parent. Few take her advice to heart.

"Having sex can open up a lot of doors for you."

With the door closed, Anna's corner office seems especially small; her big metal desk eats up most of the space, and only a few feet separate her and Debbie. Anna's walls are blanketed with messages about delaying pregnancy and warnings about sexually transmitted diseases. A black-and-white poster behind her chair declares, "Having Sex Can Open Up a Lot of Doors for You." The doors pictured lead into a maternity ward, familiar territory for many of Anna's visitors. Over Anna's right shoulder, a rainbow of pamphlets hangs, thumbtacked to a shelf; each one discusses a different kind of contraceptive. Anna keeps the real items locked in a cabinet in a corner of her office.

Anna's job is to be someone with whom these teenagers can be comfortable in talking about their lives and reproductive decisions. One problem is that girls don't get to her until they are already sexually active;

Anna cannot remember any girl coming to speak with her before having sexual intercourse. Even so, Anna begins by trying to explain the benefits of now abstaining from sex. Those conversations usually end with Anna feeling the sense of futility Epimetheus must have felt when he tried to close Pandora's box. Three years of experience have persuaded Anna that the best help she can give most of these girls is to convince them to protect themselves from both pregnancy and sexually transmitted diseases such as gonorrhea. Even this is difficult.

Debbie, like many girls Anna talks with, is steadfast in her refusal to rely on any contraceptive except condoms, and she uses those only on occasion. The last time they talked, Debbie told Anna she depended on her boyfriend to use a condom. By now Anna knows that when a teenager like Debbie says her boyfriend is the one responsible for contraception, condoms are probably not being used much of the time. Girls often worry more about the possibility of making their boyfriend angry by demanding that he use a condom than they do about an unplanned pregnancy. Debbie's attitude toward a third pregnancy seemed to Anna one of indifference. Whenever Anna mentioned her concerns about the possibility, Debbie shrugged as if to say, "If it happens, it happens."

If Anna suggested the use of other contraceptives, Debbie fired back excuses. Foam was "too messy," and she absolutely ruled out Anna's suggestion that six matchstick-sized capsules of Norplant, a time-release contraceptive, be, as she liked to put it, "stuck" in her arm. Birth control pills nauseate her. And like many girls her age, Debbie lets Anna know how "icky" it is to touch her genital area. The mere mention of vaginal inserts, a diaphragm, or contraceptive sponges was greeted by an expression mixing horror with disdain.

These days Debbie's desire for another baby, which she mentioned to Anna before her miscarriage, arose not from the wish to fit in with her friends but from the hope of cementing her relationship with Eddie, her twenty-two-year-old boyfriend. Debbie was certain that if she had Eddie's baby, he would stay in her life, unlike her first baby's father. Debbie presented Anna with her evidence: Eddie displayed his paternal responsibility by visiting with and providing for a child he'd had with another woman. Anna tried to point out to Debbie the obvious fact she was overlooking: Eddie isn't *with* his other child's mother. But Debbie saw only what she wanted to see: Eddie was taking some responsibility for his child, and he was now *her* boyfriend.

Rarely will a girl come right out and announce to Anna that she's actively trying to get pregnant. Most girls are savvy enough to know that, as close to Anna as they may feel, she will not hesitate to voice harsh disapproval if she thinks they are trying to get pregnant. It took Anna a while to learn, but by now she is adept at reading behind a girl's words and deciphering her intent. When Anna thinks she senses an intent to get pregnant, she tries to apply proper doses of frankness, empathy, and persuasion to underscore her points about the difficulties of early parenting without driving the girl away. Intricate strategizing is required over which words to use and how to phrase certain questions if Anna is to connect with these adolescents. For Anna, making this connection is her only chance, if she has one at all, of derailing a pregnancy that otherwise seems inevitable.

"Okay. I'm pregnant again."

"So, what's up?" Anna asks.

"Well, I have some news," Debbie responds. Her brown eyes remain fixed on the floor.

Anna looks across her desk at Debbie. Suddenly, she knows why the girl is here.

"Please! Please! Tell me you're not going to say what I think you're going to say!" Anna implores.

"Fine. I won't say it."

"If this is a joke, it's a very bad one," Anna goes on. "Really, what can I do for you? Why are you here today?"

"You know why," Debbie says.

These quick volleys back and forth provoke Anna to start sounding as angry as she is starting to look: "No, I don't," she snaps.

The word "pregnant" is suspended somewhere between them, unspoken but fully present.

"Yes, you do," Debbie says.

"No. You're going to have to tell me." Anna's tone is commanding.

Debbie is now also getting angry. "I don't have to say it. You know why I'm here."

"No," Anna tells her. "I remember talking with you not too long ago. And we were talking about you preventing another pregnancy. So you're not here for that." Anna can barely contain her anger.

"Okay. I'm pregnant again," Debbie declares. In deference, perhaps, to Anna's soured mood, she sounds more apologetic than proud.

Anna lifts herself up from her chair, looking as though she's ready to speak, but then sinks down again. "Let me just sit here for a second," she says, tapping her sculpted bright-red nails on her desk. She needs time to think.

"They just think this is like a Cinderella thing."

When Anna was seventeen years old, she was pregnant, too. Her pregnancy was a careless mistake, the kind an adolescent makes when sex is a forbidden adventure, advice about contraceptives isn't handy, and consequences seem far away. She and her boyfriend had discovered sexual intercourse one hot afternoon on a cot in her mother's attic. Nearly a year later, after having sex about once a week, she found out she was pregnant. Given what she knows now, Anna is surprised it didn't happen sooner, since she and her boyfriend relied on the "pulling out" method. It was, she told me, their ignorance, not some burning desire for a baby, that made her become a mother too soon.

Anna remembers one afternoon during her pregnancy with particular clarity. She cried often after she found out she was going to have a baby, but this time she cried so much her eyes hurt. She was alone in her room, praying for a signal of what she should do, and she felt something move inside her. At that moment, she says, she decided to have her baby, though she had no intention of getting married to the father. "I don't want to get married," Anna told her boyfriend's family and her own when they assembled in her living room to discuss their children's predicament. "I'm too young to get married." None of the relatives disagreed. And neither Anna nor her parents ever considered putting her child up for adoption. Somehow, they would all find a way to raise this child within their family.

Anna's daughter is now seven. They still live in Anna's mother's house, not by choice but out of economic necessity. Anna received welfare for a while when she was still attending high school and after graduation, before she found a job. Today, the salary she is able to earn without a college degree is not sufficient for her and her daughter to live on their own. She tried going to college classes to study nursing, but between her parenting responsibilities and her full-time job, and given her proclivity for procrastination, it has not worked out. Anna knows how lucky she is to have had family help with child care so she could finish high school. If she didn't have that degree, she'd be filing papers or answering telephones, and she'd be lucky to have even that job. Anna feels sadness for Debbie, who doesn't have the kind of family support she did. Anna knows that by the time Debbie wakes up to the limitations imposed by her lack of education, some opportunities to change her circumstances will have passed her by. And if Debbie continues to have more children, making progress in her own life will become steadily more difficult.

There are many times when Anna looks across her desk at a pregnant teenager and sees herself. She knows this girl cannot possibly grasp how dramatically a baby is going to change her life. She didn't. And from experience Anna knows that, even when she tries to explain this, a teenage girl, focused on impending motherhood, isn't at all likely to hear her. But when Anna shares stories of the chaos of her early parenting days, she believes her words just might reach a few girls. When she speaks with groups of teenage girls who aren't pregnant, she sometimes tells them how nighttime feedings and daytime child-care responsibilities ate up her time and made her so tired that she didn't have the stamina to stay in high school.

Anna was a good student, and her mother, who always tried to keep her focused on her studies and away from bad influences in her neighborhood, pushed her not to give up. Anna heard the message again and again: if she was to have a productive future, she needed to graduate from high school. Anna knows that many of the girls she talks with don't have someone they feel close to giving them this consistent message, so she tries to do it. But Anna knows that even though she believed what her mother told her about staying in school, parenthood overwhelmed her. Only thanks to her grandmother's around-the-clock help with child care was Anna able to graduate.

"I can sit here and preach all day about what it is like to bring up a child. These girls just have no idea. No idea." Anna shakes her head in dismay. "Their friends who have babies, they don't tell each other the bad points. They don't share the negative aspects of raising a child. Instead it's like, 'Oh, yeah, I buy him little Nike sneakers and I get a check each month and food stamps and, yeah, the baby's father is around and he's helping out.'" Anna mimics the squeaky, insincere voice of a teenage girl. "They just think this is like a Cinderella thing," Anna continues, sounding cross. "It just does not happen. It just doesn't."

But when Anna tries to explain the hard work of child-rearing, the girls' expressions often let her know the message isn't sinking in. Instead of the dismal picture her words paint, the girls see in her life a portrait of success. As impressionable teenagers see it, Anna has achieved the kind of life they can only dream of for themselves. They don't absorb the lessons Anna tries to teach them about how tough it's been for her to get even this far.

Many girls can't understand, either, how constrained are Anna's prospects for advancement: unless she goes to college, Anna won't be able to find a better-paying job. Nor can these teenagers comprehend how difficult it is for Anna and her daughter to get by on her salary. That Anna owns a secondhand car seems so exciting to a teenager that she will not take in Anna's stories about how often she has to take that car off the road because she cannot pay for a repair or the insurance. And Anna's stylish clothes, her sparkling jewelry, her exotic hairstyles and sculpted nails—all signal success in the eyes of the young who stare back at her. Teenage girls can't be faulted if they see in Anna someone who is a young and unmarried mother but whose life declares, "I'm making it." Anna wishes she felt that way inside.

Anna's pride keeps tucked away the more wrenching aspects of her single-parenting life. Her desire not to dwell on them isn't different from that of the teenage mothers she spoke of earlier, who don't share with one another the less pleasant sides of their parenting experience. Not until Anna and I have known each other for more than a year does she pull open a desk drawer at home to reveal to me a stack of collection-agency notices, many still in sealed envelopes. Why open them? She knows she can't pay the bills. Anna rarely allows herself to cry in front of me, but once she wiped a few tears away as she told me about how difficult it is to figure out how she can work full-time, attend college, find time to study, and still take care of her daughter and herself. Days are not long enough, nor does she have the perseverance she knows such an effort would demand.

She wishes teenage girls could be made to understand how hard early motherhood is, while they can still prevent a pregnancy from occurring. "A lot of them talk about this baby like it's going to be a play doll," she says, with a long sigh. "They sound like I did before my daughter was born. I never knew that babies wake you up at night."

"There's no excuse! You know I'm here."

Anna stares at Debbie, and her rage builds. She tries to mask her anger with sarcasm: "You know what's really funny? I swear I heard you say you are pregnant. Please correct me if I'm wrong."

Debbie is silent.

"What are you planning to do?" Anna asks.

"I don't know." Debbie stutters as she tries to respond. "I have to talk to Eddie and find out how he feels. I mean, I know how he feels, but now that it has happened, I gotta talk to him."

"So what do you want from me?" Anna asks abruptly.

"I want prenatal care," Debbie says to her, though she knows those arrangements are made by someone else at the clinic. It is clear to Anna that what Debbie wants most is her support.

"Go make an appointment," Anna says, with crisp finality.

"Anna, what's wrong?"

"Go make your appointment," Anna says.

"What's wrong?"

Anna inhales, deeply. Debbie's eyes now stare into hers. From somewhere deep inside Anna, words force their way up and emerge with explosive velocity.

"How could you do this? How could you? There is no excuse. I mean, you had a baby the first time because you said you wanted one. You left school. You're living in a shelter. Then you have a miscarriage. I mean, Debbie, God is trying to help you out here, but you're not doing anything to help yourself. Do not even try to tell me there was a weak moment. You know about condoms. Whatever excuse you have for me today is bullshit. You can always find me. I mean, I give you condoms. You know I'm here."

Anna's voice is both plaintive and angry. "You have no excuse," she concludes.

"I know you're mad at me," Debbie says, quietly.

"No, I am not mad at you." Anna averts her eyes from Debbie's sad face. "I'm not even going to use the word 'disappointed' to describe how I feel right now. But I'm feeling something, and it's not love. There is just no excuse. I mean, you know me. You tell me you are comfortable talking with me. I tell you about how hard my life is with one child and doing it on my own. Now you go and do this. I'll tell you what it feels like to me: like I've been stabbed in the heart. That's how I feel."

Debbie squirms in her plastic chair as Anna's verbal barrage comes at her—faster, louder, harsher than anything Debbie has heard from her before.

"You know you aren't ready to have another child!" Anna yells. "You don't have a pot to piss in, or even a window of your own to throw it out of. And you, you are going to take on another baby?"

Anna is trying to get Debbie to realize how preposterous that seems, but by now she can hear herself yelling at the girl. She doesn't mean to sound so angry, even if she feels it, so she reins her voice in. But her words still tumble out: "I mean, if I got pregnant again, I don't know what I'd do. And I have a car. I have a job. I live with my mother. Still, I have a hard time managing. One of these days maybe you'll wake up and get a dose of reality. And I hope for all your sakes it happens soon. I mean, this is your third pregnancy. There's no excuse. Just no excuse."

"I can't take care of another child right now."

A few weeks later Debbie invites Anna to dinner at her mother's house. Debbie's mother, who speaks Spanish and not much English, listens to their conversation. Eddie is there, too, and as the evening evolves, Anna begins to suspect that Debbie invited her so that she would show support for her pregnancy and make her boyfriend feel more at ease with it. However, Anna is not willing to be cast in this role, especially after she hears Eddie explain to Debbie what it feels like to him to be expecting another child.

"I'm breaking my ass right now trying to come up with money to make ends meet. It's really hard," says Eddie, a tall man with a muscular build and a mustache. He works as a mechanic. Recently he completed a general equivalency diploma (GED), an option for those who don't graduate from high school. "I can't take care of another child right now. You know I'm trying to go back to school," Eddie tells Debbie. "You know all this about me, and still you don't want to take my feelings into consideration."

Their conversation goes back and forth in patterns that Anna can tell are familiar ones. Clearly, this is not the first time Debbie has heard Eddie say this. Nor, Anna suspects, does Eddie have any hope that by repeating these concerns he'll convince Debbie to change her mind about having this baby. Each seems to be performing a well-rehearsed role for Anna.

Just as Anna spoke harshly to Debbie in her office, she now challenges Eddie. Why didn't he make sure to use a condom if he didn't want to have another child? she wants to know. While she admires his determination to be responsible for his child, she wonders why he allowed Debbie's pregnancy to happen when he has these other financial obligations as well as plans for his own life.

"I mean, you have a job, and I'm pretty sure you could've said to Debbie, 'We can't have sex until we go buy condoms,' " Anna says to Eddie. "And yet you chose not to do all you could to avoid this situation."

After a long pause, Eddie responds: "Well, I trusted her. And she knows how I feel."

"You need to stop right there," Anna tells him. "If you wanted to be alive tomorrow, would you put your life in someone else's hands, someone you weren't sure of?"

"No," Eddie says.

"Fine," Anna says. "I rest my case."

"Maybe, just maybe, this time she'll use it!"

Several months later Debbie has her second child. Her labor is long and difficult. When their broad-shouldered son arrives, weighing eight pounds, nine ounces, Eddie is in the delivery room. But when Debbie leaves the hospital, she and her baby return to live with her other child at the group home.

Before she leaves the hospital, Debbie visits Anna in her office and tells her about a hearing she has set up to try to get an apartment. Eddie is going to move in with her, she tells Anna, but the welfare department won't be informed. If welfare officials find out Eddie lives with Debbie, her assistance will stop even though he doesn't earn nearly enough to support her, the two children, and his other daughter.

Anna refuses to let Debbie leave without talking to her about preventing another pregnancy. "You know, Debbie, we've spent so much time talking about all of this, you could probably sit here and counsel *me* about this stuff," Anna says.

"I'm thinking about using Depo-Provera," Debbie replies. Her determined tone of voice surprises Anna. An injection of Depo-Provera would give Debbie three months of contraceptive protection. But Anna reminds Debbie that if she does this, she must also use a condom to prevent transmission of a sexual disease.

"One of my friends had that shot," Debbie says. "Do you have stuff that tells me about it?"

Anna reaches up to the shelf and hands Debbie a gray pamphlet about Depo-Provera. In case Debbie forgets to return for her appointment in two weeks, Anna puts together a bundle of condoms and tosses into the bag some contraceptive foam. Anna thinks to herself: "Maybe, just maybe, this time she'll use it!"

"Being pregnant. It's something that changes you inside more than outside."

When I ask Anna to reflect on what it's been like to counsel Debbie, the first thing she tells me is how regrettably typical her situation is. Debbie is like so many of the other young, unmarried girls Anna knows who are having babies. Like the others, Debbie didn't have any clear sense of where she wanted her life to go when she embarked on the road out of childhood. She wasn't doing well in school and, in the chaos and anonymity of early adolescence, she all but gave up trying. By then, too, she stopped being able to find comfort in her deteriorating relationship with her mother. Poverty surrounded her. Her father was not around. Friends became her family, and lots of them were having babies. In her eyes, becoming a mother didn't seem an abnormal thing to do.

It is, as Anna knows so well, girls whose outlook and upbringing resemble Debbie's who are likelier to engage in sexual intercourse early in adolescence and then use contraception erratically or not at all. As a result, even though teenagers from poor and low-income families account for less than 40 percent of adolescent females, nearly three-quarters of girls who get pregnant come from such economic backgrounds. And when adolescents become pregnant, girls who grew up in poverty and aren't doing well in school decide more often than their prosperous, academically successful peers to have and to raise their babies. About 60 percent of poor, pregnant teenagers, and nearly half of low-income adolescents who conceive a child, decide not to have an abortion; only a fourth of their better-off peers make the same decision.* The result of these progressive stages of decision-making—first about sexual activity, second about contraceptive use, and then about abortion—is that 85 percent of the adolescents who become mothers begin parenthood at severe economic and academic disadvantage. For these girls, giving birth is not the entry point to these problems; sadly, it is a predictable continuation.

The prevalence of births to poor teenagers who are barely able to take care of themselves leaves Anna despondent. She can try, as she did with Debbie, to persuade girls to postpone motherhood, and she can give them the means to do so. But Anna, by herself, cannot manufacture motivation. This must come from the fabric of girls' lives. When a girl doesn't receive ongoing guidance and support from family members, attention from teachers, and consistent concern from mentors, it's tough for her to construct a strong belief in her own potential and develop feelings of belonging that she will not look to a baby to fulfill. It is said that if teenagers had to take a pill to get pregnant, the number of births to them would be minuscule. This is probably true. Motivation and follow-through are key ingredients that many teenagers who get pregnant lack.

Perhaps when Debbie was nine or ten years old she, like many youngsters, still trusted in the possibility of molding her talents to meet her own goals. But early in adolescence such beliefs have a habit of slipping away,

---

*The term "poor" refers to those whose income falls below the official, federal poverty line, while "low-income" is generally taken to refer to working individuals and families whose income is close to the poverty line.

especially from youngsters who live in neighborhoods where violence is only one wrong turn away and who attend schools where their failure becomes just another in a long list of reasons why no one seems to care. Ambition can die young. And when adolescent girls let go of their dreams, as Debbie clearly has, motivating them to postpone motherhood becomes, as Anna admits, nearly impossible—especially when having a baby seems to offer an alternative route to becoming a "woman."

Anna thinks that if some of these girls knew just one adult in whom they felt they could confide, they might trust in the guidance they receive and might see a way toward a different future. A sense of belonging can push away a girl's feelings of wanting a baby who will belong to her. "Maybe if once a month they had someone to take them on a little picnic or ice-skating, just something where they are spending time together," says Anna. She reminds me of the really difficult relationships many of these girls have within their own families. "If they need advice or help, they can pick up the phone and call this person. Just someone who wants to be there and they don't have to feel obligated to. Just to have a friend's shoulder to cry on." Such relationships help girls construct ladders to the future upon which adult companions can help them advance step by guided step.

As I listen to Anna talk about all of this, words spoken to me a decade earlier by a fourteen-year-old girl named Michelle replay themselves in my head. At the time I met Michelle, I was in San Francisco reporting a *Time* magazine cover story, "Children Having Children." Michelle would become a teen mother in three weeks. Her pregnancy, she said, had done for her what nothing else ever had: it had jolted her into planning for her own future. Michelle was now earning extra money by typing, and was thinking about finding a clerical job so she could support herself and her child. "I have to get my money together and think about my future," she said. It was easy to forget she was only fourteen. "Instead of just thinking about tomorrow, now I have to think ahead," Michelle went on to say. "Like in years. I mean, I used to think, 'Ten years from now I'll be twenty-four.' Now I think, 'Ten years from now, I'll be twenty-four and my child will be ten.' " Michelle paused before she said the words that had etched our conversation in my mind: "Being pregnant. It's something that changes you inside more than outside."

Now, in talking with Anna, a woman who understands the transformative power of early motherhood, the wisdom of what Michelle told me resurfaces. Anna explains to me how much easier her task would be if the girls who come to her were carrying inside them some sense of hope about what their present and future lives hold. Anna and I are far from alone in realizing how central this inner belief in one's own potential seems to be in the prevention of early pregnancies. Leon Dash, a *Washington Post* reporter who spent seventeen months getting to know poor, black teens and talking with them about pregnancy and parenting, concluded that for many of them "a child was a tangible achievement in otherwise dreary and empty lives."

Teachers and guidance counselors—actually, anyone who spends a good deal of time with poor and unmotivated adolescents—can testify to how hope diminishes in many youngsters as they travel through adolescence. In 1995, the Carnegie Council on Adolescent Development observed in its report "Great Transitions" that, "Especially in low-income neighbor-hoods where good education and jobs are scarce, young people can grow up with a bleak sense of the future." And hope about one's own future, it turns out, is an often missing but absolutely essential ingredient if sexual abstinence is to be chosen or contraception used. As Marian Wright Edelman, whose Children's Defense Fund once led a national campaign to prevent teenage pregnancy, is fond of saying, "The best contraceptive is a real future." Anna's experience bears this out. Debbie, for example, had plenty of knowledge about how to prevent a pregnancy, and she had access to the means to do it. What she did not have was the desire and discipline to use what she knew. That hope and motivation seem so essential in this process worries Anna, for she knows that these two ingredients are not possible for her to prescribe.

"I keep saying to myself that I could have done more in helping Debbie prevent this," Anna says to me, shaking her head in dismay. "But really I don't know how. People seem to learn only by making their own mistakes. Honestly, I don't see a very bright future for Debbie. I really don't. I don't see her going back to school. She tells me she'll get a GED, but I don't think she's going to do it. Besides, a GED won't get her a good job. Debbie is like a lot of girls these days. They just don't see how important education can be. The important things to them are making sure their telephone doesn't get shut off, getting an apartment, being on their own. Sometimes I want to just shake them and shake them and scream at them, 'Don't do it. Don't do it!' "

"A good role model, that's what these girls need."

Anna's frustration is suffused with anger at her own failure. When I ask her to imagine how it might be possible to reach the girls she counsels, Anna leans back in her chair and is silent, as though she's trying to conjure up some magic formula she hasn't tried. What nags at her is the feeling she described earlier—the sense of how different things might be for the girls if, when they were younger, a parent, teacher, or coach, someone they came to trust, had planted inside them expansive visions of possibilities, then stuck around long enough to help them turn those visions into reality.

"A good role model, that's what these girls need," Anna says. "Someone who is really going to be there for them." But this is not something Anna can hand to these girls from the cabinet in the corner of her office; finding dedicated adults can be the hardest thing for some of these girls to do.

Because I am a sailor, Anna's words create for me an image of a boat settling in at anchor, its coiled line slipping loop by loop into the stormy waters of these girls' adolescent years. To me, the loops represent parts of a girl's vision of her future. If a young girl strings together enough of those loops by the time adolescence arrives, the anchor line—still attached to caring and reliable adults—will reach deep enough to dig in securely as the currents of teenage desires and pressures toss her about.

As Anna shares these frustrations, a rumbling laugh works its way up from her belly and bursts forth. I recall the meeting with Debbie when Anna's fury exploded across this same desk and landed in the chair that I'm occupying. Today the anger is gone, but the exasperation remains.

"No way you can get them to not have a baby," Anna says. "No way. No way. I know, because I've tried."

What's Changed Since the 1950s? It's Not the Number of Births to Teenage Mothers but the Absence of Marriage.

Anna's exasperation is shared by an American public grown weary of looking at the pregnant bellies of teenage girls. And Anna's anger reverberates in the reluctance now being voiced by many to transform their tax dollars into these young women's welfare checks. That streams of weariness and anger are converging in the minds of so many reflects a woeful reality: despite a hodgepodge of efforts to reduce births to teenagers, our nation's adolescent girls have babies at a much higher rate than those of any other industrialized country. Today, one in four black women and one in seven white women are already mothers by the time they reach the age of twenty. Of more concern to some observers is the relatively recent and rapid increase of out-of-wedlock births among teenage girls, and how many of these children are being raised without their fathers' involvement. Add to these ingredients the fact that increasing numbers of teenage mothers are white and are younger, on average, than their counterparts of a few decades ago, and one better understands the broadening of societal concern.

Casual observers of the rhetorical battles now being waged over teenage motherhood can easily emerge with mistaken impressions. Words and numbers get tossed around haphazardly, often for the sake of sustaining an argument. For example, the word "epidemic" is often used to describe the present-day level of teenage births. Yet "epidemic" makes it seem as if a scourge of some sort has suddenly invaded our lives. This is not the case. In fact, fewer babies were born to teenagers in 1995 than in 1950, 1960, 1970, 1980, or 1990.

Compare what we think of as a quiescent year, 1956—a year when television's most famous married couple, Lucy and Desi, slept in twin beds—to 1995, the most recent year for which data are available. In 1956, a few more than 525,000 teenage girls gave birth. Thirty-nine years later, with a larger population of teenage girls, more birth control options, and legalized abortion, 513,062 babies were born to teen mothers, more than 10,000 *fewer* than in 1956. And the rate at which teenagers give birth has also decreased. In 1956, there were ninety births for every thousand girls between the ages of fifteen and nineteen. By 1985, the rate at which teenagers gave birth fell to a low point of 50.2 per thousand. The next year, the teenage birthrate began to climb again, and by 1991 it reached 62.1 per thousand—still considerably less than in the mid-1950s. And as the 1990s got under way, the teenage birthrate dropped slightly, the first time this had happened since 1986. It is still too soon to know if the small yearly declines represent the beginning of a prolonged downturn, or only a blip in the recent climb.

What is very different today, however, from what happened several decades ago is that many fewer teenage mothers are married. In 1956, less than 15 percent of births to teenagers occurred out of wedlock. Now, in the 1990s, the figure is more than 70 percent. Most of this dramatic turnaround has happened during the last twenty-five years. In 1970, 70 percent of births to teenage mothers occurred within a marriage. Then, during each year of the 1980s, there was a rise in the rate of of nonmarital births to teens. By 1994, 76 percent of all births to teenagers happened outside of a marriage. In recent years, births to unmarried teens have increased faster among whites than among blacks. But today the proportion of out-of-wedlock births to black teenagers is, as it has always been, considerably higher than among whites.

"Few of [these young mothers] expect to marry and nearly all want at least one other child."

The reasons that young mothers don't get married are tangled up in the web of social, cultural, and economic transformations our nation has experienced since the end of World War II. Social attitudes have changed: premarital sex is now more widely accepted, especially among the young. And with the onset of menstruation occurring earlier than it did decades ago (on average, when girls are around twelve) and the age of first marriage delayed until the mid-twenties, young women today have a larger window of time during which sexual relations take place in the absence of marriage. When a pregnancy does happen, the stigma of unwed motherhood is dissipated by the existence of many similar-looking families created by divorce. And, like some older women, teenage girls express some reluctance to get married when they don't believe expectations about their partners will be fulfilled. After all, many of these girls have collected evidence during their childhoods confirming the instability of marriage and the lack of promise it sometimes holds for economic security.

Two centuries ago the statesman and philosopher Benjamin Franklin remarked on the connection between a thriving economy and the likelihood of marriage. Franklin's words apply to much that is happening today: "The number of marriages . . . is greater in proportion to the ease and convenience of supporting a family. When families can be easily supported, more persons marry and earlier in life."

Especially among young people, this economic fact accounts in large measure for why fewer are getting married than did two decades ago. Hourly wages for young male workers have fallen sharply since the 1970s, as has the ability to secure steady employment, particularly for those with only a high school diploma. The most precipitous drops in wages—and rises in unemployment—have occurred among young men, especially minorities, who have dropped out of high school; many of these men are the fathers of the children of young, single mothers.

The Census Bureau reported in 1992 that nearly half of full-time workers between the ages of eighteen and twenty-four—the age at which most men become the fathers of children born to teenage mothers—were earning less than a poverty-level wage for a family of four. A 1995 study released by the Annie E. Casey Foundation reported that from 1969 to 1993 the percentage of twenty-five- to thirty-four-year-old men whose salaries could not support a four-person family more than doubled, reaching almost 33 percent. Not surprisingly, the proportion of children who live in female-headed households doubled as fewer marriages between young parents took place. Both these upward trends existed whether the young men and families were African-American, Hispanic, or non-Hispanic white, though (as is often the case) more minority families confronted these economic realities and suffered them more severely. During these same years, women's wages either rose, or didn't fall as rapidly as men's. More women also moved into the labor force, and the gap between women's and men's earnings narrowed. These circumstances have had vast repercussions in how men and women perceive their ability to form a family and what their role within it ought to be. Young men who are not able to fulfill a breadwinning role often have difficulty finding ways to fit themselves into families and remain a consistent presence in their children's lives.

But it is not only the economic equation that is altering ways in which young people think about marriage. Views about marriage as an emotional partnership are also shifting. Young men's and women's expectations of each other, as well as their trust in each other, have been undergoing enormous changes, most of which have not moved adolescents in the direction of embracing marriage. Many young single mothers, like their potential partners, grew up during an era of intensifying marital instability. Many explain that they're willing to forgo marriage when the man with whom they've had a child is not going to contribute anything more than his name to make the child "legitimate," though no young mother I spoke with ever used this word. Teenagers often portray the young men they have children with as "selfish," more a source of problems than of benefits in their lives.

At a time when teenage mothers are eschewing marriage, broader debates are also taking place about whether marriage, as the bedrock institution of family life, is in need of a major overhaul. In the view of some, marriage—as defined by traditional gender roles—is constraining and antiquated, like a tired, squeaky vehicle in which the gears no longer shift to meet this engine's new demands. Some women feel squeezed by conventional attitudes men hold about them and by the propensity some men have to try to control what they do. One very young mother who returned the engagement ring her boyfriend gave her told me that if she'd married him she would not have finished high school. "He wanted me to be at home with the baby. That's what his mother did," she said. "He didn't want me to stay in high school." She is now in college, still unmarried.

In poor communities, both urban and rural, out-of-wedlock births are becoming a typical teenage experience. In her book *Black Teenage Mothers: Pregnancy and Child-rearing from Their Perspective*, Constance

Willard Williams, a professor at the Family and Children's Policy Center at Brandeis University, describes what she learned during extensive interviews with thirty teenage mothers. They do not, Williams writes, "view early childbearing as having ruined their lives, and they see themselves . . . as capable of rearing children without marriage or a commitment from the father. Few of them expect to marry and nearly all want at least one other child."

"Black women, illegitimately pregnant, were not shamed but simply blamed."

Nowadays one of the most noticeable changes in teen births is that white adolescent mothers usually decide not to get married *and* not to place their children for adoption, as a large percentage of them did until the 1970s. Among their black peers, adoption and marriage have always been less common responses to unintended pregnancy; instead, families absorbed the children into their lives and communities. But as the stigma attached to unwed motherhood has diminished, many more young white mothers decide to raise children they bore.

The racial disparity in such decision-making did not result solely from individual choice. Pregnant girls' decisions were often dictated by the options offered by societal institutions and by the public's perspective about why they'd gotten pregnant. As recently as three decades ago, unmarried white women were shepherded into maternity homes to receive "redemptive" care. Black peers weren't welcomed at these often segregated homes—and that fact reflected the societal myths devised to explain how and why unmarried girls of different races became pregnant. Rickie Solinger, in her 1992 book, *Wake Up Little Susie: Single Pregnancy and Race Before Roe v. Wade*, explains that white girls were regarded as having made "mistakes," which could be "cured" if they received care and counseling. However, young, unmarried black women who got pregnant were regarded as hypersexual. Among them, pregnancy was "the product of uncontrolled, sexual indulgence"; the girls themselves were regarded as "unredeemable."

As often is the case, the way something is viewed determines how it is treated. White women, because people believed their lives could be turned around, were provided with therapeutic care. To "restore" themselves, the women had to relinquish their babies for adoption. Counselors at maternity homes provided soothing words, and at times threatening ones as well, in order to convince the young women to do so. The girls were then taught proper "feminine" skills so that when they went home their lives would resume as though nothing had happened; they could begin anew the pursuit of marriage and family. On the other hand, black women who were pregnant and unwed wore the unerasable stigma of immorality, something no amount of counseling could remove. There was no reason to send them to maternity homes: their immoral behavior was construed to be biologically driven and therefore unchangeable.

During these years public sentiment about unmarried motherhood included a mixture of shame, anger, and blame, depending on the race of the girl who was pregnant. "Black women, illegitimately pregnant, were not shamed but simply blamed," Solinger writes, "blamed for the population explosion, for escalating welfare costs, for the existence of unwanted babies, and blamed for the tenacious grip of poverty on blacks in America." During the early 1960s, in various states, policymakers concocted punitive, behaviorist "remedies" to deal with unwed motherhood. Because a clear majority of unmarried-female-headed families were black, there was no doubt at whom this regulatory approach was targeted. Laws were passed with the aim of eliminating what some characterized as "subsidized immorality," a sentiment that is hauntingly similar to what some conservatives today say is the primary goal of welfare reform. Some laws cut off welfare payments when children were born to mothers who were not married. Other states cobbled together so-called "suitable home" laws in order to give authorities justification in removing "illegitimate" children from homes or withdrawing financial support. Punishing women as well as children for out-of-wedlock births was thought by some to be an effective way to get these women to alter their reproductive and marital decision-making. But the goal of ending "illegitimacy" was one these laws failed to meet; the rate of out-of-wedlock births rose steadily.

These days sentiment about unwed motherhood runs a similar emotional gamut of shame, anger, and blame, though shame has receded a bit into the background. Still, many of the discussions now taking place in state legislatures and Washington, D.C., revolve around the issue of whether—and, if so, how—assistance ought to be designed to reverse the trend toward out-of-wedlock births. Efforts to do so include designing new regulations, reminiscent of these old ones, to cut off additional support to unwed mothers when another child is born. At the extreme edge of the current debate was discussion about providing no assistance at all to children born to unwed teenage mothers. Although scant evidence exists that such approaches serve their intended purpose, anger at and blame of unwed mothers are fueling this policy debate.

"If I didn't even like him and he bought me a car, whoosh, I'd get married."

It jolts me each time I hear a teenage mother say that right now is the "perfect time to have a baby." And I am continually surprised by young moms who tell me how ready they feel to be mothers but how unprepared they are to take on the role of wife. Marriage can wait, many of them tell me, until they are older.

"It's the perfect time to have a baby," Alicia, the nineteen-year-old mother of a fifteen-month-old son, told me one morning. Alicia became a mother when she was seventeen. She and I are spending time together at her school, an alternative program for parenting teens. Several classmates join us; each one is a mother, finishing high school, and also unmarried.

At first Alicia's words seem playful. She seems to be teasing me, testing the level of my naïveté. However, the longer we talk, the clearer it becomes that she actually believes that her teenage years are the "perfect time" for her to become a mother. She tells me her mother was nearly forty when she was born, the last of a dozen children. Her father died when she was four years old, so Alicia spent much of her childhood in the care of older siblings. "My mother never did nothin' with me," she says. Her conviction that her teenage years are the ideal time for motherhood arises, in part, from her need to feel as though she belongs to something, a family, and someone, in this case her child. Alicia ran away from home many times, and it really bothers her that her mother never seemed to notice or care. She believes, as other young mothers tell me they do, that being close in age to her child will give her more understanding of his life and enhance her ability as his mother.

Alicia doesn't think about marriage to her baby's father in similarly positive terms. "He gave me an engagement ring," she says, thrusting her left hand toward me so I can see the glass "stone" she wears on her ring finger. "He gave it to me when I was pregnant, but now, I don't think so. I mean he's not bad and he takes good care of me and stuff. Buys me clothes and sneakers and stuff. Same with the baby. I don't know. I guess I wouldn't mind marrying him. I feel out of love with him but I wouldn't mind marrying him." Her son's father is seventeen years old, unemployed, living with his mother who is on welfare, and collecting his own disability check because he lost an eye in a fight. Alicia boasts to her friends about how much time her boyfriend spends with his son—and how much the boyfriend enjoys it—but she makes no mention, when I ask her about marriage, of how their being together, or at least committed to each other, might benefit her son.

"If you were to think about marriage, would you rest your decision more on your baby's father being a provider or on whether you're in love with him?" I ask.

"Oh, I don't care whether I'm in love with him or not," Alicia replies. "It just doesn't matter." Her voice is now loud and commanding. "I mean what's love? Come on, now. I mean, if he bought me a wardrobe I'd be happy because I am very materialistic. If the guy told me he loved me and all this other stuff and I didn't even like him and he bought me a car, whoosh, I'd get married. If he bought me a house or something, we're set. It isn't like I'd go out and cheat on him or something."

"Would you put up with him cheating on you as long as he was buying you that car?" I ask Alicia, struck by her blatant attraction to material possessions.

"Well, if he wasn't living there but still buying me stuff, I could handle that," she says. "Yeah, who cares?"

"Get married? I never seen marriages stay together."

Alicia's views of marriage are shared by many of her contemporaries, many of whom experienced childhoods of material as well as emotional deprivation. But, as I learned in talking with other teen mothers, the reasons why they do not get married vary enormously.

Myieka is a seventeen-year-old unwed mother of a two-year-old son. And she is also six months pregnant; the baby she is expecting has the same father as her son. Her protruding belly is covered by an oversized shirt, so when we meet what I notice most about Myieka are the silver braces on her teeth. When Myieka smiles, her mouth sparkles. Her braces make her seem even younger than she is.

"Do you think about getting married?" I ask Myieka, after we've talked for a while.

Her brown eyes bulge with incredulity that I'd even ask her such a ridiculous question.

"Get married? I never seen marriages stay together. I never seen it," Myieka declares. "You know how they put it on TV, like in marriages everyone lives happily ever after. It's not really like that. I don't really see marriages get along. My grandparents have been together forever, but they're old. That's why I think they are still together. They are old. I just don't like it. My uncle was married. He is divorced now. My mother was married once before and she's married now, but I don't like the guy she married."

Myieka tells me that this stepfather tried to abuse her sexually, so she left her mother's home when she was fifteen and moved in with her aunt. Since then, she has rarely spoken to or seen her mother. The way Myieka sees it, her mother didn't care enough to protect her from this man, nor did she believe Myieka when she told her about the abuse. And her step-father controls her mother's life. Myieka saw no choice but to leave and sever all ties to her mother. After she moved into her aunt's house, Myieka started to spend time with a man who was eighteen years old. She got pregnant, had the child, and now lives with him. At twenty-one, he still hasn't graduated from high school and doesn't have a job. And Myieka doesn't want to marry him.

Myieka fits the profile of a young woman more likely than most to have a child when still in her teens. She is the daughter of a teenage mother, raised in poverty, abused by a family member, and without a trusting connection to any adult. That she hasn't gotten married harkens back, in part, to her childhood experiences. Her own mother dropped out of high school and did not marry Myieka's father. As a consequence, Myieka grew up in a poor neighborhood where few people she knew were married. She watched those who were have their marriages fall apart. And when her mother married for the first time, Myieka's family moved to another state and her life was uprooted. To her, marriage isn't a positive event; it is disruptive and dangerous. All that turmoil also sent confusing signals to her about whom and what she could depend on. At the same time, she wasn't getting many encouraging messages from family members about the value of education, nor were opportunities being presented for a different, more promising future. All this left Myieka susceptible to seeking companionship in early sex, to using contraception infrequently—in part because of her chaotic life—and to getting pregnant.

Myieka always disliked school; by the time she got pregnant, she was failing several subjects. "I didn't really care about an education," she says. "I just had to be there."

I ask Myieka if, when she was in high school, she made any connection between the classes she was taking and the chances she might have to find a well-paid job when she graduated. "I wasn't really seeing that then," she replies, lingering on the word "then." Myieka shakes her head and repeats herself. "I just wasn't seeing that then," she says, then turns quiet for a moment. "I see it different now."

Myieka left high school in the tenth grade. "I stopped because I was pregnant," she tells me. She transferred to what she calls "a pregnancy school" and completed the year. She then took courses at a GED program and passed her high school equivalency tests. Her diploma from the City Roots Alternative High School hangs on her living room wall, a sign of the pride she feels in this accomplishment. Myieka tells me how, to get her GED, she had to learn algebra, one of the many subjects she avoided during her regular school years. "The teacher in algebra was so stupid," she says, a look of disgust on her face. "We'd go in there and he'd just start puttin' stuff on the board. I didn't know what was going on, so I just never went."

How was it, I wondered, that she'd finally passed algebra? "Were your teachers at the alternative program better?" I ask.

"Yeah, they were real good. They'd work with you individually. If you needed extra help, they'd give it to you. They were real good. I liked them." It is clear that personal attention made a big difference in preparing Myieka for the GED tests.

Myieka also tells me that her attitude about school changed a lot after she'd been at home for a while, caring for her child and depending on welfare for her income. "I want to be somebody for me and my kids. I don't want to be sitting home all day like a welfare parent," she says, scowling at how this circumstance makes her feel. "You know, I don't like that. I don't want to be nobody. I want to have a job. Be somebody."

"He wanted to get married after we had the baby. But I don't like it. . . . I never wanted to get married."

Myieka sits next to me on a small, well-worn couch. Because of its tiny size and her expansive belly, she and I are squished together so tightly that when either of us turns an elbow out, we're touching. This couch is the only piece of furniture Myieka has to sit on in the L-shaped room that serves as her living room, dining room, and kitchen. A friend gave her the couch. She can't afford to buy furniture. Another friend has offered her a round table and metal folding chairs, but Myieka has no way to get them to her public-housing apartment. When we finish talking, I drive her a few miles down the road so she can pick up the table and chairs and finally have a place to sit down and eat with her family.

I ask Myieka to take me back to the time before she became pregnant with her son, when she was in high school and living sporadically with her aunt, then with friends. It was then that she began to have a sexual relationship with William, the man who would become the father of her two children.

"Did you think about getting pregnant?"

"No. Not really," Myieka responds.

"Did you think about *not* getting pregnant and ways you might prevent it from happening?" I ask, reframing the question as a way of trying to understand how she was thinking at the time.

"No," Myieka says, dispensing another of her customary sparse replies. Rarely does she elaborate on her answers, so it always feels as though I am pulling these words and thoughts out of her.

"You didn't think about it one way or the other?" I say, again.

"Right. That's true. Yeah."

"Did you know how you could get pregnant?"

"Yes."

"How did you know that?"

"My aunt told me if I had sex unprotected I'd get pregnant," she says.

This, a complete sentence, is the first one she's spoken today. She also looks over at me. Her customary monosyllabic answers, on the other hand, are accompanied by little eye contact.

"You knew what she meant by 'unprotected'?"

"Right. But I only had sex with his father," she says, glancing over toward her son. Myieka wants to make certain I know that theirs is a monogamous relationship.

"When you found out you were pregnant, was that a big surprise to you?"

"Yeah, in a way. Yeah, it was."

"How did you react to the news?" I ask, searching for some way to elicit even a hint of what her emotional reaction was.

"In no certain way," Myieka says, dryly.

"In no certain way," I say. I echo her words, as if playing them back to her will prompt her to remember something about how this news made her feel.

"Yeah, I was just normal, just normal about it."

Her words jar me. What does "just normal about it" mean? What is the normal way for a teenager to react to such news? I remember Anna telling me how she'd cried and cried and cursed and prayed. Myieka clearly did none of these things, or if she did she's not telling me. I am still curious to find out from her what a "normal" reaction is when you are fifteen and you find out you're going to have a baby.

"Myieka," I say, tentatively trying to guide us back into this conversation, "every month of your life until then had gone by without you being pregnant." She nods her head nearly in unison with my words. "Then, this month you find out you are pregnant."

She nods again. "Right," she says, but with a weary look in her eyes as though she's worried that I'm about to sermonize about how what she did was wrong.

I speak slowly, choosing my words carefully. I know that if my words seem scolding to her, Myieka will ignore them and become more reticent.

"So, finding this out—it didn't change the way you were thinking about your life or what was happening to you?"

"No. Not really."

Myieka describes the conversations she and William had about the coming baby. But her voice sounds flat and emotionless. Her words convey no descriptive information. Perhaps because no one in her family ever shared stories with her or read to her, Myieka hasn't learned how to describe, beyond the bare facts, what is taking place in her life. Nor will she let me know how she feels. To me, she seems to believe her feelings don't matter, so there's no use in bothering to share what they are. The one exception to this appears to be the subject of marriage.

"What did you decide was the best thing for you to do?" I ask her. "Did you think about getting married?"

At the mere mention of the word "married," Myieka shoots me a pained expression, as though she smells a bad odor. She rolls her eyes, then suddenly bursts out laughing. "I never want to get married," she says. Her laughter is soon squelched by a firmness in her voice. And she surprises me by stringing together several sentences. "Never. I don't like married life. It doesn't suit me. I don't like it. He wanted to get married after we had the baby. But I don't like it. . . . I just never think about it. And I never want to get married."

"Why do you feel so strongly about this?" I hope Myieka's new verbosity will continue.

"I don't like sharing things like that. Sharing," she says, grimacing again. "I just don't like it. Sharing with someone who is not even related to you?" Myieka poses this as a sort of question to me, as though she expects me to let her know that I now understand her reluctance. When I say nothing, she underlines her opinion. "I don't like the whole point of sharing," she says definitively.

"If you get married, that means you have to share?"

"Right. Yeah."

"What would you have to share if you got married that you don't share now?"

"My home. My child. The person has to like my child and my child has to like the person. And my time. A lot of my time. I just don't like it," she insists.

What Myieka says doesn't make a lot of sense to me. After all, William is the father of her children; their son carries his first name and his last. And William moved in with Myieka soon after their son was born. Still, marriage isn't something she'll consider. Myieka tells me that William's mother gives him some money from her welfare check; also, every so often, he earns money by moving furniture. But those jobs—like any others William might get—are not consistent or reliable, so Myieka doesn't depend on him for any of the family's monthly expenses. She also doesn't rely on him for much of their child care.

"Yeah, he stays here with me," she says. This is her way of describing their family arrangement. "And it's all right. Everything is okay."

"I don't want to be dependent on him. He should understand that."

Myieka's unflappable and low opinion of marriage is not likely to change. A few months after this conversation, she gives birth to her second child, a daughter. One afternoon, after they return home from the hospital, Myieka goes with William to what she calls "the notary republic." She stands next to him and listens as he swears to this public official that he is their daughter's father. (From the state's perspective, this means William is responsible for child support. But if the Department of Revenue is going to collect, William needs a reportable income, something he hasn't had since before his son was born.) That afternoon Myieka and William return to the hospital, where he signs his daughter's birth certificate.

"Why is it so important for you that he does this?" I ask Myieka, recalling her reaction to my questions about marriage. If they were married, William would automatically be acknowledged as her children's father. But to her, it is enough that his name appear on the birth certificate.

"I think if his name's not there, your kid has no father. That basically is what it [the signature on the birth certificate] is saying," she says. "It means the baby has a father."

On the walls of Myieka's apartment, where a few months earlier there had been only her diploma and a photograph of her son, she's now hung other framed photographs of her, the two children, and their father. I ask Myieka if maybe she is changing her mind about getting married to William.

"We talked about it again," Myieka tells me, "but I really don't know. I am scared to get married. I've seen a lot of marriages fall apart. Just one day they are together, then the next day they get a divorce. I don't want to get married, then get a divorce. It's a waste of my time." She tells me that William mentions the idea even more now than he used to. I ask her why she thinks he does.

" 'Cause we have a family," she says. "We have a family together."

"Are you getting more willing to listen now to this idea?"

"Yeah, I listen but I just say, 'I don't know,' " she answers. "I listen."

Though she says she's now willing to listen to her boyfriend's proposal, Myieka is not budging in her opposition. There's one big roadblock she can't overcome: Myieka doesn't want what happened to her mother to happen to her. The first man her mother married—he was not Myieka's father—turned out to be an alcoholic. He also moved Myieka's mother away from her extended family and familiar surroundings. In time, she divorced him and brought Myieka back home, but Myieka hated having to go through all of that. Then her mother married again, this time to the man who tried to sexually abuse Myieka. To her way of thinking, all of this leads to one conclusion: don't get married.

"I think I am more smarter than that," she tells me, comparing her decision to her mother's.

Myieka is determined not to depend on anyone but herself. "If you depend on people it never gets done," she says. "You always have to do something for yourself to get it done. . . . When you're dependent on people, they think you owe them something, and I just don't want to do it."

"Does William want to take care of you?" I ask.

"Yeah, but I don't want him to," Myieka replies.

"So how does this work when you have such different views about all of this?"

"It works fine," Myieka says. "I don't want to get married and I am not going to be dependent on him. He can't force me, so we have to work it out the way I want to do it."

I'm curious to learn what Myieka thinks would happen if William also held the view that their relationship could work only if it functioned as he wants it to.

"He wouldn't be here," Myieka says, shortly. "Because I don't want to be dependent on him. He should understand that."

"Getting pregnant and having a baby gives girls control."

As I talk with teenagers like Myieka, I find that their reluctance to consider marriage often involves the issue of control. The hatred of sharing that Myieka describes is connected to her desire to retain whatever tiny amount of control she feels she still maintains over her own life. She talks with passionate anger about what it's like to feel controlled by the welfare system, epitomized for her in the demeaning ways in which she is treated by caseworkers. The caseworker she has now, she says, is terrible to her:

"He thinks I'm a lowlife and that I can't accomplish anything." Marriage, in her opinion, would simply impose another unwanted level of control and judgment upon her, forcing upon her new sets of obligations to William. This is an obligation and level of sacrifice she sees no reason to make.

The issue of control has also been found to be a relevant factor in the increasing likelihood that girls who have been sexually abused will become pregnant during their teenage years. A University of Washington study of 535 young women who become pregnant as adolescents revealed that 66 percent of them had been sexually abused as children and 44 percent had been forced to have intercourse at some point in their lives. Many of these girls told counselors or described in their diaries how sexual abuse steals from them any sense of control over their own bodies. It is, in part, this control over her body that a girl can be trying to regain when *she* decides to have sex and get pregnant with someone who is not her abuser.

Carol Sousa, a tall, dark-haired woman who directs the Dating Violence Intervention Project in the Boston area, spends her time talking with teenagers about their relationships with one another and with family members. Sousa describes to me the various ways in which girls connect having a baby with rescue from the experience of sexual abuse. Her subdued tone is disarming as she vividly portrays how sexual mistreatment—often by men who were known and once trusted by the girls—leaves these young women feeling profoundly helpless.

"I don't think for them their pregnancies are about having the child so much as they are about regaining some control," Sousa says. "They feel that getting pregnant and having a baby will give them some control in their own lives, will give them some focus."

"Is it having control over another person, like a baby?" I ask, still a bit puzzled by how pregnancy is equated in girls' minds with control.

Carol guides me toward a different way of thinking about this: "For them this is the first time they are making a decision about what they can do with their bodies," she says. "It is the first time they've had the freedom to choose and make a decision like this. And that freedom can feel very powerful."

"So before they got pregnant their body was being used by someone else, and now they've regained control."

Carol nods. "Then, when she's pregnant, a girl gets a lot of positive attention around her body. She gets prenatal care. In school, she's given special programs to attend. She uses the teen health center. People care for her and they care about her."

"Before this she was just another girl in an anonymous setting," I say, recalling how many girls, including Myieka, told me how their school environment became much more personal, encouraging, and supportive after they became pregnant. Their pregnancies attracted the sustained attention from adults that they had needed and lacked.

"Yeah," Carol responds, "particularly the focus on the physical aspect of pregnancy. For them, it is really important and really attractive."

"Boys manufacture. Girls take the blame."

Pregnancy happened to Myieka, as it does to almost a million other teenagers each year, not because she purposely set out to have a baby but because she was sexually active and not particularly concerned about the consequences. For other girls, sex is involuntary: 75 percent of girls who had sex before the age of fourteen say that they were coerced into it. But when a girl like Myieka gets pregnant, because she has engaged in sex without using contraception, then at some level having a baby might be something she wants, or at least something she is not motivated to work to prevent. Whether, in Myieka's case, her indifference to having a baby, or unexpressed desire for it, was related to her stepfather's sexual advances, or to her failure in and indifference to school, or to the lack of connection to a "real" future, or to her separation from her family—or, as is most likely, to the combination of all of these—the possible consequence of her unprotected sexual involvement was known to her. And she was not disappointed when it happened.

One finding about teenage motherhood especially bemuses me. According to surveys of teenage mothers, 85 percent of young women say that their pregnancies were "unplanned" or "unintended." But what does "unintended" or "unplanned" mean to a teenager such as Myieka? Does it mean that on the particular day when conception occurred, she was not planning to get pregnant? Or does "unintended" characterize a pregnancy that happens when sexual partners use contraception regularly and for some reason it fails? Or are "unplanned" pregnancies those that happen in a rush of impulsiveness, rendering participants oblivious to the consequences of unprotected sex? Or are girls like Myieka just not motivated to prevent pregnancy? Or is it that when a stranger like me comes by to ask her to explain why her pregnancy happened, she will tell me it was "unplanned" so as not to make it appear as though she did, on purpose, something of which she knows many adults disapprove?

Some revealing insights about this question surfaced in a study of inner-city teenagers, done at the time when they were having pregnancy tests. Only one in twenty of the young women told the interviewer that she had intentionally tried to become pregnant. Nearly half of the young women were adamant in stating that they did not want this pregnancy to have happened. The remaining teens expressed what researchers characterized as "ambivalence," not only about their pregnancies but about sex and the use of contraception. It turned out that the teens who seemed ambivalent—a category into which Myieka might well have been placed—were equally likely to have a baby during the next two years as the very few girls who said they definitely were trying.

As Anna's counseling of Debbie reminds us, whether a girl gets pregnant usually depends on how much motivation she has to avoid it. Even though young men today use condoms with increasing frequency (chiefly because of health education about AIDS), responsibility for preventing pregnancy still rests primarily with women, as do the most significant consequences of having a child. Many young women told me that it isn't easy to convince the men they have sex with to use a condom. When men say no to using a condom but still want to have sex, young women who want to hold on to the relationship sometimes decide to go along with that demand. Though most are very much aware of what can happen if they have unprotected sex, being with their partner seems, at the moment, more important. And girls are still negatively perceived as being "eager" for sex when they anticipate encounters by bringing along condoms for partners to use.

When Anna was seventeen she wasn't thinking about having a baby, but she was having unprotected sex. She remembers word for word the conversation she had with a woman at the clinic when she called to find out the results of her pregnancy test.

"Well, what do you want it to be?" the voice on the other end of the phone asked her.

"I don't want to be pregnant," Anna replied.

"What if it is? What are you going to do?"

"Well, it's not, so just tell me so I can get on with my life," Anna said, upset by this unexpected grilling and impatient to hear.

"I wish I could tell you that, but it is positive," the clinic worker said. "You are pregnant."

Anna asked her older sister to be with her when she told her mother. "I remember my mother sitting down on my bed, grabbing my hand, and saying, 'Are you sure?' And my older sister said yes."

"How do you feel about it?" Anna's mother asked her.

"I don't know," Anna said, as tears came into her eyes. Her mother hugged her and told her that whatever she decided she'd have her support.

"But I need you to help me figure out what to do," Anna said to her mom.

"I can't answer that. You are going to have to live with your decision, either way."

"Would you be mad at me if I decided to keep it?"

"No. I will be here for you whenever you need me."

How long, I ask Anna, did it take for her to make her decision?

"Three weeks," she replies. "Back then I thought I was old enough to have a baby but I was too young to get married. That was how I thought about it. I just didn't want to get married."

"People tend to forget about these girls because they forget about themselves."

There are reliable clues about which teenagers are most likely to get pregnant and become mothers, whether accidentally or more or less intentionally. Poverty; having a mother who had her first child as a teenager; academic failure; a history of sexual abuse; and feelings of detached hopelessness are prevalent risk factors for too-early motherhood. As Anna's experience attests, early sexual activity, inconsistent use of contraception, and the decision to not have an abortion characterize these girls' actions. While Myieka and Debbie's journeys into unmarried motherhood illuminate other aspects of the territory that many of these young women travel through, additional psychological dimensions, too, lead girls in the direction of early and unwed motherhood.

Gina Adams, a public-policy analyst who has spent a lot of time looking at adolescent pregnancy, explained to me as well as anyone has why some girls end up teenage mothers and why, as adults, we've done such an inadequate job in preventing it. "There are three ways to succeed in society—in school, in work, and in family," Adams told me. "These are kids who have failed in school and who see little possibility of succeeding at work. And we're trying to convince them that they shouldn't do the one thing they know they can do: have a family. We're saying to them that having a child shouldn't be an option, but we offer them nothing else."

Often, as I speak with adults who spend their time with teenagers, especially with youngsters growing up in disadvantaged circumstances, I hear from them variations on the point Adams so cogently expressed. Guidance counselors explain how they see teenagers disconnect themselves from future goals when despair overtakes hope in the battle for their attention. Teachers know that when a girl falls too far behind in school, she becomes more likely to turn to something else, such as pregnancy, as a visible, active way to move her life ahead. Only then, too, do caring adults pay attention to her—because she is going to be a mother.

At a neighborhood clinic that serves predominantly poor women and children, a parade of young and unwed mothers passes through each day. A nurse I came to know has befriended several of them. Unlike a lot of other adults whom these young mothers meet, this nurse truly believes that many of these girls have within them the ability to improve their lives and their children's. But many of the girls have found whatever belief they once had in themselves stripped away during adolescence. The immense effort necessary for the nurse to maintain these friendships and convince young women of their own inner capacities requires more time and energy than she, a mother, wife, and full-time worker, can give.

"Many times I have said to myself, 'If I could only have Shanika in my home twenty-four hours a day, even if just for a week, I think I could get her to do some things to help herself," Beverly Jones told me one day. Shanika, twenty-four, first became a mother in her late teens; she now has three children, no high school degree, no job or good prospect of getting one, and no husband. Her life seems forever stuck in a groove of inaction. There are moments when Beverly allows her frustration with Shanika's apathy to get the better of her; she hates it that Shanika seems content to be going nowhere and doing nothing. A few times she's scolded Shanika, once telling her: "Your biggest problem is that you have grown too comfortable with where you are and what you're doing." It made Shanika angry to hear this, but nothing has changed.

Shanika's path to motherhood was littered with the debris of her miserable and lonely transition into adolescence. Her father died when she was ten, and her relationship with her mother soured; often she was sent to live with her grandparents, in a different state. After a while, the grandparents would send Shanika home. No one in her family seemed to want her to stay for very long. Back and forth Shanika traveled, tossed like a volleyball. "People tend to forget girls like Shanika because they forget about themselves," Beverly says. Shanika fell behind in school, and teachers lost track of her. Friendships were impossible to maintain. Sex, which Shanika discovered early in her adolescence, became her grip on intimacy, even though the young men she was involved with tended to toss her away, too, after they'd had enough. At a time in her life when she should have been gaining confidence about who she was, what Shanika was internalizing was a sense that she was someone most people wanted to forget.

"I really didn't have a dream."

Shanika and I sit facing each other on a gray, puffy couch in her darkened living room. She keeps her venetian blinds pulled about halfway down across the double window, and her blue-flowered curtains are partially closed, so what little light there is comes from the television, which is always on. Shanika, whose round face is often concealed by a baseball cap, rarely smiles, and when she talks her voice is quiet. Often I find myself inching closer to her so I can hear better what she's telling me about her life. Her voice can be so soft that it seems as though she doesn't want me to hear. But whenever one of her children does something to upset her, Shanika's velvet voice shifts abruptly into a bellow or roar. Her stout body stiffens as her voice booms. When her children ignore these strong commands, as they usually do, she reaches out to grab one of them. Or, if necessary, she rises to chase and slap her unresponsive son or daughter.

During an earlier visit, Shanika told me how much she hoped her children's lives would turn out differently from hers. "My life is the pits," she had said, her words oozing bitterness at her predicament. "I don't want my girls to be with no one like their father, or my boy to be nothin' like his father," she'd declared. Rob, her children's father, has never lived with them; since they were born he has fathered two children Shanika knows of with other women.

Now Shanika is sharing with me a conversation she had with Rob a few days earlier, when once again he'd made her feel as though she mattered to no one. "I said to him, 'What did I do? Did I do this wrong? Or my house wasn't tidy enough? Or the bed was made the wrong way?' " It hurts me so much to listen as Shanika describes her pleading with this man, detailing the blame she is willing to accept. Trying to please him—rather than protect herself—is an impulse she has that, in part, led to her getting pregnant: Rob refused to use condoms and she didn't have the power to insist that he do so.

"Shanika, what you're doing is looking to find something to blame yourself for," I say, hoping to get her to see how she is treating herself. She ignores my observation and continues to recite her faults. "The food wasn't good? Or the lovemaking wasn't good? Or have I got too fat, to where he can't put me where he want me? I don't know," Shanika says, as she struggles to find answers that aren't within her. It's likely that Rob has accused Shanika of each of these things at some time or other. Maybe she believes that if she can fix what he says is wrong, he'll come back.

Her self-flagellation is soon replaced by despair. "Sometimes, Melissa," she says, "I get in a mood where I don't want to do anything. I just get like that." I reflect back on what Beverly, the nurse, told me about the apathy that seems to envelop Shanika. In an attempt to inject some ray of hope, I decide to ask Shanika about her dreams. Surely the land of fantasy can't be as dreadful for Shanika as the reality she is describing.

"What do you dream for yourself?" I ask. "What is it that you dream about happening for Shanika, for her life?"

I can hear myself addressing this question to Shanika in the third person, something I seldom do in conversation. But I'm doing it on purpose, fearful that if I ask Shanika to tell me what she dreams for herself, she might not respond. As Beverly told me, just as people have forgotten about her, Shanika forgets about herself.

Shanika responds instantly, though she uses the past tense to do so.

"You know," she says, "I really didn't have a dream." Her voice trails off again to a bare whisper. Shanika is crinkling her son's cellophane lollipop wrapper in her clenched palm, so it's difficult to hear her. I ask my next question by repeating what I think she said.

"You really didn't ever have a dream?" I ask. But the way I say it carries an edge of incredulity, as though I don't believe her. When I realize how critical of her this must sound, I switch my question around, trying to ask it in a way that might elicit a more positive reaction.

"Can you have a dream now?"

By now, Shanika is scrunched up in the corner of her couch. It seems my words might have pushed her there. Her expression seems frozen in neutral, neither sad nor happy. She is quiet and withdrawn.

"Why do you think there has never been a time when you've been able to dream?" I ask, but as I do I worry that maybe I have intruded too far into spaces she considers private. At the same time I don't want our conversation to end at this point.

"I never had a dream," Shanika repeats in her flat, declarative voice, which is now much louder. She's telling me to accept as fact that she's never had a vision of where she'd like to be other than where she's been and where she is. Her harsh tone makes clear that as far as she is concerned, this ridiculous conversation about dreams is over.

"I just lived day by day," she says. "It happened. It happened. That is just the way I feel about it. It happened."

Her life "happened." Shanika "never dreamed."

"What happens to a dream deferred?"

No one could hear Shanika's words that morning or look into her sad brown eyes and not think of words the poet Langston Hughes wrote:

What happens to a dream deferred?

Does it dry up
like a raisin in the sun?
Or fester like a sore—
And then run?
Does it stink like rotten meat?
Or crust and sugar over—
like a syrupy sweet?

Maybe it just sags
like a heavy load.

Or does it explode?

Perhaps Shanika's "explosion" came in giving birth. When she was eighteen, she became the mother of twin girls. In the years before, she'd aborted three pregnancies. But when she found out she was pregnant with twins, she says, she felt she was "receiving a message."

A pivotal moment in Shanika's life occurred when she was ten years old. It was then that the man Shanika grew up knowing as her father—a man she adored and who she says adored her—died suddenly. Without him in her life, Shanika's self-confidence unraveled. He'd believed in her, and without him she began to lose belief in herself. Her mother berated her and disciplined her with mean words and a heavy hand. With her father gone, there was no one for Shanika to turn to, no buffer between her and her mother. Fights became frequent and intense. After the arguments with her mother turned violent, sometimes bloody, Shanika went to live in a foster home for a time. Sometimes her mother simply sent Shanika to her grandparents. What Shanika remembers most about her adolescence is how lonely she felt. Her grandmother, she says, was too old to understand what she was going through; her mother never seemed to care.

Shanika did not finish high school, nor has she ever gotten a GED. By the time she was pregnant with her twins, she had fallen way behind in school, was older than her classmates, and frustrated by the slow pace of learning and her teachers' unwillingness to listen to her. She was also angry at discovering, midway through her adolescence, that the man she'd grown up loving, the man she knew as "Daddy," was not her biological father. This news came as a crushing blow. She thinks her birth father might still be alive. Her mother once told her his name. Shanika has no idea how to find him and has never tried, though at times she talks of wanting to.

One day when Shanika and I are together in a hospital waiting room, I offer her a section of my newspaper to read to help pass the time. The paper happens to be *The New York Times*. A few minutes later I glance over at Shanika and see that she is reading the obituary page. I ask her why. She tells me she's checking to find out if her birth father died. Later, as I drive her home, she tells me that a part of her is afraid to try to find him and learn what his life might be like. But since her mother told Shanika that she looks like him and walks like him, she's curious about him and interested in finding out if she has any brothers or sisters; if she knew she had siblings, Shanika thinks she might feel less alone. When Shanika shared this desire with her mother, she replied in her character-istically callous way, "Why find him? He never wanted you."

When Shanika was a child the man she knew as Daddy was, she says, the only person who was always there for her. He listened patiently to her pestering questions. "He told me, 'Shanika, I love you,' and he did the fatherly things with me," Shanika says. She describes her childhood as the happiest time of her life. "When I needed to be disciplined, he disciplined me. But most of all he was somebody I could talk to. I could say to him, 'Daddy, how does this go?' and he'd say to me, 'Shanika. Sit down and do your homework.' And if I wanted to get my hair done, he would take me so I would look like a pretty little girl. Sometimes I think, gee, my father could have been here to see his grandchildren 'cause I was all he had. But things didn't happen that way."

There's that word "happen" again. She uses it a lot. Indeed, her father's death was something Shanika couldn't control, but there are so many other aspects of her life over which she seems simply to have relinquished control, and now she appears content to let what will happen just happen. As I spend more time with Shanika, I come to understand that whatever she has done or said has seemed to make so little difference that she no longer believes there is anything she can do to alter her destiny.

"I had two babies in my belly. I wasn't thinking about school at all."

Shanika tells me what "happened" after her father died. "I became adolescent," she says matter-of-factly. "I came of menses." She was eleven
years old. No one talked with her about what these bodily changes meant
or what could happen if she became sexually active. "My mother, she
didn't teach me about the birds and bees. She just handed me a book. It
was called *Love, Sex, and Babies*," Shanika says. In a soft, distant voice, she
adds, "The only thing I hated is that she handed me the book and she
didn't talk to me."

By the age of twelve Shanika was, as she says, "runnin' wild." Her
mother didn't want to hear any of her adolescent back talk. Shanika found
nothing at home or at school to anchor her. "My hormones just started
runnin' wild in me. . . . It was like I would ask myself, 'Why is Shanika
going wild?' " she says. School authorities labeled her as having learning
problems, though many of her problems in school likely stemmed from her
constant moves and not from any diagnosed disability. Nevertheless, she
was always being placed in remedial classes. By the time she was seventeen, Shanika was so bored by school that she was looking for any excuse
to leave.

"I'd say to my teacher, 'I've done this before.' And she'd say to me, 'Do
it again.' So I would do it again, but I was getting tired of this. I mean you
do get tired," Shanika says, looking over at me to see if I agree. I do, and
tell her so. "It's supposed to be where you go to school and learn something
new every day. You thrive to go to school. I didn't want to do the same
thing. It was just a waste of my time. And I never did go back 'cause of
having my babies."

I ask Shanika if anyone tried to convince her to stay. After all, a high
school diploma would be essential if she was going to find a job someday.
And now that she was going to have children, completing high school
would be important. She shoots back a look of utter amazement that I
could be so foolish as to think anyone like a teacher would care about her.

"No. No one noticed," she says.

"Nobody called?"

"No."

"No letters? Nothing?"

On Shanika's face is bemusement. "I mean, there are a lot of kids that
left like I did. Just less headache for them. The school people don't care."

"What did you think about when you walked away from school?" I ask.

"I had two babies in my belly," she says. "I wasn't thinking about it at all. I'm working. I've got two kids in my belly and I'm trying to help my mother pay the rent. My mind wasn't thinking about it, really."

"Your mother couldn't convey to you that it was important for you to stay in school?"

"I'm, like, seventeen years old. What else can she say to me?"

"What do you mean by that, Shanika?"

"I'm working. I mean, I am helping out with your rent. I am doing the best I can," she replies, telling me what she might have said to her mother.

"Why did you have to help her with the rent?"

"Ain't nobody else who was gonna help her," she shoots back at me.

"She needed your extra income to pay the rent?"

"Yeah," Shanika says.

A few moments later Shanika, tired of my questions, launches into an impassioned monologue. "You get tired of moving back and forth." It's herself she's talking about, herself during those years when she was shuttled between her mother and grandmother. "Going from New York to Boston. Boston to New York. You just had it. And when I came back to Boston, I gave up. I'd had it. I went to school but I just got pissed off 'cause the points [credits] that I did have in New York, they wouldn't give me them here."

Shanika calculated that if she'd stayed in school long enough to graduate, she would have been twenty years old. "I wasn't going to do it. Twenty years old! Still being in high school! No, I don't think so."

"Now you're a mother of three children, twenty-four years old, and you're talking with me about going back to school to get your degree," I remind her, though her talk has not been transformed into action. "What's changed about you from that eighteen-year-old who couldn't wait to leave school when she was going to have two babies and the twenty-four-year-old who is the mother of three children?"

"When you are there all your life for your kids, you don't want to be on welfare for the rest of your life," she replies. "Because you look at it, my girls are growing up fast. The year 2000 I don't want to be sitting on no welfare. I want to have me a good job so my kids ain't goin' to ask me for nothin'. They don't have to go out and even steal for nothin'. They ain't gonna have to go out here and sell drugs, you know. I don't want that. I don't want to be like having to turn around and watch them put one of my kids in the ground because of the stupid situation over drugs, that they was sellin' drugs. I don't want that."

"So you need an education," I say. "You can now see links between going to school and a better life for your kids. You couldn't see that link when you were eighteen years old?"

"Yeah, it came across to me," she replies.

"You couldn't handle it then?"

"Yeah, it was too much," Shanika says.

"I'm not a virgin anymore. But I wish I was."

Shanika once believed that Rob truly cared about her. He is three years older than she, a tall, good-looking young man who treated her nicely, at first. They met at a department store where they both worked, she as a cashier. Rob drove an old yellow Cadillac and he'd often pick up Shanika at her house and drop her off after work.

Back then she considered Rob her best friend. He filled the void left by her father. "He was the first person I could really talk to about everything," Shanika tells me. She was sixteen years old when they started to date, and though she tried to pretend with Rob that he was her first lover, he wasn't. She had already had her first abortion.

"I didn't know you was supposed to have a rubber," Shanika says of her early sexual adventures. "I didn't know nothin' about protection." The book her mother had given her about love and sex and babies was Shanika's only guide. She read it, but there was a lot she did not understand. As things turned out, her experience pretty much tracked the book's title, *Love, Sex, and Babies:* "With the first guy I talk to, I love him and we have sex together and then it was I was having a baby," Shanika says.

I ask Shanika to tell me more about what was happening to her during her early adolescence. "Oh, a lot happened," she replies. "I am not a virgin anymore." Then she adds, her voice even softer now, "But I wish I was."

Shanika leads me through a dizzying maze of sexual encounters. Her story is hard to follow; she talks about getting pregnant by one young man but wanting to tell another man the baby was his. Beyond these complicated logistics, however, Shanika keeps using one word that intrigues me. Shanika employs "talk" as a euphemism for the physical act of lovemaking. I finally realize this when, in the midst of describing a convergence of physical relationships, she says, "I mean, we did talk but I had like two other guys that I talked to while I was talkin' to him."

"When you say 'talk,' Shanika, does that mean you are sleeping with him?" I ask.

"Mm-hm, it means sleep with them," Shanika replies.

After she explains this, I realize what perfect sense it makes for Shanika to use "talk" to describe her sexual encounters. For a girl who wants only to be heard, having sex gives her a physical language, with which she can "talk" with someone who will listen to her, even if his listening means only that his body is using hers. For Shanika, these "conversations" of lovemaking became her way of being heard. For her, they filled the vast caverns of emotional emptiness, places where encouraging words and caring, attentive support should have been.

Even in the early stages of Shanika's pregnancy with the twins, Rob was spending time with other women. One day when he failed to keep a date with Shanika, she called him at his house. A woman answered the phone.

"Don't you be callin' him no more," this female voice warned Shanika. "My man appreciate if you don't call his house no more."

Shanika asked a girlfriend to go with her to Rob's house. When they arrived she found Rob in bed with a woman—the one who had answered the phone.

"My girl was laying on the bed with a skirt on and no stockings," Shanika says, describing the scene. "And I am like saying to Rob, 'I know that routine. I know that routine real good, Rob.'"

Six months later Shanika gave birth to twin girls.

"They are mine and I love them with all my heart. If they don't have a father, I'm still their mother and father," she says. "I am everything to them, and that is how I feel because their father is not a full-time father. He comes. He don't. He comes. He don't."

"Now I don't imagine myself doing anything, anymore."

About a year later, Shanika and I are seated on the same couch where she told me she never dreamed. Today she is feeling sad because another relationship she was counting on seems to be collapsing. "That's why I told him I have to stop daydreaming 'cause things that you want to happen doesn't happen," Shanika says. "And he tells me, 'There is nothing wrong with dreaming in life,' but I don't think so because you always get hurt."

Hearing her say "dream" surprises me.

"Once I asked you, Shanika, if you could share with me some of your dreams and you told me you'd never dreamed," I remind her.

"I stopped dreaming," she insists. "I stopped."

"When did you stop?" I ask her.

"I stopped dreaming after . . ." She drifts into silence and doesn't speak for a few moments. "I found myself one time in a dream with a wedding dress on. One time."

She says she had this dream when she imagined that Rob would want to stay with her forever.

"So after you saw yourself in the wedding dress, and you dreamed it would be your life and then it didn't happen, you didn't dream anymore," I say, trying to put this revelation into the context of what she's told me.

"Yeah," Shanika says. "I thought that Rob was going to choose me over her. . . . Now I don't imagine myself doing anything, anymore."

"What you are is a child moving into an adult's world."

Dreams matter. Absent a vision of where one wants to go, the road there can be very hard to find. Or, as Rosetta Stith, principal of Baltimore's Lawrence T. Paquin School for teen moms and mothers-to-be, told me, "Kids need to see for them to be. If they don't see anything, they see no need to be anything." Too often, however, when teenage motherhood is talked about, the easier to quantify measures of girls' lives—how poor their families are, how far they have fallen behind in school, when their mothers' childbearing began—supply the categories we put them in to explain why this happened. Yet, many related layers of explanation can be found in the psychology of girls' adolescent development, and these reasons for why pregnancy happens and why marriage doesn't are as important for us to understand.

Judith S. Musick, a developmental psychologist, listens to teenage girls describe their inner lives and, with their permission, reads their diaries. She does this because she believes it is vital for us, as adults, to understand these adolescent girls' point of view. In her revealing book *Young, Poor and Pregnant: The Psychology of Teenage Motherhood*, Musick discusses what happens to girls like Shanika when dreams are constantly deferred. "No intervention, no social or economic or educational opportunity will change them, no 'better option' (than pregnancy) will be chosen, unless it is grounded in their psychology and their dreams." When their capacity to dream disappears, girls find it hard to build adult lives, especially lives like the ones most of us think they should have.

Adolescents long for dependable relationships with adults, something Shanika doesn't have. In its 1995 report, the Carnegie Council on Adolescent Development addressed a misperception many adults have: that when children become teenagers they no longer want grown-ups in their lives. This had been the accepted understanding of a previous generation of researchers who emphasized the inevitability of adolescent alienation. This Carnegie report, however, relied on fifteen years of new research about relationships among families and adolescents that convinced the council that "adolescents develop best when they have . . . the serious and sustained interest of their parents in their lives." Other supportive adults are necessary, too, if teens are to learn how to cope successfully with the multiple risks—sexual activity, drug use, delinquency—that so many of them face during the transition from childhood to adulthood.

Adolescents need trustworthy adults who are available for them, adults who will give them the room to form their own identities but who never are so far away that a cry for help won't be heard. Adolescents also want adults to be alongside to celebrate their accomplishments. It is when caring adults disappear from adolescents' lives that teenagers arrange other forms of what they regard as protective and dependable companionship. Had an adult been present for Shanika, making her feel wanted, respected, capable, and listened to, perhaps her unprotected sexual adventuring would not have happened.

A conversation with Dr. Bonnie Leadbeater, a psychologist at Yale University, helps me make more sense of how teenage girls like Shanika use motherhood as their stepping-stone to adulthood, especially if they haven't found another. Dr. Leadbeater's office is crammed with tilting stacks of reports on numerous interviews she's doing with adolescent mothers living in poor and low-income neighborhoods. In her interviews with primarily minority teenage girls, Leadbeater opens discussions of how they think about making a successful transition to being "women." Leadbeater offers me examples of the questions she poses to prompt such discussions: "Is it possible to be successful?" "What does it mean for a woman to be successful?" While Judith Musick tries to learn how girls feel and think about their present lives because of what has happened in the past, Dr. Leadbeater attempts to understand how they envision themselves as they head into the future.

"What is most interesting to me is the contrast between what these girls say and what we, as upper-middle-class white women, might say in response to the same kinds of questions," Dr. Leadbeater tells me. "If someone asks you what it means to be a successful woman, you or I might speak of ourselves in contrast with men. You know, things like saying what it means to be a woman is that you don't get paid as much as men, things such as that. These girls don't talk about it in this way. With them, the contrast is with what it means just to be an adult, what it is to have responsibility versus what it is to be a teenager. . . . For them, there is this other message of what it means to be a woman. It is to be an adult. To them, there are adults and there are teenagers. When you're a woman, you're an adult. You have a lot of responsibility. You have to care for everything. You have to care about everything. You have to get your apartment fixed up. Pay your bills. Know where your income is coming from. . . ." This list of defining characteristics is identical to the topics Anna said her teen moms thought most about. "These girls do not have the sense that you are compromised because you're a woman trying to fit into a man's world," Leadbeater says. "What you are is a child moving into an adult's world."

I ask Leadbeater if girls can use pregnancy as a way of becoming women.

"Some of them do," she replies. "Some of them are really identified as adults once they have had the baby. They feel like they are women." For Shanika, who was desperately looking for a way out of her miserable adolescence, pregnancy and then motherhood gave her life a definition it hadn't had.

"So how am I going to be a grown-up?"

Motherhood thrusts teens into adult roles. Even when a girl is too immature to take over full-time responsibility for her baby, giving birth still offers her direct passage into adulthood. Dr. Tesi Kohlenberg, a physician who directed the Teen & Tot Adolescent Center at Boston Medical Center, points out that no matter what age a parent is, unless she loses custody she is, by law, the decision-maker about her child. "A mother can be fourteen years old—and because we recognize parental rights, if her child needs a medical procedure, then she is the one who has the final say. [So] becoming a parent is in many young girls' minds a mark of progress to adulthood," says Kohlenberg, supporting the perceptions voiced by Leadbeater's young mothers.

The anonymity and loneliness of adolescence also can be swept aside by motherhood. Babies can provide girls with a satisfying, if only illusionary, sense of moving their lives ahead. "Many of these girls seem to be saying to themselves, 'I'm not going to make it through school. I mean, I can sit here in classes forever and not one person I know who gets out of school, even those who have a degree, has a job anybody would want. So how am I going to be a grown-up?'" Kohlenberg says. Unless adults begin by understanding how girls perceive their present lives and limited future opportunities, convincing them to consider alternative means of becoming adults can be exceedingly difficult.

Among poor, black teenage girls, in particular, mainstream messages about postponing early, unwed childbirth are tough to convey. This is especially true when the people or institutions delivering these messages are regarded by the girls as "outsiders" who aren't going to do any more than talk to—or, even worse, lecture—them about how postponing motherhood will improve their lives. Young women's suspicions about these messages are borne out by research. In a 1995 study, University of Chicago public-policy professor V. Joseph Hotz revealed that teenage mothers tended to earn more over their lifetimes and work more steadily than women who came out of the same social and economic circumstances but delayed childbearing until they were no longer teenagers. And although there is a plethora of evidence to back up claims that delaying mother-hood past the teenage years is best for children, data from the mid-1980s National Longitudinal Survey of Youth found that black teenage mothers had a greater high school completion rate than whites. This finding didn't apply to teens who didn't have a child; graduation rates of blacks remained lower than their white peers'.

"Those messages are for white people."

Naomi didn't grow up in a family that relied on welfare, though many chil-dren living in her Boston neighborhood did. Her father was a college pro-fessor who acted on his belief that a good education was essential. In the morning a school bus took Naomi to a virtually all-white public school in a wealthy suburb. The daily thirty-mile round trip left Naomi, who is a black, articulate, and opinionated woman, with anger percolating within her. "I went from blight to beauty to blight every day and that was demeaning to me," Naomi says, facing me across a table in the living room of a house on her college campus. She is now twenty-nine years old, con-vinced that she commands her destiny, and determined to succeed. She is a junior at a prestigious college, a full-time student while she and her son are supported by welfare.

"I was an intruder, an invader," Naomi says, taking me with her back to childhood. The staccato rhythm of her voice seems energized as she retrieves these vivid memories. "This made getting an education very difficult because some people in that town called me 'nigger.' They would say to me, 'Go home, nigger.' The message I took out of this was that my own environment was so deficient that I had to be removed from it to be educated. But because I was part of that environment, they were telling me I was also deficient. . . . All of this tells you that something is wrong with you. You are not good enough to receive the kind of education that white children whom you are sent to school with are getting in their neighborhood."

Naomi's confidence in her inner strength was also severely tested by events within her family. Her father moved out when she was six. Naomi describes the aftermath as "an explosion of dysfunction all across my family." Etched into her memory are times when her mother beat her with a vacuum cleaner hose or reached into the freezer and threw frozen-solid hamburger patties at her head. Naomi knows now that her mother blamed her for her horrible marriage; getting pregnant with Naomi was what made the marriage necessary. Often Naomi's mother reminded her that she was not a wanted child.

Her mother's words took root in Naomi, and when she got pregnant, just after her teenage years were over, she refused to allow this unintended pregnancy to trap her in an undesired marriage. Raising her son alone seemed far preferable to repeating the destructiveness to which she'd been exposed. She believed that, in time, she would find a man who could be a caring father to her son. None of Naomi's younger sisters, who also had children at just about the same age as she did, got married, either. "None of us were willing to give up our right to be mothers because there are not marriageable black men," Naomi says, responding to my question about whether she believes black women regard marriage as an irrelevancy. "I was in my early twenties when I had my son, and getting older," she continues. "As African-American women, we do not want to be like those yuppie women who go and have kids at thirty-five or forty years old."

"Why do you feel that way?" I ask, as Naomi delineates this clear difference between her life and mine.

"I do not want to be fifty years old and still raising a young child," she says. "It is stressful enough being an African-American woman in this world without having the added responsibility of raising a fifteen-year-old when I am fifty-five."

I am curious to learn what Naomi thinks about why so many "yuppie women" wait to have babies at such an advanced age. "I think it is mostly that they want to attain career goals and personal goals before they become mothers," she says. "There's a perception, and I think it is more common among white people than blacks, that children are a hindrance. They get in the way. So the message is, 'Don't have them until you have done enough for yourself.' It's very me-oriented. African-American women take a different position on it. Mostly because we haven't had the opportunities accorded to people of noncolor, we have had to raise children and try to achieve personal and professional goals at the same time. It's been done this way in our community since we were brought over here in the bowels of ships."

"So it is never regarded as separate spheres?"

"No, it is never separate spheres. We haven't had the luxury of making that separation. African-American mothers have always had to work, so there is no way to separate them," she says. "We figure why don't we have our children when we are younger, so when we are older we can enjoy our lives."

Listening to Naomi helps me to think more about how different the receptivity of African-American girls is to messages about postponing motherhood. "These messages don't apply to us," she tells me. "Those messages are all about white people and about white people's needs for black people to do things white people need them to do. I do think it's true that young women need to be educated and they need to attain some ability to care for themselves before they have children. And most African-American women of any stature or education agree with that. But we don't necessarily agree that the way white women have done it is the right way for us."

Given what she has already pointed out to me, I seek Naomi's guidance about how it might be possible to persuade African-American teenagers to delay motherhood until they are ready to raise children and can do so in the context of a committed relationship. Naomi believes this will happen only when African-American women who have attained what she calls "educational excellence" return to poor communities and devote time to being with the young women. "We need to go and talk with these young women. The responsibility is ours to take care of on our own, and I'm looking for a way to do that," Naomi says.

"If you cannot be a parent, then I don't want you around."

Naomi's pregnancy was not intended or desired, but when birth control failed she was firm in her decision not to seek an abortion. The father did not want Naomi to have the baby; when she refused to have an abortion, he was very angry at her. "Jack felt I put him in an untenable position," she says. At first, Naomi was willing to let her boyfriend decide whether he'd be part of his child's life. But, in time, she set out explicit stipulations: "If you cannot support him and if you cannot help me," she says, "and if you cannot be a parent, then I don't want you around."

"What did you mean when you told him that?"

"For him to 'be a parent' meant to me he was providing financial support and emotional support. And he had to be a positive role model for my son," Naomi tells me. I notice that she calls her child "my son," not "our son," a semantic point that is not without significance. "He needed to be a man who is making strides, moving forward in his own life, not someone feeling victimized by racism to the extent that he's allowing it to destroy or paralyze him. But this is not the kind of person Jack was, so I decided I didn't want him to be part of my son's life."

Even though Naomi was reluctant for Jack to remain in their lives, emotions made it difficult to let him go. She was in love with him, even if his paternal qualifications were suspect. As her pregnancy advanced, his anger at the situation intensified. Perhaps, Naomi thinks in retrospect, Jack's outward rage was actually directed at himself for his inability to meet her demands concerning what he needed to be and do if he was to be allowed into his family's life. "I still loved him, so I dealt with his behavior until I was about seven months pregnant," Naomi says. "Then, basically, I told him to go to hell."

After their son was born they found their way back to each other again, as though bound by an invisible cord that neither could cut. For a time Jack moved in with Naomi and the baby. Tensions escalated, however, until one night he exploded. "When my son was three months old, his father decided he was going to spend an entire night beating me up," Naomi says, her voice devoid of emotion. She sounds utterly detached from this memory. "That was the end of it."

Naomi was on her own.

"He's yours. You want a baby. Now you've got one."

A few years ago Naomi had a chance to try to persuade a young woman to postpone pregnancy. Her cousin Melanie, who was sixteen years old, was talking incessantly about wanting to have a baby. Naomi's aunt begged her to talk with Melanie, and Naomi tried: she talked, and she talked, and then she talked some more, about how difficult her own life had become. But nothing Naomi said seemed to diminish Melanie's desire to have a baby, now. Finally, Naomi's aunt pleaded with Naomi to do something more to change Melanie's mind. She agreed to try.

"I had Melanie come and live with me and I made her take care of my son," says Naomi.

She carefully supervised the monthlong experiment. "I handed my two-and-a-half-year-old baby to her and I told her, 'He's yours. You want a baby. Now you've got one.'" She gave Melanie complete responsibility for his care. If Melanie felt like going out with friends, Naomi would tell her, "No. No. You've got to find a baby-sitter. You can't just go out." Her cousin would protest, insisting she was going to go out. "I don't know what you are going to do, but you have got a child to think about," Naomi replied. "You have to feed him and give him a bath and get him ready for bed."

Naomi was vigilant in making sure Melanie never neglected her care-taking duties. "I did not make my child a victim of this, but I went on about my life and showed my cousin what she had and what she would be giving up by having a baby," she says. The result: Melanie enrolled in a Job Corps program and concentrated on gaining some workplace skills. Three years later, at the age of nineteen, she did become an unmarried mother. But after the baby was born, she went back to school.

"Even with all you did in giving her this hands-on experience, Melanie still had a baby on her own at the age of nineteen," I say to Naomi.

She nods. "Yeah, messages have to start when girls are really young. You can't take a sixteen-year-old and reeducate that child after years of messages that she is inferior, years of her hearing she will not be successful, years of her hearing she cannot attain a reasonable educational stature, years of her hearing she cannot be a producing and participating citizen in the economy."

"What she sees is that she can be a participating and successful member of society as a mother?" I ask.

"Absolutely. They believe that is the only thing they can do right," Naomi says. "And nobody can tell them they can't do that."

"My twenty-eight-year-old sister wants a baby so bad, she had three miscarriages and two babies dead at birth."

Naomi's observations speak to critical issues now being confronted by those who want to persuade young women to wait longer to start having children and to be married when they do. Conservative legislators argue that if public assistance is withdrawn from unmarried mothers, and other punitive consequences are set up, the rate at which teenagers give birth outside of marriage will tumble. However, there is no solid evidence that welfare payments are the primary cause of the rise in nonmarital child-bearing. Twenty years of research on this question have produced divergent findings. However, two conclusions seem apparent, according to Robert A. Moffitt of Johns Hopkins University, who evaluated the research in the 1995 "Report to Congress on Out-of-Wedlock Child-bearing." Moffitt explained to policymakers that "the simplest evidence indicates that the welfare system has not been largely responsible for the recent increases in nonmarital childbearing." And, he said, to the extent that welfare has produced such increases, it has done so more among white women than among African-Americans.

Yet it is among blacks, especially teenagers, that a larger proportion of nonmarital births occurs. Some reasons why many more black than white young women become pregnant so soon and have their children out of wedlock reside in the circumstances of being a minority and poor and growing up in America today. Arline T. Geronimus, a professor of health behavior and health education at the University of Michigan, has looked at what distinguishes these young women's experiences from those of their white peers. Her research suggests that early childbearing might be, in fact, a "rational reproductive strategy" for African-American girls from underprivileged socioeconomic environments. Geronimus's contrarian point of view is gradually gaining attention, and simultaneously a few more adherents. "In 1990, I was pilloried for raising some of these issues," Geronimus tells me. "Now I'm finding greater tolerance and interest in these new ways of thinking."

Geronimus explains that girls from varying social environments develop different perspectives about when women ought to complete their childbearing and consequently about when it is logical for motherhood to begin. Among girls she spoke with, blacks growing up in poor communities perceive the earliest cutoff time for reproduction. (Low-income whites suggested a slightly higher cutoff age; middle-class teens of both races set the cutoff even higher.) The poor, black teenagers whom Geronimus surveyed believe that women should be finished having babies by the time they are twenty-five to thirty years old. It is interesting that thirty— the age these girls marked as the upper boundary—has recently become a customary time for more prosperous, better-educated white women to start their families.

What one nineteen-year-old black mother-to-be said to Geronimus expressed much about the experiences many such girls use to frame their views about the timing of motherhood:

> My 34-year-old sister is dying of cancer. Good thing her youngest child is 17 and she seen her grow up. My 28 and 30 year-old sisters got high blood [pressure] and sugar [i.e., diabetes]. The 30-year-old got shot in a store. She has a hole in her lung and arm paralyzed. Good thing she had her daughter long ago. My 28-year-old sister wants a baby so bad. She had 3 miscarriages and 2 babies dead at birth. Doctors don't think she can have a baby no more. All my sisters weigh 250. I bet you wouldn't have believe they looked like me at my age. I'm sure I'll look like them when I'm old.

From this young woman's perspective, the delay of motherhood, even until one's mid-twenties, carries increased risks.

Other research by Geronimus supports what these young women say about their lives. Her study of health factors finds that women's well-being deteriorates faster with age when they are poor and black. And it does so in ways that affect their capacity to carry pregnancies to term and deliver healthy babies. Geronimus found, for example, that among white women, teenagers experience the highest rates of low-birthweight babies and infant death. Among blacks, however, babies born to mothers between the ages of fifteen and nineteen have a lower incidence of these adverse outcomes than babies born to women in their twenties.

"The messages coming out of their personal lives are the ones that are getting through."

It is Geronimus's belief, buttressed by this research, that the early timing of births in poor black communities is likely the result of a constellation of factors, which she places under the heading of social inequality. The hard, stressful conditions of daily life wear down young women's capacity to follow formulas designed to fit the circumstances and prospects of more advantaged peers. Geronimus labels her suspicions the "weathering hypothesis"; she suggests that these girls age sooner and that this changes how they place motherhood within the larger scope of their lives. In a paper about this hypothesis, she wrote: "Behavior patterns that appear unfamiliar or perplexing to members of advantaged populations . . . may represent collectively patterned coping strategies, not necessarily individual deviance or community pathology."

Geronimus points out, too, that the health of young mothers isn't alone in maintaining the pattern of early childbearing in poor black communities. More than in white neighborhoods, where the ideal of the nuclear family still predominates, child-rearing among poor young blacks generally leads teenage mothers to rely on help not from boyfriends but from extended-family members. If older women—generally the family members teenage moms depend on—are to assist with raising children, they need to be healthy. But first, they need to be alive. Black women don't, on average, live as long as whites, especially when they reside in poor urban environments. As Geronimus points out, the probability that a black woman who lives in Harlem will reach her forty-fifth birthday is the same as the chance that an average white woman will survive until her sixty-fifth. Given a shorter life expectancy, greater risks of bad health, and reliance on family members for help in rearing children, it does not surprise Geronimus that many girls from such backgrounds have babies young.

Marriage rarely accompanies these births, in part because childbirth often coincides with the years in young fathers' lives when few have secured an economic foothold. Also, for many young women in very poor neighborhoods, postponing motherhood until their twenties will not significantly improve the likelihood of finding a marital partner. Nor does a slight postponement of childbearing, by itself, seem to improve the early development of these mothers' children, especially if the additional years have not brought with them more education and increased job skills. In a study Geronimus undertook comparing children of teenagers with those of similarly disadvantaged older mothers, both sets of children fared just as poorly. This finding—though taken from a very small sample—leads Geronimus to speculate that factors other than the age of the mother affect the developmental outcomes of children. As she writes: "Heightened risk of poor performance on development indicators may be common to children of disadvantaged mothers in general, not peculiar to those with teenage mothers. . . . [Therefore,] a focus on altering fertility timing, per se, may not alter conditions that fundamentally affect the well-being of children."

If the poor educational, economic, and health circumstances of these young women's lives aren't addressed, Geronimus thinks it likely that early, nonmarital childbirth will persist. "Today, in the latter part of the twentieth century, poor black teenagers are exposed to strong messages that teenage childbearing is unacceptable and destructive behavior deserving of stigmatization and punishment," she says. "Yet the experiences in their own lives and that of their elders sometimes contradict this societal belief. For many, the messages coming out of their personal lives are the ones that are getting through."

"Teenage mothers certainly seem to be accepted around here."

Personal messages predominate when societal ones arrive jumbled and disconnected from daily experience. Right now, not only are mainstream messages about postponing motherhood or at least getting married first being rejected by many black teenagers, as Naomi points out, but white teens are tuning them out as well. A white teenager in Bobbie Ann Mason's novel *In Country* describes the attitude in her rural Kentucky town, highlighting a change that is evident in many communities today: "It used to be that getting pregnant when you weren't married ruined your life because of the disgrace. Now it just ruined your life and nobody cared enough for it to be a disgrace."

In many neighborhoods—not just in poor or predominantly black ones—neither teenage pregnancy nor unmarried motherhood is thought of as disgraceful, as it was just a few decades ago. Girls no longer leave school or get sent away from home to hide their pregnancies. In fact, school systems are accommodating early motherhood by setting up school-based child care and other programs targeted at teen parents. In the eyes of adolescents, pregnancy and parenthood are just things that happen to many of their friends. By the age of nineteen, one in every four black women is a mother; one in every seven whites is, as well.

A shrug-of-the-shoulders acceptance of unmarried, adolescent motherhood isn't confined to urban communities. In more rural western Massachusetts, in the former mill town of Montague, where the unemployment rate is high, especially among young workers, and nearly everyone in town is white, the rate of births to teenagers is higher than the state's average. "Teenage mothers are accepted in society and they certainly seem accepted around here," an assistant superintendent of the schools told a *Boston Globe* reporter. The school system's curriculum stressed sexual abstinence, and the town's voters rejected a plan to distribute condoms in the high school, even though students overwhelmingly favored it. When the *Globe* reporter asked teenagers how they felt about being unwed mothers, they said it was "fine." Almost all said they knew someone their age who is a parent. And girls who didn't have babies spoke admiringly of their friends' efforts to persevere as parents. Several spoke about one teen single mother in particular, a sixteen-year-old whose mother had thrown her out of the house when she found out she was pregnant. Her peers praised her for keeping her life on track and staying in school while raising her son on her own. In their eyes, hers was a profile in courage, not a life tarnished by disgrace.

Veneration for girls who have babies was voiced by many white teenagers with whom I spoke. Some of the mothers told me during our private conversations about their struggles as young parents, but when they are surrounded by friends there was no talk about hardships at all. In these moments they emphasize motherhood as an accomplishment, and their descriptions can start to sound pretty heroic. Sometimes, listening to these young women talk, I get the feeling that raising a child outside of marriage and at such a young age earns them a badge of honor. At the very least, it gives them recognition they wouldn't otherwise have.

One day *The New York Times* quoted an eighteen-year-old college student who summed up for me the attitudes I'd been hearing. Describing how she feels when she sees a young single mother, this student said, "She's a better person than me. Someone who is strong." Her words reminded me of what Anna, the family planning counselor, told me about how teen moms would rather talk about good times and the positive ways motherhood makes them feel. That's why they tell each other about putting their babies in strollers and parading them around, and dwell on those times when someone pauses to look at the baby and pays attention to them. I now appreciate more what Anna was telling me about how this personal dynamic puts one more hurdle in the way of convincing girls to wait.

"I figured if I'd had my dad that my life would have went so different."

Another factor common to many white and minority teenage mothers is the absence of their fathers from their everyday lives. Sara McLanahan, the Princeton researcher on single motherhood, calculates that children who grow up living with only one of their biological parents—this parent is usually the mother—are two and a half times more likely to become teenage mothers than are those who grow up with both parents. Single-parent families—especially those created by out-of-wedlock births—are more prevalent among blacks, so this factor is associated with their higher incidence of teenage motherhood.

Judith Musick, the psychologist who devotes much of her time to talking with teenage girls about pregnancy and motherhood, describes fatherless girls' early pregnancies as, in part, "logical outcomes of their attempts to cope with father absence." Some women who had their first child as teenagers also described their fathers' absence as leading them to early parenthood. Other teen mothers may not make this association because unpleasant memories have pushed this loss from their minds, but the effect of their paternal relationship may still be significant.

One woman who first became a mother when she was sixteen told me how she sought out an older man to date, had sex with him, and got pregnant. Jacqueline drew a direct line between much of her behavior with men and the fact that she did not know her father. "I wanted someone who was like a father, 'cause I always wanted my father. I figured if I'd had my dad that my life would have went so different. I would have felt good about myself. Be able to say, 'I had my dad.' That would have been more support. You see, I didn't have that and I didn't like that as a kid, didn't like the fact I didn't have him," Jacqueline said. Like many teenage girls who get pregnant, Jacqueline dated a much older man and then found it difficult to resist fulfilling his consistent demands for sex. "For me, having sex was just doing it for my boyfriend 'cause it made him happy, I guess," she told me. "I felt that if I wasn't ready to have sex he was going to leave."

I asked this woman, who is now thirty-two years old, unwed, and the mother of six children, what having a father would have given her.

"Strength," Jacqueline replied without a moment's hesitation. "Your father gives you strength. So as I grew up, I didn't feel like I could do anything. I was really talented. I really was. But I just felt like I couldn't do it. And I got mistreated when it came to the opposite sex for the simple fact that they knew I didn't have a father and what was my mother going to do?"

It was when she was eleven, Jacqueline told me, that she became very aware of her father's absence and how it was affecting her. As she entered adolescence, a time of heightened risks, she grew increasingly enraged at her mother and blamed her for depriving her of her father. "I was angry at her. I asked her, 'Where is this guy that is supposed to be a part of me? A part of me I don't know about,'" she said. That rage pulled her away from her mother, the one adult to whom she had been close. During adolescence, she had no adult she felt attached to.

Musick believes that young women who have not been exposed "to a consistent experience with older males in loving, protective, and other roles," both practical and expressive, can develop "a kind of learned helplessness" in their relationships with men. Especially during their teenage years, these young women can think of themselves as powerless and unable to influence their interactions with a partner, interactions that often turn out to be harmful to them.

"Things didn't go as we planned."

Susan, who became an unwed mother when she was eighteen, has only a few childhood memories of her father. She remembers one afternoon on a beach, when her father and his friends tossed her up into the California sky. Up she flew, giggling and churning her tiny legs like propellers, until she landed in the nest of his blanket. "I can remember that," Susan tells me, with a smile so broad that her dimples carve deep into her pale cheeks. She was three years old then and on a trip with her mother, Sheila, to visit her father on the West Coast. Usually Susan lived in Boston with her mother and five half-brothers and half-sisters. Sheila never married Susan's father, though she'd been married to the father of her other children. Susan can't remember him ever living with them, either. "That's about most of it," she says, referring to memories of her dad.

After that day in California, Susan doesn't remember seeing him again until her eleventh birthday. She was upstairs in her bedroom in the midst of a raucous pajama party. "My cousins ran up the stairs to tell me my father was coming. They knew he was here before I did," she recalls. "They yelled up to me he was in the house and I came running downstairs and I hugged him and everything. It was exciting to see him, but nervous. But I kind of took right to him. I remembered him right when I seen him." Susan turns silent for a few moments, as though she wants to linger privately with this long-ago moment a little longer.

Soon after that visit, Susan's father left again; "He's been around recently," she says. "Still on his own and doing his own thing, but he keeps in touch."

I'm curious about whether her father's return to Boston when Susan was eleven led her to have any expectation that he might come back into her family's life.

"No," she replies, without hesitation. "I just figured he was just coming around and see how things were. I didn't expect him to stay. And it wasn't like they would be together, because my mother has her own boyfriend and they're happy. She has her own life now."

When Susan was born, Sheila was a widow raising five children on her own. For a while Susan's father stayed with all of them, but when she was two he moved far away, to California. Her mother worked as a waitress and every so often had to rely on welfare and food stamps to get her family through rough times. In early childhood, Susan lived on the top floor of a boxy six-family house in a working-class Irish Catholic neighborhood. Close friends and extended-family members lived in many of the other apartments. When her mother went to her job, the extended family took care of Susan. With older siblings at home, Susan recalls, she never lacked companionship or supervision. On weekends, family and friends came together in her backyard to swim in their above-ground pool. Susan says she always felt safe, in part because she had four older brothers to protect her. "I'd use my brothers to scare people away," she says. "They did what a father would do. They stood in place of that."

When Susan was seven years old, her mother was able to buy a house a few miles away. She remembers her mother describing their new house as being a "good deal"; it is where she and her mother still live today, a gray, asphalt-shingled two-story house near the end of a potholed dead-end street. What Susan missed most when they moved was the safety and comfort of her earlier surroundings, but in time she found some girls her age in the neighborhood, and they became close friends. On summer days they'd play street games such as red rover or go to the beach. In the evening, they mostly watched television. During lulls in these activities, Susan and her girlfriends shared with one another their dreams about how their lives would be when they were grown-ups.

"All of us used to dream about how we were going to live in a fancy house with a white picket fence and have two kids, like everyone imagines," Susan tells me. "We all wanted to move away. We'd been here. We wanted a change. It was like a *Fantasy Island*–type thing."

"When you'd have these dreams, who did you see living in that fancy house?" I ask.

"It was always two kids, a boy and a girl. The perfect family! And the father and the dog. All of us wanted dogs. I think everyone's dream is like that. The perfect family."

"Where did you and your friends get these ideas of the 'perfect family'?" I ask. Susan has told me that some of her friends had been raised only by their moms, as she was. "I mean, your own family experiences weren't like that."

"Maybe that's why we dreamed about that, because it wasn't the way we grew up and we wanted our kids to grow up in a different way," Susan says.

"Where did your images of this 'perfect family' come from?"

"Oh, from television. *Brady Bunch* and *Happy Days*," she tells me, reminding me of how the television shows of my childhood—*Father Knows Best, Leave It to Beaver, Ozzie and Harriet*—made similar lasting impressions on me.

"What got you off track in having that perfect family?"

Susan laughs loudly. "Oh, I don't know," she says, her dimples showing again. "Things didn't go as we planned."

"Oh, I don't know if she'll get married. She hasn't mentioned that."

Susan and most of her childhood friends, each of whom is white, had babies as teenagers. Only one of them married the father, and by that time they'd already had two children. I ask Susan to tell me more about what's happened to these childhood friends who shared her dream of having "the perfect family."

"My friend Karen, she lives on the street right behind me and she has a little girl who is two weeks apart from Sean [Susan's son]. She's not with the father," says Susan, who at the age of twenty-one still looks like a high school student with her puffed-up curly bangs, big ponytailed brown hair, and a dab of red lipstick. "Karen works at Burger King, I guess she's a manager or something, and she lives with her mother. My friend Mary has a little girl who is a few months older than Sean. I don't keep in contact with her, but I knew when she had her baby. The one I really talk to from high school, Christy, she's pregnant now. She tells me, 'I'm going to be twenty-three, I've got a full-time job, and my boyfriend and I are going to move in together.' Christy works in a nursing home."

"Does Christy ever talk to you about getting married?" I ask Susan.

"Oh, I don't know if she will get married." Susan looks a bit puzzled that I would ask about wedding plans. "No. She hasn't mentioned that."

Susan never got married, either. She and her son live in her mother's house and have separate bedrooms at the top of the back stairway. Susan decorates her bedroom door with posters of muscular male models, well oiled and scantily dressed. Her older half-sister, Deanna, who at thirty-five is unmarried and childless and works as a bartender, also lives here, as does Deanna's boyfriend. Susan's mother, who is still waitressing, is on call with a catering service. Her work hours and income are unpredictable, so Susan's $486 monthly welfare checks and $114 in food stamp coupons help keep the household afloat. Susan pays $240 each month for rent; the food stamps go toward the family's grocery bill.

"I know I should save some money so that when I go to my own place I'll have a start," Susan tells me, "but it's hard for me to save. I can't take away from my mother. She lets me live here. I help her any way I can."

"Nick thought I didn't need him anymore. I had the baby."

Susan's pregnancy happened by mistake. She says she forgot to take birth control pills for a few days and then tried to play catch-up by taking a couple at a time. That month she learned a hard lesson: unless contraception is used properly, it doesn't work.

"Didn't it worry you to have sex when you'd forgotten to take the pills?" I ask her.

"No," Susan says, explaining how she figured that if she bunched up the pills they would work just as well. "But it wasn't as though I *planned* to get pregnant," she tells me, emphasizing the extent of her surprise by the exaggerated way she says "planned." "But I had to deal with it. I don't believe in abortion."

Having a baby was not something Susan thought of as a status symbol, though she remembers many girls who did. "For some girls in my school, it was cool to have a baby, even if they weren't really acting like a mother. But other girls, they were real involved with their kids," she explains, walking me through the diverse ways that girls approached their new roles as mothers. "For some girls, it happened and they took responsibility for it. A few used their pregnancies to keep their boyfriends. They'd be breaking up with someone and use this to get them to stay around, which is something you shouldn't do."

Susan's boyfriend, Nick, accused her of "trapping him" by getting pregnant. She vehemently denied it. "You don't have to stick around," she told him. "I'm not asking you to. I'll deal with this myself. If you want to, you can but I'm not forcing you." Susan met Nick at her high school, and they'd dated for about two years before she got pregnant. "We'd talked about our future, just talked. Nothing definite," she says. "I didn't want to rush into anything. I wanted to take time for us to know each other before dealing with something else."

Sometimes after school Susan and Nick went to his mother's apartment. His bedroom was off the kitchen and the door had a lock. Nick's mother was usually at home, but she was often in the parlor watching television, or in her bedroom. Susan and Nick would watch TV, eat sandwiches, "just hang out," as Susan says. However, on many of these afternoons, they'd also go into Nick's room, lock the door, and have sex.

"And that was okay with Nick's mother?"

"Not at first," Susan says, "but Nick didn't care." Susan even spent entire weekends at Nick's house.

"What about your mom?"

"My mom didn't like that, either. She'd make comments like, 'Don't you think you should just come home?' and she would ask me, 'What does his mother think?' That kind of stuff."

"When you were at your house with him, did you have sex?"

"Not at first, but yeah, after a while we did. Then he would stay at my house, too," Susan says. "And when I was pregnant, Nick practically moved in. Then, right after I had the baby, he was there most nights, too."

By then, however, their relationship was unraveling, a process that had begun early in her pregnancy. Nick's habit of trying to control Susan's activities—telling her which friends she could see and when she could see them, lecturing her on whom she could talk with at school—was no longer something Susan was willing to put up with. She'd gone along with his demands because she wanted to be with him, and to be with him meant playing by his rules. Until she got pregnant, Susan never summoned the courage to challenge Nick, even though she says now that she always felt suffocated by the way he treated her.

"It was like Nick was more of a father to me than a boyfriend," Susan explains. "I mean, I couldn't talk to anyone without him knowing who it was. At times, it kind of made me break away from him so I could have time for myself. And still he'd call me and say, 'What are you doin'?' It was as though I had to tell him. He was controlling." Had she had a close relationship with a father whom she saw every day, perhaps Susan would have known more about the way a relationship with a man could be, and might have developed more confidence in herself. "Nick put me down a lot. He'd always say I was fat or I was too short. Or I wasn't smart enough. All of this kind of pushed me away. I didn't feel secure," Susan says. "He made me feel like I was nothing." Still, she accepted his insults because she wanted the relationship with him.

Nick hit Susan a few times. On one occasion, when Susan was at Nick's house, he hit her and then locked her in his room. She was scared. She knew that Nick's father had battered his mother and that that was why they no longer lived together. Nick's mother called the police to get her son to let Susan out.

During her pregnancy the tension escalated. Susan accepted much of the blame for this; she believed that her reactions to Nick were caused mostly by mood swings related to her pregnancy. "I would get in certain moods and we'd fight. We'd have big arguments. I tried to tell Nick that my body was changing and my hormones were making moods so that on some days everything is going to get to me and other days nothing will. He just thought I was taking it out on him, trying to push him away. He just didn't understand these changes I was going through." Now, as Susan looks back on what was happening to them, she believes much of the tension arose because of Nick's increasing frustration as he gradually lost his power to control her.

However, even as they fought, Susan and Nick continued to talk about getting a place of their own after their baby was born. In their minds, having a baby meant that it was time to act like a family, even if marriage wasn't yet in their plans. "I was still working," Susan says. "So we were going to save up money. We were going to do it. But then things started going downhill for us."

A few months after Sean was born, Susan had to quit her receptionist's job because the baby was getting sick a lot and she had to take him to the doctor. And it became clear to them that Nick's job as a machine operator couldn't pay the bills they'd have if they lived together on their own. But an equally important ingredient in Susan's decision not to live with or even consider marriage to Nick was how he continued to treat her after their son was born.

"He felt my time was being eaten up by the baby and I didn't have time for him," Susan says. Her eyes roll as she says this, an indication of how ridiculous it was for Nick to imagine she'd have as much time for him once their baby was born. "Nick thought I didn't need him anymore. I had the baby. That wasn't true, but once he gets something in his head he believes it. That was one of the things that made us separate."

During the brief time Nick stayed with her after Sean's birth, Susan grew even more disenchanted with the idea of the three of them becoming a family. When Sean cried during the night, Nick would roll over and tell Susan, "You go get him." "I'd say, 'You're right there. Why can't you?' " Occasionally Nick gave Sean a bottle or played with him, but he refused to change a diaper. "He'd say to me, 'He's not going to remember me changing his diapers.' And I'd tell him, 'Nick, it's not that he's going to remember or not. It's you helping me out. Giving me some relief.' But diaper changing, feeding him in the middle of the night, that was all me. I had to do everything. Nick was here, but all the responsibility was on me. That kind of got me frustrated and cranky."

In listening to Susan, I remember conversations I've had with close friends who were new mothers. Most of them are married and their relationships solid and hearty after years of tramping together through the day-to-day sharing of lives. But Susan's stories remind me of how similar these dynamics sound. Often my friends' expectations about how parenting duties will be divided collapse once the baby arrives. For my friends, this disillusionment is usually integrated into their relationship, one more bump along a road they know they will somehow keep traveling together. For Susan, as for many other young mothers, the road that led them to parenthood is shorter, its bumps bigger, and the vehicle they travel in less durable. Often, if the pregnancy by itself doesn't end a relationship, the daunting responsibilities of parenthood will.

For Susan, being a mother changed the dynamics of her relationship with Nick. Now, when he tried to dictate what she could or could not do, Susan rebelled as she'd never done before. The daily demands of motherhood left her with no tolerance for meeting her boyfriend's demands as well. Besides, whatever time Susan found to be away from Sean, she wanted to use to revitalize herself. "I handle everything better when Nick isn't here," Susan says, offering me an example of ways in which Nick disrupts their lives. "When he wants to do something with Sean, he'll tell me, 'I'm his father.' I say to him, 'You're his father in a sense, but you don't help out.' I mean, there'd be times when Sean would be asleep and Nick says, 'I'll wake him up.' When I'd tell him he couldn't do that, he'd get mad and yell at me, 'You are trying to tell me how to raise my son.' But I'd tell him, 'No, I'm not trying to do that, but a baby has a schedule and you're not going to ruin it just because you say you are his father.' This is what makes me mad."

One afternoon, as Susan and I watch Sean play with his toys on the living room floor, I ask her how she feels about the way things have turned out in her life so far. "Does it make you sad that the fantasy you thought about as a young girl—the white picket fence, the house, a dog, two kids, and a father with you—doesn't exist for you, at least not yet?" I ask her.

"No, not really," Susan replies, shaking her head as though to convince herself of her certainty. "I mean, not everything works out in the way you want it to. So you take it as it goes."

"One person's compassion becomes another's incentive."

Neither Susan's nor Nick's mother had the energy or willpower, the personal know-how or community support, to convince their daughter or son to not engage in sexual intercourse or, at the very least, to protect themselves adequately from disease and pregnancy. Nor were the fathers even part of this conversation. Nick didn't use condoms, something he should have been doing even if Susan were properly using her birth control. Nor were the families of Susan's girlfriends able to prevent the unmarried motherhood that also became a defining event in their children's lives. Like so many other teenagers, Susan and her friends didn't set out to become parents so soon and on their own, but that's what happened.

Sex, pregnancy, and unwed motherhood are topics about which adults have a hard time communicating with adolescents. Though they're taught the biological mechanics of reproduction, girls say what they want to know a lot more about is how these bodily changes are likely to affect their emotional relationships. Girls want to learn negotiating skills that will help them resist pressure for sexual intercourse while still maintaining relationships with the young men they want to be with. Unlike their European counterparts, who talk about sexuality much more easily and provide greater access to contraceptives, American adults aren't comfortable with helping adolescents cope with their budding sexuality. In this country, sexual desire is widely regarded as something adolescent girls shouldn't have. Mention of sex and sexuality, too often, is ceded to advertisers, who are not at all shy about using sex to market products to teens.

When teenage pregnancies occur, adults find themselves in a quandary about how they should react. Should parents offer unlimited support to their teenage daughter who is soon to become a mother? Or should they treat her as an outcast and make her feel ashamed, in the hope that stigmatizing her behavior will dissuade others from following her path? But how do they shame her without hurting her and her child? And should adults demand that young, expectant parents marry, or at least try hard to convince them to do so, even when their relationship shows little promise of being healthy and sustaining? If parents' own marriages crumbled during their children's childhood, or if there was no marriage, what credibility does their advice have? Can an adult's words be more powerful than what a youngster has already witnessed or experienced? Instead of urging marriage, should adults make it easier for young mothers to continue their education so they can gain the skills they'll need to be self-sufficient? What about the baby's father? Who's watching out for him?

Decisions about how communities and families should handle unmarried teenagers' pregnancies are among the most difficult we, as a society, face today; they are intertwined with the myriad of social, economic, and cultural issues our nation now confronts. Community members who might have been among the most vocal opponents of teenage motherhood a few decades ago now find themselves, because of strong opposition to abortion, encouraging pregnant girls to give birth. Those who adamantly oppose abortion are also often similarly vocal in their demands to limit sex education and prevent schools from offering advice about or access to contraception.

A clash among these forces played itself out in the small farming and ranching community of Hempstead, Texas, during the fall of 1993. Townsfolk there wrestled with the incompatibility of a federal law that prohibits discrimination by public schools against pregnant girls, and the messages about sex and pregnancy that many of the adults wanted to deliver.* That fall four of the high school's fifteen cheerleaders were pregnant. None was married. It was the height of football season in this Texas town. Every Friday evening when townspeople turned out for the game, cheerleaders assumed a prestigious and very visible role along the sidelines.

This situation presented adults with a plethora of difficult decisions: Should the pregnant girls be allowed to remain on the squad? If they did, would it convey to the other students that school board members, teachers, administrators, and parents were sanctioning early, unwed pregnancy? Then a complicating event occurred: one of the pregnant cheerleaders decided to have an abortion. Once she was no longer pregnant, could she still be held ineligible to lead cheers? If she was reinstated, what signal would that transmit to youngsters in a community where disapproval of abortion is strong?

---

*In 1972, the U.S. Congress made it illegal for schools that accept federal funds—and every public school system does—to expel a student or prohibit her from participating in school activities because of pregnancy or parenthood.

By a vote of six to one, the school board barred all students, male and female, from holding an elected position—including cheerleader—if they were pregnant, caused a pregnancy, or had a child. However, it was impossible to take action against the boys who may have been responsible for the cheerleaders' pregnancies—one of whom was thought to be a football player—because none was identified.

The board's ruling created an uproar. The pregnant cheerleaders were benched. The girl who had an abortion was told she could cheer, but she decided to remain in the stands with her friends. But to those who opposed abortion, the decisions appeared to encourage girls to have abortions. Yet what message would be sent if the board allowed all four of the girls to resume cheering? As news of Hempstead's conundrum spread across the country, the National Organization for Women announced its inclination to file a suit, based on the federal antidiscrimination law, to reinstate the cheerleaders. Within a few days, the board voted again, this time reversing its earlier decision. The four girls were allowed to return to the cheerleading squad.

Hempstead's debate presents key ingredients of our contemporary societal dilemma. In a December 1993 interview with *The New York Times*, Alexander Sanger, the president of Planned Parenthood in New York, addressed this perhaps as forthrightly as anyone: "How much compassion and understanding should society show toward pregnant teenagers, and when does compassion become a license to do as one pleases?" he wondered. Sanger believes that because many of those who legislate public policy "really don't understand young people, . . . it is inevitable that one person's compassion becomes another person's incentive." Why should anyone be at all surprised, Sanger asked, that adolescents might interpret a demonstration of societal compassion—which is for many of them a rare occurrence—as an incentive? However, by acknowledging this dynamic, Sanger seeks neither to diminish the value of nor to negate the need for supportive services for teenagers who become parents. Instead of denying them assistance they and their children need, Sanger says, we must reframe the question: "So how do we do one [help teen parents] without the other [encouraging teen parenthood]?"

"Teenage pregnancy is undesirable and teenagers require help in avoiding it."

Sanger believes much more needs to be done by all members of a community if we are going to create environments in which "getting pregnant accidentally is uncool." What won't work, he argues, is to simply tell adolescents "Just say no" to sexual exploration. Rather, Sanger envisions creating a milieu in which "all structures of the community"—families, recreation centers, schools, and religious institutions—work in tandem not only to convey that accidental pregnancy is "uncool" but also to provide teens with the ongoing support and resources they need to construct strategies of their own to prevent pregnancy. Some might choose abstinence; others might engage in sex but become motivated to prevent disease and unintended births. Sanger proposes that adults could provide, among other things, "nonjudgmental education about sexual health." And in keeping with his birthright as Margaret Sanger's grandson, he also insists upon "no-big-deal access to birth control." This is a part of what Europeans provide for their adolescents.

Much of what Sanger urges Americans to do is what has evidently contributed to keeping teenagers' birthrates so much lower in Europe. Since 1970, teenage birthrates in Europe have fallen, while they've risen here. At the start of this decade there were 9 births per 1,000 teenage girls in France; in Sweden, 13 per 1,000; and in the United States, 61 per 1,000. Nor, as many Americans might suspect, is the difference between us and these other countries due only to high birthrates among nonwhite Americans: the birthrate among non-Hispanic white teenage girls was 42 per 1,000 in 1992, substantially higher than the rates in France and Sweden. The European nation in which the birthrate among teenagers is closest to our own—the United Kingdom—had a rate in 1991 of 33 per 1,000, only a bit more than half of ours.

In its 1985 landmark study comparing teenage pregnancy in the United States with that in thirty-six other developed nations, the Alan Guttmacher Institute found that the United States led these other nations in rates of teenage pregnancy, abortion, and childbearing. (In the 1990s the situation remains the same.) It is sobering to find out, as the study documents, that the United States' teenage abortion rate *alone* was as high as or higher than the combined abortion rate *and* birthrate of the Netherlands, Sweden, France, Canada, and the United Kingdom. The study concludes that blame for the high U.S. rates cannot be placed on the availability of welfare benefits or services: each of the five named nations is much more generous in its welfare and general social safety-net expenditures than is the United States.

The Guttmacher researchers associate several factors with the higher fertility rate among U.S. teens. These include a lack of openness in discussion about sex; a relatively inequitable distribution of income; a high degree of religiosity; more restrictions on teenagers' access to contraception; and less in-school teaching about birth control. Sweden, the Netherlands, France, Canada, and the United Kingdom all also have confidential, accessible contraceptive services, which cost nothing for teenagers. Finally, Europeans are more willing to acknowledge that most teenagers will engage in sexual activity. But, as the Guttmacher study noted, the focus of attention stays firmly on the prevention of pregnancy. "In each [country], there is a broad consensus that teenage pregnancy is undesirable and that teenagers require help in avoiding [it]," the report concludes.

"Teenage pregnancy is not so much about what happens below the waist but about what happens above it."

A few years ago I traveled to Harlem to visit a man named Michael Carrera. His parents, Italian immigrants, worked as a house painter and a pattern maker. Lessons from his own childhood taught Carrera about how a child's sense of self-confidence arises out of meaningful human connection. This ethos of closeness and caring has given him his extraordinary ability to help kids whom others have given up on seize a sense of purpose.

Mike, as he asks the teenagers to call him, grew up in an extended family that was not very well-off economically but was very attentive and close-knit. His family imbued him with a belief in himself and an ability to seize opportunities—qualities he needed to venture out of the shelter of his neighborhood and become the first member of his family to graduate from college. He went on to earn advanced degrees. At the time of our visit, Mike Carrera was Thomas Hunter professor of health sciences at New York City's Hunter College.

Each day, when his duties at Hunter were done, he went to a central Harlem community center. In the blocks surrounding this center, one in every four babies was being born to an unwed teenage mother. He went to this community because he wanted to offer youngsters what he'd been lucky enough to have during his childhood—caring, concerned adults to be there with them while they navigated through adolescence. If provided these human connections—which he believes are essential if youngsters are to find purpose in their lives—Carrera suspected, many of these young men and women would choose to postpone parenthood, finish high school, and work hard to prepare themselves for responsible adult lives.

"It was clear to me how poorly kids like these were treated," Carrera said. "But I also saw how responsive they were to being around a caring adult, how that would get them turned on to other things, such as learning." These observations form the cornerstone of the Family Life Education and Adolescent Sexuality Program that Carrera initiated in Harlem. Now, after several years of success in reducing the incidence of teenage pregnancy among the program's participants, Carrera continues his work with New York's Children's Aid Society by teaching others to replicate his approach. There are now ten other sites in New York City as well as sixteen in other communities around the country. And his program is not the only one to take this approach to preventing teen pregnancy.

"Employment, education, their own bank accounts, good health, and family involvement produce self-esteem," Carrera says, listing his program's components. Just saying these words sets his brown eyes twinkling, for he knows how powerful this combination can be. "These are also contraceptives," he says, referring to the powerful effect they have on teenagers. "It is the total fabric that is important. When kids are empowered with information and stimulated by hope for the future, it has a contraceptive effect." Although Carrera's program emphasizes abstinence as the best choice teenagers can make, birth control is available for those who become sexually active; it's prescribed (with parental consent) by an on-site doctor whom the adolescents know. Sexually active teens also have individual weekly meetings with a reproductive-health counselor.

"This is not a value-free program," Carrera says. "We have a message that delaying sexual activity is good. We are taking a stand." However, Carrera buttresses his "stand" not with punitive warnings and threats but with a whole lot of caring, which he believes cultivates the personal resources successful adolescents develop. His approach doesn't require fancy gimmicks. It does, however, require long-term commitment by caring and responsive adults who connect with youngsters and, in turn, connect them with the necessary tools and strategies.

Teenage pregnancy, Carrera contends, "is not so much about what happens below the waist but about what happens above it." Adolescents' knowledge of and access to contraception are rarely enough to prevent them from experiencing unplanned pregnancies. What adolescents need is help in finding the motivation to postpone sexual intercourse or to protect themselves from disease and pregnancy if they do have sex. Besides the program's consistent motivators—access to jobs; tutorials to help with school; sports and drama activities—there is also the promise of future educational opportunities. This is a mechanism by which hope is instilled: If they accomplish their mission as teenagers, the message to them is that they will have a chance at a "real" future. The young men and women who remain involved with Carrera's program through high school graduation are offered something many middle- and upper-income adolescents grow up assuming will be theirs: the chance to go to college. Under an agreement he made with Donna Shalala, President Clinton's secretary of health and human services, when she was president of Hunter College, youngsters who complete the New York City programs earn admission to that college. By the spring of 1996, fifty-five of the program's members were attending Hunter.

It had been twelve years since Carrera first sat down in the entryway to the Dunlevy Milbank Center in Harlem and doggedly persisted in convincing families to have their children become the first participants in his program. Though there has never been a randomized and controlled study to test Carrera's approach, an evaluation of six of the ten New York City programs, involving 200 young men and women, found the participants less sexually active than peers from similar circumstances. And, among those who were sexually active, the rate of contraceptive use—including condoms in tandem with another form of birth control—was also much higher than among comparably aged youngsters in New York City. Graduation rates were also higher than the city average.

These factors played a role in keeping the pregnancy rate among participants in Carrera's program relatively low. Just 12 percent of the girls in the program have ever been pregnant, a figure that heartens those who work with youngsters whose lives are circumscribed by a number of risk factors. Among the young women enrolled during the spring of 1995 in one of the six programs evaluated in the study just mentioned, only one in twenty-five had become pregnant during the previous year. And counselors believe that relatively few of the young men participating have become fathers.

To some observers, the fact that 12 percent of the young women have been pregnant (some before entering the program) may seem unpersuasive as evidence that such a holistic approach is doing all that much good. After all, too many girls are still having babies too young. But when considered within the context of this problem's usual intractability, Carrera's program—and others like it—are considered among the more promising strategies. However, we can be all but certain that progress in reducing births to teenagers is going to be incremental and slow, and will depend as much on the commitment of adults as on the efforts of teens.

"No way you can get them to not have a baby."

The ingredients of pregnancy prevention are precisely what too many adults don't have—the desire and willingness, the patience and perseverance, to stick with troubled youth across the span of their adolescence, and the societal will to invest resources to improve teens' circumstances so they can take advantage of opportunities that could lead them more safely and successfully into adulthood. Teens who do receive this kind of adult attention are often the ones who grow up trusting that opportunities will be there for them, and among them early pregnancy and unwed motherhood happen much less often.

No individual like Anna, working as a family planning counselor with adolescents, is going to be able to prevent a significant percentage of the teenagers she meets with from getting pregnant. It is unrealistic to expect otherwise. Factors over which she has no control drive these decisions more than anything she can say to teenagers or do for them. As Alexander Sanger suggests, all structures of a community must become engaged in this effort if American teenagers are going to avoid pregnancy and motherhood. And as many of these young mothers' families conclude, marriage to the baby's father rarely promises much of a solution to the difficulties of early motherhood. The legal union of a sixteen-year-old mother and a twenty-year-old father—to make this birth occur within a marriage—ought not to be at the heart of our debates about girls having babies too soon. Nor should efforts to make teenage pregnancy "uncool" break down over our differing perspectives on what adolescents should know about their blossoming sexuality and the ways they can address it. Although the content of messages about sexuality is very important—and access to contraception saves lives and prevents pregnancies—our focus needs to be, as Carrera puts it, not so much on what might happen below these youngsters' waists but rather on what is happening above them. If such comprehensive solutions are not embraced, then the words Anna said to me, words that epitomize our shared frustration with this situation, will continue to be prophetic:

"No way you can get them to not have a baby," Anna told me. "No way. No way. I know because I've tried."

4

Having a Baby: Unmarried Older Mothers

By four o'clock the parking lot of the white clapboard church is nearly full. The drivers of the cars are all women, many with children strapped into car seats, some without. As they walk toward the church, the ones carrying infants can barely be seen under the multiple layers of clothing and blankets they've wrapped themselves and their babies in to protect against the chill January wind. Other mothers hold the mittened hands of toddlers, leading them gingerly along a narrow shoveled path. The women who don't have children rush out of the cold to reach the church's side entrance. Inside, a short hallway leads to a spacious room where they find what they came for: the reassuring company of women gathering to talk with one another about unmarried motherhood.

"Okay, everyone, let's set up tables and chairs so we can get started," says Jessie, a forty-eight-year-old woman who put this Sunday afternoon group together after she decided to have a baby on her own several years ago. Her booming voice carries above the din of conversation and babies' crying, a cacophony the mothers, at least, are accustomed to. None of the other women seem to mind it, either; in fact, many of those who arrived without a child now are holding someone else's baby.

Jessie's command sends a phalanx of women into action. Within five minutes a large table with chairs has been set up, and the women arrange themselves around it. Those new to the group often sit near one another, seeking the comfort of proximity to others who are, like them, nervous about being here. For many of them, this meeting marks the first time they are admitting in public that they want to become mothers, even if it means doing so on their own. Coming here gives them a rare and valued opportunity to meet women who have already acted on similar desires, as well as others like them who just need to talk before deciding whether and how to move ahead.

Once Jessie is seated, her presence quiets the buzz of conversation.

"Let's go around the table and introduce ourselves," she says, reminding the women of the customary way they describe themselves: "Remember to tell us whether you are thinking, trying, already pregnant, or a mother.

"Okay, I'll start. I'm Jessie. I'm a mother, and my daughter is six years old."

The thirty or so women who are regulars at these monthly meetings pretty much know what stage of this process each of the others has reached. Many of them have developed close friendships with one another; between meetings, they meet or talk on the phone. Sometimes, however, there are surprises. Tonight, for instance, a woman announces that she's just found out she is pregnant; this elicits applause from many in the group, applause that is sustained because the women know how very long she has been trying.

As the introductions proceed around the table, another woman lifts a month-old baby out of her infant seat; her adopted daughter has been with her for two weeks. "So I'm now in the moms group officially," she declares proudly. Waves of congratulations travel her way. Occasionally, women share much sadder news, telling the group about a miscarriage, or an adoption that at the last moment did not work out. Since many among them have withstood these kinds of setbacks along the road to motherhood, they are able to extend the companionship of understanding.

Most of the women who are trying to get pregnant are doing so with the assistance of doctors and anonymous sperm donors. In their introductions many women give voice to the frustration and sadness they feel, now that another month has gone by and their inseminations have again not produced a pregnancy. "I'm a longtime trier," one woman says, describing herself with the same phrase she uses every month. She sounds exhausted and downbeat. Others tally up how many months—or, in some cases, years— it's been since they embarked on this medical path toward motherhood. Some have started to use drugs to stimulate ovulation. Since not all insurers treat fertility issues of older, unmarried women in the same way, the women trade information about receptive doctors and about insurers whose plans offer later age cutoffs for coverage and will pay for various aspects of their treatment. Sometimes a woman will ask whether anyone has fertility drugs she no longer needs and would be willing to give to her. Such drugs are very expensive, and some insurance plans do not reimburse women for their cost, so passing along medication left over after a pregnancy happens can give another woman an opportunity to try again. For example, Pergonal, an injected hormone that increases the number of eggs readied for ovulation, costs more than $1,000 each month. As the introductions continue around the table, a nurse who says she is considering adoption extends an offer to assist women with their fertility-drug shots. Because many of these women live alone, they need help with the intramuscular injections. Her offer is accepted by several women.

"I could not imagine going through life without a child."

For the women in this room, time is of the essence. They are in their late thirties or early to mid-forties, the time when a decision to pursue motherhood collides with diminishing biological prospects for achieving it. These women know this, and it worries them. "Why did I wait so long?" they'll say to one another in moments of frustration at how difficult it now is to conceive. If only they'd tried sooner, maybe they'd be mothers already.

But even as they volley such questions among themselves, they know the answer. Until recently, many had simply assumed motherhood would one day, somehow, happen. They'd meet a man, get married, and have children together. By now, they have realized that these things are unlikely to happen, at least in the usual order. They just hope it's not too late to have a baby. The man and the marriage may have to wait.

A fertility specialist, Dr. Robert Nachtigall, whose perspective is shaped by the baby-seeking women he treats, once remarked to me that it is virtually impossible for a woman to avoid run-ins with the powerful monthly signals her body sends about her reproductive capacity. Like a drumbeat, microdrops of GnRH, a hormone that the hypothalamus excretes every hour, deliver these signals. And each month the completion of a woman's menstrual cycle is another vivid reminder of her ability to nourish a fetus inside her. Today, because cultural and economic forces encourage women to delay marriage and childbearing, many more women, married and single, arrive at their middle to late thirties feeling that they've missed out on a big part of what their lives were meant to include. As Dr. Nachtigall said to me, it is difficult for childless women, no matter what their marital status, to "escape from the sensation that their bodies are telling them something about the desire to reproduce."

It is when women sense the impending demise of their reproductive ability that stronger urges to become a mother often emerge. The wish to find someone with whom to fulfill this desire usually accompanies the initial sensations of yearning for a child. But this wish—and the pursuit of it—may be shelved if too much time goes by and possible partners don't appear. At this point, having a baby may become the predominant focus of a woman's life. As I'd discovered, the dream of creating a family with a man can be pushed aside by a more powerful desire to become a mother. "A woman's biological drive to reproduce may be stronger than the social one to get married," Dr. Nachtigall suggested. More and more of his patients were single women. "Many of my single patients tell me, 'I'd rather have it the other way [with marriage], but I don't.' "

One woman described to me how her biological clock started to sound "like a time bomb" when she reached her late thirties. She'd been married during her twenties but she hadn't thought about having a child then. Her career as executive director of a national advocacy organization kept her on the road, sometimes five days a week. "During these years, I had no life," Victoria said. "I ceased to be a person." By her mid-thirties, she was divorced and pledging to change the way she lived. At first she thought of adopting a baby, but was deterred by the expense and by barriers to doing so as a single woman. A few years later, she found herself in a relationship with a man. She told him how much she wanted to have a baby and made it clear that she was ready to be a single parent if she got pregnant. When she did become pregnant, he informed her he wasn't ready for marriage or fatherhood.

"Count me out," he said in their final conversation, which took place by phone. This man has never seen his daughter.

Though Victoria might wish for her daughter's sake that the man had reacted differently, she tells me how ecstatic she is about being a mother. "I could imagine going through my life without a man," she told me. "But I could not imagine going through my life without a child."

"Sometimes when I think back on how much sperm came in and out of me, I just can't believe it."

Women who attend these monthly meetings usually don't have an ongoing, committed relationship with a man. Like the unmarried woman who was thrilled to be having a baby despite her boyfriend's departure, many of them were married when they were younger. But for a variety of reasons they postponed having children, and their marriages ended. Since then many have had other relationships, though none has found the "right" man—one who shares the desire to have a child. They exchange observations about how "eligible" men—the ones who are unmarried and roughly their age—seem to go out of their way to avoid dating them, preferring younger women. One conclusion drawn from this anecdotal evidence is that these men are worried about being cast in the undesired role of baby-maker in these women's midlife bouts with "baby fever."

A woman in her early forties tells me she had speculative conversations with men about using their sperm to conceive. None was willing, so she decided to try to get pregnant using anonymous sperm. Finally, when that didn't work, she adopted. Now that she's a mother she looks back with humor on how out of kilter her timing was. "Sometimes when I think back on how much sperm came in and out of me, I just can't believe it," she says, recalling how conscientiously she avoided pregnancy for so many years. "I mean, there the sperm was. And without paying for it!" She shakes her head. "It is just really, really remarkable how well I protected myself with birth control for twenty-five years, how stringent I was about it, and then all I went through to try to have a baby."

"Looking for Mr. Meaningful"

The round of introductions is over.

"Okay, before we break into smaller groups, I have a few announcements to make," Jessie says. She mentions an upcoming session in which a financial planner, who is herself an unmarried parent, will offer advice on how to organize family finances. Then, a few months later, an attorney who specializes in family law and is also an unmarried mother will talk about the legal implications of using sperm from "known" or "anonymous" donors as a way of getting pregnant.

"Now, does anyone have an idea about what you want to discuss in your groups?" Jessie asks. It is the custom that for an hour or so before dinner small groups of women discuss specific aspects of unmarried motherhood. At Jessie's prompting, the women toss out suggestions. One suggests forming a group to talk about using fertility drugs; another wants to talk with others who are considering adoption; some of the mothers want to get together to talk about child care. Then a woman tosses out a suggestion that no one can recall being proposed for a group discussion before:

"What about us talking about how to meet potential 'significant others'? Like figuring out how we can date when all we want to do is to get pregnant." It's as if she has taken a pin and pricked a balloon. The sudden release of pent-up emotion is palpable. Ripples of laughter circulate around the table. Conversations spring up everywhere. There is no one, it seems—not mothers, not "thinkers," not "triers," not even those who are pregnant—who doesn't have something they want to say about this.

"We should call this group 'Looking for Mr. Meaningful,' " one woman suggests.

When Jessie polls the women to see who is interested in joining which group, the overwhelming favorite—even among many of the mothers—is the hunt for Mr. Meaningful.

"I need to give up the fantasy of a man around the corner."

Chairs are hurriedly rearranged to form the "Looking for Mr. Meaningful" group. Even before everyone is seated, the conversation begins. One woman describes her current dating relationship as "mating while waiting to conceive." Another responds by saying how difficult it is to develop a relationship with a man while trying to conceive a baby with sperm from an anonymous donor. But, she admits, different emotions are driving her to want to do these things simultaneously.

"For me to start trying to get pregnant, I needed to give up on my fantasy of finding a man around the corner," says Diana, responding to these two women and their dual-track approach. Diana, who is forty years old, wants to concentrate her energies on becoming a mother. "I mean, years are going by," she says, looking around to see if others agree with her. "It's like I can't do both at once. I needed to click off one part of my brain."

Heads nod. Diana continues, reciting tales about all the years she thought she could meet the "right man." It's easy to tell by women's reactions that Diana's experiences are very familiar. In time her voice reaches a cautionary crescendo, and she says to the others: "I found out it was a crapshoot. Trying to search for a partner made me unable to head toward my goal of having a baby." Only recently, Diana turned an important corner, deciding to give up, for now, looking for a man as her partner and as a father for her child. "Now I'm putting all of my energy into getting pregnant."

There is barely time to absorb what Diana has said before others want to jump in. Sharon, pint-sized and dark-haired and also in her forties, tells the others that she had made the same decision as Diana. But for reasons that elude her, once she began anonymous donor inseminations she was suddenly inundated with dates. The timing seemed uncanny; why was this happening now, at the time when she had finally made up her mind to try to have a baby on her own? Sharon assures these women that she won't allow this deluge of relational possibilities to trick her into delaying her baby-making. She recalls all too well that for years she had relied on relationships to lead her life toward motherhood, but her hopes ended again and again with disappointment. Older now, and with her biological clock ticking ever louder, she says she is determined to focus on the inseminations and not count on a relationship to get her the baby she wants so much.

From across the circle another woman's voice enters the conversation. She's been trying for quite a while to get pregnant with sperm from an anonymous donor. This past week she'd had another insemination; then, last night she went out on a date. She describes how strange the convergence of these events made her feel. Because it was a first date, a lot of questions were asked. Her date told her about his earlier marriage, and she told him that she also was divorced. However, when he asked if she had children, she found herself caught in an awkward pause. This wasn't a difficult question, at least on the surface. She either had children, or she didn't. But she was not at all sure whether she should tell her date so soon about her desire to have children or the fact that she was actively pursuing that goal. After a few moments of reflection, she said no and left it at that. But her internal dissonance made her uncomfortable, and the evening was not a rousing success.

Sharon leans over to assure her she did the right thing: "When I told a man I was dating that I was trying to get pregnant, our relationship changed right away. And, believe me, it was not in a positive direction."

"I've had men who've said to me, 'Are you just looking at me as a sperm donor?' " Diana adds. "And in a way, it's true. Whenever I'd be looking at a man that way, he'd sense it and run."

The story line seems quite familiar to these women: She meets a man; they enjoy each other's company. They learn more about each other and, in time, sexual relations begin. Soon the man finds out that his girlfriend wants more than anything to have a child. But perhaps he doesn't share his partner's interest in procreation, at least not right away. He may start to wonder whether the woman wants him or his sperm. Of course, he can find out by telling her that he's unwilling to father a child, but such brinksmanship often means their relationship will not go on. Conversely, women caution one another to be on guard against allowing their powerful feelings about motherhood to carry them too far into a relationship that they sense is not good.

As I listen to these women, my thoughts drift back to those wrenching months in my own life when my long relationship with the man I wanted to have children with crashed into this immovable object: He didn't want to have a child. I did. I remember, too, the time when I met another man while I was trying to conceive by donor insemination, and how difficult it was to reconcile these two desires—one for the companionship of a partner; the other, to become a mother. He was in the midst of a divorce and, with one child of his own, he wasn't close to thinking about a new commitment. But now, as this discussion takes place around me, I keep wondering why I was never able to bring these two circumstances together.

As I tune back into the group discussion, a few of the mothers are discussing their sense of relief at no longer viewing men through the prism of procreation. But as their comments reveal, even after the need to find a reproductive partner goes away, a different dynamic can surface. Belinda, who had her son on her own when she was forty-two, tells the other women, "What I want now is to find a father for him." Her son is sleeping in her lap. Belinda's words express the commonality of these women's circumstances: whether they are trying to become mothers or have already done so, their relationships with partners are intricately related to what they want for their children or the baby they hope to have.

"There must be something that triggers our separation from the dream."

Sharon pulls the conversation back in the direction of making babies. "It is strange how sex seems so separate from having a baby," she says. "I mean, right now I'm making a baby with a speculum and a catheter. It's hard for me to even imagine having sex in the middle of all this. And right now I don't want to meet anyone who'd make me think of taking even a month off." She looks in Diana's direction, as though seeking reassurance. Diana nods. "At the same time, though, I also hate to think of nobody being there with me," Sharon adds.

The women's conversation meanders in this territory of absence. Occasionally they laugh together heartily. Mixed with their laughter, however, is sadness about what hasn't been or might never be. Mothers assure the wanna-be moms that having a baby—even on their own—is the best decision they ever made, even if at times they miss having a partner with whom to share the experiences of being a parent. That loneliness is tempered by memories of how much more alone they felt when they didn't have a child. Wishes for a steady companion, the women tell one another, are infinitely more bearable than the aching longing they once had to become a mother.

"There must be something that triggers our separation from the dream," one woman suggests. It is clear to everyone that by "dream" she means the "traditional family"—a married couple, two kids, a dog, white picket fence, a honeysuckle-vined house. Each of these women has had to go through her own tough reckoning in abandoning the dream. A solution many arrived at was to split the dream apart and act on the parts of it they could control: the child, perhaps the dog, maybe the house and fence. Marriage, many hope, will come later. "I mean, for me, I just know I want to be a parent," this woman continues. "I want to be a mother. I've thought a lot about what life would be like without my child having a father, particularly if I have a son." She tells the women that her decision, like theirs, was arrived at only after a great deal of internal debate. "There are a lot of women who do it," she adds, as if, by appealing to the increasing numbers, she can successfully bypass prolonged discussion about the trade-offs they all know so well.

This woman's willingness to separate from the dream was triggered by the death of an eighty-three-year-old woman friend. At the funeral she found herself envisioning the totality of her friend's long and complex life; she herself was just entering her forties. Thinking of her friend's eighty-three years made her realize how much of her own life she might have left. That day she made up her mind not to let the second half of her life pass without having a child. "Being at her funeral made me think about whether I had the strength to do this. I found myself answering yes."

"Most of these women are actually becoming single mothers by second choice."

Merle Bombardieri, married and the mother of grown children, is a small woman with a high-pitched voice. Her office exudes the cozy intimacy of an old-fashioned parlor. A large Amish quilt, patterned in earth tones of green, blue, and rust, complements the comfortable, soft-cushioned chairs and sofa. Polished wood end tables display the only visible clue to Bombardieri's occupation: a flowered box of tissues is never more than an arm's length away.

Tissues are a staple of Bombardieri's practice as a clinical social worker.

A hefty supply is needed by many women she counsels who feel stuck on the cusp of motherhood and come to her seeking guidance in deciding whether to try to have a baby by themselves. These women shed a lot of tears as Bombardieri prompts them to talk about failed relationships and regrets they might harbor about choices they made many years ago, to leave a man or have an abortion. It is Bombardieri's job to help a woman untangle the deep emotions that are now being brought to the surface by her intense focus on motherhood. "It can be heart-wrenching," she says.

"Many of these women are trying to reconcile what is happening in their own lives with their ideal image of having a child as part of a committed relationship," she explains. "For them to go ahead on their own, it is important for them to be able to grieve about the loss of what they don't have." She has discovered that many of these women, most of whom have established careers, carry with them what she calls "the new great American dream": instead of envisioning the husband/father, kids, dog, house, and picket fence, they hope for "the great career, the great husband, and the children whose care the mother and father share."

Many women have sisters or friends who've created this kind of family. Here, in the safety Bombardieri provides them to express pent-up emotions, women talk about the unfairness they feel: why do other women find this and they do not? "By going through this grieving process, they are able to deal with anger and sadness they feel about not achieving this dream. Grieving about the loss of this dream isn't saying to them they will never be married, never have this family." In fact, what a lot of these women come to believe is that they'll have a child, *then* meet the special partner. "I have been fascinated by men falling in love with women who have children rather than with ones who want to get pregnant," she says. "Men seem very scared of change. Perhaps some are also afraid of women using them as a vehicle to have a child. They may be more comfortable about making a commitment to a child they have already met and know they like, and forming a relationship with a woman who is already a satisfied mother." Bombardieri believes that in the future we may see more families being formed in reverse order: "A woman will have a child; then, later, she may get married."

Most women who become mothers on their own would, if the choice was theirs to make, have a partner. Life just has not worked out that way. "When they finally decide to go ahead and have a baby, people say they are 'single mothers by choice,' " Bombardieri says. (Single Mothers by Choice is also the name of a national organization to which many of them belong.) "But for many of these women that name does not really fit. Their first 'choice' is to be with a partner when they are becoming a mother.

When they go ahead and do this without one, most are actually becoming 'single mothers by second choice.' "

"Women don't want to just drift into childlessness."

During the past decade Merle Bombardieri has counseled more than a thousand unmarried women who are considering motherhood. Some women come on their own to talk with her, paying for one-on-one therapy. Others participate in her daylong workshops, which she advertises with the title "The Last Call for Motherhood" and offers as part of adult education programs. She keeps these groups small; they are usually sold out. She estimates that about one-third of the women she counsels decide not to pursue motherhood on their own.

At the workshops, Bombardieri explains to women how they can sometimes confuse feelings about an unresolved loss, such as the breakup of a long relationship or the death of a parent, with a yearning for a child. Grieving can lead a woman to thoughts of bringing something new into her life. Or what Bombardieri calls "baby hunger" can tug at women when the mirror reveals their gray hairs or crow's feet. Or baby hunger can hit a woman when she invites her younger sister's friends to a baby shower. Or it can occur when a birthday year is divisible by five. Turning thirty-five seems to launch a lot of single women into this pursuit. And if the urge doesn't set in at thirty-five, then by the time forty rolls along, it can hit fast and hard.

By this age a woman's ability to remain afloat amid the strong undercurrents of the biological, emotional, and social messages telling her not to "miss out on motherhood" is usually wearing down. For years now she's stood on the sidelines as friends have gotten married, announced with great fanfare their pregnancies, and then celebrated the arrival of their children. She's watched her friends' lives be transformed by parenthood, which has consumed the time they once spent together. She feels left out in this passage into middle age. And in comparison with the changes she sees happening in her friends' lives, her own seems static. Friends who are parents resume their careers with outlooks that seem more expansive; if something at work doesn't go well, at least they have a family at home. On the other hand, a childless woman begins to wonder whether her job, interests, and circle of relationships can consume the kind of connective energy she wants to express. She knows, too, that her years of reproductive possibility are collapsing into a precious few.

I remember well when "baby hunger" hit me. The symptoms were numerous and varied and burrowed into almost every aspect of my life. Everywhere I went, it seemed I was dragged into a confrontation between my wish for a family and the realization that this was precisely what I didn't have. When a mother passed by pushing a baby in a stroller, I was stung by envy. At the beach my eyes always drifted away from my book to watch parents walking hand in hand with toddlers at the water's edge. Once I returned home it was impossible to clear my head of these images. I hated feeling this way, but I was a prisoner to these thoughts. Whenever invitations to friends' weddings arrived in the mail, a voice from a place deep inside me would say, "Why can't this happen for me?"—even though my attempt at marriage had been miserable. At reunions an awkward difference surfaced whenever photographs of ponytailed and freckle-faced children were passed around and conversation touched on little else. It was hard to join these conversations, as much as my friends tried to include me. And when I went to buy baby presents, in my mind's eye I saw piles of all the tiny sneakers, rattles, and teddy bears I had bought over the years for all of my friends' babies. By now I'd given enough baby presents to stock my own store.

When baby hunger hits, a woman's first impulse may be to try to ignore it. This is hard to do, but possible if one's attention is strongly enough diverted. But in time, this urge pounds so ferociously on what might once have seemed a securely locked door that a woman has few choices but to peer inside. From that moment on, until she arrives at some resolution to these irksome questions about her reproductive future, life can feel like a spinning record, a needle stuck in its groove, circling but advancing nowhere. But there is one outcome that can be predicted with some measure of certainty: whether she becomes a mother or not, by confronting these issues she will reshape how she thinks about the rest of her life.

For women who seek out help with this decision from someone like Bombardieri, probing their "baby hunger" can be a difficult but extremely worthwhile journey through a field of emotions they were afraid to enter on their own. When they don't seek professional guidance, women usually rely on other women for advice. Rarely does a single woman get through these years without talking with someone about childbearing or being sought out by a friend to be her sounding board. "Women tell me they don't want to just drift into childlessness," says Bombardieri, whose job it is to help them be certain that they don't. Whatever a woman finally decides, she gains a measure of comfort from having confronted her choices.

"I'm going to decide. I'm going to decide."

Between the ages of thirty-seven and forty-two, Janice, a psychologist, was consumed with trying to decide what she wanted to do about motherhood. Not having a child had become for her a debilitating and painful condition. But that didn't mean that Janice acted on this desire. For her, as for many women, the decision-making process itself became long and difficult. Although a part of her felt an intense compulsion to have a child, other emotions restrained her from going ahead on her own. She desperately wanted to share the experience with a man. At times, when she thought she had convinced herself to go ahead, she would find herself debating for many more months whether she should adopt or try to become pregnant. Her decisions shifted constantly, swinging back and forth 180 degrees from week to week. Meanwhile, Janice was working full-time and trying to finish her doctoral dissertation. But these internal conflicts about motherhood obsessed her.

Janice felt miserable. The pages of journals became her reliable companion; she poured out her emotions onto them to try to relieve the pressures she was putting on herself. When Janice mentions this, I remember Merle Bombardieri explaining why she encourages women to start a journal to increase self-understanding: "The journal is a friend whom they can reach for at three in the morning. It's never too angry or busy to listen."

"I have journals and journals and journals of writing I did about how much I wanted to have a baby." Janice is now forty-five years old, and as she revisits this time in her life, her memories seem fresh; her angular face is drawn and her eyes are teary. "Every week I would write to myself about this. I'd start the week with big scrawling letters on the top of a page: 'This week I will decide!' Then I'd write out categories: 'Should I have a baby?' 'Should I adopt?' and I'd create pro and con columns. I would imagine what my adopted child from India would look like. Fantasizing. Visualizations. I'd plan to spend the weekend by myself at the beach, with a promise that by Sunday I'd decide what to do. On some Sundays I'd write to myself, 'I will adopt.' And I'd go home thinking I had finally figured it out. Sometimes I'd even give my adopted child a name. But by Wednesday, I would be back to wanting to get pregnant. It just went like that. Cyclical. It went on like this for years. 'I'm going to decide.' 'I'm going to decide.' Then I couldn't. It just went on and on. It completely took over my life."

Janice joined a support group for people considering adoption. A social worker came to her house to begin an evaluation of her fitness to become an adoptive parent. Then Janice abruptly decided to halt the process. Her former boyfriend, a man with whom she'd been for the better part of a decade, had died, and his death reminded her of how much she'd wanted to have a baby with him. She even called the morgue to find out if it was possible to retrieve some of his sperm. It wasn't.

Janice talked often with her parents about her pursuit of motherhood. They encouraged her, but each held a different view of how she ought to go about it. Her mother favored adoption because it was "more socially responsible." Her father thought pregnancy would be better; he liked the idea of his daughter passing on the family genes. He suggested that she try donor insemination. Janice finally decided against adoption after she discovered that being an older, unmarried woman made it virtually impossible for her to adopt from India. She decided to try to have a baby. "At this point I was wishing I could have a relationship, but more of me was caught up in this question of how I was going to have a baby." She asked several male friends if they would donate sperm. "I wanted my child to be connected with a father," she says. "I thought it would be really neat to get sperm from a friend. Not to have intercourse with him, but to get his sperm. I explained to the men that I'd just like the child to know that you are the father. They didn't need to give me any money or have any parental responsibilities. I just wanted there to be a father I could tell my child about." None of the men agreed to help her.

"I was so happy that I was finally taking action to get pregnant."

During all the years she spent struggling with her decision, Janice rarely missed a day of charting the small changes in her body's temperature. She did this with a thermometer accurate to a tenth of a degree, so that she could know precisely when she ovulated. If she did try to get pregnant, this tracking would be helpful to a doctor. For a few months her menstrual cycle shut down—an event precipitated, she believes, by the stress she was experiencing in making this decision. A friend suggested she go on a trip to give herself an opportunity to reduce the constant pounding of these thoughts. Janice went hiking in Nepal. In the mountains, she pledged to herself that she wouldn't allow the decision about motherhood to overrun everything else going on in her life. When she got back home, her cycle resumed. Calmer months followed, in which she worked out her feelings; she decided to move ahead. To do her inseminations, she located a doctor highly recommended by other single women.

Friends accompanied her to the doctor's office for her first insemination. "I remember I felt okay about doing it this way because I just wanted this child so badly that it was going to be okay," Janice tells me. "All of a sudden, it was just okay. I remember lying on the table and the doctor was putting the sperm into me. I was so happy that I was finally taking action to get pregnant. After all these years I was taking action to do it. I felt really, really good about it."

Janice did not get pregnant that month. By the next month, when it was time in her cycle for her insemination, Janice again found herself consumed by ambivalence. "This thing came up again inside of me, my sadness about a child not having a father. It brought up tremendous feelings of loss." She now realizes that the sorrow she ascribed to her child's potential predicament was, in part, *her* sadness at not having a partner to do this with.

However, she kept her insemination appointment that month. This time she did not ask any friends to go with her. By the time she arrived at the parking lot, her feelings of uncertainty were at a boiling point. She walked up the two flights of stairs and down a long hallway of doors leading to her doctor's office. As she approached his door, it was as if she heard warning bells clanging louder and louder in her head. "I was sweating," she says. Even now, as Janice tells me about this moment, she looks frightened and worried. "My heart was just beating." She walked back to the parking lot. "There I was, pacing back and forth in front of the stores." She went to a pay phone and called several friends, but reached only their answering machines. She couldn't talk about this to a machine.

"I went up the stairs again, but I felt like I was going to pass out."

Again, Janice hesitated at the office door. After a few moments, she returned to the telephone downstairs. She dialed her doctor's number and when his receptionist answered she said:

"I'm canceling my appointment."

Janice never went for an insemination again.

"How did you feel after you walked away?" I ask.

Janice sits silently, avoiding contact with my eyes and not answering my question. In sharing this story with me, she has transported herself back to a time and place she thought she had left behind forever. Reliving these times is not easy. Her remembrances also reawaken the ambivalence I myself experienced during the days that led up to my monthly inseminations. During some months I, like Janice, canceled appointments. But unlike her, the next month I usually returned.

"I felt relieved," Janice says. "But I also had this sense inside of me of, 'Oh, shit, when will this ever end?' "

"The absence of motherhood rurns out to be a greater disappointment than never having had a husband."

In 1994 209,000 unmarried women who were thirty or older had a baby. Out-of-wedlock births accounted for 16 percent of babies born to women in this age group. A decade earlier, births to similarly aged unwed women totaled just over 84,000. The National Center for Health Statistics reports that the birthrate for unmarried white women between the ages of thirty and thirty-four rose by 104 percent from 1984 to 1994. For black women in the same age range, the rate of increase was 31 percent. Among all unmarried women aged thirty-five to thirty-nine the increase in birthrate during this same ten-year period was 82 percent; for those between forty and forty-nine, it was 88 percent.

These large increases in unmarried motherhood reflect the life circumstances of this generation of women. If they are well educated, women can be economically self-sufficient and earn enough to support children as well. And women, on average, are attaining higher levels of education today than men. These changes in women's economic status have altered expectations about marriage and parenting. Because many women do not depend on men for their economic well-being, they can be more choosy about whom they select as both a partner and a father to their children.

These women also came of age during a time in which attitudes about male-female relationships shifted significantly. Premarital sex and cohabitation are now much more widely accepted. And in an era when close to half of all marriages end in divorce, belief in marriage as a secure, supportive relationship has greatly diminished. The Roper Organization polled four thousand people just as the 1990s began and asked whether they believed the institution of marriage was stronger, weaker, or about the same as it had been a decade earlier: 61 percent of women and 62 percent of men said it is weaker. Only 12 percent of the total sample replied "stronger." Given such attitudes, it is not surprising that many more adults than ever before now choose not to get married. Between 1970 and 1993, the number of never-married women between the ages of thirty and thirty-nine doubled. And childlessness increased. Among the subgroup of baby boom women born between 1946 and 1955, nearly one in five is childless. When compared with our mothers, by the time women in my generation reached our mid-thirties we were twice as likely not to have children. Childlessness among college-educated women is also higher than among less well educated peers; by the time they reach their forties, 28 percent of them do not have a child. And there is little racial disparity in the incidence of childlessness among highly educated women.

Previous generations of educated women found their choices more limited. Many college-educated women figured they had to choose between marriage and career. By not getting married, they also virtually eliminated the possibility of being a mother, because they faced an apparently unbudgeable barricade of societal stigma against unmarried motherhood. Half of the women who graduated from college in 1910, for example, never had children. Even if unpartnered child-rearing had been acceptable back then, many of these women would not have had the economic security they needed to make it manageable. So with stoic, generally silent acceptance, these unmarried women remained childless. Their circumstance was regarded as an inevitable consequence of their "unfeminine" ambition.

One morning I notice a newspaper announcement about the formation of a support group for elderly, never-married women. I am curious to learn how these women have dealt with the absence of both marriage and children in their lives. The social worker who organized this group explains to me that she did so because these women are usually excluded from many of the rituals associated with old age. They do not have grandchildren to visit them. They don't have children to invite them to holiday dinner with their families. Yet, by watching their friends, they are constantly reminded of what they now miss out on because of the constricted choices they had earlier in their lives.

More than a dozen women, who range in age from the mid-sixties to the early eighties, join this group. Having one another to talk with encourages them to share aloud—often for the first time—their sadness and regret about having lived in a time when women were expected to sacrifice motherhood if they didn't get married. For these women, the social worker tells me, "the absence of motherhood turns out to be a greater disappointment than never having had a husband."

"Murphy Brown mocks the importance of fathers by bearing a child alone and calling it just another 'lifestyle choice.'"

While many more older, better-educated, unmarried women are bearing and adopting children now than in past decades, in neither percentage nor numbers does the incidence of out-of-wedlock births among them come close to the figures for less well educated, poorer, younger women. Even so, there appears to be enormous interest in these mothers' lives— that is, if media coverage can be used as a reliable gauge. These days, when the U.S. Census Bureau issues reports that chart the rise in unmarried motherhood, much of the coverage steers away from data on younger moms and toward older ones. And because of former Vice President Dan Quayle's memorable speech about family values, these women have a nickname: people refer to them as "Murphy Browns," after the fictional TV anchorwoman who has an out-of-wedlock child—regardless of how closely their circumstances match hers.

The Quayle speech that triggered the initial volcanic flow of media attention was given on May 19, 1992. The vice president was addressing the Commonwealth Club of California, a well-heeled, conservative audience. The theme of his speech was the need he saw to return Americans to the bedrock of "traditional family values." The most fundamental prerequisite of family values was described by Quayle as the married Mom-Dad-kids type of family. He chastised single-parent families in inner-city America for having "a poverty of values" and sharpened his attack on the "narcotic of welfare." Quayle also called for "dismantling a welfare system that encourages dependency and subsidizes broken families." Coverage of those remarks, however, was obliterated by a stampede to report on what he had to say about *Murphy Brown*.

In sentences that took him no more than thirty seconds to deliver, Quayle, who had never seen an episode of the show, used the lead character's decision to have her baby as a way to further discredit unmarried motherhood. He referred to Murphy Brown as "a character who supposedly epitomizes today's intelligent, highly paid, professional woman." Then, in a line that would be repeated hundreds of times in print and on TV and radio, Quayle derided Murphy Brown for "mocking the importance of fathers by bearing a child alone and calling it just another 'lifestyle choice.' " The night before he gave his speech, 38 million viewers had watched as Murphy Brown gave birth to a son who'd been fathered out of wedlock by her former husband and who was going to be raised by her alone.

During the next several weeks Murphy Brown seemed to be everywhere—on the covers of national magazines, in banner front-page headlines and op-ed pieces, on nightly newscasts. Radio talk show callers wouldn't talk about anything else. Pollsters got to work tracking public opinion. Caught up in the Murphy Brown hysteria, the media devoted much less coverage to Quayle's main message, which attempted to link recent riots in south-central Los Angeles to a "breakdown in family structure."

At a White House press conference, Canada's then–prime minister, Brian Mulroney, who'd come to discuss trade, was peppered with questions about what he thought of Murphy Brown's out-of-wedlock child. When Mulroney became testy, President George Bush lectured the press corps: "I've told you, I don't want any more questions about it." After the press conference was over, President Bush pulled the prime minister aside and, shaking his head, he reminded him, "I told you this was the issue. You thought I was kidding."

By this time, "Quayle vs. Murphy Brown" was assuming a life of its own. Quayle's remarks were being interpreted by many as demonstrating insensitivity to single mothers, many of whom let him know that they were doing all they could to care for their children after their partners had abandoned them. Before long, Quayle apologized: "I have the greatest respect for single mothers. They are true heroes." Still the topic wouldn't go away. Murphy Brown's creators demanded to know if the vice president would have preferred to see Murphy Brown have an abortion rather than bear her baby out of wedlock. No, Quayle responded. At the White House, presidential spokesman Marlin Fitzwater went out of his way to praise Murphy Brown for exhibiting "pro-life values which we think are good." By the time the new TV season began in September, the vice president had selected a proper Republican gift—a stuffed elephant—and sent it to Murphy's baby boy. In an accompanying note, Quayle congratulated Murphy for her role, inadvertent as it might have been, in helping to "start an important discussion on ways to strengthen our traditional values."

"The power of this desire to have a child, when women no longer need to have a child to define themselves as women, seems to be as great or even greater than ever."

Clearly it is not the number of births to older, unmarried women that draws media attention. The attraction lies elsewhere. For one thing, the pace at which women of this age and economic status are pursuing motherhood has been accelerating rapidly. People who are these women's age—and, coincidentally, consumers the media want to attract—are curious about what motivates them to do what no other generation of women has done. And in choosing unwed motherhood, these women spark discussion about many of the hot-button gender issues of our time—women's economic independence, their diminished interest in and heightened expectations of marriage, and the "breakdown" of traditional family structures and parental roles. If women have children on their own, some men worry that they, in their customary roles, are dispensable. And mothers who are married but unhappy wonder about the path they didn't take.

Heightened interest also reflects the age and life circumstances of many of the editors and producers who decide what we read about and watch on television. Stories about older, highly educated mothers offer news editors a fresh direction in which to steer story lines about unwed motherhood, moving it away from the often-told saga of poor, young unmarried mothers. And because many editors and TV producers belong to the baby boom generation, stories about older, unwed mothers have personal appeal. If a reporter isn't herself considering this idea, it's very likely that she knows women who are, and has friends who have already become unmarried mothers. Suddenly this is no longer seen as news about "them"; it is about "us."

This is the first generation of women to have the economic wherewithal all of them need, the medical technology some of them need, and society's cautionary yellow light to pursue motherhood on their own. However, despite the changes that make unmarried motherhood feasible, women's decisions to go ahead on their own still upset many observers. Some share Quayle's view that intentionally having a baby outside of marriage is selfish, indicative of the me-generation mentality infecting baby boomers, and that the decision is made much too lightly. By satisfying her own desire to become a mother, a woman blatantly disregards her child's need for the consistent, caring presence of a mother *and* a father. Yet, as one unmarried mother said in response to such criticism, "How can this be selfish when I am saying I am now prepared to put someone else, my child, first?"

Others worry that if older unwed mothers—several of whom are well-known personalities—are allowed to escape societal sanction for their out-of-wedlock births, it becomes all but impossible to convince younger women to put aside their urge to have a child until marriage. Marian Wright Edelman, the nation's most prominent children's advocate, receives rousing ovations when she points out this dichotomy in her speeches: "If it's wrong for thirteen-year-old inner-city girls to have babies without benefit of marriage, then it is wrong for rich celebrities, too, and we ought to take them off the cover of *People* magazine."

Others regard the trend toward out-of-wedlock births among older, educated, working women with less alarm and more understanding. Some view it as a predictable concomitant of women's self-reliant economic status, particularly in a transitional time when men and women seem to be figuring out new roles and responsibilities within marriage. Until marriage adjusts itself to accommodate changing circumstances, some women who can do so will create families on their own. As social commentator Katha Pollitt wrote in *Glamour* magazine: "We can't put the genie of women's economic, sexual and social independence back into the bottle of marriage, because marriage, at bottom, is based on the absence of those things."

Today many women, by the time they reach their mid-thirties or early forties, regard their decisions about motherhood as a choice between whether they'll "do it alone" or "not do it at all." A survey done by the Institute for Social Science Research, in Los Angeles, found that half the women surveyed said they would consider having and raising a child by themselves if they were childless by the time they reached their forties. Similar attitudes are expressed by teenage girls. When asked in a 1994 *New York Times*/CBS News poll about their expectations for family life, a majority of the girls said that they'd consider becoming a single parent if they didn't get married. Girls were also more inclined than boys to say they could have a happy life if they did not marry. One can already see in these young people's responses the divergent expectations that girls and boys might someday bring to marriage: nearly 20 percent of the boys said they'd expect their wife to "stay at home," whereas close to 90 percent of the girls said they intended to work outside the home if they got married.

Betty Friedan's 1963 book *The Feminine Mystique* transformed the way many women in my generation envisioned our adult lives. Unlike our mothers, about whose generation Friedan was writing, we would make marriage and motherhood only a part of our lives. Being a wife and mother would be something we did after we'd established distinct definitions for ourselves. That focus explains, to some degree, the explosive increase in the number of women in my generation who have reached the age of forty without having had a child. But they're not necessarily happy about that. In the 1980s, when Friedan wrote a new introduction to *The Feminine Mystique*, she explored the visible conflict between women's independent outlooks and actions and the still forceful tug of motherhood. She wrote that "the power of this desire to have a child, when women no longer need to have a child to define themselves as women, seems to be as great or even greater than ever." Conversations I have with unmarried women who are in their late thirties and their forties bear out the perceptiveness of Friedan's insight. Many, including some who have achieved considerable recognition for their professional success, talk about the feelings of immense emptiness they experience because they do not have a child.

The other part of Friedan's assertion—that women "no longer need to have a child to define themselves as women"—rings less true. Some women who have devoted their entire adult lives to the world of work have a nagging sense that who they are as women has not been fully expressed. Many talk of wanting to add new layers of feminine identity to their lives. And an undercurrent in the lives of childless women is a sense that not to be a mother is to be deviant, to be caught outside the natural course of what one's life as a woman can—and should—be about. Jeanne Safer, a psychoanalyst and author of *Beyond Motherhood: Choosing a Life Without Children*, explains that women who remain childless are forced to confront different psychological tasks. "Our decision not to have children violates norms of feminine conduct," she writes.

"Now I have the right accoutrement, a baby, to prove I am a real woman."

Marsha's three-month-old son sits in a bouncy baby seat as his mother and I sip tea at her kitchen table. Her rooms have a kind of windswept look, as if a hurricane has passed through, leaving clothes and toys strewn haphazardly in its wake. An old wood side table in the dining room has been transformed into her son's changing table. Stacks of bills, unopened envelopes, and papers lie scattered on the living room floor. Chairs are so crammed with rattles and pacifiers, colorful outfits and blankets that there are few places to sit down.

Marsha is a thoughtful woman, a psychologist to whom I often find myself repeating the comments of other unmarried mothers to hear what she has to say. Today I want to talk with her about what I've heard several unmarried, childless women in their thirties say about the sense of "deviance" they are starting to feel. Some told me that people sometimes say things that make them appear as something other than "true women," since they are living neither the role of wife nor that of mother. I ask Marsha if she ever wrestled with this feeling and, if so, whether having a child has made a difference.

"Well, since I was a young child, I've always been deviant," Marsha declares. The directness of her reply appears to leave little doubt that she's content to have her life be viewed in this way. But her next words make clear that this isn't so. "There are times when it's been very painful for me. A part of me would love to have conformed. In some ways I don't have the temperament to be a deviant. I'm too anxious and wish to be acceptable. But there is also a stubborn streak in me that wants to call it as I see it, and for much of my life I've been a nonconformist. It's a central part of my identity—not one I tried to have; I just am. In some ways, when I was making the decision about having a child on my own I thought to myself, 'Well now, hold on, are you just trying to be deviant?'" Marsha laughs. "But in another way I thought, 'No, it is not being deviant for deviancy's sake. It is that I am a very strong maternal person and I want a child. And

I would do it other ways if I could. But I haven't been able to, and it looks like I won't, and I want to have a child."

"But in another sense your decision to have a child meant you'd be able to conform more closely to the normal pattern of a woman's life," I say.

"Yes," Marsha responds, agreeing with this premise. "At least, I value the thing that women are supposed to have at the center of their identity. And, in fact, yes, I think this makes things emotionally easier for me in some respects. I was joking with a friend about the 'baby-as-accessory' like we see in fashion magazines, telling her that now I have the right accoutrement, a baby, to prove I am a real woman. In fact, I wanted very much to question myself about this, to make sure that was not the central reason for having a baby. Was I needing a child to complete myself because I felt I wasn't a whole person? Or was I wanting a child to fulfill myself and to nurture another full person, another individual? Yes, it is gratifying to me to do something that society approves of, even if society doesn't approve of the way I do it."

"I'm not married, so I figure I'll never have a child. I'm stuck."

The pursuit of motherhood pulls single women through mazes of self-exploration. Many a woman compares what she had as a child with what she knows she'll be able to offer if she parents on her own. For many, this comparison presents discomfiting moments, as it did for me. It can be hard for those who grew up with a mom and dad to imagine their children living without a father, and with a mother who needs to work full-time to pay her family's expenses.

As the women navigate these difficult junctions of memory and desire, some, like Janice—the psychologist we met, who agonized over whether and how to become a mother—decide not to push ahead. Those who do keep going toward creating their own families confront other choices and challenges along the way. First they must decide whether they will try to conceive, and if so, whether they will do so with a boyfriend, with a man who agrees to be a donor, or with an anonymous donor; or if they will try to adopt, and if so, whether they will hire a private attorney to find a baby, work through a public agency, or travel overseas. Each approach carries with it a different set of issues, which women often turn to friends or family members for help to resolve. Also, because these women are older, their ability to conceive is lessened, and because they are single and older, their access to babies to adopt can be limited. To face repeated disappointment—as many women do—in the midst of trying to fulfill what has become an obsessive desire can feel devastating.

Kerry spends her days working as a research scientist. Hours at her office can easily drag into the evening, especially when there is no one waiting at home for her. The two-bedroom house she owns is in a suburban community. It has a huge backyard for her dog to play in. The neighborhood is ideal for children—safe, with almost no traffic; the neighbors watch out for one another. It seems an ideal place to raise a family.

A family—children or a husband—is something Kerry wants but doesn't have. "I never thought of myself as someone who wouldn't have children, who'd be a career person exclusively," says Kerry, whose buoyant and optimistic outlook is being buffeted by the unintended direction of her personal life now that she's reached her late thirties. Surrounded by shelves bursting with scientific journals and thick piles of reports, Kerry tells me how difficult it has become for her to spend time with friends who have children. She enjoys playing with their children so much that it becomes terribly painful when she returns to her empty house.

As more and more of her friends have married and begun their families, their lives, which for so many years ran on parallel tracks of career and friendship, now veer apart. Many of her friends have returned to their jobs after they became mothers, and Kerry notices how their daily lives assume new and complicating layers of responsibility. This is something she envies, given that the routine of her life remains much as it has always been. She yearns to have it change. Finding common ground with these friends is also no longer easy. Kerry not only misses their companionship but finds herself becoming jealous of their experience as mothers; this creates a new emotional distance.

"I love kids and I never would have said when I was younger that I would be without children. But as I look at where my circumstances have led me, I'm not married, so I figure I'll never have a child," Kerry says, in a downbeat tone of voice that contains an edge of resignation unusual for her. "I'm stuck."

"Oh, I hope you haven't abandoned the idea of having children."

Job offers often find their way to Kerry. Given her track record of accomplishment, she is much in demand. Because she's single, potential employers don't need to concern themselves with conflicts a husband's career might pose. Nor is a child's school year schedule something that would complicate a move. She's now thirty-eight, and the possibility of a prestigious shift in her career is also enticing. One offer, in particular, interests her: it's a top-level position in a laboratory where she's always wanted to work. Since she received the offer, she's thought about little else. She finds herself scribbling on scraps of paper lists of reasons why she should take the job and reasons why she shouldn't. The balance shifts day to day. The job is everything she needs to advance her career; a few years ago Kerry would have leaped at such an opportunity without the slightest hesitation. Yet, now, she's not so sure. She finds herself focusing on the commitment of time and energy that will be required, and the intense pressure she will be under, to prove herself all over again. If she is to succeed, Kerry knows, she'll need to put her personal life on hold, again.

One morning, in the midst of this decision-making, Kerry's mother, Eleanor, stops by her office to say hello. Kerry is delighted to see her, and hopes that her mother's guidance can help her sort through her conflicted feelings. A few weeks ago she told her parents about this offer, alerting them to the possibility that she might move away. She hadn't shared with them all of the personal issues that she's been wrestling with in trying to make this decision. But Kerry thinks this might be the moment she's been looking for to talk about the real reason she might not take this new job.

That she wants to have a baby instead of this job isn't easy for Kerry to admit. She's tried in the past not to let her parents know how disappointed she is about not being a mother. Often she's wondered whether her parents are disappointed in her for not giving them a grandchild, but that is one of the conversations they all seem adroit at avoiding. Now as Kerry pushes ahead, she tells her mother how wonderful this prospective job sounds but how she no longer wants to commit herself to the long, unpredictable hours that she's been so willing to work in the past. Then, words Kerry had not known how to say tumble out: "So, of course, one of the big considerations is whether I've abandoned the idea of ever having children."

Her mother hardly hesitates: "Oh, I hope that you haven't abandoned the idea of having children."

Kerry is shocked. Is her mother forgetting that her daughter isn't married? Or does she assume that if she turns down this job she will apply the dedication she brings to her work to the task of finding a husband? Kerry hasn't shared with her mother any of her thinking about having a child before she has a husband. Pausing to collect her thoughts, Kerry inhales deeply, composing just the right sentence to transport this idea on its maiden voyage outside her mind.

"Well, as a matter of fact, I've been thinking about having a child on my own," Kerry says.

Hearing herself say this startles Kerry. She feels like the little Dutch boy, but taking his finger *out* of the hole in the dike. Once these words break out, others spill out behind them. Kerry's mother listens, giving no indication that she's at all surprised by what her daughter is telling her.

"My mother was incredibly supportive," Kerry tells me later. Kerry believes that her own enthusiasm about this idea must have been contagious: "My mother got very excited about this."

"It started as me saying to myself, 'of course I can't have kids because I'm not married.' "

Kerry's parents have been married for forty-seven years. Her father still maintains a satisfying and lucrative professional life. His income alone has afforded the family a comfortable house in the suburbs and paid for Kerry's higher education and her brother's. Kerry's mother stayed at home to raise the two children. Her older brother, who is now a lawyer, bought their childhood home and lives there with his wife and child. Her parents live nearby, in an apartment.

"I come from a very nuclear family," Kerry says, to underscore the gigantic shift in thinking about family that she's going through to try to get comfortable with the idea of having a child on her own. She had expected her mother to have at least as hard a time accepting this idea as she did in arriving at it: "My mother is not at all a liberal person in terms of new social ideas."

But while Kerry views intentional single motherhood as a "liberal" idea, in the sense that it yanks her away from her own traditional childhood experience, her mother sees it through different eyes. What she cares about most is that her daughter not miss out on the experience of being a mother. If Kerry's only chance to be a parent is to do so by herself, then so be it. Besides, she knows her daughter will be a wonderful mother.

Later that day she telephones Kerry at work.

"I mentioned your idea to your father," she tells Kerry. "He was really shocked."

"Frankly, Mom, I was surprised you weren't shocked," Kerry replies. "I would have predicted that you would have reacted the same way."

Her mother all but ignores Kerry's comment in her eagerness to tell Kerry more about her father's reaction. "After I told him, he went away for about five minutes," she says, building the drama. "He was just by himself. Then he came back and said, 'I could be a grandfather again.' "

Kerry is relieved. Now that both her parents know, she is thrilled that they are so solidly in favor of this new plan. Soon she tells her brother and sister-in-law, who are jubilant: now their son will have a cousin to play with. In the next few weeks Kerry shares her thinking with some friends. No one cautions her against single motherhood. Everyone tells her it's a wonderful idea.

"My thinking evolved over a period of months," Kerry explains. "It started as me saying to myself, 'Of course I can't have kids, because I'm not married.' But then it was like, 'Well, wait a minute. Is this really true?' Once I let this idea, that I didn't have to be married, seep into my consciousness it was like I was able to hear people saying to me, 'Well, maybe you should.' Maybe they were saying things like this to me before but I'd always ignored their promptings."

Kerry refuses the job offer and turns her attention to having a baby, though she still worries about whether she, alone, can do for her child what her parents, together, did for her. Will parenting be too difficult for her to handle by herself? Will her child feel okay about her decision? Will having a child on her own make her less likely to meet a man and perhaps one day get married? After several more months of rumination Kerry concludes that, despite her uncertainties, she is ready to go ahead.

"I can let my child know there was never anybody who knew of his existence who did not want him."

Kerry's next hurdle is figuring out how she will get pregnant. Her first thought is to find a friend willing to donate sperm. That way she'll know who her baby's father is and, assuming this friend agrees, her child will, too. She doesn't intend to have sex with him but to go to a clinic for the insemination. Her friend will produce the sperm. Then, in another room, she'll lie down and a nurse will inseminate her.

When Kerry asks a couple of her male friends, she reports that they seemed flattered by her request. In her initial conversations with them, Kerry tries to be brief, leaving talk about the details for later on. She doesn't want to scare them off. She wants only to test their willingness to participate before she thinks some more about what she wants to do.

But it doesn't take long for Kerry to realize how complicated all this can become. If she and this man are friends, what might happen to their friendship if they have a child together? Would they share custody? What happens if she doesn't want him to be a steady part of her life? How does she work that out so that he can still be an active father to their child? How eager is she to involve herself and her child in such an arrangement? And what if, after the child is born, this man gets married and has children of his own and decides he doesn't want the child to know that he's its father?

Kerry asks her brother for legal advice. He explains how murky the laws and court decisions on this type of arrangement are. Even if she and the man who donates sperm sign documents in which he relinquishes his claim on the child and she releases him from parental responsibilities, there is no assurance that such an arrangement would hold up in court. If he decides he wants to play a larger role in his child's life and makes an effort to do so, Kerry can't do much to prevent it from happening.

Kerry also reads about insemination and learns that married couples sometimes mix the husband's sperm with a donor's. By doing this, a husband and wife hold open the possibility that the child who is conceived might be biologically the father's. This gives Kerry the idea of mixing together sperm from several friends. "No one would know who the father is," she says. "But I'd know he was from a small group of people whom I knew and trusted." What seems most important to Kerry is that she do whatever she can to ensure that her child is genetically endowed with intelligence, to whatever degree this is possible. To choose donors she knows are smart would make this aspect of the baby-making less worrisome than using sperm from an anonymous donor.

However, when she mentions the sperm-mixing idea to potential donors, she says, smirking, "all they did was sort of get into this fantasy notion of how their sperm would win the race." By turning the insemination into a race, the men temporarily pushed aside the reality of responding to her request. In the end, each of them declined. "I was impressed by how many of them felt it would be very hard not to know whether the child was really his and not to have a role in the child's life," Kerry tells me. "I actually thought it was very encouraging that the people I asked are such good potential father figures." By this time, she no longer figured it was a good idea, either. Confusion about paternity isn't something she thinks would benefit her child.

Kerry next considers using an anonymous donor. But she doesn't like the idea that her child will never be able to know his biological father. "I thought about that a lot," she says. "And it's an ongoing concern. In what I would say to my child I planned to emphasize how much his mommy wanted a baby and that there is no daddy. . . . I guess I try to focus from the point of view of how involved or uninvolved a father is. Whether married or not, there always has to be some sense of abandonment for the child who does not have their father with them as they are growing up. At a later time I could constantly remind my child of the generosity of this man who made this anonymous donation to bring him into the world. And [if I use an anonymous donor] I can let my child know there was never any-body who knew of his existence who did not want him." Kerry realizes that the same could not be said if a friend of hers was the man who donated sperm.

"You mean that no one abandoned him?" I ask.

"Yes," Kerry replies. "And that there is not another person on the other end of this for him to search for, no one who knew him who said, 'I don't want him.'" This differentiation carries the most significance for Kerry, and I hear other women who use an anonymous donor to get pregnant echo her thinking.

When women like Kerry hear people criticizing them for intentionally having a baby by themselves, they sometimes compare their children's situation with the trauma many children suffer when parents divorce and one parent—usually the father—abandons them. At least their child, these women say, won't have to face a beloved father's sudden disappearance.

"Probably no one's childhood is perfect," I say to Kerry, attempting to weave together some of these threads of our conversation. "I guess there are always things that can make a child sad or angry as he grows up, even when he has two parents."

She nods. "But that idea of not having two parents is such an enormous barrier when you're thinking about doing it on your own. You feel as though somehow you have to provide everything. And if you can't, you figure maybe it's not the right situation."

Kerry devotes a lot of time to talking about her decision with married friends who are mothers. They assure her that her worries about being a good mother are not unlike their own. Like Kerry, many of them have demanding careers which they resumed a few months after their babies were born. Though they have husbands, the bulk of responsibility for child care, they have discovered, rests with them. A few joke with Kerry that having a child on her own might actually be easier, a remark I hear women make again and again. After all, Kerry's friends remind her, she won't have a husband to take care of as well.

These sentiments provide only limited comfort. "You put a fair amount of pressure on yourself when you think about doing it alone," Kerry says. "You feel you need to be the be-all and end-all which, of course, you can't be."

Over time Kerry becomes comfortable with both being a single mother and using an anonymous donor to get pregnant. Her comfort level grew, she tells me, as she focused her thinking on all she has to offer a child instead of on what she can't. The stubborn fact is, however, that her son or daughter will not have a daddy unless she meets a man who wants to form a family with them. This means that her child isn't going to grow up as part of a nuclear family, which she still considers the ideal. But with the love, nurturance, and attention she knows she is ready to give her child, and with an income sufficient to pay for high-quality child care and a good education, Kerry decides not to let her chance for motherhood go by.

"If I didn't try as best I could to have a child, I would kick myself years down the line."

Kerry sets up an appointment at a clinic where she knows doctors inseminate single women. (Not all doctors will.) Her doctor explains the medical facts about the "procedure"—donor insemination—and urges Kerry to get started because she is old; at least, her ovaries are.

One of her first steps is to select a donor. Kerry tells the doctor's assistant about characteristics she is looking for. Her requisites are for the man to be highly educated and to share her religion. Once these preferences are identified, the clinic assesses potential matches from both a personal and medical perspective. (Factors such as Rh and blood type must be compatible.) A few days later, Kerry is handed a short list of potential donors and chooses one.

"Were you comfortable you'd been given all the medical information you needed?" I ask Kerry, recalling my own experience with donor selection. I became quite upset at the paltry amount of each potential donor's medical history I was permitted to see. The staff at my clinic refused to let me read the information they had about the donor's family members' medical history, or even very much about the donor. I knew, however, that the California Cryobank, a sperm bank in Los Angeles, compiled and shared with customers detailed medical and personal information about donors and their families. I demanded access to my donor's medical history if I was forced to choose from the doctor's donor list, as the clinic required me to do. Finally, after a long discussion, the doctor gave me permission to review the information. He also made me promise that I wouldn't tell other patients about this arrangement.

"Yes and no," Kerry replies, shrugging. "I would have loved to have more information, but, yes, I was comfortable." Her biggest concerns had to do with possible genetic abnormalities and sexually transmitted diseases such as AIDS, and these were automatically screened out of the donor pool. "Ultimately, what also let me be comfortable about the information I had about my donor's intellect was that someone told me that how well a child does in school tracks to the education level of the mother. And I figured I have that covered."

In Kerry's third month of inseminations, she becomes pregnant. She uses neither fertility drugs nor any other medical intervention, apart from the catheter by which her donor's sperm is placed directly into her uterus. But a few weeks later, Kerry's euphoria ends abruptly with a miscarriage. The loss is emotionally shattering, and it forces Kerry to reevaluate her thinking. "I had been concentrating so hard on all the reasons why I might be a good parent," she says. "Now I am coping with the realization that I might not be able to have a child." It is hard for Kerry to come to terms with this possibility. In the rest of her life, perseverance has always paid off for her. Now sheer willpower and hard work might not be enough.

Before Kerry can bring herself to try to get pregnant again, she forces herself to examine her responses to some tough questions: "Can I tolerate the uncertainty of what I'm doing? Can I tolerate this if I try and nothing happens?" Again and again she quizzes herself to figure out if she has the strength and desire to continue. One day, in the midst of this self-examination, Kerry realizes that she has no option but to go ahead: "If I didn't try as best I could to have a child, I would kick myself years down the line." Kerry resumes her inseminations. This time her doctor suggests that she use fertility drugs to stimulate the release of more eggs each month. But because Kerry got pregnant before without using drugs, she decides against them, preferring not to interfere with her body's own hormonal rhythms.

For nearly two years Kerry continues trying, without success, to get pregnant. Before each insemination she has to go through a series of appointments for blood tests and ultrasounds. She can't arrange her work schedule to fit all this in every month, so she ends up being able to inseminate only every few months. That bothers her, because time seems to be rushing by. As for the months when she does inseminate, the hours she misses at work are tough on her and the process drains her emotional energy.

As her failed attempts accumulate, it becomes harder for Kerry to maintain her optimistic outlook. Particularly as her fortieth birthday draws near, Kerry feels an even stronger pull to motherhood; because of this, her resistance to using fertility medication breaks down. Finally, after the arrival of her period signals another failed attempt, Kerry lets her doctor know that she's decided to try using drugs. He prescribes Pergonal and Kerry talks a friend of hers into injecting it for her. In her second cycle with Pergonal, Kerry gets pregnant.

Kerry didn't tell people at work about using donor insemination to get pregnant. So when colleagues see her belly swell, a few of them ask her about the man they assume is now part of her life.

"Do we know him?" a co-worker asks.

Kerry has decided not to share her secret with anyone at work. "No, he's not around and he's not going to be involved" is all she tells them.

No one ever says anything negative to her about having a child without being married. "Most people are able to look at it from my perspective rather than from a preconceived notion of the way society should operate," Kerry says. "Many of them have seen me with children, and no one seems to feel I'm not going to be a great parent. They are amazingly supportive." When it's almost time for her baby to be born, Kerry's mother asks if she is worried whether her colleagues might start to question her commitment to her career. "Actually I am more concerned that they won't realize that I'm going to do some things differently than I did before," she responds.

Kerry knows her decision to become a mother has altered forever her single-minded devotion to her job. How she'll adapt to motherhood remains a mystery, but there is one thing about which she's certain: now there will be someone to come home to.

"What am I going to put in the place where it asks for father's name? My sperm donor's identification number?"

Donor insemination, as a method of impregnating a woman, is not new. More than a century ago, in 1884, a professor at Jefferson Medical College responded to a plea for help from a childless married man by substituting a donor's sperm for his own. The man's wife was anesthetized and the donor's sperm was injected into her with a rubber syringe. Accounts of the event record that the man selected to donate his sperm was "the best-looking member" of the medical school class. These three men—the husband, doctor, and donor—agreed never to tell the mother how she became pregnant. When her baby was born, she and her husband raised it as their own.

In the late nineteenth century no laws, no state or federal regulations, and no ethics committees were in place to determine if what the doctor, medical student, and husband did was proper. Nor were counselors available to assist parents or children in coping with any impact of medically assisted procreation. Instead, the solution that was considered best for everyone was secrecy.

During the twentieth century, donor insemination became a widespread way of assisting couples who were unable to conceive on their own. The woman's husband became the child's legal father. Donor insemination was largely done outside of public view or scrutiny; unlike today, such services weren't advertised, in part because married couples demanded secrecy. Even in cases when couples weren't satisfied with their treatment, the veil of privacy surrounding insemination often kept them from complaining.

The way anonymous-donor insemination was designed to work protects, not surprisingly, the individuals who held the power to shape its rules. That these individuals were men speaks volumes about why the system was originally designed to work the way it usually does. To get men to donate sperm, promises were made to conceal their identity and nullify any paternal liability, such as child support. The woman's husband assumed these responsibilities. Doctors also had no obligation to keep reliable records, since the whole idea was to act as if this had never happened. (Stories still surface every so often about unscrupulous doctors who used their own sperm to impregnate patients.) A child's perspective didn't seem to matter very much; a son or daughter conceived in this fashion would never be told that a man other than the father they knew played a role in their conception. "What you don't know won't hurt you" seemed to sum up the view most adults had about the children. When children did find out (as some inevitably did), their anger was often directed at the fact that their parents had kept this secret from them.

Secrecy remains a linchpin of this system today, because many factors still work in its favor. To begin with, many more couples than single women use donor insemination to conceive a child. For those who are married, there is still little incentive for them (or their children) to know the identity of the donor. Keeping the procedure secret protects husbands from having to deal in some public fashion with their infertility, and also protects a family from the stigma still associated with medically assisted conception. If a couple is Catholic, for example, donor insemination violates church doctrine, which condemns all forms of "artificial" conception and disapproves of masturbation, a necessary step for men in this procedure. Secrecy leaves to the individual's conscience the decision about whether to acknowledge these acts.

Earlier in this century several judges articulated disapproval when asked to rule on some consequences arising out of this method of family formation. In a 1921 divorce case, a judge denied a wife alimony after her divorced husband accused her of adultery on the basis of donor insemination (to which he had consented). Intercourse, the court claimed, was not the essence of what defined adultery: this woman's "voluntary surrender" of her reproductive powers to someone other than her spouse was enough to constitute adultery. In the years prior to World War II, ethicists and scientists published dozens of scathing articles about the immorality of a couple using a donor's sperm for procreation. In 1955, a Chicago judge's ruling echoed the earlier finding that equated insemination with adultery. Since adultery was violation of public morality, this judge refused to acknowledge the husband's consent and was thus unwilling to grant him legal paternity of the child. As recently as 1963, a New York court ruled that a child conceived with an anonymous donor wasn't "legitimate."

By the early 1970s, however, court decisions began to reflect more tolerant attitudes about sexual and reproductive issues. In 1968, the U.S. Supreme Court found that many of the legal disabilities associated with out-of-wedlock births violated the U.S. Constitution's Fourteenth Amendment, providing for equal protection. At the same time, pollsters were finding that views of premarital sex were becoming much less negative. Divorce was also more common and more accepted as a way to resolve marital strife. Men and women were living together openly outside of marriage, and more open discussion about such previously off-limits subjects was creating an atmosphere in which the shame surrounding infertility was also starting to be shed. In this atmosphere of cultural change, judges became less likely to adhere to earlier rulings that characterized donor insemination as an adulterous act. With that hurdle cleared, arguments that the children conceived with an anonymous donor were "illegitimate" were invalidated. In 1968, a California judge ruled that a husband charged with criminal neglect for not paying court-ordered child support to a child conceived, with his consent, by donor insemination had a legal obligation to pay support. The judge concluded that this man, the mother's husband at the child's birth, was the child's only "lawful" father.

By the mid-1970s, the Uniform Parentage Act (UPA) had been drafted by a national commission of experts and enacted by several states. The act's key provision extends the parent-child relationship to every parent and every child, regardless of the parents' marital status. In many states, because similar statutes have been enacted, children born out of wedlock have most of the same rights as those born to married parents; for example, regardless of whether marriage has taken place, if a biological connection is established, an absent parent has a legal responsibility to support the child. In the UPA, and in several state statutes, questions about donor insemination and paternity are directly addressed. The laws say that when a married woman is impregnated with an anonymous donor's sperm under a physician's supervision and with the written consent of her husband, the child is to be treated as the "natural child" of her husband. The donor, according to the UPA, is to be "treated in law as if he were not the natural father." But only a handful of states have statutes offering legal clarification about what happens when an unmarried woman uses an anonymous donor. Those laws similarly nullify the donor's rights and responsibilities toward the child. Because the unmarried mother has no husband, she retains full legal and custodial rights to her child.

Today donor insemination, as part of an expanding array of medically assisted reproductive options, faces increasing legal and ethical scrutiny. Doctors now must maintain donors' medical records. The American Society of Reproductive Medicine also issues guidelines for screening sperm donors for sexually transmitted diseases, including HIV-1, syphilis, gonorrhea, chlamydia, and hepatitis B and C. Some clinics also test for HIV-2 and HTLV-1. And chromosome analysis is performed; sperm banks screen donors for certain genetic abnormalities, including sickle-cell anemia, Tay-Sachs, and thalassemia. One sperm bank, Xytex, also preserves donor cells that can be used, if needed later on, to develop a complete analysis of the donor's genes. During the past decade it's also become common practice to freeze and quarantine donor sperm for a minimum of six months, sufficient time for follow-up blood tests on donors to rule out the possibility that their semen carries the HIV virus.

Nowadays, too, the veil of secrecy about the donors is being lifted. Not surprisingly, unmarried women are the ones doing the heavy lifting. Fertility specialists estimate that between 10 percent and 15 percent of women using anonymous donor insemination are unmarried. Despite making up only a small percentage of the clientele, single women are having a major impact on changing the "old boy" system of donor insemination. Because of their different circumstances, secrecy about the donor's identity is not something unmarried women want to preserve. Many of these unmarried mothers' children will never have a "social" father to raise them as his own. These mothers know that, in time, their children will ask them where their "daddy" is, and they intend to be honest with them about how they were conceived. Many of these unmarried mothers also want their children—when they are older—to be able to get answers to questions about their fathers, or to get in touch with them, if they choose.

Several sperm banks have responded to these women's new circumstances and desires. They have lists of donors who agree, when their child turns eighteen, either to be contacted directly by the child or to be notified by the clinic that a child has an interest in making contact. At some clinics, donors are asked to write essays about why they are willing to become fathers in this way and to supply considerable personal detail that mothers will be able to pass along to their children. A few donors even agree to have their pictures taken, and these are made available to their children. Or, at Xytex, one of the clinics responding to the customers' changed expectations, a woman selecting a donor can send a photo of someone she'd like her child to resemble, and the staff will match this person up with a few possible donors. An eight-by-ten-inch reproduction of a childhood photograph of the donor is also available. Mothers who belong to the national organization Single Mothers by Choice are also setting up a sibling registry, so that children who are biologically connected to the same donor—and thus to one another—will be able to locate each other.

Despite these changes, when an unmarried mother gives birth after using an anonymous donor she still does not have a name to write in the "father" spot on her child's birth certificate. "What am I going to put where it asks for father's name?" one such mother asked me, her voice as sarcastic as it was sorrowful. "My sperm donor's identification number?" Some mothers write "conceived by donor insemination," but in that case this information becomes a permanent part of their child's public record. Other mothers tell me they invent a name so that their child will never have to face a disapproving look from a snooping bureaucrat, who on seeing an empty space might conclude this child's mother "slept around" and couldn't identify who got her pregnant.

"I feel a terrible heartache and anguish that I, by design, would create a person's life without a father."

For some women who feel that they've never wanted anything so much as they now want to have a child, the one big stumbling block in moving ahead is concern about who their child's father will be. Kerry was able to reconcile herself to the permanent absence of her child's father by considering everything she had to offer as a parent. Because of this she felt all right about the scanty information she could obtain about him. For other women, accepting such trade-offs is a lot harder. Some never feel comfortable, even if they decide to go ahead.

Joan launches her search for sperm donors by placing an advertisement in the personals section of several magazines and newspapers, including *The New York Review of Books*. The ad reads, "FATHER/DONOR NEEDED NOW: Jewish woman, 39, M.D., seeks healthy, handsome, bright, HIV-negative man of compassionate integrity. Various options." When she wrote this ad, Joan imagined setting up some kind of coparenting arrangement with a man who responded, but she never put together a precise vision of how such a setup might actually function.

The response is promising. Some of the men send photographs along with their letters explaining in great detail why she should choose them as a donor. A gay couple asks whether she would be interested in being a surrogate mother for them. She isn't. What Joan intends is to get pregnant and raise her child on her own. A doctor who lives with his mother writes to Joan to say he'd be willing to donate sperm but wants the child to be raised at his mother's house. She doesn't. As the number of replies approaches one hundred, Joan loses a precise tally. All she knows is that the pile of letters is getting quite high and the job of evaluating the candidates starts to fill every available moment she has.

"Why," I ask Joan, "are you willing to get involved with a stranger to do this?"

"A child has to have a father," she replies. "I want my children to know their father and to have an opportunity for some kind of relationship with him. I think children should know their biological and cultural roots. These are the feelings that shape my search. I feel a terrible heartache and anguish that I, by design, would create a person's life without a father."

Joan's light blue eyes blink often as she speaks. Her face is round and friendly, yet her voice conveys the loneliness she endures. Several of her close friends have recently moved far away. A serious relationship also ended for her. Joan's family—her divorced parents and younger sister—live in another city. Exercise and work are Joan's only reliable companions. I sense that Joan believes her loneliness will be eased by having a child. Because she is a lesbian, Joan never expected that a man might one day arrive to enable her to have a child, and to satisfy her desire that the child have a day-to-day relationship with its father. Kerry had postponed motherhood while she waited to see if marriage would happen. Only when it didn't did she consider having a child on her own. Marriage was never something that Joan wanted, but now that she is almost forty, motherhood is.

Using the telephone, Joan interviews about eighty of the self-nominated donors. These conversations help her to narrow her list to about twenty men whom she regards as "promising." She arranges face-to-face meetings with them. One man sends flowers before he flies thousands of miles to meet her; he brings along the results of medical tests he's had done on his blood and semen and assures her that he will not claim paternity rights. Even though he isn't Jewish (the religious affiliation she wants) he says he has no problem with her raising their child in her faith.

I ask Joan about this man's motives. "Well, he told me he's never had a child with a really bright woman before," she says, chuckling to herself—a welcome rarity in this conversation, which for the most part is quite serious, almost somber, and clearly agonizing for Joan.

After several months of meetings with these potential donors, Joan realizes she's arrived at a crossroads. She must make herself answer some fundamental questions, ones that hadn't occurred to her as clearly before she entered into this process. Is she willing to trust a person who is, after all, still a stranger in such a major decision that will affect the rest of her life, as well as that of her child? What if, after she is pregnant, the man she selects changes his mind and decides he wants an active role in the child's life? Or in her life? As a biological father, he'll have parental rights which neither she nor any written agreement they might reach can nullify. Joan becomes even more acutely focused on questions revolving around trust when her sister tells her that a former boyfriend of hers concealed from her the fact that he is HIV-positive. This revelation only adds to Joan's mounting sense of unease about her own situation. "It makes me pull back and question the whole thing about trust," she tells me. "Whom do you trust? How do you trust? There I was meeting strangers and talking with them about the most intimate thing anybody can undertake together. . . . I realized how complicated it was to undertake this with somebody basically unknown in my life. So I'm thinking now about sperm banks. It's sort of become like the devil you know versus the devil you don't. Something in me shifted and I worked through some of the stuff that had made me feel so passionate about the child having to have a known father."

With great reluctance Joan abandons her search for a donor she knows and decides to select an anonymous one from a sperm back. "Making this decision was absolute anguish during the last few weeks," Joan says. The tired look on her face reflects this misery. "Back and forth, back and forth I went. How can I choose an unknown donor over a real person who seems like a decent person, who can be a nice daddy, who can give me a little bit of help, whom I respect, who's got a decent profession? Then at other times I feel, well, it would be better for the child to have the father and better for me not to have that complication and not to have to consider and negotiate with somebody who has his own set of attachments and feelings about this child. It was like if I could do this with an unknown donor, I could create this whole thing more myself."

"I had a fantasy about arranging to fly out with the baby to meet him."

Though Joan accepts, in principle, the idea of her child's father being unknown, she still wants as much information about him as possible. She decides to use a donor from the Sperm Bank of California because it has enlisted many men who are willing to be identified when a child turns eighteen. These men are called yes donors. Joan also insists that her donor be Jewish. "Then I also told them I want a man who is extremely handsome and extremely bright," she says.

Once Joan receives background information about her donor, she can't resist trying to find out who he is. "I have a reputation of being sort of a detective," she says. "Any obstacle is a challenge for me." Using clues from her donor's biography, she makes "a million calls," contacting people at universities where she believes he went to school. She talks with coaches of sports he said he played and professors in his fields of interest. If she weaves together enough clues, Joan thinks, she might emerge with a logical suspect.

"What's the goal of this search?" I ask Joan one day as we talk by telephone a while after she finally abandons her search without locating the man. "I mean, what were you planning to say to him if you'd found him?"

"I was going to tell him what I was planning to do," she replies. "I was going to tell him about myself a little bit, and I was going to ask him in more detail about some medical questions. On one of his forms he did say he would like to someday meet his offspring; I was going to ask him—I mean, not to back him against a wall or anything, but I guess I had a fantasy about arranging to fly out with the baby to meet him."

"If you do get pregnant, will you resume your search for the donor?" I ask, recalling how when we first met she told me how important she thinks it is for her child to know its father.

"Yes," she says without a moment's hesitation. "But I don't feel hopeful about it. And I think my doing this is an obvious indication of how much I'm not at peace with this arrangement. My reason for wanting to find the father is for the child not only to have an image and knowledge of who the father is but to have the experience of growing up with some contact with its father."

Joan's thoughts about this are shaped by her childhood. She always felt close to her father. She remembers how the two of them would get up very early and set out on pre-breakfast adventures to places around the city before he went off to work. At night, he often sat by her bedside to tell her stories before she went to sleep. But Joan's parents divorced when she was about ten years old; her father left the house and her relationship with him became more distant and difficult to maintain.

"I felt totally abandoned," she says, though they did not lose contact with each other. "I was heartbroken. My whole life became organized around trying to get my parents back together. I developed obsessions and compulsions. I made contracts with God. I recited magical prayers. It was very painful." Now, whenever Joan thinks about having a child who won't know its father, she revisits these painful times during her childhood.

Her pursuit of motherhood also seems inextricable from the mental portrait she carries of what a "family" should be. "A family lives in a honeysuckle cottage," she says. And inside that cottage, Joan says, "there should be a mother and father and children, even if the mother and father are not bound by sexual or romantic love. At least that way there is a father. 'Your father this' and 'Your father that.' 'You look like your father.' 'Your father is coming to do this with you.' " Through Joan's eyes, this mom-dad-kids family arrangement is a fundamental ingredient of what it means to be human: "What makes somebody a person is a relationship with a mother and father." Joan knows her child won't have this, but choosing a donor who is willing to be contacted when her child is eighteen years old offers, at least, some measure of consolation. Joan just hopes that all these years from now this donor is still willing to meet their child.

On the day before her first insemination with the unknown donor's sperm, Joan and I are facing each other on a long, curving couch in the modern living room of her new home. How does it feel, I ask her, to finally be acting on her plan to become pregnant now that she's decided to use an anonymous donor? Given what I have come to know about Joan, her answer doesn't surprise me. Even now she is fantasizing about composing another advertisement, this one to run when she launches her search for a man to act as a father for her child: "MOTHER AND BABY seek uncle figure and family friend. Various options."

"Nobody's father is a teaspoonful of sperm."

"To say to a child, 'You don't have a daddy, you have a mommy' just isn't true," Los Angeles psychotherapist Annette Baran tells me when we speak about unmarried women using anonymous donors to have children "We haven't learned yet how to clone eggs and not use sperm," Baran says, her voice rising to underscore her next point. "Nobody's father is a teaspoonful of sperm. There is always a person attached to it, a real person. If there is anything I feel strongly about, it is that a child has the right to know there is a father, a genetic father if nothing more."

With Reuben Pannor, Baran has written two books outlining what in their view are the harmful consequences to a child of secrecy about his true parentage. In *The Adoption Triangle*, Baran and Pannor describe the damaging effects on children and families of sealing adoption records. That influential book, published in 1978, helped alter people's attitudes; laws have since been changed to make it easier for adopted children to locate their birth parents and vice versa. Today, adoptions are usually arranged with much less secrecy than existed only few decades ago. When Baran and Pannor wrote their 1989 book, *Lethal Secrets: The Shocking Consequences and Unsolved Problems of Artificial Insemination*, they used similar arguments on behalf of children's right to know about their genetic father. It is unhealthy, they argued, for any child to be raised amid a "conspiracy of silence" that in subtle and sometimes not-so-subtle ways can erode relationships within a family.

The authors believe that the solution to the problems they see in anonymous donor insemination is to establish more openness about the process, including the identification of donors. In *Lethal Secrets*, they recommend that "all sperm must be received from known volunteers who agree to share total identifying social and medical information. [And] the donor must agree to be available on a lifetime basis as the genetic parent. This implies updating information, permitting contact with (or on behalf of) the child, and accepting responsibility as an important genetic link for the child." In several countries, including Australia and Sweden, there are laws that make it impossible for sperm donors to retain lifelong anonymity: when the child reaches eighteen, the biological father's identity can be revealed, though his donation of sperm entails neither financial responsibility nor custody rights. In neither of these countries is there a shortage of donors, although many cite potential shortages as a reason for not establishing an open policy in the United States.

Older unmarried women don't anticipate that anonymous donors will provide financial support or participate in child-rearing. In fact, those choosing this method of conception often do so specifically to avoid potential conflicts with a man who, if he knew his child exists, might seek custody or make unreasonable demands on her or her child. Donor anonymity protects mothers from this kind of intrusion. But, like Joan, many unmarried mothers want the ability to assure their children that if they're interested in finding out more about their father, they can do so at the age of eighteen.

Two sperm banks, both in California, have been in the vanguard regarding donor identification. Not coincidentally, these two banks are used by increasing numbers of unmarried women. The Sperm Bank of California, in Berkeley, was the first to offer identification of willing donors after eighteen years and let women choose to be inseminated with their sperm. In 1993 the California Cryobank in Los Angeles developed a "Policy of Openness": when a mother or child requests additional information about the genetic father once the child has turned eighteen, the clinic promises to "make all reasonable efforts" to supply the information by either reviewing records or contacting the donor. (Files on each donor are kept indefinitely and constantly updated.) Donors' anonymity, however, will be broken only by mutual consent. Recognizing the unpredictable twists and turns that every life takes, the Cryobank doesn't ask the donor or the woman at the time of conception to specify how they will feel about this matter eighteen years later, but the door is left open for the man to at least be queried.

The Cryobank's change in policy is a response to pleas by unmarried women and by psychologists such as Baran and Pannor to take into account the child's perspective. In introducing this new policy, the clinic noted that until now the child has "not been a party to any of these arrangements." The clinic director acknowledged to me that a child has "real and legitimate needs . . . to know about his or her biological heritage."

Even before the Cryobank established its "Policy of Openness," many unmarried women selected their donors there. (Women on the East Coast often ordered sperm from the Cryobank; it was shipped in dry ice.) Compared with other places, which released only snippets of information, such as donors' eye and hair color, height and weight, occupation and education, and religious and ethnic background, the Cryobank was providing detailed though nonidentifying information about the donors and three generations of their family history. Take, for example, a sperm donor I'll call Number 874. He describes himself as "virtually ambidextrous." Purple is his favorite color and baseball is his favorite sport. Rock is his favorite music. He likes Thai food. As a hobby he enjoys medieval history. He describes himself as "laid-back, congenial, slightly introverted, yet a leader." His SAT scores total 1270, and after majoring in economics he went on to get an MBA degree and now works as a financial analyst. He wears glasses when he drives. He had cosmetic nose surgery and never has been treated for a sexually transmitted disease. I learn also that for about five years he smoked marijuana and now averages two drinks a week, though he does not drink coffee or smoke cigarettes. His father, a surgeon, has hardened arteries. His mother developed ulcerative colitis after his nineteen-year-old sister died in a car accident. His maternal grandmother, whom he describes as pessimistic and passive, had high blood pressure and suffered a heart attack that led to her death. His paternal grandfather, who he says was an easygoing, optimistic doctor, was diagnosed with Alzheimer's disease at the age of seventy-four and died three years later. "I believe I have good genes," this man writes in response to the question about why he wants to be a donor. He doesn't foresee having children of his own, so being a donor gives him "a way to pursue my own immortality."

Dr. Cappy Rothman, the director of the California Cryobank, explains to me some of the advantages of anonymous-donor insemination from the perspective of the unmarried women with whom he's spoken. "If she gets sperm from us, she's assured of innumerable things that she's usually not assured of when she falls in love and gets married," he says, referring to the close medical scrutiny that is given to the sperm. "A single mother using donor sperm is also protected from a man suing for paternity rights to her child."

"This ultra-planned-pregnancy stuff, it is not a joy."

For a variety of reasons, some women decide that using an anonymous donor will leave them too uncomfortable about the circumstances they're creating for the child. Joan, of course, initially felt this way, but in time she changed her mind—though, as she reminded me, her frantic search to locate her donor made it clear to her that she was still unsettled by her decision. Joan didn't have former boyfriends to whom she could turn to ask for help, as some women do. And though she did try to find a man to be her child's genetic father, the process turned out to be so complicated and confusing that, by the end, an anonymous donor seemed a reasonable answer. But women who feel as Joan did and have men who are willing to help them conceive a child need never exercise the less desirable option of becoming pregnant by someone they will never know.

Paula, a slender woman with a head of thick curls, knows Jason's telephone number at work so well that when she reaches for the phone to call him, she barely glances at the keypad. Her fingers move by memory. These days her frequent calls to him are driven by her intention to chart a new future for herself: Paula wants to get pregnant. Jason, a former boyfriend, told her he would help. If they succeed, she will raise their child on her own.

"Tonight, what time are you getting home?" she asks Jason when he answers the phone.

Around eight o'clock, he tells her, or maybe a bit later. When exactly he will get there is less important to Paula then the fact that he'll be available to have sexual intercourse that evening. He lives near her house, so they can rendezvous easily. Every morning Paula takes her temperature with a basal thermometer, monitoring to within a tenth of a degree the fluctuations in her body temperature. This gives her a good indication of when she is going to ovulate, and it is around this time that Jason needs to be available. This is now their fourth month, so Jason pretty much knows which nights they will be together.

"Sounds like you were on a beeper," I say jokingly to Jason, a serious-minded man who recently turned fifty.

"Pretty much," he replies, with a forced half-smile. Then his smile vanishes. "This ultra-planned-pregnancy stuff," he tells me, "it is not a joy."

"I could say to my child, 'you have a father, and this is what that person is like.' "

Paula talked with three close male friends about becoming her partner in conceiving a child. (Such a man is called a known donor.) Each of the men agreed to participate, with the understanding that Paula would raise the child and ask for no financial assistance. To varying degrees, all the men indicated that they would probably want to establish some relationship with the child. But defining what this "father-child" dynamic might be like wasn't something any of them could do. Occasional visits were the main thing the men said they wanted. When Paula and Jason talked about this aspect of their agreement, he told her he saw himself as being more of an "active uncle" than a "daddy."

In thinking about conceiving a child outside of marriage, what seemed most important to Paula was that her child have an identifiable father. She didn't want to have a child who would grow up asking lots of questions about a man she'd never known. "This was definitely a factor for me," she says. "Even if, in the end, the known donor chose to not be at all involved in the child's life, I, at least, would know what he's like as an adult and be able to tell the child. Yeah, I could say to my child, 'You have a father and this is what he is like.' That was important for me." As Paula tells me this, Jason keeps a watchful eye on their eight-month-old son, Peter, who is playing on the floor nearby. At my invitation the three of them have come to my house for dinner. Because they do not live together, they don't have dinner together often.

That Paula chose Jason—and that he agreed to father her child—is testimony to the friendship they have managed to sustain in spite of the rocky transitions they've been through as lovers. For the many years during which she and Jason were romantically involved, their relationship left onlookers dizzied by its ups and downs. Though clearly attracted to each other, they could never get along well enough for long enough to consider marriage, nor did they ever talk about having a child. Jason was not eager enough to become a parent to suggest such an idea. And Paula, because she was still in her early thirties when they were seeing each other, didn't feel an imperative to act. Given their difficulties with each other, having a child with Jason wasn't something she even considered. When they finally ended their relationship, Paula figured there was still plenty of time to meet someone else, get married, and have a child.

Her views about all this changed abruptly when she was thirty-six years old and no longer involved with Jason. An appointment with her gynecologist revealed to Paula that she had a very serious case of endometriosis, a disease of the membrane lining the uterus which can make pregnancy virtually impossible. Suddenly Paula confronted the possibility that she might never bear a child—and now she realized for the first time how much she wanted to do so. At that moment she made a pledge to herself to do whatever it took to make it happen. However, her doctor told her she couldn't even begin to try to get pregnant until the medication he was prescribing went to work to clear her uterine walls. The first drug she took triggered signs of early menopause, an unwelcome reminder of how slim her chances of having a baby were becoming. Subsequent drugs, however, rid her uterus of the diseased tissue without producing similar side effects.

Paula's relational life was not going smoothly during this time. News of her endometriosis arrived in the midst of her involvement with a man who, she says, "could have been the one." But "baby hunger" swept over her, upsetting the rhythm of growth in their relationship. The man was "so scared of the idea of having children" that the topic's constant presence broke up their relationship.

After eighteen months of drug therapy, Paula's doctor pronounced her ready to try for a pregnancy. Because she was, by then, approaching the age of thirty-eight, he suggested that she start trying as soon as possible. She was eager, too, to get started, but now an essential ingredient was missing: she didn't have an ongoing relationship with a man. And prior experience informed Paula that finding a man with whom she could establish a promising relationship, point toward marriage, and plan for having children was a puzzle she was unlikely to put together anytime soon.

Paula signed up for a ten-week workshop designed to help women decide about single motherhood. All the women in the group were about Paula's age and wrestling, as she was, with what seemed her only alternative to not having a child: having one on her own. Once a week they met to talk about their concerns, about the burden they'd assume in being their family's only breadwinner as well as their child's only caregiving parent. No one liked the idea of purposefully creating a situation in which her child wouldn't have a father. Even so, all the women decided, in the end, to push ahead. They learned about various options for getting pregnant or adopting, and picked up tips from the workshop leader on how to talk with family members and friends about their decisions. In one session Paula and her colleagues were handed crayons and asked to draw pictures of their lives, both with and without a child. Their renderings of life without a child had fewer bright colors, more vacant space, and drearier backgrounds.

As the sessions went on, Paula became more certain she would proceed. She decided early on that whatever the financial hurdles, she would not allow them to stop her. She'd worked steadily since graduating from college and had always earned a decent salary in a growth industry, computers. Already she'd saved enough to be able to buy a three-bedroom town house. Paula was certain she'd be able to support herself and a child in the years ahead. She was also willing to sacrifice the extras her income could buy her for the sake of having a child. For Paula, the toughest part of the decision resided in emotional uncertainties it seemed to present. From day to day she traveled from peaks of happiness and certainty into valleys of indecision. Having grown up in a two-parent household with a sister to whom she remains very close, she was worried by the prospect of becoming a single parent of an only child—which was all she believed she could handle and afford on her own. Would she be depriving her child of important, sustaining, even vital relationships? Her feelings about having only a daughter or only a son seemed harder to resolve than those about the absence of a consistent father. "I figured what I would do is start to live my life more with a lot of my friends' families. And with as many guys as I know who are single, divorced, or married with children, I could spend time with them," Paula says, explaining how she expected to deal with the missing-daddy aspect of her child's life. "My friends would be the male adults in my child's life." And Jason said he wanted to play some still-undefined role. But figuring out how to substitute for a missing sibling seemed tougher.

"My father is always saying he wishes I'd gotten married to some prince."

Paula thought the workshop had prepared her well for talking with friends and family about her plans. But she was wrong. Her father was furious at her for even considering the idea. "He thought it was crazy," Paula tells me. "And there was noooooo talking about it to be done." He grew so enraged that Paula pledged to herself that she would never mention the subject to him again. But this solution saddened her; her mother was no longer alive, and now her only parent would not give her any emotional support. After she left that evening, Paula cried, wishing her mother were alive. She knew her mother would have understood.

Paula's father had never played an integral role in her upbringing. Like many men of his generation, he believed the rearing of children was best left to their mother, and he arranged their family life so it worked out that way. He was at the dining room table for dinner every night but, Paula says, "he was very removed." As a young girl, Paula sensed that her mother resented her husband's attitude but went along with his dictates to keep the peace. Paula's mother never took a job outside the house, though Paula and her sister knew she very much wanted to. Her husband forbade it. "My dad says that kids and babies are just a woman's realm," Paula tells me. "I got a lot of my career orientation in seeing how resentful my mother was."

In spite of her father's conventional views about a woman's "proper role," Paula reports that he brags to friends about his unmarried daughters' professional accomplishments. Nevertheless, she says, "my father truly believes the best way for my life to go would be for me to be taken care of by a husband so I wouldn't have to work. He is on both sides of the fence: he brags about my work but he is always saying he wishes I'd gotten married to some prince."

"My father couldn't find support for his outrage about me being unmarried, so he let that one go."

In her fourth month of trying to get pregnant, Paula succeeded. This turned out, however, to be the same month—in fact, the same week—in which she was unexpectedly laid off from her job.

"My life was really well set up," Paula says, describing the circumstances she had assumed would be the foundation for her family life. She walked to work. There were plenty of high-quality day-care facilities nearby to choose from. Because she'd been with the company for so many years, Paula was counting on thirteen weeks of paid maternity leave. Suddenly all this vanished.

"I remember having such anxiety and reaction to the stress of losing my job that I didn't feel pregnant," she says. In fact, Jason told her that week, "You're much too stressed to get pregnant now." Though neither of them knew it, by then Paula was already on her way to becoming a mother.

One day Paula's happiness about her pregnancy made her break her pledge of silence regarding her father. Besides, sooner or later he'd know anyway. Unlike their prior conversation, during which they had been alone, this one took place at dinner with Paula's stepmother. Midway through the meal, after Paula told him she was having a baby, her father had managed to make both women cry. He simply wasn't willing to accept what his daughter was telling him. Paula was relieved, however, to find that her stepmother strongly supported her. "I remember her saying to my father, 'You wouldn't understand.' "

"What was it that bothered your father so much?" I ask. "Was it that you were having a child outside of marriage?"

"I don't think the institutional lack of marriage bothered him as much as the fact that the way I've chosen to live my life doesn't fit into choices he would've made for me," she says. "My choices are my choices; they are not his choices. And that's really the bottom line with him. He's got his view of how things should go, how people should act and relate, and if you make other choices then there is no room for that. It's sad."

Paula doubts that her father would have been any happier about what she was doing if she'd married Jason, of whom he didn't approve. "Anyway," she says, "the lack of marriage got tossed off his plate of objections pretty early, because so many of his and my stepmother's peers did not react with horror to what I was doing. He couldn't find support for his outrage about me being unmarried, so he let that one go."

"Which objections stayed on his plate?" I ask.

"That I am not being taken care of," Paula replies. "That I have to work. That I have taken on all of this, my job and the baby's care, alone. That I have to do so much work. That whole set of things."

"Have you said to him that if you were married you would probably be working at a job as well?"

"Oh, yeah, I told him that." Paula shakes her head to indicate how little impression any of that seemed to make on her father. "Actually we don't even talk about this anymore because it falls on deaf ears. He and I have so many land mines of conversation that we can't venture near; it's too bad. He is my only living parent. It would be nice to have more of a relationship with him. But the fact is, I never did."

Paula's father is a lawyer, and he did want to advise her about legal arrangements she should make to protect herself and her child. This struck Paula as very typical of him: he wasn't able to give her any emotional support for what she was undertaking but, when it came to dotting an "i" and crossing a "t," he was more than willing to offer guidance. She soon discovered that his primary concern was that Jason be prohibited from inheriting anything from either Paula or their child if they should both die before him. Paula agreed to put a clause to this effect in the draft of her proposed agreement with Jason about the parenting of their child, even though she knew the agreement's legal viability was questionable.

Searching for Solomon's Wisdom in the 1990s

Courtrooms have always been the destination of last resort for resolving what appear to be irresolvable family disputes. In the tenth century B.C., King Solomon employed judicial wisdom to devise a way of discovering a baby's maternal origin. Nowadays reproductive technology and variable social norms can make judges long for the relative simplicity of Solomonic times.

A child born today can have three "mothers" and two "fathers" by the time she is three days old: a genetic mother, who donated the egg; a gestational mother, who carried the pregnancy; an adoptive mother, who brought the baby home; a genetic father, anonymous or known, who donated sperm; and a social father, the partner of the adoptive mother. It isn't necessary for any of these individuals to be married. If a dispute arises, it is a judge who will be asked to sort out the rights to and responsibilities for the child involved.

For an unmarried woman who is impregnated by a man she knows, circumstances that arise after the baby's birth can turn into courtroom confrontations. The "donor" may decide that he wants to be his child's "daddy" and demand visitation or want to share custody. A mother who has told a man she was willing to release him from financial responsibility may decide that she needs his assistance in raising their child, after all. Whatever sets the legal process in motion, once the dispute enters the courtroom, a mother's and father's rights and obligations are evaluated in light of the primary responsibility: to decide what is in the child's "best interests." Judges view their task as trying to figure out what role each parent should play so that their presence and financial wherewithal will provide the greatest benefit to the child. In many instances, this means that a judge will try to provide a child with what most closely resembles a nuclear family. Thus, an unmarried mother's intention to parent on her own is especially vulnerable if a child's genetic father wants to claim shared custody or visitation rights. Many judges overlook a woman's stated desire to parent by herself when a father says he wants to exercise his paternal interest. There is only one way a woman can fully insulate her child and herself from such a paternal claim, and that is by using an anonymous sperm donor.

Courtroom encounters between unmarried parents resemble custody and child-support battles between couples who are separated or divorced. Similarities exist because the law and the courts treat paternity and child-support obligations similarly regardless of whether a marriage has taken place. Few, if any, legal distinctions exist nowadays between children who are born out of wedlock and those who are born to married parents. However, in an era when new pathways of reproduction complicate the standard legal definitions of who is a child's "parent," it is not surprising that courtroom decisions lag behind societal change.

What happens, for example, when an unmarried woman such as Paula asks Jason to "father" her child? Does Paula have the right to free Jason of financial obligation to his child? What if her circumstances change and she loses her ability to earn an adequate income? If she someday becomes too poor to support her child and has to depend on public assistance, doesn't the state have the right to require Jason to support his child? And can Jason sign away custody rights before his child is born, then change his mind if he decides to participate more actively in raising his child? Or can parents like Paula and Jason sign a contract before their child is born and have provisions such as these hold even if circumstances change?

"She is fully capable of providing for all the needs of the child she so desperately wanted."

Perhaps no case exemplifies some of the potential dilemmas involved in "using" or "being used as" a "known donor" better than what transpired between the biological parents of an Indiana child named Briley. In 1991 a lawsuit was filed on Briley's behalf by her mother, asking that her father acknowledge his paternity and assume responsibility for child support. Courtroom arguments revolved around whether this man—who had signed an agreement of understanding before he impregnated Briley's mother—could claim the same legal immunity from paternal responsibility that an anonymous sperm donor enjoys. His lawyer claimed he could. The attorney for the mother and child argued that he couldn't.

The Indiana courts agreed with Briley's mother. In January 1994, the state's Fourth District Court of Appeals ruled that Briley's "father" has a "common-law, statutory, moral and societal obligation" to support his child, which "cannot be contracted away" by her mother. This decision set a precedent in an often vague and confusing arena of family law. "Known Donor–Recipient" agreements, though increasingly popular, cannot be regarded as legally binding contracts, because the child's interests are the predominant concern once he or she is born. Attorneys advise clients who want to put their parenting intentions on paper not to depend on judges to uphold pre-birth agreements.

The saga of Briley's parents began when they met as teachers at an Indiana elementary school. The woman who would become Briley's mother convinced the man whom she later sued to help her get pregnant. This man, whom she was dating, agreed to help her become pregnant but told her that he did not want to assume the responsibilities of fatherhood. He was already paying substantial child support after his divorce. They talked about terms under which he would agree to help: his name would not appear on the baby's birth certificate; she wouldn't ask him to provide any financial support; he wouldn't acknowledge his child's birth by participating in any "daddylike" activities; she'd tell friends that her pregnancy was the result of an anonymous donor insemination, and he would not contradict her story. This secret would remain theirs. To be certain this was agreed to, he wrote a paragraph and asked her to sign it. She did.

> To Whom It May Concern:
> I, Francine Todd, in sound mind & fore thought [sic] have decided not to marry, but would like to have a baby on my own. To support financially & emotionally, I have approached several men who will not be held responsible financially or emotionally who's [sic] names will be kept secret for life.
> Signed Francine Todd
> Dec. 15, 1986

Her signature signified to both of them that they could begin to have unprotected sex. Within three months she was pregnant.

For three years after her birth, Briley was raised and supported by her mother, who relied on her $30,000 annual salary. Ms. Todd remained silent about her child's paternity and the father upheld his part of the agreement. Though they continued to see each other, he established no relationship with his daughter. However, after a few years, Ms. Todd changed her mind, filing a petition to establish paternity and force Briley's father to contribute financially to her care. The mother explained that she had decided to abrogate the agreement because when Briley was three she had begun to ask questions about her "daddy." At this point, she said, she had second thoughts about the wisdom of her decision. Briley's father claimed that the lawsuit came about only after he refused to impregnate Ms. Todd a second time. By the time her lawsuit was filed, he was married to someone else.

The court of appeals concluded that Francine could not contract away the rights of her child. Nor, the court wrote in its decision, could a parent "by his own contract, relieve himself of the legal obligation to support his minor children." The written agreement was found to be "void" because it violated Indiana's public policy, which recognizes the obligation of both parents to support their children. The court rejected this father's argument that because he was acting only as a "sperm donor," the agreement should be enforced: "We know of no medical requirements—or of any sperm donor program—that continues to give insemination injections after the donee becomes pregnant": a reference to the uncontested fact that the parents continued to have sexual relations after Briley was born. The majority then summarized its legal finding: "In this action we are not concerned with any alleged contractual rights of the parents—paternity actions in Indiana are only concerned with establishing paternity and with the rights of the child." The man was legally declared Briley's father and held responsible for child support.

One judge, J. Conover, dissented, arguing that Indiana's public policy lagged behind social change. "Today, the general public almost universally looks with understanding and approval upon a single woman's desire to bear and nurture a child without male interference," Judge Conover wrote. "A financially responsible modern woman, at her option, has an unqualified right to do so. . . . In other words, our declarations on this subject are currently incorrect. They reflect policy which has been dead since the 1960s." Because Indiana's constitution was amended in 1983 to provide for women's equal rights and responsibilities, Conover concluded that "Women are now irrevocably bound to perform the obligations they incur when contracting just as men are. . . . Thus, in my opinion, the contract in question is valid and enforceable because it is conversant [sic] with current public policy. . . . Quite simply, she bargained away the right to file a paternity action against this man and to publicly name him as the child's father . . . [and] she is gainfully employed and fully capable of providing for all the needs of the child she so desperately wanted."

This judicial debate, influenced as it is by societal views of women's changing roles, reminds us of the complex mesh of factors that influence our judgments about these new ways of forming families.

"Isn't it extraordinary that we live in a time when this is not only attainable but acceptable?"

Molly, a forty-three-year-old adoptive single mother, heads out of her parents' house one day for a walk in the woods with Sandy, a childhood friend. As young girls living in this tiny island community, they'd been inseparable. Now, as women at midlife, each is home for Thanksgiving to visit her family. It's been several years since the two have seen each other, and it's a bit strange for them to discover the many similarities in the paths their adult lives are traveling. Neither woman has been married, though not because either lacks the desire to be. Now each is a mother. Sandy gave birth to a daughter, conceived with an anonymous donor, about a month after Molly had adopted hers. Their babies are less than a year old.

The two women walk for a long time, sharing thoughts about their lives as unmarried mothers. When Sandy tells Molly she's been thinking a lot about whether she can find out who her child's sperm donor is, Molly doesn't know how to reply; she isn't able to reassure her, as she wishes she could. For a brief time Molly had tried to get pregnant through such inseminations but stopped when she became concerned, as her friend is now, about her inability to identify her child's father. ("I didn't like doing it," Molly tells me later. "I felt continuously sad.") As it turned out, Molly knows her daughter's birth parents, and the child will always be able to find out what she wants to know about them.

Soon the friends' conversation moves on to other topics. Like Molly, Sandy is thrilled to be a mother at last. Neither woman's parents had disapproved of what their daughter had decided to do. All had joyfully welcomed their granddaughter's arrival. Though Molly and her friend admit to each other that parenting is hard and they miss the company of a partner, both now define happiness as belonging to the family each has created for herself. Deciding to go ahead and have a baby, even if it means raising her without a partner, is, they agree, the best thing they've ever done.

After a while they circle back to Molly's parents' house, where they left their daughters napping. With the house in sight, Sandy stops for a moment. "Isn't it extraordinary," she says to Molly, "that we live in a time when this is not only attainable but acceptable? If a woman wants to have a baby badly enough, she goes out and finds a way."

"I just wanted to have a child so badly and it just didn't seem to make any sense to me that it was going to be this difficult to do."

Adoption is usually the very last stop a woman makes on her road to parenting. Usually, by the time she applies to adopt a child, she will have exhausted the biological means of achieving motherhood. It is hard to separate the strong cultural signals that compel women to push adoption into a distant corner from women's internal desire to biologically reproduce. But for a mixture of these reasons, women appear willing to pay huge amounts of money to infertility specialists and devote years of their lives to trying to get pregnant, even when the odds against success are high. And they'll do this long before they'll register with an adoption agency, though doing so will virtually assure them of one day achieving what they say they want: parenthood. And today the biological options married and single women can pursue are expanding. An older woman who is desperate to achieve a pregnancy can use eggs donated by a younger woman and made fertile by donated sperm. While she is the one who gives birth, her child—just like an adopted child—has no genetic link with her. Scientists recently announced the medical possibility of removing eggs from an aborted female fetus and implanting them in women who can't produce eggs; if this technique is ever used, women could then give birth to a child whose genetic mother will never have lived.

One woman I spoke with, Carol, endured four years of medical procedures trying to get pregnant during her marriage. When that marriage ended, she was in her late thirties. After some time passed, she realized she still wanted to have a child, but she couldn't bring herself to return to a doctor's office knowing that this time she'd have to use an anonymous donor. Despite assurances, she didn't feel entirely comfortable about the risks of disease from using donated sperm. By this time, Carol was in her forties, so her chances of becoming pregnant were probably even slimmer than they had been during the years she'd tried and failed with her husband. Also with him, she was using his fresh sperm which improves the chances for conception. (Donor sperm must be thawed before an insemination.) "I thought to myself about how this donor sperm is frozen." "So I just didn't want to put myself through all that stuff," she explained.

Friends suggested that Carol think about adoption, but she wasn't convinced it was what she wanted. Despite her reluctance to use an anonymous donor, she was finding it very difficult to give up on her lifelong dream of giving birth to her child. To help sort through her feelings, Carol signed up for a decision-making group for single women considering adoption. She'd run into hurdles that she knew she needed help getting over. Initially Carol thought of trying to adopt a white, American infant through a privately arranged "open" adoption but, she says, "I realized that financially I couldn't afford to do it": the cost could run as high as $30,000. And she, a single woman, would be competing against couples for a pregnant woman to select. "I knew that, yes, it was possible for them to select me," Carol says, but she was discouraged by how high the odds seemed stacked against her. Another public agency told her that because she was single, she'd most likely be able to adopt an older, handicapped child. "I wasn't opposed to that, but it just didn't make any sense. A handicapped child needs much more attention than a full-time working, single mother can give." By the time Carol started attending the adoption-decision group, "I was very discouraged because I just wanted to have a child so badly and it just didn't seem to make any sense to me that it was going to be this difficult to do."

There were six other women in the group. Five of the seven had never been married. Carol was the youngest; the oldest woman was fifty years old, and for her, only extreme medical interventions could make biological motherhood possible. For the rest, pregnancy was theoretically possible but by then each had tried unsuccessfully for many years and was too exhausted by the disappointment to keep going. Each had, for one reason or another, become willing to relinquish the biological link she'd once felt strongly about in exchange for becoming a mother through adoption.

As weeks went by, one by one the women announced their decisions to adopt. They shared with one another their good and not-so-good experiences with various agencies. They tutored each other in the rules of international adoptions; some countries, they found out, welcome older single women while others disallow adoptions to women who are unmarried or over forty. For a time Carol considered adopting from Russia. But when one of the women in her group went to China and returned with an infant girl, she changed her mind. "I was just stunned to see her with this baby," Carol says. "I couldn't believe it. I said to my social worker, 'I'm changing my program to China.' "

"I had achieved other things that were difficult. I could and would achieve pregnancy, even against all odds."

Elizabeth Bartholet is a Harvard Law School professor, an unmarried, single mother of two Peruvian-born boys, and the author of *Family Bonds*, published in 1993. In this book, and in her other writing about adoption, Bartholet argues that societal messages about the primacy of biological parenthood lead women who are having trouble becoming pregnant toward medically assisted procreation and away from adoption as a route to parenting. Writing in the *Duke Journal of Gender Law & Policy*, Bartholet observed how cultural messages "glorify procreation and childbirth, while at the same time stigmatizing infertility and adoption. . . . We do it by subsidizing procreation through health insurance, tax laws, and employer benefit packages, while at the same time making adoptive parents pay every step of the way for the adoption costs created by restrictive regulation. . . . Ultimately, these policies may deny many women what they most want—the parenting experience." Slowly, messages like Bartholet's are getting through to policymakers: beginning this year adoptive parents receive a $5,000 tax credit, and some companies are instituting practices to support adoptive parents.

Betsy, as Bartholet prefers to be called, knows very well from personal experience how easy it is to fall under the sway of societal messages and be carried along by ingrained incentives. When she was in her thirties, divorced and the mother of a teenage son from an early marriage, she decided to become a mother again. She underwent surgery on her blocked fallopian tubes in the hope that she could get pregnant again. The surgery failed. For a time Betsy felt as though her chance to have another child had disappeared. She had waited too long. Now her body was telling her that what she wanted was no longer possible. But Betsy still felt an intense desire to conceive. In retrospect, she believes her urge to reproduce was influenced as much by external messages about the primacy of biological family relationships as by her own instincts. However these two forces merged within her, together they kept pushing her to find some way to make a pregnancy possible. And she is someone who has a hard time giving up.

Betsy's rise to the rank of tenured professor at Harvard Law School had been, like the accomplishments of many other women of her generation, a test of skill, perseverance, and fortitude. In that and other realms of her life she'd grown accustomed to finding ways of getting around supposed obstacles. "I had achieved other things that were difficult," wrote Betsy in

Family Bonds. "[So] I could and would achieve pregnancy, even against all odds."

While she was recovering from the fallopian tube surgery, Betsy started to save articles she read about adoption. But the feelings she had when she thought about adopting were not in any way comparable to the excitement she felt in envisioning herself pregnant. She could find nothing to push her toward an equally aggressive pursuit of adoption. In fact, the more she read about adoption, the less encouragement she found for a single woman like herself. Betsy let the idea of adoption fade away.

In the early 1980s, in vitro fertilization (IVF), an infertility technique in which a woman's fallopian tubes are bypassed by bringing sperm and eggs together outside her body, was becoming more widely used in the United States. Betsy read about its success and wanted to try it. But she had two strikes against her. One was her advanced age, nearly forty-three. Back then most IVF programs did not accept women older than forty. Betsy pleaded with doctors at several U.S. clinics offering IVF until a few of them let her try. The other issue was her marital status; IVF clinics, at that time, restricted their services to married couples. Whenever Betsy went to an appointment she made sure to wear a wedding ring she'd bought for these occasions. A friend agreed to provide the sperm.

"No one [at these clinics] ever suggested I consider adoption as an alternative to further treatment," Betsy writes. "All of this was entirely understandable. These were medical programs, and the people involved thought in medical terms. They were working to press beyond the frontiers of knowledge and make it possible for the patients knocking down their programs' doors to achieve what they desperately wanted to achieve: pregnancy." Pregnancy was certainly what Betsy still wanted. She enrolled in programs in three different states to avoid losing valuable time on waiting lists.

Medical insurance didn't then pay for infertility treatment, as some policies do today. So Betsy spent more than $5,000 a month in her attempt. Month after month, IVF failed. Yet she kept trying. "Then I got lucky," Betsy says; "I ran out of money." Five months after she ended her pursuit of biological motherhood, she was in Lima, Peru, holding a baby boy, her son Christopher.

"Obviously, there was a powerful compulsion at work inside of me."

The National Adoption Information Clearinghouse describes "a steady, sizable increase in the number of single parent adoptions" during the past two decades. The Clearinghouse finds, for example, that a quarter of those who adopt children with special needs are single men and women. This high percentage of such adoptions among single parents is due to the hierarchical sorting that takes place in most public agency adoptions; as Carol discovered, two-parent families remain the most likely destination of babies who present the fewest problems and therefore are most in demand. The Clearinghouse also estimates that 5 percent of all other adoptions—that is, of children without special needs—are by single people. There are some who can afford the high cost of hiring private attorneys to help them locate a woman who wants to place her child for adoption. But many single women do as Betsy and Carol did: they go overseas. In the expanding arena of international adoptions, more and more American adoptive parents are unmarried women. This is true especially of adoptions from China, which has a surplus of adoptable girls and welcomes older parents and single women.

One day, as Betsy and I sit in a Chinese restaurant sharing a lunch of cold spicy noodles and fried tofu, I ask her to describe her shifts in thinking about becoming a parent. I first met Betsy when I was a student in her "Alternative Parenting" class at Harvard Law School. She helped students explore ways the American legal system intersects with how people are creating and trying to define "family." Our classroom discussion included topics such as surrogacy, donor insemination, foster care, and adoption. After that class ended, Betsy and I became friends. Now I want to know how she'd managed to keep herself going back time and time again to the clinics, enduring all sorts of medical procedures, taking all those fertility drugs, and how she dealt with the emotional consequences of her failures. At one point I use the word "courage" to characterize what I applaud as her determination.

Betsy looks at me with a quizzical gaze. "It wasn't courage," she says. "No. Courage would not be the way to describe it." She sits back in her chair, sweeps her hand through her tightly curled hair, and thinks about how she can explain what was happening. It was, she tells me, her compulsive drive, born of her obsession with giving birth to her child, that kept pushing her to attempt more and more high-tech methods of procreation. Each one offered a bit more hope of success. Once she set down this path, Betsy says, only her eventual lack of money convinced her to stop. What I'd called courage, Betsy views quite differently: "It felt to me as though I was being swept along to any length to make pregnancy happen." If there was courage, she says, it was in her finally turning away from trying to become *pregnant* and realizing that what she really wanted was to be a *parent*.

It's now been nearly eight years since Betsy returned from Peru with her second adopted son. "What kept pushing you so strongly toward motherhood on your own even after you realized you couldn't get pregnant?" I ask her that day during lunch. Betsy is surprised by my question. Time has erased so many of the painful memories of desperation that she says it is hard to reconstruct her feelings. "Usually when people ask me about this, I say that I'd always wanted more children and I got to a point where I realized I had to do it or not do it and I just did it," she replies. "And that's true." But there is more: "Then why did I do it against such odds? Why did I insist on doing it? Obviously, there was a powerful compulsion at work inside of me." She smiles.

I appreciate Betsy's willingness to push herself to remember. The questions she is trying to answer are ones I've asked myself many, many times. I explain to her how the breakup of my relationship, the one in which I'd hoped to have children, prompted me to try to have a child by myself. I ask Betsy if she can remember what her catalyst was.

"In some ways, I think, I'd always thought of children separately from relationships," she responds. "Raising a child largely on my own after my divorce seemed in some way entirely natural. When people would say to me it must have been so hard for me to be divorced and have a child, I'd just think to myself, 'What would be hard would be not to have the child.'" Even so, Betsy still hoped that during her thirties she'd meet someone with whom she'd want to have more children. But her thirties went by, and nearly half of her forties, and her hope wasn't realized.

"When I hit my forties I faced up to mortality. Infertility makes you face up to your mortality. Dealing with it gave me the really clear sense that my time is not limitless and I had to get on with it in terms of what I wanted to do." This reminds me of how Paula's decision about single motherhood arose out of suddenly learning about her possible infertility. Like Paula, Betsy wanted to have a child whether she was married or not. "By then I was very conscious of the limited likelihood of finding 'the right man,'" Betsy says. "And with my son from my marriage now older, I was living a life where there was not an intimate daily connection with another human being. I just had a very powerful sense that the real me was not being lived."

What does she mean by "the real me"?

"The 'real me' being an emotional, caring, and loving person," Betsy answers. Neither her work, her friends, nor her relationships were providing her with the outlet she wanted to express herself in this way.

"And you didn't have anyone to give that to?"

"Yeah, I could go through the motions. I could go to work, but that felt like I was going through the motions. I had a sense inside of me, 'Is this the rest of my life? I mean, what is the rest of my life?' I'd never asked myself this before. When I thought about it, what I wanted to do for the rest of my life was the thing that has been most satisfying and real to me," she says. "And that was being a parent."

When Betsy left for Peru for her first adoption, her emotions were still scrambled. Soon she would be holding a baby, who would become her child. This was what she wanted, but it also terrified her: "I still had lots of anxieties when I got on that airplane. I was worried that maybe there was something about the biological connection that explained the unconditional love and commitment parents have toward children, something that in adoption you don't get." Betsy wondered whether she'd feel toward a child who was a stranger the way she'd felt about her son, to whom she'd given birth two decades before.

It was two weeks after she had held her son for the first time that Betsy realized "it had happened. I had become his parent and it had happened without me even knowing it was." At that moment, Christopher was sick, with a terrible hacking cough deep in his chest. "I remember calling my friend and hearing her assure me that he would be okay. Tears were pouring down my face as I held him. It was then I knew I was as connected to this child as I could imagine ever being."

5

Raising Children: Unmarried Adolescent Mothers

The alarm clock next to Sarah's bed jolted her out of her first sound sleep of the night. The time was five, and darkness had not yet lifted. Because David, Sarah's son, rarely slept through the night, only now, early in the morning, did Sarah feel she was starting to get a restful sleep. She reached from under the covers to smother the clock before it woke up her mother, whose room was next to David's. Sarah wanted to roll over and go back to sleep, but that that was impossible. Classes began in about three hours. Fifteen-year-old Sarah and her infant son had to ride several city buses to reach her high school, a trip that usually took an hour and a half. And after they arrived, Sarah had to get David settled at the child-care center before she could join her classmates.

David cried when Sarah reached into his crib. She hated to wake him when he was sleeping soundly, but she needed to change his diaper, feed him, get him dressed, and pack his tote bag with diapers and bottles, as well as finish getting herself ready for school. Every morning she made a last-minute search of the apartment to round up any school papers she might have overlooked the night before. Despite her early alarm, Sarah had barely enough time to get the two of them ready to leave.

Bundled against the morning's chill, Sarah's strong, athletic shoulders were draped in bags. Her elegant features barely visible beneath her scarf, her snugly wrapped baby in her arms, she looked like an overloaded

Sherpa setting off on a mountain climb. During the snowy months, the waits between buses made the trip feel a lot longer. The school, on the other side of the city, was not the one Sarah would have attended if she had not become a mother. She had enrolled there because it was the only school with on-site child care, something she needed if she was going to continue her education.

"You will take care of the baby. It's your baby.
I will take care of you."

Like thousands of other teenage parents around the country, Sarah brought her child to high school with her. To have her son well taken care of while she went to class gave her the comfort that allowed her to concentrate on her studies. Still, it was hard. Each day she got reminders of how different her life was from the lives of those who sat next to her in class. She found their conversations hard to relate to; girls were consumed with gossip about boyfriends, which couldn't be a priority in Sarah's life. Even if she'd wanted a boyfriend, she had no time to spend with him. While other students' lives seemed filled with adventure, Sarah's could be summed up in one word: responsibility. When she won $200 in a lip-synching contest at school, Sarah was asked by a school newspaper reporter how she was going to spend her money. "I'm buying my son some underwear," she replied.

I asked Sarah to pinpoint a moment when she truly understood how different her life had become. She told me about the day when tryouts for the basketball team were taking place. "It hit me: I can't do this because of my child. Playing basketball was so important to me, because when I get stressed out I don't scream or yell. I do physical things. Basketball was a real release."

But if Sarah had played basketball there would have been no one to watch her son. Her thirty-six-year-old mother, Judy, who was divorced when Sarah was two years old, worked full-time as a secretary, and on weekends had a part-time job waitressing. Sarah's father, mentally ill and homeless, wasn't involved in her life. When Judy was rearing Sarah, she attended college classes at night so she could find a job that would pay enough to get them off welfare and keep them off. Judy knew she served as a valuable role model for her daughter. Quitting her job to take care of David would have meant returning to welfare, something she was unwilling to do for her own sake and Sarah's. Because Judy wanted her daughter to appreciate the enormous responsibilities that go along with being a parent and also to understand the rewards of hard work, going back on public assistance would have been disastrous.

There was another reason Judy was reluctant to be at home with David while Sarah was in school: she believed that even though Sarah was extremely young to be a mother, it would be best for her to learn how to be her son's primary caregiver. Unless Sarah assumed this role—with Judy's support and guidance in doing so—the years ahead would be harder for her and her son. In a few years, they would leave Judy's house to live on their own; it was important that before then Sarah establish herself as her son's parent.

Before David was born Judy explained to Sarah, with as much clarity as she could muster, how their household would function. "I told her, 'You will take care of the baby. It's your baby. I will take care of you. I'll take care of the house and the cooking and the bills and your laundry and all of those other worries. You'll take care of the baby. And you will finish school.' " Judy's expression when she tells me this is one of utter serious-ness, a reminder of her determination that Sarah's unintended pregnancy would not doom her.

Sarah's son was born in May of her freshman year of high school. She was thirteen when she got pregnant. The baby's father, Terry, was an after-school playground buddy, someone her age with whom she played basket-ball. Sarah has never told Terry how much his friendship meant to her, but on the day before she met him Sarah was feeling so despondent that she wrote a suicide note and sealed copies in three envelopes, addressed to friends. "That day I was looking for anybody," Sarah told me. "If I'd come across a worm on the ground and it talked to me, I'd have said okay. Terry was somebody who was showing an interest in me."

One afternoon about a year after they'd met, Sarah and Terry sponta-neously became lovers instead of playing basketball. This was the first time Sarah had intercourse. Sarah remembers how much she enjoyed making love with Terry, even though it was her first time. She did not shy away from his advances; instead she admits that she urged him on and that her curiosity shoved worries aside. Only in a remote outpost of her mind could Sarah hear faint echoes of her mother's voice warning her not to be doing what she was about to do.

Judy had known the day would come when her daughter was tempted by sex. So for several years, as Sarah approached adolescence, she had talked with her about how babies are made. When the biology lesson ended, Judy would always remind Sarah: "All I ask of you is not to get pregnant and to finish high school." Judy knew too well the hardships inflicted on a young woman who didn't at least graduate before taking on motherhood. She asked Sarah to tell her if she ever believed there was a possibility that she might become sexually involved. If she couldn't persuade Sarah to postpone sex, Judy was prepared to take her to a doctor and get birth control. On the day she got pregnant, Sarah hadn't expected to have sex, so she'd never taken her mother up on the offer.

"Rather than help me out with his son, Terry spent all his money on sneakers and fixing up cars."

During the summer months after David was born, Sarah worked as much as eight hours a day as a waitress at Dunkin' Donuts. She wanted to earn money to avoid going on welfare. The baby's father didn't have a job so he stayed at Judy's house with the child. On weekends, Terry, Sarah, and their son traveled to his parents' house in a nearby city. The baby's grandmother would baby-sit while Sarah went to work at another Dunkin' Donuts from four in the morning until four in the afternoon. Often when she returned to their house after twelve hours at work, Terry's father would impatiently tap his cup on a table as a way of getting Sarah's attention: "He wanted me to get up and refill it for him." Sarah refused be his servant, something she soon discovered that the women in Terry's family were expected to do. "I wouldn't do it," she says with forceful determination. "I think that's why they don't like me."

Attitudes such as these also contributed to the deterioration of Sarah and Terry's relationship. Even as she was working, Sarah tells me, Terry was receiving checks from what he said was the welfare department. She doesn't know why. All she knows is that he received some money from the state but none of it went to her or the baby. "Rather than help me out with his son, Terry spent all his money on sneakers and fixing up cars." Even now, several years after their breakup, Sarah's anger about Terry's behavior rises as she talks about his unwillingness to assume parenting responsibilities. She calms herself down before continuing: "Sometimes he'd borrow *my* money." This time she laughs.

It did not take long for Sarah to grasp the immensity of her responsibilities as a mother. She resented Terry's failure to help with their baby's expenses. Though he stayed with David while she worked, it angered Sarah that she was expected to organize every detail of their son's care so that Terry would be able to handle it. Whatever fun the two of them once had together vanished under the weight of these new tensions. The presence of a baby in their lives demanded a very different, more supportive arrangement between them. As months went by it became clear that

Sarah and Terry, like many other teen parents, could not sustain a close relationship with each other.

Nevertheless, Terry wanted to get married; he gave Sarah an engagement ring two months after their son was born. Sarah kept the ring for three months even though, as she tells me, "I never felt like I was engaged." One day she told Terry she could no longer keep it. "I remember him banging his head against the wall and crying and telling me he'd drive his car into a tree. He begged me to just keep wearing it or even keep it in my pocket. But it didn't mean anything to me. To wear something like that it should mean something and it didn't."

Soon after Sarah's return of his ring essentially ended their relationship, Terry dropped out of high school.

"We'd go to see the legislators and some would tell us they're too busy and can't listen to us now."

Terry moved to the city his parents live in, about sixty miles away from Sarah and their son. Now Sarah could no longer work after school, since no one was available to watch the baby and her earnings would just barely have covered the cost of a baby-sitter. While she was at school, David was cared for at her high school day care center because the state government provided Sarah with a voucher to pay for it. Without a voucher, she couldn't afford it.

Getting her son child care was the primary reason Sarah applied for public assistance. When David was an infant, Sarah's biweekly $170 check was part of a state welfare program called General Relief. This program—known primarily for its support of indigent men—was also designed to assist young mothers who lived at their family's home. The voucher was essential, but Sarah didn't need the cash assistance that went along with it. So she returned what she considered excess to the state agency.

"I didn't care what they did with the cash," she says. "It was off my shoulders."

After a while the amount of her check was reduced to what Sarah told them she needed. Within the year, however, a new Republican governor set out to fulfill a campaign promise to reduce government spending. One of his early targets was benefits for the poor—in particular, General Relief. When word of his proposed cuts arrived at Sarah's school, the young mothers understood the implications immediately: many, like Sarah, were suddenly in danger of losing their cash benefits and their precious child-care vouchers.

Several of the young women decided to try to fight the cuts. They organized themselves to go door-to-door to obtain signatures on petitions urging legislators to do something about their situation. In talking with people about the cuts, Sarah was surprised to learn how little they knew about what the governor's proposal would do to the child care she depended on for her education. When she explained that her child-care voucher enabled her to stay in school, many no longer hesitated to sign the petition.

"I refuse to say that I would have 'quit' school if I didn't get a voucher," Sarah tells me. "I think of it as me being *laid off* from school because this program is what's keeping me there."

Sarah and her friends took their petitions, with hundreds of signatures, to the gold-domed statehouse in Boston. They wanted to tell legislators about their situation. If these policymakers understood how valuable the vouchers were, how they enabled young mothers to finish high school, Sarah felt certain they'd vote to save them. But she was unsuccessful in her efforts to speak with many of the representatives and senators directly. "We'd go to see the legislators and some would tell us they were too busy and couldn't listen to us now." Sarah's face tightens into a scowl. "This kind of angered me because the next day I might not be able to go to school. But they just couldn't listen to us."

One day a newspaper reporter interviewed Sarah as she sat outside the governor's office. "If that voucher is cut, I'll be forced to quit school," she told the reporter, slipping into the word "quit." "If I quit school I won't be able to go out into the working world because I still won't have day care. And without school, there's no way for me to climb up the financial ladder. I will have to go on welfare full-time. What people don't understand is that once I'm working full-time, I will be putting money back into the system. I just need a stepping-stone." During this legislative debate Sarah wrote a letter to the editors of her city newspaper as well. It read, in part: "Without General Relief and child care we will become even more dependent on the state, and believe it or not, for an even longer amount of time. Not a smart move."

"What was the result of your activism?" I ask her.

"I graduated," Sarah says, flashing me a big smile.

"But were you able to keep the child-care vouchers?"

Sarah nods. "The young mothers who already had vouchers through the General Relief program were able to keep them until they completed high school. However, during Sarah's junior and senior years, she did not receive cash assistance because she continued to live with her mother. "If I'd left my mother's house and moved into a shelter with my son and then gotten emergency housing, I would have qualified for welfare," Sarah says. "But the best support for me was in my mother's home. Why would I want to leave my mother, my only support, my only real family, and go to a shelter when I am in high school and trying to pass final exams and stuff like that? Why would I want to do that? It's just ridiculous." Sarah knew girls who did exactly that: they moved into shelters because it was the way to secure a welfare check to help with the baby's expenses.

Like any young mother who's trying to get an education and does not have family members who can baby-sit, Sarah depended on reliable, subsidized child care. Yet, in her experience with the welfare system, securing this crucial assistance always seemed to be a struggle. This is so for many women. There never seem to be enough vouchers to meet the demand, and in any case vouchers often provide less reimbursement than many good-quality child-care centers charge, so it's difficult for mothers to locate dependable and well-trained caregivers. After Sarah finished high school and enrolled at a local college, she applied to the welfare department for a voucher so David could be well cared for while she went to class. "I told the welfare people that I didn't need any money but my son needed a voucher," she says. "But they said they couldn't give me a child-care voucher unless I was on welfare. I sat there and I said to them, 'You mean you want to give me four hundred and eighty-six dollars a month for me to get a piece of paper to pay for my son's child care?' It's like they won't give you a little bit of help unless you take the whole cake. So that is what I had to do. I mean, I'm not ashamed to go onto welfare, but I didn't need to, at least not for that year."

"So the welfare system spent money on you that you told them you didn't need?" I ask her, making certain I understand what she's telling me.

"Yes. I told them I didn't need it. But that's the system. Because they'd already cut General Relief, they couldn't give me a lesser amount. It was really crazy. It really was." Sarah shakes her head in disgust.

Sarah managed to make the system work for her and David, but her experiences with the legislators who devise public assistance and with welfare officials who operate it left her incredulous at the stupidity of their decisions: "We had to fight the system, just so we could go to school." She shakes her head, and her brown eyes, usually so alert, stare into the distance. It is as though she wants her anger to fly away.

David is sitting with us as Sarah and I talk about these hurdles. He is now nearly three years old, and as inquisitive as he is talkative. Sarah always takes the time to answer whatever questions he has. She is a loving and attentive mother.

"Mommy," David says, as he nudges her with his elbow. "What is 'fighting the system' mean?"

"It's a figure of speech," she tells him. "What Mommy had to do to stay in school."

"Mommy went to school," David says.

A smile crosses his round, happy face while he mimics her words, savoring the sound of his own voice. A moment later, he turns his attention back to the stack of pancakes he is eating, content at having his question answered.

"Schools are navigating a tricky path, as they try to help teen parents without giving the nod to teen pregnancies."

Sarah is a fighter and, she says, a perfectionist. Her life isn't something that just happens to her; it is something she constructs. She says her mother tells her that a stubborn, determined streak has always been embedded in her. The person she's become—the petitioner, the activist, the pragmatist—emerged out of her determination to prove wrong the many people who doubted her capacity to get herself and her son over the hurdles of early parenthood.

"When I got pregnant everyone said to me, 'Oh, my God, what are you going to do?' I never said, 'Oh, my God, what am I going to do?' And I didn't say, 'This is great.' I was just adjusting to everything, going with the flow," Sarah told me once we knew each other well. "Lots of things I did, I did to prove to people I *could* even though I was a young, young, young parent. Then it got to the point where I doubted myself, because I heard so much about all that I couldn't do. All those extra things, like getting on the honor roll or being on the basketball team. I had to do that to prove myself. And it sort of has turned into that. I am trying to prove things to other people but I'm trying to prove them to myself, too."

But as important as determination is for Sarah and other young mothers, it is not enough to enable them to surmount on their own all of the obstacles that early motherhood puts in their paths. Young mothers need safe, dependable, subsidized child care if they are to remain in school or go to work. And if their children are going to get the stimulation they need to develop their social and educational skills, the caregivers must be well trained. Yet, in a survey of more than 150,000 single-parent families in Illinois who were receiving welfare or had recently gotten off the rolls because of finding work, 42 percent of the teenage mothers reported that difficulties in securing child care had forced them to quit school within the past year. As for the mothers who worked, they were able to earn, on average, no more than the minimum wage. For child care, most of these young mothers had no choice but to rely on relatives or friends. As the survey revealed, "those who relied on informal child care arrangements reported more work and school-related problems due to these arrangements than those using center-based care."

There are some who argue against setting up school-based child-care centers of the kind Sarah relied on. Providing child care in school, these critics say, sends precisely the wrong signal to youngsters: that if a pregnancy occurs, someone else will care for their babies. If there are child-care centers in the schools, one of the few remaining social sanctions against teenage parenthood vanishes. Messages about the need to accept personal responsibility for one's actions, some argue, get lost when youngsters see that others will assume some of the most basic parental obligations.

Those who favor in-school day care contend that providing child care is often the only way of keeping teenage mothers in school. And they must complete their education if they're to become capable of supporting their families, as many of them will have to do. (Federal welfare reform now requires teenage mothers to finish high school or lose benefits.) To punish young women once they've become mothers is foolish, proponents of such assistance contend, since to make their lives as mothers more difficult only ends up hurting their children during the most important developmental years. If such care is not provided, the alternative arrangements these young mothers find—and can afford—are likely to be less good and much less dependable. And when a young mother leaves school—as too many still do—because she can't find child care, she and her children are virtually certain to suffer the detrimental consequences of poverty for longer than they otherwise would.

A 1993 article on the front page of *The Wall Street Journal,* "School Day Care Helps Teen Moms, but Risks Condoning Pregnancies," highlighted this debate. Does providing child care for teen moms promote early motherhood? Does school-based child care "really [keep] teen parents in school"? The writer, Gabriella Stern, reported finding limited and conflicting evidence. "No comprehensive studies exist," she wrote, "meaning both proponents and critics can wave their own sets of conflicting data." Consequently, she observed, schools "are navigating a tricky path, as they try to help teen parents without giving the nod to teen pregnancies."

While it is exceedingly difficult to isolate one factor, such as the availability of child care, in trying to determine what motivates certain young women to have babies early and out of wedlock, fairly good evidence does exist about the effectiveness of comprehensive services in keeping teenage mothers in school. A 1992 study by the Alliance for Young Families, a not-for-profit Massachusetts consortium dedicated to preventing adolescent pregnancy and expanding quality services for teenage parents and their children, revealed numerous benefits associated with providing child care, parenting education, and other services for teenage mothers. (This statewide study—the first of its kind—had been released by the time of Stern's story, but she did not cite its findings.)

The Alliance report compared teenage mothers who had child care and other supportive services with those who did not. Young mothers who did not have access to these comprehensive services had much lower rates of completing high school: 80 percent failed to graduate, 69 percent were on welfare by the time their first child was four years old, and 40 percent of them were likely to be on welfare for a decade longer. Teenage mothers who had dependable child care, along with counseling, parent education, and transportation, seemed to have more promising futures: 80 percent of them earned a high school diploma; a quarter of those graduates went on to college, and 65 percent would go on to earn incomes above the poverty line.

The report also found that taxpayers accrue quantifiable, long-term economic benefits from keeping young mothers in high school and ensuring that their children have quality day care. The average cost of these services for each mother and child was calculated by the Alliance to be about $10,000 a year. It is estimated that taxpayers would save three times as much per family during the subsequent decade; costs potentially avoided include Medicaid, cash assistance, and housing subsidies.

Many conversations I've had with teenage mothers lead me to believe that while the availability of child care may be one of many factors that influence a girl's decision about whether to continue a pregnancy, it is not high on the list of reasons why she becomes pregnant. As for young women who decide to carry their pregnancies to term, their decisions usually have more to do with their personal circumstances than with strategic thinking about child care. The everyday lives of most girls who continue their pregnancies are enmeshed in the chronic effects of poverty, failure in school, and difficult family relationships. Sarah may seem to be an exception to this pattern, and to some extent she is. But it is worth recalling that when she became pregnant and decided to continue the pregnancy she was exceedingly lonely, not doing well in school, and living in public housing. As her mother reminded me, "Junior high was a rough time for Sarah. She had friends who had gotten killed. She went from being an A student in grammar school to getting F warnings. Her teachers told me she had an attitude problem. They didn't like her questioning their authority, which was something she would do."

I've listened as many teenage girls tell me about wanting to have a baby.

But the amount of time most give to connecting their vision of being "Mommy" with the reality of what a child's care will actually entail is just about zero. These girls' reasons for wanting to have a baby rarely extend much further than a powerful wish to secure a loving relationship.

For us, as adults, to get stuck on the "incentive" argument is to be blind to the short-term, reactive nature of many adolescents' decision-making. Risky behavior characterizes this developmental time in young people's lives, especially among youngsters who do not have a close, trusting relationship with an adult who can offer them strategies and reasons to resist the temptations they face. If adolescents decide to leap into parenthood, in very few cases will their primary reason be the availability of child care at school. After all, the presence of rescue boats at the dock is not what motivates someone to jump off a bridge. There are far more constructive ways to frame this debate about child care's impact on early parenthood. It would be more worthwhile to consider whether the availability of high-quality child care, the consistent involvement of mentoring adults, the creation of supportive learning environments for the children and young parents, and access to medical care can offer promising ways to help young mothers to "rescue" their lives and those of their children. When the question is put this way, the answer is undoubtedly yes. In fact, as long-term findings of the Perry Preschool study* indicate, enriched learning environments and family support services are related to positive outcomes: not only did this high-quality intervention lead to improved school achievement and higher rates of school graduation for participants in general, but women who attended Perry Preschool as toddlers had higher rates of marriage and fewer out-of-wedlock births by the time they were twenty-seven than peers who didn't have this early attention.

Sarah's mother, Judy, has no doubt that similar ingredients, plus her daughter's individual effort, enabled her to turn her life around and give David a promising start. Judy remembers one year when she had to postpone her return to college because she wasn't able to find child care for Sarah, then a toddler. "I was very bored and needed to be stimulated," Judy says. "And Sarah was bored, too, being at home with me." Because of her own experience, Judy was delighted that Sarah and David received the help they needed. "Sarah took advantage of everything that was offered to her, from counselors to support groups. She went for it all. She was like the ideal single parent because she reached out for everything."

---

*Perry Preschool was an experimental, high-quality education program for poor youngsters which took place during the early 1960s. These children's lives have been studied since then and compared with those of peers who did not receive these intervention services.

"Another unplanned pregnancy further cements them into this life path."

The Alliance report found—as other studies have—that providing comprehensive services for teenage mothers offers another important benefit: young mothers who have this kind of support are more likely to postpone the birth of a second child. That decision turns out to have enormous ramifications for a young family's future success as well as for the costs of public assistance, which are picked up by taxpayers. Young mothers who have fewer children are more likely to finish high school and less likely to remain dependent on welfare; their children, on average, do better in school.

In the Alliance study, somewhat fewer than one in four adolescent mothers who didn't have good and reliable child care and parenting education gave birth to another child within two years. A quarter of these second babies had to stay in neonatal intensive-care units because they had low birthweights; the Medicaid expenditure alone exceeded $28,500 per baby. However, among the mothers who had child care and additional support services, only about one in nine had another baby within two years, and many fewer of their babies had such severe and costly problems at birth. A long-term study of primarily black teenage mothers in Baltimore found that young women who had two or more babies within five years of their first child's birth were "almost four times as likely to be on welfare and 72% less likely to be economically secure" seventeen years after their first child was born than mothers who had no other children during that five-year window. Mothers who didn't have an additional baby for at least five years attained, on average, more education and lessened their family's reliance on welfare.

A Yale study of teenage mothers in New Haven, Connecticut, who received such services also found that delaying the birth of another child has an enduring positive effect on the child the mother already has, especially if that child is a boy. When mothers waited at least five years before having a second child, their sons performed significantly better in school than did boys who had younger siblings when they were in preschool. By the time these young women's firstborn children were twelve years old, their school performance turned out to be closer to national norms for children of their age, even though they had been raised by teenage mothers, most of whom were unwed. With firstborn girls, similar effects were found when mothers postponed a second birth for just two years. As the researchers note, these cases "suggest the possibility that, for children of teenagers, the experience of being an only child during the pre-school years is so powerful a protective factor that, to some extent, it can override very negative events later in the child's life."

Results such as these demonstrate what casual observers might suspect: by postponing another pregnancy, a young mother enhances her future prospects and her child's. Sarah's situation was manageable, in part, because she had only David. She and her mother viewed her pregnancy as a onetime mistake, and afterward she used contraception diligently. Sarah is not willing to contemplate having a second child until she graduates from college. She tells me she imagines getting married when she is twenty-five years old. "David will be eleven then," she says. "He'll hand me the ring." Only then will she think about having another child.

The direction a young mother chooses to move in during the first year or so after her baby is born does much to determine the trajectory of her life and her child's. When no one from school—no teacher, counselor, or administrator—reaches out to reengage a girl who has had a baby, when no one in her family works with her to alleviate the stresses of parenting, it is more likely that she'll disconnect from school as the burdens of new parenthood overwhelm her. When this happens, her identity as a mother roots itself in her. From this vantage point, a young woman becomes less and less likely to regard the arrival of another child as disrupting her own future; instead, as Debbie's story illustrated, another child seems to be a natural continuation of the new life that her first pregnancy set into motion.

The Yale psychologists Victoria Seitz and Nancy Apfel, who followed the life course of the New Haven adolescent mothers mentioned above, watched what happened to the mothers who went on to have other children soon after their first. These young women, Seitz and Apfel wrote, "often appear to become overwhelmed with their multiple responsibilities and [thus] are more likely to abandon hope for personal achievement. One consequence of this attitude is likely to be another unplanned pregnancy, further cementing them into this life path." In their study of a school-based program that offered young mothers and their children comprehensive, supportive services, Seitz and Apfel discovered that mothers who remained in the program for at least seven weeks after giving birth considerably lessened the likelihood they would have another child within two years. What was surprising—and encouraging—about this finding was that a relatively small investment of time and resources appeared to make such a big difference. That led Seitz and Apfel to suggest that the two months after her child is born may be "a critical time" during which an adolescent mother "begins to make crucial decisions affecting her fertility," a time in which adult guidance can truly make a difference.

"We are cannibalizing our own children."

School-based child care, like the kind Sarah had, is often of high quality. But young mothers who are no longer in school or who live in places where schools do not provide it have a hard time finding good care. Many young mothers are also suspicious and fearful of out-of-home child care. They hear stories, which several shared with me, about children being molested or physically hurt when placed in the care of strangers. These fears also arise out of their own experiences—they've seen or heard of abuse or neglect, or were themselves victimized. Unless child care is integrated into her own school day, many a young mother will be reluctant to entrust the care of her child to anyone else. If the choice is between continuing school (something many of these girls didn't enjoy even before they got pregnant) or making certain their child is not hurt by a stranger, some will choose to stay home with their babies.

Besides, young mothers' fears about the safety of child care are not unfounded, especially since many can't secure high-quality care. A 1991 federal investigation of child-care programs found that some had inoperable toilets and raw sewage in play areas; dangerously high tap water temperatures (exceeding 110 degrees); locked fire exits; roach infestations; and bug spray, broken glass, alcoholic beverages, and sharp knives left where children could get to them. In all, the investigators reported dangerous conditions at nearly a third of the facilities they visited, and unsanitary conditions at nearly a quarter.

In another study, published in 1995, psychologists and economists from four universities evaluated how well child-care centers were serving the needs of children and how their quality was related to their cost. Of the more than 200 infant or toddler programs visited, 40 percent provided less than minimal levels of care. Only 8 percent were judged to be of "high quality." This meant that most of the children were not having their needs for cleanliness and safety met; nor were the children receiving appropriate stimulation and nurturing from adults who cared for them; nor was learning being enhanced. The psychologists expressed concern that these children's cognitive and emotional development was being stunted by the care they were receiving. The economists determined that the most important factor in the quality of child care is how generously parents' contributions to its cost are supplemented by employers or government programs. The more expensive care is, the more likely there will be well-trained child-care providers who know how to care for children in developmentally appropriate ways and who will remain their caregivers for more continuous periods of time.

The fact is that too many children are being taken care of by adults who are inadequately trained and poorly compensated. Television can become a daylong baby-sitter when caregivers have neither the skills nor the resources to offer other essential experiences. Child care, when done well, is constantly demanding. Burnout is common and turnover among caregivers is high. Child-care workers' salaries average less than $10,000 per year, placing this among the lowest-paid jobs. In some centers more than a quarter of the adults upon whom children have learned to depend leave within a given year. This revolving-door care negatively affects children's ability to develop trusting attachments, which are related to how well children learn and develop social behaviors. Dr. T. Berry Brazelton, a pediatrician well known for his advice books and TV shows about babies and children, observed that high turnover among child-care workers "is why we have children who cannot form attachments, who grow up with shallow relationships. . . . The price we pay is all the violence among young people." Unless adolescent mothers receive adequate subsidies or vouchers, the child care they can afford for their children is not likely to give their infants and toddlers a promising start.

Often young parents decide to leave their children with relatives or neighbors who operate what is commonly referred to as family day care, because the care is available near home and is relatively inexpensive. But this choice also presents risks, in part because oversight and training are lacking. Even though informal arrangements seem more homelike than centers, a recent study by the Families and Work Institute found that some 40 percent of such providers planned no activities for the children they cared for. The researchers found that in more than a third of settings they visited the care being provided was "so indifferent" that it might actually be harmful to children's development. Only 9 percent of these home settings were rated as providing good care.

Edward Zigler, Sterling professor of psychology at Yale and an architect of Head Start, the nation's early education program for poor children, is worried about infants and toddlers in "subpar" day care, where they are not receiving the nurturing and stimulating human interaction they need. Like Dr. Brazelton, Professor Zigler worries about the relationship between low-quality child care and the increases he observes in depression and violence in children and adolescents. "We are cannibalizing our own children," Professor Zigler told me in his customarily blunt way. "What many of these kids are experiencing every day is dooming them."

If we want to produce the factors that we know increase the likelihood that a teenager will become a mother—academic failure and antisocial behavior—there's no better way than to deprive at-risk infants and toddlers of the high-quality learning and social environment every child needs. By ignoring, or even worse, harming the development of the children of today's teenage mothers—by not improving child care—we are making it more likely that a decade and a half from now these children will be having children too, most likely out of wedlock.

"This label of 'teen parent,' it doesn't wear off."

Sarah's son, David, received at his child-care center the kind of stimulating play and attention that infants and toddlers thrive on. For his mom, too, David's child-care center offered a security blanket, one she relied on often. It was her son's caregivers to whom Sarah turned for advice about what she could do after high school. To these adult women she also confided things about herself she couldn't tell anyone else. Without their practical and emotional support, Sarah wonders if she would ever have made it through the mine field of negative comments and attitudes she encountered in high school.

Sarah believes that some teachers went out of their way to make derogatory remarks about girls who'd become mothers. She describes a time when she showed one of her teachers her report card, which bore several A's. Sarah was proud of her accomplishments. Her teacher's only comment was "But you have all easy classes, don't you?"

"There always had to be some excuse, because no one could accept I could do the level of work the other students were doing and be a teen parent," Sarah says. "I mean they figure, 'How can she get A's and be a single mother?'" Remarks like this teacher's reinforced Sarah's propensity for self-doubt. Despite her amazing capacity to persevere and outward display of self-confidence, as I came to know Sarah I realized how easily she allowed negative comments to stick to her. "I'd get disgusted and depressed," Sarah tells me of such run-ins. "They blew my whole day." After a while, however, she'd turn these remarks around and use them to energize herself. "They'd become a reminder for me to push on." Other teen mothers who did not have Sarah's combative and resilient temperament seemed to allow disparagement to settle in on them, adding one more reason to resign themselves to failure. After all, if failure was expected of them, at least it was something they could provide.

Sarah tells me about the day a friend who was also a teenage mother came to her in tears after meeting with a teacher. She'd gone to get help after she'd received an unexpected C on a paper. She told her teacher: "I don't know what I'm doing wrong. I'd really like to improve my grade and

I'm trying so hard." The teacher targeted her reply like an arrow from a well-aimed bow: "Well, you didn't seem to be trying too hard when you were lying on your back." Sarah's friend left the classroom sobbing.

There were plenty of times Sarah cried a lot, too. "This label of 'teen parent,'" she says, rolling her eyes as if to draw my attention to some imaginary spot on her forehead where the words might just as well be stamped. "It does not wear off."

"What do people conclude about you if you are a teen parent?"

"Oh, when people first find out, they say you'll drop out of school and that you'll be on welfare for the rest of your life and that you won't ever accomplish anything and that your hopes and dreams are gone." Sarah recites these items like someone reading a grocery list. "And it is not as though you are sitting there imagining that they are thinking these things. They say them to us!" Often, too, Sarah thinks that her light brown skin—the product of her parents' interracial marriage—encourages people even more to underestimate her abilities or doubt her determination.

"How can you break out of this cycle?" I ask her.

"Well . . ." She pauses. "I am in this situation, so I need to do what I can to be a good role model for my son. And just to survive. Because I don't want to be a stereotype, it just drives me to rebel against that. I guess the message I want to give out is that being a young mother is not easy. People see me and I am graduating from high school and going to college. And they see that my son is a great kid but they don't see the times that I'm home in tears and my son is comforting me."

Sarah is still bitter about the attitudes she felt school administrators displayed toward students like her. I ask her to explain. "Oh, like, 'We're getting them through high school. Let the welfare department deal with them afterwards.' I mean, that was their only goal," she says. "They didn't help us set further goals." Sarah showed up for the college entrance exams only because a friend had asked her to take them with her. No adult at school bothered to explain to Sarah the importance of college board scores, so Sarah didn't prepare for the tests. She remembers leaving about half of the answers blank. Her scores were not good.

"College isn't in your future," a guidance counselor told her when she went to discuss what she should do after high school. Sarah's grades were pretty good, and she was senior class president—but still no teacher reached out to her with words of encouragement about future academic pursuits. Sarah assumed her life would be like her mother's: she'd find an apartment, get a full-time job, and take college classes at night. She had a plan: the caregivers at David's child-care center told her about an internship program for teenage mothers. Because Sarah enjoys science, she decided to apply to a local biotechnology company. The program was designed to last for a year; if there was an opening at the clerical level after her internship was over, she'd get the job.

One day, a few weeks before her high school graduation, Sarah received an invitation to interview for a college scholarship. A woman on the scholarship committee had heard Sarah speak in favor of mandatory sex education in the public schools and was so impressed by the gutsiness of her presentation that she invited her to apply for this money. "I had never heard of this scholarship," Sarah tells me. The only thing she knew about scholarships was that when she asked counselors or teachers at school about applying for one, they'd discouraged her. Now she was being *asked* to apply. At her interview, the panelists' questions bespoke very different attitudes about her prospects. "They asked me why I wasn't going to college," Sarah says. " 'Why wouldn't you go?' they wanted to know. I ended up in tears because up until that moment everyone said to me I couldn't go and now these people were saying, 'Of course you can go. Why aren't you?' "

On graduation day Sarah learned that she'd been selected for this generous college scholarship. Even then, it was difficult for her to adjust her thinking about the future. "It was hard to think about going to college when I had the job security" of the paid internship. Judy's emphasis on the security of a paycheck had left an imprint on her. "But when I thought about it, I figured if the biotech park blows up, then I am jobless. But if the world blows up, I'll still have my education at college."

Sometimes Sarah imagines being invited back to speak with students at her high school after she graduates from college and has embarked on a career. Perhaps the administrators will decide to parade her before students as one of their success stories. Remembering how badly most of them treated her, Sarah says that if she ever has that chance to speak to students, she has a pretty good idea what she'll say. "The people who never helped me will know who they are when I go there. I'm not going to say, 'Ha, ha, I made it.' But I am going to speak directly to the students who are now being put down by those same people. And I'm going to say to them, 'I was told by people here I couldn't do this and I did it, so you can too.' "

"David lays down on my lap and goes to sleep."

A few years later Sarah and I get together to talk again. David, now six years old, is a delightful boy with a bountiful vocabulary, an effervescent personality, and a streak of stubbornness definitely inherited from his mother. From the time David was very young, Sarah learned how to set well-defined limits for him. She's always disciplined him with her voice, never with her hand; in fact, she rarely raises her voice to him. Sarah also follows through on warnings of punishment if unacceptable behavior continues. Her word is something David can depend on.

Sarah is now a junior at a prestigious four-year all-women's college, where she is the youngest member of a special program to enable mothers to attend college full-time. She and her son live in an old wooden house in a low-income section of a town near the campus. Her monthly rent on this two-bedroom house is low, but it still devours most of her welfare check. To pay for expenses her scholarship does not cover, Sarah takes out student loans. She also has a work-study job at school as part of her financial aid.

Even though David is older now, being a single mother still means that Sarah has to figure out how to keep pushing her life forward while taking care of him. During her first semester, she and David spent many evenings at the school's computer lab. To do her math assignments, Sarah needed to work on a particular computer program. But because she didn't own a computer, she had to return to campus most evenings to do so. "I pick David up at his school, go home, get something for us to eat, do something with him for about an hour or so. Then I dress him for bed and we drive back to school," Sarah tells me when I ask how she juggled classes, a job, and motherhood and still found time to study. "We stay at the lab until about midnight. David has a chair right next to mine and he lays down on my lap and goes to sleep."

"So you get home after midnight? And would you still have other schoolwork to do?"

"Yeah." Sarah's tone is matter-of-fact. "I usually go to bed about three."

"And get up when?"

"Oh, about six. But it works. I did it."

In the spring her mother, Judy, uses her tax refund to buy a personal computer for Sarah. As Sarah tells me, "The quality of my work is so much better because I'm not always rushing."

Young Mothers' Children: Early Development

Sarah's ability to manage so well the nurturing and disciplining responsibilities of motherhood so early in her own adolescence, and to steadily progress through school, is an anomaly among girls of her age who have babies. For young mothers, whether they're married or not—and especially for the majority who have no option but to rear their children in poor, often unsafe neighborhoods while they grow up themselves—the job of being a parent is, at best, exceedingly difficult. The job becomes virtually impossible for a young mother when she doesn't receive assistance from family members, friends, counselors, and her school.

Few young mothers succeed, as Sarah has, in rearing a child who possesses the inquisitive nature, attentiveness, and agreeable disposition that make David eager and ready to learn. Often the result of young mothers' immaturity, poverty, and disaffection from learning is that their children, by the age of five or six, display various problematic behaviors that are likely to make schooling more difficult right from the start. The common convergence of early motherhood and disengagement from education is particularly unfortunate for such children. Just at the time these young mothers pull away from learning, their babies and toddlers are relying on them to be their first teachers. While young mothers can resume their education later on—and many do—children go through crucial stages of cognitive and emotional development in the first three years of life. If they miss certain opportunities then, they will have a more difficult time mastering many of the educational and behavioral challenges they confront later.

When a young mother leaves school, she separates herself not only from the content of her classes but from the structure and discipline of learning. An increasing sense of failure may easily be stirred up in her, as may anger at the educational system that she blames for letting her down. Whether she intends to or not, she can easily transmit this attitude to her child. Unless young mothers are given help in understanding why learning experiences are vital for children's early development, as well as hints about how to provide that stimulation, they won't know what they ought to do or how to do it.

Every adolescent knows babies must be fed. What many mothers, particularly younger ones, don't know is that infants and toddlers also require a high-calorie diet of interactive communication and age-appropriate play to nourish their developing brains. When young mothers are engaged in their own chaotic adolescent struggles or are depressed—as studies show large numbers of poor and young mothers are—they are unable to emphasize the activities and initiate the verbal exchanges that babies require if they are to lay a solid foundation for a lifetime of intellectual exploration. Without an enriched environment during these early years, children have a hard time living up to their inborn potential.

Research tells us, too, that there is a very strong relationship between a mother's level of education and her children's achievement in school. In 1995, for example, a study revealed new findings about linkages between mental retardation of children and the social and economic characteristics of their families. The strongest sociodemographic risk factor— stronger than either racial differences or marital status—was a mother's inability to complete a high school education. Even children born to high school dropouts who were twenty years old or older at delivery are impacted. The researchers concluded that "mothers with less than 12 years of schooling at the time their children were born were four times more likely to have their children diagnosed as mildly retarded by age 10 years than were mothers with 13 or more years of education." The Carnegie Task Force on Meeting the Needs of Young Children had highlighted similar evidence one year earlier, in its 1994 report "Starting Points."

"If you fail to learn the proper fundamentals at an early age, then you are in big trouble."

The Carnegie task force reported in 1994 that by the time most healthy infants are a year old their weight will have tripled since birth, their length doubled, and their brain will have achieved 80 percent of its total growth. By then, trillions of vital connections among brain cells, linkages that influence an individual's intellectual, behavioral, and emotional abilities, will have been made.

Babies who receive good nutrition and medical care, who live with parents (or a parent) diligent in providing stimulating and nurturing environments, and who aren't exposed to extremely stressful events such as family violence tend to construct solid foundations. This is probably why Sarah's son, David, is doing so well. But if a child grows up in a home where harsh discipline is combined with chronic parental unresponsiveness, that vital foundation will be severely weakened.

A young child's brain acts like a super-sponge, absorbing external stimulation as a way of guiding its intricate internal formation. During infancy, brains are as pliable as they will ever be. Everything the brain will involve—learning, memory, emotions, an individual's reaction to stress— is influenced by what happens during these early years. If children don't get appropriate stimulation (such as interactive language, warm and responsive caregiving, and instructive play) by the time they reach school age, the brain will be less likely to assemble all the connections necessary to prepare them for the challenges ahead. Scientists now estimate that the number of connections made in a baby's brain can go up or down by 25 percent depending on whether he is raised in an enriched and stimulating environment.

"It is just phenomenal how much experience determines how our brains get put together," Baylor College of Medicine neurobiologist Martha Pierson told *Chicago Tribune* reporter Ronald Kotulak, who wrote a 1994 Pulitzer Prize–winning series on early brain development. "If you fail to learn the proper fundamentals at an early age, then you are in big trouble. You can't suddenly learn when you haven't first laid down the basic brain wiring."

When young children are exposed to extreme stress or ongoing conflict among family members, their brains may react by creating networks of "diseased" pathways. The stress hormones that normally protect individuals by making them alert to dangerous situations can become over-stimulated by exposure to persistent stress; when this occurs, aberrant networks of connections among brain cells can be made, and the brain can become unstable. Scientists are now studying the potential for such stress-filled environments to encode destructive patterns of reactiveness into children's brains. Some hypothesize that one result of these structural aberrations may be that some children grow up less able to control aggressive or violent reactions to stress. In other children, the damage may produce susceptibility to depression or other mental illness. As neuropsychiatrist Bruce Perry explained, "These kids are doubly at risk. They don't have the opportunities to learn the traditional currency by which we normally get along in our society, and their brain systems that are involved in mood and impulsivity are poorly regulated. As they get older, these kids have fewer coping skills and fewer ways to solve problems. That predisposes them to use aggressive and violent strategies to try to solve problems. . . . If we don't change those developmental experiences . . . we'll end up building more prisons."

A child's mother is usually at the hub of these early experiences, so much of the responsibility for a child's development rests with her. She is also usually the primary figure to whom a child forms an emotional attachment. Attachment to the mother goes a long way toward determining how comfortably a child will experience the environment she lives in. When a child enjoys what psychologists call a "secure" relationship with her mother, she is more likely to explore, and exploration is a key ingredient in healthy development. When a young mother feels depressed about her own life or is distracted from her relationship with her child by other pressing issues—as so many adolescent mothers are—her attachment to her child is less likely to be secure. Instead, the relationship may be "ambivalent" or "avoidant"; children with maternal relationships of these types do not seek out their mothers for comfort because they are afraid of or uncertain about the kind of response they will get. Children who experience ambivalent or avoidant maternal relationships are also less able to attend to the primary developmental tasks of infancy.

When children don't hear words of praise and encouragement from their caregivers, they don't learn how to offer such sentiments to others. As a consequence, their interactions with peers and teachers are likely to suffer. Many teenage mothers, who themselves hear plenty of put-downs, are less likely to compliment their children. And because teenagers tend to fixate on their own emotional turmoil, as mothers they can find it hard to differentiate between their internal struggles and the distinct emotional needs of their children. And because they've often had so little encouragement themselves, many of them are unable to appreciate the profound effect this detached approach to parenting can have.

Parents who use physical punishment as the primary means of discipline—something I have watched several young mothers do—can also set up their children for greater aggressiveness as they grow up. Dr. Richard Tremblay, a Canadian psychologist, undertook a longitudinal study examining this issue in the lives of boys. He found a relationship between early, harsh discipline and subsequent aggression and violence by adolescent boys. The most aggressive boys came from families that "tend[ed] to be more physically punitive with their children, beating them or using other physical punishment," Dr. Tremblay said.

Often, parents who are physically punitive also don't frequently engage in more tranquil parent-child experiences, such as reading or telling stories to their children. I noticed this absence among some of the teenage mothers whose homes I visited. When a young mother doesn't consider reading relevant to her own experience, she's not likely to engage her child in it unless someone convinces her of its value to the child and shows her how to do it; many poorly educated moms don't know how to read well themselves and have no idea how to do so with their children. And someone must be there often enough to reinforce her efforts with praise. Many of the teenage mothers I visited had no books at home. The Carnegie task force reported that only half of infants and toddlers are routinely read to by parents. It should not surprise us that many of the children not being read to are among those whose mothers have less than twelve years of education.

"He won't sit and let me read a story to him."

Myieka, the young mother who adamantly refuses to get married to her children's father, has a two-year-old son, a newborn daughter, and less than twelve years of school, though she did receive a GED. She's almost eighteen years old, though her winsome smile always makes me think of her as younger. She lives with her children and their father in a third-floor, two-bedroom apartment in a Boston housing project. A scribble on the stairwell wall tells me something I'm already too aware of: "These stairs smell."

It takes a few moments for Myieka to respond to my knock, but then she welcomes me in and directs me to the one place in the living room where it's possible to sit, a small couch with a patterned cloth tossed over it. As I look around her small living room, I see the TV and stereo system she rents. The only other piece of furniture is a bookcase set along one wall. It is empty. She has no books, not for herself or for her children, Matt and Chandra. Nor are there toys for them to play with.

High school all but ended for Myieka in tenth grade, when she found out she was pregnant. "I went to a pregnancy school," she'd told me. She finished her sophomore year there, but never returned to her high school, instead choosing to take a few courses and pass a high school equivalency exam. She spends most of her day in this overheated apartment, watching television and listening to music.

"I didn't really care about an education," Myieka admits. She says that she cares more now, but the plans she has tried to make to go back to school have gotten bogged down in her inability to secure child care. "Welfare won't benefit me for it" is how she puts it. "I was supposed to go to school in September but they didn't have child care."

"How did that make you feel?" Remembering how hard Sarah fought to retain her child-care voucher, I expect Myieka to be angry. Instead, she seems willing to accept what she feels she cannot change: "I wasn't feeling any way. I knew I had to wait and there was nothing I could do about it." Perhaps Myieka has not learned to fight for what she needs because she never had anyone in her life who seemed willing to fight for *her*.

While Myieka waits to go back to school, she remains one of the mothers the Carnegie task force described, who don't read to their children. Her mother never read to her when she was growing up; she can think of no reason to do so with her children.

"Do you do some reading yourself?" I ask Myieka.

"No. I don't read a book. I did so much reading when I was in school," she says. The clear implication is that reading is a burdensome chore, something she'd do only if required to.

"Do you have books for your son?"

"No, because he won't sit and let me read a story to him."

"He won't?" I say, revealing how startled I am to discover a child who doesn't like hearing stories.

"No," Myieka insists.

"He never has?"

"No."

"So how do you put him to bed at night? Do you tell him a story, if you don't read to him?" I ask.

"I say to him, 'Lay down and go to sleep.' "

"Did you ever have stories read to you or told to you before you went to sleep when you were little?"

"No," Myieka says, staring at me quizzically.

I tell her how my father would sit between my bed and my sister's every night and weave a make-believe story about a man he named Leo. She is incredulous. "So that's why I'm asking you about telling your son stories or reading to him," I explain. "But you don't do this with Matt?"

"He won't listen. Even if I try to tell him a story, he won't listen," she says.

I ask Myieka whether she thinks the absence of such nighttime rituals or daytime reading or storytelling will make any difference when her son is old enough to go to school. She doesn't think so, nor does she think she should force something on her children that they don't like: "I'm not going to force him to read if he doesn't like reading. If he doesn't like it, he just doesn't like it." Her voice is firm; it is clear that without encouragement and help to do this, her way of thinking and acting is not going to change.

Myieka goes on to explain that getting an education is something her son will either want or not want to do. There is very little she thinks she, his parent, can do to influence Matt's decisions. "He has to want to do it for himself. I'm not going to make him. I mean, I am going to want him to go to school. He's going to get out of here. I'm not going to beat him or anything because . . ." She stops abruptly, then picks up just where she left off a moment before: "Because he has to want to do it himself."

"Would you tell him there's value for him in getting an education?" I ask.

"No, I will tell him that he would need one. That he needs an education to get somewhere," she says.

Maybe Myieka is agreeing with me; perhaps "getting somewhere" is her way of stating the value of education. But just as I begin to digest her words with this interpretation in mind, Myieka, who is shaking her head, adds weight to her overriding conviction. "No, I don't see a value in it," she says.

Myieka's parenting situation is made more difficult by the fact that she's had another child. Her second pregnancy was intentional. "I wanted to have a daughter," she explains. It is a bit unclear what she would have done had her child not been a daughter.

When I asked Myieka why she didn't wait longer to have a second child, she replied, "I think it's better to have kids when you are young."

"Tell me why."

"Okay, what I think is I want to have kids when I am young so I'll be able to go out when they get older," she said. "Like go places. When I am twenty-one I get to go out and party, and they will be kind of older and people will want to baby-sit for them. They won't be babies anymore."

I asked Myieka if she believes it is easier for a baby-sitter to take care of a five-year-old than a baby.

"I think people baby-sit kids when they are older because they'll go to sleep," she answered.

Having a baby and a toddler taxes even the most prepared parent's ability to meet each child's different developmental needs. But no parent can respond appropriately to children's needs when she doesn't even know what to expect of a child at a particular age, or when her expectations about their behavior have nothing to do with the reality of children's natural progression. Teenagers, in general, are much more likely than older mothers to be quite inaccurate in predicting what a child will be able to do at particular age or what behavior can be expected; adolescent mothers tend to expect children to reach developmental milestones earlier than they ever will. When they don't, frustration or irritability can set in, whether this ill-prepared mother is married or not.

"I think when I give him a couple of licks he listens better."

During my visits to her house, Myieka displays her willingness to use physical discipline to manage her son's bad behavior. First, she yells at him. Loudly. When he doesn't react to vocal commands—he rarely does—she threatens him with a belt. When he still doesn't conform his behavior to Myieka's shouted commands and threats, she sometimes applies the leather belt to his bottom.

Today Myieka holds a doubled-up belt in her hands. Every so often she interrupts our conversation to threaten Matt with it. This morning her son is kicking Chandra's bottle from wall to wall on the cold linoleum floor. He is wearing only a diaper. Myieka does not get up from her seat to take the bottle away from him, nor does she find something else for him to play with. She simply commands him to stop.

Punitive patterns like the one Myieka has established with her toddler—harsh words; no attempt to find alternatives to inappropriate behavior; threats; doses of physical punishment; and an absence of positive stimulation—are likely to perpetuate problem behavior now. And this is likely to happen regardless of whether a young mother is married, single, or, like Myieka, living with her children's father. Sadly, Myieka's parental strategies may also be jeopardizing her son's brain development in ways that may cause him greater difficulties later on in social encounters and in school.

I am curious about how Myieka learned to discipline her children. I know her childhood was punctuated by the arrival and departure of several men with whom her mother lived, two of whom she married. Myieka's mother was sixteen when Myieka was born, and they moved often as her mother's circumstances changed. Because of all these changes in her family life, as well as her mother's youth, Myieka probably never experienced consistency, either in how she was treated or in the lessons of acceptable behavior she was taught. When Myieka was nine years old, one of her mother's boyfriends took her along with him when he stole things. Her mother's first husband was drunk most of the time; her second, Myieka's stepfather when she was in her early teens, tried to sexually abuse her.

"Oh, I just learned as I went along," she tells me, indicating that most of her parenting lessons come out of her own experience and not from special guidance. Myieka's voice is boastful. Clearly, she is relieved that I am finally asking her about something—parenting—at which she believes she excels.

"You can't just talk to a kid sometimes," she tells me. "You see me trying to talk to him and he's not listening." Myieka is referring to exchanges she had with Matt this morning: she stayed seated on the couch, yelling orders at him. "Put that back," she screamed at him when he took his sister's bottle. "Put it back! Put it back! Did you hear what I said?" When he did not respond, Myieka yelled at him some more, and warned him: "I'm going to have to get the belt, then!"

"Tell Daddy belt," Matt responded. "Tell Daddy belt."

"What does he mean by that?" I asked.

"It means he will tell Daddy that I got the belt after him," Myieka explained.

"In his mind, what does that mean?"

"That I'm not going to do it."

"Because if you do, what will happen?"

"He will tell his daddy."

What her son says about telling his daddy, Myieka assures me, makes no impression on her; her boyfriend—her children's father—shares her views about how children should be disciplined. He'd do the same thing if he were here, she says.

"How often do you end up hitting him with the belt after you tell him that you will?" I ask.

"Fifty percent of the time I will do it."

A few moments later she is angry again. "Don't do it or you will get it," she warns her son. By now Matt has moved closer to her and is hitting her leg. "You are definitely going to get it, buddy," she tells him. Myieka tells me that when Matt notices that she is moving toward him with the belt he will start to cry.

"He'll say he is sorry and he won't do it again and he'll go lay down." This time, she insists, even if he goes through that routine, which he uses to garner her sympathy, "I am still going to beat him."

A few minutes later Myieka taps Matt's leg with the leather belt. Her son slinks away and lies whimpering on the floor.

"Stop it!" she yells at him. "Go sit down somewhere."

He whimpers even more, starts to cry, and rolls himself into a fetal position.

"Be quiet," Myieka commands.

Still he cries. Still she sits.

"Did you get through to him?" I ask her.

"Yeah, if I use the belt," Myieka says, smiling and nodding.

"How long will it be until you have to face this same thing again?"

"One or two times a day I have to do the same thing."

Her son is still crying, loudly.

"You get up and get out of here," she says harshly. "Go into your room. Go in your room. Go into your room. Get out of here. Be quiet there."

He silences his crying but remains huddled on the living room floor.

"I think when I give him a couple of licks he listens better," Myieka says.

A Grandmother's Role

Myieka and Sarah each experienced young, unmarried motherhood. That fact is all they share. While Sarah fought to keep herself and her son in school, Myieka was in a hurry to get out. Sarah looked forward to time she could spend with her son when her classes were over. During evenings when she had a test to study for or a paper due, her mother was there to help with David. Myieka, who hates to go outside, especially when it's cold, stayed cooped up day after day in an small apartment with a young child who demanded much of her, though as the hours went by she had less and less to give. There was no older person in her life to give her a respite from her parental responsibilities. Sarah rarely raised her voice to David; she never used physical punishment and always followed through on the consequences she'd warned of when her son did something he knew was wrong. Myieka relied on a belt to get her son to do as she wished; she threatened him often, but her follow-through was inconsistent.

How Sarah and Myieka adjusted to early motherhood had everything to do with the kind of developmental start their children received. Much about these young mothers'—and most teenage mothers'—adjustments has at its core the quality and durability of their relationship with their own mother or with another adult on whom they can depend. Sarah and Judy were close, and Judy acted swiftly and aggressively to line up the support her daughter needed to meet the challenges presented by her unintended pregnancy. Judy's use of education to better her life and her daughter's was a model, which Sarah emulated. Myieka was estranged from her mother, who had failed to protect her, and no one stepped in to assume a grandmotherlike role when she herself became a parent very young. The chief lesson Myieka learned from her mother was that nothing and no one can be depended on.

What we can learn from these contrasting lives is that how well a young mother does in rearing her child is related to several factors: her temperament, how she has been raised, the support she's able to find in the larger community when she becomes a parent, and the role her own mother— or another adult who is consistently available to her—plays in her life.

No matter how old a girl or woman is when she becomes a mother, it is usually her mother to whom she turns for guidance and support in how to care for her child. For women who are older, highly educated, and married, their mothers often play peripheral roles: visiting the grandchildren, helping out in emergencies, and, when asked, giving advice from afar. (Some are more directly involved in their grandchildren's care.) However, for unwed teenage mothers, a majority of whom live with or near family members during the early years of their children's lives, the role a grandmother plays is often central.

Several decades ago fewer women of grandparenting age were in the paid labor force, and thus many more were available to provide auxiliary or surrogate child-rearing. Sometimes a young mother's own mother (or the baby's paternal grandmother) actually assumed the day-to-day tasks of parenting. In black families, skipped-generation child-rearing (with grandmothers taking on the mother's role in their grandchildren's lives) was widespread. Such arrangements do exist in African-American communities today, though their frequency is diminishing. One reason is that nowadays many of the grandmothers—and teenage mothers' mothers are often in their thirties or forties—are in the labor force and therefore unavailable for child care. In other households, grandmothers balk at starting over again as primary parents. So households seek new ways of rearranging themselves to care for the child.

When a young mother comes home with her baby, her family relationships enter a period of redefinition. Not only has a new family member, a grandchild, been added but the daughter, only recently a child herself, is now a parent. Old patterns must change to make way for new ones. Perhaps no relationship undergoes such intense pressure and painful transition as that between a teenage mother and her own mother. But the style and tenor and content of these interactions provide the framework for the young mother's parenting success and her child's developmental well-being. No one formula for how a family arranges itself can be labeled "the best," though family strategies that prepare a young mother for self-sufficiency as a parent are generally more successful. But when young mothers are teenagers, their own difficult developmental task of creating a separate identity may be compromised by the pressing need to rely on their mothers for child-rearing help. Unless grandmothers are able to deftly handle the different psychological roles involved in supporting their daughters' autonomy while also assisting their parenting, conflict can easily arise and can lessen the ability either woman has to cooperatively parent the child.

At present, extraordinary changes in welfare regulations are being implemented by the states. Unwed mothers who are eighteen or younger are now required to live in a household with "a responsible adult, preferably a parent," if they are to receive any benefits. (Someone like Myieka, who was young enough to be subject to such a requirement but is estranged from her mother and has fought with relatives with whom she's tried to live, would have to live in some kind of adult-supervised group home.) For families who absorb their parenting daughters into the household, how to make the situation work constructively for these young mothers and children is an important issue. But few researchers have studied it, and the legislators who are dictating these welfare changes have ignored it.

"There were distinctly different approaches to how these families coped."

Two researchers who have examined in detail the dynamics among teen mothers and family members are Yale psychologists Nancy Apfel and Victoria Seitz. They observed the family lives of more than a hundred teenage mothers and the babies' grandmothers in New Haven, and they interviewed the participants.*Apfel and Seitz intended to use these close-up portraits of grandmother–teenage mother parenting to draw some conclusions about the benefits and drawbacks of various family setups.

"In talking with these mothers and grandmothers, we could see that there were distinctly different approaches to how they coped," Nancy Apfel told me when I visited her at Yale to discuss her findings about how these mother-grandmother families were faring after eighteen months. She began by describing four basic approaches to two-generational parenting that the study identified. "Parental replacement" occurs when a grandmother assumes total responsibility for rearing her daughter's baby; a young mother who is a "supported primary parent" is primarily responsible for her baby's full-time care but also receives support from family members; in "parental apprenticeship," the grandmother acts as a mentor to her daughter, whom she regards as an "apprentice mother"; and the term "parental supplement" characterizes situations in which care of children is shared by a grandmother, her daughter, and other family members.

Few family arrangements fit snugly into one of these four categories. And because family dynamics are fluid, interactions among family members change as time goes by; families sometimes shift from one childrearing arrangement to another. Hybrids are common. For instance, sometimes a grandmother replaces the young mother as the primary parent so the girl can finish her education, but at the same time treats her as an apprentice to prepare her for when she will once again take over. Nevertheless, the four approaches are a useful entry into understanding the important impact family dynamics have on the success of teen mothers and their children.

---

*The few young mothers in the study who were not with their families identified a woman who was participating in her life as a grandmother might.

At the time Apfel and Seitz visited with the young mothers, nearly half the families described situations in which the care of the child was shared among family members. Another 20 percent of the families had arrangements in which various family members—mostly the grandmother—occasionally helped take care of the child, but the young mother had primary responsibility. In equal but smaller percentages, the researchers found examples of grandmothers who took over full-time child-rearing and grandmothers who purposefully worked with their daughters to tutor them in how to be competent parents. Young mothers were most often enabled to make a successful transition to self-sufficiency when grandmothers tutored them as apprentices or when families effectively supplemented the young mothers' care.

Apfel and Seitz concluded from their research that grandmothers and other family members are an invaluable resource, which ought to be better understood and more effectively utilized. In visiting with these families, they realized that it would be a good idea to provide some kind of education and services for grandparents to help them "manage the developmental challenges of adolescent parenting." Grandmothers, Apfel and Seitz wrote, "can be apprenticed into becoming effective teachers of the parenting role to their daughters." Yet parenting programs for young, unwed mothers rarely focus with any intensity on the actual, daily parenting dynamics of multigenerational families.

"Sometimes I felt the young woman was losing not only her child but her mom."

In "parental replacement" families, a grandmother assumes the job of rearing the young mother's child, and in the process sometimes becomes the baby's "psychological parent." When this happens, she, not the child's mother, becomes the person this child turns to for sustenance, protection, and encouragement. In some families this might be a good solution, particularly if the young mother is not interested in or capable of taking care of her baby. But in other families, a grandmother's usurpation of a young woman's maternal role will not be welcomed by the mother and will pose additional difficulties for the child.

When an adolescent mother agrees to turn over full parental responsibility to her mother, her relief from the obligations of motherhood can give her a chance to finish her education and secure a job. When there is agreement about this shift in responsibility, conflict between mother and daughter is less likely to develop, because the path of parental decision-making has been clarified and accepted. The grandmother in this case might be better able to offer the child consistent and experienced care-giving, something the teenage mother might not have the patience, ability, or desire to do. Children can prosper in this arrangement if it means they avoid the predictable mishaps of a young mother's uninformed and unsupported attempts at parenting.

But having a grandmother take over full-time care doesn't always work out well for the baby or the young mother. Situations in which young mothers become overwhelmed by the tasks of parenting, and grand-mothers simply take over the job without reaching any agreement with the child's mother, can be damaging for everyone. Some young mothers told Apfel and Seitz they resented their mothers' intrusion. By the time some grandmothers took over the dominant parenting role, they had already spent so much time criticizing their daughter's maternal incompe-tence that they'd created deep fissures in the relationship. When that hap-pened, "the risks are higher that the child has suffered and that the mother could feel loss, anger, guilt, and depression," the researchers observed.

An escalation of emotional tensions between mother and daughter can affect the child's sense of well-being by hampering his ability to make the secure attachments he needs if he's to explore his environment comfort-ably. Such tensions can also lead to estrangement between a young mother and her family just when she most needs adult guidance in coping with troubling issues in her own adolescent development. "Sometimes I felt the young woman was losing not only her child but her mom," Apfel said. "And this was happening when she critically needed her mother. She was still a child."

"I felt inside that my mother wanted my daughter to be my sister."

Lavina, the oldest daughter in a family of primarily sons, was always given household responsibilities by her mother. From the time she was nine, she spent weekday afternoons baby-sitting for younger siblings and cleaning the house.

"I couldn't go outside," Lavina tells me. As she describes her childhood, Lavina rubs the back of her hand beneath her eyes to sweep her tears away. Her features are delicate, her straight black hair tugged back tightly off her forehead. All her feelings show in her expressive brown eyes. "I couldn't do anything. I never could do any activities with my friends after school. All I did was baby-sit and clean." Her eyes look sad. "I just had no life."

We're talking in the corner of an office where she now works as a manager; Lavina speaks in a soft voice so others can't hear. She is the never-married mother of four daughters, who range in age from fifteen years to five. From the time she was very young Lavina imagined herself going to college one day; finally, at twenty-nine, she is a student at a state university. This part-time job helps her to pay off her financial aid. Welfare supports her daughters.

At the age of fourteen, Lavina became sexually involved with a twenty-one-year-old man. In the neighborhood she lived in, lots of girls she knew were hanging out with older guys; being with them, however, meant having sex. What Lavina didn't know was that by having sex she could get pregnant. No one ever talked with her about what the changes going on in her body meant.

"Now, when I look back, I realize I had no clue," she tells me. "All my mother kept saying to me was 'Don't open your legs.' She'd say it again and again, 'Don't open your legs.' That's all my mother ever said to me, 'Don't open your legs.' Nothing more."

When Lavina did get pregnant, her mother could not accept the news. "I had just started my freshman year at high school. My mother took me to a family planning place and she talked to this woman. I didn't do much talking." By the way she rolls her eyes, Lavina makes it clear she wasn't invited into the conversation. "They examined me and we went home. The next day my mother told me somebody from the clinic was picking me up and taking me somewhere. She didn't tell me anything else."

The next day, a Friday, Lavina skipped school—something she'd never done before—to go back to the clinic and find the woman with whom her mother had spoken.

"Didn't your mother tell you we're taking you to have an abortion?" the woman asked.

"No, she didn't tell me," Lavina replied. She remembers the hard plastic chair she sat in, and how she cried and cried. She had never been more angry at her mother. "I don't want to have an abortion. I don't want to."

She and the counselor talked for a long time, and it became clear that Lavina could not return to her mother's home and be pregnant. That afternoon Lavina moved in with a foster family.

After she'd been there a while, her mother visited—but, Lavina says, her mother's eyes never focused on her belly. She did promise Lavina that when the baby was born she could come back home. This turned out to be a promise her mother didn't keep. She was still unwilling to accept that her only daughter was having sex at such a young age and now was going to be a mother. So she arranged for Lavina to travel four hundred miles away to live with her father, whom Lavina didn't remember, and his new nineteen-year-old wife. That arrangement didn't work out, so a few months later Lavina's mother reluctantly agreed to have her oldest daughter and her grandchild move into her home.

Lavina also rejoined her classmates in the tenth grade. Her mother took care of the baby, essentially replacing Lavina as the girl's mother. As usual between Lavina and her mother, there wasn't any communication. Lavina's mother simply took over.

"I had no money," Lavina explains. "My mother had the money and she bought whatever my daughter needed." Lavina tried to work after school, to earn her own money so she could buy things for her baby. That way she could at least feel some connection to her child. But she could find only work, such as cleaning houses, in which people paid her cash and not much of it. Sometimes she worked from three in the afternoon until eleven at night and arrived home having earned only twenty dollars. While she was at work her mother took care of her baby.

"I would come home, do my homework, and go to sleep," she says. "I didn't get to see my daughter all day and all night. My baby was sleeping with my mother in her room. My mother said it was so I could get some sleep. Then I'd get up at six o'clock and do this all over again."

By the time her daughter was a year old, Lavina felt she was losing her to her mother. "I felt inside that my mother wanted my daughter to be my sister," she says. "She wanted her raised to think she was my sister. When I found that out I moved out."

Only during the last several years has Lavina gained enough emotional distance to be able to reflect more objectively on what was happening with her mother. She now believes her mother was motivated by the immense shame she felt because of her daughter's early pregnancy. After Lavina refused to have an abortion, her mother's strategy was to "pretend" that Lavina wasn't actually a mother. But this interfered with Lavina's early maternal attachment to the baby. So strong were Lavina's feelings about this that at the age of fifteen she took her daughter and left her mother's house, determined to live on her own.

After leaving her mother's home, Lavina dropped out of high school. Taking care of her child meant that she couldn't go to school. Within a year—during this vulnerable time, when Lavina did not have the structure or sense of future that going to school might have given her—she became pregnant again.

"Didn't you get scared for yourself in terms of how you could handle another child?" I ask.

"You know, while all this was going on I just did it," Lavina replies.

"You didn't ask yourself, 'How is this going to work?' You just did it day by day?"

"Yeah, right," Lavina says. "I was a kid. I had no idea what life was about. I just took care of my babies. I loved them so much and I'd made the decision to have them, so I took care of them. And I was happy doing that."

"Did you think you were doing a good job at taking care of them?"

"Well, I was sixteen years old and I had two kids. One had a crib. The other had a bed. I had a table and chairs. I had a bed and bureau. I had a couch. I had my own place. I had thought I was doing pretty good," she says, with a hint of the pride she still feels at managing to raise her children as well as she has. "I mean, I bought their food. Their clothes. Yeah, I just didn't think back. That was my way of surviving, I guess. I didn't think about what had happened. I just kept on going."

"It didn't seem like I had no baby 'cause my mother took over."

Lavina's story of having her role as young mother usurped by her own mother, then giving birth to another child, is a sadly familiar one. Looking back on their confusing early years of motherhood, women tell me that failing to establish the close relationship they'd expected to have with their first baby prompts them to have another. The second baby, they promise themselves, will be theirs, not their mothers'.

One morning I visit with a group of five mothers at a contemporary version of a settlement house, located in a low-income Boston neighborhood. Its mission: to help families—many of which are headed by single parents—help themselves.

None of the five women I meet, all of whom are in their early thirties, is married, though two of them tell me they are currently living with a man. Among them, they have twenty-seven children. Each was a teenager when she had her first child. And each, along with her children, recently completed the Nurturing Program, a fifteen-week series of classes in which families are given help in improving their home environment. Parents who don't know how to discipline their children without using physical punishment learn ways to talk with them. They work out alternative strategies to yelling and hands-on discipline. (The women I meet tell me they needed such lessons.) Family members also learn how to express empathy toward one another, in place of scolding criticism and uncontrolled anger. When the classes were over, these mothers didn't want to let go of one another's supportive company. Every few weeks they meet here so they can keep talking. Today they agreed to let me join them.

The women are swapping stories about when they became parents.

Each of them was sixteen years old. "Most times when young children go havin' babies, it is because they want someone to be with them who loves them," Cyndi declares. "That's what I did." Cyndi now has six children.

"I did that, too," says Nora, who's raising four children on her own. " 'Cause with my first baby, it didn't seem like I had no baby 'cause my mother took over. So I went out and I had *me* one." Nora emphasizes the word "me" to underscore her belief that her first baby might just as well have been her mother's. She describes how painful it was to watch as her first baby grew more attached to her mother than to her. She became determined to have another baby. This one, she says she figured, would be her own.

"You did the same thing?" I ask Cyndi, who'd been nodding while Nora spoke.

"Yeah. My mother did what grandmothers do," she replies. "My daughter called her 'Mom' and that just ate me up. I was like, 'Why she call you "Mom"?' My mother and I had a big thing over that."

Another woman, Daniella, enters the conversation. "That happened to me," she says. "But I didn't let that bother me." Daniella seems to want her friends to believe that whatever disappointment she might have experienced as a teenager long ago faded away. However, as she tells us more about what happened, it becomes clear that things probably went less smoothly than she now would like to admit.

"For the first two kids, I lived with my mother," Daniella says. "My mother helped me raise those kids."

"So you didn't learn what it was really like to raise a child?" I ask.

"No. I didn't until I left home. My oldest girls were like eight and nine years old then. And they were good kids. So when I was getting ready to leave, my mother told me, 'You aren't going nowhere with them.' So I said, ' 'Bye. Keep 'em.' "

"So your mother kept your daughters?"

"Yeah, she raised them. She raised all of us. She was raisin' me. I was young, only sixteen when I had 'em, and she raised us together. So I left them there."

"Your other children," I ask her, "you raised them on your own?"
Daniella nods.

"What was the difference between having your mother raise them and you doing it?"

"Oh, a lot of difference." Daniella laughs heartily. That I would think of asking this clearly amuses her. Soon the other mothers are laughing, too.

"Oh, I can't go out. I got to take care of those kids," Daniella says. "What are you talkin' about? A big difference. Like *boom!* This is reality."

Her friends' uproarious laughter continues as she speaks, making it hard for me to hear. Later, when I listen to this conversation on tape, it occurs to me that shared hilarity is perhaps the easiest way for these women to shield themselves from remembering how unprepared they actually were for parental responsibility.

When the laughter subsides, Lisa joins the conversation. "I was young when I had my kids. I was lookin' at it as playin' house. Now it is hitting me." Like the others, she has reached her mid-thirties and has never been married. She has six children.

Daniella picks up on this thought: "Like I said, I probably would've ended up having a couple more kids, but I wouldn't have had all them more 'cause it would've finally sink down into me." Daniella has seven children. "Like if the first little baby I'd had to raise by myself, it would be like, 'Oh my God, this is it.' "

Perhaps, I suggest to the group, there ought to be a way to give teenagers some sort of reality check about what motherhood actually entails, as a way of persuading them to avoid it so early in their lives.

"That's right!" Daniella says. "I mean, you have entered a different world."

Each of these women now has a child who is the same age she was when she became a mother. So far none of these women has become a grandmother. Each says that she tells her adolescent daughter how much she doesn't want to become one anytime soon.

"I had no idea what I was doing. I was depending on my mother."

A family member's takeover of the day-to-day care of a baby gives some young mothers a chance to concentrate on their education. A few years down the way, when she is better able to handle the responsibilities, she can be helped to establish herself in the parenting role. How productively a young mother uses her respite from parenting—whether she completes her education or has another baby—often hinges on the messages and support she receives from family and friends and from adults at school and in her community. How well she and her child handle the shift in parental responsibility also depends on several factors: whether the decision to turn over the child's care to someone else is mutual and has been discussed; how much contact the young mother maintains with her child; and whether and how well she is taught to eventually assume full-time parenting responsibilities.

Anna, the young woman who now works as a family planning counselor for adolescent girls, was just about to turn eighteen when her daughter was born. The month was August; that gave Anna only a few weeks to adjust to motherhood before starting her senior year of high school.

"Those first few months of Tina's life were very difficult for me," Anna tells me one afternoon, as she and I sit in her very pink bedroom at her mother's house. "I had no idea what I was doing. I was depending on my mother. I remember how I would say to her, 'I can't deal with this.' Thank God my mother was very understanding."

A framed photograph of Anna in a fancy white prom dress sits on the corner of her desk next to her typewriter. On her bedroom walls Anna has hung big framed photographs of herself with her daughter's father, whom she long ago stopped dating. He still spends time with Tina, but the day-to-day responsibility for their child's care has always been Anna's.

A king-sized bed, covered by a frilly pink bedspread, dominates the room. Anna spends much of her time in her room; she regards it as her sanctuary within her mother's house. This is where Anna, whose daughter is now seven years old, retreats when she craves privacy. It is frustrating and difficult for her to be twenty-four years old and still living in her mother's house. But she and Tina simply can't afford to live on their own.

Anna tells me what it was like when her daughter was only a few days old. In those days Tina's crib was next to her bed. "I remember the first night when Tina woke up crying. It was two-thirty in the morning. I was so tired, and I remember saying to myself, 'What can she possibly want? She's dry. She just ate a few hours ago. Why is she crying at this time in the night?' I remember getting up and going over to her crib and looking down at her. I'm like, 'What's wrong?' I am touching her and looking at her and watching her cry for maybe ten minutes, not knowing what to do. Then my mother, who heard her crying, got up from her bed and came in and asked me what was wrong. I told her I didn't know."

Her mother asked whether Tina was wet, when Anna had fed her—and then why Anna didn't pick her up. "And I am, like, saying to her, 'I didn't think about that.' So my mother says, 'She wants you to hold her. She has been in your stomach for nine months. She needs to feel your heartbeat. She is used to your smell.' I didn't think about any of that. So I picked her up, and when I did, she stopped crying. Pretty soon we went back to sleep and I woke up at five o'clock when she was hungry. It took me a long time to figure out how to respond to my daughter's different cries."

There was no child-care center at Anna's school, so Anna would drop Tina off at her own grandmother's house for the day. (Anna's mother worked.) "Either I had to drop out of school or do this with my grandmother because I didn't have enough money to put her in day care," Anna recalls. Every school morning was the same. She had to leave the house by

6:15 to drop Tina off and get to her job, which was how she started her school day.* Her morning trip involved four buses in all and usually took her an hour and fifteen minutes. Day by day Anna became more and more exhausted. "After my job was over, I'd go to school in the afternoon and finish at about four o'clock. Then I'd go back to my grandmother's to pick up Tina, get home, and try to get my homework done. But I had to take care of Tina, and that meant trying to keep her calm. Wash her bottles. Wash her clothes. Get Pampers and formula. It was really, really tough. I'd have Tina in one arm and my pen in the other. After about four months of this my mother and grandmother saw how stressed out I was becoming. I was missing days of school. I was getting sick a lot. Finally I said, 'I can't do this anymore,' and that is when we came up with the idea of my grandparents keeping Tina at their house." As Anna had told me earlier, this was her grandmother's idea. "I was at the point where I could not function. I thought it was a wonderful idea." So Tina moved in with Anna's grandparents.

Even though Anna's grandmother "replaced" her as Tina's primary parent, this arrangement began with a clear understanding that Anna would resume full-time parenting when she finished high school. To make this transition work for Tina, it was agreed by all that Anna needed to be taught how to assume the responsibilities of being her parent. So each day after school Anna went to her grandmother's house. She was given the manageable task of maintaining supplies of Pampers and formula. On evenings when Anna's grandmother went out to play bingo, Anna would stay with Tina until her grandfather could drive her home.

Anna's family combined the best ingredients of two different approaches: her grandmother "replaced" her as the primary parent so that Anna could concentrate on her schoolwork; she also "apprenticed" Anna in how to be a responsive and responsible parent. When Tina was two years old, she moved back in with Anna. By then Anna had graduated from high school and had found a full-time job as a receptionist at an insurance company. She received a state-subsidized voucher that enabled her to enroll Tina in a high-quality child-care center.

It was back at home that Tina's care became a bit confusing. It became apparent to Anna that she had not been handed back all the parenting reins. Her mother and grandmother were still involved, and that made it difficult for Anna to figure out how to reestablish herself as Tina's mother. "Anything I had to say as far as my daughter was concerned, if my mother disagreed, then my grandmother took her side," Anna explains. "When

---

*The high school Anna attended offered a work/study program in which students spent half of each school day at a paid job.

Tina came back home it seemed like every other day I would play mom, then my mother would play mom. And I'd actually hear my daughter call my mother Mommy."

That stung Anna. "At times, I mean, I could understand," Anna tells me, but her voice sounds unconvincing. She takes a deep breath. "No, I really couldn't understand why, and I would get upset. I would say, 'I don't like this.' But neither my mother nor grandmother would ever correct her. They'd say, 'She knows who her mother is and it's just a nickname she gives her.' And I'd say, 'If she calls you Mommy I think you should say to her, 'I am not your mommy. I am your grandmommy. That is your mother.' "

"What would Tina call your grandmother?" I asked.

"Nanna."

"So that was pretty clear?"

"Yeah, Nanna was Nanna," Anna replies. "And Grandma was either Grandma or Mommy."

"And you were . . . ?"

"I was always Mommy," Anna says. "But it got to the point I wanted to move out. No one else could see why I was so upset. And to be honest with you now, I don't even know why I was."

Anna realizes now that if her grandmother had not helped her as she did, if her mother had not been there to offer guidance, she might not have finished high school and found steady work. If she hadn't accomplished those two things, Anna might have lost her sense of initiative and found herself, like many of the adolescent mothers she now counsels, having another child and making her future and her daughter's more difficult.

"Daughters would not romanticize the responsibilities of motherhood and make the same mistake again."

In some families an unmarried adolescent mother assumes primary responsibility for taking care of her child, though her mother and other relatives are often called upon for help. Apfel and Seitz call the young woman in this arrangement "the supported primary parent." Most such mothers live in their family's home. Some live separately, but in the same apartment building as their families, or a few doors down the street. They receive varying amounts of family support, including help with household chores, baby-sitting, regular communication to break their isolation, and, when a family can afford it, a few dollars to help them get by.

Implicit in this setup is a belief that this young mother is able to make a rapid transition to full-time parenting. "In talking with these grand-mothers, what interested me is how many seemed to feel that their fifteen-year-old daughter knows how to take care of her baby," Apfel tells me. "They thought being a mother came naturally and were sort of baffled when some things were not working out." One grandmother explained to Apfel that she thought her daughter's baby-sitting experience adequately prepared her for being a mother: "Kids know this already. They are around kids and raising them all their lives." The grandmother seemingly didn't account for the difficulties posed by the demanding pace of around-the-clock care and responsibility.

Several grandmothers told the researchers that they favored the "sup-ported primary parent" arrangement because it provided a kind of "tough love" approach to their daughter's situation. They seemed convinced that if their daughter had to really take care of a child she wouldn't be so eager to have another. Their daughter would not "romanticize the responsibili-ties of motherhood and make the same mistake again." However, there is a risk that while this point is being proved the child may not be well cared for by her young mother, who really needs more adult guidance. That was the primary risk Apfel and Seitz associated with this arrangement. Espe-cially when the young mother lives on her own, problems can develop, which a visiting grandmother may not detect. And when a teenage mother is a full-time parent, it can become very difficult for her to move her own life ahead.

But there are also strengths in supported primary parenthood. Because the boundaries of caregiving responsibility are well drawn, maternal roles tend not to get blurred. The teenage mothers who do best as supported pri-mary parents are the ones who can rely on their mothers as part-time con-sultants and sometime companions. For example, after a young mother has taken care of her child during the day and her mother arrives home from work in the early evening, the older woman's companionship pro-vides a welcome break from the young one's isolation. And the baby's grandmother may be willing to offer her daughter a needed respite from child care. Apfel and Seitz compare this mother-daughter parenting dynamic with that of married, at-home moms who look to their husband for this relief when he gets home from work; of course, in both situations, how well that works depends on the other person's willingness to assume the supportive role.

Of course, living with your family while trying to be your child's primary parent can be hard, even if some family members are willing to play sup-portive roles. Young mothers get upset because of their lack of privacy. Not only do they have a child to take care of, but they find they can no longer just walk out of the house when they don't want to be with their family. Their child is an anchor, tethering them to household situations they might not want to be a part of. Young mothers may also be made to feel as though they are not really doing the job of parenting because they are not living on their own. This lack of recognition for their efforts often makes them angry.

"It's like Sean has four parents. He's got everyone telling him what to do. And then I do, too."

Too many cooks, the adage says, can spoil the broth. The same might be said about what goes on in a household in which a young mother doing her best to raise her child is bombarded with more advice from family members than she knows what to do with. On some days all she wishes for is that no one else will tell her how to be her child's mother.

Susan, twenty and unmarried, is the mother of Sean, an only child who is twenty-two months old. The past week has been a particularly rough one for her. Sean's acting as though he's already entered the "terrible twos," and Susan's family can't seem to resist reminding her at every moment what she ought to be doing as his mother. Susan is grateful for her mother's and sister's occasional assistance with Sean's care. In fact, she depends on their support and help. But she is her son's primary parent, and she often wishes they'd just let her do her job.

"There are days when I just want to get out of here," Susan says to me. We are sitting in the small square living room in her mother's house. The room functions more or less as a hallway. She is wearing a Mickey Mouse sweatshirt and jeans, her usual outfit. Ever since she came home from the hospital with Sean, this tiny room has been the hub of Susan's parenting life. It is here that her son watches television and plays, and here that Susan watches him play—all day long, every day. In the evenings, she often falls asleep on the couch as she watches TV. On days when she feels restless, Susan moves the living room furniture around, giving herself a change of scenery without leaving home.

"Like, last week I was ready to go to a shelter," she says. She even looked up the telephone numbers of city shelters and started to pack up her and Sean's things. "I wanted to get out of this house." By the acid tone of her voice I sense how miserable and angry she must have been. "Like, the people in this house would try to tell me how to do things with my son. And I'd say, 'Let me do what I want to do.' I'd been holding it all in and I ended up blowing up. Like, I would yell back at them, 'Why don't you take care of him? You see how you are since you think you're so perfect!' And I ran upstairs. I was crying. Exploding. I started to pack my bag. I'm leaving. Then I said to myself, 'I've got to deal with this until I figure out a way to get set in my own place.' But some days I just explode. It's too much."

It is unusual to hear Susan sound so angry. On most afternoons when we talk, her mood seems resigned, as if in acknowledgment that the way things are is just the way they are and nothing she does will change them. Living at home is just something she has to do until Sean is old enough to start school; then she can find a job and move out. Besides, Susan is very close to her mother, Sheila. When her family isn't criticizing her, Susan enjoys her mother's company. She admits she'd probably be very lonely living on her own with her son.

When Sean was born, Susan's mother had agreed to take care of him during the day so that Susan could go to her job as a receptionist. Susan enjoyed being out of the house and earning money to take care of her baby. However, when Sean was a few months old he started to be sick a lot. Since Susan had to take him to doctor's appointments and then stay home with him, she and her mother decided it would be best if she left her job. Susan's mother, who had raised six children of her own, also wanted to get back to her own part-time job as a waitress: she'd realized within a few months of Sean's birth that she did not want to be stuck at home taking care of him. So Susan went on welfare and has been at home with Sean ever since.

What bothers her most are the criticisms of her parenting that she hears from her family. "If I do something wrong, they're on my back. Even when I do something right, they're on my back anyway. There's always someone on my back."

"Do they tell you these things because they think they have more experience than you do?" I ask.

"Yeah, I think that's what it is. But I try to say to them, 'Just let me make my own mistakes.' Like Sean, he'll try to get up when he's done eating. He will stand up in his high chair and you can't force him to eat. He has an excellent appetite. But if he doesn't want to eat any more, I let him down. My sister's boyfriend who lives here, he says to me, 'You should make him eat. Sit him down and spank him on his bottom and tell him he's not done yet.' But when he doesn't want to eat, I can't force him."

"Does your sister's boyfriend have children?"

"Yeah, he's got two children. But he's not with them." Susan shakes her head to indicate how little she values his opinion. But it's apparent how much it still bothers her when he expresses it.

"So how do you deal with that?"

"Sometimes I blow my stack and sometimes I just walk away," Susan says. "Some days, because I let it build up inside of me, one more thing happens and I will just blow up. I try to just ignore it, but it's hard. It's like Sean has four parents. He's got everyone telling him what to do. And then I do, too."

Susan's voice is weary, her eyes tired and distracted. Her downcast demeanor seems mismatched with her appearance. Her thick ponytail rises like a volcano on her head, and high-curled bangs frame her dimpled face. With her pint-sized body, Susan, in another setting, could pass for a bouncy high school cheerleader on homecoming afternoon. Today, however, her sullen mood keeps her dimples hidden. Susan has neither enthusiasm nor energy. She tells me she is bored. It's hard to engage her in conversation. She tells me that what she enjoys most is being with people; it was what she liked best about working as a receptionist. Being at home with Sean sometimes makes Susan feel like a prisoner.

She knows that her being with Sean is important for him, and from what I observe, she is doing a good job of parenting. They read together. He enjoys TV shows like *Sesame Street* and gets excited about learning letters and numbers. But as good as things may be for Sean, his mother is not satisfied with how things are working out in her own life. Since she left her job, Susan has neither gone to school nor looked for any kind of paid work. The repetitious routine and isolation of her daily life seem to sap the willpower she needs to move in a new direction. She doesn't have a car; she depends on her mother to drive her places. Nor does Susan have money, so she can't take Sean to museums or movies. Most of their waking hours are spent in this small room, sitting in front of the television.

"Would you like to get back to work?" I ask one afternoon. She and I had been talking about welfare reform proposals that will require recipients to go to work.

"Yeah," she replies. "I know I am getting lazy. It's like I don't even want to get up and get dressed anymore. Same old thing. The same schedule every day. I get tired of it. I just need something different."

"When you say you feel lazy, what does 'lazy' mean?"

"Unambitious," she says. "Not every day, though. There are days when I'll get up and go for a walk. Walk to the store. Just do something. But other days, it's like there is nothin' to do outside. Why bother? I don't know."

Whatever initiative Susan once had is evaporating amid the boredom and discouragement she feels about how her life is going.

"It's like I have to have Sean on my hip every five minutes or I am not doing my job."

A few months later Susan and I discuss her future plans; Sean is getting closer to an age when he can attend preschool. "When Sean gets into preschool, and I can count on him being there each day, then I can get out and do something," she says, but she can give me no concrete sense of what that "something" will be. "But I just have to wait for that, because I'm not going to depend on anybody else to take care of him because they always let me down."

Susan tells me what happened a few weeks ago: she went upstairs to take a shower, asking her mother to watch Sean. While she was in the bathroom Susan heard the telephone ring. When no one answered, she jumped out of the shower to pick it up. She heard Sean on the other end. Dripping wet, Susan yelled for her mother. There was no response. Wrapped in a towel, she ran downstairs, to find Sean teetering on his high chair: he'd climbed up on it to answer the phone. She grabbed him and set him down on the floor.

"I'm like, 'Where *is* she?' " Susan says. "When I open up the front door, my mother is outside starting up her car because I have an appointment to go to. I say, 'Mom, the phone's for you and Sean is answering it.' And she's like, 'Oh, that kid.' After she gets off the phone I say to her, 'I asked you for fifteen minutes while I take a shower to watch him and you go outside and start the car.' I was upset at her. It's like I have to have Sean on my hip every five minutes or I am not doing my job. I have no freedom." This is yet more evidence to Susan of how little she can really depend on anyone, even her mother, to give her the kind of help she needs.

It will be another year or so before Sean can start preschool. Born in November, he missed the age cutoff this year. "I could do day care for him, but it's so expensive," Susan says. "I mean, welfare would probably help out. But it is too expensive."

"You could probably arrange to get a sliding fee," I suggest.

"Yeah, welfare would probably help me pay for it, but I don't think it's worth their money and my money to send him to day care when he's going to school next year," Susan replies. "I'll just let him stay home this year."

"What about you? Might it be worth it to you in terms of feeling less trapped?"

"I can wait. I can wait."

"But aren't you feeling depressed as you wait?" I ask Susan this because I know that a mother's mood is bound to affect how she acts with her child.

"Yeah, a little every day, but that is just something I am going to have to deal with," she says. "I'm just going to wait until he can go to school. I think it is really the only thing that I can do. Once I get him in school I want to get a part-time job. I don't want to be on welfare. That is depressing itself. Just being on welfare. I can't stand it."

While she says she hates welfare, Susan nonetheless seems resigned to living on it, at least for the foreseeable future. She is also resigned to remaining at her mother's house, despite her complaints about the lack of privacy and her family's interference. Sometimes Susan tells me she doesn't move out because she wouldn't be able to find a place she can afford in a safe neighborhood. But the longer we talk about this, the clearer it becomes that, as with other aspects of Susan's life, unhappiness with her present situation isn't enough to motivate her to actively seek change.

Her reasons for staying are also woven into the complex fabric of her family's finances and her relationship with her mother. It turns out that Susan's welfare checks and food stamps help keep the entire household afloat. Out of Susan's biweekly $234 welfare check, her mother gets $120 as rent for her and Sean. This money enables Sheila to pay her mortgage and heating bills; her income as a waitress for a catering company is sporadic. The $114 Susan gets each month in food stamps also buys food for the entire family. Besides, if she were to move into her own place, Susan says, she would hurt her mother's feelings: "We're buddies." Susan is her mother's youngest child, and also the only one of Sheila's six children who was born out of wedlock; perhaps because her father wasn't a part of their lives, she and her mother grew to be especially close. "My mom and I do everything together," Susan says. "Wherever she goes, I go. Wherever I go, she goes. Siamese twins. We're pals. When I was pregnant I used to always wake up between three and five o'clock in the morning and we'd watch TV together."

So even though Susan complains a lot, most of the time she is grateful to have her mother as her companion, someone who relieves her when she's exhausted from taking care of Sean. It's hard for Susan to imagine how she'd manage if her mother wasn't a part of her young-parenting life.

"My brother, he tells Sean to call me auntie, like I am not his mother."

One day when I stop by to see Susan, her mother is away on a trip to Canada with her boyfriend. It is rare for Susan and Sean to be by themselves, but because her older sister is also away Susan has been basking in a few welcome moments of privacy. Only an unexpected visit from her brother John—a visit that ended just moments before I arrived—had spoiled her day, reminding Susan of what she puts up with because of her parenting arrangement. It seems to her that no one, least of all John, is willing to give her the credit she thinks she deserves for being Sean's full-time mother.

Whenever John drops by, he makes it his goal to be certain Susan is in a bad mood when he leaves. He goes out of his way to provoke unnecessary tension between Susan, her son, and their mother. "He will come in and say to Sean, 'Where's your mother?' Then he'll point to my mother and say, 'Oh, there's your mother.' It is his way of putting me down, like she's the one who takes care of Sean and I don't do anything with him. Sean knows I'm his mother. He knows that. But my brother, he tells Sean to call me Auntie, like I am not his mother. Like I don't do anything for him."

Susan becomes increasingly agitated. "He does this to aggravate me," she says, trying to dismiss his remarks. "All he wants to do is make everyone else miserable because he's miserable," she concludes. "But it's things like this that get to me. If I was out of here, I wouldn't have to deal with that anymore because they'd know I am doing it all by myself."

"My mother had control of telling me what to do with my babies. I hated that. But I guess all mothers do that."

Yet Susan stays at her mother's home. Everything's a trade-off, she figures, a trade-off she's willing to make. The support she has in her mother's home seems better than what she'd get if she and Sean were living on their own.

However, for some unwed teenage mothers, their family's home becomes unwelcoming and potentially harmful for them and their child. There may be abuse in the family, or relationships may be so strained that conflict is constant. Even so, a young mother might stay simply because she has nowhere else to go. As time goes by, the fissures may grow deeper, until it becomes clear that she has no choice but to take her child and go. Sometimes she ends up in a public shelter. From there she might move in with friends or find a subsidized apartment.

A young mother in this situation is, almost by default, her child's primary parent. Sometimes a grandmother maintains a walk-on role despite the fact that her presence isn't always helpful. This is what is happening in Shanika's life. Now in her mid-twenties, Shanika—the young woman we met who had lost the capacity to dream—is the mother of three young children. Her unreliable and volatile relationship with her mother contributes to making her life as a single parent chaotic and difficult.

Shanika's health is not good. High levels of stress inhabit her everyday life. Shanika also has asthma. On some days her asthma attacks are so bad that her ribs hurt when she tries to take a breath. Often she can't afford to pay for the medicine doctors prescribe. These infirmities combine to make her seem older than her chronological years. Her hard life writes itself across her pudgy, downcast face; she speaks of herself as depressed. Though Shanika has a warm, engaging smile, she seldom shows it. Her life doesn't give her much to smile about.

Shanika stayed on at her mother's house after she gave birth, at the age of nineteen, to twin girls. She'd dropped out of high school when she found out she was pregnant. As her pregnancy advanced, she also stopped going to her packaging job on an assembly line: she couldn't stay on her feet as long as the job required. After her daughters were born, she received $524 each month from welfare. Her mother insisted that Shanika give her $200 for her share of the rent. She also told Shanika she was responsible for paying the heating bill. That ate up a lot of her check during the winter months.

Shanika relied on her mother because she had no one else to turn to. By then, Rob, the father of her twins, was living with another woman, who was soon to give birth to a daughter. Occasionally he would stop by Shanika's apartment to see his twins—but, as Shanika says, "he was just a person who dropped in." When she says this, her voice displays little emotion. This is a hint of what I will learn as I spend more time with her: Shanika tends not to express anger when people treat her badly, because she expects nothing different. "Rob had another life," she says matter-of-factly. From talking with Shanika I know his absence hurt her terribly: there was no one she cared about more than Rob. But: "He was with somebody else," she says.

There were other reasons why Rob's visits were difficult for Shanika. Every visit escalated the already high level of tension between Shanika and her mother, who did not like Rob. Her advice to Shanika was to not bother having him come around: "What good is he to you?" She told Shanika that Rob wasn't the kind of man she should want to be with. Shanika insisted that her children would have a father, even if he was not going to be her husband or even her boyfriend. So Rob came to see the children, and whenever he did, arguments erupted between him and Shanika's mother. Her mother's anger would reach such a peak by the time Rob left that she would vent it, foul-mouthed, on Shanika.

"My mother was a lot of help to me," Shanika tells me as we talk about these early parenting times. I am not surprised to hear Shanika say this. Although her mother criticizes almost everything she does, Shanika tries to defend her, always portraying their relationship as though it is better than it is. But the longer we talk, the more the rough edges of their strained and difficult relationship come into focus. Nothing Shanika tries to do, no man she wants to be with, will satisfy her mother, who seems to have been born angry at the world.

"What would your mother do when you and the girls were living with her?" I ask. As always, Shanika's impulse is to protect her mother, as though she'll be severely punished otherwise. Initially she says things worked out okay, but then she reveals some things that led to her leaving. "The only thing I hated was, it was like she had control, telling me what to do with my babies," Shanika says. "I hated that. But I guess all mothers do that."

When I explain that some mothers actually work in constructive ways with their daughters, gradually and patiently teaching them how to parent, Shanika stares at me, wide-eyed.

"My mother, she was like, 'No. You should do it this way.' " Shanika mimics her mother's irritated and demeaning tone. " 'You should give them this. You should give them that.' And she'd say to me, 'You don't know how to take care of no babies.' It was stuff like that, and it got on my nerves." However, when Shanika's daughters woke up in the middle of the night, her mother was nowhere to be seen. Shanika was on her own—but no one had taught her how to soothe them. They'd sometimes cry for hours.

"Did you feel like you knew how to take care of your kids?" I ask Shanika. "I mean, two babies is a lot to take on. Did you think you could do it?"

"It was hard, but I did do it," Shanika says. In her mind, she's always been her girls' primary parent. That point made, she backs down a bit from her earlier statement about how she did it: "I tried," she says. Her voice is quieter now.

Her mother's put-downs and scoldings became too much for Shanika. She was depressed, too, because Rob was moving on to be with other women. Shanika felt herself losing whatever capacity she'd thought she had to function as her daughters' mother. When her twins were less than a year old, Shanika applied for public housing. She had to get away. But the waiting list had hundreds of names ahead of hers. It would be years before she could get an apartment of her own. She also foresaw a stumbling block: "Me and my mother having so many fights and stuff, I just knew I had a police record," she says. "We had called the police lots of times." Neither Shanika nor her mother had been arrested, but she was afraid she had a police record, so she withdrew her application. Shanika stayed at her mother's house until her mother ordered her to leave.

"Why did she kick you out?" I ask Shanika.

"Because of Rob's mouth. He don't know how to bite his tongue."

"Did he say something you got in trouble for?"

"They were arguing, she and Rob. She felt he should bite his tongue."

"Did you defend him?"

"No, I didn't defend anybody. I didn't defend her. I didn't defend him," Shanika says. I can tell she is becoming exasperated by my questions. "They'd have arguments. I didn't defend anybody."

"So this left bitter feelings between you and your mom?" I say, trying to guess at what happened. "And she threw you out?"

"Yeah," Shanika says, staring down into the puffy gray sofa on which we sit. "I had to leave."

By moving into a homeless shelter, Shanika got her name up toward the top of the waiting list for public housing. Five months later, she and her daughters moved into a subsidized apartment. By then, her daughters were nearly two and Shanika was pregnant with her third child, a son she'd also conceived with Rob.

"I know if I let what they do bother me, I am going to hurt them."

Her twin girls are now five years old. Her son, Rob, is three. Shanika's mother stops by her apartment often, and she frequently stays over, sleeping on Shanika's living room couch, though she lives only a few miles away. Sometimes when Shanika needs to see a doctor, she asks her mother to stay with the children. Or Shanika leaves them at her mother's house at times when she simply needs to be apart from them for a little while. In return for this help, Shanika's mother asks her daughter for money or food stamps.

But her mother's help is undependable. A word misspoken by Shanika can instantly ignite a heated argument between them. When that happens, arrangements Shanika has made with her mother can fall apart at a moment's notice. This is what happened when Shanika signed up to begin training for a job she wanted, as a nurse's aide. Her mother had promised to watch the children. But when Shanika's original class schedule had to be postponed because she had to testify in court regarding a restraining order against Rob (he'd cut her face by throwing a kettle at her), this window of opportunity shut down.

"Why couldn't you start your training a few weeks later?" I ask Shanika.

" 'Cause it was a two-week course," Shanika responds. This, of course, fails to answer the question.

"Is it being offered again?"

"Yeah, but now I don't have a baby-sitter."

The moment she says this I know that once again she and her mother are fighting. But as soon as Shanika starts to explain, young Rob begins to cry. He has caught his hand in the iron grate of her fish-tank stand, on the other side of the room. He tries to pull it out but can't get further than his wrist. Shanika doesn't move. In fact, she tries to ignore his cries. But I'm worried that if he pulls any harder the heavy glass fish tank may tumble down on him, so I get up to help.

This incident and our subsequent discussions about discipline explain much about how Shanika's parenting style is shaped by experiences with her mother. Had she gone over to her son at a time when she was angry about something else, it's likely she would have lashed out at him rather than helped. A few minutes earlier, she'd been screaming at him about not throwing his toys on the floor. He had ignored her, which irritated her, and when his hand got stuck her rage at him had not yet subsided. Even though Shanika tells me how much she hates her mother's temper, she realizes that she has inherited some of her mother's less pleasing characteristics. Therefore she tries to employ protective strategies. "I don't let anything bother me," Shanika told me once when I'd said something about the harshness of her discipline. "I know if I let what my kids do bother me, I'm going to hurt them. So I don't let anything bother me." The problem with this strategy is how poorly it seems to work.

One consequence of Shanika's "containment" approach is that she's emotionally detached. Her children get her undivided attention only when they annoy her so much that she finally erupts. They know this, so they provoke her, just to be sure she notices them. The protective distance Shanika has put between herself and her children is one reason why, by the age of three, her son is not yet capable—as he should be—of expressing himself in sentences. She talks with him only when he is doing something wrong, and then her anger spills out in a flurry of fast-spoken words.

After I return from helping Rob untangle his hand, she resumes our conversation as though nothing happened, explaining why her mother can't baby-sit:

"We are not like how we were." This verbal shorthand means they're not speaking to each other. Maybe they'll be back in touch next week, but no one, least of all Shanika, knows for sure. All Shanika knows is that plans she made to find a job have fallen apart again.

"Motherhood is so hard."

When Shanika and I get together a month or so later, her mood is extremely downcast. "A lot of things going on right now make me sad. I get depressed all the time," she tells me. "A couple of days ago I felt like I had nothing to live for." Shanika has found out that her new boyfriend, a policeman, is seeing another woman. A few months earlier he'd talked with Shanika about moving to another city together. She was very excited when she told me they might get married. Now, as she sees it, she's been deceived. Again.

"I'm in a spot now where it is just me," Shanika tells me, wearily. She pauses, then looks right into my eyes and declares, "Motherhood is so hard."

Shanika's mother is still, to some extent, propelling her daughter's emotional roller coaster. "What I also have is a war between my mother and my children's father," she says. She wants her children to know their father; her mother, who has been staying with her again, has ordered Shanika to keep him away. The court put a restraining order on him when he injured Shanika with the kettle, but that hasn't stopped her from wanting him to spend time with his kids.

"My mother and him, they don't like each other. But what happens between me and Rob, there is nothin' my mother can do," she says. In the next instant, she is putting her customary positive spin on her mother's behavior: "But she is trying to make up for what she did when I was little."

"So she's trying to help you?" I ask, not sure what Shanika's implying.

She nods.

"But does it end up creating tension?"

"A lot of tension," Shanika says. "Now my mother is staying here all the time so I really can't date other guys."

"Then why isn't she here right now?" I notice that Shanika's mother's belongings seem to be gone, too.

"Oh, she's mad that Rob came and brought groceries."

"Isn't there a restraining order against him?" I'm reminding Shanika that there might be a good reason for her mother to react this way.

"The court put it on," Shanika says. The police did that; had it been up to her, she continues, she wouldn't have asked for the restraining order.

Shanika never knew her biological father, and the man she thought of as Daddy died when she was very young, so she is insistent that *her* children will spend time with *their* father. She puts up with Rob's physical abuse and his liaisons with other women—even with his fathering children by other women—because she cares more about her children being with their father than she does about how he treats her. Anyway, she assures me, she can protect herself. "I don't care what we go through," Shanika says. "I want him to be there for his kids. Anyway, today Rob brought his mother when he came."

"So that's okay?"

"I guess so," she says, unsure whether it would be so in the eyes of a judge. "As long as he brings his mother, I don't see anything wrong with it. He didn't try to bother me."

"But he upset your mother, and she left?"

"Yeah."

As usual, Shanika doesn't know when her mother will be back.

"I have to be actually crazy if I let a five-year-old rule my life."

There are a lot of days and nights when Shanika says she feels "miserable." She hates her own life, though she tells me all the time how deeply she loves her children. To her, they are who she is. Without them, she would be no one. With them, she is someone, their mother. But on this particular day she feels frustrated by what she says are her failures at being what she is—a mother.

Shanika is puzzled because one of her five-year-old daughters is acting up in school. Nearly every morning during the past several weeks, the assistant principal has called to ask Shanika to come to the school and take Rosa home. The administrators tell her that Rosa has hit, scratched, or bitten her kindergarten teacher, torn up a student's paper, thrown a chair. Rosa tells her mother that a nurse at the school yelled at her, saying that she "gives a person a headache." What seems to upset Shanika most is hearing that her daughter is being spoken to in this way. But Shanika is also angry at her daughter, not so much because of her behavior as because of what she had told the school nurse.

"She told her that I hit her with a belt," Shanika says.

"Did you?"

"No," Shanika says, quietly, as she turns to face me. "The nurse told me she had a ring around her eye. I mean, she had a red mark around her eye from where she and her sister were fighting. I'd slapped her on the face, but the mark wasn't from that. But I was like, 'I don't know where the red mark come from. Between her and her sister, they fight, so I couldn't tell you.' Now it's from this report that they're bringing the social workers in on me."

Because the school nurse reported possible child abuse, several social workers have visited Shanika's house to assess whether any action needs to be taken.

"What's it like for you to have social workers come by your house?"

"It's nothin' like when I was little," she says.

"You mean when you went to a foster family?"

"Yeah, when I went for six or seven months."

"That happened to you when you told someone at school your mother had beaten you up?" I say, checking that I'm recalling correctly what Shanika told me.

Shanika nods. "A person gets tired of being hit on, you know, for no reason," she says, referring to her childhood. "I mean, with my daughter, there's a reason. She's doing things. She's acting out. With my mother, well, the difference is, when I hit my daughter, I am not abusing her, like leaving any marks or anything. I'm going to hit her on the behind because that is where you're supposed to hit her. But my mother, she'd pick up anything. Hit me on the eye. Or hit me, or scratch me, or bite me." Perhaps Shanika is forgetting the slap she said she'd given her daughter's face, the one that might have left that red mark.

"The social workers asked me, 'Would I hurt her?' And I told them, 'It's like this. If I didn't hurt my daughter after she stuck that pipe down my son's throat, I am not going to hurt her now.' I mean, he had to be in the hospital for three days after she did that. The pipe was that long," she says, extending her hands until they are about eight inches apart. It's hard to believe that Rosa put something that big down little Rob's throat.

"Do you think your daughter was intentionally trying to hurt him?"

"It was like she told me, she wanted him to leave her alone," Shanika says.

"And that is how she tried to do it?"

"Yeah."

I ask Shanika what the social workers are saying to her about her style of discipline. She says they want her to force her children to stand in the corner after they've misbehaved. She says she's tried that and it doesn't work.

"If I do that, they'll just be there crying and crying. They won't stop crying. And the walls around here are so thin and people will think I'm hurtin' my kids because they'll be crying."

Shanika seems convinced that the ways in which she disciplines her children work well enough. She assures me they are learning right from wrong. As long as she doesn't leave marks or scars on them, Shanika says, social workers have "nothin' to complain about." For now, she has no intention of changing her ways, grounded as they are in what she's learned about what a parent should expect from a child and what consequences go along with receiving any less.

"I'm the mother. You are the child," Shanika says when I ask her to describe her view of roles a parent plays in the lives of her children.

"You do what I say. I don't do what you say. If you feel you're goin' to run over me or talk out at me, I don't think so. You get old enough to get your children, they're goin' to have to do what you say. . . . I have to be actually crazy if I let a five-year-old rule my life."

"I didn't want history repeating."

Many months later, during one of our more tranquil moments of conversation, Shanika huddles under her down jacket in the corner of her couch and talks about her wish that she could avoid what she sees as her mother's patterns. Rob Senior is now in jail, serving a year-long sentence because he threatened a man Shanika was dating after he saw the man with his children. Shanika has not told the children about their father's imprisonment: she doesn't want them to think of their daddy as being behind bars. But it's been three weeks and they are starting to ask where he is. In time, they'll surely find out. Shanika says if it were up to her Rob would not be in jail, even though her phone call to his probation officer initiated the legal process that put him there. She calls his imprisonment "the most difficult thing that's happened to me in my whole life."

"What makes it so difficult for you?" I ask.

"For my kids. I want him here, regardless. I don't care what we go through. I want him to be here for his kids. 'Cause I went through a whole lot with my mother. I argued with her so my kids can know their father. The reason why I did is 'cause I grew up without knowing my father. My mother grew up without knowing her father. So it was history repeating, and I didn't want that to happen with my kids. I understand you can be mother and father and all of that. But it's hard. It's hard, especially since I have a son. Later on down the line I want my son to say, 'Dad, how is such and such, blah, blah,' and to go fishing and stuff. His father, he does a lot of things with fishing. I want him to do that with his son. I don't want my son to ever say to me, 'Mom, who's my daddy?' You know."

Shanika looks up to see if I'm following. I nod, and she continues. "I feel

so strongly about my kids knowing their father, 'cause I do not want history repeating. I just don't because everything happened to me was history
repeating. I didn't go to my graduation from elementary school 'cause my
mother didn't go to hers. I didn't finish school. My mother didn't finish
high school." Shanika's voice, usually so soft when we're talking by ourselves, now rises to a loud, insistent pitch. "I didn't want to do all that. I
didn't want history repeating, you know. I got pregnant young. My mother
got pregnant young. I was saying to myself, 'This has to stop down the line
here.' When I carried my babies, my mother did not want their father to
be around, just like my real father wasn't. From the beginning she did not
want him around. But I tell her, 'You can't control me. You did not give
me these kids.' "

Shanika may have left her mother's home and taken on the sole responsibility for rearing her children, but the ghosts from her past unfortunately
persist.

"The goal of these grandmothers was to nurture and mentor their daughters into parenthood."

Shanika's mother has neither the inclination nor the ability to purposefully guide her daughter in how to be a nurturing and responsive mother.
Being a parental apprentice was never an option for Shanika, since no
adult in her life stepped forward to be her teacher.

In other families—some which Seitz and Apfel observed—grandmothers did act as positive mentors for teenage mothers. These grandmothers did not presume that, because their daughters were old enough to
have had a baby, they had the know-how or skills to be good mothers.
However, unlike grandmothers who responded to similar beliefs by
usurping the daughter's maternal role, these women applauded their
daughters' best efforts, then demonstrated other approaches, sometimes by
example, other times by explanation. Anna's mother teaching her to pick
up her baby to soothe its crying in the middle of the night is an example
of how a grandmother can "apprentice" a teenager in her job of being a
parent.

Some grandmothers lead their daughters rung by rung up the ladder of
parenting competencies; they make parenting more manageable by
breaking apart into workable units the numerous tasks that as a whole
might appear overwhelming. As daughters gain in confidence and competence, grandmothers gradually withdraw. As Seitz and Apfel note, "These
grandmothers acknowledge their daughters' inexperience and youth, but

also articulate a belief that their daughters can become capable parents. . . . The goal of these grandmothers was to nurture and mentor their
daughters into parenthood." The "apprentice" approach is the only two-
generational parenting arrangement in which grandmothers make a conscious, calculated effort to pass along parenting skills to their daughters.

The potential benefits of such an approach are numerous. A young
mother feels more confident about her ability to take on her new tasks if
someone has explained to her why and how they're done. Using this
approach, grandmothers can improve the chances that the child will form
a secure attachment to his mother, instead of undercutting this maternal
bond by establishing a competing relationship with the child. When
apprenticeship works well, tensions between the young mother and her
own mother are reduced through their cooperation. It is also much less
likely that a well-mentored young mother will jeopardize her child's development and well-being through either neglect or abuse.

There are a few risks in the apprenticeship approach. One is that a
young mother's schooling can suffer if her life is consumed by her mother's
emphasis on teaching her how to parent. Also, because the apprentice
arrangement relies on good personal interaction between the two
mothers, the daughter must be receptive and her mother must communicate well. If these ingredients are not present, the apprenticeship is likely
to fail.

"All a baby is is need, need, need. And these teenage mothers are so needy there is a real conflict, but they don't realize it."

Judy relied on aspects of the apprenticing approach in educating Sarah
how to be a parent. But Sarah actually had many teachers; her mother is
the first to suggest that without the guidance and support Sarah received
from caregivers at her son's child-care center, what she was able to do in
"apprenticing" Sarah at home might not have made the lasting impression
it did. Having her mother's words backed up by these women helped convince Sarah that Judy's advice was worth listening to.

Sarah was fourteen when she became a mother. Despite her youth, Judy
firmly believed her daughter could learn how to be a good and reliable
parent. But she knew she'd need a lot of help. The day after Sarah told
Judy she was pregnant, her mother says, "I went to work." That "work"
involved unstinting efforts to prepare Sarah for her new life as a parent.
Judy rearranged just about everything in their lives to provide Sarah the

physical and emotional environment that would give her and David the best chance for success.

"The most important thing for me to do for Sarah was to maintain her self-esteem, because that's really her basic foundation," Judy explains. "If Sarah didn't have that, everything else would fall apart." It had taken Judy most of her thirty-six years to awaken her confidence in her own abilities. She remembered that when she was a teenager her family treated her like a misfit, and she heard nothing but criticism about everything she tried to do. After she finished high school, Judy didn't hesitate to set out on her own. Soon she was married; when her marriage fell apart, her parents did little to help her even though she was struggling as a single parent. Only years later, when friends at college complimented Judy on her perseverance, did she begin to believe in her strengths. "After a while it got to be like, well, maybe I am strong," Judy tells me. "Everyone else says I am, so maybe I am."

Her familiarity with the pain of self-doubt gave Judy plenty of reasons to want to protect Sarah from it as much as she could. Judy knew criticism and blame would only make Sarah's transition to motherhood more difficult. On the day after Sarah's announcement—after Judy had spent a restless night crying in her bed—she went to the city school's administration and enrolled her at a special school for adolescent mothers and mothers-to-be. Judy wanted her to spend time with other young mothers so she could learn what it was going to be like to have a baby. She was also eager for Sarah to work with teachers whose job was to keep her focused on her studies and also to help her to learn how to be a parent. Judy knew another big benefit of the program would be to shelter Sarah from discomfiting stares and comments by her peers. She knew her daughter's adjustment to motherhood would be tough enough without taunts about her very youthful pregnancy.

Judy also arranged for a loan and found a part-time waitressing job on weekends to supplement the family income. This way she could afford to move them out of their apartment, which was in a public housing project. "When I found out Sarah was pregnant, I wanted to get her out of this depressing environment where a lot of girls were having babies." Judy knew Sarah didn't set out to become pregnant, as she suspected some of the other girls had. But now that her daughter was going to be a mother, Judy didn't want Sarah to start thinking about herself or her baby the way she believed many of these girls do. "Oh, these girls think, 'A baby who will love me,' " Judy says sarcastically. In an instant, her tone is utter seriousness. "A baby is full of needs. All a baby is is need, need, need. And these teenage mothers are so needy there is a real conflict, but they don't realize it. All they think about is how they'll find somebody to love them and how they'll give the baby all their love," she declares. "But what happens is, babies take from you. They are not giving much unless you don't have many needs yourself. If you have no needs yourself, then you can get everything you want out of a baby."

Judy realized she and Sarah would also no longer have only their mother-daughter relationship to work on. Being a single parent of an adolescent daughter was tough enough, but now Judy would also be a live-in grandmother, an event that was happening long before she'd expected or wanted it to. Judy knew that strenuous parenting of Sarah lay ahead if she was to enable her strong-willed daughter to gain the skills and confidence she'd need to rear her own child successfully.

"All I could give Sarah was her mother, and that had to be good enough."

That Sarah persevered—and that her son has prospered despite his mother's youth and her circumstances—is a testament to her inner resolve, which was strengthened by adversity. It is also a testament to her mother. Judy became a buttress for Sarah: while she was willing to help Sarah learn how to be a mother, she neither assumed responsibility for raising Sarah's baby nor abandoned her equally essential role as Sarah's mother, in which she saw her primary task as that of helping Sarah make the difficult transition to womanhood.

As many adolescent daughters do, Sarah tested her mother constantly. Often she ignored or ridiculed what Judy said. At times, she laughed when her mother tried to discipline her. Judy would then yell louder in futile attempts to gain Sarah's attention. A few times she shocked herself by swearing at Sarah, something she had never done before. When nothing seemed to work, Judy told me, she sat in her room and tried to figure out why she wasn't getting through to her daughter. "I realized I was trying to be a man, or at least my perception of what a man was," Judy says. "Men raise their voices. They yell. They swear. I guess I felt a man was what Sarah needed then for discipline. Because Sarah and I lived together and I was a woman and we knew each other so well and I'm a soft kind of person, I felt she needed something hard and firm. So I transformed my personality into what I thought a man could provide for her."

This approach did not work. Tensions between mother and daughter escalated until the apartment seemed ready to explode. Judy knew she had to do something. After a while Judy realized that by trying to discipline her daughter as she thought a father might, Sarah wasn't getting what she, as a mother, knew how to give. A few days later, Judy sat down with Sarah and apologized. "I've tried to be a father to you because I'm kind of scared," Judy told Sarah, who listened without any of her usual combativeness. "I don't know what's going on here but I will not tolerate disrespect," she told Sarah in a calm, firm voice. "We have rules and I thought you needed a man, a father, to enforce them."

Sarah laughed. It wasn't the mocking kind of laugh Judy was accustomed to hearing. Rather, Sarah's chuckle signaled relief. "You know," Sarah said, "you really did look ridiculous trying to do that." Now they laughed together. That evening Judy and Sarah talked for a long time, reestablishing their relationship as mother and daughter. "All I could give Sarah was her mother," says Judy, "and that had to be good enough."

However, Judy's continuing uncertainty about how to mother an adolescent daughter who was also a mother convinced her to seek help from a counselor at her employee assistance program. "She presented me with a whole lot of theories that I didn't have much time for," Judy tells me. "I wanted something practical." She pushed the counselor to give her a workable solution. Finally the technique of developing a contract with her daughter surfaced, and Judy leaped at it.

Sarah wasn't nearly as enthusiastic. "It's a stupid idea," she responded.

"I know," Judy said, trying to lure her in, "but just do it. Let's just try it."

Each drew up a list of what they expected the other to do. They compared lists, bartering until they created a "compromise list." Judy typed it so it looked like a real contract, which she and Sarah signed. Consequences were clearly spelled out, so that failure to live up to the agreement would not lead to an argument about the punishment. "If Sarah stayed out too late and didn't let me know, then for two weeks I wouldn't do her laundry or give her her allowance or do baby-sitting for her," Judy explains.

One night Sarah did stay out too late. Upon her arrival home, Judy was waiting for her, contract in hand. "I know," Sarah said, wearily. "Consequences."

"I didn't have to think about her punishment," says Judy, "and that was such a relief. There was no screaming or yelling. I didn't have to say a word."

Finding this comfort zone of understanding provided Judy and Sarah with the confidence that together they'd be able to make this unanticipated situation work out well for everyone. And once she had a secure base at home, Sarah had the strength to prove wrong the many adults who doubted a teen parent's ability to succeed.

"Sometimes the baby gets lost in the shuffle with so many people taking care of it."

Of all the ways families reorganize themselves when a daughter brings home a baby, Apfel and Seitz found by far the most prevalent was what they called the "parental supplement" arrangement. Such families don't arrange themselves in any one way, nor do individual members follow the same roles as parental assistants, but there are some common identifying factors: many people involved and the rules governing the arrangement are flexible enough to accommodate the mother's and child's immediate and changing needs. "This is a sort of crisis management approach," Apfel says. Members of the young mother's family—sometimes neighbors and friends, as well—share in a child's caregiving.

In some households, each person has a different task; for example, Grandma might feed the baby, but when it is nap time a cousin might take over. In other families, caretaking tasks are turned over to whoever is on duty when a baby needs something. Whatever system is used, the distinguishing characteristic is that caring for a child is regularly shared. A family's employment of these arrangements is premised on the belief that the young mother needs a lot of help, often because she is in school or at work.

There is, as with each of the other two-generation models, the potential for difficulties. "Sometimes the baby gets lost in the shuffle with so many people taking care of it," Apfel says. "It was not always clear to us who was feeding the baby, or even if a baby was receiving the right amount of formula. And there's a sort of blurring of the role of who really is the child's mom." Another possible downside is that a young mother may not learn to nurture and care for her child effectively as the primary parent, even when everyone acknowledges that at some later point she will assume this role. Similarly, her child may become more emotionally attached to another family member who plays a significant parenting role than to her mother. Because of this possibility, Apfel and Seitz warn: "The question of 'Whose baby is this?' is apparent in some families that feature this shared care approach."

How many caregivers share parenting responsibilities and how a family organizes its child care have implications for how well the adolescent mother and her child are likely to fare. When confusion or tension exists, the child may have a difficult time identifying with a primary psychological parent. Discipline styles may vary greatly, confusing a child. Daily care may become inadequate because tasks either overlap or are forgotten.

However, when the number of people taking care of a child is small and their relationships are "relatively harmonious and predictable, [and] . . . the caregiver feels strong affective ties to the child and takes primary responsibility, the likelihood is high that a child could thrive in such an arrangement," Apfel and Seitz conclude.

Though Apfel and Seitz limit their observations to the early years of a child's life, these shared parental patterns can persist as new demands, such as employment, are placed on young mothers. Now that welfare reform requires young, single mothers to move quickly into the labor force, reliance on "shared parenting" with other family members is likely to increase. And since few of these young women will earn enough money to establish a separate household or be able to pay for full-time child care, many will continue to depend on family, friends, and neighbors to help care for their children. But having this kind of family assistance doesn't mean a mother's worries about how well her children are doing ever go away.

"I just want my kids to know, 'yeah, my mom did it on her own. She went to college and got her degree.' "

The hastily typed pages of Morena's class assignment are spread across the kitchen table. Morena takes a sip of coffee from a chipped white cup while she contemplates her next step in finishing her term paper about writer Maya Angelou. Morena is dissatisfied with her effort and embarrassed to show it to me because she knows how littered it is with misspellings and garbled sentences. More distressing to her, however, is the fact that themes she wants to highlight have somehow gotten lost in the writing. She's feeling frustrated: she knows what she wants to say, but with the crush of time she was barely able to get this sloppy draft typed. She is so disappointed by her effort that she's doubting her ability to think critically about Angelou's books. Yet as she talks with me, Morena expresses her ideas cogently. I can hear the excitement she feels at having discovered an emotional kinship with this writer.

Morena pours herself another cup of coffee from the pot she keeps constantly brewing. She relies on coffee to keep her going because she gets only a few hours of sleep each night. "I don't know if you know this," Morena tells me. "But Maya Angelou had her first child when she was sixteen years old. She was raped. She went through a whole lot to get where she is now. It's like, if she can do all that, I can do what I want to do, too."

Angelou's words resonate with Morena as they never could with someone like me who has not experienced what it was like to become a mother at a young age. Morena was, at nineteen, a bit older than Angelou when she had her first baby. She hadn't been raped, but neither did she like the idea of staying with her daughter's father. Though Morena also had a son with this man three years later, no binding relationship, either as parents or with each other, ever took hold. Now twenty-six, Morena lives at her mother's house with her seven-year-old daughter, Kendra, and four-year-old son, Daniel.

What connects Morena most intimately to Angelou is her determination to "be somebody," a person to whom her children look with pride, someone they'll know and trust will always be on their side.

"I really don't look at me as living for me. I look at what I'm doing now and how it is going to reflect back on my two kids," Morena told me the day I met her. I remember that morning well, because of the sweltering humidity that enveloped us. The apartment where Morena pays her mother rent for a small bedroom she shares with her children is on the top floor of a three-story house. That morning it seemed to me that every molecule of heat had risen to settle in this upstairs kitchen. Morena wore a sleeveless, loose-fitting purple jumpsuit. With her freckled face, straight shoulder-length hair, and manicured pink fingernails, her look was a whole lot perkier than her spirits.

The neighborhood is so crime-ridden that Morena refuses to allow her children to go outside by themselves. This means that when no grown-up is available and willing to be with them, Kendra and Daniel must be content to ride their bicycles up and down a narrow corridor. One hard push on the pedals and they reach the end. Nor does Morena want her children to go to school in the city; she worries not only about their safety but also about the inferior education they're likely to receive. When Kendra was just two months old, Morena went down to the city's main school office to put her daughter's name on a waiting list for a special program that buses children to suburban schools. Kendra was accepted.

"Someone I work with, she has a fifteen-year-old daughter, and she called me into her office to tell me her daughter is pregnant. And I mean, Melissa . . ."

Hearing Morena say my name startles me. In telling me about her colleague, she seems also to be pleading for me to offer her words of reassurance about Kendra. I do my best to comply. "That is my worst fear with my daughter," Morena says, as a look of horror settles on her face. "My worst fear," she repeats, pausing to give the words plenty of time to sink in, before she tells me what she's doing now to counteract this possibility. "So now I have got to pave the way and make the rules and do the right thing and to make sure she sees me doing the right thing so when she reaches the ages of fifteen and sixteen I am not just saying to her, 'You can't go out.' What I want her to know is that I am doing something with my life. That my life is not going to be all about playing and hanging out with friends and not getting into school. It's an example for her."

Setting this example, however, involves various trade-offs. For Morena to attend college while working to support her family means she cannot be at home with Kendra and Daniel much of the time. It also means she must rely on family members—most of all, her mother—to supplement her own parenting. Concern about what might go wrong while others are looking after her children is the baggage Morena carries every day. She chose to pursue this course rather than relying on welfare, which would have allowed her to stay home with her children. Her brief experience with welfare, which she used only once, when Kendra was very ill and she needed public medical insurance, convinced Morena that it wasn't good for her or her family; she knew she needed to be moving her life forward. "I felt like if I didn't get off welfare, I would fall into a hole so far where I didn't think I could pull myself out," Morena says. But despite her determination to carve out a more dependable future for herself, Morena is never certain that what she has decided to do in her own life is really best for her children. She can only hope it is.

"My biggest fear is that my children will resent what I am doing."

Morena has worked for the past several years at a clerical job, filing medical records. She works full-time so that she can get medical benefits for herself and her children, earn enough money to afford day care for her son, and still pay her other bills. Her shift begins at three o'clock each weekday afternoon. She does not get home until after midnight. These work hours enable her to attend college classes during the morning and early afternoon. Morena earns just $19,000 a year. Her paycheck is barely enough to pay for her family's expenses.

I ask her to run through her monthly budget. "It costs a hundred and twenty-five dollars a week for Daniel's day care," Morena tells me. "And I need to pay even when he is sick." When Daniel is sick, Morena not only misses her own classes but must use a vacation day from work to stay at home with him. "I also pay two hundred dollars a month for my daughter's after-school program. My mother, she gets seventy-five dollars a week for our rent. There's also my school fees and books and groceries. When I started going to school, I did a budget and I came down to having eigh-teen cents each month I can save."

Morena is studying to be a nurse, with the expectation that when she graduates she can find a well-paid job with benefits. She intends to earn enough so she and her children can move into their own place, and Morena plans to find a job whose hours allow her to be at home when her children get back from school. If she manages to stay on her schedule, Morena tells me she'll have her nursing degree when Kendra completes fourth grade and Daniel second. "I want to be there when I can really, really help, like at the age when Kendra is getting older," Morena says. "That is the time I really feel I have to be there for her, when I really have to start putting my foot down on guidelines."

Morena realizes, however, that if what she wants to say to her children a few years from now is to have any meaning for them, she must build trust with them when they are young and keep the lines of communication open. It's hard to do, when she is away from them so much of the time. "That is why from when they were little I've tried to get my kids to talk to me," Morena says. "I say to them, 'Anything you want to talk about, Mommy's here to listen. If you don't want me to say anything, I'll just listen.' "

There are times when Morena's confidence in herself as a parent is boosted. She recalls one night, in particular, when Kendra called her at work.

"Mommy, Mommy" was all Morena heard when she picked up the phone. "Mommy, I don't know how to tell you what happened."

"Kendra. Just calm down and tell me," Morena said, afraid her daughter might be hurt. She was relieved to find out that Kendra had accidentally spilled a bowl of soup on their bed.

"Now, did Mommy yell at you?" she asked Kendra, reinforcing the mes-sage that it was good for the child to call and tell her truthfully what had happened.

"No."

"Did Mommy call you names?"

"No."

"You see. You did the right thing by calling me and letting me know what happened. You don't hide things. You don't go off and act like you are adult and handle things your own way, because you are still a child," Morena told her daughter, who listened intently. "I am really proud of you for doing this because it shows me you are listening to Mommy. And that makes me feel proud of you more than anything else."

"Mommy," Kendra said, "I'm glad I told you."

"I'm glad you told me, too," answered Morena.

"That is what I want them to be able to do," Morena tells me now. "To call me and talk about a problem."

Sharing this story seems to offer Morena reassurance that what she is doing is working out okay. But a few weeks later, when I give Morena a ride to her job, she sounds a lot less confident. At a stoplight a few blocks away from where she works, Morena blurts out how worried she is about this life she's trying to lead. "My biggest fear is that my children will resent what I am doing," she tells me, her voice choked with emotion. "I know what I'm doing now means we will be able to be together later. But what if my children by then say to themselves, 'Mommy hasn't been a part of our lives. Why should she be now?' " She looks away from me as she says this. Her eyes are filling with tears.

When we get to her office, Morena reaches down to grab her heavy black book bag. As she steps away from the car, I see her thick microbiology textbook tucked under her arm. Last night she stayed up until nearly daybreak to study for an exam. When she finishes her job at midnight, she'll take a bus home, put coffee on to brew, and settle in at the kitchen table to work on her term paper. At 6:30, she will wake up her children and spend an hour or so with them while they get ready for school.

"I miss my kids. I miss them terribly. I see my kids only two hours each day."

Often Morena doesn't know how she can manage the demands of work and school and still be the mother to whom her children will turn when they need to be comforted. But each day she soldiers on.

For Morena's and her children's lives to work, family members must be willing to help. Morena refuses to allow her children to be home alone, so she stitches together an elaborate network of around-the-clock care. Usually her system works well, but if one person is unavailable, her schedule can unravel. The toughest part of each day for her comes when she knows Kendra and Daniel are returning home, while she is just in her first few hours of work. "I miss my kids," Morena says. "I miss them terribly. I see my kids only two hours each day." And that is during the chaotic rush of school preparation in the morning. Daniel is often cranky, hard to get out of bed. His sister, meanwhile, moves quickly through her tasks, gulping breakfast so she can catch her school bus. Kendra is walked to the corner by her godfather, who waits with her until the bus arrives. Morena stays with Daniel, because he has to be ready to leave with her. Kendra's godfather meets her when she returns in the afternoon, since his son comes home on the same bus. Kendra stays at her godfather's until Morena's mother arrives home, shortly after seven o'clock.

Daniel's schedule is different. Morena walks him to his preschool on her way to classes. Then each afternoon her younger brother picks Daniel up on his way home from work and feeds him a snack before Morena's mother returns. It isn't until about 7:30 that the food Morena prepared during the weekend gets heated up by her mother and served to the children. After dinner, Kendra and Daniel often call Morena at work to talk about their day; at other times when they call, it seems they just want to listen to her voice. On the rare occasions when Morena's mother can't resolve a problem involving the children, Morena takes a bus home, tries to work things out, and then returns to the office.

Morena's mother, Selma, is in her mid-fifties, an age when she no longer has the energy or patience to deal with the nonstop needs and demands of children. One Saturday morning when Morena and Selma are sitting at the kitchen table, Kendra and Daniel start to giggle loudly in a hallway only a few steps from the kitchen. Suddenly Selma rises and approaches them.

"Will you kids shut up?" she screams. "I am sick and tired of this damn giggling. You are giving me a headache. You are driving me crazy. Just shut up."

Morena jumps in. "Ma, they are laughing."

"Well I've had enough."

Morena knows that she asks a lot of her mother and other family members during the week, so on weekends she tries to take over the care and discipline of her children. It is hard for her to observe how impatient her mother is with Kendra and Daniel, and to know that these patterns probably persist in her absence.

"Ma, the kids are feeling good about something. Leave them alone."

"No, I won't," she says angrily. "They're making too much noise."

Morena gets up and goes over to embrace Kendra and Daniel, leading them quietly into their bedroom.

"I felt really bad because here are my kids, at home, and they can't even laugh," she tells me. "When they run around their footsteps are making too much noise. Or they watch TV and someone doesn't want to watch what they are watching. It's all those things. When this happens, I get upset." Morena has been thinking of taking a job on the weekends so she can save enough money to move out. But if she did that she'd have no time at all with her kids. So she decides against it, even though it's the only way she could earn enough to move out. "I am just tired of being around so many people without having privacy. Sometimes I just want to give up. I don't care no more. I'm not going to school. I am not going to work. I don't want to do this anymore. I hate this. I hate the way things are going. I hate the way my life turned out. It is like, 'Why me?' "

But Morena's deeply held belief that what she is doing will work out best for her children keeps her going. "I think about everything," she says. "I think about the effect of me being away from them so much. About what it's going to do to them. How close we will be. How far apart we might be. If they might have any psychological problems because their mother was always away from them. I just don't know. . . . I want to be able to notice the little things, like if something . . ." Morena's voice drifts away. "I mean, now I look at Kendra and I'm not here all the time but I know when something is wrong. And I say, 'Tell Mommy. You can talk to me.' But I want to be here when she comes home. I want to know what is going on in her life. I don't want to be an outsider. I feel like at least she'll be able to come to me and talk and tell me whatever is on her mind. Same with this little one over here." Morena looks over at Daniel, who is drawing on paper she's spread out on the kitchen floor.

"Sometimes I feel as though if I was there more it probably never would have happened."

"Mommy, I need to talk to you."

"Okay, go ahead," Morena tells Kendra. "Let's talk."

"No, Mommy. Not here." Kendra and Morena are sitting in their bedroom. Because of a teacher's conference at Kendra's school, Morena has taken the day off from work.

"Where do you want to go?" Morena asks.

"Can't we go for a walk?" Kendra says, pleading in a way that Morena is not accustomed to. Her daughter sounds scared.

They walk to a church around the corner, where they sit next to each other on a large rock in a secluded spot in the yard. It is here that Kendra tells her mother a secret she's been keeping, a secret that will change everything.

Morena's voice is shaky as she tells me the story. Tears well up in her eyes. We are sitting in a nearly deserted cafeteria at her college. It is a bit after two o'clock. In an hour, Morena must be at work.

"It was such a nice day outside. It wasn't cold, and we sat there on that rock behind the church." Morena inhales long and deep. "It turns out someone in the house has been molesting Kendra and it's been going on for a year. When she told me this I just remember feeling numb and getting dizzy. I remember feeling tears coming down my face but I don't remember actually crying." Morena starts to cry again.

When Kendra saw the look on her mother's face, she shouted that she knew she shouldn't have told her this. "You're mad at me!" Kendra cried. "I got you all upset. You're mad at me."

Morena was hearing her daughter's words, but at the same time she felt strangely distanced from them.

"I could feel Kendra grabbing me," Morena tells me. "She is like, 'Mommy, Mommy, Mommy,' and it is like, um, like I am trying to believe, not believe."

"To believe Kendra?" I ask.

"Not even that," she says. "But trying to believe this was actually going on with my child. That someone actually took it upon themselves to do this to my child."

"Did she tell you who did this to her?"

Morena shakes her head. "Kendra won't say. She won't tell me whether the person lives in the house or comes to the house. All she says is 'he.' That's all I know, is 'he.'"

That afternoon Morena moved all their belongings out of her mother's apartment. "I called my sister at work and told her she had to leave and come home. I met her at my house with my kids and a couple of bags." Her sister, Beth, helped bring Morena's children and their suitcases to her apartment, then Morena went back to her mother's house. "When I got in that house, the feelings overwhelmed me. I started punching walls. I started knocking things off my dresser. I went berserk in that room," she tells me. "Then all of a sudden my bedroom door opens and my sister is standing there. She'd come back just to be sure I didn't hurt myself. I kind of just collapsed in her arms. I kept saying to her, 'Who could do this to my little baby?'"

The next day Morena took Kendra to a pediatric gynecologist. "When I was sitting there with her, all I could think about is that I am watching my seven-year-old daughter go through a gynecological exam," Morena says, dabbing at her tears. "It took us like an hour to coax her to take her underwear off."

Everything about Morena's life changed at the moment when Kendra told her about being molested. No longer could she rely on family members to be with her children. Her support system crumbled. Because Morena didn't know who did it, she suspected everyone—her brother, her stepfather, her brother's friends, every man who'd ever come into their house. "I literally think about going to that house and torturing people to find out who did this to my child," she says. But Morena restrains herself from violence; as her children's only active parent, she knows her job is to be here for them. She cannot risk getting hurt. "I am like, 'I can't do this because anything happens to me, what's going to happen to them?' That's all I keep thinking. I have not let them down before. I can't let them down now, especially at a time like this, when my daughter has to have me around."

Since Kendra's revelation, Morena has had to miss a lot of classes. "Certain mornings Kendra wakes up and she does nothing but cry," Morena says. "She is like, 'No one loves me anymore. I should never have told. I should have kept my mouth shut.' " Because sexual molestation has taken place, the child protection department is also involved. Social workers are trying to get Kendra to reveal who molested her but, as many girls would be, she is embarrassed that so many people now know and refuses to talk about it any more. She tells Morena she wishes it would all just go away.

"Right now, Melissa, I am just so glad Kendra told me, glad that she felt she could come to me with something like that," Morena says. It validates all her efforts to make certain her children feel good about talking with her. "And I am glad she's not in that environment anymore . . ." Obviously distracted, Morena doesn't finish her thought. "Sometimes I sit here and ask myself, 'How? Why? When? Who?' " Morena shakes her head in disbelief.

"Do you start blaming yourself for not being there?"

"Yeah," Morena says, without hesitation.

"That would seem a natural reaction, although I'm sure you've been told that you shouldn't do that."

"Right. But it's hard. Sometimes I feel as though if I was there more it probably never would have happened. And if I was there more, maybe she could've come to me sooner. She might have come to talk to me the first time. I try not to dwell on that, but sometimes when I look at her and see how upset she gets over the simplest little things now, you know at times I blame myself."

"I beat up on myself because I feel like I am not being a mother."

Morena found out about Kendra's molestation in April, just a few weeks before semester's end. Doing well is particularly important because Morena is in the midst of applying to transfer to a four-year college to finish her nursing degree. But everything that's going on with Kendra seemed too much for her to handle. Morena tells me she considered dropping out of school.

"I'd get another job or two more jobs," she says, describing what she saw as her options. "See how much money I could come up with to get us into our own place. I don't know. I feel just like when I finally start to be on my own, to be independent and do the things I know I have to do, something comes up and knocks me like five feet back." Her expression is of disbelief combined with anger.

Beth convinced her sister to stay in school and agreed to help with the kids so that Morena could complete the semester. But she urged Morena to consider going on welfare so she could quit her job and spend time with the children. As much as Morena wanted to be with her kids, she told her sister she couldn't go on welfare. "I just can't do welfare again. I really can't. I can't. I mean, there is not enough money there, and it's just more of a hassle than what I have right now. You've gotta prove this and prove that. It's just a plain-out hassle—and the attitude in those offices! Well, I just don't want to deal with it. I don't want to deal with it." Morena repeats the phrase as if memories of welfare are circling like nightmares inside her head.

That summer, when neither Morena nor her children are in school, she spends the days with them. In the evenings, when she works, her sister is at home with them. But Morena worries about whether she and her sister can handle these responsibilities once the school year begins. She can no longer rely on her original network of support. And her schoolwork will be even more demanding in the fall, because she's been accepted into the nursing program at a four-year university. So when Morena's godmother, who lives in Trinidad, where Morena was also born, suggested that Kendra and Daniel come to live with her and her husband, Morena agrees. She realizes there is no perfect solution, but this is the best one she can think of, at least for the upcoming school year. One thing Morena can count on, because she's watched her godmother's own children thrive under their parents' care, is that Kendra and Daniel will be well taken care of.

"It is very, very quiet where the children are living," Morena tells me a few weeks after taking them to their new home. "Where they're living is like the suburbs up here. It's safe," she says, smiling. "My godmother doesn't have to worry about them going out into the yard, because there aren't kids out there using foul language. And there aren't kids carrying guns. The type of environment they're in is not one in which everyone is at home not doing anything and having no goals. These people are businesspeople. They're working. They have grown children who are out doing things on their own. It is pretty much, how should I say it, a functional family. This is the type of environment that I always wanted my kids to be in."

By now it is September and Morena has begun classes at her new college. She and I sit along a brick wall in the middle of the campus and, as usual, she sips from her constant cup of coffee and smokes a cigarette. She tells me that by the time she graduates, she'll owe $46,000 in student loans. She knows it will be difficult to make the monthly payments on those loans and still live in the kind of place she wants for her children, a safe community with good public schools. But if she let such future obstacles halt her progress, Morena would not have gotten this far.

"Oh, I see the obstacles," Morena admits, "but I can't let myself worry about them anymore. I just have to go over one hurdle at a time. And after I get over that one I have to keep my concentration up so that when I get close to the next hurdle I can jump high and do what I can do to get over it and land on my two feet on the other side. That's all I've been doing. I'm taking it one step at a time."

She misses Kendra and Daniel painfully. On Sunday nights, she talks with them by telephone. She stays on the phone with each child for about fifteen minutes; this is as much as her budget will allow. Daniel recently told her about a "boo-boo" he got on his foot because he went outside without his shoes on. "I feel a little included, a little bit part of their life when I can find out about them having little boo-boos," she says. "And my daughter says she's having a little hard time in school because the reading is difficult." Morena encourages Kendra by reminding her about the stories they used to read together. "So I kind of feel like I am away but I still know what is going on," she says. "It kind of makes me feel good. Kind of does."

"It must be hard to imagine bringing them back here where they will have a lot less freedom to simply go outside and run around," I say. "How do you reconcile within yourself what their life is like now compared to what it will be like back with you?"

"I don't know yet," she says, with an awkward laugh. "All I hope is when it's time for them to come back home they'll just be happy to be here, no matter where they are or what the environment is, because they want to be with me. That's all I think about now. It's just like, I don't know, you lay in your bed on a Sunday evening and tears start coming because you want your son to give you a hug or for him to come in and complain that his sister isn't doing this or that. Then you get beyond it. You don't look at where we're going to live or what we are going to do or what the environment is. I look at it this way—we are finally going to be together. And right now I can't wait for that to happen."

Morena mentions that time seems to be passing very slowly for her, even though she is as busy at her job and at school as she's ever been.

"Is that because your kids are not part of your life right now?"

"Right."

I remind her of something she'd said to me before any of this happened, that she hoped her children would not look back and resent what she is doing. "You must feel that even more strongly now," I say.

"Yeah. That's why I call them as often as I can. And Kendra has my number at work. She knows how to call me at work collect and if I am away from my desk, she knows the call will be accepted. She leaves the message 'I got to talk to Mommy' and I will call her right back.

"I let them know no matter where I am I will be there for them. If something happens, if I have to sell my feet to come back home, I will be home."

At three o'clock one morning Morena was awakened by her ringing phone. She leaped out of bed.

"Mommy," she heard Kendra say.

"What's wrong? What's wrong?" Morena was instantly wide awake.

"I can't sleep," Kendra said.

Morena felt her body relax. "Just hearing that was wonderful. She'd asked my godmother if she could call me when she couldn't sleep. We talked for about fifteen minutes and then she told me she was getting tired and wanted to go to sleep. It made me feel so good that she'd called me. I couldn't go back to sleep after talking to Kendra. I had a really good day after that, as I kept thinking about how she had called me. She needed me, and she called me. I felt good."

Morena rarely feels very good about the choices she has had to confront in rearing her children. She works full-time so that she can lift them out of poverty. She is in college so she can improve her ability to provide her family's income, since no one else contributes. But the emotional trade-offs are hard on her; the future consequences of her decisions are unknown. Choosing who will stand in for her as caregivers is always the hardest decision, especially after what happened to Kendra.

I ask Morena what keeps her going.

"I have to," she responds. "It's like people who have kidney problems who need to have dialysis. If they don't have dialysis, they will die. In order for my children and me to survive I have to do this. It is like my dialysis treatment. I have to do this. I admit I am missing a part of their childhood. I am not there like I should be for them. And I beat up on myself because I feel like I am not being a mother. But if I don't keep on doing what I'm doing, what will the future hold for us? What will happen to my children? What will their lives turn out to be?"

6

Raising Children: Unmarried Older Mothers

Carol's return from China with her newly adopted daughter, Amy, was uneventful. Amy spent most of the time asleep, nestled in Carol's arms. Her mother's curly blond hair and light complexion presented a sharp contrast with Amy's olive skin, silky black hair, and rounded face. But during the brief time the two of them had spent together, their physical differences vanished from Carol's mind as she discovered the deep emotional bonds involved in becoming Amy's mother.

Mother and daughter had spent four delicious weeks living in a Chinese hotel, becoming comfortable with each other. It had been a magical time, during which Carol transformed herself from a woman who'd always wanted to have a child into one who was now a single parent. Sometimes, while Amy napped, Carol found her mind drifting back to the years when she was married. She remembered how long and hard she and her husband had tried to become parents and how painful it had been when they failed. Now, on her own, at the age of forty-one, she was Amy's mother.

The time they spent together in China had felt like a vacation. Since they were staying in a hotel, Carol didn't have to cook for herself, just prepare bottles of formula. She had no dishes to wash, no apartment to clean, no job to rush off to. But on this vacation, instead of catching up on rest, Carol discovered how tired she could feel after a few nights of not getting a solid sleep because of Amy's frequent waking. But she didn't mind: to Carol, lack of sleep simply confirmed she was a mother.

"I was so used to living alone and doing things just for me. I didn't know how to adjust."

Back home it didn't take long for the less magical realities of single motherhood to sink in. In China, Carol had had the luxury of focusing her energies solely on establishing a relationship with her daughter. Now that she was back in her three-room apartment, there was no one else to shop for food or to prepare meals or to wash dishes or to launder the clothes. Carol's mother had died several years before; other family members lived far away and were not available to help her. Friends stopped by, but the time they spent with Carol and Amy was not the kind that got household tasks done. Also, because Carol had taken so many weeks away from work just to get to China and carry out the adoption, she would soon have to go back to her job as an administrative assistant.

Within days, Carol was overwhelmed by the scope of what she'd taken on. Adjusting to this other person in her life was proving harder than she had imagined. "I was so used to living alone and doing things just for me. Then all of a sudden I had this little baby who was taking up one hundred percent of my time and I had no time for myself," Carol tells me one evening as we sit in her living room amid a hurricane of toys and puzzles and books that one-year-old Amy has been playing with. Amy is now asleep. "I didn't know how to adjust to it," admits Carol, whose slender, athletic build seems to give her the stamina she needs to keep up with the onslaught.

Some nights Carol collapsed into bed so exhausted that she fell asleep in her clothes. Often it was not until her stomach growled that she realized she hadn't eaten dinner. "I couldn't figure out why it was already evening and I hadn't done anything. Emotionally, I think I was adjusting to really being here by myself and doing this all on my own." There never seemed to be a moment when her daughter did not need her, a moment when Carol might do whatever needed to be done to keep the household running. When Amy slept during the day, Carol napped, too, trying to reenergize herself for the next round of activities.

One day Carol wrote out a schedule, one that built in the extra time she needed for various tasks like food shopping now that she had a child. Instead of dashing out to the store to buy a few items, Carol had to figure in the time it took to get Amy and herself organized for a trip. Every task was like that. What she'd been able to do with ease before now involved complicated and often unpredictable delays. But by drawing up a more realistic timetable, Carol helped herself come to terms with these logistical difficulties. Most of all, by writing her schedule down, Carol came to accept in a way she hadn't done before that she was doing this by herself; there was no one on whom she could depend for help.

"I realized this is it." Carol nods to emphasize the point of self-understanding at which she had finally arrived. "This is your responsibility. You're here with this baby. This is your daughter and there is going to be no one here to help you."

Fortunately, Carol had had the foresight to arrange for child care before she left for China. If she'd had to begin that search now, with Amy consuming every ounce of her normally bountiful energy, she could not imagine how she would have coped. Choosing a place to leave her baby while she went back to work had been hard enough without the daily pressures of motherhood weighing on her. After working out a family budget, Carol had realized that with an annual income of just under $40,000 she couldn't afford to spend more than $600 a month for Amy's care. The child-care referral agency told her that finding full-time care for an infant at that price would be difficult. This did not surprise Carol; her friends with children had warned her how expensive high-quality infant care can be. Despite her financial limitations, Carol was determined to find a child-care provider who was loving toward the children she cared for and with whom she felt absolutely comfortable leaving her daughter. After all, this person was going to be spending more waking weekday hours with Amy than Carol would.

Even if Carol found a caretaker she liked and could afford, however, other aspects of her life would need to change: "I knew I couldn't pay all that money each month in rent *and* day care." Carol would have to find someplace less expensive to live. Rent on her one-bedroom apartment was $875 a month, reasonable considering the high cost of housing in areas of Boston where she felt comfortable living. However, what was reasonable when she was on her own was now prohibitively expensive. To find a suitable and affordable apartment, Carol figured she'd need to move many miles away from the downtown office building where she worked. What she worried about most was that if she moved so far away her few precious free hours, which she wanted to spend with Amy, would be eaten up by driving between work, day care, and home.

"I had a few weeks of sheer panic," Carol says. "I'd find myself wondering, 'What am I going to do if I can't afford to support this baby? What am I going to do?' Then I told myself just to calm down. And I was able to work it out. I mean, now I don't have much money left over, but I can do it."

Carol was able to "work it out" because people who were neither family nor friends decided to help her. When she told her landlord why she might need to move, he reduced her rent to $625. Now monthly expenses for day care and housing would be $1,225, an amount her carefully calculated budget could handle, though just barely. So that her monthly expenses did not exceed her income, Carol used a flexible spending account her employer had set up to deduct $96 of pretax earnings from each paycheck. Child care and medical expenses are two personal areas that this account can, by law, be used for. Carol put these pretax dollars toward Amy's care. Had her employer not offered this benefit, Carol would not have been able to pay even $600 each month for child care.

"My monthly take-home pay, with dependent care taken out, is almost eighteen hundred dollars," Carol tells me. "And right off the top goes the money for my rent and my daughter's day care. Then there is car insurance, at eight hundred dollars a year. And I don't spend anything on myself. I don't go anywhere. I don't go out to dinner. I don't go to the movies. I knew when I set out to adopt her that it was going to be very close. I knew I was going to have to give up those things, but I didn't care because they didn't make any difference to me. What bothers me most is I'm really living paycheck to paycheck, and I really don't like to do that."

Carol used up her savings, plus more, to adopt Amy. The cost was about $12,000. Carol had reached a time in her life when she was willing to forgo personal indulgences if it meant she could have a child, but her month-to-month financial precariousness bothers her. She's keenly aware that she already needs to be thinking about putting away money for Amy's education; those are savings she doesn't have. At the same time, she sees around her increasing job insecurity. Some of her friends are already dealing with the impact of downsizing and layoffs; she worries about what would happen to her and Amy if her job was eliminated.

"You have no choice but to manage," I say to Carol.

"I have no choice," she replies.

"I am now prepared to put someone else first—my child."

Older, unmarried women who set out to raise children on their own are quick to separate their own circumstances from those of what people think of as typical unwed mothers with "illegitimate" children. These mothers reject vociferously and vehemently any label suggesting that their children are less "legitimate" than any others. No children could be as wanted, as cherished, or as loved, these mothers say, as our sons and daughters are; look at how much soul-searching and sacrifice we went through to have them. Outsiders sometimes describe these women's nonmarital parenthood as a selfish act, one in which women who have eschewed marriage set out to fulfill their own desires for motherhood to the detriment of the children they will raise alone. When seen, however, through the mothers' eyes, the decision to parent can be construed as representing the opposite impulse. One older unmarried mother explained her outlook to me: "This is an unselfish act in the sense that you are now willing to put aside the I-come-first way of living you've been used to and say, 'I am now prepared to put someone else first—my child.' "

Unlike poorer, younger, and less well educated women who have children out of wedlock, these older mothers are, for the most part, college-educated, many having advanced degrees; they're well settled into careers and earn decent salaries. Many own their homes. They are also quite willing, as Carol was, to trade away the quiet solitude of their home lives for the midnight crying of a child who wants to be comforted by her mother. Because of the lives they have led—both as individuals and as members of a generation who charged through the gender barricades that held their own mothers back—these older unmarried mothers are confident they can and will do well in raising their children, even if they do it on their own.

These women believe that whatever stacks of studies say about the potential harmful effects on children of growing up with one unmarried parent, these conclusions don't apply to their families. After all, they say, the unwed mothers whose lives have usually been studied don't look or act like them and generally have many fewer resources, not the least of which are money and education. Most of them haven't gone to college; in fact, many never finished high school. They don't have professional skills that allow them to earn good salaries or hold on to steady jobs with good benefits such as health, life, and disability insurance, tax-free flexible-spending accounts, and retirement pensions. Nor do their children usually attend good schools; too many grow up in poor communities, living in neighborhoods where other families look just like theirs. Few of their friends have fathers who live with them. In fact, there aren't many men around, especially men who have steady jobs and act as good role models for children. As Dr. Deborah Prothrow-Stith wrote in *Deadly Consequences*, a 1991 book about adolescent violence, "Regardless of the race or class of individuals, when large numbers of men are out of work and larger numbers of families are headed by women, the rate of crime and violence in that community rises sharply. The fact is as true for whites as for blacks."

So when older, unwed mothers say their lives—and their children's lives—will be different from and more successful than the usual experience of unmarried motherhood, they are probably right. Their children will be part of communities in which large numbers of men will be employed and large numbers of families will have two parents present in the home. However, so recent is these older single mothers' emergence that long-term studies of their children's development and social adaptation have simply not been done. One reason is that the number of children over the age of ten (that is, old enough to be part of such long-term investigations) whose older mothers entered parenthood unmarried is relatively tiny. Early in the next century, when the babies who were born or adopted during the past fifteen years mature, there will be many more of these families to study. Then their experiences will be able to provide us with better-quantified information about how well children in these families are doing.

Even as their numbers grow, however, these older mothers and their children are less likely to be studied than are families created by unmarried teenage mothers. There are several reasons why. Since the older mothers' lives rarely intersect with governmental policies and funding, there is less reason to support studies of them. And because older unmarried mothers do not often end up in welfare offices or public health clinics, are rarely visited by state caseworkers, and do not reside in housing projects, recruitment of large numbers of them for studies is more difficult. These mothers and children tend to blend into the fabric of middle-class communities, looking not much different from the families of divorced or separated mothers. The women are also very protective of their and their children's privacy, and more cautious than younger mothers about allowing people to snoop around in their personal lives. My experience with both older and younger unwed mothers taught me that teenagers, in part because they crave attention, are less reluctant to open up their private lives for an outsider's inspection. Also, many of the teenage mothers were raised in households whose members, dependent on outside assistance, did not have the luxury of keeping personal issues off-limits from intrusive questioning. Answering personal questions is something they've gotten used to.

More financially secure, older unwed mothers are often regarded as a sort of derivative form of divorced mothers. Through this lens, the only fundamental difference is that these mothers never had a partner to be divorced from. (Of course, this also means some of their children will never have known a father.) Otherwise, their single parenting is thought to pretty much mirror that of mothers who raise children on their own after a divorce.

But this point doesn't fully acknowledge the two groups' differing realities. Marriages that collapse often leave children emotionally scarred by their parents' animosity. Mothers often find it difficult to reconcile themselves to their unanticipated life as a single parent. And fathers must find new ways to remain engaged parents. Conversely, a woman entering parenthood on her own doesn't usually carry the emotional baggage of a failed partnership with the father of her child. In fact, many older unmarried women raising children by themselves favorably compare their unfettered circumstances with the trauma they've seen many of their friends with children suffer through divorce. Many unmarried mothers say that while it may be lonelier and more difficult day by day to do without a partner, their parenting is predictable and constant. And this consistency, they contend, is something children like and need.

"A single parent has to earn twice as much."

Unlike younger mothers and many of their divorced peers, these unwed mothers take on family responsibilities with the expectation that their own money-making abilities will support their children. They have no husband's salary to fall back on, no child-support payments. And like Carol, most of these older, unwed mothers don't have extravagant salaries like that fictional poster girl of unmarried motherhood, Murphy Brown. Most of them earn enough to guarantee themselves a comfortable, middle-class lifestyle, but they need to worry—and do worry, a lot—about their ability to stretch their budgets to cover the additional expenses the child brings. Sometimes they formulate a financial plan well before the baby arrives. One woman described her strategy to me: "It's time for Operation Baby," she said. "This year is equity year. The next year is pregnancy year." Another unwed mother, a psychologist who works in private practice, summed up the feelings of many unmarried mothers when she told me, "People are silly if they think money isn't an issue in having a family."

Family finance is one topic these mothers have a voracious appetite for discussing. At meetings of Single Mothers by Choice, when the participants are asked to suggest speakers, they often select investment advisers or bankers who describe savings strategies for children's college educations. Even though most of these women know they will be dealing with squeezed finances well into the future, this awareness rarely becomes an insurmountable roadblock to having a child. "I decided early on that financial reasons wouldn't be what stopped me," one mother said. "I knew I could make that work. It was the emotional issues that went up and down." For this woman and many others, the much tougher hurdle to get over is dealing with their feelings about giving a child just one parent.

When it comes to finances, a lot of the women believe that solutions to financial problems they run into will present themselves when needed. Sometimes they do, as when Carol's landlord cut her rent. And sometimes they don't, as happened to Angela, an unmarried mother of two, when she applied to her children's school for a scholarship.

Like other older, well-educated mothers, Angela wants and expects her children to have opportunities like those her parents gave her. Growing up in New York City, Angela attended private schools, from kindergarten through law school. Her family wasn't wealthy, and tuition was expensive, but her mother and father believed that education was the key to their children's happiness and success. Angela remembers the admonition her parents gave to her and her brother: "You get the best education possible, and you pay for it no matter what it costs. You never compromise on that. That is what you do." Now, Angela tells me, "I do this for my children."

This means Angela sends her children to a private elementary school even though the public schools in her town are considered by many parents to be pretty good. But paying tuition for her two children—and also paying for the nanny she employs to help run her household—eats up quite a hefty portion of her six-figure annual salary. One day she told me about a letter she'd written to her sons' school asking them to consider her family for scholarship assistance. Although Angela knew that her salary put her way over the usual income cutoff, because she is a single parent of two children at the school she thought she had a legitimate case to present. Angela wrote, in part:

> *There is no father to provide any portion of the children's support. [This] means that I must provide, through life insurance and other means, for their support in the event that something should happen to me. It also means that in order to care for them and work for the income I need to support them I must have extensive child-care support at home. I am also an older parent—fifty-one years of age. This means that both for my children's sake and my own I cannot afford not to have a retirement fund. I also have had extraordinary expenses in the last couple of years, related largely to required deleading of my house for my kids. I work as hard as seems to me consistent with being an adequate parent—I put in significant time doing work outside my regular work commitments in order to earn extra income. I have very few expenses related to what I would see as discretionary matters. I pay out virtually all my income for the essentials—tuition, mortgage, child care, life insurance, and the like.*
>
> *I have avoided asking for scholarship assistance in the past because I have very much not wanted to do it. But I feel that I have no alternative. As I*

review my records for the last decade I can see that I have steadily borrowed increasing amounts from my home equity credit line in order to keep up with my expenses. I am now at the end of my borrowing capacity. . . . I have no assets to call upon—no savings, no stocks, nothing except my house. At the present time I am a month behind in paying for a child-care bill and a month behind in paying school tuition because there are simply no funds for me to draw from in paying these bills.

I do feel that if I could obtain scholarship assistance for a few years I would get to the point where I would be able to do without it. I anticipate, among other things, that my child-care expenses will go down as the children get older. . . . I hate to ask for scholarship assistance, even for a few years. But I feel that I have to, and hope very much that you will be able to provide it.

Angela's request was rejected; she juggled her finances so her children could stay at the school.

Angela knows that to anyone who isn't trying to rear children alone on one income—and even to poorer single mothers—her high and dependable income makes her application for a scholarship laughable. But she knows what it costs for her to provide the kind of high-quality substitute care for her children that mothers who can stay at home provide for free. "A single parent has to earn twice as much to keep the household running," Angela says. She has to earn money for all the usual costs associated with a family, a house, and school, and she has to pay for the person who takes her place at home—all on one income. She gives me an example. In the summer, when Angela is at work, her boys go to sports camps; these camps come with a good-sized price tag. But she also has to keep paying her nanny to run the household and be certain the boys get wherever they need to go.

"So during these summer weeks you're paying double again, just like you do when they are in school? Two camp tuitions plus a nanny?"

"Right," Angela replies. "And I pay for my nanny's vacation time. But my children are five and eight years old. What am I going to do? Have them stay home all day? I mean, they might stay home if there was a non-working wife there to get them together with friends."

Though the issue of what amenities her budget can support is pressing for Angela, none of the options she confronts put her children's well-being in jeopardy. For young mothers, many of whom are raising their children in poor, unsafe neighborhoods, the inability to stretch a meager monthly budget can result in inadequate substitute care, improper nutrition, and poor schooling for their children, each of which can have catastrophic consequences.

"Is it really right to go all the way to China and then to have someone else really raise her and take care of her?"

When older unmarried mothers discuss their financial concerns, they include worries about who will be taking care of their children when they can't. Some who can afford the expense, as Angela can, hire a nanny whom they can count on to be available whenever they aren't. What most clearly separates unmarried mothers from their married friends is that they don't have another parent to call when a last-minute appointment or crisis arises at work. Otherwise, older, unmarried mothers resemble their married peers both in the daily child-care arrangements they make and in the fact that they, not their partners, are responsible for making them. Mothers, whether they are married or not, assume the bulk of the work in arranging and providing—and often paying for—their children's care. And mothers' daily lives, regardless of their family configuration, are laden with worry about the impact day care might have on their children and on their relationship with them.

Carol remembers worrying about whether Amy, who spent so much of her time in someone else's care, would know who her "mommy" really was. Her hunt for child care had taken several months and, even before she met her daughter, had given her a glimpse of how complicated their daily life was going to be. Carol looked first at child-care centers near where she worked. When she imagined her life as a working mother, she envisioned herself walking out of her office at lunch to see her daughter. That way they'd get to spend more time together, and their day away from home would be broken up by a playful visit. But Carol soon learned that the cost of high-quality city-based care was way beyond her limited means: the lowest price she could find was $850 a month; the highest was $1,200.

"I was appalled. I couldn't believe it," Carol says. "I couldn't afford to pay that." It was one thing to know in theory how much high-quality infant care costs, but with each of these early visits the different-than-she-imagined reality of her situation began to sink in. "But I knew it was possible because I knew mothers who were doing it," Carol says, referring to her search for a $600 placement that she would feel comfortable about. However, the places her friends recommended had no openings. For the next few weeks, Carol turned her attention to a list of family day-care providers—women, usually mothers, who care for small numbers of children in their homes. One day she discovered Sally, a woman who was raising three children after her husband had left her. By taking in other people's children, Sally was able to stay at home to be with hers. Carol liked her and could imagine her daughter enjoying Sally's companionship, too. Carol told Sally about how she was going to China to adopt her daughter. That day Sally became the third person—after her landlord and her employer—who helped Carol make her parenting arrangement work out well for her child. Sally told Carol she would reduce her usual fee by $200 each month; Carol could pay $600 and be assured that her daughter would receive wonderful care. "Sally was interested in what I was doing," Carol says. "She had been adopted herself. I was very lucky."

Amy is now one of six children to arrive at Sally's house every weekday morning. She spends nine hours there, five days a week, except when her mother is on vacation. Amy has been in Sally's care for several months, and Carol is delighted by the motherly attention Sally heaps on her daughter. "That Amy is as warm and loving as she is has a lot to do with Sally," Carol says. "I don't know how she would be if she were in a big child-care center all day. I don't think she would be the same child." Even so, Carol realizes that nine hours is a long time for any child to be in someone else's care and away from home. But with her eight-hour workday, plus the commute, Carol can't make the time any shorter. She did manage to rearrange her work hours; Amy now begins her day with Sally earlier so Carol and she can get home at a more reasonable hour and they can share more time together before Amy goes to sleep.

"In the beginning I wasn't getting to pick her up until six o'clock," Carol says, "and that was too late." Even with the revised schedule, it's still quite a long day for the two of them. Each morning Carol gets up at 5:30. As tired as she feels at that hour, she has come to realize how valuable this time is, since she spends the rest of her day taking care of other people's needs. This is the only time she has alone, by and for herself. By the time she wakes Amy at 6:50, Carol is ready and eager to be with her.

"I really want to have time to feed her in the morning. I don't want to take her to day care and have her get fed there," Carol says. Like many working mothers, Carol tries to preserve rituals of care from her own childhood, when she had breakfast with her mother every morning. "I want to have this time with her because I am getting so little with her as it is."

I ask how Carol feels about not having more time to spend with Amy after going to the effort she did to adopt her.

"It's hard." Carol is pensive, tucked away in her own thoughts. Stalling while she collects her thoughts, she fluffs a pillow on the sofa where we sit. It's clear that my question touches on difficult aspects of Carol's decision. A few moments pass in silence until she turns to face me and reveals at least some of what she's feeling.

"Is it really right to go all the way to China and then to have someone else really raise her and take care of her?" Carol says. "No, it's not the ideal situation. I always wanted to be home and raise her, be home with her all day long. But that is not the way it's going to be. I feel sad, because I am not really going to see a lot of the things Amy does that Sally sees every day."

Often Carol stays to talk with Sally for a few minutes when she picks Amy up. She digs for nuggets of information about her daughter's day. Sometimes she chats with Sally about her own confused reactions to this setup. "When I brought Amy to her in the beginning, I said to Sally, 'She's not going to know I'm her mother. She's going to think you're her mother.' " Sally assured Carol that despite the many hours she had to be away from her daughter, Amy would not be confused. The two of them, Sally assured Carol, had complementary roles to play in Amy's healthy development.

"Sally told me Amy would know the difference. And she does," Carol says, smiling. "She knows I'm her mother." Her relief is palpable.

"It is still not acceptable for a mother to leave a small child."

Going to her job was something Carol had no choice about. She and Amy had no one else to support them. Unlike married mothers, who can sometimes take a leave from their jobs, or quit altogether, or cut back their schedules to part-time, unmarried mothers need a steady paycheck. They must do what it takes to hold on to their jobs. They do not, however, always feel comfortable about the trade-offs entailed.

In the June 1993 issue of the Single Mothers by Choice newsletter, Jessica Curtis, who is raising a child on her own, explored the sense of guilt evoked by discussions about substitute care for young children. "The assumption that if you don't stay home with your children, they won't be your children, won't have your values, won't know what it is like to have close family relationships, a 'one to one' maternal tie, is at the root of the dilemma," Curtis wrote. Though millions of mothers—married, divorced, single—need to leave infants and toddlers in the care of others while they go to work, Curtis observed that "it is still not acceptable for a mother to leave a small child."

Curtis urged unmarried single mothers to be honest with themselves about their feelings. "All of us, as prospective single parents, knew we were going back to work soon after giving birth," she wrote. "[But] how do we handle the conflict and guilt we inevitably feel?" In speaking with unmarried mothers, Curtis had found, not surprisingly, that how they felt about child care was very much influenced by beliefs about parenting that were shaped by their childhood experiences. How they were raised—most of all, whether their mother was in the labor force and who took care of them—set their comfort levels about the choices they face in rearing their children.

What can make these choices discomfiting for older unmarried mothers is that the families they've created bear little resemblance to the ones most of them grew up in. Most of the older, unmarried moms I've talked with have siblings; but most have only one child themselves, and acknowledge with sadness that their financial wherewithal will prevent them from raising another. Most have parents who are married; but many of them have never had a husband, or if they have, they don't now. These women grew up during the 1950s and early 1960s, so their mothers mostly stayed out of the workforce, at least until the children went to school. Now they themselves must go back to work before their child even crawls. So as much as these women might like to rely on road maps from their childhood, they can't.

Unmarried mothers are hardly alone in their concerns about juggling career and family. A majority of married mothers—including those with infants—now work outside the home and rely on substitute caregivers for at least a part of every week. During work hours, the lives of many married and unmarried mothers are virtually impossible to tell apart.

There is much speculation—a lot of it informed by beliefs about what a mother's family role *ought* to be—concerning how well children do when their mother works outside the home. In 1989 Lois Hoffman, a University of Michigan psychologist, reviewed fifty years of research on this much-studied topic; she found that anticipated negative effects had not materialized. When demographic backgrounds were accounted for, the children of employed and stay-at-home mothers did just about the same on standard measures used to assess their development. One consistent difference was found: among both sons and daughters of employed mothers, the review found fewer sex-stereotyped views about how families and the world operate. This result is one that many mothers, and increasing numbers of fathers, would regard as a definite benefit.

Some studies, of course, highlight specific cognitive and behavioral problems that can arise when children spend too much time in day care at very early ages, especially when the caregivers are poorly trained and the daily environment fails to provide the stimulation young children need. It is the poor quality of child care, and not the fact that a child is in day care per se, that makes developmental delays more likely. A large research study of the effects of early child care, financed by the National Institute of Child Health and Human Development (NICHD), reported in 1996 that placing an infant in day care is not, by itself, likely to jeopardize the mother-child bond. A mother's sensitivity turns out to be the best predictor of attachment.

Another significant factor in how well the children of employed mothers do is the women's level of contentedness about their life choices. "Going back to work can reduce financial stress on women and enable them to approach mothering more relaxed and less depressed," says Marsha Weinraub, a Temple University psychologist who was a researcher on the NICHD study. Generally speaking, mothers who are employed while raising families have been found to be in better physical and mental health than those engaged in only one of these roles. And being involuntarily out of work is a major risk factor for depression in women, just as in men. In a University of California–Berkeley study that followed women for twenty-two years, researchers found that mothers who stayed home seemed more "disillusioned and frustrated" than those who were juggling additional roles. Mothers who wanted to have a job but remained at home with their children scored high on tests for depression and stress. *Lifeprints*, a study done in the early 1980s, also found that housewives had higher levels of stress than mothers who were maintaining dual roles. Caryl Rivers, a co-author of *Lifeprints*, explains: the housewives "were not able to say no to any demands. They had no 'time off,' but were always at everyone's beck and call."

Careers can bring women sweet rewards of recognized accomplishment and independence. As for less-educated women, whose jobs are likely to be more routine and less pleasurable, earning a paycheck still gives them the release many say they want from dependence on others. Also, mothers often forge bonds of friendship and support at work, bonds that are especially important when women are raising children on their own. Maureen Perry-Jenkins, a researcher at the University of Illinois–Champaign, noted this phenomenon when she interviewed single mothers working in low-paying jobs.

"Their support groups at work were what were keeping these mothers alive," Perry-Jenkins told me. "They relied on each other and used each other's help. Some of these mothers worked at jobs where they had mandatory overtime; if they didn't stay, they were docked a day's pay. Among themselves, they worked out a system in which some do the overtime and others take care of everyone else's kids. Fellow workers were their lifesavers." Older, more prosperous single mothers rely on one another, too. Though the work lives of these unmarried mothers don't necessarily bring them into daily contact, they make an effort through meetings and informal get-togethers to set up networks of support.

What cannot be ignored is the substantial role that a steady, good income and a high educational level play in how well a mother and her child do. Having ample money, of course, does not guarantee good parenting, but having enough to afford reliable, consistent, and developmentally appropriate care increases the likelihood that a child will receive a solid foundation when she is young. The hardships of an unmarried mother who has a low-paying and unstimulating job are worsened by her accompanying realization that she has few good, reliable child-care options. Low-wage workers are not able to purchase optimum care. On the other hand, the child of a well-educated single mother is likely to end up with high-quality substitute care—and to receive attentive, bountiful, and stimulating care at home. Given these advantages (which are the ingredients most research points to as buffers against developmental problems), it wouldn't be surprising to find that school-age children of older, well-educated unwed mothers are, on average, as cognitively prepared and as behaviorally well-adjusted as their peers being raised by married, employed parents with similar incomes and educational status. But no such comparison has yet been done.

"I was very ready to return to work."

If there was ever an era designed for these women to have children on their own, the 1990s appears to be it. If these unwed mothers must have jobs to support their children, at least they have plenty of company, as well as encouragement from many sectors of society. At no other time in the twentieth century have so many Americans supported so strongly, at least in their rhetoric about public policies, the belief that a mother's role includes having a paid job. In the national dialogue about changing the welfare system, for example, few topics receive as much attention as the desire to get poor mothers, even those with infants, into the workforce. States seem to be competing to see which can get its welfare mothers into the workforce quickest. Of course, similar sentiments don't attach themselves to discussions about middle- and upper-income mothers, who are often criticized for "shirking" parental responsibilities by heading back to work too soon after a child is born, or spending too many hours at their jobs.

For Kerry, the research scientist we met earlier, who is now an unmarried mother of two and in her mid-forties, her workplace routine has not changed much. Eleven weeks after her first son, Adam, was born, she returned to her full-time job; her maternity leave was scheduled to last for twelve weeks, but when colleagues needed her back early, she obliged without a trace of resentment. After she had her second child, Nathan, Kerry was back at work even sooner, because complications with her pregnancy had forced her to use some of her maternity leave before his birth.

After all of Kerry's drawn-out decision-making about whether to have a child on her own, and then her discovery of how wonderful it felt to be a mother, I wonder how she reconciled herself to her speedy return to work. Many of my friends—albeit married ones—decided after their children were born to take a long break from their careers. Like Kerry, these women, who had postponed parenthood for so long, had quickly fallen in love with being a mother. Most told me they intended to return to a job someday, but were now expecting to do so part-time, at least for a while.

But Kerry—like most women who decide to have a child on their own—couldn't afford such a leisurely reentry. Kerry's job is her family's only means of support; without her weekly salary, they wouldn't be able to live in their big house in a suburban neighborhood. Nor would she be able to hire the kind of household help she needs to make her single-parenting life work. And without her full-time job, Kerry wouldn't receive employee benefits such as affordable health insurance for her family, a good retirement and savings plan, and access to on-site high-quality child care.

Kerry tells me she could have taken more time off without pay, but she didn't want to: "I never considered lengthening my maternity leave." Kerry's voice is full of certainty, her brown eyes full of contentment. "In part it's because I always realized I was the kind of person—I mean, it didn't matter whether I was connected with someone else or not, I was always going to work. That would have been a part of what I would've been as a mother regardless of whether I was married or not," says Kerry, who at midday is sitting behind a large desk in her small, light-filled office. Her children are in day care. Behind her, a computer screen blinks. "I think in a sense having to go back helped me to be fairly unconflicted about it," she goes on. "I didn't feel I was depriving my child by going back. I loved the time we had together, but I was ready. I was very ready to return to work."

There will be vacations and weekends to spend with her children, but for much of each workday, Monday to Friday, Kerry's sons will be in someone else's care. This is a fact of her parenting life that she, like every other unpartnered mother who goes to work, has to accept and then figure out how to manage. Kerry's "other" job—the one motherhood enrolled her in—is to decide at each phase of her sons' lives who that someone else will be, and to find the money to pay for the high-quality substitute care she will always demand.

"I get a lot of help at the fringes."

When her children were babies, Kerry hired a nanny to stay at her home. Now that her younger son, Nathan, is going to day care, as he started to do when he was ten months old, Kerry no longer has live-in help. With the $250 she pays each week for her sons' child care, having an around-the-clock helper at home would strain her finances too much. But if Kerry had no help preparing meals or food shopping or bathing one child while the other is being read to each night, she wouldn't have the time she wants at home to be with her children. Instead of playing with her boys, she'd be consumed by the tasks that need to be done just to keep her household running.

Kerry devised a solution, a system that she can afford and that provides assistance at precisely the times she and her sons need it. As Kerry says: "I get a lot of help at the fringes."

Morning, noon, and night, but not in between, Kerry relies on different part-time workers to be at her house to help with what she calls "crunch" times—when she and the kids are getting ready each morning, when grocery shopping and meal preparation need to be done, and around dinner, when playtime, eating, more playtime, baths, reading, and bedtime take place over an extremely hectic two and a half hours. The best thing about Kerry's arrangement is that there has never been a day when none of the three women she hired has shown up for work. When one woman is sick, Kerry can easily adjust to her temporary absence. Knowing she won't have to scramble at the last minute to find a substitute—as she might need to do if she were relying on one person for everything—gives her an emotional boost.

Kerry's alarm goes off at 6:00. Her sons are still asleep. Kerry uses this time to shower and to prepare herself mentally to meet the day. At 6:30 her first part-time helper arrives. She lets herself in and starts work downstairs with the laundry, then prepares Adam's lunch and puts formula in Nathan's bottles. Then it's time for Kerry to wake up the boys. She helps her three-year-old decide what he wants to wear, while her helper diapers and feeds Nathan. When the boys go downstairs for breakfast, Kerry retreats to her bedroom to get dressed.

"It's not impossible," Kerry says of the few mornings when no one has been there to help. "But if I have an early meeting, it's a lot easier to move the boys along when I have an extra pair of hands."

"I have the luxury of spending extra money so I can have this time with my kids, because that's why I had the kids."

Kerry and her sons leave the house by eight. Her helper leaves a half-hour later, after she folds and distributes the laundry and cleans up from breakfast. Several days a week, a second woman arrives while Kerry is at work. Kerry leaves her a grocery list; the woman shops for and then cooks meals that she and the boys enjoy eating and that can be easily reheated. A big advantage of this arrangement—aside from all of the time and effort Kerry doesn't expend on food preparation in lieu of seeing her kids—is that the family eats lots of fresh fruit and vegetables. They never eat prepackaged meals. Nor are Kerry's sons becoming accustomed to the taste of nutritionless fast food, the kind of food many moms with little time to cook depend on.

Another unmarried mother with whom I spent time referred to dinnertime as "the arsenic hour." Tired after her day at work, she wants to spend time with her child, whom she hasn't seen all day. Dinner must somehow be prepared, but she hardly has time to get it under way because her son, tired and cranky after his long day away from home, demands her full attention. Time is spent on comforting hugs and playful companionship instead. Consequently she has no time to unwind from her day at work, nor can she retreat alone to her bedroom or talk with friends or family on the phone. No matter how busy her workday has been, she knows that when she and her son arrive home, her second shift—for which she needs to find lots of new energy—is just beginning.

To avoid this dinner-hour routine, Kerry hired a third helper to arrive at her house each workday about thirty minutes before she does. "I knew both boys would want something at the same time and I'd go nuts. So I said to myself, 'I don't have to either go nuts or feel incredibly frenzied.' " For this two-and-a-half-hour-a-day job, Kerry hired a college student, Cheryl, who arrives at 6:00 and stays until 8:30 each weeknight; by that time her sons have been bathed and read to, and are in bed.

"When we walk in, Cheryl is here, just like in the morning we leave home and Bonnie is here." While Kerry unloads the boys from their car seats, Cheryl is already warming their dinner. Kerry hands the boys over to her and heads upstairs to change out of her office clothes and into a baggy sweatsuit more suitable for playing with her boys. Having this time to unwind by herself lets Kerry make the emotional transition between her job as a scientist and her role as her boys' fully engaged mother.

"By the time I come down, the boys are already at the table and eating," she says. "This leaves us a lot of time for play, and that's very important. It is our playtime together that would disappear if I was just attending to all the household business that has to be done. I mean, I've done it on evenings when Cheryl couldn't be here, and what happens is there is very little time for us to just play. Despite the fact that both boys spend most of their day playing, they want this playtime with me. That is the way they like to unwind. So rather than plunking them down in front of the television set, it is a time for all of us to sort of get together." After Cheryl finishes clearing the table and doing the dishes, she joins them.

These hours together give Kerry's sons the kind of opportunity many children don't have to simply enjoy a parent's company. "I have more time for both kids than I would have as a working parent with a spouse," Kerry says, not to advocate single motherhood but simply as an observation about what she's come to view as an advantage that many of her married friends don't have. "If I had a husband I'd have to spend some time thinking about what I would be doing with him. And so I guess my sense is that all of these things compensate. No one could look at my children and fail to think that they were well adjusted. They are great kids. And some of that has to come from the way I deal with them and what I can give to them and the attention I pay to them."

Kerry redesigned her house with evening playtime in mind. The construction took several months, but the expense and inconvenience were worth it. Now, when the boys' dinner is over, they need only take a few steps and they are in a wide-open space with their toys and games. Kerry can eat her dinner while her sons play nearby. From across the room her older son peppers her with questions, which she answers between bites of dinner. She is never out of their sight. After she eats, Kerry joins in with whatever activities her sons have chosen, getting down on the floor with them as a sort of elder playmate. But—as their mother—Kerry can't resist punctuating her childlike participation with plenty of congratulatory clapping and words of encouragement.

When Kerry announces that it's time to go upstairs and get ready for bed, Adam offers little resistance despite the fun they're having. The reason: Kerry spends a lot of time gently reminding him, as the time draws near, of what to expect. When he asks for just one more round of a balloon-tossing game, Kerry, who has already calculated this request into her timing, is happy to agree.

During bath time, Cheryl sits with Adam as he plays in a tub occupied by more toys than water. Down the hall, Kerry rocks Nathan to sleep. When he is settled in his crib, she heads to the bathroom to relieve Cheryl, who goes home.

"Then I do bedtime stories," Kerry says. She and Adam spend a lot of time searching through his extensive library, selecting a bunch of books he wants his mother to read with him before he goes to sleep.

"I have the luxury of spending extra money to get peace of mind, and that's what I am doing," Kerry says. "It's also spending money so I can have this time with my kids, because that's why I had them. Otherwise, I would just be frazzled all the time. The important thing for me to remember is that the needs the boys and I have will be constantly changing. What works now isn't going to work when they are in elementary school. The arrangements I need to make will continue to change."

When both boys are asleep, Kerry heads to her own room to work or simply relax in her bed with a book or watch a television show. If she has the energy, she might return phone calls to friends or her parents or her brother; when she and the boys are playing, the phone is always answered by her machine. But her nightly quiet time does not last long: sleepiness quickly sets in. Kerry arranges her pillows and sets her alarm. Six o'clock will come soon.

"Do you feel like you have your family now?"

Kerry's financial situation not only enabled her to hire help and redesign her house but also made it possible for her to afford to have a second child. Most older unmarried mothers feel fortunate to be able to meet the expenses and time commitments required by one child. When the cost of substitute care, health insurance premiums, and clothes and toys and food are added up, many mothers conclude that neither their budgets nor their energies can be stretched to cover a second child.

Reaching this conclusion is one of the great disappointments these mothers talk about. Very few of the older, unmarried mothers I spoke with were only children. They wonder—and sometimes worry—about what it will be like for their son or daughter to be an only child *and* to have only one parent. Will their mother-child relationship grow too close and too emotionally dependent if there is no one else to serve as a buffer?

When Kerry was growing up, her brother was a very important person in her life. They remain extremely close. After she had Adam, Kerry thought long and hard about what it had meant to her to have a brother. She tried to imagine her life without him in it; she saw herself standing in the center of a big, empty circle and feeling very much alone. She didn't want Adam to feel that way. Even so, she hesitated to conceive another child on her own. She would be able to handle the added costs, but being a family of three would squeeze any cushion she had out of her income, and that felt scary. Friends also warned her that having a second child didn't "add to" the challenges of parenting—it multiplied them. Kerry questioned herself hard: Would she be able to manage all the demands of two children by herself? Did she want to?

"Initially I thought, 'Well, if someone comes along who wants to be involved with me and my son, then it would be nice to have another child with him,' " says Kerry; as she thought about having a second child she was reminded of how much she'd always wanted to share family-making with a man.

But two factors convinced her to go ahead on her own. One was her son's strongly expressed wish to have a sibling. Teachers at his child-care center told Kerry how much time Adam was spending with the infants, how he'd tenderly pat their heads and ask if he could help rock them to sleep. One day at home Adam announced to his mother that he was going to go on a trip and return with a baby for their family. "How are you going to do that?" Kerry asked. "I'm going to take a plane to New York and pick up a baby," he replied. When Kerry finally told Adam that she was pregnant and explained that soon he'd have a brother or sister, he was ecstatic. "Now we'll have a family," Adam said.

"Even though he would still like very much to have a daddy, somehow it does seem like having a brother is going to make things a bit easier for him," Kerry told me after Nathan was born.

The other factor, the one that finally convinced Kerry to go ahead, was her own mother's experience. Because Kerry's mother, Eleanor, is an only child, when *her* aged mother entered her final illness, Eleanor was the only one with a family responsibility to care for her. The great strain this put on her made Kerry think about Adam's future. She didn't want him to be burdened by the sole responsibility for her care, or to have no relatives when she was gone. And even though her health was excellent now, the fact that she was relatively old when she had him made her aware of how precarious her long-term well-being was.

When Adam was two, Kerry decided to try to have another baby using an anonymous donor. She used fertility drugs and within a few months she was pregnant. She was forty-three when Nathan was born.

"Do you feel as if you have your family now?" I ask Kerry soon after she returns from her second maternity leave. I'm intentionally echoing her son's declaration about finally having made a family.

Kerry laughs heartily and nods. "Yes. Yes. And Adam agrees, although he'd vote for more. He's sort of said to me, 'Mommy, when are we getting our girl baby?' "

"To which you reply . . ."

" 'I think we've stopped, honey,' " Kerry says. She laughs even louder. "He should feel lucky he got a brother."

I wonder, though, if Kerry is completely content with her family con-figuration, or if, like many of the older moms I've met, she still feels she wants a husband for herself, a dad for her sons. "How about you? Do you feel like you've completed a family? Or would you still like there to be a man as part of it?"

"Certainly I have completed my family in terms of children," she responds. "But, I mean, I could be sixty-five years old, or fifty, and I could meet a wonderful man and end up having a relationship that means some-thing to me. That is clearly not a time frame when I'd consider having kids, but there is no time limit to when I could meet a man. So I never abandon the idea. It may happen. And I think it would be wonderful for all of us if it did. But he'd have to be the right person."

"Have this 'right man's' qualifications changed since you've had children?"

Kerry chuckles. "Yes. There is no question it would take a special kind of person to be able to insert themselves into this. Sometimes I wonder if I've complicated finding a partner by having two children. There probably are men who'd tolerate one child who might not tolerate two, or who might feel intimidated by what seems like more of a family unit. But when I had all that construction done on my house, I had it designed so it could accommodate another person."

In the master bathroom, Kerry installed a second sink next to hers. For now it goes unused. It is a sink-in-waiting, a place being saved for a member of her family who has not yet arrived. "I have always felt that it would be more fun to share all this with a man than to not," Kerry explains. "And if someone comes along who can see his way through all this and wants to be part of this, I suspect I'll be open to it."

As our conversation continues, though, it becomes clear that Kerry does not actually believe that there's much chance she'll find someone to complete her ideal family. "With two kids, it would be very short-sighted of me not to have it more than enter my consciousness that something like that may never happen for me," she admits.

"So it's like your son says—for now, you have your family?"

"Right," Kerry says, her voice upbeat and definite.

A few moments later she remarks contemplatively that she's still amazed at having been able to create her family in this way. The path Kerry has traveled to purposeful unmarried motherhood is one that few would have imagined passable when she was born, four decades ago. Women now can make reproductive choices unavailable when she was growing up; unwed women can use medical assistance to conceive a child without having a partner. Women are encouraged to pursue professional careers, and they can earn salaries that enable them to support a family on their own. Because of these changes, as well as greater acceptance by society of women as breadwinner-mothers, women like Kerry have been able to define for themselves what it means to create a family.

"I mean, I passed along my family name," Kerry says, a look of amazement settling in her eyes. "That's not supposed to be something a girl could do."

"Since we don't have husbands, we are dealing with only two of the three competing demands."

In her Single Mothers by Choice newsletter column about the range of emotions these mothers experience about child care, Jessica Curtis also observed a tendency older unmarried mothers have to keep to themselves how difficult parenting on their own really is. Only in one another's company—one of the few situations in which they feel protected from the scornful "I told you so"s they know strangers are eager to heap on them—do these mothers air the complaints, worries, and frustrations that accompany this choice. It is in such settings, Curtis wrote, "that one is likely to hear a different story . . . stories about the emotional guilt that accompanies this new lifestyle. . . . Will our children resent us? What will they tell their shrinks when they are grown? What will they shout or whine at us when they get to be teenagers and are cataloging all of our faults?" Such questions are many, but their experiences are so new that answers are few.

At other moments, however, the tenor of conversation switches and mothers remind one another about what they regard as some advantages of parenting alone. "Married women must meet the demands of children, husband and job," Curtis wrote. "Since we don't have husbands, we are dealing with only two of the three competing demands. Perhaps we can do a better job at two enterprises, work and child, without the stress of a third relationship." This is a refrain heard often among unmarried older mothers—Kerry, for one, articulated it. The way many of these women look at their everyday lives, raising children by themselves can mean less household work and domestic annoyance and more emotional energy going to their children than would be the case if they had husbands.

Studies of what men and women generally expect from marital relationships seem to back up this perception. Men do tend to rely on their wives for emotional comfort and support, as many women say they can't rely on their husbands. Essayist Anne Taylor Fleming echoed this research when she observed that "married American men have the best mental health because their wives shield them from emotional distress." The energy women expend to support their partners sometimes amounts to more than they have to give, particularly when children also require their similar attention *and* when they are juggling responsibilities and relationships at work. And for these unmarried mothers—most of whom say they want to find a partner—the difficulty they have after they are mothers is finding the emotional energy (not to mention the free time) to pursue and enter a steady romantic relationship while they are working and raising a child.

Christina, a medical technician who is forty-two, unmarried, and the mother of six-year-old Nancy, discovered some of the downside of trying to bring a man into her family life. By the time her daughter was almost three, Christina was spending quite a bit of time with one particular man. Usually this meant that he participated in things she wanted to do with her daughter. At one point he convinced Christina to let him take over some of her household tasks. She had hired a nanny to be at her house when she went to work, but she herself handled the rest of what needed to be done around the house. "I remember Tim saying, 'Let me take your garbage to the dump. Let me mow your lawn,' and how reluctant I was to give up all those jobs I'd been doing," Christina says. "The only thing I hadn't done was clean the house. I had hired a young woman who came in and did that. But I mowed the lawn and I went to the dump. Whatever had to be done, I did it. But Tim was so insistent about wanting to help me, I finally agreed to let him."

For a year or so he performed these "husbandlike" jobs for Christina, even though he didn't live with her. She liked the fact that he seemed to enjoy contributing to her and her daughter's life in ways that came naturally for him. And it didn't take long for Christina, an energetic woman with a solid, athletic build, to grow accustomed to his help. She spent the extra time with her daughter. "It was great," she admits.

Other adjustments Christina had to make to fit this relationship into her parenting life were not as easy. One ongoing challenge that seemed to have no right resolution was how to balance her daughter's need for her as a mother with this man's desire for her attention and companionship. "When he'd be here for dinner, I felt like I had to cut my time short with my daughter upstairs and not spend the time doing all of her normal bedtime things like reading and talking, in order to take care of him," she explains. Her voice is, by now, packed with exasperation. "It's always the woman who gets pulled in ten different directions taking care of everyone." She shakes her head.

After nearly two years, the relationship ended. In the wake of the breakup, Christina was angry at herself for having let this man take over many of the responsibilities she had managed so well on her own before he came into her life. "When he walked out of our relationship, it was like 'Ooooooooo, how do I incorporate all of these jobs back in?' It was very difficult for me to do." Christina never did manage to rebuild into her schedule the time to do everything she once had. She guesses that perhaps she has more trouble fitting things in because her daughter is older, with different needs and desires. When she was younger, Christina would strap her in the car seat and take her wherever she had to go. Now that she is six, Nancy has definite opinions about what she wants to do; going with her mother to the recycling center is not high on her list. Nor is there naptime any longer, which used to be a time when Christina could sneak outside and mow her lawn.

"So I've learned how to delegate tasks," Christina says. "What makes it easier for me than for some single parents is not really having to worry financially. Having a secure job, I am able to hire people." She now pays a youngster in the neighborhood to mow her lawn. "It's not that I don't like to mow my lawn or clean the house," she says, "but there's only a certain amount of time each day, so you need to divvy up some of these jobs."

"I simply stopped expecting anything from him. Now I can't be disappointed."

When a single woman has a child on her own, she avoids the possibility of tension or anger surfacing with a partner about who does what and when. She knows that she is the only one responsible for seeing that everything gets done, all the time. And since there is no marital relationship that must realign itself to fit the new rhythms of family life, there is one less set of emotional expectations with which she must contend.

Satisfaction with marriage has been shown in some studies to decline among about half of all couples after a first child arrives. One study showed that, in two-earner couples, the more baby-related chores a father did, the more likely he was to become dissatisfied with the marriage and to say his love for his wife had diminished. Fathers who were their family's sole breadwinners tended to quarrel more frequently with their wives after they became parents, and their wives became more likely to find reasons to criticize them and argue with them. On the other hand, women with the most realistic expectations of her partner's involvement with child-rearing tasks were least dissatisfied with what they got—even if what they got was a husband who contributed little to the baby's care.

To some degree, the reasons for such patterns involve the differing self-images men and women develop of themselves when they become parents. Research shows that when a woman becomes a mother, her sense of herself as a wife and employee (or employer) tends to diminish. Men, however, tend to hold on even more tightly to images of themselves as workers and providers. These self-images can get in the way when it's time to reorganize the household with a child's care in mind. There are other reasons, as well, for the disappointments and disagreements some couples experience in dividing parenting responsibilities. Many women want to believe that work and family roles played by men and women have changed more than they actually have. But as Pennsylvania State University psychologist Jay Belsky, who researches parenting roles, once explained, "Our ideology has outpaced our practice by leaps and bounds."

A married friend once reminded me of what being realistic about a partner's participation actually means. After several years of trying to figure out ways to cope with her husband's erratic pattern of assistance—years when her feelings rotated among anger, annoyance, and frustration—she announced one day that her situation had been resolved.

"How did you fix it?" I asked.

"I simply stopped expecting anything from him," she declared. "Now I can't be disappointed."

Gloria Steinem, a leader of the modern women's movement, was reminded in a conversation with a top-level businessman of the chasm that still separates the promise of change from the reality of the status quo. This man could not give her enough compliments about the women's movement she'd helped to lead. He told her how impressed he was, in particular, with the extraordinary number of women who now held very good, well-paying jobs. As he said this, Steinem contemplated how few of these women, particularly the ones who were mothers, were likely to rise as high as he had. So she decided to ask him about the flip side of the progress he claimed to be so delighted about.

"Do you think that men are doing housework and raising children as much as women are?" she asked.

"My God, no," he replied, looking appalled. "Is that what you want? That will never happen."

"Women continue to do two to three times as much non-wage family labor as their husbands."

Raising a child alone doesn't seem that difficult to women after they take a close look at the lives many of their married friends lead. In terms of taking care of the children, they don't see much difference, especially when the husbands of their married friends travel a lot or work extremely long hours. In her book *The Second Shift*, University of California–Berkeley sociologist Arlie Hochschild pointed out how much is still expected of women in couples after they get home from their jobs. And the family tasks mothers are usually assigned are ones in which they are expected to respond to consistent and immediate needs (feeding children, cleaning up after them, responding to them), whereas the fathers' primary responsibilities (such as mowing the lawn or taking out the garbage) are ones he accommodates to his schedule. Nor do mothers get much credit for performing child-related or household duties; fathers, however, get all sorts of kudos when they undertake almost any aspect of child care.

Studies of actual family dynamics tell us that less has changed in the arena of domestic labor than images in the popular media would suggest. After examining how household labor is divided by occupants of four different kinds of households (first-marriage families, stepfamilies, divorced mothers, and never-married mothers), sociologists David H. Demo and Alan C. Acock reported discouraging findings—discouraging, that is, if in their role as mothers, women expect more. Demo and Acock note that "many women may be confused and distraught because of the contradictions between the images and messages in the popular culture that portray contemporary relationships as egalitarian and the burdensome, oppressive reality of their own lives."

Husbands, the data showed, produce about the same amount of additional work for wives as they perform for the household. The absence of a husband does not appear to significantly increase the time a mother in any kind of family grouping spends on household tasks. Across all family types and regardless of women's employment, "women continue . . . to do two to three times as much non-wage family labor as their husbands or partners." Their customary tasks also remain universally defined as "women's work," even when their male partners occasionally agree to "help." ("Help" is, of course, a word many mothers resent because it implies that certain tasks are basically theirs to perform and their husbands graciously agree to "help.")

Joseph Pleck, a family studies expert, finds in some of his research that women associate their level of marital and personal happiness with their partner's willingness to share in household labor. Men, he discovers, don't make similar associations. Demo and Acock speculate that many men—particularly those who are better educated—think of themselves as holding egalitarian beliefs, and are, in fact, doing more housework than their fathers did, so they have a difficult time understanding their partners' complaints. But, as Arlie Hochschild told a *People* magazine reporter, "the measure these men are comparing themselves with is the wrong measure. They should compare themselves with women."

Knowing—or at least sensing—that such disparities exist does not mean most unmarried mothers would not still prefer to have a partner. Most would. Despite their delight at becoming mothers, among themselves they talk openly about the loneliness of unpartnered family life. Many wish for the kind of household setup their happily married friends have. But if they had to choose between raising a child on their own or doing it with someone who wasn't willing to help, many would vote for doing it just the way they are—on their own.

"To have someone who you know is capable of helping and isn't—I would go out of my mind."

To hear Christina talk about parenting on her own is to be in the company of someone whose experience gives her increasing confidence in her ability to make it work. When I tell her this, Christina giggles, accepting the compliment while assuring me she didn't always feel this way. As we talk she stretches her lean body out across one of her living room sofas. Her legs, bedecked in colorful flowered leggings, dangle over one end of it. She props her head up on a pile of soft, matching pillows, and her sandy hair, gathered in a ragged ponytail, spreads out behind her. It is nine on a Friday night, and she is where she usually is at this time each week—at home, at ease, and glad to have this quiet, restful time to spend by herself. Her daughter is asleep upstairs. Only my presence disturbs Christina's routine.

Christina's mother came to stay with her for a few days after Nancy was born. Christina remembers the morning when she stood in her front yard with Nancy in her arms and watched her mother drive away: "There she was driving away in this huge station wagon. She was honking and waving at us and saying to me, ' 'Bye, honey. You'll do fine.' I stood there sobbing and thought, 'What have I done? What am I going to do?' "

What helped Christina most was becoming a member of a mothers' group. Most of the mothers she met with had been in birthing classes with her. When the babies got to be a few months old, they arranged play dates among the kids so they could find time to spend together. Over the years these play dates dwindled as each mother's schedule changed and became more crowded, but the women made a point of meeting once a month just to talk. Out of the eight mothers, Christina is the only unmarried one. The others, as she says, are part of "conventional relationships." She is also the only member of the original group who has not had another child. Even though her parenting life differs from theirs in many ways, there is still much about their experience of motherhood that provides common ground. The companionship of these mothers makes Christina feel less alone.

And, Christina tells me, she derives a measure of comfort about her situation from conversations the other mothers have about their parenting experiences. "They'll start moaning and groaning about how their husbands don't do anything, how they sit in front of the TV set like couch potatoes and don't help out and then moan and groan to them about something. These women will say to me, 'Oh, you're so lucky you don't have to deal with that.'" Christina chuckles, as though absorbing this observation anew. "Yet I see the other spectrum, too," she says, her tone of voice much subdued. "I see where they are going off and doing things like a little family unit." There are many times when she'd like it if she and her daughter had another person to do things with, as they did during those years when Christina's boyfriend, Tim, was a part of their lives.

Christina continues: "A lot of people ask me, 'How do you do it?' And I say to them, 'Well, what do I compare it to?' It's not like I did this for ten years with a spouse who helped me. The way I see it, if you don't have a supportive partner, then it would be one hundred times harder than what I am doing. To have someone who you know is capable of helping and isn't—I'd go out of my mind."

The absence of a "capable" partner in her family life is something Christina is very aware of. But it is also a topic she tries to avoid thinking about, since she does not believe that she's very likely to find such a relationship. Besides, on most Friday and Saturday evenings, like this one, she's just too tired to go out looking. "I probably should try to get out, but I don't have the energy. I go to bed. My head hits the pillow and I am out. I'm gone."

"So it's not as if you are kept awake at night wishing someone else was here?" I ask, half-jokingly.

"You mean, 'Where is that prince'?" she responds, with more than a hint of sarcasm. Her experience with Tim makes her wary of trying again. "I suppose it would be wonderful if you believe in the knight on the horse riding in who will say, 'Oh, where have you been all my life?' But the real thing is an awful lot of work. When Tim left, I was angry at him but I also thought, 'This is one less thing I have to deal with.' "

Christina also recognizes that just as she needs to do things for and with Nancy, she needs to do things for herself, too. Realizing this, however, is not the same as being able to fit these moments into her hectic schedule. "The times I do go out and do things with friends, it's so exhausting just trying to get everything ready, especially on a work night. I come home, get dinner ready, go out and get the sitter and bring her back and explain everything to her." When her evening activities are over, Christina still has to drive the baby-sitter home. Since she can't leave her daughter in the house by herself even for the five minutes it takes to get the baby-sitter home, she has to lift her out of bed and carry her into the car—and try to do this without waking her up. That rarely works. When Christina finally gets them back home, it can take a long while for her daughter to get back to sleep. By the time Christina gets herself to bed, her visit with friends seems but a distant memory, hardly worth the effort.

"Basically, I'm happy to stay home," Christina says. "I really don't need to be going anyplace."

"There's a lot of loneliness."

Women do not become mothers on their own without being aware at some level of the emotional trade-offs likely to follow. That awareness, however, rarely matches precisely with the feelings she experiences after her baby arrives. For some women, those whose loneliness has to do with not being a mother, having a child does soothe that feeling. But raising a child can start to feel lonely, too. A different kind of loneliness may begin to creep into a woman's parenting life.

Angela—the unmarried mother whom we saw applying for a scholarship for her boys—says she is "very conscious on a very regular basis about the absence of this man." It is not so much that she misses his presence in her day-to-day life. When she is busy and engaged in her daily routine of work and being with her children at home, she manages to bury thoughts about "this man" beneath the fullness and general contentment of her life. Awareness of what she and her children don't have, but that other families do, hits hardest when they are involved in activities in which mom-and-dad families usually participate. When she sees mothers and fathers and children together, comparisons with her situation surface and loneliness more easily sets in.

Angela experienced this feeling on a ski vacation with her children during the winter holidays. "We managed to have a lot of fun," she says, as though she is forcing herself to sound upbeat. What she remembers most about the vacation is that "it was me with two kids, getting them organized to ski, loading the car by myself, driving up there alone. I mean, there's a lot of loneliness." At the ski lodge where they stayed, nearly every other family had a mom *and* a dad. Seeing them gave Angela an inescapable point of comparison, reminding her—especially since this was the holiday season—of what she and her sons do not have.

She also told me about the time she took her children to Disney World. Surrounded by mom-and-pop families, Angela was struck again by how much she missed not having a partner to share these experiences with. "I kept thinking to myself, 'How do I make this fun?' "

Angela's feeling of aloneness, a feeling she has even when she is with the children she loves dearly, resembles what Sara Lewis, in her novel *Heart Conditions*, about an unmarried mother, called the "interior reality" of loneliness. This feeling is not the same as the painful emptiness Angela felt during those many years when she desperately wanted to have a baby. That aloneness is gone. Now, on certain occasions, Angela experiences a different loneliness, the kind that kicks in when she is reminded of the partner and family she does not have.

"What is hardest for me emotionally is the incredible responsibility of doing this on my own."

By the time an older single woman decides to have a child, the chances are good that she no longer lives near her parents. Even when she does, she usually has set up a household of her own. When Angela adopted her children, her parents and sibling lived some distance from the community in which she had rooted her adult life, so she could not routinely count on their help or company. She was truly on her own. The contribution Kerry's family makes to her parenting life is somewhat larger. Because her parents and her brother's family live nearby—and enjoy one another's company—they spend time together. It delights Kerry to watch her boys develop layers of close family relationships with their grandparents and cousins. Her sons have an especially tight bond with her father. He often takes them to a park where they spend hours just hanging out together. When Kerry and her sons go to a restaurant with her parents, her sons like to parade beside their grandfather, keeping several steps ahead of her and her mother. Since one of Kerry's concerns in having children on her own was the absence of a male in their life, she is delighted by their developing closeness to her father.

Even though older mothers usually lead very separate lives from their parents, becoming a mother often refreshes the bonds between them. Because they don't have a steady adult companion, unwed mothers sometimes rely on family members for support, guidance, and just plain bucking up when the solitary responsibility looms too large. "If my mother was not helping me out from time to time, I wouldn't be able to do it," says Bethany, a forty-two-year-old mother of twins whose outward composure conceals the tumult of her life. Each month her mother makes a car trip of several hours to stay with Bethany for a week or so. She cooks dinner for everyone, takes care of the dishes, and occupies one grandson while Bethany bathes the other. Bethany can't afford to hire someone to help out at night because so much of her salary pays for the woman who stays with her sons eight hours each day while she works as a teacher. Yet evening is when she is most depleted of energy. Her mother's visits make a substantial difference in moderating her accumulated exhaustion.

"Mostly my life feels like I'm on a careening roller coaster," Bethany says. "Every hour is filled, and I always feel like I'm racing to get everything done. I can't do anything for myself." She is constantly pushing all sorts of things to the side. Bills eventually get paid, but always late. Applications for professional courses she wants to take are set aside until long past the due date. Papers she needs for work get lost in the hectic shuffle between her office and home. Bethany can't remember when she last read a novel or finished a magazine or relaxed with a newspaper, things she enjoyed doing before she became a mother. "There's never anyone to take up the slack," she says.

One day I ask Bethany how she manages to make her family life work. She rolls her eyes and sits silently for a moment. "The reason I made a face was that I don't always feel that I make it work so well," she says. "And when I do, it is at great cost. It is really hard. There are times I feel overwhelmingly anxious. Or very depressed. Often, it's just because I'm tired. What I experience now as depression is not like what I felt before I had the kids. Then I felt I didn't have what I wanted in my life. Now it's more like, I take a breath and say, 'I can't keep doing this.' It's hard, it's that gut-level, bone-wrenching exhaustion when it's nine o'clock at night and I've worked all day, come home and bathed the boys and put them to bed. Then one screams for an hour, and I still have to pick up their toys. And somewhere in there I have to make my dinner and eat. There is no give. It is hard work. I don't know how else to put it."

When Bethany's mother visits and relieves her of some of these everyday tasks, it's a big help, but her mother's emotional presence means much more. "What is hardest for me emotionally is the incredible responsibility of doing this on my own and not having anyone to share it with in an ongoing way," Bethany tells me. "To have every decision be mine and just knowing these two little beings are completely dependent on me and I don't always feel so competent and so whole. Sometimes I do, but sometimes I feel like I need to be taken care of, too. I don't sit and think about it a lot, but there is something about the aloneness of responsibility."

This "aloneness of responsibility" is accentuated because no other adult is at home with Bethany on a regular basis. There is no adult at the end of the day with whom she can share news about the children. Friends are willing to listen for a while, but Bethany knows she can't expect them to care about her kids the way she does. She needs someone to talk with, a person who is as eager as she to hear about what's going on with her children. For now, this person is her mother. When she's not at Bethany's, they talk on the telephone twice a day, at eight A.M. and nine P.M. Bethany has always been close to her mother, but they never spoke so frequently until she became a mother too. Now, each morning at eight, Bethany is eager to share stories about what has transpired since she and the twins got up about two hours earlier; one morning, after one of her sons kept Bethany awake most of the night because he was teething, she needed to complain to someone who has an empathetic ear about how tired she was. Her mother is a good listener. And when her sons laugh at funny faces she makes, Bethany enjoys sharing those moments with her mother as well.

"It's like I am aware that my mother is someone who cares about my boys the way I do. It's the sharing of them with someone who loves them the way I do and will be interested in these little things about them," Bethany explains. "Talking with my mother fulfills a need I didn't have when it was just me. I think we talk so that I can share with her the responsibility and the pleasure of raising my children."

"Women around the country are groping for a new definition of the good mother."

The willingness of older, educated mothers—like Carol, Kerry, Bethany, and Christina—to undertake nonmarital childbirth and solo parenting fuels the roaring flames of an unceasing debate about what a mother's responsibilities are to her children and how she can best perform them. Can she be a "good mother" when her parenting life constantly faces the pressures of full-time employment, as it does for so many single mothers? Many people insist she can't, despite decades of evidence showing that maternal employment has few, if any, negative effects on children, especially when high-quality substitute care is provided. However, the evidence has a tough time competing with ideology when motherhood is the subject. This particular topic of motherhood remains a lightning rod for societal views about how women, in all aspects, should lead their lives.

When the task of defining a "good mother" is taken over by men—as it often is in public policy debates about how to curtail "illegitimacy," reform welfare, or subsidize child care with taxpayer dollars—threads of discontent with changes in women's lives weave their way in. Some men are angry about all that has been altered in their personal and professional lives as women gain more-equal status. In the minds of many, chief prerequisite for being a "good mother" is marriage, then a job that leaves the woman at home more than it takes her out (unless the mother is poor, in which case it's better for her to work outside the home as soon as she can). Such views about "good motherhood" are by no means confined to men, though men do seem more likely to vocalize them.

No matter what mothers do—whether they remain at home, work part-time, or choose or need to have full-time employment—they are made to feel as though they bear ultimate responsibility for how well or how poorly their children's lives turn out. It is within this complicated arena of feelings about themselves and their maternal responsibilities that mothers wrestle with decisions about how to arrange their lives. When a mother remains at home but longs to be at a job, her resentment is likely to surface and can negatively affect her child. If she returns to her job, and her child is unhappy when she picks him up at child care, she worries that her decision might be making his childhood miserable. Finding the proper balance can be especially difficult when a woman is also tugged by memories from her own childhood. In a 1992 *New York Times* story, "New Realities Fight Old Images of Mother," reporter Susan Chira explored some of these dilemmas. She observed that many women who are mothers today are to some degree trapped, as I felt I was, by their childhood images of TV motherhood—Harriet Nelson, June Cleaver, and Donna Reed—images it's often impossible for them to replicate. "Caught between a fictional ideal, changing expectations of women's roles and the reality that many mothers now work because they must, women around the country are groping for a new definition of the good mother," wrote Chira.

In a society as diverse as ours, it is unlikely we will arrive at any universal definition of what a woman's life should look like if she is to be a "good mother." Nor is there any one formula that can guarantee mothers an escape from worries such as "Am I doing the right thing for my child? If I do this, will I be a good mother?" A mother's assessment of how well she is raising her children seems destined always to be overlaid with her own second-guessing and societal judgments. For unmarried mothers, most of whom have no option but full-time employment, this jagged territory of self-judgment is vast.

"I believe there is an implicit judgment of single motherhood as being less than adequate."

In Sue Miller's popular novel *The Good Mother*, a newly divorced woman, Anna, is forced to obliterate aspects of her own life to prove her worthiness as her daughter Molly's mother. Even before events compel Anna to uproot her life so she can restore her maternal relationship with Molly, she has wondered how, now that she is divorced, she can be the kind of good mother she wants Molly to have. In an opening scene when Anna comforts her frightened daughter, she reveals her fears about her inadequacies as a single mother: "I sat hunched in the back seat with her in my arms until she was still, feeling only that I could not do this alone. I was not strong enough, good enough to do this alone, I could not do this."

Over time Anna finds within herself the strength, confidence, and ability to make her single-parenting life work. "It was good for Molly," Anna tells a psychiatrist, describing the life they'd built together. It is the psychiatrist's job to evaluate her mothering in light of what her former husband regards as inappropriate parenting resulting from Anna's relationship with a boyfriend and their daughter's proximity to him. "I know that," Anna tells the doctor confidently. "I was . . . I was busier. Less focused on her, but we were like a family. We had fun. I didn't fuss as much about her every little . . . You know."

"You relaxed your vigilance about her life," the psychiatrist replies.

"Yes. I just didn't spend as much time as I had right after the divorce, imagining her every feeling, worrying about her," Anna says. By creating what she believed was a healthy distance to give Molly room to grow, Anna believed, she was becoming a better mother.

However, when Anna's mothering is placed under the microscope of courtroom scrutiny, her ability to be a "good mother" is evaluated not in terms of the objective evidence she offers but against society's image of what a "good mother" is supposed to be. By this standard, Anna is judged a failure. The price of such justice is steep: Anna forfeits her right to Molly's custody.

Marsha, who is in her early forties, is an unmarried mother with a young son. She's never read *The Good Mother*, but, like many women of her generation, Marsha is familiar with its theme. She recalls that in the mid-1980s, when the book was popular, she avoided reading it. She didn't need to read a book to be reminded of such wrenching emotions and events in mothers' lives. Each day in her work as a counselor of disturbed children, she witnesses similar dynamics. Her work with these children and their families offers her plenty of insight into the hard grip the concept of the "good mother" has on all of us. Marsha remembers many occasions when she watched a mother absorb like a dry sponge the full blame for her child's condition, even though Marsha tried to explain the many other forces at work.

Marsha confronts such uncertainties about her own single motherhood as she tries to maintain her career, raise her son, and preserve aspects of her personal life as well. One morning as she and I are sipping herbal tea at her kitchen table, I mention the series of *New York Times* articles entitled "The Good Mother," of which the Susan Chira story was a part. This leads us into a discussion of the phrase, and in a few moments Marsha is describing to me how this affects her now that she is a single mother.

"Those words, 'the good mother,' say something about the vulnerability one feels doing the nontraditional family as a woman in a patriarchal society," Marsha begins. It surprises me to hear her speak of herself as feeling vulnerable. In my mind, her petite stature and delicate features have always stood in stark contrast to the strength of her forcefully voiced opinions. I'd thought of her as someone who would not allow the judgments of others to stand in her way. And she hasn't, at least not in her decision to go ahead with her donor-inseminated pregnancy. But Marsha seems to be revealing how concerned she is that she and her son, because of how their family was formed, will be exposed to quickly arrived-at judgments based on nothing but unsubstantiated assumptions.

"I believe there is an implicit judgment of single motherhood as being less than adequate," Marsha says. "I do a lot of consultations in schools and with parents and social service agencies, frequently at places in which kids are having trouble. And I hear all the time single mothers being talked about as the cause of the kids' distress."

"But haven't mothers of all kinds always been targets of blame when something goes wrong with their kids?"

"Right," Marsha responds, but in her intonation I can sense a lingering, "Yeah, but this is different . . ." waiting to come out. I urge her to go on. "There's an underlying belief that as a single mother you don't have financial resources. And, in fact, the vast majority of single mothers have fewer resources to provide for kids' needs. But people also assume you don't have a network of emotional support or you don't have the knowledge or energy to take care of your child properly." Marsha's voice conveys frustration. "So, yes, I think there's this kind of assumption about single motherhood, an assumption you are less than adequate, less than good, and that someone should step in and make sure you are being a good enough mother."

Marsha never liked it when she heard these assumptions being voiced about other single mothers. Now resentment of a more personal nature bubbles up inside her. She realizes similar judgments will be made about her and her ability to be a "good mother," for no other reason than that she is doing it without a husband. Though Marsha is not at all reluctant to admit she'd prefer to be raising her child within a good, solid marriage, that obviously can't happen with the anonymous donor who fathered her son. Besides, Marsha says, even if her son's father were with them, his presence would neither add to nor detract from her own ability to be a "good mother." As things are, she feels she's doing the best she can, and that, she believes, is "good enough."

"To do a good-enough job of parenting means being in touch with a child's developmental needs."

At a Sunday afternoon meeting of unmarried mothers and single women who are considering motherhood, Marsha discusses the concept of "good-enough" mothering, which she describes as a more realistic and healthy approach to parenting than the idea of a "good mother." These women had invited her to speak about the developmental needs of young children and how they, as single mothers, could be most responsive. After Marsha's presentation, the mother of a seven-year-old girl asked her guidance in sorting out the confusion she and other single mothers have about whether it's okay for them to hire a baby-sitter when they're *not* at work. "I think our confusion arises because most of us think we should be spending all of our 'free' time with our children," this mother told Marsha. "But is this healthy for us and for them?" Implicit in her question was, of course, her concern about whether she is being a "good mother" if she spends any time away from her child when she *could* be with her.

Marsha responds by explaining what it means, in psychological terms, to be a "good-enough" mother. One aspect of this includes the idea of creating environments for children of what Marsha refers to as "manage-able or tolerable frustration." As soon as Marsha mentions this, several mothers who have toddlers lean forward attentively. Marsha explains that when, as a mother, "you're always hovering over your child or always doing everything for her, as you did when she was an infant, you can thwart opportunities for discovering her own capacities. I mean we are talking about being good-enough but not being so perfect about meeting a child's every need that the child isn't being encouraged to develop herself."

To the evident relief of these women, Marsha urges them to set aside time for themselves occasionally, and to do so without punishing themselves for being "bad mothers." The maintenance of this delicate balance between self-care and child-care is, she tells them, essential. However, as Marsha observes, a child's needs can never be discounted as mothers figure out how to balance the competing demands of their solitary parenting lives.

Marsha is aware of the razor-thin boundaries between what various people believe constitutes good mothering and not-so-good mothering. As she attempts to keep herself on the more positive side of this line, Marsha draws comfort from academic knowledge she has acquired about child-rearing. Her experience and professional training remind her there is no single proven path to successful parenting. But there are essential components, each of which she makes certain her son receives. "To do a good-enough job of parenting means being in touch with a child's developmental needs," Marsha says. "No parent is a textbook, nor a parenting machine. But each is a human being who is in relationship with this other human being." It is, she says, "the closeness and certainty of that relationship that make a difference." Marsha, like many unwed mothers, may not be able to be with her son as often as some other mothers are to respond to every one of his needs, but a central part of her job as his mother is to be certain his needs are being met in safe, loving, developmentally appropriate environments when she can't be with him. It's a job she and the other older unwed mothers I spent time with take very seriously.

That afternoon, Marsha offered advice that applies to every mother's life. But she suspected that these unmarried mothers, in particular, were carrying in their minds "an idealized vision of what a mother is," a vision their circumstances would never allow them to live up to. Marsha advised these women to use this "idealized vision" to shape the broad contours of their parenting goals, but suggested they define their day-to-day situation in more practical terms. "Do a reality test with someone else whose situation is like yours," she told them. She urged them to compare notes with one another in striving to find a comfortable middle ground between what is most desirable and what is possible. "Then I think you need to forgive yourself for being a human being," Marsha said. "And you need to be resourceful enough so that if things aren't going the way you reasonably should expect, you can find external resources you need so you can feel more comfortable about your parenting."

At the meeting, as Marsha talked about this "idealized vision" of motherhood, I was reminded of a conversation she and I had had about a year and a half earlier, when she was a brand-new mother. That morning we sat on the screened-in porch of her house while she nursed her six-week-old son. Looking down at him as he lay against her, Marsha said she knew that even if their lives weren't "ideal," because she didn't have a partner and her son didn't have a father, she felt confident that they were going to be okay. "I feel very competent as a mom," Marsha said as she hoisted him to her cloth-covered shoulder for his burp. "I have lots of experience with young children and babies. I have a sense of what babies need and what they don't need. Like they don't need perfection from their mothers. . . . But I also feel like I have the same anxieties any new mother has in meeting her baby. It is an adventure. He is six weeks old tomorrow and I feel we've made a very good start. . . . Motherhood is less intimidating than I thought it might be. I had a notion I might not be well enough organized to take good care of a baby. But I found out I am very able to just say, 'Oh, well,' and deal with whatever needs to be done whenever things are not ideal. Like the day we moved into this house. On one trip I forgot to bring his diaper bag so I ended up making a diaper out of toilet paper and a clean rag. It was like, 'Oh, well!' "

"I felt really guilty about it. Not spending enough time with Peter—I mean, awake-time with him."

A mother's ability to do her job well depends largely on the circumstances of her daily life. Without reliable child care, her ability to earn a dependable income can be compromised. Finding such care—and then needing to find it again and again when a caregiver leaves or her job changes—is, without doubt, one of the emotionally toughest aspects of these women's lives. And when a woman spends all day at a job, is at home with her child in the evenings, and spends weekends making up for all that didn't happen during the week, it can be difficult for her to form the close, supportive connections she might long to have with neighbors or community groups. It's these relationships, however, that can help to break a mother's sense of isolation and offer her reassurance and help in moments when she has nowhere else to turn.

*　*　*

By the time Paula's son, Peter, was one and a half years old, he'd been with three different day care providers. It was not by Paula's choice that this happened. The first day care provider, whom Paula liked enormously, decided to quit taking care of children. After a few weeks of frantic searching for a replacement, Paula found one; she wasn't as satisfied with the new setup but it was the best she could find near where she worked.

"One thing about motherhood is you learn nothing ever stays stable," Paula said to me after this switch. "If you ever think you've got your whole world set up, one piece is going to cave in. Learn to enjoy the rare days when everything goes smoothly."

A few months later, after her son had adjusted to his new situation, Paula had to move him again. This time her company had relocated to a place that made the second child-care site impractical. By now, Paula had developed antennae that enabled her to tell almost instantly whether a place would work out for him. Her standards are high: She will not leave him at a place where he will watch a lot of television. And she wants the person taking care of him to be someone who has training in early childhood development, who can help him learn how to get along with other children. She was displeased that her son had to make so many transitions at such a young age. Each change, Paula said, "was a very anxiety-producing ritual" for both of them.

As Peter became older, his sleep patterns changed. He no longer liked to take a long afternoon nap, at least not when he was at day care. At the same time, Paula's work hours were increasing. By early evening, when she was able to pick him up, they were both exhausted, and Peter usually fell asleep in his car seat on the way home. Paula missed his playful chatter. This had been one of the fun times they had with each other every day. "We'd get home and I'd feed him and just put him into bed and then I'd work for two more hours," she says.

"Did you depend on those two hours at night as part of your workday?"

"Yes," Paula says. "And it was terrible. I hated it. I felt really guilty about it. Not spending enough time with Peter—I mean, awake-time with him. We had two hours in the morning and that was it. Then he was at day care the whole rest of the time."

Paula is telling me this as we sit in a park near her house. It is a weekday morning and Paula, small-waisted and slender, is wearing faded blue jeans and a colorful T-shirt. It is far from the tailored-suit look of her usual executive life, but, as Paula told me on the phone, her employer recently fired her. She was now collecting unemployment. When we arrived at the park Peter, who is now two years old and loaded with energy, bolted out of his stroller and began to dash madly from one piece of equipment to another. Paula had followed him around to be sure he was safe and to make sure he knew how to climb or swing or twirl. There is no need to share these big toys with other children. Even though it is a beautiful spring morning, we are the only ones here.

Nowadays Paula and Peter spend a lot of time visiting this park and going on other outings. It has been like this for the past few weeks, ever since Paula's boss called her into his office at the end of a workday to tell her, "I find it necessary to terminate your job." The announcement shocked Paula. After several minutes of awkward conversation, her mind focused on Peter, and she suddenly realized it was past time to pick him up. With the termination letter in her hand, Paula left. As she drove home, her emotions raced back and forth between shock and denial.

Within a few days her primary feeling was anger. A month earlier she'd put herself and her son through the anxiety-provoking switch in child care because of the company's move. She'd been given no indication then that she should consider a shift in her own employment. "I got really pissed off that they'd put me through all of this reorganizing of my life, finding new day care, dislodging my son, everything I did, for just three and a half weeks in this new location. I mean, couldn't you see this coming?" Paula says, addressing me as though I'm her boss.

At this point Peter interrupts his mom to tell her he's ready to try the big shiny slide on the opposite side of the playground. She lifts him out of the swing and follows close behind as he runs toward it. As he climbs the ladder, Paula makes certain he sets his feet squarely on each rung. Then she places herself at the base of the slide and assures her son that she's there to catch him when he comes down.

"It's really nice to be able to spend time with your kid. I mean, you go to all this trouble to have a kid."

Last week Paula's four weeks of severance pay ended. She is redoing her résumé and has already sent out job-inquiry letters. She also took her son out of day care, which was many miles away from their home and cost her $150 a week. Now she is looking for part-time child care so she can go on interviews. Right now, being away from work—angry though she remains at how her employer handed her release—feels better than she'd imagined it would. In fact, she tells me she is not in any rush to find a new job.

"To tell you the truth, I don't want to find a job tomorrow," she says, reaching into her backpack to produce the bag of grapes she packed for Peter. "For the first time, I am spending time with my son. And it's really nice to be able to spend time with your kid. I mean, you go to all this trouble to have a kid."

I reminded Paula of an earlier conversation, in which she told me how ready she'd felt to return to work after her ten-week maternity leave. She admits that, yes, she was relieved back then to be leaving Peter with someone else for much of the day. The caregiver was a woman in whom she had the utmost confidence. "Taking care of him was so much harder than going to work. I was exhausted," Paula had told me then. She tells me how different things are now, how much fun she's having with Peter now that he is walking and talking and trying new things instead of crying and sleeping most of the time.

"Especially since I was working so hard in the last few months, and I was only seeing him for like two hours a day," she says. The sadness in her voice connects me with a wellspring of unspoken feelings about how unsatisfactory aspects of this arrangement have been for her. "It was almost like I wasn't even bringing him up," she says. "So to have time with him now is fine. Financially I can stay not working for a few months before it will become an anxiety-provoking situation. Right now, I'm happy to spend time with him rather than be at work. But don't tell the folks at unemployment!" She winks.

In her ideal reemployment scenario, Paula will start a new job about six months after losing her old one. "I want to have the summer to play with my son, to get to know him. Maybe I'll do something part-time," she says. "That would be ideal."

"You've certainly had a lot of changes in your life in the past year or so," I say.

"Yeah." Paula positions herself to catch Peter, who is readying himself to slide again. "Three jobs. Three day-cares. One baby." She shakes her head as though she has a hard time believing all the experiences they have gone through in such a short time. I tell Paula how I've talked with several other mothers who, like her, collected unemployment after being laid off and how they, too, had exulted in the unexpected time off. They described it as being handed a gift. "Yeah, it really is a treasured time," Paula says. "I mean, your kid is little only once. Being unemployed is a very mixed blessing. You are mad and angry and unhappy and a little bit anxious about not having a job but, geez, if you're not going to have a job, when is a better time than when your kid is little?"

"Being the full-time, at-home mom was not ever something I saw myself being."

As we follow Peter on his romp around the playground, Paula talks eagerly about all the things she looks forward to doing with him this summer. There won't be any early-morning commutes or tired, cranky evening rides home. Instead, she imagines, they will take day trips to the beach or to the Boston Children's Museum and spend lazy afternoons walking by the Charles River. Paula is also happy that, for the first time, her son will have plenty of time just to be home and play with his toys.

When Paula and I get together about five months later, a few weeks after she has started her new job—right on her "ideal" schedule—she reports on her summer as an at-home mom. Peter, she thinks, had a wonderful time. But it proved very hard for Paula to adjust her self-image so that she could feel really good about being a full-time mother.

"First, I became aware of the sense of isolation you feel," she says. "Then there is this feeling of the loss of the contribution that all of those external forces make to forming your identity. Those things went away for me. I was no longer a worker. I was no longer part of a company. No longer did I define my role in life by what I was paid to do. I mean, that was gone, so my sense of my identity felt very threatened. I had to redefine that, so I'd be reminding myself, 'Okay, so you are temporarily out of work.' "

Being a full-time mother was a role Paula never expected to play, especially after she'd decided to take on the responsibility of unwed single motherhood. But, she says, even if she had a husband, full-time motherhood wouldn't likely be her choice of how to live. "Being the full-time, at-home mom wasn't ever something I saw myself being, even if I'd gone the American Dream route. Growing up, I saw my mom as being frustrated in that role, and I told myself I was never going to do that. But here I was in that cubbyhole. There was that component. And then there was this sense of isolation. I mean, when you are at a job you have all these built-in contacts. You're plugged in. You attend meetings. Now my time was completely, completely unstructured. The only thing that had to happen was to feed and diaper and play with my son. How was all this extra time going to be spent? It was terrifying. I felt really at sea. I wasn't used to structuring the day of a mom and a toddler. This was not something I'd practiced. It took me a good number of weeks to be able to say, 'Okay, this is the pace. This is the flow.' I guess I found out that I'm a person who needs structure."

Paula surprised herself by taking naps when Peter did. They revitalized her, just as they did him, providing fresh energy for the remaining hours of what turned into busy days. In fact by the time Paula returned to full-time work, she was so accustomed to having an afternoon snooze that she wondered how she would get through her day at the office without one. "It turns out sitting at a desk is a lot less exhausting than taking care of a toddler," Paula says, laughing as much at her rediscovery of this as at her early bewilderment at how she'd fill the day at home. Now she regards both of these things as reminders of how little actual experience she'd had as an active parent during the time when she was employed.

I ask Paula to speculate on how making these adjustments might have been different for her if she were married. "Well, in our case there wasn't another person's life that we had to incorporate into our schedule. It was really a clean slate for me to decide what our life was going to be like," Paula replies. She pauses for a moment to reflect. "It wasn't like two-thirds of a triangle had collapsed and there was this one-third that remained pinned in place." She makes a V with her hands and collapses it to show me what she means. "If you think of two points as defining a line, well, my son and I, we are going to define our line. We didn't have to worry about a third point still being on our plane," Paula explains. "So I guess it was almost in some sense easier."

As soon as this word, "easier," escapes, Paula pauses, just long enough to catch her breath. Like almost everything about life as an unmarried mother, when one part of it gets easier, another part is almost sure to be more difficult. "The negative side of this story is that there wasn't any relief from parenting. I mean, this is what every single mother faces. I would spend the entire day with my son and, by the end of it, I would have seen no one else. He'd been my sole focus and he would remain my sole focus until eight-thirty each night when I'd finally get him to sleep. There is nobody arriving home to say, 'Okay, you're off duty for a while.' "

"Two people who are married are expected to do it all on their own. But nobody expects me to do it all."

Asking for help was an important lesson Paula learned during her summer of full-time motherhood. But it wasn't easy. Like other women I spent time with, Paula entered motherhood with the belief that since it was her choice to have a child alone, it was also her job to make it work without help from anyone else.

When I hear Paula describe this attitude, the words of another unmarried mother arrive back inside my head. At the age of forty-three, this woman had adopted an infant daughter. In describing the attitude she thought mothers like her had, this woman told me, "We are not even people who should be asking for help because we have made this step on our own." That comment led us into a broader discussion of how Americans seem to want to extend their national ethos of individual responsibility to families, expecting each family to raise children as a self-reliant unit. "I know I buy into that idea," the woman told me. "I do it all the time. Every day I act like that. I find it very alienating. I don't like it." This mother admitted that on more than one occasion she'd felt herself bump up against the American myth of total self-reliance. Instead of reaching out when she needed to, this mother refrained from asking others for help and tried to manage on her own because she believed others thought she should.

Many unmarried mothers learn out of necessity—as this adoptive mother eventually did—how to ask for help. Often they discover that by involving others they not only ease anxiety about their ability to be a "good-enough" mother, but create welcomed layers of adult companionship for themselves. And being on their own sometimes makes it easier to ask for help.

One fortyish, unmarried mother of a two-year-old boy explained this to me when we had lunch one day in a coffee shop near where she works: "I look at women who have children, any woman who has a child, and I think, we are all in the same boat. I mean, a lot of people say I am really brave to be doing this by myself, but I don't believe that. I believe I'm doing the best I can. Just because you aren't married does not mean it is easier or harder. In this society two people who are married are expected to do it all on their own. But nobody expects me to do it all. I can call people and say, 'I'm not feeling well. I really need help. Can you help me?' If I was married and I did that, people would think I was really weird. They would say—or, at least, they'd be thinking—'What's the matter with your husband or your partner? Why can't he do it?' "

Becoming a single mother and learning how to ask for help—and give it to others—helped improve this mother's relationships with her friends. "I used to think of myself as a very selfish person. I was like, 'Don't ask me to do that.' But either I really misunderstood myself, or other people are much friendlier," she says. "Being a mother has really taught me something. Now whenever I meet people who have young children I say, 'Here's my phone number. Call me if you need to talk about anything or I can help you.' It doesn't bother me if someone calls and says, 'My child was up all night. Can you come over and play with us so I don't have to be the only adult here?' I understand."

"It's okay. I want you to be able to think of me as your backup. You're doing this alone."

Paula missed having adult companionship during her stint of unemployment. She didn't know how to bring such company into her life without sacrificing too much of the precious time she had right now to be with Peter. She didn't feel comfortable about getting him a baby-sitter just so she could spend time with another adult. Besides, most of her friends were at their jobs. And because she'd been a commuter, Paula knew very few people in her neighborhood. "All we did was sleep here," she says, referring to their town house. In the evening, when she was home, parents were occupied in feeding and bathing their youngsters and putting them to bed. As for Peter's friends, they were children he played with at day care, so she hadn't met other parents in the neighborhood through him.

One day when Paula and Peter went for a walk, a solution presented itself. She struck up a conversation with a mother who told her about a group of neighborhood women who got together often and talked while their toddlers played. She invited Paula to join them. This seemed perfect: Paula would get the adult company she wanted, and her son might find new and nearby playmates. From then on, she became a regular member of the group.

Spending time with these mothers made Paula realize how isolated she'd been from the local networks of support that mothers create for themselves. These were precisely the kind of connections Paula had wished for when she was employed but had never made. As she thought back and wondered why she hadn't, Paula remembered that, apart from her time constraints and her commute, she'd felt, a bit stubbornly, that she alone had to make her family situation work. It never occurred to her to seek out mothers who were married as sources of help and friendship.

When she got to know the local mothers, and they her, Paula discovered to her delight how wrong she'd been to think this way. After the summer, their relationships remain strong even though she is back at a full-time job. Paula now realizes how valuable it is for her, as a single mother, to have a reliable network of support and friendship within her community. Her new job is within walking distance of their home, and Peter's child care is nearby as well, so if an emergency arises, Paula no longer needs to feel totally on her own in responding to it.

During Paula's second week back at work, her new connections got an early test. One afternoon she received a phone call from one of Peter's caregivers: her son had a fever and had to go home. Paula left work immediately to pick him up. Because her son had to be fever-free for twenty-four hours before he could return to child care, he'd need to stay home the next day. But Paula had an important meeting at her new job, one she couldn't miss.

Between 4:30 and 8:30, as Peter slept, Paula made phone calls to her neighborhood friends. At first, she felt a bit reluctant to ask for help, in spite of the closeness they'd developed. She realized that mothers who stay at home with their children are said to resent being asked to do things for those who go to a job; they may feel that a mother who "chooses" to go to work ought not to turn to those who don't to take up the slack in caring for her children. But Paula remembered being pleasantly surprised when one mother urged her to call if she needed help now that she had a new job. "It's okay," she told Paula. "I want you to be able to think of me as your backup. You are doing this alone and I know you have to be an example to others." Her encouragement and offer of help touched Paula deeply. "She was expressing admiration, but at the same time she had this sense of empathy for what I am up against," Paula tells me. "It is really great to know people are so generous." Paula thinks that the lack of resentment from these at-home mothers arises partly from the fact that she is a single mother, who has no choice but to earn her family's income.

By the time Paula went to sleep that evening she knew her son would be well cared for the next day. The other mothers had woven together a baby-sitting schedule, so that Peter would always be in the care of a woman he knew. Paula would reciprocate by inviting their children to her house for dinner so the women could enjoy an evening to themselves or have dinner alone with their husband. This reciprocal arrangement worked out well for everyone: when Peter has a friend over for dinner, Paula is relieved of her job of playing with him. She can cook dinner with fewer interruptions.

"Peter and I have become so much more connected to the neighborhood," Paula tells me. "Now I know what the neighborhood resources are. And I know the people who live on this block and on that block, something I never knew before in the five years I have lived here. Never knew anybody!"

Now that Paula does know people, it's hard for her to believe she ever considered trying to parent without establishing these personal connections. That they are essential was underscored for her when she took a trip with Peter to visit some married friends. Their house is at the end of a woodsy road, in a suburban cul-de-sac they share with three other families. In all, the couples have ten school-age youngsters. "There is always somebody watching out for each other's kids," Paula says, envy creeping into her voice. It is not, she says, each family's arrangement of a husband, wife, and kids, but rather the mutually bolstered caregiving, that most impresses her. "There is such a free-flowing exchange of toys and clothes and care and concern that they don't even remember any longer whose toys belong to whom. Everything is like this big communal pot. It was just so amazing for me to see. And so wonderful! There is not enough of that around anymore. My romantic notion says to me it used to exist more in the olden days. But I don't know if it did or not." This is the kind of child-rearing environment, Paula declares, "I aspire to being a part of."

"There is so much more uniting us than distinguishing us."

Her summer as a neighborhood mom took Paula at least partway toward this goal of creating an urban version of the life she'd seen at her friends'. Befriending the neighborhood's stay-at-home mothers eased any discomfort Paula had thought might exist because of their different choices about employment. "There is so much more uniting us than distinguishing us," she says. "I mean, me as a mom relative to them, well, we have much more in common. There was one mother, in particular, whose husband travels all the time. Her life was my life for the summer. Totally. Everything was the same. She had the full twenty-four-hour responsibility."

What separates Paula from this mother is less the daily routine of their mothering lives than the image each has of herself. "I had a real clear image that I'd be back at work and this was temporary for me," Paula says. "For the woman whose husband traveled, this was going to be her life for quite a while, because she thinks it is really important to stay home with her child during these formative years and her husband's income allows her to do so. It pains me even to say this to you because I have an element of that belief, too, and it is sad for me to think I am not doing that. But on the other hand"—her voice suddenly sounds upbeat—"I did get to do it for five months. And it was a treat."

"It must help you be able to push your pain and guilt aside, knowing you don't have a choice."

"Yeah, I can," she replies. "And I remind myself that there are going to be lots of important times for me to spend with Peter, but right now I was lucky enough to be offered a very well-paying job. It's important for me to earn money this year, particularly because I didn't earn any during the past five months. Now I'll be able to save a lot and I'm getting great health-care benefits. I'm doing the breadwinner stuff for us right now. That is my emphasis now, as opposed to mommying. As I did with this summer, I am now viewing this job as a chapter, not as a permanent condition."

7

Where's Daddy? Unmarried Adolescent Mothers

Morena's seven-year-old daughter, Kendra, knew that Steve, a man her mother had been dating for several years, was not her father. That didn't stop her from wanting him to be her daddy. Morena remembers how Kendra would rush to the door to greet Steve when he came to their house.

"Daddy! Daddy! Daddy!" she would cry. "Come and see what I did in school."

Steve barely had a chance to take off his coat before Kendra lined up her drawings on the floor. She'd stand next to him, shy and eager, awaiting his encouraging words. On a few afternoons, when their schedules permitted, Morena and Steve would meet Kendra at her school bus. When Kendra saw Steve she'd skip down the steps of the bus with an extra bounce, and always with the same request. "Daddy," she'd say, her voice ringing with pride, "show Tommy your muscles." Kendra loved these opportunities to show off her "daddy" in front of her cousin, Tommy, especially since it was Tommy's father who usually picked them up.

But one day, something important changed in Kendra's happy relationship with her "daddy." It wasn't because Steve vanished from Kendra's life or from Morena's, although, in some ways, it might have been easier if he had. Instead, during an especially rough spot in his relationship with Morena, Steve declared that he no longer wanted Kendra to refer to him as Daddy. "I am not her father," he told Morena. "Tell her to stop calling me Daddy." He insisted that Kendra call him by his name. It was her job, he ordered Morena, to let Kendra know about this change.

Steve's command stung Morena deeply. That night she lay across her bed and wept—not so much for herself, she says, as for her children, who clearly enjoyed having a "daddy" even if he didn't live with them all of the time. Morena recalled how hurt Kendra had been when friends in preschool teased her because she didn't have a daddy. "I'd tell her to let them know it wasn't that she didn't have a daddy but that her daddy just isn't with her mommy," Morena tells me. But that reasoning must not have been enough to satisfy Kendra. Being teased hurt, but so did not having a father to spend time with. "I guess through all of this, and with Steve around, Kendra figured it was okay for her to call him Daddy," Morena says.

Morena wasn't there the first time Kendra called Steve Daddy. However, she remembers the evening when Steve told her about it, and how proud playing a fatherly role seemed to make him feel. Now, suddenly, he wanted the practice to end. "You never mentioned anything to me about not liking it," Morena reminded Steve. "We are in a relationship. If you had problems with it, you could have said something to me. I mean, why would you let it go on so long, and then all of a sudden be like, 'Oh, I should have stopped it from the beginning'?"

Morena had never seen or heard anything to indicate that Steve wasn't enjoying himself in the role Kendra gave him. "He never once said anything to me like, 'Hey, I'm not those kids' father. I don't think she should be calling me Daddy,' " Morena explains. "And he always responded to Kendra when she called him by that name."

From the beginning of their relationship, too, Morena made it clear to Steve that even though she was single, she wasn't unattached. "I come with two kids," she'd say to him, to emphasize not just the obligations that attachment entails but her emotional connections as well. "If you can't accept this, you let me know, because I cannot give up my kids for you or anyone else. It's a total package: Morena, Kendra, Daniel." Now, three years into their relationship, Morena was astonished by Steve's demand.

As Morena lay on her bed crying, she didn't want to wake her children, who were asleep in a nearby room. If Morena screamed the explosive anger she felt inside, then surely Kendra and Daniel would hear. So she contained her rage, repeating again and again words about the betrayal she felt. It was problems between her and Steve that sparked this; why couldn't he leave the children out of it, she wanted to know. "If you want to hurt me, hurt me," she kept repeating plaintively to herself. Tears kept coming, too. "Hurt me. Hurt me," she pleaded, pretending Steve was there to say this to. The internal conversation went on most of the night. "Why my kids? What did they ever do to you?" she asked herself. "They never did anything to you but show you love."

Now, pausing only long enough to take a breath, Morena breaks off her remembrance of that awful, restless night and speaks directly to me. "My kids, Melissa, they'll tell you in a minute they love this man." Morena's voice breaks as she strains to find some way to make sense of why this has happened and what its impact on her children has been. "My daughter, that was the biggest thing for her, to have a daddy and especially her daddy who had such muscles and he was a policeman, too. That was something that made her feel like she was on the top of the world." Morena's tone of voice lifts momentarily, only to tumble again. "When he took that away from her, oh man, Melissa." There is such sadness in Morena's eyes. "Oh, I mean, it was like I don't believe this."

"I'm not really a daddy. I'm Mommy. How can I be two people at one time?"

Kendra rarely sees her birth father. He and Morena never married, though they lived together for a while after Kendra was born. Amid the strain of trying to be parents, their relationship collapsed. Morena especially resented his family's expectation that she not only care for her child and her child's father, but also clean up after and care for his many brothers as well. By the time she discovered she was pregnant with Daniel, Morena knew that she would not marry this man. Their attraction to each other had, by then, evaporated. Marriage, she believed, would only have exacerbated the numerous problems that living together had brought to the surface.

Her children's father lives on the Caribbean island where Morena's family originally came from. Since she moved back to the United States with Kendra and Daniel, he's never come to visit; he doesn't send money, and he rarely telephones his children. Daniel has never lived with him, so unlike Kendra, he has no memories at all of the man who is his father. Sometimes, when they'd go to the island during the summer to visit family members, Kendra would see her father. But these infrequent, casual visits with a man she didn't really know weren't enough to make her think of him as her "daddy." She yearned to feel attached to a daddy who was present in her daily life.

"When I had to tell Kendra what Steve said, it broke my heart," Morena says, averting her eyes and staring at the red checkered cloth on her mother's kitchen table. She fingers the tiny gold cross she wears, then wraps her arms around herself and squeezes tightly. The gesture reminds me of how alone Morena feels in coping with her daughter's pain. Hardest for Morena were Kendra's questions.

"Kendra was like, 'Mommy, why? Doesn't he love me anymore? I thought he loved me, so I thought I could call him Daddy. Doesn't he want us anymore? Doesn't he want to be my Daddy anymore?'" Morena assured Kendra that Steve still loved her; she tried to explain that his decision had more to do with herself than with Kendra. Then Kendra asked, "Mommy, who is going to be my daddy?"

"Kendra, you know what? You've got Mommy and Daddy right here," Morena replied, trying to sound as upbeat as she could. "If you want to call me Daddy, you go ahead. I'll answer you. I'll be your daddy."

"But you're not a man," her daughter replied.

"That's okay. I can still be your daddy. I'm being your mommy. Right?"

"Yeah," Kendra said, puzzled by what her mother was trying to get her to understand.

"Well, if you want me to be your daddy," Morena insisted, "I'll be your daddy, too."

Even as she spoke, Morena knew her remedy wasn't going to assuage Kendra's longing for what she did not have. But at that moment she didn't know what else to say or do.

The idea of Morena becoming her daddy never did catch on with Kendra, though she did teach herself not to call Steve Daddy. Every so often, however, she asks her mother if Steve still loves them, and she lets Morena know she still wants somebody whom she can call Daddy. "It's hard because you want to give them something they can hold on to, a daddy who is going to be there," Morena says. "But then there is no one there for them because there's nobody here for you."

I ask Morena if, when she tried to have Kendra pretend she was her daddy, too, she believed her parental love, by itself, could be enough for Kendra to overcome her longing for a "daddy."

The still-sad look in her eyes lets me know that my question is already on her mind. For a moment Morena is pensive, as if trying to reconnect with how she felt before this happened. It seems to her like another lifetime. As she begins to speak Morena nods, as though to try to convince herself that she'd believed this. "I did think I'd be able to overcome it. But now I can honestly say that anyone who is a single parent, they have either gone through this or they are going to find out that they cannot be both Mommy and Daddy because these kids are going to want Daddy somewhere in their lives. Like me telling Kendra to call me Daddy. I mean, that might satisfy her for a little while, but I'm not really a daddy. I'm Mommy. How can I be two people at one time? In a sense, though, I'm doing that. During the week, I have to be like a father. I have to provide. I have to make sure they are set. Then come Saturday morning, I have to change over and be their mother, because I am here all day with them. So I just have to be able to switch myself to and fro. But to Kendra, it is not the same. She wants a daddy who can say, 'Come on everybody. Let's get in the car and go for ice cream.' "

"There's a fat man down here who keeps telling me he's my daddy and I keep telling him no."

After Kendra told her mother about being sexually molested, Morena made the tough decision to send her and her brother to live with her god-mother, who lives on the Caribbean island the family's from. Because Morena was determined to finish her nursing degree, something she would have had to set aside if she moved to the island, too, she decided to stay in the United States. She planned to concentrate on finding a new place for them to live, then bring her children back as soon as she could.

Living with her godmother, Morena realized, Kendra and Daniel would be near where their father, Anthony, lives. They were bound to see him; in fact, she knew he'd want to spend time with them. During the several weeks Morena spent with her children at her godmother's, she eased them into accepting their temporary new home and talked with them about their father. In particular, she wanted Daniel to talk with her about the man who'd made him cry during a previous summer visit, the man whom Daniel, when he was younger, called the fat man, the man who is his father.

"How did your son respond?" I ask Morena.

"He told me, 'No, Mommy. He is not my daddy. He's not my daddy. If he was my daddy, how come he wasn't with me when I was a baby? How come he never called me?' "

Morena wanted to give Daniel answers he could understand, but explaining to such a young child why everything is the way it is was diffi-cult. "I mean, Steve was still with us," Morena says. "He'd go on trips with us. He never said anything bad about the kids. He never showed them in any fashion that he didn't like them. I think that is what Daniel was clinging on to. How should I say it? The portrait Steve painted for Daniel as far as being there. I think Daniel values that and sees that as being

'Daddy.' " Morena struggled to find words to explain to Daniel why a man who never acted like a daddy was actually his father. And it was impossible for her to forget how angry her son had been the previous summer, when he unexpectedly saw his father and spent some very unpleasant moments with him.

Morena found out about this encounter from Daniel himself; he called her right after it happened. Just the way Daniel said "Ma" let Morena know he had something on his mind that he very much needed to talk about.

"What? What is it?"

"Ma. There's a fat man down here who keeps telling me he's my daddy and I keep telling him no," Daniel told her. "I keep saying Steve, he's my daddy. But he says no."

While her son talked, Morena was asking herself: "Oh, God, what am I going to do? How can I explain this to Daniel? What am I going to tell him?"

By now her son was pleading with her to help: "Mommy. You just call him up. Tell him to stop telling me he's my daddy. He's not, and I don't like him."

Morena promised Daniel that she would telephone the man.

Immediately after she and Daniel hung up, she called her cousin, who lives next door to Anthony. The cousin was able to give Morena details about Daniel's unexpected encounter with his father. Kendra and Daniel had come to her house for a weekend visit at a time when Anthony was supposed to be away. But it turned out he wasn't. Kendra and Daniel were playing with some neighborhood children on her porch, when she heard Kendra yelling, "Daddy, Daddy, Daddy!" When Morena's cousin came outside, she found Daniel and his father engaged in a loud volley of words.

"No. You're not my daddy," Daniel was shouting. "I don't know you. How can you be my daddy? My mommy doesn't even know you."

By that time Kendra was also involved, shouting at her brother, "That *is* your daddy. He is your daddy!"

"No he isn't!" Daniel yelled back. "No! My daddy's a policeman. My daddy's got muscles. My daddy isn't fat like you. I don't know you."

Now Daniel was crying, but his father kept trying to convince him. "Yes, I am your daddy," he insisted. "I am your daddy."

At this point Morena's cousin intervened, taking Daniel in her arms and carrying him inside.

As her cousin described what had happened, Morena started to boil inside. When she hung up, she paced the corridor of her mother's apartment, smoked a few cigarettes, drank a strong cup of coffee, then dialed

the number she had for her children's father. It was the call she promised
her son she'd make.

"You absolutely amaze me," Morena told Anthony the moment he
answered the phone. "I mean, you are going on thirty years old. How are
you going to argue with a three-year-old about who's his father? Does he
even know you? Did you even take the time to be his friend before you try
to force it down his throat that you are his father? No. You just come up
to the kid, he's never seen you, and you just start telling him that you're
his daddy."

She paused only long enough to sip her coffee.

"This poor kid," she continued. "You probably got him so confused."

"So what?" she tells me he replied. "So what? He's my child and he's
going to know he's my child."

As she reenacts their conversation, Morena's anger surges again, along
with resentment at how insubstantial Anthony's efforts at being a father
have been. Recounting the conversation to me, Morena spits fire.

"I'll tell you something," she told him. "You're 'Daddy' biologically and
biologically alone. Other than that you've never ever done anything for
him. You've never been up nights when he was sick and throwing up and
having to take him to the hospital when you found out he had asthma. I
mean you were never around. You never even changed a Pamper on him.
You are not his father."

From where Morena sits, such moments are the ones that transform a
person who creates a child into one who is a *parent*. To her, the fact that
Anthony wasn't around for any of them—didn't even bother to ask about
them—disqualifies him from claiming that he is her children's "daddy."
Even when they were living together, taking care of baby Kendra was
something he expected Morena to do. In fact, that rigid view of her caretaking role was one of the things that drove them apart. One thing
Morena didn't mention in her dressing-down of Anthony was the fact that
he'd never helped to support his children after he and Morena split up.
The reason she didn't mention it is that she is less concerned about his
failure to provide money than about his long-standing lack of concern
about his children's well-being. Now, suddenly, he wanted his son to call
him "Daddy."

Morena and Anthony argued back and forth, circling in predictable
patterns. Finally, exhausted by the pointless exchange of recriminations,
Morena brought the conversation to an end by issuing an ultimatum: "If I
find out you are telling Daniel this one more time, I will pull the mat out
from under your feet," she warned him. "I have the authority to bring my
kids back home anytime I please, so please leave them alone." And
Anthony did not try to convince Daniel of his paternity again.

After Daniel returned home, he occasionally asked Morena about the "fat man." "Mommy," he'd say, "I don't think that fat man is my father."

"Well, one day when you are older and you can really understand, Mommy will explain things to you," Morena would reply.

"The fat man is being nice. He doesn't ask me to call him Daddy anymore."

When Morena was making arrangements to move her kids to the island, she talked with their grandmother about Anthony's behavior with Daniel. Morena's biggest worry was that, with Daniel older and living nearby, his father would again try to "push himself on his son."

"I told his mother, 'You have to understand that he hasn't been around, and Daniel isn't going to realize he is his father,' " she tells me. Anthony's mother, Morena learned, shared her concern. "She didn't like the way he was forcing himself on Daniel that summer, either." She told Morena she'd already spoken to him about it and set down rules for how things had to be: "I will stop you from coming to the house if when this child comes here you continue to do that." She assured Morena that he had agreed to change his ways. "She is the type of woman who is firm-fisted," Morena says, so their conversation gave her reason to believe that someone who shared her perspective would be keeping an eye on the situation.

Because Morena's godmother and her husband both had full-time jobs, they couldn't be home when Kendra and Daniel got out of school. Anthony agreed to pick them up and keep them at his house until Morena's godmother was finished with work.

"How does this arrangement sit with your son?" I ask. "Have you resolved some of his questions?"

"Well, we did. And then again, we didn't. I mean, how should I say it? My son is now five years old. Because he really didn't know his father, he still believes Steve is his father. But this man, his father, is somebody who likes him and wants to help him out. He still doesn't call him Daddy. Now he calls Anthony by his name. I don't think he can really accept him as Daddy. But at least his father doesn't push the issue anymore. They are developing a close relationship."

Morena describes her most recent phone conversation with Daniel: "The fat man is being nice to me," Daniel told her. "He doesn't ask me to call him Daddy anymore."

"How do you feel about that?" Morena asked him.

"I like that," Daniel said. "But I don't think he is my real daddy."

Morena says her life feels empty without her children in it, but she is comforted by knowing how well they are doing. And in moments when she can let go of her own disappointment at the man with whom she had her children, she is happy that they are getting to know him and that things seem to be working out: "It makes me feel good that my son feels comfortable with him now. That he doesn't feel pressured and pushed. Daniel tells me that maybe in the future he will start to call him Daddy, which is what his father really wants. For me, I could care less, because to me their father plays. This is what Anthony does. He plays Daddy when he has the children, but once they are away from him he forgets he has them."

"Do I have a daddy? Who is my daddy?"

Millions of children in America grow up without knowing anyone as "Daddy." Others have a "daddy" who once lived with them, but whom they no longer see. Still others find someone they'd like to be their "daddy," only to have him disappear from a parent's life, and therefore from their own. Kendra and Daniel came to love Steve as a "daddy," but various circumstances pulled their relationship apart, then placed them in a new environment to try to build another. Each of these situations—and others in which children experience either the absence or loss of their birth father or a man they come to know as "Daddy"—carries the potential for difficult emotional transitions, some with lasting consequences.

No child who travels along a daddy-less road toward adulthood does so without stopping every so often to ask for directions. Early in children's lives, they usually turn to their mothers for guidance. By the time a child is a toddler, the absence of a father becomes inescapably clear: she notices that other families include men, or she sees daddies as part of families on TV. One mother told me it wasn't until the day when some fathers arrived to pick up their children at day care that her daughter asked her, "Mom, where's my dad?" Her daughter, this mother told me, was not panicked about this absence, just curious about where this missing man was.

Toddlers who haven't grown up with a father often ask their mothers, "Do I have a daddy?" or "Who is my daddy?" As they grow older they begin to wonder why their families look different from their friends'. Sometimes a youngster will imagine things about a man who might have been her "daddy" and wonder what he might think of her. "Does Daddy love me even if he's not here with me?" she might ask. If a man who is not the child's father becomes a consistent figure in her mother's life, as Steve became in Morena's, a child's inquiries are likely to keep pace with the changes that his presence brings. Many unmarried moms tell me that their children worry about how a man's presence might alter their own relationship. "Why does he have to be here, Mommy?" one child asked when he felt that his mother wasn't paying enough attention to him. Other children actually tell men to leave. But if a child becomes accustomed to and delighted by a particular man, as Morena's children did, they might want to know, "Is he going to be my daddy?"

Discussions with youngsters about missing fathers and disappearing/drop-in daddies are among the more unforgettable—and important—conversations unmarried mothers can have with their children. Yet mothers, especially younger ones who don't know what kinds of information children of certain ages are able to absorb, often don't know what to say or don't understand why they must help a child to cope with this absence. Many young single mothers grew up either not knowing their fathers or disliking them. If no one helped them to process their feelings, how are they to know how to comfort or respond to their children now? In Morena's case, her father's departure from her family when she was eleven years old was painful for her. However, unlike her children, she had lived with her father for some time before he left. Whether she had a father or a "daddy," or who he was, never was a question for Morena, as it is for her children. Another aspect of her children's situation is different, too: Kendra and Daniel are much younger than she was when her father left, so their level of comprehension is going to be different.

Young mothers' lack of knowledge about how best to respond does not mean that they don't empathize with their children or wish things had turned out differently. The young mothers I visited with told me that the absence of their children's father is something they worry about a lot, and this was true even among the young women who were angriest at men whom they say abandoned them. "Leave me, but pay attention to your children" is how young mothers put it. Acknowledging children's sadness about their father's absence does not fulfill their children's missing emotional needs, however, as Morena found out.

No woman, whatever her age or level of education, possesses a magic wand that, when waved, resolves children's disappointment or dissolves their sadness or anger at having only one parent to depend on. Unmarried mothers usually rely on a blend of personal experience and intuition to arrive at combinations of words and actions which they hope will help their children adjust. Sometimes they call upon therapists for assistance. But when mothers are very young they are less likely to have either the knowledge to assist them in figuring out when and how they should seek such help, or the financial resources to pay for it. So they muddle along, doing what they can with little more than homespun advice, much of which can be confusing and misguided.

Young mothers talk about feeling torn between what they want to do for their children and what others tell them they ought to do. When a young mother resides with her family, the child's father may not be welcome in the home. For example, Shanika, the unwed mother of three whose own "daddy" died when she was ten, feels adamantly that her children ought to know and spend time with their absent father, but her mother strenuously disagrees. When Shanika lived with her mother—and even now that she doesn't—this disagreement is a constant source of friction between them. "If my mother had her way, my kids would never know their father," Shanika told me. "But I don't think that's right. They should know him." Even Myieka, whose childhood track record with men who acted as her "daddies" left her with bitter memories, wants to have her children's father as a part of their daily lives, although she refuses to marry him.

The typical child-rearing manual does not deliver parental advice about absent fathers or disappearing daddies. Nor is adequate preparation for dealing with these situations only a matter of study. Questions about "Daddy" arise out of a child's individual experience, anger, or longing; mothers learn one approach to deal with a particular circumstance, and then another situation presents itself. Kendra and Daniel grew up together, but the questions they asked Morena about "Daddy" surfaced for different reasons and sprang out of circumstances Morena could not necessarily have predicted or controlled. In each instance, Morena tried, as well as she knew how, to help her children adjust. She is extremely hard on herself, as those hearing her story might be too, about how she failed to protect her children from "Daddy" problems. Nor did answers she was able to offer Kendra and Daniel contain the wisdom she wished they did. Several times Morena sought advice from her children's physician, but even when she relied on this doctor's suggestions she never felt well enough versed in all that she sensed she needed to know.

Morena blames herself for not preparing Daniel for the possibility that he might see his father during that first summer vacation. But how could she? Daniel was three years old and wanted so much for Steve to be his "daddy." How was Morena to get him to understand that some man he might meet was actually his father? What would the word "father" mean to him? Because Morena didn't know how to do this, she didn't try. There are other moments she regrets. As she thinks back, Morena wonders why she didn't keep her boyfriend from letting Kendra call him Daddy. At the very least, she should have made certain he understood what it meant to

Kendra to think of him as her daddy. Perhaps even that, however, was asking too much of herself; at the time, all Morena wanted was for her daughter's pain about not having a daddy to be taken away. Kendra's happiness in finding a "daddy" made Morena temporarily oblivious to the possible consequences. Now there are so many things she wishes she'd done differently, so many more helpful words she wishes she'd been able to say to Kendra and Daniel. But it's impossible to alter what happened.

For parents like Morena, who are raising children without the help of a "daddy," emotional dilemmas such as these are piled on top of the overwhelming and exhausting tasks of parenting on their own. They also get mixed up with whatever complex feelings a woman has about the man who is her child's father. If he has abnegated all parental responsibilities, she may be so enraged at him that it's difficult to work to include him in his children's lives or even speak positively about him to them. When he helps out financially but rarely makes an effort to see the children or participate meaningfully in their lives, she may resent the emotional trouble he's left to brew inside her home. Her own emotional turmoil can make doubly difficult the job of guiding a son or daughter through the briarpatch of questions they will one day ask about the missing "daddy."

"Men, in general, and fathers in particular, are increasingly viewed as superfluous to family life."

Fathers help their sons identify what's masculine within themselves. If a son does not develop a close, warm relationship with his father, his search for male identity can lead him to look outside of the family. Sometimes this results in what has been described as hypermasculinity, an aggressive and danger-seeking attitude among young men who assume the souped-up masculine credentials they see depicted in the media. As for a daughter, her father, through his relationship with her mother, offers a close-up view of what relationships with men might one day be like for her. Her ability to regulate her adolescent and adult sexual behavior can be affected by the relationship her father has with her and her mother.

Combine these widely accepted psychological norms with the economic contributions expected of fathers, and one better appreciates how the diminishing presence of fathers kindles fiery rhetoric about the consequences associated with the splintering of American families. Though Morena and other young mothers do not, in the midst of their hectic parenting lives, spend much time debating the theoretical pros and cons of how "family" turned out for them—and how it may affect their children—

most are aware of the intense anger many people feel toward them. Nowadays, few discussions about America's economic and social predicaments take place without someone pointing to unmarried mothers and fatherless children as the leading indicator of our nation's declining values and the primary cause of its deteriorating well-being. Usually, it is mothers who get blamed, though absent fathers are starting to be publicly admonished and punished.

"Men, in general, and fathers in particular, are increasingly viewed as superfluous to family life," declared David Blankenhorn, founder of the Institute for American Values, in an influential speech he delivered to family policy experts on January 13, 1993. Subsequently, Blankenhorn wrote about the catastrophic consequences he ascribes to this trend toward fatherlessness. In his 1995 book, *Fatherless America: Confronting Our Most Urgent Social Problem*, he argues that nothing is more dangerous to our societal well-being than the millions of children being raised without fathers. The consequences of this all-too-typical circumstance are, Blankenhorn asserts, myriad and haunting. Teenage pregnancy and premarital birth are more likely to occur among daughters without fathers, thus perpetuating the cycle of fatherless families. Fatherlessness, Blankenhorn said in his 1993 speech, "is the most important predictor of criminal behavior." It is "not race, not income, not religious affiliation" but "boys who don't grow up with their fathers" that is the determining factor in the upsurge in adolescent aggression and violence.

There is general agreement—and cumulative evidence—that the absence of a father is, in general, accompanied by increased risks for children. Those who grow up without their fathers score lower, as a group, than children from two-parent families on tests of cognitive ability and academic achievement and are less likely to graduate from high school. They also have a higher incidence of antisocial behavior and delinquency. Girls who grow up living apart from their fathers are more likely to give birth when they are young and unmarried. But researchers who produce such findings caution that the absence of fathers is embedded in a complex web of debilitating circumstances that inhabit the lives of these children. Father-absence, on its own, can be difficult to pinpoint as *the* cause of children's troubles. Nor is every child who lives in a father-absent family at equal risk of negative consequences, just as children who grow up with both of their parents are not automatically protected from them. Nor would it be correct to say that our social problems would be solved if only fathers remained with their families, though it is hard to argue that this wouldn't help. But Princeton sociologist Sara McLanahan points out that if every child lived with both parents, the high school dropout rate would be predicted to decrease from 19 percent to 13 percent: that is, problems associated with deficient education would be far from eradicated. "If we want to know whether living with one parent increases the risk of dropping out of school, the answer is clearly yes," McLanahan writes. "On the other hand, if we want to know whether it [father-absence] is the primary source of school failure, the answer is clearly no."

It should be no surprise that social scientists find that other factors—family and neighborhood poverty, emotional trauma, harsh discipline, ignorance of or neglect of children's developmental needs, and family conflict—have similarly robust relationships with the likelihood that children will experience difficulties. For example, Joan McCord, a professor of criminal justice at Temple University, studied boys who grew up in one- and two-parent families. The findings she published during the 1980s and 1990s provide evidence that the primary factor in whether these adolescents fell into deviant and delinquent behavior was not the absence or presence of a father but how the adults in the children's lives handled conflict.

Criminal justice expert John Laub and sociologist Robert J. Sampson have come to similar conclusions about just how complicated the ascription of cause can be. In a 1993 book, *Crime in the Making: Pathways and Turning Points Through Life*, they examine a range of family variables that turn out to be good predictors of children's problem behavior and delinquency. They cite a comprehensive 1986 review* that identified four dimensions of how parents—married as well as single—actually function in raising children. These categories of influential parental behavior emerged again and again:

1. Parent-child relationships: the quality and level of parental involvement with children and supervision of them.
2. Discipline practices of parents, and whether patterns of parent/child and child/parent rejection are established.
3. Parental history of criminality, and parental attitudes that reinforce deviant behavior.
4. Marital conflict and parental absence.

All four factors, it turns out, are associated with children developing aggressive and delinquent behavior. But each exerts a different degree of

---

*This review was done by Rolf Loeber and Magda Stouthamer-Loeber and was published by the University of Chicago Press in a book entitled *Crime and Justice*, vol. 7, edited by Michael Tonry and Norval Morris.

influence. For example, listed among "powerful predictors" are the effectiveness of parental supervision, the degree of parental rejection, and the amount of parental involvement in a child's life. Parents' marital relations, and criminal engagement by a parent or parents, rank as "medium predictors"; among factors labeled "weaker predictors" are the lack of parental discipline, and parental absence.

Laub and Sampson further examined the relative impact of these "family process" variables. Laub explained their results to me: "What we found is that once you begin to take into account how families raise children, the direct effects of family structure on delinquency or some sort of deviant outcome are mediated by what goes on within the family. That becomes important. Basically, this is a hopeful message, but it also can be a pessimistic one because single parents tend not to be able to supervise or monitor children as well, they are less likely to use consistent styles of discipline, and they are less likely to have strong, secure bonds of emotional attachment." This indicates that although family structure by itself is not the major determinant of children's deviant behavior, the kinds of interpersonal relationships that this family arrangement tends to bring about remain at the hub of the spokes connecting this circle of factors.

Weak social bonds between children and their families and communities turn out to be a very reliable predictor of antisocial behavior. Strong "emotional bonds of attachment," even when sustained with only one parent, can be a crucial protective factor for any child. As Cornell developmental psychologist Urie Bronfenbrenner says, "Every child needs someone who is crazy about him." Similarly, consistent connections with adults in the community add more layers of protection. Laub and Sampson describe how "socially integrated forms of monitoring and discipline" within communities also go a long way toward improving children's well-being; the process is similar to how these relational dynamics play out in families.

One reason children raised by single parents are more likely to exhibit behavioral problems is that a single parent simply has a much harder time monitoring children than two participating parents would. Likewise, communities where a majority of families are headed by single parents tend to be poorer and more dangerous; fewer sets of caretaking eyes watch over children; and positive male role models, which are extremely helpful, are lacking. As Robert Sampson said, "It is almost a threshold effect: once you reach a certain proportion of homes in a neighborhood where there is a single parent, it becomes much more difficult for a community to maintain a certain level of control or supervision over kids. A lot has to do with the ratio of adults to kids. It doesn't really matter whether the parents are married or not. . . . What I am really saying is that it is the overall context that perhaps matters more than the individual families. If you take a child in a one-parent family and put him into a community with a high rate of intact families, the probability of delinquency will be reduced."

"What can you expect from these poor kids who come from families in which there isn't a father?"

The popular media—unschooled in the complicated nuances that ought to inform discussions about father-absence—are too often content to depict children's family structure as the primary predictor of failure. Consequently, in the minds of many, father-absence offers a satisfactory explanation for why so many youngsters aren't doing well. The logic goes like this: a child raised without a father will do worse than another child whose parents are married. But research helps us understand that a very large percentage of children who don't grow up living with both parents turn out to confront a wide array of other obstacles—obstacles that these children would probably face even if *their* fathers lived with them. Their mothers are usually poorly educated, and maternal education is the primary factor in how well the children are likely to do in school. Their communities are mired in joblessness, concentrated poverty, and violence, all of which affect how children perceive their efficacy and assess their opportunities. And the schools many of these children attend don't do much to change the outcomes these external circumstances tend to predict.

In patterns that can quickly become self-fulfilling, adults attach their unexamined beliefs about the inevitability of failure to these children very young. Many are branded "less than promising." (Just as Sarah felt her own promise was threatened by the imaginary brand of "teenage mother" others wanted to put on her.) Unfortunately, the next step in this all-too-common pattern goes something like this: if growing up with an unmarried mother (and without a father) "causes" these dire outcomes, then neither teachers nor child-care providers nor government policies nor community supports can do much to alter what is inevitable. A damaging dynamic sets in: don't expect much of this child; you won't get much in return.

This scenario is played out in too many schools. An elementary school principal in Boston told me that some teachers she's worked with base expectations about children's ability to learn on little more than the structure of their families. Abilities are presumed to be lower in children whose families do not include two parents. (Seventy percent of the students in her school live in families where just one or neither parent is present.) I asked her to tell me how teachers express these attitudes. " 'What can you expect from these poor kids who come from families in which there isn't a father?' " she says, making little effort to conceal her contempt for this prejudice. This principal views her primary leadership role as that of convincing teachers to reexamine their assumptions about each child's capacity to learn. "Spend time with a child before rushing to judgment," she advises them. She also works with teachers to develop new techniques to highlight the multiple range of children's intelligence and to look for ways to involve parents (who are often not well educated themselves) in the process of learning. This principal believes—because her experience shows it to be true—that when at least one parent acts as a steady beacon for a child's academic pursuit, that child remains eager to learn. That faith was affirmed by James Coleman, a University of Chicago sociologist renowned for his findings on the value of parental involvement in education. Coleman observed that the "social capital"* in the family that is "available to aid children's learning is not merely the presence of adults in the household, but the attention and involvement of adults in children's learning." Coleman's research also suggests that children from single-parent families are no more likely than children from two-parent families to drop out of school *if* their families are supported by community, educational, and religious networks.

Do children who live with both parents have educational advantages? When fathers play an active role in their children's learning, the answer is undoubtedly yes. Even when a father is not directly involved with his children's academic pursuits, his income can still enable his children to attend higher-quality schools and give them access to more educational resources, such as books and computers in the home. In its 1993 report "America's Smallest School: The Family," the Educational Testing Service highlighted a well-known finding: children who live with both parents generally do better academically. But beyond the headline there were interesting revelations. Family structure, it turns out, was found to be just one of the major variables affecting how well students perform on standardized tests. For example, the more time students spent watching television, the lower their math scores; that relationship was stronger than the one between test scores and how many parents a student lived with.

Researchers are now trying to more accurately identify what it is about father-absence that affects how well children master a variety of skills. It is one thing to point out that children who live in one-parent families do worse, on average, than those who are with two parents. But a more constructive approach involves asking *why* this is so, then using what is

---

*"Social capital" is the relational and psychological resources present in a child's environment.

learned to ease hardships for children who grow up in such families. For example, is it a lack of fathers' paychecks or their physical and emotional absence from their children's lives that has the more detrimental impact on children's well-being?

"A poor relationship is worse than no relationship at all."

The difficulty in figuring out what fathers contribute to their children's lives—and what difference the various contributions make—stems from the fact that fathers' roles are less culturally scripted than mothers'. While there is a societal expectation that fathers support their children financially, what else they are meant to do is unclear. But if men better understood and appreciated their beneficial paternal contributions, their inclination to be more involved in their children's lives—even when they couldn't provide much financial support—might be spurred.

Some research is already unraveling stubborn stereotypes about young fathers. Often it is assumed that when a father is not present in his child's home (as so many younger ones are not) he is also absent from his child's life. In Morena's case, this was true, but many other young fathers play at least peripheral roles in the lives of their children. Some are very involved; others want to be. One sixteen-year-old unmarried mother told me that her baby's father "is trying so hard to be a father." As she put it, "his father wasn't much of a father figure, so I guess he's kind of figuring out that he doesn't want to treat his child that way." They are experiencing difficult times in being parents, she says, "but he is there for me all the time."

Frank Mott, a psychologist at the Center for Human Resource Research at Ohio State University, studied children aged four to seven who didn't live with their fathers. The majority didn't have an ongoing relationship with their biological father, but in many cases other men had entered their lives as father figures and were maintaining consistent fatherlike involvement with them. For white children, this father figure was likely to be a man who moved into his mother's home. Among black families, not only had a larger percentage of the children's birth fathers remained in continuous contact with their children—even when their relationship with the mother had "become more ambiguous"—but also relatives and other community members were more likely to take on aspects of the paternal role.

Despite these diverse relationships between children and their "absent fathers," research on these families still tends to take a "bunch 'em together" approach when effects of fatherlessness are being assessed. Children whose parents are divorced are lumped with those whose parents have never married, even though the relational dynamics are likely to be dissimilar. By not better differentiating the various relationships fathers maintain with their children, and the emotional effect of their absence or departure, research can obscure important information about *how* men affect children's well-being. Mott urges his fellow researchers to develop more precise definitions of "fatherlessness" and to collect data in a way more sensitive to the wide variety of actual father-child relationships.

Some researchers are already doing this; their studies offer varied findings. Some show positive linkages between how often children see fathers who live apart from them and how well the children do on some developmental measures. Others don't find such strong connections between time spent together and improved outcomes. However, researchers generally agree that when fathers work to maintain "very close relationships" with their children, the youngsters usually do better. The message seems clear: the quality of the paternal relationship—like that of the maternal relationship—matters. When University of Pennsylvania sociologist Frank Furstenberg, Jr., for example, looked at the impact a group of young black fathers had on their children over the course of seventeen years, he found that "contact, even regular contact, with fathers outside the home had little effect on positive outcomes for the adolescent children." Children, he wrote, "only benefit from a close paternal relationship." Furstenberg found that the children who were doing best were those who'd lived with their biological father *and* had established a close bond with him. The youngsters who lived with their biological fathers but did not have a close relationship were actually doing worse than the average of all the children in his sample, which included many who had never lived with their fathers. "Our data show that a poor relationship is worse than no relationship at all," Furstenberg explained.

The inconsistency of findings about the impact of nonresident fathers' relationships with their children casts doubt on what some assume is always in the child's best interest—more contact with his father. In their book *Growing Up with a Single Parent* Sara McLanahan and Gary Sandefur provide an explanation for why contact with nonresident fathers doesn't, on average, enhance children's well-being. Only when parents get along with each other do children appear to benefit from contact with their fathers; otherwise, contact with the father tends to renew family tension and conflict, and this can work to children's detriment. "The positive and negative effects on these two types of contact cancel each other out," the researchers assert.

In the 1990s it is not possible to speak about the absence of fathers and assume that we know how a particular father came to be absent from his child's life, how "absent" he truly is, or what his absence means from an individual child's perspective. As more women give birth out of wedlock and raise children apart from the fathers, the ways in which social scientists assess the economic, cognitive, and psychological impacts of father-absence will no doubt try to capture more accurately the dynamics of various father-child interactions. For example, now that so many children never do live with their fathers, it is important to examine specific issues that affect these children's lives, beginning in infancy. Their experiences are bound to differ from those of children whose parents divorce. What degree of contact or involvement do never-married fathers maintain with their children? What aspects of their involvement are most beneficial? How do children perceive this paternal engagement? And how does a father who moves in and out of his child's life compare with one who totally disappears? If another man settles in as father figure, what can *he* do to improve a child's prospects? What are the main contributions nonresident fathers make as children become adolescents? What connections, if any, are there between a father's involvement with his children and his willingness to provide financial support? How does an "absent" father's relationship with his children's mother affect his paternal connection?

Researchers will be offering more guidance on these and many more such questions as we move toward the twenty-first century and fatherlessness maintains its rightful prominent place on the public policy agenda.

"Hey, I'm Daddy. Daddy's here. Try to see you as much as I can."

Young mothers and fathers wrestle with personal issues that social scientists cannot quantify. The measures researchers use don't address the gut-wrenching moments of everyday life when children want to know about "Daddy" or wish they had one, or when fathers try to figure out how to fit into families when they have no model to show them how, or when mothers and fathers try to reconcile their mutual anger and distrust with their desire that their children be close to both parents. When I asked young unmarried mothers "Where's Daddy?" and listened as they told me how their children's fathers affected them and their children, it soon became apparent that important voices were missing: young fathers'. Many children of unmarried young mothers don't know their father, or rarely see him—and often their fathers have that experience in common with them. Hearing from young men what this absence felt like to them as children and how it affects them now seemed essential if I was to fully appreciate the family experience of these young mothers and their children. I was fortunate to be introduced to some young men whose childhoods didn't do a very good job of preparing them for the role of father, and their experiences and insights complemented what I was learning from young mothers.

The grin on Oscar's face must be a mile wide when he tells me how good it makes him feel when he hears the word "Daddy." "It makes me happy," says this twenty-one-year-old father of two girls. "Hearing your child call you Daddy. It's wonderful. You can't help but stand right when you hear her call you, Daddy, Daddy. Can't help but smirk. You are trying to hold the smile in, but you can't. And you give her a hug. Thank you."

Oscar doesn't hear the word "Daddy" every day: He doesn't live with his daughters. He never has. And each time he drops by to visit them, Oscar wonders if they'll remember to call him by the name he wants to hear. "My oldest daughter, she'll call me by my name or she'll call me Daddy. Sometimes she'll say, 'Where's Oscar? Where's Oscar?' and I don't say nothin'. But my youngest one, she call me Dada. It feels good, feels good."

Along with several other young men, Oscar is spending time with me, trying to explain what it's like to be a father. After hearing many young mothers, like Morena, disparage their partners for their inability to act as they say a father should, I now have an opportunity to listen as these young men tell me how hard it is for them to try to be fathers without being husbands. (One young man is not yet a father, though he will be soon.) All of them have thought and talked with many other young men about fatherhood, thanks to their involvement with a Boston-based program aimed at helping men like them assume their paternal responsibilities.

The young men who participate are employed irregularly, always in low-wage jobs that rarely provide benefits such as health insurance and offer no security. They don't have the kind of education or training they'd need to get better-paid jobs that would enable them to support families without relying on public assistance. Their children's support comes primarily from welfare, though each of the men I'm talking with makes it a point to tell me that when he has money he "provides" for his children. "Providing" means stopping by their children's house with a box of Pampers or a toy.

"Even though I don't see my daughters that much, I want my daughters to know, 'Hey, I am Daddy. Daddy's here. Try to see you as much as I can. And I love you and I always want you to try to love me,'" Oscar goes on to say. The other young men nod as he speaks. "I try to do as much as I can for them," he says.

Oscar didn't graduate from high school, and only now, at twenty-one, has he earned a GED. His daughters are one and three years old. Right now he has no job and lives with his mother in a tough, dispirited neighborhood that offers plenty of temptations, such as selling drugs, which he knows could earn him money but also pull him down. After their first daughter was born, Oscar often stayed overnight at his girlfriend Anita's apartment. But as the months went by and their relationship soured, he spent more days and nights at his mother's. "Back and forth" is how he describes his present nomadic life.

By the time Anita told him he was going to be a father for a second time, their relationship had disintegrated. When his second daughter was born, little affection remained between him and Anita. They had never considered getting married. To do so made no sense financially. With the low hourly wage Oscar occasionally earns he could not support his children, and to be married would jeopardize their support from welfare, Anita's rent subsidy, and possibly the medical care his daughters and their mother receive. Oscar can think of no way—even if their relationship were going well—that he could pay $650 a month in rent (the cost of a tiny one-bedroom apartment in the city), not to mention buy diapers, clothes, and food and pay medical bills.

When Oscar does work, the state's department of revenue deducts child-support money from his paycheck. Because Anita didn't tell him that she'd given his name to welfare officials, Oscar was shocked and angry when his paycheck suddenly shrank. He says supporting his children is not what bothers him; that is something he says he will always try to do. What upsets Oscar is the impersonality: the state has now become a middleman between him and his children. This makes it harder for him to visit his daughters—and maintain a "daddy" relationship with them—since he no longer has the money to buy them a special gift or even a package of disposable diapers. Instead, the state sends his support in a welfare check.

"It's okay," Oscar says. That's as enthusiastic as he can be about the wage-garnishing, which is at the heart of recent get-tough-on-absent-fathers initiatives. To get nonresident fathers to pay their fair share, states are devising strategies to identify them early in their child's life and then force them to devote a portion of their earnings to support. "I mean, I don't have to worry about it coming out of my pocket," Oscar says, an admission that at least this way it's easier for the money to be set aside.

Automatic payroll deductions provide a consistency Oscar acknowledges he does not maintain on his own. The last time Oscar had a job, $25 was taken out of his paycheck each week—but out of the $100 deducted per month, his daughters received only $50. Even if $200 had been deducted from Oscar's paycheck that month, only $50 of it would have passed through to his children. Under the old federal welfare rules, the government kept the remainder to recoup taxpayers' costs for welfare. (The 1996 federal welfare reform eliminated this $50 "pass-through"; now each state will decide how to deal with the garnished money.) The disparity between what these fathers give and what reaches their kids angers many of them, including Oscar. He feels as though he's paying but his children aren't getting the full benefit. Nor do they—or their mother—connect him directly with this contribution to their support.

It's now been three months since Oscar was laid off from a job packing boxes. "It's really gettin' harder and harder," he says, grimly. "I'm trying to be supportive of my family, trying to help out with the bills as much as I can. It is really hard." A few moments later, his eyes averted, Oscar continues: "What good are you to anybody if you ain't got yourself together? I mean it's like we say to each other here, 'What good am I to my daughters?' I'm trying to get a job. It's hard being turned away." Oscar sees other young fathers make different choices as they try to get more money so they can act like "daddies" and construct a sense of worth for themselves: "For some of the brothers out here who are fathers, they see selling drugs as the only means of supporting their children." Oscar claims this is something he'd never do. But he knows "never" can be a big word when each day he wonders what he can do to give his daughters a better life.

"I needed Dad. 'Dad, yo, Dad. Where are you?' "

None of the men I'm speaking with has a close relationship with his own father. One of them never knew who his father was; the others saw their fathers only sporadically when they were growing up. Though their fathers' absence created painful moments during their childhoods, until they became fathers these young men did not think about their paternal relationships in the way they do now. When they are together, they help one another make sense of the connections between what happened then and what's happening now, with their children. By sharing stories and discussing their feelings, they are trying to stop history from repeating itself.

What motivated these young men to become fathers at an age when they weren't prepared to assume parental responsibilities is, by now, a blurred memory. When they had no children and were having sex, thoughts about what fatherhood means were a million miles away. Of course, there are young men who believe that making a baby is a part of transforming themselves from boys into men. This perspective isn't unlike the one girls express when they talk about having babies as a way of becoming women. Becoming a father can also make young men who feel they are marginalized, ridiculed, demeaned, and ignored by much of society feel as though they matter to someone. This desire to belong seems to account, in part, for why the men I am talking with find themselves being fathers so young.

During the months that Oscar and his friends have been meeting, they've talked about how being a "father" is not the same as being a "daddy." The difference, as they see it, is that fathers biologically create children and support them financially, while dads stay involved in their children's lives. They have come to appreciate that these two aspects of being a parent are often embodied in the same person but that they demand different skills.

Sid, the twenty-two-year-old father of a sixteen-month-old son and a one-month-old daughter, explains to me how he views the difference between a "dad" and a "father." His son lies, eyes closed, against Sid's chest, sucking loudly from a bottle. "Being a dad means being there for him when he needs a friend, when he needs someone to talk to," Sid says, glancing down at his son. "Like I couldn't always go to my mom to talk about something. I felt uncomfortable going to her talking about sex. I needed Dad. It was like, 'Dad, yo, Dad. Where are you?' I winded up having to talk to Unc." Sid shakes his head to indicate how unsatisfactory this was. " 'Father' is sort of the provider of money and just teaching him the way to go. And if he needs chastisement, he's who chastises him. He is the corrector. 'Father' is the parent part of being a parent, but the 'dad' is like the friend. Like I am the dad right now," he says, reaching down to check on his son's bottle. "But if he gets out of hand, I'm going to turn into the father." Listening to Sid and watching him, I realize how hard it must be to define and then assume roles he never experienced while growing up.

Sid met his own father only twice: he disappeared just after Sid was born. "The second time we met," he says, "I went bowling with him. But it's like I'm bowling with a man I don't even know. I mean, you know." His companions howl with laughter. What Sid is describing, each of them can visualize from his own life. "And he expect me to call him Dad, and I don't know this man!" Heads nod in agreement. The men realize, as Oscar had told me earlier, that if they want to be called Daddy they have to find ways to be involved in their children's lives. It's hard though, Sid says, to figure how to be involved when a woman suspects, as he says many of them do, that fathers aren't going to help out and are likely to disappear.

"Yeah, like my girl," Sid says. "The first thing she asked me wasn't, 'Are we going to get married?' but 'Are you going to take care of this kid?' She was afraid to tell me she was pregnant. Her mother had to tell me because my girlfriend thought the first thing I was going to do was pack up. 'See ya, I ain't comin' back. I ain't got no kid. It's not mine.' That's what they expect." Sid didn't leave his girlfriend or his children, though as far as the welfare department is concerned he doesn't exist in their lives. Welfare officials certainly don't know the day-to-day role he plays in his family's life, and Sid prefers that things remain just this way. "I ain't going to pay no system," he says, referring to the child-support enforcement system in which Oscar is a reluctant participant. The mother of Sid's children has not given officials his name. When they ask her, as they do, she lies and tells them she doesn't know who the father is.

"The reason I don't want to be in the system is that I want to take care of my child. I don't want to pay anybody else to take care of my child. I want to do it myself, you know. And the simple fact that I'd pay, like, all that money and only a part of it go to him, it just don't make sense to me. Why not just give them the whole money?"

"So you are a full-time parent, but you aren't registered as your children's father?" I ask Sid.

"Nowhere," he responds, proudly. His name is neither on his children's birth certificates nor in the computer at the welfare department. "I just want to do it myself." Sid doesn't mention that at this time welfare actually pays most of his family's bills.

"So your children's mother, she's not scared someday you'll just take off?" I ask Sid. "I mean, you've convinced her you'll stick with your responsibilities?"

"Yeah, I convinced her by showing her what I was going to do. I did it. I paid for the boy's diapers. I bought most of his clothes. Most of the things in the house come out of my pocket."

"Are you working now?" I ask.

"No, I just got laid off. I was working as a security officer in the welfare office," Sid says. A grin like the Cheshire cat's creeps across his face as he chuckles at his job guarding the camp of his enemy, whose scouts want to track down fathers like him to garnish their wages. "Now I get unemployment."

Sid's loss of his job coincided with the birth of his second child. Since then, he has spent a lot of time taking care of his son while he looks for another job. His girlfriend spends most of her time with their infant daughter. "Wherever I go, you'll see him," Sid says, smiling at his son. His proud-papa look reaffirms how glad he is to have his little buddy with him.

I ask Sid whether he and his girlfriend are considering marriage now that they have two children. "Marriage is not like the highest priority," he responds. "The highest priority I have right now is being a father, you know, watching over them, making sure they have a role model, making sure I keep myself in line, making sure I don't do things I used to do before they came along that were bad and negative, and just try to be totally, one-hundred-percent positive, as I want them to be. That's my perspective."

"Some noncustodial parents are themselves having trouble making ends meet."

Among these young fathers, only Sid seems satisfied with how his life as a dad is turning out. The others wish they could find ways to play a more central role in their children's lives but feel constrained by forces over which they believe they have little control. Securing an income resides at the top of any list of what the fathers know they need if their family lives are going to work out.

Today's economy is less forgiving toward young men, especially less-educated ones, than it was during earlier decades when our country was enjoying greater economic growth. As recently as the early 1970s, young men who had not graduated from high school could get factory work at wages that made it possible to support families. Research cited in the Children's Defense Fund report "Adolescent and Young Adult Fathers: Problems and Solutions" confirms that in 1973 nearly 60 percent of men aged twenty to twenty-four were able to earn enough to lift a family of three above the official poverty line. By 1984, 42 percent of young male workers could do this, and among those who had not finished high school, only 32 percent earned enough. During the 1990s, the ability of poorly educated young men to earn the kind of wages they need to support a family continues to diminish. And the earning of young, minority males from disadvantaged backgrounds—consistently lower than those of their white peers—have dropped even more dramatically.

When young fathers can't do what they believe a "good father" should do—provide financially for his family—their relationships with children and girlfriends often unravel. As one mother said to me, "Welfare becomes the man." The incapacity of many young fathers to provide the income and housing and health security that women and children receive from public assistance often dooms the possibility of knitting together a married family. In a 1995 report, "Fathers, Child Support and Welfare Reform: The Missing Link," Northeastern University economist Andrew Sum explained that the yearly value of welfare's cash assistance and food stamps was equivalent to half of the average gross earnings of unmarried twenty- to twenty-nine-year-old men. For men who dropped out of high school, the welfare assistance equaled 89 percent of their average earn-ings—142 percent if the men were black. These evaluations do not take into account the added cost of housing and health insurance that public assistance often provides.

Gordon Berlin, an expert on child support, testified at a 1992 congres-sional hearing that a key ingredient in reducing child poverty (and thereby potentially improving children's well-being) "is to collect more child support from noncustodial parents." He acknowledged, however, that "at least some noncustodial parents are themselves having trouble making ends meet." When these young men don't have a steady income, it is difficult to obtain the amount of support children need in a timely and consistent way. Nor are their contributions likely to make a significant dif-ference in moving children out of poverty.

It is also a disheartening fact that, in the mid-1990s, nearly one in every three young black men is in jail, in prison, on probation, or on parole. Fathers who are in jail aren't earning money, and their prospects for doing so in the future are not as high as those of men without criminal records. Nor do young men whose "jobs" involve illicit activities have paychecks which the state can trace; what they do have is a greater likelihood of dying early and abandoning their children forever. Because of increasing violence the death rate for young men who live in poor communities has risen alarmingly, which also contributes to the growth in fatherlessness of children. Rates of incarceration and death are lower among young white males than they are among black and Hispanic men. But for young white men whose job skills and education leave them woefully unprepared to find jobs in today's changing economy, bleak prospects are luring more of them down similar paths, albeit at a slower pace.

When young men can't earn enough money to make a real economic contribution to their children's lives, they are less likely to claim paternity. And—as Sid's case illustrates—unless paternity is established it is difficult to legally force a father to support his child. Even with laws and policies in place to better identify fathers, only about 40 percent of children born to unmarried parents have established paternity. Researchers who inter-view young unwed fathers discover that many do not know how to legalize their paternity, even if they say they want to. (Some states require a judge's approval even when the father signs a form admitting paternity.) How-ever, fathers say they do know something about how various options for acting on their paternity stack up. If a father marries his child's mother, the child won't be as likely to receive public assistance—which, given the father's economic circumstances, she might need. And if his support pay-ments flow into "the system," the mother of his child will give him "no credit" for contributing financial support. One consequence of these assumptions is that just 37 percent of mothers receiving welfare have paternal support orders; of those women, only a third receive formal payments.

"You never see a black man taking care of his child."

After a while what began as an interview with these young fathers evolves into a more free-flowing conversation. These young men want to give me—a highly educated, never unemployed, older, white woman—some sense of how susceptible their lives are to shifting economic winds and how discomfiting this uncertainty is, especially at a time when they are trying to find beneficial ways to act as fathers. They also want me to know how their ambitions are stymied by societal attitudes about them, and by the stereotypical images and words that they say are hard to ignore.

"The media are always communicating that black men don't take care of their children," Sid says. The others again nod in agreement. "They make the man look as though he don't take care of them. On TV, a father is never around. You never see a black man taking care of his child. And you are not going to see that on TV. You know why?" I say nothing, not wanting to interrupt by debating with him whether *The Cosby Show* counts. Sid continues: "Because that's not going to sell. People don't want to hear that. The system doesn't want a black man to succeed. So the best thing for them to do is keep us down on the lower level, make it look like we are just the bottom. So all the time in the news media, we're going to come out on the bottom and have a black woman floatin' on top."

Surfacing in Sid's comments is a sentiment I hear a lot of young people express: when young men and women talk about one another, considerable animosity gets targeted at the opposite gender. This is, of course, not unlike conversations that go on among my peers; these days, men and women seem to find much to criticize about each other. Similarly, young mothers are convenient targets for these fathers as they vent their frustrations at not finding ways to fit into their children's lives: it's the mother's fault or it's the system's fault, they seem to say. Sid suggests that much of his and his friends' animosity gets stirred up because of all the attention society pays to mothers' lives while virtually ignoring theirs. His friends agree. "I mean I'm glad they have many programs for the poor mothers, but what about the dads?" Oscar asks, tossing his question out to no one in particular. "You've got many fathers like Sid who is walking down the street with the child in his hand. Or he's holding him and taking him with him. But you never hear nothin' about it. It is always, 'The mother. The mother. How is the mother?' " Oscar's soft voice turns louder and more mocking in its tone as he continues. "What about the father? I mean, this is a place we can come and talk and say, 'Look, I'd like to be noticed, too!' I mean, it is not just the mother." Oscar insists that his presence should be paid attention to. "I, for one, as a father, would like us to be recognized," he declares.

The recognition these young fathers say they are looking for rarely comes to them, even from members of their families. Girlfriends ridicule their awkward efforts to act as they think a father might. Such criticism sounds to these young men like an unwelcome echo of what their own mothers used to tell them when they were growing up. "Some mothers, they say, 'Oh, you look just like your dad. You're going to wind up just like your dad,' " Sid tells me. The others assure me they heard the same.

"So that's negative?" I ask.

"Yeah, my mom, like when I didn't get up early enough in the morning, her words were, 'You are going to end up a bum, just like your father,' " Sid explains.

"Was that something you heard all the time?"

"All the time." He shakes his head as if to try to toss away the bad memory.

"How does it leave you thinking?" I ask. "Does it leave you fearful of growing up and taking on these responsibilities?"

"It did when I was in high school," Sid replies, looking around to see where his son is wandering and make sure he's okay. "It really did, because when I tried to do something to better myself all I could hear inside of me was, 'I'm going to wind up a bum anyways, so why am I doing this?' "

Oscar is nodding vigorously. "My mother was the same thing, too," he says. "You get up late one day and your mom was always joggin' down your back, 'You ain't goin' to do nothin'. You ain't goin' to do nothin',' she say to me. And you are like, 'Ma, I will do it, will do it.' And she says, 'No, you ain't goin' to do it. You keep sayin' you goin' to do it.' Mom was always joggin' me out." Because Oscar never knew his father, he had no way of knowing what the man did or did not do. Maybe he was someone who "did nothin'," and that's why he never was around. And maybe Oscar's mother was right: as his father's son, he might "do nothin'," too. That thought scared him when he was younger and bothers him still.

"Now, in my situation, you tryin' to be a father to a child when I never had a father," he says. Oscar tells me he has no siblings, either. "My mother . . ." He pauses. "My mother was my mother and father. She told me about my father, as much as I know about the man. She told me his name, but that's about it. I never seen him or nothin'. As far as I know, by callin' himself father, if I ever come to meet him, it could just be that, words."

I am curious about a particular phrase Oscar uses: "My mother was my mother and father." It's one I hear from a lot of young mothers. I remember when Morena tried to calm Kendra by saying she'd be both her mother and father, although, as Morena and other mothers figured out, this approach usually doesn't work. When young mothers say this their words are not to be taken literally but rather as a way of describing their parenting burden and their wish that someone else was there to share it. When I ask mothers to show me how they act as "fathers," frequently they lower their voice and reenact an occasion when they disciplined their child. A manlike voice, they tell me, seems to grab a child's attention. But, as Sarah's mother, Judy, learned, trying to act like a man served only to detract from what she knew how to give her adolescent daughter as a mother. And the attributes fathers bring to parenting are ones that mothers are unable to replicate.

"My mother cooked. My mother cleaned. She did everything she could for me," says Sid. "And when I was bad she chastised me. When I did seriously wrong, she beat me. I was almost afraid to do things if my mother finds out. She was both that, a woman and a man." But although his mother acted out these dual roles for Sid, she was unable to set aside her perspective as a woman. "It wasn't so much the fact of how my mother raised me but it was the words she said," says Sid of the way his mother put him down, treating him as though he were and would always be a replica of his father. "When you're young, words computerize in the back of your mind," Sid says, "and then they come back when you want to do something to help better yourself."

"The words stuck?"

"Yeah." But, realizing how critical he sounds, Sid defends his mother from what he senses is my misconception of how he feels toward her. "I mean, my mother, it was amazing." Renewed excitement enters his voice. "She took me out. She taught me how to play football and, I mean, she taught me about sports. She was everything to me when nobody else was. I have no complaints about how she raised me. The only thing I have complaints about is the negative things she said when I was a child."

"So if you were not a part of your son's life, he'd be okay? A woman can handle both roles?" I ask Sid, following what he's just said to its logical conclusion.

"No. I'm not saying that," he insists. "I'll put it this way. It is not for all women. Lots of women out there are totally dependent on men. And there are a lot of independent women out there who can do both."

"I guess what I'm getting at," I say, "is when seen from a child's perspective, is there a need to have that man around?"

"There is a need to have a man," he says, without any equivocation.

"My mom did the best she could, but there is a need for a man in a little boy's childhood. And in a little girl's childhood, too." That Sid can't put into words exactly what this need is speaks to how new his discoveries are about what it means to be a father.

While Sid and I are talking, I see out of the corner of my eye that Vince, a twenty-year-old father-to-be, is shaking his head.

"What are you thinking about?" I ask Vince. "Are you thinking that a woman can't be both a mother and a father?"

"No, she can't," Vince declares. His mother and father have been together off and on, but he describes their relationship, as well as many others he's been around, as just "one catfight after another."

"A woman, right, especially like my mother," he says, "all the men she had in her life, her brothers, her husband, her father, they all sort of let her down in her life as she was growing up. So you see, as for bringing me up to be a young man, to be a man, she couldn't, because she had no idea herself what a man is or what a man should be because her father let her down, her brothers let her down, her husband let her down. So the most she did with me is she brought me up with manners and to be obedient and how to deal with people on a social level."

"So when a mother puts her son down, you can understand it as being a natural reaction to the anger she feels?" I ask.

Vince nods, but it is Sid who speaks up. "The simple fact is the women can't hide the truth," he says. "They can't hide that feeling. They aren't going intentionally to put it on the child, but it's going to be there 'cause you're going to see it. It's written on their faces. You can tell a woman who's been hurt a lot just by the way she acts towards you."

In becoming fathers, these young men discover they have to construct relationships with their children without having been given the bricks they need to build them. Having one another to talk with helps, but it doesn't erase all the words they've heard and the images they've seen that tell them fatherhood is something they are bound to fail at, if they even bother to try.

> **"The mothers, they don't call and say, 'The baby
> took his first steps, let me call the father.'
> They don't do that."**

In a while the fathers' conversation shifts to their current relationships with the mothers of their children. They explain how they are trying to remain a part of their children's lives, but how difficult this is to do. It can be, they say, like maneuvering through a mine field. Communication breaks down and turns nasty, particularly when the romance and sexual attraction of a relationship fade away. Anger moves in.

The only time Oscar hears from his children's mother, he says, is when she "wants something" from him. "Like when they want you to baby-sit," he says. "They don't call to say, 'Your child did this today or did that. I wish you were here to see it.' That's when my frustration happens."

Sid is with his children's mother, so this isn't an issue for him. But he hears the same complaint from many of his friends. "He's right," Sid says. "That is where a father's frustration comes in. I mean, the mothers, they don't call and say, 'The baby took his first steps, let me call the father.' They don't do that."

"So they call only when they need you?"

"Some of the women out here, they're really no good," says Sid. "They'll be like, 'I want to go to the club so let me call your daddy.' They ain't called daddy in more than a month and the kid has started walking, grown three teeth, and started eating solid food. The father, he don't know none of that, so he makes an infant bottle because he is not informed about what is happening in his child's life."

"Some of the mothers, they don't want the father to know." Oscar's remark reminds me of what experts say about how some mothers become gatekeepers of the father's relationship with his children.

As my conversation with these young men draws to a close, I notice Sid is staring at me from across the table. This time, however, it is Vince who speaks up—to let me know how uncomfortable it makes him to be sharing his insecurities about fatherhood with me, a white woman who until a few hours ago was a stranger.

"It's a shame to sit here and tell you all this because, as black men, we are in a very sad situation where we don't know ourselves," Vince says. "We don't know where we came from. Even if we did know, we are not ready to accept it. We are like a patient in an emergency ward, suffering from amnesia. To sit here and be telling you these things about our women, about ourselves, is just sad because if you study history you understand that this did not start today. In generations way before ours, this has been going on. And it's not our fault, but it would be passing the buck if we say this is not our fault, that it is the system's fault. I refuse to go along with it. I have to find the answer."

"That is how it goes down the ladder from child to child," Sid adds. "People will go, 'Black men ain't nothin'. They never goin' to be nothin'.' It's never going to change."

" 'They create 'em, then they leave 'em,' " Vince says. "And young black men, they just take this to heart and it becomes part of them 'cause it's already there. Now it is time for us to say, 'Okay, it's not our fault but it is time for us to do something about it.' And that's why we're here. We are trying to tell the world, 'Black men, you ain't got to be like this. Black women, you have to stop talkin' like this. You got to let us all work together so we can all find out who we are.' "

"Failure to support one's children is experienced as a loss of manhood."

Who men are as fathers begins—and ends, for some—with the income they can provide. As the young fathers I spoke with told me, neither they nor the women they've had children with can easily ignore their inability to be good and stable financial providers. Money defines for men much of who they are and want to be in the lives of their children. As Mercer L. Sullivan, an anthropologist who spends time talking with young fathers in low-income neighborhoods, said, "Failure to support one's children is experienced as a loss of manhood." Other paternal roles sprout off this breadwinner trunk. In its absence, the roots of parenthood are hard to firmly plant. Even if a father's income is adequate, his paternal desires may be thwarted by family members' attitudes and by how social institutions treat fathers, either ignoring them altogether or assuming they are unfit. Certainly Sid, Oscar, and Vince were trying to deliver these messages to me.

James Levine, who directs the Fatherhood Project, a national research and education initiative to find ways to support men's involvement in child-rearing, often hears young men describe the obstacles they confront as fathers. From fifteen years of experience in trying to help fathers, he knows these hurdles are very real and very daunting. "Assumptions about young fathers are all negative," Levine told me. "People who make policy, people who develop programs, people who deliver services to families— all of them need to be thinking about family as mother *and* father and not assuming, as many do now, that just because the father's not visibly present, he isn't available or interested."

Levine is encouraged because within the past few years, as societal interest in fatherhood has increased, there has also been a dramatic growth in the number of programs to help young fathers assume responsibility for their children and participate in their lives. Such attention will no doubt help, but as Levine acknowledges—and fathers I spoke with alluded to this fact—scattered programs go only so far in bringing about the fundamental changes necessary to engage large numbers of unmarried young fathers in family life. "The fundamental issue involves changing the mind-set of people who make policy," Levine explains. "What we do at the Fatherhood Project is work with what I call the mediating institutions of our society—schools, workplace, community organizations, and public programs—to try to change the attitudes and practices of people who work with families. It has been our experience that when you change the way these institutions deal with families, you can start to change the way family members behave."

Consider the Head Start program. Even though this national preschool program for low-income children—a majority of whom live in single-parent families—makes a point of stressing "parental" involvement, fathers are routinely overlooked as participants in their children's school activities. Levine's 1993 article "Involving Fathers in Head Start" pointed out that "No established line or cohesive body of literature exists on the involvement of fathers in Head Start or other early childhood programs." And out of hundreds of studies of Head Start, Levine could locate only one survey focused specifically on father involvement in the program: it found overwhelming agreement among mothers, staff people, and fathers that fathers' participation was important. However, specific strategies for increasing paternal participation aren't being used at most Head Start programs.

Indeed, getting fathers to participate in Head Start and other everyday child-centered activities can be difficult. As Levine pointed out in his 1993 article, it's necessary first to break through the thick layers of feelings many young fathers develop about the inadequacy of their parenting skills, and to ease their fear that their ineptitude will be exposed if they try. Second, mothers (who, as the young fathers I met pointed out, assume gatekeeping roles) often resist fathers' actual engagement in early child-rearing even though they say it's a good idea. In the survey about Head Start, researchers reported that "mothers did not tell fathers about, or encourage them to participate in Head Start activities." And other research suggests that unless what the child is doing interests them, fathers tend not to remain involved for long. For example, Levine found that fathers find educational toys "feminine and juvenile," don't feel comfortable playing with them, and so don't stay engaged in their children's activities.

Clearly a wide spectrum of attitudes must change if fathers—particularly younger ones—are to play significant roles in their children's lives and be invited by mothers to do so. It is unrealistic to assume that such shifts can occur in a vacuum, apart from progress in helping men address their financial obligations. True, some men will still avoid paternal responsibilities; however, filling the "Daddy" niche is far more difficult when one is not a wage-earner.

One stated goal of welfare reform is to decrease out-of-wedlock births. To achieve this will require that attention be paid not only to adolescent girls and teen mothers but to circumstances in boys' lives that predispose them to early fatherhood and to the decision not to marry the mother of their child. The young fathers I visited with offered worthwhile guidance when they suggested that unless their problems are addressed—with better schools, with job training focused on fathers' employment needs as well as mothers', and with programs to help them learn to be fathers—the proportion of children born to unmarried couples isn't likely to lessen dramatically. Clearly, as with young women, the best strategy would be to convince young men to postpone parenthood until they're prepared to handle its responsibilities. But as our attempts to persuade similarly situated adolescent girls to delay motherhood demonstrate, unless adults are willing to invest substantial time and resources in achieving this goal, babies will still be born to young people who aren't ready to be mothers or fathers and don't think of marriage as an option.

"Because he pays, he thinks he can come by whenever he wants and see the baby, which isn't right."

The day-to-day care of children is confusing for many young parents. After listening to these young men tell me about how their mothers and girlfriends ridicule them in their roles as sons and fathers, I was reminded of a conversation I had with Susan, the unmarried mother of toddler Sean, about a run-in with Sean's father, Nick.

Occasionally, Nick takes care of Sean. But, sounding exasperated, Susan tells me that what this means is that she drops Sean off at Nick's house and his mother actually does most of the caretaking, relieving her son of the responsibility that should, after all, be his. Susan doesn't ask Nick to take care of his son very often, but when she needs his help she expects him to provide it. After all, she tells me, he constantly reminds her that Sean is *his* son, too, and when he worked money was taken out of his paycheck for Sean's support.

It was on a Sunday morning that Susan learned about her grandmother's death. Determined to attend the wake and funeral, she telephoned Nick to ask him to take care of their son. She was tired of him always complaining to her about how little time he got to spend with Sean. This would give him the opportunity.

"I have a really big favor," she told Nick.

"Well, the only time you call is when you have a favor to ask," he replied, curtly.

"This is really different," she said, trying to avoid a fight right at the start of the conversation. "My grandmother passed away."

"Oh, I'm sorry." His tone of voice changed. "Tell your father I'm sorry."

Susan explained that her grandmother's wake and funeral would probably be on Tuesday and Wednesday.

"That's fine. I have nothing to do." A disability now prevents him from going to his factory job.

"Okay," she said. "But I'll call you again to let you know."

The next day Susan found out that the wake could not take place until Thursday. She called Nick back. His manner was gruff. "I hope you bring him on time, 'cause I have things to do on Thursday," he told her.

"But I need you to take Sean all day," she said. "I can't have him with me. This is my family. I have to be there all the time."

He became angry. "Don't you try to run my life!" he yelled at her. "Don't try to schedule me around what you have to do."

"I can't plan this!" Susan screamed back at him. "I can't put my grandmother's wake on hold because you have to go out and cash a check and pay people back or whatever you have to do. This is really important."

She hung up, fuming. She hated Nick's attitude. When she settled down, she tried calling back, but he wouldn't come to the phone. Finally Susan told his mother what was going on. "I don't know what his problem is," his mother said. "He has no sense of responsibility. He really needs help."

At ten o'clock on the evening before the wake, Susan finally reached Nick by phone.

"I'm not doing it," he told her. "Don't think you can run my life. Just go to hell." And he hung up.

What Susan hates most about these exchanges is how Nick always tries to blame her for controlling *his* life. Actually, the way she sees things, just the opposite is what happens. A day or two after a fight, Nick usually shows up at her house without letting her know he is coming and tells her he has a right to be there anytime he wants because "his son" lives there. "I mean, how does he know I don't have company?" Susan says, referring to her new boyfriend. "It's like I am always having to work around him and he couldn't just work around me for that one day when I needed him! So it's like he does what he wants and I have no say over it. Whenever we get into a fight about this, he's like, 'Oh, you're going to tell me when I can take my son and when I can't.' "

His refusal to take care of Sean when her grandmother died so enraged

Susan that she removed his photograph from Sean's bureau. "If he can't do that much for me, I am like I don't want Sean even referring to him any-more as his daddy until he comes and explains why he did this to me."

Susan can't tell me exactly what she expects of Sean's father if he's to be a "daddy" for a son with whom he doesn't live. But she believes he regards his parental responsibility as being fulfilled by occasional payments of child support. "That is what he does, and that is all he has to do," she says, her voice now thick with resentment. "And because he pays, he thinks he can come by whenever he wants and see the baby, which isn't right. I mean, I pay money, too. And I have to still go about my schedule by what my son does. I can't just say, 'Oh, I don't want Sean to take a nap. Let's go out.' I can't stay out until ten o'clock at night, because Sean goes to bed at a certain time. But his father doesn't realize there's this kind of responsibility. His responsibility is that he pays money and that's all he has to do. He doesn't have to come by and take him out and do things with him. He has a responsibility in his mind. But in my mind it's not a respon-sibility at all the way he is doing it."

Between young mothers and fathers lie vast gulfs of disagreement regarding who does what and who *should* do what. Some fatherhood orga-nizations attempt to help men gain clearer understanding of how relations with women affect their roles within a family. For women, similar forums for such introspection are also valuable. Unless young parents are given guidance in overcoming what one researcher calls "gender mistrust," the absence of a "daddy" can become its lasting by-product.

"They have learned to fear, perhaps to expect, failure in fatherhood."

"Gender mistrust" is what Frank Furstenberg, Jr., a preeminent researcher on adolescent pregnancy, discovered when he talked with young mothers and fathers about what keeps them apart. Gender mistrust, he writes, "pervades the cultural setting in which these young people are growing up" and infects their attitudes toward each other. The young men Fursten-berg talked with spoke of feeling "locked out" of their children's lives by women who display "nasty attitudes" toward them. The young mothers drew their criticism about their children's fathers from a wider set of beliefs about how men, in general, cannot be trusted.

Furstenberg contends that children internalize this pervasive gender mistrust as they grow up; one consequence is that by the time young men become fathers, they have internalized a "double script." "They want to do better for their children than their fathers did for them, but they have learned to fear (perhaps to expect) failure in fatherhood," Furstenberg says. Childhood experience too often teaches youngsters that, sooner or later, fathers leave families. Certainly this lesson had been learned by the young men I spoke with. It should not be surprising that, as Furstenberg writes, these young fathers get "caught in a pattern of reproducing the circumstances of their own childhood."

Nevertheless, the young mothers and fathers Furstenberg interviewed each assured him that they valued "the ideal of establishing a marriagelike relationship." However, neither sex held out much hope of achieving this ideal. The men didn't foresee having the means to provide a steady income, and thus saw themselves as powerless—particularly in comparison with mothers, whom they view as having control over their children. The young mothers echoed what Susan told me about how "being a father" has to mean more than "just paying money": they placed a high priority on fathers offering emotional support to them in their caretaking roles, but lamented how often they'd been let down in this expectation. Furstenberg asked young fathers about this complaint: as they saw it, even if they figured out how to do what the young mothers said they wanted, they would never be "fully credited" with being a father unless they backed up these personal interactions with financial support. As one young father said, "If you don't got money, mothers don't want to deal with you."

"It was like, 'I think that's my daughter' and 'I think that's my dad.' He gave her some money and that was it."

Fathers complain, as the young men I spoke with did, about mothers who make it difficult for them to see their children. However, in my conversations with young mothers I learned there's a lot these women try to do—and a lot they put up with, such as Shanika's tolerance of abuse so that her children can know their father—to keep fathers who might otherwise wander away involved in their children's lives. If mothers didn't value children's paternal connection, fewer children than do now would spend time with their fathers. One reason is that when men exit relationships with the mothers of their children, they tend to disengage from their sons and daughters as well. The same cannot generally be said of women: after their breakup with the father, their involvement with their children usually continues.

Reflecting on what young mothers and fathers said about their interpersonal dynamics, Frank Furstenberg wrote: "It is almost as if many
fathers saw their child care responsibilities as part of an umbrella contract
with their children's mother." Many young men, he believes, regard
fatherhood as a "quid pro quo for [women] continuing an emotional
relationship that involves caring for them as well." For example, had
Morena in the early years of motherhood been willing to devote herself to
taking care of her children, their father, *and* their father's brothers, Kendra
and Daniel might have grown up knowing Anthony as their father. But
since she wasn't willing, he separated himself entirely from his children's
lives. He sent them no letters, placed very few phone calls, paid them no
visits, provided no money, and didn't get them any gifts.

For adolescent mothers, in particular, the personal demands placed
upon them by the fathers of their children can be overwhelming. To begin
with, many of these fathers are more than a few years older than the
mothers; two-thirds of teenage mothers have children with men who are
over twenty. This age difference can make even more brittle the already
delicate balance of power in their relationships. Many men soon vanish,
but even when fathers try to maintain the romantic relationship, young
mothers find they have little power to bring about a paternal relationship,
especially when the man doesn't want one. And the personal sacrifices
sometimes demanded of women if they want to keep fathers present for
their children can be an unfair burden for them to bear.

At the age of sixteen, Lavina, already the mother of two girls, waited in
line overnight at the welfare office. The next morning she received what
she'd camped out for: a housing voucher that enabled her and her two
daughters to move into their own apartment. Her mother's house was not
working out as a place to raise her children. Lavina's five siblings were in
trouble more often than they were in school; alcohol and drug use were
rampant in the neighborhood and now family members and friends were
bringing the ugliness inside. Besides, the apartment was crowded and
Lavina ached for privacy.

Her children's fathers, both of whom were in their early twenties, were
not involved in Lavina's decisions or in their daughters' lives. This was not
Lavina's choice; both men were imprisoned soon after their daughters
were born. "I thought I was a jinxed person," Lavina says.

These difficult times are now a dozen years in her past. Today Lavina's
brown eyes sparkle with such confidence that she belies her earlier self-
portrait. Everything about her childhood—her father's disappearance, her
mother's lack of a high school education, her family's reliance on welfare,

the crime-ridden neighborhood in which she was raised, the arrival of her first child when she was fourteen, then of a second one within two years, the fathers of her children ending up in jail—all portended dire outcomes for her and her children. Yet today, at the age of twenty-nine, Lavina is in college, has a job at the school as part of her financial aid, and soon plans to be off welfare forever. Her four daughters are all progressing well in school. When Lavina tells me about her life today, her rose-red lips shape themselves into an ebullient smile.

During her teenage years, when motherhood came unexpectedly and quickly, Lavina felt anything but confident about herself. She'd gone looking for love from men who were much older than she; what she got was babies. The father of her first daughter, a baby conceived when she was thirteen years old, was twenty-one. "He went to jail, so that's why I had nobody else there," Lavina says. "I used to write him and he'd write me. And I spoke to him a few times on the phone. I asked him if we would, like, get married someday. And he was, like . . . well, he didn't say no but he didn't say yes. So I got real disappointed and I never called him or wrote to him again."

"And he never saw his child?" I ask.

"He did. A long time after, not then," Lavina says matter-of-factly. "Then the same thing happened with my second child, when I was two or three months pregnant. These guys were older guys so they were doing stuff I did not know about. Selling drugs. He went to jail for a year. I was going to visit him in jail until one day another girl came when I was there. I just looked up at him and I said, 'Do you want to make a choice here?' And when he didn't say a word, I just walked out. I didn't see him for a long time after that." The father of her second child initially even denied his paternity. He finally acknowledged it to Lavina, but no legal documents were signed. She doesn't know where he is today.

"He doesn't even have a relationship with his daughter. The first one, he always said, 'Yeah, that's my daughter.' But he never did anything for her. I was very proud so I wasn't going to ask anybody for anything. I always felt it was on him. He should come to me and see her. I should not have to chase him because this is his daughter." Later on, when Lavina developed more confidence in herself, she did assert herself as an advocate for her children and work hard to keep her other daughters' father involved in his children's lives even after their own relationship ended. But when Lavina was young, this wasn't something she thought a lot about, nor was it something she believed she had any ability to influence.

The result was that her two older daughters have never spent time with their fathers. When Lavina's oldest daughter was fifteen, she bumped into her father at a convenience store. She'd seen him only a few times when she was growing up, but something about him made her look again. "She looked at him and he looked at her," Lavina says, recounting the scene as her daughter described it to her. "It was sort of like 'I think that's my dad' and 'I think that's my daughter.' He gave her some money and that was it."

"Do your daughters' fathers remember their birthdays or call them on Christmas?" I ask.

"No, no," she says, emphatically. Her expression lets me know she is surprised by my question.

I ask whether the state has tried to get either of these men to pay child support.

"Oh, it tried," she says, exhaling resignedly. "The state needs their social security numbers and I don't have them. The revenue department did find the oldest one's father and made him pay. It would send me a check for fifty dollars once a month. But that only happened twice. After that, nothing happened again."

"Did they ever find your second daughter's father?"

"No."

"He'd tell me nobody would want me and I'd better stay with him because who was going to want me with all these kids."

Babies and bad relationships defined Lavina's adolescence. She never resumed relationships with either of her children's fathers after they got out of jail. But before she was twenty Lavina moved in with a man—again someone a lot older than she—and, with him, had two more children. When her third child was a baby, Lavina, who had passed her GED, tried to go back to school. But the father of her child, Juan, ordered her to stay home with the baby, and in those days she did as men told her to do. "I didn't stick up for myself," she says.

"Did you consider marrying Juan?"

"No," she responds, firmly.

"Did he consider marrying you?"

"No."

"This wasn't an issue?"

"Um, um, no." Lavina hesitates. Her eyes, which were looking into mine, now turn away. Lavina is quiet and pensive, as she debates whether she should go on. We are sitting in an alcove of an office she shares. Even though no one else is in the room, her voice becomes soft and secretive.

"Juan was involved with drugs," Lavina says, and after living with him for a while, she was, too. "At first he'd just get high and I would see that he was. It didn't bother me. But then he started bringing the drugs home and I said, 'Well, I want to do it, too.' So I started doing it."

"Even with the kids around!" I'm surprised to hear this, because during her early teenage years, when pressures on her were immense, Lavina had not given in to the lure of drugs or alcohol.

"I didn't do it in front of the children, but they were around," she says. Lavina explains how she would get high after her daughters were asleep.

I ask her why she decided to use drugs.

"I felt different when I did it. I didn't feel so uptight and boring. I'd always felt so boring. I would always say, 'I have nothing to say. Nothing exciting ever happens to me. I never do or say anything exciting.' I felt so boring and so ugly that when I did do the drugs, I felt happy." Soon, however, Lavina realized what the drugs were doing to her—and to her ability to function as a mother. She wanted to escape from the drugs and from the man who had introduced her to them, but she discovered this was hard to do. Loneliness and physical addiction kept bringing Juan and his drugs back into her life, even though each time he returned their relationship worsened. He abused her physically. "He was mentally abusive to me, too. He'd tell me nobody would want me and I'd better stay with him because who was going to want me with all these kids." In a voice that emphasizes her disbelief, she says, "And I put up with that!"

Although Lavina didn't notice it at the time, her children, particularly her oldest daughter, were starting to act more motherly to her than she was acting toward them. Between her drug use and her anger at what her life was becoming, Lavina's ability to be a parent was compromised. Her fourth child was conceived with her partner while she was in a residence house for battered women, recuperating from his abuse. This pregnancy kept them together for a while longer, but as time went by all she wanted was for him to leave. Finally he did.

"My daughter wasn't very old when he left," Lavina says, referring to their second child. "I didn't tell him he couldn't see the children. I just told him he couldn't be with me."

"You and I don't have to have any kind of friendship or relationship. It is just you and them."

It's now been several years since Lavina found a way out of her downward spiral. Eventually, drug treatment worked for her, and her dream of one day going to college is now being realized. But I am curious to know what happened to the father of her third and fourth children and what, if any, relationship they now have with him. "Do the girls ever see him? Does he pay anything to help support them?" I ask.

"Yeah, he picks them up," she says. "He takes them places. He's clean now, too." Lavina's wide smile returns. But soon her tone grows harsh again: "For a while he wasn't taking the girls. Everything else was his priority but them. And I was worried about my daughters. I don't want to see them suffer. The little ones, they were really close to him. They grew up with him. He was always around."

Lavina resolved that her younger daughters would not lose touch with their father even though he was no longer involved with her. They let her know how sad it made them not to be able to spend time with their father. And they were also hurt by Juan's inability to follow through on his promises to do things with them. Lavina suggested that they speak with him about how his behavior was making them feel. But her daughters told her they didn't know how to say these things to him. They delegated Lavina to deliver their message.

She did. "I got angry at him and I said, 'Look. I don't tell you that you can't see them, but I am getting upset. You tell them you're going to come and then you don't. You need to take a hard look at that.' " It was difficult for Lavina to get Juan to understand that his paternal relationship with his children could, and should, continue to develop even though they were no longer together. "You and I don't have to have any kind of friendship or relationship," she told Juan. "It is just you and them." After a while, her words sank in. Juan began to call more often and when he arranged get-togethers he'd arrive when he'd said he would to take them to the movies and out to eat.

"Now he's got a girlfriend," Lavina says. This woman's presence seems to have helped by shifting Juan's focus away from Lavina and on to his children.

"Does he pay child support?" I ask.

"He gives me money. If he was to give it to them [the child support enforcement system], they would only give me fifty dollars a month. So I would get less money than he gives me now." But Juan recently started to work at a steady job, and Lavina suspects the state will eventually catch up with him and start to deduct child support from his wages. "I'm not protecting him," she says, with a shrug. By this she means she hasn't hidden his identity from the folks at the welfare department. "Right now," she says, in a display of her emerging self-confidence, "I am protecting myself."

I ask Lavina whether her two older daughters—who are not biologically linked to this man—think of him as their father. After all, during most of their childhood they lived with him.

"No," she replies, firmly. "I have never told my daughters that he is their father or that they had to call him Dad. 'Call him by his name,' I'd tell them. They know he was with me, but they didn't like him too much for a long time. But he is good to the girls."

"There don't have to be two parents there if you meet their needs."

As our conversation winds down, I ask Lavina to respond to the frequently voiced comments connecting unmarried mothers and families, such as hers, with society's most intractable problems.

"It has nothing to do with being a single parent," Lavina says in a determined voice. "I know families with two parents and they have all these kids who are messed up. It has to do with how you bring up children. I know I have made a lot of mistakes, but I must have done some things right somewhere along the line that my kids are the way they are right now. It is up to the parent. There don't have to be two parents there if you meet their needs, and I've tried. Their needs that I can't meet, I have let them know I can't. I don't lie about it. I don't make my daughters false promises."

Lavina realizes that many people who don't know her or her daughters are likely to blame her and others like her for the unraveling of our society. She knows that a lot of people would probably say that she hasn't been a "good mother" to her children. In class discussions in college, she hears her fellow students say plenty of derogatory things about unmarried mothers on welfare, women like her who are rearing children apart from their fathers. "They think everybody is on welfare because they want the money and that we have a lot of kids just to keep getting money," says Lavina. At first, she just listened to what her classmates were saying. "They said that we're nothing. That we don't think. That we aren't smart. That we are content. We are happy being on welfare." After a while, Lavina spoke up: "Well, I am not content or happy about being on welfare." Lavina tried to help her classmates understand a bit more about the circumstances under which fathers vanish and women end up taking care of the children on their own.

Her parenting life, Lavina admits, "would have been easier" if she'd found a reliable partner. But she knows herself well enough now to realize that a parenting partnership will only work if the man can be a positive contributor in emotional as well as financial ways. Lavina refuses to ever again enter into a relationship with a man who tries to tell her what she can and cannot do. "If this family can't have that"—the supportive involvement of a father figure—"then we have to do it on our own, and we will do the best we can. But that doesn't mean we are doing a lousy job because we're doing it on our own. I don't think I'm doing a lousy job. In fact, I think I'm doing a pretty good job."

"I'm not going to try to keep the ties if he is just going to be gone the next day."

Many young mothers told me of efforts like Lavina's to keep their children's father engaged in their lives. When Lavina saw her children's father growing detached, she stepped in. The role she played—trying to convince an unattached partner to remain involved with his children—is one many mothers realize they must play if their children are not to lose touch with their fathers. When women don't make such efforts, men are more likely to disappear, as the fathers of Lavina's first two children did. But when—because of exhaustion or anger—young mothers stop trying to encourage fathers to participate in children's lives, long-lasting disconnection often follows.

Lavina's recollections of her efforts to keep the father-daughter connections strong reminded me of conversations I'd had with Sarah, the woman who, like Lavina, had a child at the age of fourteen and is now in college. Sarah told me about the things she'd tried over the years to keep her son, David, and his father, Terry, in each other's lives. At first, Terry came around all the time; but, as is often the case, as months and years went by his visits became much less frequent. But Sarah was willing to do whatever she required to get Terry to spend more time with David. Sarah's mother, Judy, once explained to me why this seemed so important to her daughter: "Because Sarah didn't have a father who was active in her life, a father is very important to her. So Sarah puts up with a lot of stuff with her son's father."

Terry never paid child support, but that didn't keep Sarah from wanting him to stay connected with his son. When Terry left school and moved to a different city, Sarah would take David to see him. When Terry had a child with another woman, Linda, Sarah established a close relationship with her. She believed that was the only way her son's connection with his father—and with his new half-brother—would not fade away. And she was right. He remained involved with David because Sarah and Linda combined their efforts to make sure of it.

During Sarah's first year at college, when studies and work and David's care consumed all of her time, she ran out of energy to keep after Terry. "I've been really busy with school and not able to see Linda," Sarah said. "And because I haven't been able to make the effort to go over there and maintain a friendship with her, his father hasn't made an effort to stay in touch with his son." David's relationship with his father was, she said despondently, "dwindling away." At the time we had this conversation Sarah was also getting ready to move about sixty miles away to attend a four-year college she had transferred to. Ordinarily she would have been thinking about making arrangements for David to remain in frequent contact with his father. But it was clear that she had reached a point of exasperation with juggling all her responsibilities and trying to keep Terry involved; she now seemed willing to simply let Terry fend for himself and see what happens.

"I'm basically starting over," Sarah declared, referring both to her impending move and her change in attitude about her son's father. "I'll explain to my son that when his father comes, he comes. But right now his father is even talking about moving to Florida. I mean, he can just up and leave whenever he wants to. I'm not going to try to keep the ties if he is just going to be gone the next day. So I'm going to go on and build our life on us two. If Terry comes by, great. I will let my son take what he can out of his father when he does come. But other than that, I am not going to have my son depending on him."

"It is extremely important, particularly for a male child, to have a father image."

Mothers sometimes give up on trying to keep fathers involved with their children and decide it's better for the children and them to be on their own. But as time goes by and children grow older, some women start to wonder if their children need someone else, a man, as part of their daily lives. This is especially so in the case of sons. But finding men who will not only accept the independent spirit some of these mothers have carved out during their single-parenting experience, but also agree to be active in the lives of children they did not create can be difficult. Weaving these two relationships together is important because, as research points out—and as many mothers know intuitively—if her personal connection with the man doesn't work out, his interaction with his children is likely to suffer.

Naomi's son, Michael, is almost nine years old. His father, whom Naomi left when her son was an infant, has never been involved with him. It is time, his mother figures, for him to have a "dad." Marriage is something she is now, at the age of twenty-nine, seriously considering for the first time, in part for herself, but mostly for her son. "It's extremely important, particularly for a male child, to have a father image," Naomi says one morning when I join her at a house for older students on her college campus.

Unlike most of her younger classmates, Naomi doesn't live in a dormitory, roll out of bed to a ready-made breakfast, and then walk a few hundred yards to her first class. By 8:40 in the morning, she's woken her son, tried to get him to eat a good breakfast, checked to see that his homework is in his backpack, walked him to the school bus, organized herself for her day of classes, and driven a half-hour to get herself to school. She had to postpone schooling when her unintended pregnancy made unmarried motherhood a part of her life during years when she should have been in college. While we talk, she drinks a cup of coffee and eats a doughnut. For her, food is consumed on the run.

I ask her to describe to me how her son is getting along without a father. "I don't negate the need for a father image, and no one who has a child will," Naomi says. She sounds defensive, as though she's responding to some criticism I didn't make. I wonder whether she thinks that a white person, like me, assumes that black women, like her, don't worry about the absence of a child's father. By the firmness of her response, Naomi leaves no doubt that that absence bothers her a lot, just as it does other black single mothers she knows. "But women don't usually come to this conclusion until after they have their child and they see that this child needs a father," she continues. "Male. Female. Children need that other person to tell them what it's going to be like from the perspective of an African-American man. I cannot tell my child what it is going to be like to be an African-American male. I am not an African-American male."

Even though Naomi wants to bring a man into her and her son's lives, she tells me how hard it is to find a "marriageable man," one whom she knows they will be able to count on. She explains that when young black women look around and see a dearth of dependable men, many aren't willing to put motherhood on hold and wait around, hoping to meet men who, the odds tell them, will never appear. (Her explanation makes me think of the single women my age who decide to have babies on their own when "marriageable men" don't seem likely to materialize.) The result for Naomi and her peers is that a lot of black children grow up living apart from, and in many cases not knowing, their biological fathers. I know that the inability of Naomi's former boyfriend to curb his drinking led her to leave him, even though they had a child together.

As I listen to Naomi, I restlessly scribble in my notebook. When I glance down at the page, I see swirling lines creating incomplete circles. I show them to Naomi. "None of these circles is complete," I say, pulling the page back; my hand seems to want to keep drawing them. "In some way, these incomplete circles make me think about the end result of what we've been talking about. I mean if women continue to raise boys within mother-only families, then how do future generations emerge out of this cycle to produce marriageable men?"

"There is a tremendous amount of pathology left in the African-American community," Naomi says. I'm startled at hearing her use the word "pathology," which Daniel Patrick Moynihan was so bitterly criticized for using three decades ago when he discussed out-of-wedlock births in black communities. Even today, the word is seldom used in this context. But Naomi goes on to describe how she makes historic connections with the present. "Tremendous damage has been done to our community by our experiences on this continent for the last four hundred years and by the history of racism in this country," Naomi says. "To remedy it, white people are going to have to abdicate the privilege that comes along with being a white person and give up the notion that they have certain inalienable rights because their skin is white. Until that happens, nothing is going to be accomplished. I mean, we've said as a society that we'll train African-American males, but we have not said we will employ them."

Naomi stops talking, abruptly. Her silence leaves the emphasis where she wants it, on what she's just said about how men whom she might have married when she was younger couldn't find the secure footholds they needed to prepare themselves to be husbands and fathers.

"My son needed me and I couldn't be there. I had to make a choice."

It has been tough for Naomi to raise Michael on her own. She hated being on welfare, but she's stayed on it, she says, for her son's sake. She did not want to be at work all the time, leaving him without any parent in his daily life. Nor did Naomi want to become stuck in a dead-end cycle of low-wage jobs. Naomi now uses the support she gets from welfare to take care of her son while she earns the college degree that will enable her to launch herself in a career and support both of them. She plans to go on to law or business school, as well.

When Michael was younger, Naomi did try working for a while, at a marketing job that paid a decent salary. She says it could have led to better-paying jobs and a good career, but it also demanded a huge amount of time, as many potentially well-paid, entrepreneurial jobs do. The hours became so long, her workload so heavy, and the pressures on her so intense that Naomi realized her son wasn't getting the attention he needed from her. "He was very unhappy," Naomi says. "My son needed me and I could not be there. So I had to make a choice. I gave up my job. That was an extremely difficult decision. For the next few years, I went through a rough period. It was very painful. I was very angry and resentful, not only toward myself but toward my son for a while after that." What was tough for Naomi to reconcile was the fact that her internal drive to work and her desire to better herself clashed sharply with her son's needs. Postponing her ambitions for the sake of her son's well-being was one of the most difficult things Naomi has ever had to do.

Naomi harbored no such ambivalence about her decision not to marry Michael's father. Marriage to him would have meant trying to get through the days and nights sharing her life—and her son's—with an alcoholic, a man who expressed his anger and frustration about his own circumstances by physically abusing her and upon whose salary she knew her family could not depend. Given that alternative, Naomi thinks her decision to be an unmarried mother was the right one. Since then, she has tried to do whatever it takes to make things be as good as they can be for Michael. Because she always wanted him to be around positive male role models, she moved away from the neighborhood where he was born. That was a community in which most of the families had only mothers. The few men hanging around were not ones she wanted her son to emulate. Now, when she can't be home, Michael attends after-school programs in which she makes certain male teachers and counselors are involved.

Naomi also does what she can to prepare her son for encounters he, as an African-American male, will undoubtedly experience. There have already been times when Michael has asked her why classmates who are white don't want to play with him when the school day is over. And he wants to know why some older boys are pressuring him to do things his mother tells him are wrong. That her son talks with her about these things, and that he appears to trust what she tells him, Naomi believes is a mark of the close relationship she's worked hard to construct. Her concern now, as her son gets older, is that her word alone will no longer be enough. He will need, she suspects, to hear similar advice from a man whom he trusts.

"If I was to try to be his father, it would negate my femaleness."

Her son is in the third grade. Naomi says that, from what she's read and observed, it's during the third and fourth grades that many children lose their way academically—and then never catch up. "This is when black boys start to disconnect themselves from the process of education," Naomi says. "It is when they begin to recognize that their world is set to destroy them. They begin to recognize that they are not supported, that they have no father, that there are no men in the community and that uncles and cousins, all of these men, have failed. They are standing on the corner. They are not going to be anything. And a boy says to himself, 'I am not going to be anything either. I'm going to be just like them.' And when they look in the mirror, they see the men who are standing on the corner. By this age, boys know their world. Most people don't give kids that age that much credit, but they recognize their world."

Studies back up Naomi's speculations: if youngsters have fallen too far behind by fourth grade, they can become permanently blocked in their educational progress. To counter this, Naomi thinks it is vital for Michael to develop a close, trusting relationship with a man who can become his "dad," a man who'll commit himself—as part of marriage with Naomi—to being very much involved in her son's daily life.

Naomi realizes that she may not be able to meet, on her own, the upcoming tasks of raising her son. "Women are not men," she says, stating what's obvious but often seems to be overlooked. "Black women do not know what it is to be a black man. Regardless of what you hear women say—'I am both father and mother'—that is impossible. A woman cannot be expected to take the man's role. Young men need to see other men. They need to learn from other men what it is to be a man. And women simply don't have the tools to teach young men that. If I was to try to be Michael's father, it would negate my femaleness. And I don't want my son to think that women have to be both men and women. They can't be. And I don't have a problem with that. I'm not threatened by that prospect. I have no desire to be both. I like being a woman. I have things about me that men don't have. Those are the things I want to concentrate on showing my son."

Certainly the young fathers I spoke with—and others I read about—echo the sentiments Naomi expresses about fatherless childhood. Their mothers failed them not so much because they didn't try mightily to fill in for the missing family member, but because it was never possible for them to succeed. So much about becoming a man will always remain mysterious to women. And when mothers don't know these things—*and* when, in addition, their opinions about men are biased by bad personal experiences—how can they convey positive messages to their sons?

Her son, Naomi says, is already sharing with her his confusion about what it is men and women do in families. She believes his confusion arises out of the steady onslaught of images and messages in the media about relationships between men and women. She wants him to be able to watch a man and a woman interact in real day-to-day experiences, to create for him a visible counterweight.

But Naomi wants more than this. She is unwilling to introduce Michael to a relationship built on what she considers outmoded gender roles. "Our societal norm," she complains, "has been that men are in control of women. So if a boy is listening to his mother, he is thought not to be in control of women. Okay. By the time a boy is in the third grade, they have been socialized in school, by the media, by their peers on the street—I mean, no matter how they got it, they learn to reject femininity and to begin to take control over women in their lives. They go to play with their friends on the streets when they are eight. By the age of ten or eleven, they've bonded so closely with their friends that they are on their way to being in a gang by thirteen or fourteen. That is how gangs form. It starts very young."

Naomi believes—as many experts do—that the boys most attracted to gangs are the ones who are left too much on their own to define manhood. "These boys take their images of manhood from the only source they can find," she says. "The media. And what do they see on television? Violence. Violence is manhood. That is what being a 'man' means. And they take images from their own fathers. Being a man means having babies. It doesn't mean taking care of babies, but it does mean having them. And it means conquering women. It means controlling women. It means controlling the community. 'My father was not able to be in control. I am going to be in control,' boys will say. And this is the way they get to be in control: if they're violent and if they scare people. These boys feel 'scared' and 'respect' are the same things. But it doesn't necessarily mean people care about you and like you in terms of this kind of respect."

I find Naomi's insights intriguing, as I do so much of what she tells me. "These young men, they might be looking for that other kind of respect as well?" I ask.

"Well, yes," she replies. "They wanted that respect from their fathers. They wanted their fathers to respect and love them enough to be there, and they weren't. These are some very angry children. They grow up angry. They have tremendous frustration. A lot of times their mothers are unable to take care of them in the way they need to be taken care of, physically, emotionally, financially. They are in poverty. They feel they are being oppressed. Then they get all these messages from blacks in the community who've failed and who are saying, 'The man got me down. I am angry and this is what I'm going to do.' "

Naomi wants her son to be around men whose lives offer more positive messages. And if she gets married, she wants her husband's actions and words to paint a similar portrait. She wants her son to be exposed to experiences in which "he sees other black men be successful." Most of all, what Naomi thinks Michael needs now is active reinforcement from black men for the "things he is learning at home about education. Unless black boys see this valued consistently and are taught to believe it is real and tangible for them so they can say, 'I can do this,' they're not going to buy into it. They need to be sold these messages from birth or soon after, at least within the first eight years of their lives. After that, it starts to be too late."

"I think that having a strong relationship with his own father is an indication of the father he is."

A few months later, Naomi tells me that she is going to marry Darnell, the man she's been dating. They'll be getting married this summer, before Michael enters the fourth grade. A big part of her decision to marry Darnell, she says, is "the kind of influence he will have on my son." If Michael weren't part of the equation, it's likely she would have selected, in her words, "an entirely different person." But Michael *is* very much involved, and she believes Darnell will be good for *him*.

"He is a loving, caring, unselfish type of man who can love my son as his own," Naomi says. "I wanted to marry someone I knew was going to adopt my son." She and Michael will take her husband's last name. This signifies to her that, if they have a child together, Darnell will regard Michael as equally his son. Naomi insisted that her future husband have other qualifications, too. "I wanted to marry someone who is true to his blackness, who doesn't do anything to negate it. Another man I dated, and for a time considered marrying, was very assimilationist, and I hate that. I don't want to assimilate, where you have to negate your culture to be successful. I don't think anyone should have to do that." More important, she did not want Michael to grow up believing that was what he had to do.

Naomi is somewhat concerned about what might happen to her marriage when it is time for her to launch her career. She admits to being very ambitious. One day she told me she wants to be the first black person to chair the U.S. Senate Finance Committee. At this point she is planning to become a lawyer. Naomi is aware that, like many black female professionals, she's likely to earn more than her husband whatever career she pursues. Already her education level is higher than his. Naomi wants Darnell to be able to accept this disparity and not expose Michael to unnecessary conflict between them about who earns what.

But the fundamental requirement her prospective husband had to meet was that he would be a good "daddy" to Michael. Naomi's decision to marry Darnell was based, she reminds me, on the "existence of this little human being who I absolutely adore and would die for." Naomi delights in telling me how playful Darnell is with her son: "He's like a big kid." Aside from his playfulness, Darnell also spends a lot of time helping Michael with his math homework. This has been a great relief to Naomi, who has a learning disability that leaves her with the same frustrations her son experiences with numbers and has made working with Michael on his math homework difficult for both of them. "I have no patience," she admits. "So I don't want my son to fall through the cracks while I am off doing my thing and for him to be failing when I can't help him."

Naomi's fiancé has no children of his own, so they have spent a lot of time talking about how each thinks children should be raised. And Naomi has watched carefully to see how he behaves with Michael. Fortunately, their styles and perspectives turned out to be similar. There was another man whom Naomi dated and considered marrying, but when they talked about parenting, she realized how much work it would take "to train him how to train my child." Darnell, Naomi boasts, "is already trained." And she's convinced that his ability to relate so well to her son has to do with his own close connection with his father: "I think that having a strong relationship with his own father is an indication of the father he will be."

"I don't want any man to think they have the right to father children and walk away from responsibility."

As well suited as her fiancé seems to be, Naomi is mindful of how marriage can turn oppressive for women. Spending so many years raising Michael on her own has made her protective of her needs, as well as her son's.

"My fiancé and I have this argument all of the time about how I no longer want to be a slave to my husband or to society," Naomi explains to me one evening. She's invited me to visit her in her cramped two-bedroom apartment. Her living room is crowded with boxes and bicycles; stacks of books and notebooks teeter on every available tabletop. Her kitchen runs along the back wall of the living room; her son's bedroom and hers are squeezed next to each other. Darnell will be home soon. As though prepping me for the moment when I'll meet him, she assures me that he's not at all chauvinistic. But she also lets me know that any man who lives with her needs to have an extra dose of self-confidence mixed in with plenty of patience and understanding.

"Right now I am helping him to understand why I am so driven," Naomi says. "And I need him to see the biases that exist for me. I mean, forty or fifty years ago, women like me would have been given lobotomies because we would have been deemed crazy. Or we would have killed ourselves. Or people would have called us deviant." She laughs as she hears herself say "deviant." Surely a lot of people still consider her deviant, Naomi says with a chuckle.

The night before our visit she and her fiancé were awake until three A.M., going over and over what is by now familiar territory. "I spent four hours last night telling him that I am not going to become a domestic servant when we get married. I'm not going to be entirely responsible for the household. I told him how I have goals and dreams of things I want to achieve." A look of determination fixes itself on her face. "I'm serious," she says. "He needs to understand this about me before we go into this. I told him, 'I'll walk out on you. I will. Do you understand what I am saying to you? I will leave. If it's a choice between me maintaining my sanity or maintaining my marriage, I'll choose my sanity.' I told him he'd better take a real hard look at whether he wants to be with somebody who is telling him, 'Yes, I am a woman, but I am going to be in control of what happens to me. If you can handle that, fine. If you can't, there are other brothers waiting for you to screw up.' "

I ask Naomi why, if she feels this way, she is getting married.

"I found the right person to father my children," she declares.

"But why not be with him and have children with him and not get married?"

"Because I've been through too much as a single parent, and because I don't want any man to think he has the right to father a child and walk away from responsibility. Because many women choose to be single parents, most men feel that way. That bothers me. I want my children to have a father, a man to look to. In the African-American community, this is very important. But this doesn't mean I'm in favor of the traditional nuclear family. I have thought about these things since I was nine years old [when her parents' marriage broke apart]. Ever since then I wanted to create my own version of family."

I ask Naomi what her family life is like now that this man is becoming an integral part of it.

"He cleans up in here now or he doesn't stay here," she says. "He goes to the grocery store. I can't remember the last time I went. He does all of the so-called women's things that most men are uncomfortable admitting they do. And he does it with no problem because he realizes how important this is to our relationship. He takes care of my son. He takes him to get his hair cut."

"At this point in your life, this is what you want?"

"That's right. That is what the women's movement was about," Naomi says. It is interesting to hear Naomi speak of the women's movement in the past tense, as if no such entity exists any longer. For her and her contemporaries, perhaps that is so. It is true that to many of her generation the idea that there are universal women's causes doesn't seem as clear as it did to me at her age. "It was about choices," Naomi says, referring again to the movement. "And I have chosen this life for myself." Unlike many of her contemporaries, Naomi isn't reluctant to attach the word "feminist" to herself. I ask her to tell me what she means by it.

"It means having our own voices and controlling our own bodies and our own destinies," Naomi replies. "That's what being a feminist is. That is what I am. Just like I made a choice not to be married before I was ready and not to be married before I'd found the right person. Now I'm making a choice to be married. It's a choice for me. It's not an obligation. And that is the important thing."

8

Where's Daddy?
Unmarried Older Mothers

When it is bedtime for Bethany's three-year-old boys, they sometimes say to her, "Mommy, read us the Daddy book." Its actual title is *Do I Have a Daddy?* It is a story about Erik, a boy a little older than they are who wants to ask his mother many questions about his father, a man he doesn't remember, a man his mother never married.

On the day the story takes place, Erik's friend Jennifer is angry at him for dropping a pan on her foot, even though it was an accident. Jennifer tells him she's going to tell her daddy what he has done. Erik says he'll do the same.

As Bethany reads to her sons, she assumes the voices of the book's characters.

> "But you don't have a Daddy," Jennifer said.
> "I do, too," replied Erik.
> "Where is he?" asked Jennifer.
> "I . . . I don't know," said Erik.
> Then he decided to go home.

Bethany sits in a rocking chair between her sons' beds while she reads to them. Occasionally she lifts the book over her head and, holding it open with three fingers, shows each of her boys the illustration. Noah and

Mark especially like to see the one in which Erik's mother is comforting him. On most evenings the children are content just to listen, but a few times they have stopped her to ask questions about their daddy, a man their mommy never met, a man she'll never marry, a man they'll never know.

"Do we have a daddy?" Mark asks.

"No," Bethany replies. Her tone is comforting but the words she uses are intentionally direct. She wants to leave no ambiguity in their minds. "In our family, we just have a mommy."

Bethany's sandy shoulder-length hair is flecked with a few strands of gray, reminders to her that motherhood didn't arrive until she was in her early forties, and then only after considerable planning and effort. But being an older mother, she believes, gives her a degree of confidence about parenting that she wouldn't have felt if she'd had children when she was younger.

She's comfortable in talking with her sons about how every child has a father, but not everyone has a "daddy." Right now, with her children as young as they are, Bethany tries to convey these complicated ideas simply. A few years from now, when they're five or six, she'll explain the circumstances of their birth with different words, but the core of her message will remain the same: in their family, they have only a mommy. Her graduate training in psychology provides Bethany with a foundation of understanding about the ways parents can best help children to cope with such circumstances. She believes that if she responds forthrightly and calmly to her sons' questions about their "missing" father, Mark and Noah will accept their family as it is even if they also miss having a daddy.

In *Do I Have a Daddy?*, Erik gets home, where he talks with his mother.

> Suddenly Erik started crying.
>
> "Where's my Daddy?" he asked. "Do I have a Daddy? Jennifer says I don't have a Daddy."
>
> "I'll tell you about your Daddy," Mother said. "You had a Daddy in the beginning. It takes both a Mommy and a Daddy to make a baby."
>
> "But Jennifer's Daddy lives with her," said Erik. "I've never seen my Daddy."

"Why don't I have a daddy?"

Bethany has never known her boys to cry about not having a daddy. Whenever they want to know something about their family, she encourages them to ask her. She always offers them as clear an answer as she thinks they can understand. Bethany knows that if she were to make the subject of the missing "daddy" appear secret or off-limits, what her sons might imagine about him—who he is or where he is—could be harder for them to cope with than the facts she shares and the little talks they occasionally have. Her boys' curiosity about their father surfaces only in spurts, then fades away for a while after she responds to whatever they want to know.

Bethany is certain that as Mark and Noah grow older their conversations will return to this subject many times. "As they get older, what they want to know will get more complex," Bethany says, and lists some new questions she anticipates: "Why don't I have a daddy? Did I ever have one? Can I find him? Do you know who my daddy is?" If she starts now to try to dispel the mystery, Bethany believes, it will be easier for them to accept their father's permanent absence from their lives. Because their mother used sperm from an anonymous donor—and one who did not agree to be identified—her sons will never be able to know any more about their father than the little bit of information Bethany received when she selected his sperm from a catalog. However, she wants to avoid a situation in which her boys feel ashamed of who they are because of how they came to be.

On some nights, instead of reading to them, Bethany tells her sons a fairytale-like story about a mommy having children, a story that crisscrosses with facts about their origin. She tells them about "Mommy," a woman who wants to have a baby very, very much, and a doctor, who she tells them is a wonderful person and helps Mommy make her biggest wish come true. There is also the "donor" in this make-believe story—just as there was in real life—who is portrayed as a generous man whom Mommy's doctor found for her. This donor gives Mommy what she needs to be able to have her babies, whom she loves very, very much.

"This story is a vehicle by which the kids can say, 'Gee, that's like me,' " Bethany says.

Bethany's custom-made story helps Noah and Mark to think about how their mommy made them, a biological process they're still too young to understand. Bethany knows it will be a few years before she can explain to them about a mother's egg and a father's sperm, how they meet, and what sometimes happens when they do. In the meantime, she tells them things such as "there was not a daddy, but there was a man who gave your mommy sperm." She wants them to be able to embrace this idea that a special man—their father—did something to help their mommy create them. Occasionally, Bethany shares tidbits of information she has about their father, such as the fact that he is a dentist.

Even when Bethany's sons don't appear to respond to the information, she believes that they're storing it away, like squirrels hiding acorns for the winter. Every so often one of her sons reminds her of something about their father that she'd mentioned a long time before, so she knows they are processing what she tells them, however they can. And on the evenings when she reads to them, Noah and Mark "eavesdrop" on Erik's questions. A lot of what this fictional character asks is on their minds.

Bethany reads on:

> A few days later Erik asked, "Will my Daddy come back?"
>
> "I don't think so," his mother answered.
>
> "But I want a Daddy like Jennifer's," Erik said.
>
> "Perhaps you will [have one] some day," said his mother.
>
> "You see, there are different kinds of Daddies. Sometimes a Daddy goes away as yours did. He may not see his children at all. Other Daddies live with their children and help take care of them—like Jennifer's Daddy.
>
> "You might have a different Daddy someday. If I get married, the man I marry will be your Daddy, too."

Bethany doesn't know if she'll get married. Right now the possibility seems remote. The solo parenting of her young children, a full-time work schedule, and the accompanying exhaustion make it hard to imagine how she'd be able to develop a relationship that might bring a "daddy" into her sons' lives. Like many of the older women I met who decided to have children in the absence of marriage, Bethany accepts that the way her family life is now is the way it's likely to be, at least in the foreseeable future. However, she can tell Noah and Mark, just as Erik's mother told him, that "perhaps some day you will have a daddy." She hopes someday they do.

"I've always said I couldn't have a relationship now because I have no time or energy. And it turns out I was right."

Recently, for the first time since her sons were born, Bethany has been spending some time with a man. Alan is divorced and soon to be a grandfather. He comes over to their house; Noah and Mark and their mother visit him at his. On weekends, the four of them often do things together. Bethany likes having a man as a part of her life again, and thinks it's good for her boys. But she realizes how different it is, now that she's a mother, to fit dating into her life.

"Seeing Alan is taking up time and energy," Bethany tells me, disheartened by her observation. "I have always said I couldn't have a relationship now because I have no time or energy. And it turns out I was right. Time I have with him gets taken from my sleep." She points to her eyes, which do show evidence of her exhaustion. "Often Alan comes by after the boys have gone to sleep at night, and he's here sometimes until midnight," she says, reminding me that the automatic alarm clocks that are her children ring early.

When Alan is with Bethany and the boys, Noah and Mark alternate between enjoying his company and letting him know they'd prefer to have Mom all to themselves. Though they like having a man to play with, they are disappointed when Alan won't get down on the floor and play with them the way their friends' fathers, who are younger, do. And the weekend hours—when Alan is around the most—are also ones Noah and Mark consider precious because of the long stretch of time with their mother. Bethany can tell this is so because of their refusal to take an afternoon nap, something they do without fuss when the baby-sitter is with them during the week. Bethany tells me about the time Mark ordered Alan to leave. "This is my house," Mark announced. "Go away." Another evening, Alan came over for dinner; as the boys' bedtime approached, Noah headed for Alan's shoes, picked them up, and carried them to him. "Here," he said. His commanding tone left little doubt that Alan should be heading home.

Bethany admits to feeling ambivalent about how her companion fits into her boys' life. Having a man in her life is something she'd thought about before this relationship began. She wasn't sure how to go about balancing the little time she had with Mark and Noah against the desire to spend time with a man she was dating. If she went out with a man and did not include the boys, Bethany would feel that the additional absence from their lives would be unfair to them. Nor was more time away from them something she wanted. Yet if she tried to weave her relationship in with her family activities, her children might be confused by the man's presence. And if they became close to him and enjoyed having him around, what would happen if he stopped seeing her?

Alan sometimes accompanies Bethany to school when she picks up her sons. The boys' teachers know him, and though they realize he isn't the boys' biological father, they know him as someone who is involved in their lives. For an assignment on "Life Stories," a teacher suggested that Noah and Mark bring to school photos of their mother, their grandmother, the nanny who'd taken care of them, and Alan.

"I was very ambivalent about him becoming such a real part of their lives because I knew he wouldn't always be, and what would that be like for them? Or," asks Bethany, who sensed early on the likely impermanence of this relationship, though she adored having Alan in her life, "is it better for them to have some attachment to a man for some period of time?" Bethany doesn't know how to answer these questions, at least not from her sons' point of view. However, because of what she observes, what Noah and Mark tell her, and the emotional boost Alan's presence gives her, she regards him, on balance, as a positive addition to their family. "The thing that makes it work is he has lots of time and not a lot going on in his life," Bethany says. "And I have too much going on in my life and no time." These divergent circumstances mesh in ways that have allowed the relationship to work, at least for now. "I guess I see this as a time of need in my own life," Bethany says. "I don't think it's going to be the same in five years and I don't know that I'll feel satisfied then with the kind of balance I have now. I don't think the kind of relationship I have with Alan would have worked ten years ago or even five years ago."

"It wouldn't have been what you were looking for five years ago?"

"Oh, definitely not someone I was looking to have kids with," she answers, recalling those times when becoming a mom was all she thought about in any relationship she considered. "Absolutely not." Bethany shakes her head.

"Now that you have children you see a very different kind of relationship as a possibility."

"Oh, my needs are completely different. I don't mean it to sound like I'm using Alan. I'm not. I genuinely care about him and I feel he loves me."

Despite Bethany and Alan's current closeness, I judge from the way Bethany describes their relationship that there will probably come a time when Alan is no longer an integral part of her family's life. But unlike the permanent absence of her sons' biological father, Alan's departure—if it happens—will be a visible and palpable loss for each of them, suffused with real-life memories of times they spent together.

For unmarried women who use anonymous donors to aid them in becoming mothers, "daddy" questions can eventually arrive in other guises. There will, of course, always be the psychological adjustment children make to the realization that they may never know the person who supplied the other half of their parental heritage. But when mothers bring other men into their children's lives, and include them in family activities, as Bethany did, it is inevitable that new dimensions of this "daddy" inquiry will surface, and that, like Bethany, mothers will wonder what is best to say and do.

"Well, Grandma, where's our daddy?"

When she was trying to get pregnant, Bethany did a lot of thinking about how her child would feel about the loss of paternal identity she'd accepted as part of his creation. Because her own mother, Kathleen, was very troubled by this aspect of Bethany's decision to have children on her own, the two of them had what seemed like endless conversations about it. Kathleen, a widow, was worried that any child conceived with an anonymous donor's sperm will be profoundly sad about not having a father he can know or a daddy he can play with. "My mother raised all of these questions with me," Bethany says. "She'd make me wonder if I was doing something terrible to bring these children into the world, and kept asking whether they would be mad at me."

"Could you answer her questions?"

"Well . . ." Bethany takes a breath. "I took what's probably a somewhat defensive and philosophical position, which is that all kids are mad about a lot of things with their parents. Either they're mad because their parents are too old or too young or they're too rich or too poor or too religious. I have no illusion this isn't going to be an issue and that we are not going to have pain and unhappiness and anger. But my perspective on life is that one deals with lots of things no matter what, and it is how you deal with it that matters."

Bethany's perspective hasn't given her mother much comfort. Even now, despite her great joy at having grandsons, Kathleen remains certain that the boys will eventually be grieved by the way their mother chose to have them. And Kathleen has told Bethany she wants no part of trying to explain it to them. "My mother's worst fear is that I'm going to leave her with the boys one day and they will ask her, 'Well, Grandma, where's our daddy?' " says Bethany, who tries to diminish this concern by instructing her mother to avoid answering and tell Mark and Noah to ask their mom. "I've tried to explain to her a number of times that one does not have to be profoundly sad about difference," Bethany says, relying on her study of psychology. "A person is sad about loss. I have tried to explain this to her. Yes, there may be a time when the boys have some difficult feelings to resolve about this, but we cannot project our feelings on to them.

"My mother has some vision of her grandsons one day sitting and talking together, like, 'Where is our father?' " Bethany chuckles a little, but as she continues her tone stiffens and becomes more serious. "They may just do that, you know. Maybe they will say to each other, 'Do I look like Dad?' I don't know." Right now, neither Noah nor Mark looks a lot like his mother, nor do they much resemble each other.

It does seem likely to me that Bethany's mother is right about the boys one day trying to puzzle such things out together. They will probably wonder which of them looks more like their father. Mark might decide he does. Maybe Noah will argue that *he* does, remembering information their mother shared with them, such as the color of their father's eyes. Whatever conclusion each of Bethany's sons arrives at, neither will be able to say with certainty that the other isn't right.

"I don't think my sons have an idea that the 'right kind' of family is a mother and father and children."

Bethany realizes that her mother's concern about her grandsons' potential sense of loss arises out of her experience as a widow. Bethany's father died when she and her brother were teenagers. Her mother comforted them in the aftermath of his death, so it is only natural that she thinks of children as being very sad about a father whom they miss. However, Noah and Mark aren't in the same situation; their sadness, when it comes, will not be about the intimate loss of someone who was always with them but about reconciling themselves to not knowing the man responsible for their births. They—and Bethany—will face a different psychological challenge. By talking with them about this, as she's doing already, Bethany is trying to build a firm foundation of understanding so they will have some solid ground to stand on when they cope with whatever distress they might one day feel.

Like other older unmarried mothers I visited with, Bethany also tries to ward off inadvertently hurtful comments or questions from those outside the family, queries that would needlessly remind her boys of what they do not have. She meets with her sons' teachers to explain that her sons don't know their father. That way, when classes take on projects like constructing family trees, teachers are aware of how her sons might feel upset or saddened by watching "Daddy" branches sprout from friends' trees. Also, by the time her sons are in kindergarten, Bethany wants to have written a personalized storybook about how they came to be with one another, so that Noah and Mark will be comfortable when their classmates start to talk about families.

Bethany's maternal instinct to protect her sons from these potentially painful moments is strong, but she knows that her ability to do so has limits. As they get older, she knows, they're bound to confront comments and questions about their unusual family configuration, and neither she nor her caregivers will always be present to shield them. So it's a relief to

Bethany to know that her children are already learning in preschool that not every child lives with a mother and a father. While most of her sons' classmates are growing up in "Mommy-Daddy" families, two of them are being raised by lesbian couples. Other children live apart from their fathers because of divorce. Because of her sons' exposure to these families, Bethany thinks they are better able to accept the differentness of their own family life. "What really helps is that I don't think my sons have an idea that the 'right kind' of family is a mother and father and children," she says. "They know there are a fair amount of those kinds of families, but because many of my friends are single mothers, they also know as many children who have only a mother." On weekends, Bethany and the boys often join other single mothers and their children. "I think in their minds it's like, well, there are many different kinds of families. I think they'd say that most children do have a mommy and a daddy but a lot don't. They're pretty matter-of-fact about it." Once, on vacation, she and the boys bumped into one of the lesbian mothers whose child was Noah and Mark's classmate; later on her sons described her to Bethany as "the other mommy." "The boys didn't ask me why their friend had two mommies, any more than they ask me, 'Why don't we have a daddy?' " Bethany says. "So I think they're sheltered by living in an area where they are exposed to kids who live in a lot of different kinds of families."

Questions about her sons' missing father still arise at unexpected times and from unexpected sources. One day, when Bethany took her boys to buy sneakers, the clerk who measured Mark's foot looked up at Bethany with an amazed expression and said, "Wow. His father must have big feet." Bethany was so startled that for a moment she didn't know how to reply. She, of course, has no idea how large her sons' father's feet are, but courtesy required some response, and the longer she waited the greater everyone's discomfort would be. Finally, Bethany nodded. "Yes, he does."

That same afternoon, just after Bethany told me this story, she and I set off, with Mark and Noah in their stroller, to get ice cream. Having another adult along gives Bethany an opportunity to to do some errands that are normally hard for her. With me there to watch her children, she doesn't need to try to maneuver a double-seated stroller through the narrow aisles of stores. So she dashes in and out of a few shops while I wait outside with her sons. Strangers passing by offer me a quick lesson in what it is like for Bethany to confront some of the customary expectations about family. Twice in the ten minutes I'm with the boys, several people approach and, after inquiring how old Noah and Mark are and doing a fast assessment of their large size, remark on how big and tall my sons' father must be.

"Who is going to teach them how to pee like boys? I don't know how to do that."

Bethany's job, as she sees it, is not to dwell on questions she cannot answer but to attend to what she can and needs to do for her sons. This means concentrating on how she can best teach them to be well-behaved little boys who will grow up to be good-hearted men. And she has to do this without all that many easily accessible male role models in her sons' day-to-day lives. They don't have a grandfather, since Bethany's father is dead and there is no "other side" of this family to gather male relatives from.

Bethany tells me she always saw as one of her prime maternal responsibilities the job of "nurturing for them as many relationships with men as I can." Though this urge might well have been spurred by the fact that she has sons, the older mothers I met—regardless of their child's gender—were looking for ways to bring male friends and relatives into their children's lives. This desire is no different from what I'd observed among their younger counterparts; however, many of the older moms had no actual father to try to keep involved, and they looked outside their family for help. When Bethany's sons were infants, she thought about hiring male baby-sitters for them but, as unfair as her concerns might seem, she admits that she worried what a boy who wanted to baby-sit might do with her sons. She has also gotten in touch with the Big Brother Association and learned that when her boys are six years old she can sign them up; she hopes each will be paired with a man who will spend several hours a week with them. In addition, she intends to enroll them in Boy Scouts, Little League, and community soccer teams. When they were two years old, Bethany hired a teenage boy to spend time with the three of them on weekends. An extra set of eyes and hands helped since Noah and Mark were so active, but the biggest benefit she saw in this arrangement was that it provided her sons with a boy a few years older to whom they might become attached.

Bethany wishes she had more close friends who were men. Most of her male friends are either the husbands of her women friends ("For the most part they are not into kids") or they are gay, like her friend who probably spends the most time with her sons. "He is more female in how he relates to babies," Bethany says of him. "He tends to be playful and whimsical but also tender and gentle with them." She tells me she noticed a big difference in how her sons reacted when a friend's husband spent time with them during an afternoon visit. "He's a big bearlike man and gets down on the floor and does more kinds of roughhousing play. Noah really enjoys it.

Having that kind of interaction clearly thrills him. Mark gets a little anxious. He doesn't like it as much. By nature he's a little quieter and gets put off by the rougher playing."

Figuring out who her sons' male role models will be and what place they will have in the boys' lives is an ongoing project. "I really do want them to know men and to feel good about being men," Bethany says. "I mean, like who is going to teach them how to pee like boys? I don't know how to do that." Bethany's mother pointed out that her brother learned by watching their father. So when the time came for Bethany to potty-train her sons, she asked her brother for help. "I had them watch him," she says.

"Your brother volunteered for that?"

"Volunteered, nothing," Bethany responds, laughing. "When he was around I said to him, 'Go pee in front of my children.' Of course, my brother is a bit shy, a private person and modest. But my boys stood in there and watched him and we talked about it. I also had a friend of mine come in and pee for them. And I told Alan he was free to pee in front of my children." So far Alan has not taken Bethany up on this offer.

The lessons are apparently working. "The teachers at the boys' school take the children to the bathroom in boy and girl groups," Bethany explains. "After Noah started to wear his big-boy underpants, he came home one day and announced to me, 'I peed in the urinal.'" She mimics his exaggerated pronunciation of "urinal." "He was so excited that the next day he made me come to school and watch. What is so odd is that the teacher told me he just stood there and did it as though he'd seen this his whole life. But he's never seen a urinal! He's never been in a boys' bathroom. If he'd gone with his father he might have seen one, but he hasn't."

Bethany shakes her head, awed, it seems, by the mystery of how all this seems to be working out. Raising sons on her own has made her very aware of all the things boys pick up from having a daddy around. Recently, when she and the boys were at Alan's house, he had to shave before they went out. "They had never seen a man shave," she says. Mark and Noah stood near Alan, spellbound by his every movement. They walked from side to side as he slid the razor around his face. They asked to touch his face, first feeling his whiskers, then his smooth skin when he had finished. "It is such a common little-boy experience to watch Daddy shave, but since they have never lived with a man, they'd never seen what a man does in the morning," Bethany says. "I was just really struck that they didn't know what he was doing." It was another reminder to Bethany of how easy it is to forget the differences between her sons' early years and those of many of their friends.

"With boys, I think the issue is how do they feel masculine, or how do they get a sense of themselves as men," Bethany says. She believes her sons will come to understand a lot about men through comments and ideas she presents to them, as well as through the images of men they'll see on television, read about in books, or hear about in various media. They'll also absorb impressions of what it means to be a man from the men to whom they're introduced. "What is important is that I have a pretty clear idea about men and that I like men and don't have a narrow view of what male behavior can be," she tells me. Bethany accepts as an ongoing parental obligation the job of offering her boys a rich variety of experiences with men and insights about them, to help them learn what it's like to be a man. But she ruminates on the limitations imposed on her because she is a woman raising sons on her own. "They can take in my view of men," Bethany says, "but they can't take in my maleness."

"A number of studies over the past decade have provided a clear portrait of the father as playmate."

Parenting on her own means that Bethany not only earns her family's income, arranges for her children's care while she is doing that, and spends time with them whenever she can, but also that she tries to expose them to emotional and physical experiences they might have had if their father were present. Some observers—especially those who believe every child needs the joint participation of a mother and father to grow up healthy— assert that this cannot be done and should not be attempted, and that mothers who try to do all and be all to their children are bound to fail. Yet for centuries, as fathers have died or deserted, leaving mothers on their own with young children, women have had no choice but to try to compensate for men's absence. Often they've succeeded admirably.

Now older, highly educated women like Bethany are choosing to try to raise children in the absence of their fathers. In my conversations with them, these mothers make clear that their decision to do without a father is based on several intermingled beliefs and circumstances. As discussed earlier, older women's obsessive yearning for motherhood can, and often does, override other considerations, such as whether they can really afford children and what it might mean for their children not to have a father.

With one another, older unmarried women don't spend a lot of time speculating on what impact the absence of a father might have on their children's lives. Instead, they tend to focus on practical aspects of achieving motherhood. That doesn't mean, however, that these women are not concerned about this aspect of their decision. Often, the avoidance of a topic is a signal that the emotions attached to it are very strong, too strong sometimes to want to discuss. Because of my own experience of considering unmarried motherhood, I can appreciate why women don't tend to raise this topic with one another even if, on their own, they worry about it a lot. Few subjects are as explosively painful for potential unwed mothers to confront, encumbered as this one is by memories of their relationships with their own fathers.

Among any group of women there is a wide variety of father-daughter relationships. Conversations about the potential absence of a father from their children's lives blend in imperceptibly with memories of the women's own childhood experiences. If a woman has had a terrible relationship with her father, or even just an emotionally distant one, she may be less concerned about the prospect of parenting on her own. In fact, she might feel some sense of relief for her child that a father will not be around. Other women, whose relationships with their fathers remain close and supportive, are likely to express different views; as I did, they might worry a lot about whether it is fair to intentionally create a fatherless family. Few of the discussions I've heard among these women converge on what social scientists or psychologists have learned. It is extremely difficult for these women, as it would be for just about anyone, to detach themselves from their personal experiences and discuss the subject factually and dispassionately.

Even if these women could detach themselves from their emotions, unearthing the facts about a father's actual effect on children is not easy to do. As I pointed out in the preceding chapter, compared with the mountains of studies about mothers' involvement with children, relatively little is known about what being a "good father" entails from day to day. More often, fathers' influence on children is gauged indirectly—in terms of how effectively a man supports his partner in her caregiving role, for example, or how well he provides financially for his family. Even when prospective single mothers comb the research on fathers' roles in children's lives, they can't find many agreed-upon conclusions about what children miss by not having a father involved in their upbringing. This is especially true if studies of poor, younger mothers and those without much emotional support don't seem relevant.

Since the early 1980s there has been more investigation of fathers' roles in children's lives, but these studies still lag far behind work done on mothers. In a 1992 article, "Where's Poppa? The Relative Lack of Attention to the Role of Fathers in Child and Adolescent Psychopathology," University of Connecticut psychologist Vicki Phares highlighted the disparity between research on mothers' and fathers' influences on children's behavioral problems. Having reviewed eight journals in child and adolescent research, Phares found that 48 percent of studies published between 1984 and 1991 involved mothers exclusively; just 1 percent focused solely on fathers.

There is, however, a prominent exception to this relative dearth of information about fathers. One thing researchers tend to agree about is that when fathers are involved with young children they spend more time than mothers do playing with them. When mothers pick up their infants, they usually do so to provide care or comfort, whereas fathers tend to hold babies when they're going to play with them. Psychologist Ross D. Parke and social historian Peter N. Sterns observed that "a number of studies over the past decade have provided a clear portrait of the father as playmate." And these studies find that when mothers and fathers play with their children, their styles differ. Fathers tend to be more physical in their play than mothers, so fathers' play can be more arousing for the child; certainly Bethany was aware of this difference when her friend's husband "roughhoused" with her boys. There is recent evidence to suggest that the way fathers play with infants and toddlers may, in fact, offer children important guidance about how to regulate stirred-up emotions, and thus may offer invaluable lessons for children as they prepare to engage socially with their peers. On the other hand, when mothers play with children, their interactions tend to be more verbal and didactic.

In the end, common sense, personal experience, and educated knowledge leave little doubt that from a child's perspective having two parents who are committed to each other and fully engaged in their children's lives is the best possible family circumstance. But lacking this possibility, many older, unmarried women are depending on an inner faith that without a husband, but with an abiding commitment, with love and support, with help from others, and with knowledge about what children need, their sons and daughters will thrive.

"At the top of their list of concerns was what and how to tell children about their origins."

Faith in themselves is just about all these women have to go on. Social scientists know virtually nothing about how well the one-parent families being created by older, better-educated, and more financially secure women are doing. Nor do researchers yet know much about how these children are reacting to not knowing their fathers, or to the absence of "Daddy" from their lives, or to the part-time participation of men who are their mother's friends, or, in the case of some children conceived with an anonymous donor, to learning at age eighteen who their biological father is. It is quite possible that factors such as their mothers' advanced level of education and higher income, the middle-class neighborhoods in which they are surrounded by Mom-and-Pop families, and their mothers' efforts to help them adjust to their father's absence will guard these children against consequences commonly associated with mother-only families.

The primary reason that there are so few findings about the long-term impact of fathers' absence on these children's lives is the newness of this phenomenon. A glance at the lists of birthdays in Single Mothers by Choice newsletters reveals many infants, toddlers, and young children, and not so many offspring approaching adolescence. Though some older, unmarried women chose to have children during the early 1980s, more noticeable increases in such births began in the middle and late 1980s. As these children age—and particularly as they enter into adolescence—it's likely that more studies will assess how well they are doing.

Besides the fact that such families are relatively new, another factor makes the absence of fathers among them somewhat tricky to measure: the man is absent for a variety of reasons. Older, single women conceive their babies with donated sperm, or with the help of a friend, or through adoption. Or, just as happens with many teenagers, a woman's partner announces after a pregnancy is revealed that he doesn't intend to remain part of her or their child's life.

Each kind of father-absence presents a different emotional dynamic, which can affect how well both mother and child adjust. Of the very few studies published about families created intentionally by single women, one, done in the late 1980s by clinical psychologists, examined the concerns that older, unmarried mothers had about their family life. The study was called "Single Mothers by Choice: A Family Alternative." Half of the twenty mothers interviewed conceived through intercourse with a man who was not involved with the child's upbringing, four used an anonymous donor, and six adopted.

From the perspective of their children (who averaged four and a half years of age), the common factor was that no father was present in their lives. Though these mothers reported that none of their children seemed "distraught" about the father's absence, the women worried in varying degrees about how his absence might affect the child's well-being. Not surprisingly, the mothers' concerns were closely related to their method of conception. Some of the women who chose to get pregnant by having intercourse with a friend expressed regret because of their disappointment with their child's biological father. Even limited expectations about his continued involvement with them or with the child had not been met;

this upset them, and in turn made them worry more about how their children would react to having a known father who did not want to spend time with them. It was among these mothers, who wondered aloud if it might have been better to use an anonymous donor, that the researchers found "the greatest sense of disappointment."

As a group, unwed older mothers placed the issue of "what and how to tell children about their origins" at the top of their list of concerns. In second place were their worries about the impact the absence of a "daddy" from their children's lives would have. The list of worries went on to include social isolation and financial difficulties. These concerns are ones I hear expressed constantly by older, unmarried mothers.

As Bethany has done for her sons, fifteen of the twenty mothers interviewed for this study said they'd sought out men—often relatives, sometimes close friends—to become involved in their children's lives in "intentional and active ways." Most of the women also said that they wanted to be married but found that between parenting and work they had very little time to date; fewer than half were dating at the time of the study. Ruth Mechaneck, one of the researchers, told me that as she continues to speak informally with these mothers as well as others in similar situations she finds that few have formed a permanent relationship with a man.

These researchers acknowledge that their investigation, being limited in scope and time, left many questions unanswered. As an agenda for future studies, they suggest looking more closely at the effects of single motherhood on the psychological development of the child; looking for any noticeable effects on the child's ability to form relationships with the opposite sex; and examining other potential consequences of having no identifiable father on the child's formation of his or her own sense of identity. Since their interviewees' children were so young, the researchers could not explore these issues.

"Is it possible that you are feeling guilty that you have not provided a dad for your son?"

The belief that fathers matter in children's lives produces the worry and anxiety and guilt that permeate the thinking of many single mothers.

> "My son is two months old, and although he does not yet understand that he has not got a Daddy, I now that he soon will realize it. I feel terrible knowing how hurt and upset he will be about this fact, and I want to do everything I can to help him deal with it."

Letters like this one, written by the mother of a child who doesn't have a daddy to an audience of mothers just like her, offer windows into these concerns. Correspondence like this has appeared in the Single Mothers by Choice quarterly newsletter since 1993. The newsletter gives these mothers a chance to connect with one another, to share experiences, and to offer others whatever experiential wisdom they've accumulated. In September 1994, responding to requests from readers, Jane Mattes, a psychotherapist who edits the newsletter and wrote *Single Mothers by Choice: A Guidebook for Single Women Who Are Considering or Have Chosen Motherhood*, announced that she was instituting a column, "The Daddy Issue."

To the mother worried about how upset her two-month-old son might be when he finds out how she arranged for him to be born, Mattes suggested:

> Is it possible that you are feeling guilty that you have not provided a dad for your son? He has never known his father. They have not had a relationship of any kind, so his feelings would not be the same as those of someone who had a relationship with a dad who was then taken away. However, if he picks up from you that not having a dad in the home is a terrible thing, he will feel that way, too. . . .
>
> By resolving your feelings, you will be able to better allow him to have his own feelings about this matter. He may feel sad at times, or he may feel, as many of our children do, that this is just the way it is, and not a big deal. As my son said recently, "I never had a dad, so how can I miss him?"

Because so little research has been done on how well such children are adjusting to life without a known father, or on how mothers can help children cope with this circumstance, individuals such as Mattes emerge as experts. The media seek her out for comment, and women who are considering or engaged in unmarried motherhood rely on her for advice. Mattes's credentials include her professional knowledge as a psychotherapist and the personal expertise accumulated in nearly fifteen years of unwed motherhood. After hearing hundreds of older unwed mothers, Mattes's ears have become fine-tuned to their concerns. Since 1990, she has also been a co-researcher on a ten-year longitudinal study of the impact these mothers' decision to parent on their own has had on their children's well-being. Mattes is not alone in her ability and willingness to speak about what this family experience is like. Many older, single mothers are involved in education or social work or are therapists; their academic training and professional work with children and families make it more legitimate for them to assume a podium from which they can write and talk about their experience.

Though the discussion these women have with one another is sprinkled with bits of personal experience and some measure of academic expertise, many of the questions they pose to one another don't have definitive answers. So when they ask one another for advice, such as what to tell their children about a missing father or absent "daddy," what they're looking for is guidance and emotional support, not a perfect solution.

"How do I protect my child from the pain he may unwittingly be inflicting on himself?"

Some women decide to be frank with people who are curious about how they got pregnant. They figure facts are preferable to the gossip that inevitably travels around an office, for example, when an unmarried woman is pregnant. However, many women—especially those who use anonymous donors—prefer to maintain a realm of personal privacy about their reproductive choice; many share their experiences only with close friends and family members. (Often, women's concerns about what to reveal to whom about their pregnancy reflect their desire to shield children from public judgments about their origins.) The mothers realize many people do not look favorably on what they are doing. Indeed, in the "Family Alternative" study cited earlier, the researchers also surveyed the public's opinions of the methods by which older unmarried women become mothers. They discovered that adoption had the most positive ranking; conception with a known or anonymous donor fell in the middle; and having sex with a man for the purpose of conceiving a child without his consent received the least.

Dilemmas arise later for these mothers, when their children become old enough to want to know where they came from. Mothers want to be honest with their children, but this doesn't mean they want news about their conception to be broadcast to others, lest their children face teasing and ridicule. Yet, as every parent knows, it is just about impossible to tell children something in a nonsecretive way and then convince them to keep "the secret" from others. The contradiction between knowing and not telling doesn't make sense to youngsters. While such dilemmas can sound trivial to those of us who aren't involved, this difficulty is one unmarried mothers ask one another about frequently, seeking advice from those who have faced it.

In a 1993 issue of the Single Mothers by Choice newsletter, a mother wrote about her four-year-old son. She'd told only her closest friends and family how she became pregnant. And when her son was old enough, she'd created a bedtime story about his origins, not unlike the one Bethany told her boys. Building his understanding from an early age, she believed, would help him, later, accept how he came to be.

> Once upon a time there was a lady who had a very nice life and was very busy and very happy, except for one thing—she wanted to have a child to care for and love. She didn't have a husband to be a Daddy for this child because she knew a Daddy had to be a very special person. Although she had looked and looked for just the right one, she could not find anyone special enough to be the Daddy. So she went to the doctor and asked him to help her. The doctor gave her a seed which grew into a baby, and the lady was happy at last.

After telling her son this story, she'd ask him, "Do you know who the lady and the baby are?" Now that he was four, she wrote, "he tells me in the middle of the story I'm the mom and he is that baby. He seems to accept the story with no problems."

Now this mother anticipates new issues. Her son is reaching an age at which, as she wrote, "he tells everybody everything he sees, hears, and thinks." She knows it is only a matter of time until he shares this story with his friends. "I'm uncomfortable," she writes, "because inevitably comments and questions will come from kids and the families they bring their version of the story home to. I remember too well how very cruel kids can be to anyone who is slightly different. How do I protect my child from the pain he may unwittingly be inflicting on himself by sharing this information without making him feel that we have a shameful secret he must keep?"

Responses to her question were not published in the newsletter. But Jane Mattes addressed this dilemma in her guidebook for unwed mothers. She wrote: "Most children assume that if something is a secret, that means it is somehow shameful or bad, so you will want to talk about information being 'private' rather than secret. You need to convey that the facts about his origin are private, and that they are not something to discuss with just anyone, but that it is definitely okay to discuss them with close friends or family." As Mattes points out, no child can be expected to be able to keep information private until he reaches a developmental stage that allows him to understand why and how to do this; this usually occurs at about the age of seven or eight.

Holding back information about their origins from children was not considered a viable option by any mothers I've met who used an anonymous donor to conceive. To some extent, these mothers are guided by what psychologists have discovered in their study of children who are adopted: keeping secrets about their origin from children can become emotionally harmful to them. Also, when couples used an anonymous donor to assist with conception, many children who later found out that their "social" father was not their biological father became angry at learning that this secret had been withheld from them.

These mothers acknowledge that they are alert to signs that their children are angry at them or disappointed in them. But for the most part, they try not to allow the focus of their family lives to reside in the things that make them different from other families. Their attitude can be summarized by what one mother said to me: "I did what I did to create a family. Now we're going to be one." Another woman, the forty-one-year-old single mother of a toddler, told me: "Oh, I know my son's going to be mad at me for some of these things I did. But that's just like I got mad at my parents. Well, I'm not mad at my parents anymore, and my life is what my life is. All of us have things we are upset about. But part of every life is going through those things and moving on."

"Wasn't my dad silly not to want to be a dad? He's missing out on all this fun."

Mothers tell me their children were two years old, sometimes three, before they even began asking questions about their father. One reason for this timing is that by then most children are developing the vocabulary they need to verbalize these questions. Children are also hearing their friends use the word "Daddy." By then, it's usually only a matter of time before a child who does not have a "daddy" will ask about his absence. But when a child is this young, her cognitive abilities will only allow her to process a response that fits within the context of concrete facts of daily life. Usually when a toddler asks about a "daddy," she's simply asking if her family has one. However, mothers—who have been anxiously anticipating this question—might be inclined to try to explain too much too soon. Mattes advises them that an appropriate response for a child of two or three is the one Bethany used with her boys: "No, our family does not have a daddy."

As the years go by a child learns how to absorb more abstract ideas. It is then that a mother's ability to address the distinctions between the absence of a "father" and the lack of a "daddy" becomes possible. How successful she is can be gauged not only by how well her words suit the child's ability to understand but also by how she says them. If she is nervous and upset by what she's saying, her emotional tenor can be picked up by her child. Mothers can respond to their children's questions well only after they've reached some degree of comfort within themselves about how they created their family.

But even many mothers who have done so, and think they are ready to handle their children's questions, are surprised by how, why, and when they decide to ask. Carolyn's son, George, was three years old when he first asked his mother about "Daddy." Carolyn had tried to prepare herself for the moment when she would have to explain to George that his father decided, after she became pregnant, not to be involved in his child's life. But she never expected to be asked to do this while standing shoulder-to-shoulder with her neighbors in the apartment-house elevator.

"Where's my daddy?" George asked, loud enough so that everyone present could hear. Carolyn looked to see what floor they were on and calculated that she could wait until they got off to answer him.

"Where is he?" George asked again, after his first request had been greeted by silence.

"Could we talk about that when we get upstairs?" she said.

Once they were safely inside their apartment, Carolyn sat down with her son. The first thing she did was try to find out why he was asking this question now. Having studied child psychology, she knew that when children are her son's age, the information they want often isn't the information adults think they want. Why, she asked George, did he want to know about his "daddy"? It turned out that George was concerned not about his birth father but about a man who had just left their lives after a lengthy relationship with his mother. "George wanted to know 'Was this my father?' and 'What happened to him?' " Carolyn explains.

Even though her son had never referred to the man she was involved with as "Daddy," and despite Carolyn's persistent attempts to make clear to George that this wasn't his father, George either wanted him to be or believed he was. Carolyn responded now by repeating what she'd said to him then. "No. He is not your father," she said, answering directly what George wanted to know—and could understand at this age.

This experience taught Carolyn a valuable lesson, which she shares with mothers like her: "I realized it didn't really matter what I'd said to my son about his father. You can tell them whatever you want, but they'll make up their own version."

This lesson was reinforced for Carolyn one day when she was walking behind George and his friend and heard this exchange:

"Where's your dad, anyway?" George's friend asked.

"Oh, my dad's in New Rochelle," George replied, referring to a suburb near to where they lived.

Carolyn tells me she nearly fainted. She couldn't imagine where her son had come up with this idea. "It took all my self-control not to scream out, 'What are you talking about?' " she says. "But I didn't say anything."

Several years later, when George was about ten, he again asked his mother where his father was. This time she knew he meant his birth father.

George was surprised by the answer.

"You mean he's not in New Rochelle?" he said.

"I don't know where you got that from," Carolyn answered.

"You told me," George replied. He was quite insistent on this point.

"I never told you that," Carolyn said. "Why would I tell you that, since he's not there?"

As they discussed the mix-up, Carolyn remembered that when George was younger he had taken a bus to a day camp in New Rochelle. "That was a faraway place for him, and since he had the concept his father was somewhere far away, then, in his mind, his father must be in New Rochelle," she told me.

Over the years Carolyn learned, by talking with her son, that what he found most difficult to understand was why his father did not want to be part of his life. This isn't something she understands well, either, so she finds it hard to explain. "Why a man doesn't want to be a daddy is a hard concept to communicate to his child," Carolyn says. "I think you have to be an adult to understand what the responsibilities of being a parent are and why someone wouldn't want to do that." When she talks with George about this, Carolyn tries to accentuate the positive: she tells him how much she wanted to be his mother and reminds him that not every child grows up with two parents. Occasionally, she hears George talk about his father's absence as though the loss belongs less to him than to his father.

"Wasn't my dad silly not to want to be a dad?" George asked Carolyn one day. "He is missing out on all this fun."

Being his mother, Carolyn couldn't disagree.

"The only similarity among us is that our children have questions."

On a Sunday afternoon a few years ago, Jane Mattes, the founder of Single Mothers by Choice, came to Boston at the request of a group of unmarried mothers and mothers-to-be to talk about ways to navigate this uncharted "missing daddy" territory. Though the fifty or so women who came to hear her talk had arrived at motherhood by various routes or were pondering a variety of ways to get there, they had a common link: their children were facing, or someday would face, the issues brought about by the absence of a father/daddy.

At this time Mattes was parenting on her own, eleven years after her son was born out of wedlock. In her presentation, she intended to do what she does so well when she responds to women who seek her advice through the newsletter: by combining personal insights with professional judgment, she wanted to provide not answers but experiential guidance.

"This is a very difficult thing to talk about," Mattes began. "I know because I have changed my mind about this eleven times in eleven years. I want you to know I can't help but make some generalizations for the sake of our discussion, but they are all subject to change and to disagreement. They are my opinions. Today. At this hour. And I am constantly finding that I am learning more. We are basically pioneering. There isn't much known and we are still learning. Nothing I am saying is gospel. . . . One reason why this is so difficult to talk about is there are so many different situations. Even when two women start out with the exact same situations, six months down the road it may be different: one suddenly has a boyfriend, or she moves in with her child's grandparent, so there is all of a sudden a "daddy," even though it may be a granddaddy. . . . The only similarity among us is that our children have questions."

In her talk, Mattes, a heavyset woman in her early fifties, explored some of the questions children ask most often, the response mothers frequently give, and how both parties tend to feel about these exchanges. In the hour or so that she spoke, Mattes passed on to her audience many stories mothers had told her about how they'd handled various situations. It was an effective way of communicating how complicated the "daddy issue" can be. She told them how late one night she answered her phone to hear the distraught mother of an eight-year-old girl. Years before, this woman had told her daughter that she had used an anonymous donor in her conception. And her daughter's response had led the mother to believe her child was comfortable with what she'd been told. But now, all evening long, the child had been sobbing because she knew nothing about her father, didn't even have a photograph to look at. Between sobs, she assured her mother she loved her, but she also demanded to know how her mother could have hurt her in this way. After embracing her sobbing, screaming daughter for hours, the woman called Mattes to find out what more she could do.

Mattes told her audience that what left a lasting impression on her was how well this mother had accepted her daughter's feelings, and in fact shared with her her own feelings of sadness. Mattes saw in this mother a parent who was effectively teaching her child the valuable lesson of accepting that disparate feelings can coexist. She'd wanted to have this child; she loved her daughter very much, *and* she could share with her the sadness they both felt about the person who was absent from their family.

"This concept of mixed feelings is something that at times we all forget," Mattes reminded her audience. "You don't feel just one way about most important things in your life. . . . To hold on to this mixture of feelings together is a big accomplishment and a very important developmental task we can help children with, and that is where I am on this right now. My son doesn't have to say that this is perfectly fine. Neither is it perfectly terrible. To be honest, the truth is somewhere in the middle, and at different times it ebbs and flows to different degrees and in different directions."

Mattes had given her son a book called *Double-Dip Feelings*, which soon became one of his favorites. Even before she described the story, many of the mothers were writing down the title; clearly, they want to know about anything that might help their children. "Like double-dip ice cream cones, you can have two flavors on the same cone and you can have two feelings at the same time about something and that's normal and fine," Mattes said. "This topic is something that is complex, about which children have mixed feelings and about which we have mixed feelings. . . . And children can work it out. The biggest concern I have is that we are going to shut the children up, tell them this isn't an issue, and they'll not be allowed to go through whatever they have to go through at a young age when they are able to do this fairly easily. Then later on, there are going to be all sorts of reactions if their questions and concerns were not dealt with."

"The hardest thing for me to bear in my life is that I can't see an image inside of me of my father's face."

In the absence of concrete information, children may develop fantasy images of their "daddy." Sometimes even after a mother tells her child all that she knows about an absent father, the child exaggerates certain characteristics or makes up others, as Carolyn's son did when he had his father living in New Rochelle. Psychologists have suggested to me that children's "daddy" fantasies can be quite strong and that children can create idealized male images when no real man is close to them during their early lives. If children latch on to fantasies of how men behave, as they grow older they may have trouble understanding the complex web of men's actual emotions and personal interactions. Fatherless girls entering adolescence may be confused about how to relate to men, and may be intimidated by them. Some young women seek out relationships with older men who appear to offer the security their own fathers aren't there to give. Boys who grow up without observing men's daily involvement in work or family life may emerge from adolescence unready to participate in either.

One group of children who face a tough job of dealing with what Mattes calls double-dip feelings are those who will never have a chance of meeting their father because their mother never knew him. This is the situation of most children conceived with an anonymous donor. For them, there will undoubtedly be moments of profound sadness about the inability to connect with their paternal roots. So it becomes, as Mattes explained, a mother's job to figure out ways to help her child cope. To know something about what might be at play in a child's mind can help a lot.

One afternoon, as Marsha mixes chocolate chip cookie dough in the kitchen of her three-story suburban house, she and I discuss her concerns about the "daddy" issue. Her son is too young to have asked her any questions about "daddy," but she often thinks about this aspect of their lives. In the past, Marsha and I have talked about what it's been like to bear and raise a child on her own, but until today I didn't know how agonizing her decision to go ahead with anonymous donor insemination had been.

As we talk, Marsha's two-year-old son, Henry, wanders in, refreshed by his afternoon nap and curious about what his mom is up to. Because Marsha knows that at his developmental stage Henry wants to be involved in whatever she's doing, she lifts him into a chair and invites him to help her by pouring chocolate chips into the creamy batter. Satisfied by his moment of inclusion, Henry soon heads off to the living room to play. As he settles in with his toys, Marsha explains the origins of her ambivalence about whether and how she should become a mother by telling me about an encounter she had at work. This experience, she says, temporarily convinced her to set aside her plan to use an anonymous donor.

"I remember I had just about got to the point four or five years ago of deciding I was going to go ahead with donor insemination. Then one day at work I had a conversation with an adolescent boy who had been separated from his father during infancy. The man was very disturbed and violent and had abused this boy and his mother. But now, as an adolescent, this boy was telling me he had no memory of his father and that this was something he regretted intensely."

Marsha pauses. "I remember him telling me, 'The hardest thing for me to bear in my life is that I can't see inside of me an image of my father's face.' " That remark provoked Marsha to think about the decision she was making. From the age of thirty she'd been determined to become a mother. As years passed by and no permanent partner came along, she'd grown increasingly comfortable with the thought of going ahead on her own. However, this young man's words made her aware of what it might be like for her child to grow up without a father with whom he could experience a "real relationship."

"Did this set you back in term of going ahead?"

"Oh, it did." Marsha nods, emphasizing its effect. Even though her child's situation would not be similar in most respects to this boy's, the potential psychological dynamics surrounding a father's absence might be. "Absolutely," Marsha says. "I thought, 'Oh, my God. How can I do this?' "

For several years Marsha resisted the idea of conceiving her child with an anonymous donor. Nor did a man come along to help her reach her goal. Approaching her fortieth birthday, she was still childless, so she changed her mind and decided to use anonymous donor sperm. "I came to terms with the fact that yes, every child is going to have something they really long for that they cannot have and my child is going to have this as an issue," Marsha tells me. After several months of inseminations, she became pregnant.

During one of our previous conversations Marsha described her decision-making process as causing her "incredible angst." This afternoon, she tells me more specifically about some of the considerations that tipped the balance in favor of going ahead. "I was confident my parenting and the network of people with whom I am connected would make the absence of a father a manageable frustration for my child," she says. Marsha concluded that even though not having a known father or a "daddy" would definitely matter a lot to her child, she was willing to trust that, along with people she was close to, she'd be able to help her child cope with these issues. "I believed my child could develop adequate internal resources even though there wasn't a daddy living in his house."

When I ask what she knows about the donor, Marsha admits that she is "not satisfied" with the amount of personal information she was able to get from her sperm bank. But she is philosophical, regarding this disappointment as another of life's "manageable frustrations." What she does know, she says, is just enough so that "when my son hits school we will be able to do some of that family tree stuff."

Like other women who create families on their own, Marsha realizes that whatever the circumstances of her son's conception they would have entailed emotional trade-offs. Had she become impregnated by someone who refused any involvement with his son, or by a man whose presence does little but bring havoc into all of their lives, her son's ability to resolve his feelings would also be tested, though in different ways. Using an anonymous donor presents her and Henry with a set of untested psychological challenges, and she is doing her best to prepare herself to face each and every one of them with her son. As Mattes had said at the meeting, Marsha, and women like her, are "basically pioneering."

"A part of me would very much like my son to have a dad as a part of his life, an ongoing part of his life, instead of him having to create a father in mental imagery, which I'm sure he'll do," Marsha says. "But also, yeah, I'm glad not to have to be dealing with some of that other stuff."

"He's not marriage material."

Rachel, an unmarried mother in her mid-thirties, knows what it's like to be dealing with "some of that other stuff." Her twenty-two-month-old daughter's father, Tony, is a man whom she dated for quite a while. But Rachel is not certain that his on-again, off-again presence in their family life actually benefits their daughter, Emma. She *is* certain about one thing: her own life would be much simpler and more enjoyable if Tony were not coming in and out of it to see Emma.

Rachel was both shocked and thrilled when she accidentally became pregnant at the age of thirty-three. Four times during her marriage, which ended in divorce, she endured the searing emotional pain of a miscarriage. She had wanted to have a baby since getting married at the age of twenty-one, but after many medical problems and the miscarriages, she and her doctors had lost hope. So when she discovered she was pregnant by Tony, Rachel had little doubt about whether to have the baby. She was certain, too, that she was not going to marry her baby's father. Tony is a rock musician, whom she describes as immature, irresponsible, and self-centered. When it was just the two of them, Rachel tried to ignore or tolerate these traits and concentrate on the good times they had together. But with a baby on the way, Tony's faults seemed magnified in her eyes.

"He's not marriage material" is how she puts it, in words reminiscent of Naomi's.

Though she would have preferred motherhood within marriage, Rachel tells me that if she'd reached the age of forty still childless and unmarried, she would have tried to find some way to raise a child on her own. So the idea of parenting a child by herself did not frighten her. What was toughest for Rachel was reconciling her desire to break with Tony completely,

and her rock-solid belief that Emma had the right to know her father and
spend time with him.

"Her father has this sense that being involved with a family is bad news."

As Rachel and I sit and talk in the small, comfortably furnished living
room of her quaint house, Emma calls out for her.

"Mommy! Mommy!" Her exasperated tone leaves no doubt that
Rachel's attention is required.

Rachel rises from the sofa and her straight brown hair, which falls
halfway down her back, swishes as she walks. It turns out Emma is having
a hard time maneuvering her sock around her heel.

"You did a good job putting it on yourself," Rachel says in a reassuring
voice that sounds like the high-octave chirping of the birds outside. She
and Emma live on what looks like a back-country road but is actually in a
woodsy suburban town no more than a forty-minute drive from Boston.

"You really did," she tells Emma again, bending down to help pull the
sock all the way on. Emma smiles at her mother as they tug on her sock.
"It's not an easy job, you know; socks are hard to put on."

When Rachel returns to her seat on the couch, Emma remains on the
floor, munching with evident delight on slices of apple Rachel had peeled
and put in her plastic cup. While she eats, Emma flips through books she
and her mother checked out from the library that morning.

"He wanted me to have the baby," Rachel tells me, responding to a
question about Tony's attitude toward her unplanned pregnancy. "But
what he didn't want was to be responsible," she adds quickly.

Rachel remembers telling Tony when she learned she was pregnant that
she would assume all responsibility for their child. Though she didn't have
a steady job, she did have some money from an inheritance and was
working toward becoming an interior designer. "If you want to be a father,
fine, but I'm not asking you to do anything like a regular father," she told
him. Rachel wasn't specific about what role, if any, Tony might play. Part
of the reason she didn't ask for an assurance of more participation—such
as financial or caretaking assistance—is that she feared he'd respond by
pressuring her to have an abortion. She didn't want to deal with that additional strain.

When Rachel was three months pregnant, her doctor stitched her
uterus shut to try to prevent another miscarriage. When she continued to
bleed, Rachel was hospitalized and given hormones intravenously to pre-

vent premature labor. Because Rachel's parents had died several years before, and she had no family members who lived nearby to help her, she found herself depending more and more on Tony, even though she didn't want to. He had agreed to pick Rachel up the morning she was released from the hospital, but he never arrived. Upset and exasperated at him, she found another way to get home. Later that day she discovered why he hadn't been there: out late the night before, he had slept well past the time he had promised to meet her. "He must have gotten drunk or something." Rachel's voice is as angry as it is sarcastic. "He said he was too tired. And when I talked with him, he was really grouchy." Rachel was furious.

During the later stages of her pregnancy, Rachel was under doctor's orders not to do anything strenuous. With winter coming on, she worried about how she'd manage to handle things like shoveling snow. Tony moved in when she was seven months pregnant, and that relieved her of many day-to-day household concerns. However, Rachel realized quickly that these practical bonuses did not come close to outweighing the enormous emotional toll his presence took on her.

"There wasn't a good sense of cooperation," she says, in a tone designed to emphasize the understatement. At three o'clock in the morning, when she was trying to sleep, Tony would be in her living room practicing his music. That she was trying to get a good night's rest, and having a hard time getting comfortable enough to do that, never seemed to occur to him; or if it did, he didn't care.

"I'm lying in bed thinking, 'I'm pregnant and I'm going to have a baby and I have to get my sleep. How dare he be singing this song at three in the morning?' " Rachel says. Tony also repeatedly demonstrated his undependability at moments when she was relying on his help. So Rachel decided that one of her friends, not Tony, would be her birthing coach. She wanted Tony to be with her when their baby arrived, but she was no longer willing to trust that he would show up when needed. As things turned out, both her friend and Tony were with her when Emma was born.

Tony didn't stay with his new family for long. A few days after Emma's birth, he was given a chance to audition for a band. It was an opportunity he'd been waiting for, and when he was offered the job, he leaped at it. By the time Emma was two weeks old her father, who put plugs in his ears so he could ignore her crying, was fully occupied with his new band. "Now he devotes his life to his music," Rachel says. "He has this sense that being involved with a family is bad news."

"I think it is better for her to know as much as she can about her father."

Trying to deal with Tony's self-centeredness and meet Emma's needs, not to mention her own, has not been easy, but Rachel has been resolute in her commitment to have Emma spend time with and get to know her father. So whenever Tony does or says something that upsets Rachel, she tries to focus not on her anger at him but on his importance to Emma.

Rachel knows her belief about the importance of Emma's relationship with Tony was shaped during her own childhood. A psychologist once reminded her that, more than most people, she carries within herself an intimate appreciation of how knowing or not knowing her father might affect her child.

Rachel was adopted when she was five and a half months old. She grew up knowing neither the man whose sperm played a part in creating her nor the woman who gave birth to her. She doesn't want Emma to wonder who her father is, or to be harmed emotionally by not having a chance to develop a relationship with him.

Her adoptive parents—whom she loved very much—told Rachel that her birth mother visited her in the foster home and had wanted to keep Rachel and raise her. But the young woman was nineteen, and unmarried, and this was thirty years ago. Raising a child was not something a young unmarried woman did. Rachel did not search for her birth mother as she was growing up, though she often thought about her. Only when Emma— who became the only blood relative Rachel ever knew—was the same age as Rachel had been when she was adopted, did she start looking for her birth mother. "I kept looking at Emma and thinking, 'She is five and a half months old and I knew if I, as her mother, had to give her up now I'd never forget her,' " Rachel says. "So I knew my mother must remember me and think about me."

By this time, too, her adoptive parents were dead. As Rachel set out to raise her daughter on her own, she developed an intense desire to connect with her "other," unknown family. She went to court to gain access to her birth records and was surprised by how rapidly she was able to track down her birth mother. Only a week after she started making phone calls, they spoke by phone and set up their first meeting. Within a few months Rachel was introduced to four half-siblings from her mother's marriage.

Rachel is delighted to have found her birth mother, and they remain in touch, though they live in different states, thousands of miles apart. But after her initial euphoria at their reunion, Rachel discovered that there was considerable emotional strain involved in trying to relate to each other as mother and daughter, when they hadn't spent years developing such a relationship. Realizing that reinforced Rachel's belief in how important it was for Emma to retain a consistent connection with her father.

Rachel still knows nothing about her biological father. "She went roller-skating and got pregnant," Rachel says, relating what her birth mother told her. Her birth mother doesn't remember the man's name or know anything about him. She has no photograph. "All the court records say is, 'The alleged father was a married man of English extraction,'" Rachel says. "I would like Emma not to have to go through this enormous shift when she is whatever age and might have to look for her father. I think it is better for her to know as much as she can about him."

Rachel turned to a psychologist for help in making her daughter's relationship with Tony as good as it can be. At weekly sessions, Rachel explored the feelings she and Emma have about Tony's visits. She talked about how upset Emma seems to be each time her father leaves; the psychologist attempted to ease Rachel's concerns by explaining that at Emma's age children get upset even when a parent who they know is coming back leaves to go to work. "It hit me that I feel this way because I'm a single mother and I'm thinking there are these things I am just not able to give my child," Rachel says. "I was forgetting that married people have these struggles, too." She also talked with the psychologist about what often happened when Emma spent time with friends whose parents were together: she would mimic the other children by saying, "Daddy, Daddy," to their fathers.

As Rachel tells me this, she imitates the way Emma would say "Daddy"; Emma begins to echo her, until a chorus of "Daddy" reverberates in this tiny living room. "Emma is always trying to get me and Tony to hold hands," Rachel goes on. Suddenly she seems quite aware that her daughter, despite the library books, is listening to us. "I keep watching Emma's pain at us not being together," Rachel tells me, looking over at her daughter. "So I asked the psychologist, 'Is it worth it?'" Was it worth the pain she watched Emma wrestle with, to keep up her contact with her father? "The psychologist told me, 'Well, yes, it's better.'" He also described what Rachel could do to help: "I can help her through this pain, because when Tony leaves I tell her, 'It's okay. He's going to come Sunday and, while he's gone, we can look at a picture of him.'"

Rachel appreciated—and used—the psychologist's advice. "For the moment, I think this makes sense," she tells me. "But it's not easy. For me it would be much easier to just forget about Tony." As soon as Rachel says this, Emma starts to repeat the word "Daddy" in a sort of rhythmic chant.

"I am confused at this point," Rachel admits. "What I am trying to say is that when, as a child, you don't have a father, you think of that as being a logical explanation for any pain you are experiencing, and yet there is plenty of pain in two-parent, happy households. But it's so easy to blame yourself for what you are not giving your child and forget that a lot of that has nothing to do with this. I am trying to remember that now."

"The biggest thing missing is going to be the father they didn't have."

Since Rachel is someone who has never known her biological father, I ask her to help me understand what it might be like for families in which the children's father can never be known.

"For the mothers, it is easier not to have a father involved when a child is young," Rachel says, without a moment's hesitation. "And I am clear about that. But I don't think it is easier in the long run. I think it's only a short-term gain. But for the child—I mean, I know from being adopted, what a child wants to know is the biggest thing that's missing. These children aren't going to have the big thing missing that I had, their mother. So the biggest thing missing is going to be the father they didn't have. Then the grandparents, the aunts, the uncles. And I bet they'd feel as strongly about their father as I did about my birth mother, because he is the biggest thing missing from their lives. As a child, you do get this sense of outrage. I mean, to not know what nationality you are!"

I tell Rachel that children conceived with an anonymous donor can find out their father's nationality and other biographical information about him and his family, much of which she couldn't learn from her adoption file. Since she never considered donor insemination, she didn't know these things. "Wow" is her reaction. "But," she adds, "that still isn't a person. Once I had that information, I would still have wanted to know more." In contemplating what donor insemination might have been like, Rachel tries to think of it from Emma's perspective: "One thing I can give my daughter is that I did love her father. He is not an appropriate person for me to depend on, but I did love him," she says. "And I can still feel that and describe to her what I loved about him and what I felt he loved about me. Whether she cares, I don't know, but it is comforting to me to know that I had that."

When I tell Rachel that some sperm banks let a child learn her father's identity when she turns eighteen, Rachel grabs the information as the bedrock for a policy she'd like to see devised. "If I was a person who made laws, I wouldn't allow anyone to do donor insemination without the father saying he'll be available when his child comes of age. I think every child has a right to know their parents. If a parent doesn't want a relationship, fine, but I do feel parents should be willing to meet their child and answer the questions they have. To protect an adult is not fair when you're infringing on a child's right. That's how it feels to me."

Rachel fidgets in her seat. By now, Emma is cuddled against her mother. She holds a covered cup of juice in her hand, and a book is open across their laps. Rachel flips the pages every so often and draws Emma's attention to the pictures. "I don't think I can ever describe to anyone who has not felt the way I have what it feels like not to have any knowledge of your parents," Rachel says. Her eyes are staring directly into mine. "You really feel as though someone has taken something away from you that is yours."

"His judgment is geared to his needs, not her needs."

There is a lot of anger these days between Rachel and Tony. Some of it is still residue from the breakup of their relationship. It upsets Rachel each time she remembers the weeks after their daughter's birth, when Tony left them to join the band. And Rachel believes Tony is still angry at her: "He feels betrayed that I didn't meet his needs," she speculates.

Tony sometimes wants to spend time with Emma on his own, away from the house. "I won't allow it," Rachel says. That she dictates where he sees his daughter doesn't sit well with Tony. But she claims he has sometimes arrived with marijuana in his jacket pocket. "He will do things I feel are not predictable." Rachel's tone is scolding. "His judgment is geared to his needs, not to her needs. I don't expect I will trust him alone with her until she's much older."

When I ask whether Tony's name appears on Emma's birth certificate, Rachel unloads another diatribe about how the band won out—again— over fatherhood. "He said he'd put his name on her birth certificate," Rachel says. "We were going to go to Boston to do it one afternoon, but his band had a gig that night and he decided he needed a haircut." Several times after that she pressed him to complete the birth certificate, but after a while she got tired of asking. "I got some lawyers to draw up paternity papers and I gave them to him." A look of disgust dominates her narrow face. "They have to go to a notary and he never did that, either." Then, in a whisper, Rachel tells me how at moments like these she actually envies mothers who used an anonymous donor. "They don't have to deal with this.

"However, at some point, they *will* have to deal with the child wanting to find the father."

"If you try to take me to court for child support, I will disappear so fast you'll never find me."

Nine months later Rachel and I unexpectedly bump into each other. She tells me that Emma's visits with her father are becoming "more and more problematic," and she invites me to come to her house again to talk.

When I visit her, Rachel tells me how Emma used to want to see Tony immediately whenever someone said the word "daddy." She would cry for a long time if this wish to see her father wasn't fulfilled. Because that worried her, Rachel had asked her friends to try to avoid saying things like "We have to go home now because Daddy is coming" when Emma was around. If she didn't hear the word, Rachel believed, Emma would less frequently have to confront her feelings about missing her own daddy.

During this period, Tony was visiting Emma twice a week. He and Rachel agreed that he was to stay for about two hours each time. But if Emma got cranky and cried, which she often did, Tony would simply get up and walk away from her; sometimes he would leave. On some occasions this meant he would stay with Emma for only half an hour. "There was an abrupt exit if she was fussy," Rachel says. "Then she'd be crying and saying, 'I want him. I want him.' And her father would be running away."

Tony's visits also started to become more impromptu, accommodating his schedule rather than Emma's. If Emma was asleep when Tony got to the house, he'd demand that Rachel wake her up. "Nothing was according to what might make sense for a child," Rachel says. She tried to tailor her own decisions to fit Emma's needs. "And he always acted toward me like, 'You're trying to control me. I'm not going to let you tell me what to do. I am going to make my own rules.' It was kind of like a little kid acting up." Rachel tired of this routine and insisted again that Tony come at specific times when Emma would be well rested, eager to play, and less likely to be cranky. "Come or don't come," she told Tony. "Here's your slot." So he sometimes arrived a half-hour late, insisting that he stay longer to make up for it. "No. We have plans," Rachel would tell him. She made him accept responsibility for his behavior, something many younger mothers—like Susan, whose child's father didn't heed either her schedule or her son's—don't have the confidence or willingness to do in similar situations. "I was rigid about it. And after a few months he managed to come on a consistent schedule. I think this helped Emma."

Just as these problems of consistency and reliability were being resolved, other issues sprouted. Tony's temper would erupt at Rachel, often in front of Emma. He also left vitriolic messages on her answering machine. Often,

Emma would hear the beginning of these messages, and would say to her mother, "Daddy's mad." Rachel forbade Tony to leave such messages and told him she would no longer permit him to yell at her in front of Emma. "You come for your visits," she told him, "and if anything is not appropriate, Emma and I are going to leave." For three consecutive weeks she interrupted Tony's visit, telling Emma it was time for them to go to get ice cream, because of his outbursts or remarks he made about Rachel.

It wasn't easy for Rachel to assert herself in this way with Tony; she never had before. "When it had been just him and me I could be totally self-sacrificing and convince myself I was still happy. But when it's my daughter, I can't let her not get what she needs," Rachel explains. "I became much more courageous about sticking up for what's right instead of trying to keep the peace."

As Rachel began demanding certain kinds of behavior from Tony, he rebelled even more. He told Rachel he wanted to take Emma to his girlfriend's house, something Rachel was uncomfortable about since she had never met the woman. When she refused, he accused her of punishing him for their breakup. He also demanded that Rachel ask Emma a series of questions and tape-record her answers for him.

I ask Rachel if she remembers any of Tony's suggested questions. She recites them: "Do you want to see Daddy?" "Do you know Mommy won't let you see Daddy?" "Do you know that Daddy wants to take you to pick apples with his girlfriend?"

"He wanted me to do this just to see what she would say. And she's only two!" Rachel says. "It is not appropriate for her to be making these decisions." Rachel refused, telling Tony that asking his daughter to do this made it appear he wasn't trying to help Emma as much as he was trying to prepare a case against Rachel in court. Tony assured her he wasn't, but at the same time he warned Rachel against taking him to court, either.

"If you try to take me to court for child support," Rachel says he told her, "I will disappear so fast you'll never find me."

The mutual snarling didn't abate. Finally, at Rachel's urging, they went together to see a child psychiatrist. She wanted them to try to understand things from Emma's perspective. It happened that these sessions coincided with a period in which Emma told Rachel she wasn't interested in seeing Tony. It wasn't easy for Rachel to tell Tony that his daughter wasn't eager to see him right now, and to have him believe that it wasn't Rachel's anger at him that was preventing it. It helped when the psychiatrist was able to explain that children go through stages like this; it didn't mean Emma wouldn't want to see him again soon. The psychiatrist urged Rachel to assure Tony that Emma still talks about him whenever she remembers things the two of them did together. That way Tony will know what he wants to know: that Emma has not forgotten him.

"I really feel bad that I got us in this situation where she doesn't have a decent father."

Recently, Rachel has been wanting to date again. She tells me about her new and somewhat aggressive approach—including placing a personal advertisement in a newspaper—and explains how it is linked to her concerns about her daughter. "I feel like Emma deserves a father and she deserves one now. And I really feel bad that I got us in this situation where she doesn't have a decent father. So I am kind of willing to humiliate myself." Rachel chuckles at what she seems willing to do in this quest for another parent.

Because of the way her life has worked out, with a marriage at the age of twenty-one, her long relationship with Tony, her accidental pregnancy, and now motherhood, Rachel hasn't dated very many men. Unlike some single women she knows who chose motherhood on their own and might not think of themselves as functioning well within a marriage, Rachel has a strong image of herself as being married and raising children in a two-parent family. Only on days when she feels especially gloomy does Rachel despair of ever marrying again.

Rachel has also, for the first time, undertaken a search for her biological father. She went to court to try to find out his name but it didn't appear on any documents, so now she's hired someone to help her learn his identity. Rachel says she's doing this because she believes that if she can resolve some of her feelings about her unknown father, she might become less anxious about Emma's situation. She admits to feeling twinges of envy whenever she hears an unwed mother say she is not worried about the father's absence from her child's life. She has a friend who adopted a South American child, and another who got pregnant by a man in Europe who has no contact with his child. "Neither woman feels the least bit guilty that their child's father is not involved," Rachel says, looking puzzled, as if wondering how it's possible to feel this way.

"They feel guilty about other things, but not about that," Rachel says. "And I just feel so bad about it. I think everyone needs a father and it's really important."

"Is this father material?"

Rachel's quest to find a "daddy" for her child and a partner for herself is not unusual among older unmarried mothers. These women's desire for adult companionship does not vanish with the arrival of a child, although parenting tasks and job responsibilities don't leave much time for socializing to meet a man, or for getting to know him. Many mothers also told me that they were attracted by different characteristics than those they focused on before becoming parents.

In those earlier times, "baby panic" often guided these women's relational antennae. It was difficult for them to commit to staying with a man who didn't want to have a child. Now that they are mothers, what makes men more desirable is the likelihood of dependable companionship for her and an involved "daddy" for her child, although a man who thinks about fatherhood only in terms of creating and taking care of his *own* progeny would not be well suited. However, a man who will enter into a family relationship knowing that his partner's child's needs might supersede his own becomes a treasured find. When a man already has children, as many older, divorced men do, an unwed mother can assess his fitness as a partner by observing what kind of father he is to his own children, as well as how he treats hers.

Molly is the unwed forty-five-year-old mother of a daughter, now a toddler, whom she adopted at birth. For the first year or so of maintaining her full-time work schedule as a midwife, spending time with her daughter, and coping with her exhaustion, dating was just about the last thing she wanted to do. Recently, however, she has started again. A good friend had to push her to arrange a time to meet the man she's just begun to see. Molly says it's still much too early to know what, if anything, might happen with him. "I've always wanted someone who is nurturing," she says. "But now he absolutely *has* to be. I can't make do with less."

Molly rubs her hand across her forehead. "Having a child allows me to try to enjoy myself in dating, to have a nice time," she says. "I don't have to worry about having another child, so there is great relief in that. But now there's this other thing of how serious I should be. Should I just have a good time and have some dates? Or should I get right into this with questions to myself such as 'Is this father material?' I really would like to give myself a break and just have a nice time. But we torture ourselves, don't we?" she says, then pauses for my reaction. I laugh in agreement.

"I know my daughter needs a father. I know that. And I actually don't seriously doubt I'll find someone," Molly says, even though she has never been married. How this will happen, and whether, when Molly meets "the man" she wants to be with, she will marry him, are treated by her as questions for another day. But Molly is certain that because she has a child her search for a partner will proceed "more effectively" than her relationships have in the past.

"Why 'more effectively'?" I ask.

She chuckles. "Because my daughter will force me to do that. She makes it clear I need to choose a healthy person, not a person who's just like my sex dream or who is fabulously intellectually stimulating but emotionally distant and God knows what else. Now, with my daughter, I have to think more practically. That is the major wonderful thing she's doing to help me to be a little more healthy about my choice. It's wonderful!"

"If you think we're cute, you should see our mothers."

Figuring out ways to be meet potential "daddies" poses a challenge for women who lack time and energy. Sometimes the only way individual inertia can be overcome is through collective action. Just as many women offered one another support along the way to motherhood, a few of them do the same when the search for a suitable "daddy" begins.

"We're going to have a brunch and everyone who comes to it has to bring an available man," an unmarried mother of a seven-month-old son gleefully announces at a meeting of Single Mothers by Choice. For the past year or so a group of new mothers has been getting together, apart from this monthly meeting, to talk about things new mothers talk about— babies' feeding and nap schedules, their own exhaustion, the hunt for good and affordable child care, and their delight at finally being mothers. One usual topic they did not talk about was their husbands. None has one. Their babies were always with them during their meetings; the first few months of these gatherings the infants slept or nursed while their mothers talked. As months went by and the babies started to crawl, the house where they met began to look like a train station at rush hour. Perhaps it was these early signs of mobilized independence that prompted these mothers to start comparing notes about the absence of men in their lives. But whatever the motivating factor was, one day their conversation turned to how they could meet men.

Now Valentine's Day is a few days away, and the upcoming brunch with "available men" is a gift they are giving one another. One woman asks for a more precise definition of "available." Her question elicits laughter.

"It means eligible," the woman who made the announcement responds.

"He should be eligible, not gay and not married, as well as being someone who is open to meeting women like us."

No one asks for a more precise explanation of "women like us." Another woman who's been in on planning this brunch observes that many of the women are having a hard time thinking of a man they can bring. A woman who knows someone like that—someone who is "eligible" and open to "meeting women like us"—might not be all that eager to share him with others.

"Next year we'll have a group wedding," another mother says.

"Dream on, Donna. Dream on," says a woman sitting on the other side of the room.

The brunch sets off a buzz of conversation around the table.

"Wait," says the woman who mentioned the brunch idea, trying to rein in the group's attention while she shuffles through papers in her backpack, "we're also planning to take out a personal ad in a couple of newspapers."

"All of you?" someone asks, knowing there are a dozen or so women in this group.

"Yeah. Fifteen of us are planning to have a party and we're going to place a personal ad inviting men to come to it," she says.

"How will you advertise yourselves?"

"Oh, we'll say we are a diverse group of attractive mothers who want to meet men."

The mothers envision taking out a personal ad that asks men to write letters about themselves, explaining why they want to attend this party. From these letters, the women will put together a guest list. This idea is greeted with as much enthusiasm as the brunch.

But by the next meeting, the women have learned that newspapers refuse to publish a group personal ad. Undaunted, a few of the women toss out another idea—a fantasy, really, since to execute it would cost far more money than any of the women has to spend: they want to rent a billboard along the major highway leading into Boston. They know the picture they'd paint on it and the tag line they'd write.

"Once, when we were all together, we lined our babies up on the couch and we took a photograph," says one of the mothers. "There they are, our babies all in a row. So we'd take that photo and put it on the billboard, and across it we'd write: 'If you think we're cute, you should see our moms.'"

"We were going to have to rely on a lot of faith in each other that we would do the right thing and cooperate."

Few of the mothers who attend these meetings know the father of their child. Most either adopted their children or used an anonymous donor to get pregnant. So the children must grow up before they can search for their birth father, if they choose to do so. Sometimes even that won't be possible. In the meantime, their mothers talk about how they want their children to get to know men with whom they can develop close and secure relationships. But beyond this common desire, there is a lot that differs in these families' lives. Because Bethany's boys can never find out who their father is, she makes it an integral part of her parenting to bring male role models into their lives; as they get older, she plans to take advantage of community mentoring programs. On the other hand, Rachel's daughter knows her father, but neither mother nor child is always sure she wants him around. And Rachel would like to get married, but she worries about how her husband's presence will sit with her daughter's father. Molly adopted her daughter and knows who her child's birth father is, but so far has not made any arrangement for her to meet him. It is Molly's hope that motherhood will act like a divining rod, leading her to a man whom she and her daughter will both love.

Some women, when faced with the "daddy" question, decide on a different route to motherhood: they find "known donors," men who agree to help them conceive. This will enable them to tell their children about the father; if he agrees, the father may also play an active role in his child's life. Also, by selecting men with whom they are not romantically linked, these women hope to avoid the messy entanglements mothers like Rachel are dealing with. Some of these women work out written agreements with the potential father, establishing their responsibilities and codifying the relationship the father will have with the child. But this can be tricky territory; not only are such agreements legally suspect, but no one—including longtime married couples—can know before a baby arrives exactly how having a child will affect their lives and their relationship. And sometimes, as the child grows, an unattached father and mother discover that the notions they'd once had about their intended involvements are not working out quite as they imagined.

This is what happened with Paula and Jason.

Paula asked her former boyfriend Jason to help her get pregnant. Jason was approaching fifty, had no children, had not been married, and was not involved in a relationship. After thinking hard about Paula's proposal, he agreed. In fact, from his perspective, becoming a father without assuming an obligation to support or care for the child seemed to suit him well. He had a steady job but not much savings; since it seemed unlikely that he would be settling into a committed relationship, this would at least enable him to have a child. This was also the arrangement Paula had in mind when she asked for his help: she was willing to assume all responsibility for raising the child in exchange for his willingness to help her get pregnant.

After Paula became pregnant, she and Jason went to see separate attorneys for advice on what, if anything, they should do to legally certify their arrangement. Each was told the same thing: that even if they agreed on everything, any papers they signed were unlikely to have standing if, once the child was born, either parent changed their mind. Even so, the attorneys urged them to put their views on paper. "We were both given a sort of homework assignment to write a draft of what each of us wanted," Paula says. "Then we were supposed to try to put them together."

Jason never wrote anything. When I asked him why, he replied: "I was saying to myself, 'I don't know. I don't know.'" He felt he had no way of knowing the kind of relationship he wanted to have with a child who was not yet born. "Certainly, I felt all the things that evolution has arranged for me to feel in terms of being protective of Paula and the baby," Jason told me, referring to his belief about how males in nearly every species are expected to react to an impending birth. At times he told Paula that he imagined his role would be something akin to an "uncle's." But only during the last few months of Paula's pregnancy did Jason acknowledge to himself the extraordinary emotional pull of this event. When he saw her just before their baby was due, Jason says, he realized for the first time that "that is mine."

Paula completed a first draft of what she wanted to see in their agreement. However, because Jason never wrote a draft, he and Paula became parents without agreeing on how they were going to act as parents. As her due date drew closer, Paula tells me, she realized that "we were going to have to rely on a lot of faith in each other that we would do the right thing and cooperate."

Paula reads to me from her original draft:

> J agrees to donate sperm to impregnate P with the understanding:
> 1. That J is not obligated to assume parenting responsibility.
> 2. That P does not expect financial contribution toward myself or the child by J.
> 3. That P is not going to prohibit contact between J and the child,

the amount and nature of such contact not even attempted to
be defined here because J continues to say that he is ambivalent
and doesn't know how he is going to feel about it or how much
involvement he is going to want.

"I wasn't going to try to prescribe how much time each week Jason
would have with the child or anything like that," Paula says.

Paula is reading her draft nearly three years after she wrote it. She had
to search her house to find it, and she tells me how strange it seems, given
how differently their relationship has turned out from anything either of
them could have predicted.

> I, P, have sole legal and physical custody of the child, and in the event
> of my death or inability to care for the child, my sister is appointed
> the guardian.

I ask Paula if she has also included this in her will. She nods, but is eager
to draw my attention to the next item. "This is an important clause":

> Under my sister's guardianship, there would likewise be no attempt to
> prohibit contact between J and his child.

Paula explains why this clause was so important to her. "My family—
well, my dad in particular—had been so negative in reacting to my pregnancy, and he never really embraced Jason. He saw him as the one who
perpetrated this thing on me. My dad never recognized the baby as being
my choice. He always thought Jason did this terrible thing to me. It was
completely illogical, but he was being my dad. If I was out of the picture,
I know Jason would've thought my dad would step in and say he couldn't
see his child. So I put this in there to protect Jason."

Paula continues reading.

> P may reside in any city, state or country with the child.

"You wanted to have the freedom to move without having to ask Jason's
permission?" I ask.

"Right."

"By your choice alone?"

"Yeah."

When I remind her of my interest in finding out what her thinking is
about these items today, Paula laughs heartily.

"Oh, yeah," she says with a smirk. "That one gets a whole lot more complicated today."

Her recitation goes on.

> Even if one or the other of us [the adults] gets a new family of some sort, that the statements of intention still hold:
> That J donated sperm to P to get pregnant because that was her choice. That P doesn't expect financial support from J, and that J does not assume any automatic parenting rights or responsibilities just because of his biological connection.

"That's one part that would be totally not legally binding," Paula points out. "I couldn't say that Jason did not assume any parenting rights, but that is where my head was at that time."

I ask her whether she believes Jason's thinking was similar then.

"Yeah; if I had put in that he was obligated to X, Y, or Z, or that I expected financial compensation in exchange for visiting, he probably would have had a fit."

At the conclusion of this handwritten draft, Paula had added language her father insisted on. Before reading it aloud, she scans it herself. "This is hysterical," she says:

> That J will not inherit any estate from the child if both P and the child predecease him.

"My father, the lawyer," Paula says, folding up the paper to put it away. "I mean, my father really wants to shut Jason out completely."

Reminded of this family animus, Paula looks sad.

"He's made a decision to stay somewhat involved, and I guess I've made a decision to let him."

Peter, their son, is now two and a half years old.

"Have you and Jason revisited these arrangements?" I ask Paula.

"No," she says. "It just sort of happens. But as things have evolved, it becomes more and more emotionally . . . charged," she says, trying to find the best word to describe the current climate. "As the months and years go by, Jason's psychological investment in Peter increases to the point at which it is a very emotionally loaded thing for him. It would be harder now than ever to write up an agreement. It was certainly a lot easier to do it in the abstract. When I talk to other women who are thinking of doing this, I tell them that if they take this route, it is really better to do an agreement before the baby is born."

If Paula and Jason were to try to create a parental agreement now, it would be very different from the document she has just finished reading. "Jason wouldn't be content with me simply saying I won't prohibit him from seeing the child," Paula says. "He would want a guarantee of a minimum amount of time with him. Also, the clause about me being able to move anywhere—he probably would want to say, at the very least, that if that happens there are going to be two-week blocks of time he spends with Peter. He's just so emotionally attached to Peter now. And I think it has gotten even more so in the past three months, since Jason's father died. You know what that does—especially since Jason was his father's only son, and Peter is Jason's only son."

Jason's closeness to Peter began to intensify when the baby was a few months old. "His fatherhood didn't happen on the day Peter was born," as Paula puts it. However, it wasn't too long before Jason's prebirth notion of being an "active uncle" in his son's life was replaced by wanting to be his "daddy." Peter's smiles captured his heart. That Peter also started to look very much like Jason seemed to make their connection even tighter. Paula would hear Jason refer to Peter as "my little clone." When Paula saw Jason's baby photographs, she was brought face-to-face with the striking resemblance between father and son. She really liked the fact that she could go through Jason's childhood scrapbooks and connect Peter so concretely with his father's past. These moments made her feel relieved that she hadn't used an anonymous donor, a method she'd considered briefly but rejected.

As soon as Peter uttered sounds that approximated words, Jason prompted him to say "Dada." Paula was a bit taken aback by this, and at first suggested that Peter call Jason by his first name. Being called "Dada," Paula felt, came with a lot of responsibilities, including maintaining a consistently close relationship. Was Jason willing to commit himself to that? Paula wasn't yet certain, but Jason insisted that "Daddy" was the name he wanted Peter to call him. "He fell in love with Peter and discovered that he is a wonderful father," Paula says.

There was no rekindling of strong emotional attachment between Paula and Jason; what cements their relationship is Peter. When medical problems brought him to the hospital during his first year, both his parents were with him. Paula remembers how comforting it was to have Jason there, as someone who cared about Peter as much as she did. At such moments Paula reminded herself of how different things would be if Jason had decided not to be involved with Peter. "The thought of going through all of that by myself was really scary. It made me wonder how anyone can undertake parenting by themselves," Paula tells me. "How did I think I could do this alone, when things like this can happen?"

On an everyday basis, however, Paula does act as a single parent. Although Jason buys Peter toys, he does not contribute financially to his support, nor to the expense of Peter's high-priced day care, nor to his health insurance premiums. Nor does Jason put money into a savings account for Peter's anticipated college costs, though his salary is roughly equivalent to Paula's. Jason doesn't help Paula in arranging any of the nonparental care that their work schedules entail. Nor does he rearrange his work schedule to stay with Peter when he is sick. Jason usually spends time with Peter on weekends, though if Paula knows she needs to be out on a weekday night she will check with Jason to see if he can come to her house and stay with him. Often, he does.

"Paula is a single parent day-to-day," Jason told me one evening, when he and Paula and I met for dinner. "But from my view she is not a single parent who has to feel like she has no place to turn for help. If Paula feels that way, that has more to do with our relationship than the reality of my feelings about or my willingness to deal with Peter. . . . He is a child who, right now, has one and a half single parents. If there is a crisis in his life, there is no question there are two full-time parents for him, at least as long as that lasts. It's not necessarily a full-time two-parent family, but two people who are going to be there as caring providers."

Much of the time, until quite recently, their parenting arrangement resembled what might exist between an amicably divorced couple. Paula believes one reason it worked so well is that she entered motherhood with few expectations about Jason's involvement in his child's life and without the idea that he would share the parenting responsibilities. Never having expected that the three of them would act like a nuclear family, Paula was not disappointed when Jason did not perform in a familylike way, either as her partner or as a father to their child.

During an earlier conversation with Paula, I was abruptly reminded of this. I mentioned how she and Jason had "decided to do this together."

"No," Paula reminded me, pointedly. "*I* decided to go this way and Jason helped me out. That's a very different thing. If we had decided to do this together, then I think I'd feel differently about Jason and how I want our lives to be set up. But we didn't decide together. I decided and he went along to help. Now he's made another decision, to stay somewhat involved, and I guess I've made a decision to let him."

"To me it becomes kind of like this game of pretending we are a family. And I don't see us as a family."

Paula's decision to let Jason "stay somewhat involved" has resulted in moments that have been neither easy nor always friendly. Recently there has been more tension than usual between them—including angry words, which, to Paula's regret, Peter hears. "I can see that Peter is absorbing these things and I don't want him witnessing this," she tells me. "I mean, that was expressly the point of having a household I could control. I didn't want him to grow up in that kind of an environment. For this to start happening just flies in the face of my most cherished goal."

Whether any child can, or should, be fully protected from observing conflict among adults is a question psychologists argue about. My reading, and my conversations with psychologists, suggest that it is crucial for children to see men and women resolve conflict in nonviolent and constructive ways; it is by watching adults resolve disagreements that children learn how to do the same. But if conflict festers, if it remains unresolved and erupts too often, it can be detrimental to a child's well-being. Parental conflict, after all, is identified as a leading predictor of behavioral problems in children.

Paula and Jason's conflict arises out of differing visions they have of their relationship. "It's very important to Jason that we try to do things as a threesome, he and me and Peter," says Paula. On weekends he plans activities for the three of them. "To me it became kind of like this game of pretending we are a family. And I don't see us as a family. We are, Jason and me, coparents. We are coparenting an individual. But we, as adults, have our different worldviews and our own homes and our different styles. To try to meld those and create this unified façade, I mean to me it seems dishonest."

Paula told Jason she wanted them to work on clarifying their relationship. Jason preferred to use a counselor, and Paula agreed. In her view, these visits to the counselor are to help them find a way to separate their own relationship from their parenting roles in Peter's life. "I wanted some definition of what our relationship was going to be so that he wouldn't be constantly trying to have it be family, family, family." Paula's voice climbs to the upper octaves as she repeats the word. "And so I wouldn't be constantly trying to pull it apart. Independent, independent, independent." She lowers her pitch again. "I want us to be able to define something that we can both live with."

For nearly a decade before Jason helped Paula get pregnant, sparks of attraction had pulled them back to each other every so often. But their inability to sustain a relationship had, by the time they conceived Peter, doused Paula's interest in trying to rebuild one. When Jason was trying to impregnate her, Paula certainly never considered the arrangement as indicating a resumption of their romantic relationship. "Ours were continual experiences of not being in synch," she says. Her face brightens. "Amazing I got pregnant! Right?

"I want to put a label on our relationship and say, 'Okay, Jason, you're going to be part of my life forever. I accept that. And you are a wonderful father to my little boy, and I am grateful for that. And that is fine. But I don't want it to keep holding me back from getting on with the rest of my life." Paula wants to finally be able to move away from the pull-and-tug of Jason's presence in her life as a potential partner. She wants to be able to start a relationship with some other man when an opportunity presents itself, instead of being stuck in what she considers this nowhere land. She wants to feel she has the freedom to commit herself to building another relationship.

I ask if she is seeing someone else now.

"No," Paula replies. "It's not that there's any person X on the horizon. But there couldn't be, because an intelligent male would see this as a situation where there is no place for him."

"So it's hard to get yourself to the point of seeing someone while you're in the middle of this?"

"Right. Nothing could happen under these circumstances. I have been attracted to people, and people have been attracted to me. But nothing can proceed for me. Nothing can proceed for Jason, either, but for him it's more because he is still emotionally wrapped up in me and has not given up a hope of making a family out of this situation. We are in very different places."

Jason didn't say anything about this to Paula when she was trying to become pregnant. Perhaps, Paula speculates, he just figured it might happen. What seems more likely, however, is that having their son as a bond just served to strengthen whatever feelings Jason had for her.

"Is Jason's objective to make the two of you into a couple?" I ask Paula. They've been in counseling for several months now.

She nods. "That is his hope. That is what he would like as an end point. He has even said, 'I want the white picket fence and the house in the suburbs and happy, happy kids playing in the yard. He wants this image."

The image is not something Paula rejects, but at this moment she doesn't see the two of them heading toward it together. "I mean, we've been together and apart, together and apart, for so long; if we were destined to be a couple, we would have worked out these differences. We are just such fundamentally different people that it's really like trying to put a square peg in a round hole to say this is going to work."

"We really do keep Peter's interests foremost."

Usually Peter stays over at Jason's house on Friday nights. Paula likes this arrangement. It gives her a night to herself and lets Jason have a more realistic experience of what it is like to be a parent. But there is one problem: every so often Jason calls her to say that he just isn't feeling quite up to taking care of a rambunctious two-year-old.

"Like this weekend," Paula says, volunteering a recent example. "I'd told him about an event at Peter's day care and asked if he wanted to come along and look after Peter while I helped out the other parents." Jason agreed. The event. was to take place on Saturday morning. As the weekend approached, Jason let Paula know he wouldn't be taking Peter for his Friday overnight. "He didn't want to use up Friday night, get burned out on patience or energy or whatever, or feel that he had to wake up at seven o'clock like Peter does, if he was going to be taking care of him that morning," Paula says.

"It is interesting what happens when a person has a choice about this, isn't it?"

She laughs at my comment as heartily as I've ever heard her laugh.

"Yes, isn't it?" she replies. "And it cracks me up because as I am listening to him I am thinking, 'What do you think I'm doing every day?' " Paula stretches the word "every" like elastic. "But I know what he'd say: 'Well, it was your choice to have the baby in the first place.' And he's right. It was my choice. I signed up voluntarily."

Paula sometimes wonders whether she may be shielding Jason too much from the tougher aspects of parenting. He does not see the many times when Peter's needs take precedence over Paula's. The way Jason views it, Peter fits into his schedule; he sees him when and if he can, and for relatively short blocks of time. Paula's life, on the other hand, is organized around her son. "Am I protecting his father too much by making Peter available to him when it is convenient for him instead of saying, 'Okay, you get Fridays and Wednesdays. You miss one, you miss it. There is no rain check. So you work out your schedule so that you can be there.' " Paula says this as though rehearsing with me words she might like to say to Jason. "It's not real life for him." Paula shakes her head. "Right now, he's got a pretty good deal."

Though these problems are now troubling their relationship, Paula still has no regrets about having a child with Jason. She's glad that Peter has a father whom he knows and who wants to spend time with him, even if, as Peter gets older, the situation is sometimes confusing to him. Paula takes solace from what their counselor recently told them: "The therapist has been supportive and complimentary to us, because he says he is hearing from each of us that we really do keep Peter's interests foremost. We are not trying to use our son as a weapon against each other, or any of those things that could happen in a classic divorce. At least, there is that."

"The word 'illegitimate' needs to be discarded just like other hate words have been discarded."

While Bethany, Rachel, and Paula do their best to answer their children's questions about "Daddy," they—and tens of thousands of women like them—are also hearing "Where's Daddy?" from society at large. Increasingly, these queries carry a harsh irascible edge.

One afternoon some of the women at the Single Mothers by Choice meeting decide to talk about social acceptance—or, more often, lack of acceptance—of unmarried motherhood. One woman raised this topic by recounting a story she'd read in a newspaper about a pregnant teacher in Florida who, school administrators learned, did not intend to remain with her child's father. "They told her she could either get an abortion or marry the baby's father," this woman reported to the group. Of course, the teacher had at least two other alternatives, neither one pleasant: she could sue to keep her job, or she could quit.

None of these women has experienced any comparable intrusion into her personal life. However, the teacher's treatment prompts a few of them to talk at greater length about the mean-spirited and punitive attitudes they hear in public discourse. What upsets them most is the reemergence of the word "illegitimate" to describe babies like theirs. After all their years of agonizing decision-making about having a child on their own, after all the medical treatments they endured or the thousands of miles they traveled to adopt their babies, it is upsetting to hear folks toss around a derogatory term like "illegitimate" to describe their children. Their children, these mothers say, are as wanted and loved and nurtured by them, and by a community of friends and extended family, as any child in any other family. Should their children—should any child—be talked about like damaged goods because their mothers were not married when they arrived?

These older, educated, relatively well-off, and mostly white mothers realize that the harshest rhetoric is reserved primarily for young, unwed mothers, many of whom are nonwhite and poor. Knowing this, however, doesn't make the word "illegitimate" less distasteful. Most of the mothers here recognize that people who are trying to reintroduce "illegitimate" into common usage are doing so as a way of reinstituting stigma, in the hope of making such births less common. The older mothers discussing the subject today don't believe that a punitive and stigmatizing approach will achieve this goal; it would not, they contend, have stopped them, because they do not accept the underlying premise that by having a child out of wedlock they're committing a socially destructive act or predisposing their children to criminality or deviant behavior, as much of the current rhetoric about unwed motherhood asserts.

A few weeks before this meeting, the Single Mothers by Choice newsletter carried an article about the resurfacing of the "illegitimacy" debate. It was written by an unmarried, pregnant woman, Susan Eshleman, and headlined "The Bind." Eshleman wrote: "It is not single parenting that is the problem. It is, perhaps, an overall lack of resources. As Americans grow more frustrated with the decline of our country's world power, poor economics, and ineffective governing, an increasing number of people are willing to engage in scapegoating. . . . Hopefully not too many people will jump on the latest bandwagon attacking what they refer to as 'illegitimate' children and single mothers. I, for one, don't want my child to be the focus of a hate group. The word 'illegitimate' needs to be discarded just like other hate words have been discarded."

But as Eshleman and the women at this meeting in a Boston suburb know very well, in the mid-1990s the word "illegitimate" is making a comeback. And neither these mothers' complaints nor the discomfort their children might feel is likely to stop it.

"Who do you think you are to bring a child into this world who is going to have a stigma?"

Laura's workday went as it usually did. Memos for her to type and distribute piled up on her desk. One of her bosses asked her to go down the street and bring him a sandwich just as she was about to go on her lunch break. During the afternoon the telephone didn't stop ringing long enough for her to get as much work done as she would have liked. It never does.

One of the calls that afternoon was from her mother. She wanted Laura to reconsider an invitation to have dinner with her aunt and uncle, who were visiting from out of town. When the event was first mentioned a few weeks earlier, Laura had told her mother that she'd rather skip it. "I don't think so, Ma," she had said, offering no explanation. "I'll pass."

Laura's mother hadn't pressed her then. She knew Laura didn't enjoy spending time with these relatives. And she knew why. Laura's relationship with her aunt and uncle had soured about a dozen years earlier when, at the age of twenty-seven, she became pregnant by accident and made three decisions: to have her baby; to raise it; and not to get married. As word of Laura's various decisions traveled to other family members, they were ridiculed. Laura's mother angrily tried to convince her to have an abortion. When Laura refused, her mother stopped seeing her. Nor would she speak to Laura: "Until my son was born, if I called her on the phone, she'd hang up on me," Laura says. When Laura gave birth, her mother did visit her in the hospital, and over time they patched up their differences about her having Sam outside of marriage. But Laura is still bitter over a letter one of her mother's sisters wrote, at her mother's urging. As she recites it, I can tell that her aunt's letter is as fresh in her mind as the day she received it a dozen years ago.

" 'Who do you think you are to bring a child into this world who is going to have a stigma, a child who you are not going to be able to support?' " Laura's voice is forceful as she enunciates every word and re-creates for me the sting each one must have borne. "You're going to be on welfare and people like me and my husband who have been working for thirty-five years, we're going to have to support you," her aunt wrote.

"I was flabbergasted by this," says Laura.

When Laura, a tall, trim woman whose brown hair falls straight down past her shoulders, graduated from high school, she went out and found herself a job. She'd always wanted to go to work, and was happy to be able to support herself as a secretary. She didn't go to college; back then, she had neither the desire nor the financial resources. But she had always found steady work that paid a decent salary, and she had no intention of going on welfare once she had her baby. She believed strongly that her decision about marrying her child's father ought to turn on the quality of their relationship, not on whether she had some duty to protect her family from whatever shame they or others might associate with an out-of-wedlock birth. Would her family really want her to marry him even though she knew their relationship would not last?

Her aunt's letter reached Laura at a time when she was vulnerable and would have welcomed even the tiniest hint of support from her family. Instead, the letter served only to push them farther apart. As the years went by, Laura tried to be cordial whenever she encountered her aunt and uncle at family gatherings. But forgetting or forgiving wasn't something she'd been able to do.

"Please come with me tonight," her mother now asked Laura. "They really want to see you and Sam." Laura doubted this, but hearing in her mother's pleading voice that her company and her grandson's would mean a lot, Laura agreed to go.

When she left work at five o'clock, Laura was tired. More than anything she wanted to go home and collapse onto her living room sofa. There, she'd read or watch TV or sew curtains, and when twelve-year-old Sam wanted help with his homework, he would bring his books and sit next to her. Since Sam had started attending an academically demanding private school on full scholarship, he needed every waking hour to get his assignments done. As soon as Laura agreed to go to dinner, she made sure to telephone Sam at home so he could redouble his afternoon studying.

When she got home, Laura put on one of her fancier outfits. At her urging, Sam slung a school tie around the collar of his white shirt and found an unrumpled jacket to wear. Because Laura had never told Sam the history of her troubled relationship with these relatives—she believed it wasn't necessary for him to hear what had been said before he was born— he knew nothing, either, about his mother's reluctance to attend this family gathering. Bundled against the evening's chilly wind, they walked to a nearby subway stop and traveled to the center of Boston.

"When we got off the subway, we bumped into my mother." By this point Laura's mood was starting to shift from reluctant participation to almost giddy excitement at a rare evening out. But her upbeat mood lasted only until they reached the door of her relatives' hotel room: "Oh, Laura, we didn't know you were coming," her aunt said. Out of the corner of her eye Laura saw her mother trying to maintain a smile.

"So I say to myself, 'Oh, great, that's a nice greeting,' " Laura tells me. "But I've learned to try to let what is said by them just roll off my back, so we just went on in."

"Oh, well, the illegitimate kid isn't so bad after all."

Laura was determined not to let anything spoil the evening. After everyone caught up on family news, Laura's mother ordered Chinese food; they sat in a circle sampling the dishes. Conversation was lighthearted and, in spite of the awkward greeting, Laura began to feel very much a part of her family's evening together. She was having a pretty good time, and as far as she could tell, Sam was enjoying himself as well.

"All of a sudden my uncle made a crack," Laura tells me. "He sort of announced to all of us, 'Oh, well, the illegitimate kid isn't so bad after all.'"

Laura stared at him, not quite believing what she'd heard. "My instinct was to kick him in his mouth," she tells me, "but I held myself back." She took in her uncle's words as a dazed boxer might absorb a punch. She was reminded of who she was with, and everything they'd once said came rushing back. For an instant, she felt as though this moment were a dozen years ago; all their nasty words whirled around inside her again. She realized that no matter what she or Sam did, she was unlikely ever to escape the stigma her family put on her for choosing to bear her son without marrying his father. Her aunt and uncle had not expressed these feelings for many years, but it was clear to Laura now that neither the passage of time nor her son's achievements would overcome his "illegitimacy" in their minds.

No one would make eye contact with Laura. Though the silence was uncomfortable, none of the adults knew how to end it.

"Ma," Sam said, turning toward his mother as the rest of her family listened, "if I was born thirty years ago, would he be talking about me?" It struck her that Sam knew what the word meant, but that he thought it was too out-of-date to apply to him.

"Yeah, if you were born thirty years ago, he would," Laura replied.

As she and Sam talked, Laura noticed that her uncle's usually confident expression had been replaced by one of embarrassment.

"That's a terrible word," Laura's uncle said, looking at her. "People shouldn't even use that word."

Laura was relieved to hear him say this. She nodded and looked directly at him. "You're right," she said. "It's a terrible word and people shouldn't use it."

No more was said on the subject.

"I am not willing to consciously spend the rest of my life beating myself up because I am a single mother."

Several days after this dinner, when Laura and I first get together to talk, she tells me what happened. The dinner conversation reminded her of how she and her son "will never quite be accepted." Laura realizes that in the eyes of many people she and Sam are likely to be thought of more as "what" they are—a mother without a husband and a son without his father to live with—than as "who" they are and what they have accomplished as a family and as individuals.

"No matter how well Sam is doing or what a marvelous person he truly is, or how well I am doing—I mean, I just went to school at nights and got a promotion, and I consider myself a decent woman—we are still *what* we are." Laura reaches up to push her straight hair away from her face. Her words tumble out, propelled by her frustration at being defined so narrowly by others. "In my own family, my aunt and uncle are pillars of their church—which is such hypocrisy," Laura believes, because of their failure to show her the care and concern she thinks religion teaches people they should.

Being a single parent does not prevent Laura from instilling in Sam what she believes are life's fundamental lessons and values. She resents insinuations that because she isn't married, she won't be able to raise Sam to be a good and successful person. Laura knows she can. However, living in a climate so critical of unmarried motherhood, Laura says, sometimes makes it very hard for her to retain faith in her parental abilities. "I'm going to have to put out that extra effort to prove myself to everyone except Sam," Laura says. "I mean, I don't have to prove it to him because I am all he knows. Being an unmarried mother is not something I get up and think about every day, but from time to time, it gets to me for one reason or another. At this point, I have to honestly say there is no way I am going to be able to do everything and do it perfectly. My attitude is I have one opportunity to raise Sam and I am going to do the best I can with what I've got. Beyond that, I can't whip myself for what I did wrong. And I think I have a right to pat myself on the back for what I do right. I'm not willing to consciously spend the rest of my life beating myself up because I didn't marry before I became a mother."

"If you want to get the stigma back, you have to make this behavior punishable again."

Whatever measure of comfort Laura develops about herself, just when she starts to feel okay about her situation, it seems as if someone comes along to put a dent in her confidence. Sometimes voices conveying this stigma travel into her life from faraway places, as when politicians use the word "illegitimacy" to display their support for "family values." Now, after several decades of disuse, the word "illegitimate" is legitimate again. Single mothers—particularly younger, never-married mothers—on welfare are the word's most visible and intended targets. But its reemergence also gives Laura and other unmarried mothers unwelcome reminders of what others think about them.

If we think of the word "illegitimate" as being like a refurbished battleship, long ago mothballed but now recommissioned to wage new political wars, then Charles Murray is the person who broke the champagne bottle across her bow. Murray, a social scientist at the American Enterprise Institute, a conservative think tank in Washington, D.C., launched the reentry of this word into mainstream dialogue when his highly influential op-ed piece "The Coming of the White Underclass" appeared in *The Wall Street Journal* in October 1993. Murray's article did for "illegitimacy" what former vice president Dan Quayle's complaint about Murphy Brown had done the year before for "family values": Murray gave people the green light to reemploy the term as a way of delivering an emotional punch.

"Illegitimacy is the single most important social problem of our time," Murray wrote. He claimed that illegitimacy feeds the nation's deepening roots of poverty, crime, and ignorance. Of particular concern to him was the rapid escalation in out-of-wedlock births among white women. (By 1991, more than one-fifth of white babies were being born to unmarried women.) During the preceding decade, the birthrate among unmarried white women increased by 82 percent, compared with a growth of 12 percent among blacks, though the out-of-wedlock birthrate among black women continued to be higher than among whites.

Murray delivered a warning not unlike the one that Daniel Patrick Moynihan issued in 1965, when he focused attention on the rising numbers of out-of-wedlock births in black communities. Moynihan and Murray each claimed social calamity would follow. However, though their statistical analyses illuminated similar trends, their recommendations for remedies diverged widely. While Moynihan (then a Labor Department official, now a U.S. senator) argued for investment in black communities to bolster the economic foundation on which the formation of two-parent families depends, and is still fighting strenuously against the dismantling of the federal safety net for families with children, in the mid-1990s Murray called for a withdrawal of all cash welfare assistance, a reestablishment of orphanages for poor children, and societal stigmatization of those who have "illegitimate" babies.

In his *Wall Street Journal* article Murray emphasized what he said is the connection between out-of-wedlock births and the breakdown of social order. "The historical fact is that trendlines on black crime, dropout from the labor force, and illegitimacy all shifted sharply upward as the overall black illegitimacy rate passed 25 percent," Murray wrote. What received significantly less attention was Murray's admission that evidence for this cause-and-effect linkage is "murky." But he used this "murky" evidence to predict that the same trends will soon show up among white Americans, because more illegitimate children are being born to them.

Murray's concerns about white illegitimacy captured the attention of many policymakers who were looking for a blunter way to talk about this aspect of the breakdown of families. Conservatives, who at that time were gaining considerable political power, widely embraced Murray's ideas and language. Because Murray framed his arguments about illegitimacy in terms of white women, he offered valuable cover from charges of racism to those who took up his position. Murray's strategy was not dissimilar to Dan Quayle's: though Quayle's famous speech was primarily about poor, unmarried black mothers, he turned Murphy Brown—an upper-class, white unwed mother—into the symbolic target of his nascent "family values" campaign. If white women are used as visible symbols, criticism of their marital and reproductive choices can be more easily debated in the political arena. Once the criticism is made, however, its actual target can often be understood to be somebody else. Many who now use the word "illegitimacy" are aware that most listeners associate this phenomenon with young, minority women and their children, even though more white children are being born out of wedlock each year.

Murray's approach certainly made commentators less inhibited about using the word "illegitimate." Tim Russert, host of NBC's *Meet the Press*, was acknowledging this when he began a February 1994 interview with black newspaper columnist William Raspberry by saying, "We are finally able to talk about illegitimacy." Newspaper and magazine columnists, editorial writers, and reporters also started to sprinkle their copy with the word "illegitimacy." For a few months such a feeding frenzy ensued that it would not have seemed all that shocking if someone had issued a call for unmarried mothers to wear scarlet "I" 's.

Murray was thrilled. One Sunday morning, when he appeared on *This Week with David Brinkley*, his sense of victory was palpable. President Clinton had been asked by network news anchors to comment on Murray's thesis; the president had praised Murray's analysis though not endorsed his solutions. Soon Clinton, who until then had avoided using "illegitimate" to describe children born to unmarried women, started, on occasion, to let the word slip into his speeches. Murray regards use of this word—especially by the president—as an essential step toward restoring societal stigma and thereby, he believes, reducing the number of such births and restoring marriage and two-parent families. Of course, to do what Murray envisions requires companion steps as well.

"If you want to get the stigma back, you have to make this behavior punishable again," Murray argued during his appearance on the Brinkley show. "And it has to be punishing for someone. It has to be punishing for the parents. It has to be punishing for the boyfriend who is faced with a shotgun from somewhere. It has to be punishing to the community. And until you're ready to restore these walls of penalties that used to constrain sexual behavior, you are not going to get stigma back."

"God doesn't believe there are any illegitimate children. Only white males do."

At the dawn of the conservative realignment on Capitol Hill, the new speaker of the House, Newt Gingrich, set out to do precisely what Murray advised. Stigmatizing language and punitive government strategies entered the legislative debates about welfare reform, and the Republicans' "Personal Responsibility Act" endorsed a package of reforms designed to take direct aim at illegitimacy. A menu of punitive consequences was put forth for families in which children were born out of wedlock. Under this proposal—which failed in these particulars to become law—no cash assistance would have been provided for children whose paternity was not established, who were born to unmarried teenage mothers, or whose mother was receiving welfare at the time of conception. For a few weeks even Murray's idea of setting up orphanages for children whose mothers could not support them was tossed around, but its popularity faded when people found out the extremely high cost of such communal care.

Senator Moynihan—who, like Murray, had decried unwed motherhood—became one of the staunchest opponents of these proposed changes. He pointed out that no one could produce any evidence to show that such a harsh approach would reduce illegitimacy. But instituting it, Moynihan argued, would make one thing certain: more children would be thrust into poverty. "It was," Senator Moynihan told me in the spring of 1996, "a very open assertion that the only way to deal with the problem of illegitimacy is to make it an absolute horror. But what you would be doing is making the child's life so awful that the mother will change her ways." To Moynihan, this approach presents an absolutely unacceptable gamble.

At congressional hearings on such legislation, witnesses as well as legislators uttered the word "illegitimacy" many times. On one occasion then-Congressman Mike Kopetski, a Democrat from Oregon, tried to engage a witness in a discussion of whether this word retained any actual meaning in an era when children born to unmarried mothers are accorded essentially the same legal rights as those born to married parents. Kopetski contended that the word was now being used for only one purpose, and that was to make these mothers appear blameworthy and their actions shameful. The witness, conservative scholar Michael J. Horowitz, refused to back away from the use of "illegitimacy." His refusal speaks to the visceral power this word still packs. Its force as a tool of political persuasion outstrips its accuracy in describing children's actual legal situation. Exasperated by the exchange, Kopetski looked at Horowitz and concluded his remarks thus: "God doesn't believe there are any illegitimate children. Only white males do."

Older, more financially secure unmarried mothers don't depend on direct government assistance, so they are not as directly affected by what the Congress, state legislatures, the president, or governors do. It is poor mothers who reside in the political bull's-eye. But many political marksmen are not disappointed when a few of their arrows land in the outer circles of unwed motherhood, where women like Laura reside. In this era, when the phrase "family values" is political shorthand for the heterosexual, two-parent family, the word "illegitimacy" has become an evocative stand-in for the calamitous consequences that many people associate with out-of-wedlock births. And as long as the word is perceived that way, many unmarried mothers such as Laura believe that even if they're diligent parents their efforts will be derided and their family circumstances will still be viewed by many as detrimental to their children.

In the present climate of judgment and condemnation, it isn't easy for mothers like Laura to ignore sound-bite pronouncements about how "illegitimacy" shepherds children's destinies. Yet, as observed in the previous chapter, a burgeoning supply of research on families and communities informs us that many other factors make it more or less likely that a particular child will thrive. Whether a child grows up in poverty, for example, can affect his path through life; so can how well children and parents interact, the values families convey, and how effectively the community supports its youngsters. Does a parent set appropriate rules and ensure that children adhere to them? Is communication among family members comfortable and encouraged, or is unresolved conflict present in the home? Are parental messages about values and behavior reinforced by the community in which the family lives? One problem in all this talk about "family values" and the essentialness of two-parent families is that such vital ingredients as parents' dedication and skills and children's family and community environments are often overlooked in the facile political and media debates about unmarried motherhood.

In his televised interview with David Brinkley, Murray didn't once express concern about any impact that the resurgence of the word "illegitimacy"—and the punitive actions he'd like to see attach to it—might have on children or parents. Nor did he indicate that he was troubled about any emotional ramifications that might befall children being taunted or demeaned because of the circumstances of their birth.

"Never ever be ashamed of who you are and what you are, or of who I am and what I am."

On the morning I listened to Murray talk about illegitimacy, I couldn't help but recall a conversation Laura and I had about when she prepared Sam for his transfer to a private school. Buying appropriate jackets and ties and books and devising new schedules were easy compared with helping Sam feel as comfortable as he could about personal differences between him and most of the students in his new environment.

When Sam attended public schools, his family looked like many of the other families. In fact, the part of the city he lives in, South Boston, is a working-class, nearly all-white neighborhood. Recently, the U.S. Census Bureau found it to be among the nation's most densely populated hubs of female-headed families. In his neighborhood and at school, Sam never needed to explain why his father wasn't around. Many of his friends do not have a father who lives at home. But at this private school, finding classmates whose families looked like his would be a lot harder. Laura wanted to protect her son, as much as she could, from whatever pain his new classmates might cause him, however unintentionally.

"Sam," Laura told him one evening as they were talking about his new school, "this is going to be a new world for you. The public schools are loaded with people like us, but this school isn't. There may be times when things will be said to you that are hurtful. One thing that's important is for you to face what we are. We are not the norm. Our family doesn't look like most of theirs. One thing I want you to understand is never ever be ashamed of who you are and what you are, or of who I am and what I am."

In offering her son this advice, Laura was drawing on her own experience. She remembered how hurt she'd felt when Quayle went after Murphy Brown and tangentially hit her. Laura didn't like being ridiculed for her decision to have Sam on her own. It angered her that she was being treated as though her situation—and that of millions of other women—proved her a less competent mother and transformed Sam into a target of demeaning comments. She recalled, too, how uncomfortable she'd been made to feel by Republican party leaders during the 1992 convention. On "Family Values" night, speaker after speaker emphasized the wholesomeness of the traditional two-parent family; to Laura, these people seemed to imply that only members of such families could possess so-called family values.

"At first I was hurt by it, but very quickly I got angry." That, Laura tells me, made her feel much better. Her voice assumes a defiant tone I haven't

heard before. "When I get angry, it is almost as though my head starts
clearing from the hurt feelings. Anger strengthens me."

But the potential consequences of anger also frighten her. Laura knows
that if someone makes her feel ashamed, the shame can arouse rage. She
doesn't want Sam to lash out at anyone who might make him feel
ashamed. "What became most painful for me was to think of the kind of
things my son's going to hear and feel through the years," Laura says. "My
skin is a lot more thickened than his is, so I'm concerned about how he's
going to internalize all of this." For Sam to protect himself without
resorting to fighting back, Laura knows she must help him to build a
strong, internal pride about who he is. "When Sam gets hit with something, it's going to come at him straight," Laura says. "So if some kid says
to him, 'Where's your father?' or 'Are you broke?' I do not want him not
to be prepared for it. And what I don't want to happen is for him to be dev-
astated by it because he hasn't had the opportunity to think about who he
really is and how valuable he is as a human being. One of the reasons why
I keep sending my son to church is because he learns he is a child of God
and how that makes him more valuable than anything on the face of the
earth. I think he believes that."

"No society builds the arch of social experience without the keystone of marriage. . . . children 'out of wedlock' are ill-fitting stones."

The notion of illegitimacy has been around for centuries. During the
Middle Ages, children born to unmarried mothers were called "filii nulii,"
or those who were "sons of no one." These words were less a statement of
biological fact than a designation of undesirability. Illegitimate children
were linked to their mothers because of their birth, but not to their fathers
by any social arrangement. In later centuries, governments created civil
laws to protect a man's property against inheritance by an illegitimate
child. Similarly, church doctrine preserved the sanctity of marriage by
stigmatizing children born outside it. A baby born to an unmarried mother
was commonly referred to as a "bastard." The French called such children
fils de bast, which means "child of the saddle bag"—a rootless, deviant
outsider.

According to David W. Murray, author of an article entitled "Poor Suffering Bastards: An Anthropologist Looks at Illegitimacy," the most
hideous stigma a group can attach to an individual is the charge that "he
acts as if he has no relatives." A person disconnected from family bonds
doesn't fear bringing shame or dishonor on his family and therefore has

less reason to control deviant impulses. David Murray—no relation to Charles Murray—is also a conservative who believes that having such cultural stigmas serves as powerful and necessary prods, persuading people to form and maintain recognized kinship relationships. Family bonds, certified by a ceremony such as marriage, accrue benefits to society by preserving standards of moral behavior, he asserts. "Anthropology records an interesting variety of marital form and family structure," David Murray writes, "but no society builds the arch of social experience without the keystone of marriage. Let the stakes be clear: When American society experiments with ever-higher numbers of illegitimacies and single adults, we risk being crushed by our own roof. Children 'out of wedlock' are ill-fitting stones."

David Murray, not surprisingly, predicts disastrous times ahead. At the top of his list of destructive forces is the breakdown of the nuclear family and the absence of marriage. Without well-functioning and lasting marriages, society loses the institution that, in his view and others', is the means by which women perform the socially prescribed and essential task of domesticating men. Murray and those who share his views argue that because fathers are more "culturally contingent" to family than mothers, and thus leave families more easily and more often, there is a need for "ceremonies of commitment" to bind them to women and children. Marriage anchors men as a necessary part of the family's necessary structure.

David Popenoe, a professor of sociology at Rutgers University who co-chairs the Council on Families in America, is another in a long list of well-educated white men who write a lot about illegitimacy and fatherlessness. His book *Life Without Father* was published in 1996. Popenoe has observed that "every society must be wary of the unattached male for he is universally the cause of numerous social ills. The good society is heavily dependent on men being attached to a strong moral order centered on families, both to discipline their sexual behavior and to reduce their competitive aggression." In focusing on the need to bind men to marriage, Popenoe and others leave virtually no room for the possibility—or the actuality—that in some families fathers may be a destructive force and that there are many unwed mothers like Laura who are rearing children successfully on their own. As David Murray writes, "In a home where there has never been a Father/Husband there is, no matter how valiant and strong the Mother, a crippled unit, condemned to isolation from society's opportunities and to predation from society's brutal." To manifest such views about children born to and raised by unmarried mothers is to suggest that a child's trajectory is ordained at birth by the structure of her family and can't be improved by either the process of parenting or the engagement of supportive community forces.

"Some women have decided a child is more important than a husband. Who can blame them?"

For the institution of marriage to be revived at a time when more adults eschew it than ever have before, women must be persuaded that it offers them and their children emotional and financial benefits. Nowadays many women don't regard as sufficient benefit the pat on the back society gives them for "domesticating" a man and bearing *his* children in a legally sanctioned way. Women entering a marriage nowadays must also think cautiously about what might happen if the man, after she has done the job of "domesticating" him, decides to wander off, as many do. And when wives become mothers, many of them are disappointed to learn how little caregiving responsibility some men assume in raising "their" children and in taking care of "their" household even when both spouses must hold jobs outside the home. Some wives and mothers also worry about whether a husband will mistreat them or abuse their children.

Katha Pollitt, an editor at the liberal journal *The Nation*, raised such questions in an October 1993 essay, "Motherhood without Marriage." As the subhead pointed out, "Some women have decided a child is more important than a husband. Who can blame them?" Pollitt wrote, "Maybe marriage no longer serves women very well. . . . With rare exceptions, marriage was the only path to female adulthood: a home of one's own, community standing, a sex life, children. Barred from professional training and a good job, threatened with disgrace and loss of her baby if she got pregnant, mocked as a spinster if she stayed unwed past her early twenties, a woman was pushed into marriage by just about every social institution: family, religion, neighbors, custom, law, school, the workplace, doctors of soul and body. None of this is true today."

Not surprisingly, it was another female commentator, *Boston Globe* columnist Ellen Goodman, who issued a call for a time-out in unwed-mother-bashing, by reminding readers that marriage has not always been the best answer for pregnant women. "In a society focused on the current disaster of single parent families, we seem to have developed a cultural amnesia about the earlier disaster of forced marriages," she wrote.

One question many women raise today is whether, after the massive social, economic, and cultural changes that have transformed their lives, they can fit into the old bottle of marriage. Or will women continue in increasing numbers to be unwilling to commit themselves to marriages that they perceive as demanding much more from them than they expect to receive in return? If reformulations of marriage and parenthood do not take seriously women's altered expectations and the increasing importance of shared parenting responsibility for children, it is likely that more, not fewer, out-of-wedlock births will occur. And it seems obvious—but nonetheless ought to be reiterated—that unless a woman finds a comfortable and supportive relationship with a man, her children are more likely to spend their childhood years living without a "daddy" in their home.

"My attitude was, 'I really don't need you.' "

Laura asked Sam's father to leave their home when their son was a toddler. She wasn't in love with him, just as she hadn't been in love with him when she was careless about contraception and got pregnant. Having Sam did not alleviate their difficulties with each other. "I was so unhappy in the relationship," Laura says, though she was neither abused nor mistreated. "I just didn't want to be with him, and I felt his contribution was not enough for me to want to stay with him. So I asked Paul to leave and he did."

Their relationship had been rocky for a long while. Before Sam was conceived, Laura had left Paul to attend army basic training. "I never would have admitted to myself that leaving him was the reason I joined the army, but it was," she says. "I wanted to get as far away from this guy as I could get. That was a safe way to do it and I loved it. I absolutely loved the army." When training ended, Laura came home and found Paul pressuring her to resume their relationship. Laura admits she was not strong-willed enough to resist his persistent efforts, though even then part of her was sure it wouldn't work.

"Very quickly, I became pregnant," Laura says. "And Paul was pleased by the news." Though Laura wanted to have her baby, Paul's encouragement played a part in keeping her focused on becoming a mother, even when members of her family made her feel ashamed of having a baby out of wedlock. Laura now believes she understands one source of Paul's delight at her pregnancy: "Getting me pregnant was a kind of conquest for him, because I'd left him to go into the service and now here I was, home and pregnant and having his baby and he was very proud of that. He sort of felt he had me now, and although he never said that to me, I think it is what went through his mind." Laura remembers worrying about the prospect of having a baby in the midst of their unsettled relationship, though she does not recall that Paul seemed similarly concerned. "He was a pretty self-centered guy," she says, explaining that her pregnancy didn't signify to him the enormous impending changes that it did to her. After Sam was born, she realized why: "Paul was not really ready to change his lifestyle." And, for the most part, he did not.

There was, however, one noticeable change for Sam's father: because of their different job schedules, each tended Sam while the other was at work. This meant they didn't need to pay for child care, but also they rarely saw each other or spent time together as a family. And despite Paul's contribution to child care, the overall responsibility for Sam's care and for the housework fell squarely on Laura, even though she had a full-time job as a driver for a courier service. Nor did their financial contributions to the family seem equitable to Laura. "Yeah, he certainly brought money in," she tells me. "But Paul kept most of his money for himself."

Laura admits that much of the fault for the relationship's failure rests with her. She identifies the primary problem: "I showed this strong independence from the beginning, like by bringing home a paycheck. And my attitude towards him was 'I really don't need you.' " For this reason Laura absolves Paul of blame for his inability or unwillingness to adjust to changes in their family situation. "He never really filled the traditional father role I think he would like to have filled if I had let him," she says. Similar patterns of self-recrimination continue to visit themselves on Laura in other relationships with men.

With one man, in particular, whom Laura met at her church, she tried for a long time to conceal her independence so she could better fit into his view that women should play submissive roles. By doing this, Laura hoped she could finally build a committed relationship so she wouldn't need to be a single parent any longer. It didn't work. "He and I had so much conflict, because I was not in a position to let go of my decision-making and my activities and my work. I had to maintain my household," Laura says. "I had to pay my bills. I had a growing son and still no marriage and no commitment from him. And here was a man asking me to display to him that I am willing to submit to him and leave it up to him. And I am saying to him, 'Well, that is fine, but we are not married and I am not sure you can take all of this on, anyway.' I did not see a lot of evidence. All I heard from him was a lot of talk. And finally I told him, 'You just have this big ego that says I am a man and because I am a man, and the Bible tells me so, you're supposed to do what I tell you to do.' It turned out he dumped me, hard and fast, and started to see another woman at the church. She was very soft-spoken and timid, the complete opposite from how I am."

To steer our conversation back to Paul, I ask Laura whether she was afraid that, if Sam's father "filled the role he would like to have filled," he might also have wanted to control her. "Oh, yeah," she says, nodding. "For me to be dependent on him, I would have had to compromise a lot of things, and I was not willing to do that. To this day, I am still not willing to do that, so that's why I'm still single. Truthfully, I don't necessarily still want to be single. I'd like to be mated. I feel lonesome and I'd like to have someone. But what bothered me twelve years ago about my relationship with Paul bothers me still."

"Without a man, how do you think it's going to be, for crying out loud?"

Laura was relieved to be on her own. However, for her son, who was two years old, the transition turned out to be a lot more difficult. Teachers at his day care center told Laura that Sam was becoming more aggressive when he played with other children. Laura believes his behavior reflected her worries about what the future held for them. Being apart from his father was what she'd wanted, but being on her own as a parent was really difficult. "I was tense. And I was lonesome and nervous because less money was coming in. My hours at work were long. I was scared. So I'm sure it showed in my behavior around Sam. I was quick with him and I was just miserable much of the time. And Sam missed his father."

A psychologist at the day care center called Laura and told her in more detail about the problems Sam was having. She recommended counseling, and Laura agreed. I ask whether Sam's father participated in these meetings at the school, or in counseling. Laura shakes her head. "He'd have nothing to do with it. He was asked but he flat-out refused. Paul wouldn't do it."

Laura and Sam saw a counselor for about six months. When Sam showed signs he was doing okay, Laura stopped taking him, but she continued to see the therapist for another year or so. Times were tough. Finances were tight. Her rusting water heater burst. Problems with tenants were becoming nightmarish. At one point, her house was infested with cockroaches. "One night I sat in my bed and cried for this man and I said to myself, 'I should never have ended this relationship. I really need him,'" Laura tells me. But in a few minutes her crying stopped and her thinking seemed clearer. "'Wait a minute,'" she lectured herself. "'You are crying because you're broke and your house is falling apart and you are having a bad day and you're lonesome. That's why you're crying.' That was the only time I ever missed Paul."

Difficulties were apparent to her family as well. Unfortunately, her relatives reacted with more criticism. "I was getting a lot of 'I told you so' from my mother and my poison-pen aunt," she says. Laura recites some memorable remarks: "'Your life is hard because that's the way you wanted it.' . . . 'This is the choice you made. You know you do not have a man, and without a man, how do you think it's going to be, for crying out loud?' . . .

'Let's face facts. Women have been dealing with this for centuries. What do you think? You're different?' "

By now, too, many of Laura's friends were getting married. Some were taking trips and enjoying weekend recreations with their children and husband—as a family. When she was invited to parties at her friends' homes, Laura felt uncomfortable going by herself. Whenever she ran into problems with her own house or at her job, problems she figured a man could solve more easily than she did, she found herself mimicking something she heard others say: "It's so obvious that I need a man." But whenever she found one, it seemed only a matter of time before some issue she felt strongly about divided them. One evening, Laura had explained to a man she was dating why she thought Sam's father ought to contribute to the cost of raising his son.

"But Laura," her date said to her, "why should he pay you child support? He was never married to you."

"What are you talking about?" Laura said, incredulous. "What am I? A second-class citizen?"

"Well, you don't have any right to ask him for anything," the man insisted. "He has his own life now."

The conversation ended when Laura realized there was no use talking with him about this. Each held a viewpoint, and neither was likely to convince the other to change. Soon the relationship was over as well.

"So here I was lonesome again," Laura says, exhaling as though to breathe out her frustration at her solitary life. "But I kept thinking about what he had said: 'You don't have a right to ask for child support.' I guess internally that is what I believed. I think the reason that for so long I did not ask for Paul's support for Sam was that I said to myself I really did not want Paul in my life and I decided to have Sam, even though we discussed it and it was a joint decision. So I thought maybe I really shouldn't ask him for anything because I wanted to end the relationship. I beat myself up like that for a long time before I finally got the nerve to go for it."

One day Laura brought this subject up with a friend who is a lawyer. Without a moment's hesitation, he told Laura, "What, are you crazy? Get the child support."

She decided to try.

"It has ruined my son's relationship with his father."

It cost Laura nearly $2,000 in attorney's fees to take Sam's father to court. "A lot of mothers don't have two nickels to rub together," she says. "How are they going to pay some lawyer eighteen hundred bucks like I did? And then you don't know if you'll get it."

For Sam, the emotional cost turned out to be high as well. "Paul was furious at me," Laura says. "And his father's girlfriend was furious. Everyone was furious at me. A friend said to me, 'Laura, where do you get the balls to do this?' And I said to her, 'Where does he get the balls to not send me a cent?' " I ask Laura if she thinks Sam's father believes that because they were not married he shouldn't help her with Sam's support.

"I don't think in his heart he believes that. I think he battled with me because I had wounded him. In his bitterness, the fight about child support was the only thing he had left to make life difficult for me."

Laura won a judgment obligating Paul to pay regular child support and to enroll his son in his employer's health care coverage. But their court-room days were not yet over. The judge had offered Laura the option of relying on Paul to send a check every week, or having a court order that money be deducted from his paycheck and sent to her by the state. Laura opted for the "honor system." That turned out to be a mistake. Often, she says, the check would not arrive promptly. At times, it wouldn't arrive at all. After two years, the acrimony between Laura and Paul about how much money he still owed became so intense that she felt she had no alternative but to return to court. "Not only did I get his wages attached," she says, "I got more money."

Laura went to court to get her former partner to do something she believed fathers should do automatically for their children. But the battles over child support left deep scars. After each court date, Paul seemed to back further away from contact with Sam. It was as though Laura had entered a trap: as Sam gained his father's financial support, he was losing something else—their relationship. "It's ruined his relationship with his father," she says. "I mean, his dad still is decent to him when he talks to him. But he hasn't spoken to him in more than six months."

"You know, Ma, Dad got married . . . and he didn't even tell me about it."

Laura guesses it's been about a year since Sam saw his father, though Paul works only about a mile from where she and Sam live. "Sam used to call him," Laura tells me. "He'd say, 'Hi, Dad. I haven't seen you. How you doin'? What's going on?' Sam would call his father to wish him Merry Christmas. He'd remember to talk with his father on his birthday, and telephone to wish him a happy Father's Day. Sometimes Sam just called him when he wanted to talk."

It upsets Laura to talk about this; she knows that if Sam could have a good and steady and predictable relationship with his father, he'd be happier. Even in the years when Sam's father visited more frequently, on occasion he'd call to cancel, sometimes just twenty minutes before Sam expected him to arrive. "He'd call to say he couldn't come, but he wouldn't set up another time to see Sam," Laura says. It became her job to soothe her son's disappointment.

"Sam won't chase after his father," Laura tells me. A while ago, Sam decided to stop calling him. And when Sam doesn't initiate calls, communication between them all but ceases. Last year, when Paul married the woman who's been his girlfriend since Laura broke off their relationship a decade earlier, he did not invite Sam to the wedding. He didn't even tell Sam about it in advance. Sam learned about the wedding a few weeks after it occurred, when Paul came by one day after school.

That evening, when Laura came home from work, she could tell Sam needed to talk about something. "You know, Ma, Dad got married," he finally blurted out, when they were in the kitchen.

"He did?" she replied, turning to look at Sam. "When was that?"

"Oh, a couple of weeks ago," Sam said. Pausing for a moment to collect his thoughts, he averted his eyes from hers and resumed speaking. "And he didn't even tell me about it."

"Well, honey, he must have had his reasons. Maybe he had just a little small ceremony," Laura said, attempting to ease Sam's hurt.

"Yeah, that's what he said."

Laura could tell Sam wanted to bring this awkward conversation to a close. But she also knew that Sam wondered how his father's wedding party could have been so small as not to include his only child. It pained her to see him struggling with this.

Laura suggested that he buy a gift for his father and his new wife and offered him fifty dollars out of her savings. Sam tried to come up with an idea of what to buy but nothing sprang to mind.

"How about sending them a really nice floral arrangement?" Laura suggested. "And a card."

Sam liked his mother's idea. That's what he did.

"What I hope Sam will learn from him is that you can trust someone; you can trust a man."

Three years ago Sam was introduced to Jerry, an environmental engineer with an interest in helping children. Through a school mentoring program supported by corporate donations, Jerry was paired with Sam to help nurture his early interest in science and math. Now, even though Sam has left the public schools and is officially no longer in the program, he and Jerry remain friends. This has become a vital relationship in Sam's life, especially as he gets older and his father drifts away.

"He and Jerry really hit it off with each other," Laura says. "And this man is such a reliable and regular good example for Sam." Last year Jerry helped Sam with a science project. Not only did Sam win his school's prize, but at the regional science fair, he won a prize for his age group and grade. "Jerry was right there with him through the whole thing," Laura says. "He came to the fair and he saw Sam get his award and everything."

What Laura likes about Jerry's friendship with her son is the example he sets. When he needs to rearrange a visit, he gives Sam plenty of notice and suggests an alternative time to meet. This kind of communication and consideration are things Sam's father doesn't demonstrate to him. "Jerry always has an explanation for Sam." He has also invited Sam to help him do things such as paint his apartment. And he is a man who Sam knows will be there if he ever wants to talk. "He's just a reliable, decent guy," Laura says. "What I hope Sam will learn from him is that you can trust someone; you can trust a man."

Laura is grateful that Jerry is in Sam's life to fill in gaps in what she as a single parent and a woman can offer her son. "It is a heavy load to be a single parent, and Sam has no buffer between me and him, and vice versa. A lot of people say the father is the disciplinarian and the mother is able to step in and soften the blow. Or the other way around. But there is none here. And it is exhausting for me and him sometimes." Having a male influence helps to relieve her concern that without the good guidance of men, Sam might grow up to be too easily "pushed around by women" because she is the only authority figure he knows. "It's not that I think it's a bad thing for a woman to have authority," Laura says. "But what I am afraid of is I don't want Sam to be unable to make decisions or take initiative or to step forward or to have control in certain situations."

Laura sets consistent, well-articulated limits, which Sam has learned from an early age to adhere to. If her rules mean he has to come home before the neighborhood children do, that's okay with her, even when he gets upset. "Sam has become so accustomed to these limits that when he stays within them, he knows I'll usually extend them. Those times when I don't, he won't buck it." She's never spanked Sam: "I've never needed to. But it has never been difficult for me to bark at him or speak firmly to him. Sometimes I yell at him, but that is only when my frustration mounts."

When she left Paul ten years ago, Laura thought she'd find someone to settle down with, and the two of them would raise Sam. When she looks back it's hard for her to believe she's managed to parent Sam by herself for all these years. "I could not have imagined then I was going to stay single until my son grows up." But given the men she's met, Laura says, "unless I'm willing to tolerate the kind of impatience and selfishness that will accompany trying to bring a man into this house and dealing with his insecurities, I'll be on my own. That is, unless a miracle happens and God sends me the most perfect guy in the whole world."

9

Unmarried Mothers: Who We Are and Where We're Headed

Late one spring afternoon, I headed up to Capitol Hill to speak with U.S. Senator Daniel Patrick Moynihan. With movement to restructure the nation's sixty-year-old welfare system well under way, Moynihan's ardent support for retaining the federal safety net for the most vulnerable children, many of whom are being raised by young, unmarried mothers, found him swimming against the surging tide of public opinion and congressional votes. By late in the summer of 1996, control of welfare was handed over to the states.

Being a contrarian on the issue of unmarried motherhood—and what social institutions can do about it—is not a new role for this senator. This is, after all, a subject he has studied with professional acuity for more than half of his seventy years. His views are shaped more by scholarly judgment than by the shifting winds of popular opinion. These days, as escalating anger at mothers who rely on government assistance for their family's support propels policy changes, the senator rarely allows an opportunity slip by to remind folks that children are the ones the welfare program was designed to protect.

It is a bit past six o'clock, the scheduled time of our appointment, when Senator Moynihan walks into the reception area of his suite to find me. Rarely do senators escort guests to their offices, nor do they give interviews without aides sitting close by. Moynihan does both. As we enter his office, he directs me to a chair facing his, in front of his wooden desk. For roughly the first ten minutes our conversation focuses solely on children, in particular the several million or so who, some experts predict, will be left without adequate resources when welfare is withdrawn.

"There is a new point of view in Congress," the senator tells me. "It's a very open assertion that the only way to deal with the problem of illegitimacy is to make it an absolute horror. A horrible experience. What you would be doing is making the children's lives so awful that the mothers will change their ways. In effect, cruelty to children becomes an instrument of social policy."

Those who disagree with Moynihan—and there is a powerful, vocal majority in Congress that does—assert that there is an urgent need to put into place restrictions and penalties that will alter the irresponsible behavior of women who have children out of wedlock. In testimony before a congressional committee, Charles Murray, a proponent of such change, articulated this viewpoint: "Stigma and shotgun marriages may or may not be good for those on the receiving end, but their deterrent effect on others is wonderful—and indispensable."

"This growth in illegitimacy has been like a jet plane taking off."

Senator Moynihan reaches over to his desk where a collection of graphs his office has compiled awaits his hand. "Here's what we are up against," he says, bringing the sheaf of papers to rest in his lap. "About a year ago I decided to go back and look at the growth of illegitimacy. You know I've been looking at this stuff for a long time, but when I saw this I said to myself, 'My God. That is a straight line.'"

The senator holds up his first graph, "Births to Unmarried Women (All Races) 1970–1991." The story this graph's straight line tells begins in 1970, five years after Moynihan issued his controversial report, "The Negro Family," in which he highlighted the soaring rate of out-of-wedlock births in black families. "We ran a little correlation on these figures and we found it was .99 with a slope of .86. Not bad," Moynihan says, tossing out these statistical references with the expectation that I understand, though I do not. But the graph he is holding is quite simple to interpret: the line that represents out-of-wedlock births is climbing relentlessly year after year.

"The story this tells us is what?" I ask him, hoping he'll move beyond slopes and correlations.

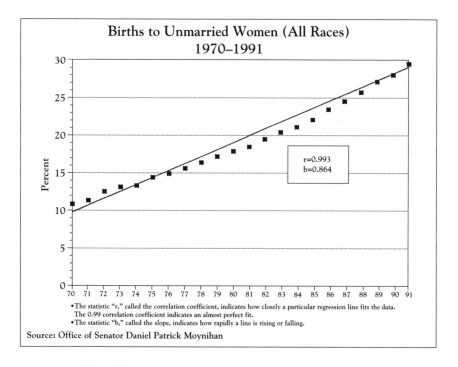

Births to Unmarried Women (All Races)
1970–1991

r=0.993
b=0.864

• The statistic "r," called the correlation coefficient, indicates how closely a particular regression line fits the data. The 0.99 correlation coefficient indicates an almost perfect fit.
• The statistic "b," called the slope, indicates how rapidly a line is rising or falling.

Source: Office of Senator Daniel Patrick Moynihan

"That these births go up and up and up and up at a rate of almost one percent each year," he replies.

Quickly, he goes on. "So then we went back to 1940 to take a look and we got this curve." He hands me his next graph.

"That straight line we saw when we began in 1970 is now more of a curve which after a few years starts going whoooosh," he says. The graph again makes it easy to see the steepening sweep of the curve, illustrating the acceleration of these births as decades ticked by toward the twenty-first century.

"Now, if you want to see where all of this takes us, look here." Moynihan directs my attention to another page. "If this curve stays growing at the same rate, it will take us to half of all births being illegitimate by the year 2004. It's like a jet plane taking off."

My eyes settle on the line of tiny dots that represents the senator's projections. They climb steadily, year by year bringing us closer to the big black dot, the one that marks 50 percent. The year is 2004.

"Nothing like this has ever happened in history. In two thousand years of recorded history, nothing like this has ever happened," Moynihan says, shaking his head and expressing in one compact gesture his amazement,

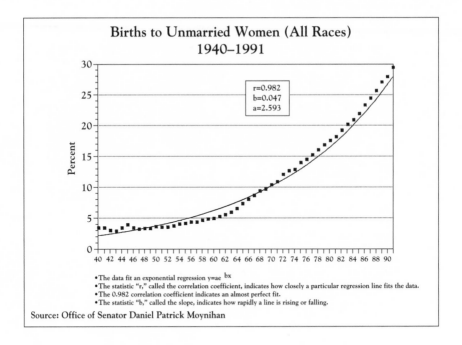

Births to Unmarried Women (All Races) 1940–1991

r=0.982
b=0.047
a=2.593

• The data fit an exponential regression y=ae^bx
• The statistic "r," called the correlation coefficient, indicates how closely a particular regression line fits the data.
• The 0.982 correlation coefficient indicates an almost perfect fit.
• The statistic "b," called the slope, indicates how rapidly a line is rising or falling.

Source: Office of Senator Daniel Patrick Moynihan

dismay, and concern. He is, after all, the person who once wrote that when large numbers of young men grow up in families dominated by women the community "asks for and gets chaos."

Senator Moynihan then hands me his final set of data. A bar graph displays various countries' increases in out-of-wedlock births since 1960. "It's happening all over the North Atlantic," Moynihan says. "Look there at France and the United Kingdom and Canada."

France, the United Kingdom, and Canada are bunched with the United States at the upper end of the graph. In all four countries the percentage of out-of-wedlock births had been multiplied by about six in just three decades. The senator's point is well illustrated. The surge of out-of-wedlock births in our country has also occurred in nearly every democratic, industrialized nation. Japan is alone in experiencing no increase during the past three decades.

"The species has no experience with this," Moynihan says, drawing his argument back around to where we began. "So I say again, we must be very careful what we do to the children."

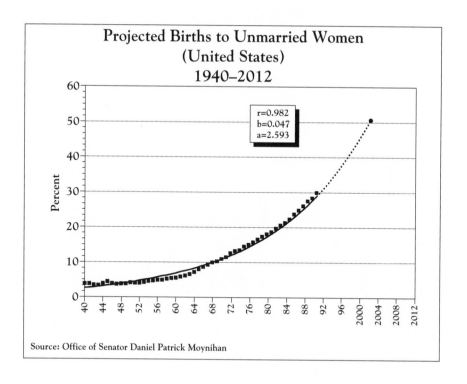

**Projected Births to Unmarried Women
(United States)
1940–2012**

r=0.982
b=0.047
a=2.593

Source: Office of Senator Daniel Patrick Moynihan

"The causes of this change are not entirely understood."

No scholar or study can tell us definitively why what Moynihan observes here and abroad is happening, or whether the proportion of out-of-wedlock births his graph projects will actually occur in our country. Some think it might, though in which year of the twenty-first century one of every two American babies will be born to an unwed mother remains pure speculation. Of course, in a few American cities and in clusters of poverty-stricken neighborhoods, half the babies born today do not have married parents. But there is, of course, the possibility that at some time the percentage of out-of-wedlock births will reach a plateau, or perhaps even begin to decrease. In fact, national statistics on U.S. births in 1995 contained evidence of a downturn. Not only did the rate at which teenagers are giving birth decline for the fourth year in a row—since 1991 the teen birthrate has fallen 8 percent—but for the first time in nearly two decades, the overall birthrate for unmarried women decreased as well, by 4 percent.

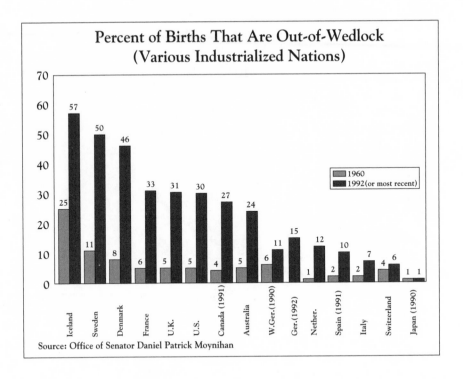

**Percent of Births That Are Out-of-Wedlock
(Various Industrialized Nations)**

Legend: 1960 / 1992(or most recent)

Source: Office of Senator Daniel Patrick Moynihan

What happened to out-of-wedlock births in 1995 marks the first time since data were first compiled in 1940 that the number of such births, their rate, and their proportion of total births all declined. We know, too, that the rate of increase in these various measures of nonmarital childbearing had already begun to slow from 1989 to 1994, compared with trends during the early to middle 1980s. Whether these recent changes represent the beginning of a long-term directional shift or only a blip on Moynihan's graph is not possible to know at this time. Nor is it possible to point with confidence to any one factor or government policy that can account for these changes.

James Q. Wilson, Collins professor of management and public policy at the University of California–Los Angeles, wrote in 1993 that "We are witnessing a profound, worldwide, long-term change in the family that is likely to continue for a long time." What is happening in the United States in terms of the disintegration of the once durable, two-parent family, Wilson concluded, "cannot be entirely the result of American policies or peculiarities," since the phenomenon is so globally widespread.

"The causes of this change are not entirely understood," Wilson conceded, though he indicated that shifts in the family's economic function and in the larger culture are responsible for it.

Indeed, the causes of these profound contemporary changes in how families are formed and how they function are not very well understood, even as patterns of shifts in family structure are well documented. In its 1995 report "Families in Focus," the Population Council, an international organization that studies reproductive health, highlights five global trends in family change. The universality of these trends supports the views of scholars who, like Moynihan and Wilson, try to arrive at an understanding of what might be unique to the American experience, but don't assume that any nation's policies are solely responsible for the changes in families that we now observe. The five trends are these:

1. Women's average age at first marriage and childbirth has risen, delaying the formation of new families.
2. Families and households have become smaller.
3. The burden on working-age parents of supporting younger and older dependents has increased.
4. In both developed and less-developed countries the proportion of female-headed households, in which mothers are the primary or sole economic providers, has increased.
5. Women's participation in formal labor markets has increased while men's has declined, shifting the balance of economic responsibility in families.

The Population Council report asserts that in many countries, including the United States, women's roles have evolved to accommodate these new family responsibilities. Men's roles have not. Fathers, no matter which country they live in, tend to divert large portions of their income to personal use; this habit is one many of the unmarried mothers we've met have had to cope with. And the council's review of ethnographic studies from 186 societies found that in only 2 percent of these societies do fathers have "regular, close relationships" with their infants.* (This increases to 5 percent during early childhood.) In every country in which interactions between parents and children were observed, fathers, on average, "never provided more direct care than mothers." Once again, this report demonstrates that the universality of contemporary family experiences is often more striking than our national differences.

---

*The term "societies" is used instead of countries, because many of these studies explore family relationships within tribes or specific ethnic groups rather than countries.

"You have a baby because you think it
will make things different."

Shifting economic and societal roles of women are clearly at the core of any attempt to explain the precipitous rise in out-of-wedlock births. But as the unmarried mothers in this book remind us, a complex web of related issues radiates from this core; this web encompasses personal and emotional issues that range from gender mistrust to evolving expectations women have of men as fathers, from what it means to be a woman within a particular environment and at a particular age, to concerns mothers have about ceding control of their lives and decisions in the partnership called marriage. Here, within the personal dimensions of women's reproductive and parenting lives, we find large patches of common ground over which adolescent girls and older women travel on their way to and through unmarried motherhood.

Having a child, at no matter what age, fills a woman with feelings unparalleled by any other experience. Many older women who are single and aren't mothers talk about how their lives, professionally accomplished as they might be, feel sadly incomplete. Marriage, while desired by many, does not evoke the intense longing that children do. A child is regarded by many as a connecting wire to the charge of emotional energy they want to give. For many, professional achievement has brought them some measure of satisfaction and an income large enough to obtain the accoutrements of an independent life—their own homes, their own lines of credit, and social status, things that women of their mothers' generation usually had to marry to secure. Yet the desire to give something of themselves to another compels many of these women to want to have a baby. But as we've learned from mothers in this book, having and raising a child on her own is not usually a woman's first choice. Rather, it's what some decide to do after years and years of anguished consideration. As one unwed mother said, describing her perspective after she finally abandoned her lifelong hope of starting a family in the conventional way, "The nuclear family's relevance should be respected, but not necessarily idealized."

Adolescent girls' descriptions of their attraction to motherhood don't come in the mature, philosophical tone one hears in conversations with older, more highly educated women. But the emotional pressures driving some of them toward becoming mothers so early in their lives are not so different. Many younger girls who have babies—primarily the girls who are already failing in school and feeling battered by an unsupportive environment—are wrestling, too, with a sense of incompleteness in their lives. In their eyes, a baby can seem like the one person capable of making fuller and more meaningful their lives, which seem, in the disquieting moments of adolescence, to be dismal, empty, and devoid of embracing love. "You have a baby because you think it will make things different," one teenage mother said. Psychologist Judith Musick writes that "Motherhood offers these girls a ready-made role with ready-made functions, what to be, what to do." Motherhood can become a seductive route by which girls become women.

Among older, single women, motherhood can be a way to fulfill what society expects of them as women and what many of them, in the sunset years of their procreative ability, come to expect of themselves. It is impossible for women to escape mainstream cultural messages on television, in movies and magazines, and, most persistently, in advertisements, reminding them that to express themselves fully as women they must be mothers. Personal fulfillment is not possible, nor is success truly within a woman's grasp, unless she experiences motherhood. In a *New York Times* op-ed piece, Jeanne Safer, author of *Beyond Motherhood: Choosing a Life Without Children*, explained how her decision to not have a child "violates norms of feminine conduct." Without motherhood, women can find it difficult to fully express their femininity. And public sentiment supports the conclusion, which many women reach, that motherhood without marriage at least brings with it the comfort of feminine expression. It used to be that spinsterhood was the mark of a woman's discontented life; now the absence of motherhood has displaced this earlier paradigm of women's deviance.

Among teenage girls, too, decisions about motherhood can be impelled by the fear of being deviant, in their case within communities in which young parenting and unwed motherhood are the norm. The desire to have, as their friends do, "a baby in a stroller" to parade around the neighborhood is not unnatural for a dispirited girl whose narrow vantage point allows her to see only the attention—and the treatment as "women"—her peers receive once they are mothers. And these observations occur at a phase in her psychological development when she's desperate to find ways to be like her peers. To work hard to *not* have a baby—something an adolescent must be strongly motivated to do—can mean that she finds herself on an unfamiliar path, heading in a direction she is worried will end in loneliness and discontent.

There are few role models in these girls' daily lives who present accessible alternatives to early motherhood or who can offer believable assurance about the benefits of postponing childbirth. Messages many girls hear about how their adult lives will be better if they don't have a child right now aren't easily verified by experiences they observe around them. Instead, young girls who are losing hope for their future think about what it is they *can* "be": one possibility they know they can achieve is to be a mother. As the director of a program for parenting teens told me, "To have a baby gives these girls a purpose."

The messages about sexuality that mainstream culture sends to young women are as pervasive and intrusive as the ones advertisers employ in marketing motherhood to older women. Commercials used to sell adolescents even the most mundane products—toothpaste, for example—exude images of enhanced sexuality. These messages emphasize for girls the sexual nature of their emerging bodies and relationships. Then, as if trying to put the genie back into the bottle, adults promote sexual abstinence and lecture them about personal responsibility. Sarah Brown, director of the National Campaign to Prevent Teen Pregnancy, describes the result of this confusing juxtaposition: "We are sitting in the midst of a media environment where everybody does it, right, left, and center and there are no consequences to anything. And everybody is unmarried. It's very hard to create responsible behavior by adolescents in environments that give exactly the opposite message."

In "We Could Be Your Daughters," a report by Radcliffe College's Public Policy Institute, low-income girls describe how their environments cultivate in them sexual personae before they are either socially or emotionally prepared to cope with potential consequences of sexual involvement. It is a difficult fact of life that girls today grow up in an era in which the potential for becoming pregnant outside of marriage extends over a longer period of time than it ever has before. As the average age at which girls become fertile has dropped to its lowest point ever, 12.5 years, the median age at which women get married has risen to 24.5 years. These circumstances combine to stretch a difficult passage to about a dozen years, longer for many women. And girls contend that they're not being counseled by adults how to successfully resist what can seem overwhelming and coercive forces of sexual pressure. Many girls told the researchers of this report that they'd welcome such help from women with whom they could develop close relationships and talk confidentially about such things.

When the Carnegie Council on Adolescent Development asked low-income girls between the ages of eleven and fifteen what they most wanted from adults, the younger girls—who experience the greatest confusion over the messages they hear and the feelings they have—said an "ideal" approach by adults would revolve around having "someone to talk to about problems and feelings," the things they label girl talk. Absent this opportunity, girls admit to being lost when it comes to handling men's sexual demands. Many pregnancies occur not because young girls want to have sex (most of them say they don't enjoy it) or purposely set out to have a baby, but because they lack the ability to resist sexual pressures. Then, if a pregnancy occurs, many of them decide to proceed to motherhood and become "women."

Older women also seek the help of other women in puzzling through reproductive decisions. However, unlike girls, whose questions about their budding sexuality are often ignored by embarrassed grown-ups who'd rather pretend the issue doesn't exist, these older, single women find plenty of outlets for their inquiries. Bookstore shelves bulge with resources covering every aspect of parenting, including guides for single women on how to conceive and raise children on their own. Therapists are available for counsel, and these women have enough money to pay for their advice they might need. At organized meetings, women can meet others contemplating similar questions. They communicate with one another by electronic mail from the comfort of their homes and the convenience of their offices. For these women, whatever "girl talk" and information they need are available to them, in forms that respect and protect their privacy.

All this means that amid the emotional and social pressures that buffet younger and older women, at least the older women have many opportunities to fully consider the consequences and adequately prepare their lives for a child's arrival, if they decide to try motherhood on their own. Many younger girls never do find anyone with whom they feel comfortable talking about what might be about to happen.

"Dan Quayle may have been right, but Murphy Brown is definitely winning."

From the perspective of many younger and older women, marriage can seem a more precarious undertaking than motherhood. Teenage girls, many of whom have witnessed the rancorous dissolution of their parents' marriage or have grown up without ever seeing a marriage work, say they are too young and too unprepared to be wives, though they consider themselves neither too young nor too unprepared to be mothers. From a teenager's perspective, having a baby suggests the welcome possibility of gaining a new measure of control over her undirected life even if her view is illusionary. Motherhood can appear to offer her the chance to define herself anew. To get married suggests just the opposite; marriage seems to offer the likelihood of being defined by someone else, of ceding control to the baby's father, and of surrendering the opportunity for self-redefinition. Marriage will come later, the girls say.

Maggie Gallagher, author of *The Abolition of Marriage: How We Destroy Lasting Love*, observed last year during her visit to a rural Indiana high school that unwed motherhood seems to be not only accepted, but widely admired, by youngsters. Single motherhood epitomizes women's strength for girls who haven't had many opportunities to view themselves as strong. "Any assertion that marriage and fatherhood are important meets with their vehement opposition," Gallagher observed. Girls at this Indiana school applauded those among them who had and are raising children on their own. "Dan Quayle may have been right" about the importance of marriage and fathers, Gallagher surmised, "but Murphy Brown is definitely winning."

Many young women find no evidence within their families or neighborhoods that a marriage will be secure or that their child's father will stick around. Even when he does, he's not considered likely to make parenting easier. As young moms explained to Yale's Dr. Bonnie Leadbeater, "Why get involved with someone who will just tell me what to do?" In general, these mothers want fathers to participate in their children's lives but not to control theirs or claim command of decision-making. When young fathers meet these expectations—as well as provide some level of financial security—these young families stand a better chance of remaining together. But among young parents it is rare for these emotional and financial ingredients to come together satisfactorily. If all this adds up to men being viewed as "superfluous," as some observers suggest, it is not they, young mothers contend, who make men so. Rather, men's attitudes about how family relationships ought to work, combined with their lack of financial resources, make it difficult to bring and keep these unintended threesomes together.

Similar views of men and their participation in family life can be heard in conversations among older women, many of whom don't need a spouse's income to be able to raise a family. Many married mothers of my generation complain about the unequal burdens of parenting and how their "partners" turn out to be anything but what that word implies. Without a man as a part of a mother's daily life, the relentless demands of taking care of her children, her career, and her husband would be reduced by a third. In hearing such complaints, women who aren't married but are contemplating parenthood sometimes decide that not having a husband seems tolerable, whereas not having a child is not. As further justification for deciding to begin their families alone, women suggest that in an era when roughly half of all marriages end in divorce—with potentially devastating consequences for children—at the very least they can give their offspring homes without parental conflict.

Unmarried motherhood is for many of its younger participants a repetition of how their own families began. A large number of teenage moms are themselves the daughters of once young, unwed mothers. For them, this formation and structure of family is the one they know best; entry into it seems natural, ordinary, and predictable. However, for older women, unmarried motherhood often represents a discomfiting departure from how the families they knew as children were begun. It can be wrenching for these women to emotionally bridge the chasm between what many of them experienced and believe is best for children—a married mom and dad—and the family they are thinking about creating. To them, unmarried motherhood can seem strange, frightening, and untested.

In a conversation I had with sociologist Amitai Etzioni about unmarried motherhood, he suggested that "in their heart of hearts, these older women know what works better. So there is a split between what reality forces them to do and what their values are." Such a split is not so readily apparent to many younger women who become unmarried moms. Thus these younger moms are less likely to treat their decision to start a single-parent family with anything like the concern and extra preparation that older women bring to it. In fact, many younger women frame their view of this circumstance thus: "I grew up in this kind of family and I survived. My kid will, too."

Within both groups of unmarried mothers, most would like their children to experience an ongoing relationship with their father. Even in the case of children whose father's identity is not known, mothers want to bring dependable men into their children's lives, men who will be trustworthy, reliable companions. Desire to do this cannot always be translated into reality, as women's experiences in this book have shown. Sometimes circumstances prevent such relationships from forming or lasting. But among both young and older unmarried mothers, there is acute awareness of how strongly children want to have a "daddy" in their lives. Daddy's absence is not something about which unmarried mothers are callously indifferent, which is often how their attitude is characterized.

Mothers who are financially self-sufficient want from fathers not money but ongoing, personal engagement with their children. This requires time, patience, and reliability, things that seem sometimes hardest for men to give. As the twenty-first century approaches, it's apparent that women's expectations of fathers are changing faster than many men appear willing or ready to respond to. And when men don't measure up, it seems, women today are willing to move their family lives ahead without them. As for younger mothers, many of them, too, go to great lengths to persuade a partner not to abandon his children, even when their own relationship hasn't endured. Some young mothers appear driven to do this by remembrance of the emotional pain they felt in losing, or never knowing, their fathers. But, like their older counterparts, younger mothers tend, over time, to lose patience with the pursuit of reluctant paternal involvement, especially when cooperation they expect is not forthcoming. Once again, if men don't measure up, these younger women move ahead on their own.

"We walk a thin line when we attempt to promote matrimony as a public good."

There have always been out-of-wedlock births. However, it is only during the last half of the twentieth century—as Senator Moynihan points out—that such a significant and ever-increasing proportion of American babies has been born to unwed women of all ages and racial and economic backgrounds.

The varied and possible consequences of this trend can be devastating for children, especially those being raised by young, unwed mothers, the vast majority of whom enter parenthood poor, inadequately educated, and emotionally bruised. Less well understood are the effects unmarried motherhood has on children born to older, more financially secure, and better educated women. And it is also possible that in the twenty-first century, the proportion of older women deciding to have and rear children on their own will decline. After all, many of the circumstances that impelled my generation of well-educated women to eventually decide on unmarried motherhood will not be repeated. Already, career-minded women no longer feel as constrained in their marital and reproductive decisions as we once did. Many career women now refuse to pay the personal costs that a lot of my contemporaries accepted as part of pioneering the transition to workplace equality. Watching my generation deal with infertility and unmarried motherhood has made many younger women more aware of the personal difficulties awaiting them if they allow their lives to slide into similar circumstances. But when some of these women nevertheless do start families on their own, their decision will no doubt be, as it was for us, arrived at after much deliberation and with children's needs uppermost in their minds.

Of course, many observers will question how women—no matter how gifted they might think they will be as mothers—can claim to hold children's needs uppermost while at the same time not providing them with a two-parent family. This paradoxical assertion lies at the heart of these women's internal debate, a debate all but impossible to reconstruct or adequately explain to anyone who has not worked her way through this agonizing decision. Nor do any two women resolve this turmoil in quite the same way; some enter motherhood feeling enormous conflict about their decision, while others find ways to reconcile themselves to circumstances their decision might create.

Will the children now being raised by older, unwed moms long for the fathers they never knew or don't have? Yes, and their mothers know it. Will this parental absence be associated with the behavior problems and lack of achievement common among children of poorer and younger unwed mothers? Possibly, but given the enriched environments in which many of these children will grow up, it is unlikely that a large percentage of them will show up in the juvenile justice system or have babies when they are teenagers or drop out of high school. In fact, as a group, the children of older unwed mothers will probably more closely resemble those who grow up with widowed mothers. And, as Princeton sociologist Sara S. McLanahan concludes, "growing up with a widowed parent is almost never associated with poorer child outcomes."

Despite disparities in how well children do in various unconventional families, when people talk about unwed mothers they tend to carelessly toss their circumstances into one gigantic pot. The rhetoric heats up, of course, when words such as "illegitimate" are attached to all their children, along with dire predictions about those children's well-being. Sadly, many children who are born to single mothers do experience debilitating difficulties. But it's not certain which factors lead to what outcomes; nor do we know which problems the children might have avoided had their parents been married. Many experts regard poverty—and in particular, dependence on welfare—as the primary suspect in the preponderance of difficulties in these children's lives; the father's absence is the key culprit in the view of others. Of course it's not a simple task to disentangle these factors, since low income is often a by-product of the father's absence. But after evaluating the most current and reliable research on the relationship between family structure and children's well-being, McLanahan, arguably the nation's leading expert on such matters, recently wrote that she "suspects that family structure is more important than poverty in determining behavioral and psychological problems, whereas poverty is more important than family structure in determining educational attainment."

For the millions of children who are poor *and* are growing up without fathers, escape from this range of anticipated problems is not all that likely. However, it seems fair to ask whether circumstances would improve a great deal for vast numbers of these children if pregnant teenagers married, thereby avoiding an "illegitimate" birth. After all, a bystander hearing the conversations now taking place about unmarried motherhood and its consequences—conversations which often dwell foremost on the babies' illegitimacy—could easily come away with the impression that if fifteen- and sixteen-year-olds simply married the fathers of their children, many social problems would go away.

This is not necessarily so. For some of these children, marriage would not eliminate family poverty. Unfortunately, many young parents don't have the skills necessary to find jobs with wages sufficient to enable them to live in communities where their children will encounter fewer risks to their well-being. Few jobs for which these younger workers qualify come with family health insurance, so children often don't receive well-child care unless their family's income is low enough to qualify for Medicaid. (Several decades ago, when pregnant teenagers married more often, labor force conditions were quite different. Young parents—even those who hadn't completed high school—had a fairly good chance of finding jobs in which wages were adequate, growth in family income was predictable, and benefits were available.) Additionally, when teen mothers today try to make a go of it as part of a nuclear family, they sometimes lose out on valuable caregiving assistance from family members. Responsible for caring for a child, a husband, and a household, young mothers have a hard time moving their own lives ahead by completing their education and joining the labor force.

This effort by young mothers is necessary even if they are married when their babies are born. The reason: within a few years, a high percentage of teen marriages are dissolved. One study found that one-third of pregnant adolescents aged fifteen to nineteen who were married before childbirth were separated or divorced by the time the infants were six months old. Unless mothers have improved their skills by then, they're in no better position to find jobs or to parent well once they're on their own. Their children are probably living in poverty *and* experiencing parental conflict—that is, confronting two well-known risk factors during a crucial stage of development. On the basis of extensive research on adolescent parenting, the sociologist Frank Furstenberg writes that "clearly, marriage is not always in a woman's best interest or the best interest of the child. Unstable marriages and conflictual relationships within marriage elevate the chances . . . [that a child will have] a poor relationship with a father outside the home. Our data show that a poor relationship [with the father] is worse than no relationship at all. . . . Consequently, we walk a thin line when we attempt to promote matrimony as a public good if many or most marriages turn out to be unstable or conflict-ridden."

For children whose adolescent mothers do marry and go on to develop a solid economic and emotional foundation for the family, having a mom and dad in their lives can be enormously beneficial. It lessens children's likelihood of experiencing problems generally associated with out-of-wedlock birth. However, as the turn of the century greets us, economic circumstances, personal pressures, and cultural messages conspire to make such outcomes less likely.

"There is a mismatch between adolescent development and infant developmental needs."

Marriage also does not erase the fact that teenagers who become parents are rarely prepared to handle the tasks involved in child-rearing. In combination with family poverty and the tension and conflict already so common in their relationships, these young mothers' usually low level of competence in child-rearing during these critical early years presents another big obstacle to their children's long-term well-being.

The list of personal and developmental tasks adolescent mothers typically confront is long, and it offers significant clues as to why so many of the children born to teenagers do not develop the cognitive and social skills necessary to do well in school and avoid behavioral problems. Compared with other teens, adolescent mothers, as a group, have a less certain sense of their own identities, are less able to make decisions for themselves, demonstrate more difficulties with trust, are more depressed, and have lower self-esteem. When compared with adult mothers, teenage moms demonstrate less understanding of children's development, display more punitive attitudes toward their children, and perceive their babies' temperament as being more difficult. Teen moms also expect their babies to be able to do things earlier than they're developmentally able, so when their children don't respond to their commands, the younger moms become very frustrated. They also talk to their children very little, issuing curt disciplinary orders rather than engaging them in instructive patterns of conversation. These traits are not reserved only for those mothers who do not get married.

Joy D. Osofsky, a pediatric psychologist who has studied adolescent moms and their babies, writes that "there is a mismatch between adolescent development and infant developmental needs that interferes with teenagers' parenting abilities." Add to young mothers' personal characteristics the increased likelihood of living in a dangerous neighborhood and experiencing frequent moves (both of which are strongly associated with diminished child well-being) and there seems to be less mystery about why so many children of adolescent mothers are not doing very well.

It isn't the absence of marriage or, as many commentators choose to put it, the child's "illegitimate" birth, that creates this developmental mismatch. Rather, it is the precariousness of these adolescent mothers' emotional grounding and their ignorance of children's development. If we could set aside the ideology through which we usually view non-nuclear families, and instead see teenage motherhood through the lens of developmental needs, we'd create more constructive strategies to assist young families and improve the well-being of the children. And it's likely that, over time, we'd, in turn, lower the number of adolescent births.

Where might such a developmental perspective lead us? For starters, it would convince us to dedicate resources to buttressing teenagers in their parenting, and children during their formative early years. By learning what to expect as a child develops and discovering the extraordinary positive influence they have on their children, adolescents can, with ongoing support, improve their parenting. Such awareness is necessary if constructive pathways are to be built for the children, and building those early pathways will reduce the social costs of remediation and punishment as the children grow up. When infants and toddlers don't consistently receive cognitive stimulation, when they are punished abusively, or when proper attention isn't paid to their basic needs, their road to adulthood becomes littered with giant obstacles, which in time can become immovable.

It is often these early deficits that transform themselves into destructive adolescent behavior and academic failure and become the identifiable precursors of the next generation's slide into early parenthood. By now we know which girls are most likely to have babies very young and out of wedlock: those who aren't doing well in school, who have difficult social adjustments, who live in poverty, and who have not found adults who provide the love and support they need. And the male partners they become involved with often display similar characteristics.

Kristin Moore is a prominent expert on adolescent childbearing and president of Child Trends, Inc., a nonprofit research organization that focuses on children and families. She is often asked by welfare administrators what they ought to do to reduce the influx of mothers onto public assistance. Her answer: "Invest in high-quality preschool child care and education." Indeed, when researchers followed children who attended Perry Preschool, a high-intensity intervention program for low-income parents and their at-risk children, they found positive effects on academic achievement and social adjustment during the children's elementary and secondary school years. And a follow-up study done when the former Perry students were twenty-seven found that they had a higher rate of marriage and fewer out-of-wedlock births than did a comparison group of peers. As Hirokazu Yoshikawa, a psychologist who has analyzed dozens of such studies on the long-term effects of early childhood and parent programs, concludes, "There is evidence that a good relationship with one parent, marked by warmth and absence of severe criticism, can have a substantial protective effect against the development of later antisocial behaviors." That so many children grow up without such protection is not an irresolvable circumstance. But to affect these life trajectories requires targeted investments in the high-quality early approaches that evidence suggests can work.

"The importance and scope of decisions to be made in early adolescence is greater than at any other developmental period."

Applying what researchers have learned about adolescent development could also help us devise more effective strategies for preventing adolescent pregnancy and thereby reducing out-of-wedlock births. Right now, pregnancy prevention efforts usually begin too late, focus too much on what goes on "below the waist" rather than what happens above it, and don't do a good job of reaching or assisting the youngsters most in need. In its evaluation of community youth programs, the Carnegie Council on Adolescent Development reported that "without exception, the young people in greatest need had the least access to support and services." Not surprisingly, teenagers from all racial and ethnic backgrounds who are disconnected from adult support and guidance are more likely to have a baby on their own.

The early years of adolescence—ages ten to fourteen—are a time of unparalleled developmental growth, when youngsters form fundamental assumptions about society and their potential roles in it. "The importance and scope of decisions to be made in early adolescence is greater than at any other developmental period," wrote Beatrix A. Hamburg, a physician who served on the Carnegie Council. Dr. Hamburg went on to observe that "even for the most competent individuals, early adolescence is a period of added stress, impoverished coping skills, and consequent vulnerability. . . . It has become painfully clear that severe problems such as

school dropout, drug abuse, alcoholism, inappropriate pregnancy, and suicide now have their initiation and show rising rates in these youngest adolescents—these problems are indicators of unmet developmental needs."

Because early adolescence is the time when children's concrete
thinking expands into realms of complex, abstract understanding, the
steadying guidance of adults is needed if youngsters are to learn how to be
prudent decision-makers. Essential skills such as learning how to resist
sexual pressure and make what might be lifesaving decisions must be
passed on by adults whose advice children have reason to trust, upon
whom they can depend in times of need, and who will be there to celebrate their accomplishments.

These preteen years offer us a window of opportunity to help youngsters
strengthen their inner foundations before potentially destructive behavior
patterns take hold and before adolescents become less willing to listen to
much of what adults try to say. Unfortunately, this opportunity is one that
we, as family members and as community members, routinely fail to take
advantage of. By the time youngsters reach preadolescence, many parents
who might have cut back work schedules during their children's earlier
years have resumed full-time employment; they now have less time to
spend with their children and less energy to expend when they *are* present.
Nor do many parents understand the essential role they play in helping
early adolescents meet developmental challenges. Instead, emphasis in
contemporary times is placed more on letting children establish an earlier
sense of independence.

In the book *Beyond the Classroom: Why School Reform Has Failed and
What Parents Need to Do*, Laurence Steinberg, a psychology professor at
Temple University, discusses the results of a ten-year study of families with
adolescent children. It turns out that at least a fourth of the parents were
basically passive, preoccupied, or just plain negligent of their children.
Only one in three youngsters said they had conversations with their parents every day, and half the parents did not know what their children did
after school. By the time youngsters arrive in high school (and often
before), Dr. Steinberg reports, parents are "seriously disengaged" from
their children's lives.

However, in surveys and focus groups, adolescents—in particular
younger ones—lament the lack of parental attention and reveal how
much they want and need adult guidance as they start to leave childhood.
But as we prepare to enter the twenty-first century, adolescents are
spending considerably less time with adults than their counterparts did
even a few decades ago. Video games and television are more consistent
companions and, more than in the past, young people's activities do not
involve either parents or other adults.

"We have to give them a reason, a context, and motivation for doing the best for themselves."

Social environments might have changed, but the needs of young adolescents have not. To successfully navigate the teenage years, every child must have certain fundamental needs met. These include finding ways to earn respect; securing a sense of belonging to one or more highly valued groups; establishing close, sustaining relationships; and constructing a sense of personal worth. These developmental challenges cannot be met without the engagement of adults in the family and the community. And when these needs aren't met within the company of adults, some girls will mistakenly assume that motherhood offers an alternative route to achieving them. After all, having a baby gives her someone to "belong" to, an accomplishment she can claim as her own, and a way to see herself as valued and strong.

The longer we, as a society, wait to respond to these girls' circumstances the more costly it becomes to help them and the less successful we are likely to be. And if we wait too long, there are their children to complicate our task. Nowadays, as our efforts offer too little, arrive too late, and therefore fail too often, we find taxpayers growing frustrated and angry at girls who become parents out of wedlock so early in their lives. That anger is then transformed into reactionary politics and policies that constitute not constructive prevention, but potential harm to these children.

Rebecca Maynard, a professor of education and social policy at the University of Pennsylvania, recently completed comprehensive reviews of state-of-the-art efforts in pregnancy prevention, as well as other programs that attempt to train and employ teen parents. Two of her central findings underscore the need for us to pay attention much earlier and much more comprehensively to girls who we know are likely to have a child in adolescence. Maynard found that "none of the pregnancy prevention programs has proven to have major impacts on the teenage pregnancy and birth rates," and "none of the employment or welfare-focused programs succeeded in helping young mothers take control of their fertility." In fact, participants in the Teenage Parent Welfare Demonstration, which involved employment opportunities and job training, experienced high rates of repeat pregnancies: more than two-thirds were pregnant within two and a half years of enrollment, despite family planning counseling. Clearly, this research highlights how remedies become progressively more difficult—and much more costly—when we overlook early warning signs and postpone our assistance until after childhood and early adolescence, even until after a teenager has already had one child.

In the late 1990s, debates about pregnancy prevention still revolve in predictable, often irresolvable, circles around the topics of contraception and abstinence. That it's vital for teenagers to hear messages about both seems to get lost in the bickering that goes on between adult proponents of each perspective. And that neither message, as it is now delivered, is sufficient or seems capable of altering the behavior of great numbers of adolescents is often forgotten. Sarah Brown, head of the National Campaign to Prevent Teen Pregnancy, believes that when we look back twenty years from now at our current debates about and approaches to preventing early births, "we will say we learned in the 1990s and the early twenty-first century that we can't just tell kids 'Don't have sex,' and we can't just say to them 'Here is a pill. Use it,' but that we have to give them a reason, a context, and motivation for doing the best for themselves."

Brown suggests that some of the more effective approaches to achieving the latter probably reside in programs that were not designed to prevent teen pregnancy, although they clearly do. "Girl Scouts learned years ago that you start with eight- and nine-year-olds and carry through," Brown says. "I do not know if the Girl Scouts had developmental psychologists working with them, but they had an intuitive understanding that if you want to make a difference in a seventeen-year-old's life, you have to start when they are seven." The Big Sister program, which brings together women and girls in long-term, one-on-one relationships of friendship and support, is another promising approach. Because a close and trusting relationship exists, the girl has help in facing developmental challenges, and is more likely to overcome them.

A 1995 report about the impact of Big Sisters/Big Brothers on youth between the ages of ten and sixteen found that Little Sisters and Little Brothers were less likely than their peers to use drugs or alcohol; they felt more competent in doing schoolwork, attended school more, got better grades, and had better relationships with their parents and peers. Neither pregnancy rates nor birthrates were measured. But what is known about the web of behaviors strongly associated with teenage births suggests they were also reduced, since behaviors tend to cluster in particular lives. As the Carnegie Council on Adolescent Development reminds us, "Crime, school dropout, teenage childbearing, and drug abuse typically are considered separately, but in the real world they occur together . . . and once educational failure occurs, then other adverse events begin to take hold."

"Adults are the ones who are supposed to be responsible for us."

I met my Little Sister, Andrea, just after she had celebrated her eleventh birthday. She and I, strangers until that day, were brought together by a social worker at Big Sisters who had spent many hours talking with each of us about our expectations of our relationship. As the person who was about to assume the role of adult mentor, I'd gone through training and learned about ways to handle situations that might arise. I also made a commitment: for four hours every week, for at least a year and a half (longer if we wanted), my Little Sister and I would spend time together. We wouldn't follow any script. Rather we'd create out of our experiences a solid and unique friendship.

This we have done. Andrea and I talk a lot, but we laugh together a lot more. I have also been with her when tears flow or frustration rises to the surface. I offer her a receptive ear and advice that, perhaps, helps her get through the rougher times. We swim and bicycle together and go to museums and to movies. Andrea shows me her neighborhood and tells me all about her aunts and cousins and her grandparents, the special people in her life. She knows my cats, and I've met hers. When I go away, my stuffed-animal collection stays in her bedroom, where she watches over it for me. It is one of the ways we remain connected even when we can't be together. When I am away, we write each other letters; we have taken a three-day long-distance trip together, too.

I am not Andrea's parent, nor does she need me to be. Though her parents never married, both remain vital presences in her life, as do other extended-family members. What I am is Andrea's friend, an adult who will be there for her whenever she needs me. As such, I'll be there to help her meet some of the developmental challenges of her adolescent years. Does my presence guarantee that she won't become pregnant during her teenage years? Or that she won't give birth out of wedlock, as her mother did in having her? Or that she'll graduate from college, something no one in her family has ever done? No. But I know that by being a reliable person in Andrea's life I am giving her an added layer of protection against forces she says she wants to resist, and I am boosting her up so she can try to meet the goals she says she wants to reach.

On the day we met, our social worker explained to Andrea that even though I was going to be her friend, if I heard or saw things in her life that I felt would be detrimental to her well-being, I'd have to share what I knew with others. Andrea, who was seated at a kitchen table with her father, stepmother, and two young stepbrothers, looked toward her family, then at me, and finally said to our social worker words I'll never forget, words I wish every adult could hear and heed:

"Yeah, I understand," Andrea said. "Adults are the ones who are supposed to be responsible for us."

It is when we, as adult members of our community, fail in our responsibilities as protectors and nurturers of children that too many of our children grow up to fail themselves.

"Will I ever be a mother?"

I met Andrea when I was forty-three years old, still single and childless, but no longer so compulsively driven as I'd been during my late thirties to have a child of my own. In those years I'd spend month after month going to a fertility clinic, selecting an anonymous donor to provide sperm, ingesting drugs to spur my body to produce more eggs, and basing my happiness on whether my period arrived each month. It always did, and it always made me sad. One month, after experiencing particularly miserable side effects from drugs I was taking, I decided to walk away from the quest for a pregnancy. I wrote my doctor a letter instructing him to remove from the icy cylinder the sperm I'd ordered from a sperm bank in California and stored for my use in Boston.

Since I made that decision I haven't met a man with whom any serious long-term involvement seems promising. Nor have I changed my mind and returned to seek help from medical specialists in getting pregnant on my own. Now I live by myself—that is, if one doesn't count my two feline companions. They arrived a while after I abandoned my inseminations. My niece, Zoe, then eleven years old, wrote me a note one day urging me to adopt a cat, or, as it turned out, two. She told me she didn't want her aunt to be "lonely and sad."

Now, in my mid-forties, I feel neither lonely nor sad. In fact, I've shared with many friends the sense of relief I began to feel once the obsessive urge to have a baby began slowly to diminish. That doesn't mean that I haven't at times thought about whether I would ever have a child, or felt pangs of regret that a pregnancy didn't happen as I once wished so fervently it would. From friends who are mothers, I hear of the unparalleled joy children bring, and I know this kind of rapturous love is something I want to find ways to express. Once, when I sought my mother's counsel about this, she wrote to me that being a parent "has been mainly responsible for what meaning my life may have." Her words—and others I keep hearing from friends—made me wonder about where I, a childless woman, should look for my life's meaning.

In 1996, as I celebrated my forty-fifth birthday, I found myself exploring again some old questions about whether I should try to become a mother, this time through adoption. My return visit to this previously abandoned territory of thought isn't that surprising. After all, Merle Bombardieri, the counselor I met who advises older women about single motherhood, once told me that we focus with renewed intensity on questions about motherhood during years when our birthdays end in zero or a five. This had certainly been true for me: at the age of thirty-five I'd first visualized my relationship with my boyfriend heading toward parenthood; when I turned forty, I was mentally exhausted by my attempts to pursue a pregnancy, but still consumed by the desire to be a mother.

Now, when I was forty-five, this internal debate was surfacing again. But this time it felt very different. The powerful emotions that once dominated my decision-making were now partnered with concrete evaluations about whether adopting a child was the only, or even the best, way for me to express my "mothering" desires. The numerous interviews I've done with women my age who are rearing children on their own only reinforced an appreciation for the unceasing commitment that parenting, when done well and done alone, requires. I'd heard single mothers my age describe the immense responsibility they have assumed, and how time-consuming, difficult, and exhausting being a single parent can be.

The limitations of any one person trying to raise a child are something I now understand as I did not six or seven years ago, when my inner obsession with being a mother was pushing me to try to conceive. Both the passage of time and the acquisition of knowledge have helped to situate me on a more solid base from which I've been able to think again, long and hard, about my decision. These days the decision-making seems more comfortable for me, and that comfort gives me confidence that what I choose to do will work out well. This time around there is an absence of the constantly churning internal and external pressures I felt when I was in my thirties and driven by "baby hunger."

Now motherhood doesn't seem as much an answer to loneliness or unhappiness as it does a natural and positive extension of my contented life. To decide not to raise a child would no longer devastate me as I once thought it would. Perhaps I feel this way because I finally allowed myself, some years after I'd walked away from the monthly inseminations, to grieve fully the loss of the dream of one day creating a family of my own. I wept for days at what I then thought would never happen for me. And when my weeping and grieving at last ended, I set about the tough but necessary job of constructing purpose and meaning in my solitary life. In time my happiness returned, and it was no longer predicated on motherhood.

Interestingly, once I was able to envision my life as purposeful without a child, I became more comfortable with revisiting the idea of bringing a child into it. None of the compulsiveness about motherhood that consumed so much of my vitality during my younger days is with me now. In its place are calm yet intense feelings and a belief that I am now ready to welcome a child into my life. In the spring of 1997, before my forty-sixth birthday, I plan to travel to China to adopt a baby girl.

I am quite aware that some people will regard the decision to raise this child on my own as one I should not have made. Perhaps because I am adopting a child who would otherwise grow up in a Communist orphanage, my detractors will be fewer. But if, instead of adopting my daughter, I were pregnant and having a baby on my own, there would be many who would be angry at me, some who would question my judgment, and others who would worry about my child's life without a father. Few among us, including myself and most unmarried mothers I've met, would not wish, if it were possible, that every child experience the loving attachment of parents who stay committed to each other. Yet, as my journey into the lives of young and old unmarried mothers shows, what is desirable is, for a wide variety of reasons, not always achievable.

If by traveling in the footsteps of these unmarried mothers it's possible to gain fresh understanding of why their lives and mine took the various twists and turns they did, then perhaps the conversations that we, as an American family, engage in will embrace these new and helpful dimensions of insight. If so, then together we might arrive at ways to devote our resources and ingenuity to making better the lives of these families and their children, rather than continuing to allow our anger at them to lead us into actions we, as a nation, will regret.

Acknowledgments

My indebtedness begins with the women and children who welcomed me into their private lives so their stories could inform the public debate about unmarried motherhood. Though these women's real names do not appear in the book, many of them will recognize their contributions. In reading about their own lives, I hope they know how grateful I am to them for allowing me to borrow some of their most personal moments. However, I also visited with women whose stories and observations don't receive specific mention. To them, I want to express my deepest gratitude: to devote the time, which these women did, and then not see the details of our conversations here might lead them to believe that the time they gave me was not well spent. To the contrary, each woman's words became building blocks upon which I constructed this book.

For bringing me together with so many of the mothers, I want to thank Dr. Linda Prine, a family practitioner who came to know many of them through her work at a community health clinic in Boston. Dr. Tesi Kohlenberg, who was the director of the Teen & Tot Adolescent Center at Boston City Hospital, was also very supportive of my efforts and helpful in introducing me to adolescent mothers. The Single Mothers by Choice group in Boston, in particular Marilyn Levin, its guiding force, provided assistance and introduced me to older, unwed mothers. Jane Mattes, the founder of the national organization of Single Mothers by Choice, was also very helpful. It is not easy to step into a mother's daily life and ask her to share her innermost thoughts and private moments, especially when I am a stranger to her and want to share her life with other strangers. It was only because of the deep respect these mothers have for the women who introduced us that I was able to establish strong bonds of trust. I am grateful for the introductions.

I am also appreciative of the professional support Linda S. Wilson, president of Radcliffe College, gave me. Through her efforts, I was provided with an academic home at Radcliffe for two years, as a visiting scholar at the Henry A. Murray Research Center and then for one year as a fellow at Radcliffe Public Policy Institute. While at the college, I received research assistance from students in the Radcliffe Research Partnership Program. For their legwork on my behalf and their insights, I thank Harley Guttman, Anne Harkavy, Joyce Kuo, Theresa Loong, Ishani Maitra, and Shiri Sella. The Columbia Graduate School of Journalism also served as an invaluable home base during the final year of this project: Because of this school's leadership in recognizing the importance of press coverage of children and family issues, the Prudential Foundation supports at Columbia a fellowship for Coverage of Children and the News, one of which I was awarded. The Casey Journalism Center's conference on "Protecting the Welfare of Children," which I attended as a fellow in the spring of 1995, also gave me the opportunity—through the superb efforts of its director, Cathy Trost—to become acquainted with the work of numerous experts on adolescent pregnancy and unmarried motherhood, including Elijah Anderson, Douglas Besharov, Leon Dash, Donald Hernadez, Rebecca A. Maynard, Sara McLanahan, Lawrence M. Mead, Judith Musick, and David Popenoe and Nicholas Zill.

During my fellowship at Columbia University and an earlier Nieman Fellowship at Harvard, I was privileged to study with professors whose scholarship in related topics has proved invaluable. I would like to thank, in particular, Elizabeth Bartholet at Harvard Law School, David Ellwood at Harvard's Kennedy School of Government, Carol Gilligan at Harvard's Graduate School of Education, Maria Brassard and Jeanne Brooks-Gunn at Teachers College, Columbia University, and Laurie S. Miller at the Division of Child Psychiatry, Columbia University School of Physicians and Surgeons.

Scholars, practitioners, and opinion-makers gave generously of their time and expertise. To them, I express my appreciation. Though many of their names don't appear in the book, their thoughts, guidance, and assistance were invaluable. I offer special thanks to Stephanie J. Ventura, a research statistician at the National Center for Health Statistics, and to Kristin A. Moore, president of Child Trends, Inc.; each is thanked for the help she provided me in finding my way through the numbers but also for the careful attention she gives year after year in shepherding this information to the public. Their research is vital in informing public debate that too often is overloaded with inaccurate perceptions. Others to whom I turned for advice, information, and insight about social implications of unmarried motherhood include Mary Jo Bane, Allie Bledsoe, Benjamin Binswanger, Stevens Clarke, Ann Crouter, David Blankenhorn, Ronald

Ferguson, Olivia Golden, Ellen Guiney, Beverly Jones, John C. Pannell, Mary Russo, Steve Savner, Theda Skocpol, Janice Walsh, Barbara Dafoe Whitehead, and Barry Zuckerman.

At the time I began this book, welfare reform was reemerging as a key political and legislative issue. Though this book does not directly address how the states are now changing their welfare systems, it was important to acquaint myself with varying views of how government can or should respond to structural changes in families. Senator Edward M. Kennedy, who was then chairman of the Senate Labor and Human Resource Committee, kindly introduced me to members of his committee as well as to other members of Congress who are involved with legislation that impacts upon the lives of children and families. Harriett Woods, who was then director of the National Women's Political Caucus, also made introductions for me. To those with whom I spoke, I say thank you: Senators Carol Moseley Braun, Christopher Dodd, Nancy L. Kassebaum, Patty Murray, and Jay Rockefeller; the staff assistants of Senators Dan Coats and Orrin Hatch; and Representatives Henry Hyde, Cynthia McKinney, George Miller, Connie Morella, Patricia Schroeder, and Lynn Woolsey.

I felt it was important also to be exposed to an international perspective on changes in family formation, since out-of-wedlock births are increasing in other industrialized nations as well. Thanks to the remarkable assistance of my friend Martin Gehlen, a newspaper reporter in Berlin, Germany, I spent several weeks visiting with unwed mothers there, many of whom once lived in East Germany. I also spoke with members of the German parliament and with experts in family policy who were able to describe to me the very different ways in which Europeans think about these family changes and shape their governmental responses to them. Once again, to the German mothers with whom I visited, I say thank you: your stories opened windows through which I'm able to look more expansively at the family lives of American women and our society's response to them.

In moving from the company of journalists to the solitary pursuit of writing a book, I came to rely on a steadfast group of friends, many of whom are writers. They have been invaluable sounding boards for my ideas as well as brutally honest and helpful critics. For their contributions, I thank Leslie Dreyfous, Ellen Fitzpatrick, Kathleeen Hirsch, Sara Rimer, and Elizabeth Weld. Also, for their assistance with various sections of the manuscript, I am indebted to Nancy Apfel, John Laub, Victoria Seitz, and Richard Weissbourd. For their constant encouragement, embracing friendship, and reliable support during the years of this project, I thank Deborah Amos, Bailey and Tori Bishop, Jack and Diane Caldwell, Tom

Callahan, Mary Jane Checchi, Hillary Rodham Clinton, Sally Cottingham, Peter and Michelle Cross, Chris DeGraw, Christine DeLisle, Bill Eglinton, Jack and Toni Fallon, Mary Fulham, Richard Goodwin and Doris Kearns Goodwin, Stan Grossfeld, Bill and Robie Harris, Therese Hattemer, Ellen Hume, Stacey Kabat, Joan Kennedy, Kara Kennedy, Sheila Kennedy, Bill Kovach, Ronald LaBrecque, Meryl Langbort, Janice Litwin, Janet Ludtke, Elizabeth Mehren, Emily Mezzetti, Ann Marie Mikols, Kay Mills, Terry Muilenburg, Jim Owens, Leslie Sandberg, Elizabeth Shannon, Blue Tabor, and Kathleen Kennedy Townsend. The daily pep talks I received from my dear friend Deane Lord, who died while this book was in its infancy, kept me going during difficult times.

Special words of gratitude go to Olga Seham, whose unwavering belief in me and in this book, as well as her keen insights about how to connect these women's personal stories to the larger societal debate, sustained me; to Philippa Brophy, my agent, whose perseverance, desire for excellence, and can-do attitude are wonderfully infectious; and to Susanna Porter, my editor at Random House, whose guiding hand helped me to knit all this together.

My family has been, as always, my rock. Their love and concern for me and their enthusiastic support of this project gave me strength I needed each day to keep going. To my parents, Jim and Jean, my sisters, Leslie, Betty, and Rebecca, my brother, Mark, my cousin, Elizabeth Edwards, and my nieces, Zoe and Allison, I say, with all my love, thank you.

Bibliography

Books

Aaron, Henry J., Thomas E. Mann, and Timothy Taylor, eds. *Values and Public Policy*. Washington, D.C.: The Brookings Institution, 1994.

Acock, Alan C., and David H. Demo. *Family Diversity and Well-being*. Thousand Oaks, Cal.: SAGE Publications, 1994.

Baran, Annette, and Reuben Pannor. *Lethal Secrets: The Shocking Consequences and Unsolved Problems of Artificial Insemination*. New York: Warner Books, 1989.

Bartholet, Elizabeth. *Family Bonds: Adoption and the Politics of Parenting*. Boston: Houghton Mifflin, 1993.

Blankenhorn, David. *Fatherless America: Confronting Our Most Urgent Social Problem*. New York: Basic Books, 1995.

————, Steven Bayme, and Jean Bethke Elshtain, eds. *Rebuilding the Nest: A New Commitment to the American Family*. Milwaukee: Family Service America, 1990.

Brazelton, T. Berry. *Touchpoints: Your Child's Emotional and Behavioral Development*. Reading, Mass.: Addison-Wesley, 1992.

Chase-Lansdale, P. Lindsay, and Jeanne Brooks-Gunn. *Escape From Poverty: What Makes a Difference for Children?* Cambridge, England: Cambridge University Press, 1995.

Cherlin, Andrew J., ed. *The Changing American Family and Public Policy*. Washington, D.C.: The Urban Institute Press, 1988.

Coontz, Stephanie. *The Way We Never Were: American Families and the Nostalgia Trap*. New York: Basic Books, 1992.

Dickerson, Bette J. *African American Single Mothers: Understanding Their Lives and Families*. Thousand Oaks, Cal.: SAGE Publications, 1995.

Dornbusch, Sanford, and Myra H. Strober. *Feminism, Children, and the New Families*. New York: The Guilford Press, 1988.

Ellwood, David T. *Poor Support: Poverty in the American Family*. New York: Basic Books, 1988.

Engber, Andrea, and Leah Klungness. *The Complete Single Mother: Reassuring*

Answers to Your Most Challenging Concerns. Holbrook, Mass.: Adams Publishing, 1995.

Garfinkel, Irwin, and Sara S. McLanahan. *Single Mothers and Their Children: A New American Dilemma*. Washington, D.C.: The Urban Institute Press, 1986.

Hacker, Andrew. *Two Nations: Black and White, Separate, Hostile, Unequal*. New York: Ballantine Books, 1992.

Hochschild, Arlie, with Anne Machung. *The Second Shift: Working Parents and the Revolution at Home*. New York: Viking, 1989.

Kamerman, Sheila B., and Alfred J. Kahn. *Starting Right: How America Neglects Its Youngest Children and What We Can Do About It*. New York: Oxford University Press, 1995.

Kissman, Kris, and Jo Ann Allen. *Single-Parent Families*. Newbury Park, Cal.: SAGE Publications, 1993.

Luker, Kristin. *Dubious Conceptions: The Politics of Teenage Pregnancy*. Cambridge, Mass.: Harvard University Press, 1996.

Maynard, Rebecca A., ed. *Kids Having Kids: A Robin Hood Foundation Special Report on the Costs of Adolescent Childbearing*. New York: Robin Hood Foundation, 1996.

McLanahan, Sara, and Gary Sandefur. *Growing Up with a Single Parent: What Hurts, What Helps*. Cambridge, Mass.: Harvard University Press, 1994.

Majors, Richard G., and Jacob U. Gordon, eds. *The American Black Male: His Present Status and His Future*. Chicago: Nelson-Hall Publishers, 1994.

Mattes, Jane. *Single Mothers by Choice: A Guidebook for Single Women Who Are Considering or Have Chosen Motherhood*. New York: Times Books, 1994.

Miller, Sue. *The Good Mother*. New York: Dell Publishing, 1986.

Musick, Judith S. *Young, Poor, and Pregnant: The Psychology of Teenage Motherhood*. New Haven, Conn.: Yale University Press, 1993.

Nightingale, Carl Husemoller. *On the Edge: A History of Poor Black Children and Their American Dreams*. New York: Basic Books, 1993.

Noble, Elizabeth. *Having Your Baby by Donor Insemination: A Complete Resource Guide*. Boston: Houghton Mifflin, 1987.

Popenoe, David. *Life Without Father: Compelling New Evidence That Fatherhood and Marriage Are Indispensable for the Good of Children and Society*. New York: Free Press, 1996.

——, Jean Bethke Elshtain, and David Blankenhorn, eds. *Promises to Keep: Decline and Renewal of Marriage in America*. Lanham, Md.: Rowman & Littlefield, 1996.

Prothrow-Stith, Deborah, with Michaele Weissman. *Deadly Consequences: How Violence Is Destroying Our Teenage Population and a Plan to Begin Solving the Problem*. New York: HarperCollins, 1991.

Sampson, Robert J., and John H. Laub. *Crime in the Making: Pathways and Turning Points Through Life*. Cambridge, Mass.: Harvard University Press, 1993.

Sherman, Arloc. *Wasting America's Future: The Children's Defense Fund Report on the Costs of Child Poverty*. Boston: Beacon Press, 1994.

Skocpol, Theda. *Protecting Soldiers and Mothers: The Political Origins of Social Policy in the United States*. Cambridge, Mass.: Belknap Press, 1992.

Solinger, Rickie. *Wake Up Little Susie: Single Pregnancy and Race Before Roe v. Wade*. New York: Routledge, 1992.

Weissbourd, Richard. *The Vulnerable Child: What Really Hurts America's Children and What We Can Do About It*. Reading, Mass.: Addison-Wesley, 1996.

Williams, Constance Willard. *Black Teenage Mothers: Pregnancy and Child Rearing from Their Perspective*. Lexington, Mass.: Lexington Books, 1991.

Wilson, William Julius. *The Truly Disadvantaged: The Inner City, the Underclass, and Public Policy*. Chicago: University of Chicago Press, 1987.

Articles and Reports
Unmarried Motherhood: A Half-Century of Change

Chase-Lansdale, P. L., and M. Hetherington. "The Impact of Divorce on Life-Span Development: Short and Long Term Effects." In P. Baltes, D. L. Featherman, and R. M. Lerner, eds., *Life-Span Behavior and Development*, vol. 10, pp. 105–50. Hillsdale, N.J.: Erlbaum, 1990.

Child Trends, Inc. "Facts at a Glance." Washington, D.C.: Child Trends, Inc., 1993, 1994, 1995, 1996.

Children's Defense Fund. "The State of America's Children, 1994." Washington, D.C.: Children's Defense Fund, 1994.

Duncan, G. J., J. Brooks-Gunn, and P. K. Klebanov. "Economic Deprivation and Early Childhood Development." *Child Development*, vol. 65 (1994), pp. 296–318.

Jones, Elise S. *Teenage Pregnancy in Industrialized Countries*. New Haven, Conn.: Yale University Press, 1986.

McLanahan, Sara S. "Parent Absence or Poverty—Which Matters More?" In *Consequences of Growing Up Poor*, Greg Duncan and Jeanne Brooks-Gunn, eds. New York: Russell Sage Foundation Press, in press.

National Center for Children in Poverty. *One in Four: America's Youngest Poor*. New York: Columbia School of Public Health, 1996.

National Center for Health Statistics. "Advance Report of Final Natality Statistics, 1991." *Monthly Vital Statistics Report*, vol. 42, no. 3. Hyattsville, Md.: U.S. Public Health Service, Sept. 1993.

———. "Advance Report of Final Natality Statistics, 1993." *Monthly Vital Statistics Report*, vol. 44, no. 3 Supplement. Hyattsville, Md.: U.S. Public Health Service, Sept. 1995.

———. "Births and Deaths: United States, 1995." *Monthly Vital Statistics Report*, vol. 45, no. 3, supplement 2. Hyattsville, Md.: U.S. Public Health Service, Oct. 1996.

———. "Births to Unmarried Mothers: United States, 1980–92." *Vital and Health Statistics*, series 21, no. 53. Hyattsville, Md.: U.S. Public Health Service, June 1995.

————. "Trends in Pregnancies and Pregnancy Rates: Estimates for the United States, 1980–92." *Monthly Vital Statistics Report*, vol. 43, no. 11 supplement. Hyattsville, Md.: U.S. Public Health Service, May 1995.

Tilly, Chris, and Randy Albelda. *It'll Take More Than a Miracle: Income in Single-Mother Families in Massachusetts, 1979–1987.* Boston, Mass: The John W. McCormick Institute for Public Affairs, University of Massachusetts at Boston, March 1992.

U.S. Bureau of the Census. "Fertility of American Women: June 1994." *Current Population Reports*, series P20-482. Washington, D.C.: U.S. Department of Commerce, Sept. 1995.

————. "Household and Family Characteristics: March 1994." *Current Population Reports*, series P20-483. Washington, D.C.: U.S. Department of Commerce, 1995.

————. "Household and Family Characteristics: March 1995." *Current Population Reports*, series P20-488. Washington, D.C.: U.S. Department of Commerce, Oct. 1996.

————. "Income, Poverty, and Valuation of Noncash Benefits: 1993." *Current Population Reports*, series P60-188. Washington, D.C.: U.S. Department of Commerce, 1995.

U.S. Department of Health and Human Services. *Report to Congress on Out-of-Wedlock Childbearing.* DHHS pub. no. (PHS) 95-1257. Hyattsville, Md.: U.S. Public Health Service, Sept. 1995.

U.S. General Accounting Office. "Families on Welfare: Sharp Rise in Never-Married Women Reflects Societal Trend." Report to the Chairman, Subcommittee on Human Resources, Committee on Ways and Means, House of Representatives. GAO/HEHS-94-92. Washington, D.C.: U.S. General Accounting Office, May 1994.

Walker, Henry A. "Black-White Differences in Marriage and Family Patterns." In *Feminism, Children and the New Families*, Sanford M. Dornbusch and Myra H. Strober, eds. New York: The Guilford Press, 1988.

Having a Baby: Unmarried Adolescent Mothers

Bernstein, Jared, and Lawrence Mishel. *Trends in Low-Wage Labor Market and Welfare Reform: The Constraints on Making Work Pay.* Washington, D.C.: Economic Policy Institute, 1995.

Bluestone, Barry. *The Polarization of American Society: Victims, Suspects, and Mysteries to Unravel.* New York: Twentieth Century Fund Press, 1995.

Boyer, D., and D. Fine. "Sexual Abuse as a Factor in Adolescent Pregnancy and Child Maltreatment." *Family Planning Perspectives*, vol. 24 (January/February 1992), no. 1, pp. 4–11, 19.

Burtless, Gary, and Lawrence Mishel. "Recent Wage Trends: The Implications for Low Wage Workers." Memorandum prepared for the Social Science Research Council Policy Conference on Persistent Urban Poverty. Washington, D.C.: Economic Policy Institute, 1995.

Carnegie Council on Adolescent Development. *Great Transitions: Preparing Ado-*

lescents for a New Century. New York: Carnegie Corporation of New York, 1995.

Carrera, Michael J. "Preventing Adolescent Pregnancy: In Hot Pursuit." *SIECUS Report*, vol. 23, no. 6 (1995), pp. 16–19.

——— and P. Dempsey. *New York Replication Evaluation Update*. New York: Philliber Research Associates, 1995.

Annie E. Casey Foundation. *Kids Count Data Book: State Profiles of Child Well-Being 1995*. Baltimore: Annie E. Casey Foundation, 1995.

Child Trends, Inc. "Facts at a Glance." Washington, D.C.: Child Trends, Inc., 1994, 1995, 1996.

Furstenberg, Frank F., Jr., Jeanne Brooks-Gunn, and Lindsay Chase-Lansdale. "Teenaged Pregnancy and Childbearing." *American Psychologist*, vol. 44, no. 2 (Feb. 1989), pp. 313–20.

Geronimus, Arline T. "Black/White Differences in the Relationship of Maternal Age to Birthweight: A Population-based Test of the Weathering Hypothesis." *Soc. Sci. Med.*, Feb. 1996, pp. 1–9.

———. "Clashes of Common Sense: On the Previous Child Care Experience of Teenage Mothers-to-be." *Human Organization*, vol. 51, no. 4 (1992), pp. 318–29.

———. "The Weathering Hypothesis and the Health of African-American Women and Infants: Evidence and Speculations." *Ethnicity and Disease*, vol. 2 (summer 1992), pp. 202–221.

———. "What Teen Mothers Know." Paper presented to the Working Group on Anthropological Demography, Brown University, Feb. 6, 1996.

———, Sanders Korenman, and Marianne M. Hillemeier. "Does Young Maternal Age Adversely Affect Child Development? Evidence from Cousin Comparisons in the United States." *Population and Development Review*, vol. 20, no. 3 (Sept. 1994), pp. 585–609.

Gorov, Lynda. "An Acceptance of Young Mothers: In Tiny Montague, Many of the Teenage Parents Have Neither Spouses nor Stigma." *The Boston Globe*, Feb. 20, 1994.

Alan Guttmacher Institute. *Facts in Brief*. "Teenage Reproductive Health in the United States." New York: Alan Guttmacher Institute, 1994.

———. *Issues in Brief*. "Teenage Pregnancy and the Welfare Reform Debate." New York: Alan Guttmacher Institute, Feb. 1995.

———. *Sex and America's Teenagers*. New York: Alan Guttmacher Institute, 1994.

Hotz, V. Joseph, Susan Williams McElroy, and Seth G. Sanders. "The Costs and Consequences of Teenage Childbearing for Mothers." Maynard, Rebecca A., ed. *Kids Having Kids: The Consequences and Costs of Teenage Childbearing in the United States*. New York: Robin Hood Foundation, March 1995.

Institute of Medicine. *The Best Intentions: Unintended Pregnancy and the Well-being of Children and Families*. Washington, D.C.: The National Academy Press, 1995.

Johnson, Clifford, Andrew M. Sum, and James D. Weill. *Vanishing Dreams: The*

Growing Economic Plight of America's Young Families. Washington, D.C.: Children's Defense Fund, 1992.

Kaye, Jacqueline, and Susan Philliber. "Comprehensive Adolescent Pregnancy Prevention Programs: Are They Working?" New York: *The Children's Aid Society Newsletter*, summer 1995, pp. 1–4.

Lehman, Jeffrey, and Sheldon Danzinger. "Ending Welfare as We Know It: Values, Economics, and Politics." Cambridge, Mass.: Electronic Policy Network, 1995.

McLanahan, Sara S. "The Consequences of Single Motherhood." *The American Prospect*, no. 18 (summer 1994), pp. 48–58.

Thomas, Emory, Jr. "Is Pregnancy a Rational Choice for Poor Teenagers?" *The Wall Street Journal*, Jan. 18, 1996.

U.S. Department of Health and Human Services. *Report to Congress on Out-of-Wedlock Childbearing*. DHHS Pub. no. (PHS) 95-1257. Hyattsville, Md.: U.S. Public Health Service, Sept. 1995.

Verhovek, Sam Howe. "Pregnant Cheerleaders Bringing Turmoil." *The New York Times*, Oct. 4, 1993.

Zabin, L. S., N. M. Astone, and M. R. Emerson. "Do Adolescents Want Babies? The Relationship Between Attitudes and Behavior." *Journal of Research on Adolescence*, vol. 3, no. 1 (1993), pp. 67–86.

Having a Baby: Unmarried Older Mothers

Bartholet, Elizabeth. "Beyond Biology: The Politics of Adoption and Reproduction." *Duke Journal of Gender Law and Policy*, vol. 2, no. 1 (1995), pp. 5–14.

California Cryobank, Inc. "CCB's 'Policy of Openness,' " *CCB News*, vol. 2, issue 2 (1992).

Dale, Michael J. "The Evolving Constitutional Rights of Nonmarital Children: Mixed Blessings." *Georgia State University Law Review*, vol. 5, no. 2 (1995), pp. 523–55.

Donovan, Carol A. "The Uniform Parentage Act and Nonmarital Motherhood-by-Choice." *Review of Law and Social Change*, vol. 11 (1982–83), pp. 193–253.

Drexler, Madeline. "The Baby Bank: How Donor Insemination Is Helping the Stork." *Good Health Magazine, The Boston Globe*, Oct. 7, 1990.

Goldin, Claudia. "Career and Family: College Women Look to the Past." Washington, D.C.: National Bureau of Economic Research working paper, pp. 51–88, July 1995.

Karmel, Marianne M. "Creating Nontraditional Families: A Legal Guide to Family Planning for Unmarried Women." Unpublished paper submitted to Professor Elizabeth Bartholet, Harvard Law School, Jan. 21, 1991.

Lewis, Sara. *Heart Conditions*. New York: Harcourt Brace, 1994.

Mattes, Jane, ed. "The SMC 2000 Study—Who Are We? Report #2." *Single Mothers by Choice Newsletter*, March 1994.

National Center for Health Statistics. "Advance Report of Final Natality Statistics, 1993." *Monthly Vital Statistics Report*, vol. 44, no. 3. Hyattsville, Md.: U.S. Public Health Service, Sept. 1995.

―――. "Births to Unmarried Mothers: United States, 1980–92." *Vital and Health Statistics*, series 21, no. 53. Hyattsville, Md.: U.S. Public Health Service, June 1995.

O'Keefe, James J. "A Shot in the Dark: Law, Society, and Anonymous Sperm Donors." Unpublished paper submitted to Professor Elizabeth Bartholet, Harvard Law School, Dec. 1991.

Patton, Stephen M. "Risks and Regulation of Donor Insemination." Unpublished paper submitted to Professor Elizabeth Bartholet, Harvard Law School, May 1990.

Sorosky, Arthur D., Annette Baran, and Reuben Pannor. *The Adoption Triangle: The Effects of the Sealed Record on Adoptees, Birth Parents, Adoptive Parents*. New York: Anchor Press, 1978.

Straub vs. Todd. Decision of Honorable Daniel Donahue, Judge, Clark Circuit Court, Court of Appeals of Indiana, Fourth District. No. 10A04-9302-JV-53.

Straub vs. Todd. Legal brief of appellant, in the Court of Appeals, Fourth District, State of Indiana, No. 10A04-9302-JV-53.

Straub vs. Todd. Legal brief of appellee, in the Court of Appeals, Fourth District, State of Indiana, No. 10A04-9302-JV-53.

Straub vs. Todd. Legal reply brief of appellant, in the Court of Appeals, Fourth District, State of Indiana, No. 10A04-9302-JV-53.

"Survey. Murphy Brown: Are You Against the Idea of Single Women as Mothers?" *Glamour*, Oct. 1992.

Tucker, Belinda. "The Southern California Social Survey, 1989." Los Angeles: Institute for Social Science Research, University of California at Los Angeles, 1989.

Uniform Parentage Act (UPA) 9A *Uniform Laws Annotated* 587, 1979.

U.S. Bureau of the Census. "Fertility of American Women: June 1992." *Current Population Reports*, series P20-470. Washington, D.C.: U.S. Department of Commerce, 1993.

Xytex Corporation. "The Xytex Donor." Xytex Home Page, www.xytex.com (1996).

Raising Children: Unmarried Adolescent Mothers

Aber, J. Lawrence, Jeanne Brooks-Gunn, and Rebecca A. Maynard. "Effects of Welfare Reform on Teenage Parents and Their Children." *Critical Issues for Children and Youths: The Future of Children*, vol. 5, no. 2 (1995), pp. 53–71.

Apfel, Nancy H., and Victoria Seitz. "African American Adolescent Mothers, Their Families and Their Daughters: A Longitudinal Perspective Over Twelve Years." In *Urban Girls: Resisting Stereotypes, Creating Identities*, B. J. Leadbeater and N. Way, eds. New York: New York University Press, 1996.

―――. "The Firstborn Sons of African American Teenage Mothers: Perspectives on Risk and Resilience." In *Developmental Psychopathology: Perspectives on Risk and Disorder*, S. S. Luthar, J. A. Burack, A. Cicchetti, and J. Weisz, eds. New York: Cambridge University Press, 1997.

————. "Four Models of Adolescent Mother-Grandmother Relationships in Black Inner-City Families." In *Family Relations*, vol. 40 (Oct. 1991), pp. 421–29.

Bronfenbrenner, Urie, and Stephen J. Ceci. "Nature-Nurture Reconceptualized in Developmental Perspective: A Bioecological Model." *Psychological Review*, vol. 101, no. 4 (1994), pp. 568–86.

Brooks-Gunn, Jeanne, and P. Lindsay Chase-Lansdale. "Adolescent Parenthood." In *Handbook of Parenting*, vol. 3: *Status and Social Conditions of Parenting*, M. Bornstein, ed. Hillsdale, N.J.: Lawrence Erlbaum & Associates, 1995.

————. "Children Having Children: Effects on the Family System." *Pediatric Annals*, vol. 20, no. 9 (Sept. 1991), pp. 467–81.

Burton, L. M., and V. L. Bengston. "Black Grandmothers: Issues of Timing and Continuity of Roles." In *Grandparenthood*, V. L. Bengston and J. F. Robertson, eds. Beverly Hills, Cal.: Sage, 1985.

Carnegie Council on Adolescent Development. *Great Transitions: Preparing Adolescents for a New Century*. New York: Carnegie Corporation of New York, 1995.

Carnegie Task Force on Meeting the Needs of Young Children. *Starting Points: Meeting the Needs of Our Youngest Children*. New York: Carnegie Corporation of New York, 1994.

Chase-Lansdale, P. Lindsay, Jeanne Brooks-Gunn, and Elise S. Zamsky. "Young African-American Multigenerational Families in Poverty: Quality of Mothering and Grandmothering." *Child Development*, vol. 65 (1994), pp. 373–93.

Cost, Quality, and Child Outcomes Study Team. *Cost, Quality, and Child Outcomes in Child Care Centers*. Denver: University of Colorado at Denver, 1995.

Crockenberg, Susan, Karlen Lyons-Ruth, and Susan Dickstein. "The Family Context of Infant Mental Health: II. Infant Development in Multiple Family Relationships." In *Handbook of Infant Mental Health*, Charles H. Zeanah, ed. New York: Guilford Press, 1993.

Dawson, Deborah A. "Family Structure and Children's Health and Well-Being: Data from the 1988 National Health Interview Survey on Child Health." *Journal of Marriage and Family*, vol. 53 (Aug. 1991), pp. 573–84.

Dorn, Stan, and Colleen Fee. "Teen Parent Day Care in Massachusetts: Helping Young Families Help Themselves." Boston: Alliance for Young Families, Dec. 1992.

Duncan, G. J., J. Brooks-Gunn, and P. K. Klebanov. "Economic Deprivation and Early Childhood Development." *Child Development*, vol. 65 (1994), pp. 296–318.

Furstenberg, Frank. *Adolescent Mothers in Later Life*. Cambridge, England: Cambridge University Press, 1987.

Galinsky, Ellen, Carollee Howes, Susan Kontos, and Marybeth Shinn. *The Study of Children in Family Care and Relative Care: Highlights of Findings*. New York: Families and Work Institute, 1994.

Goleman, Daniel. "Early Violence Leaves Its Mark on the Brain." *The New York Times*, Oct. 3, 1995.

Gunnar, Megan R. "Quality of Care and the Buffering of Stress Psychology: Its Potential Role in Protecting the Developing Human Brain." Paper delivered at Zero to Three Conference, Dec. 7, 1996.

Kotulak, Ronald. "Unlocking the Mind." *Chicago Tribune,* April 11–15, 1993.

Office of the Inspector General, U.S. Department of Health and Human Services. "Review of Health and Safety Standards at Selected Facilities Memorandum." CIN: A-03-91-00550, Aug. 1991.

Paikoff, R. L., J. Brooks-Gunn, and N. Baydar. "Multigenerational Co-resident in a Sample of Six- and Seven-Year-Olds, National Longitudinal Study of Youth." Paper presented at biennial meeting of Society for Research in Child Development, March 1993.

Rutter, Michael. "The Growth of Social Relationships." In *Developing Minds: Challenge and Continuity Across the Lifespan.* New York: Basic Books, 1993.

Satcher, David. "Annotation: The Sociodemographic Correlates of Mental Retardation." *American Journal of Public Health,* vol. 85, no. 3 (1995), pp. 304–6.

Seitz, Victoria, and Nancy H. Apfel, "Adolescent Mothers and Repeated Childbearing: Effects of a School-Based Intervention Program." *American Journal of Orthopsychiatry,* vol. 63, no. 4 (1993), pp. 572–81.

————, and Laurie K. Rosenbaum, "Effects of an Intervention Program for Pregnant Adolescents: Educational Outcomes at Two Years Postpartum." *American Journal of Community Psychology,* vol. 19, no. 6 (1991), pp. 911–30.

Siegel, Gary L., and L. Anthony Loman. "Child Care and AFDC Recipients in Illinois: Patterns, Problems and Needs." Division of Family Support Services, Illinois Department of Public Aid, Sept. 1991.

Schweinhart, Lawrence J., Helen V. Barnes, and David P. Weikart. *Significant Benefits: The High/Scope Perry Preschool Study Through Age 27.* Ypsilanti, Mich.: The High/Scope Press, 1993.

Wakschlag, Lauren S., P. Lindsay Chase-Lansdale, and J. Brooks-Gunn. "Not Just 'Ghosts in the Nursery': Contemporaneous Intergenerational Relationships and Parenting in Young African-American Families." *Child Development,* vol. 67, no. 5 (1997), pp. 2131–2147.

Waldron, Ingrid, and Jerry Jacobs. "Effects of Labor Force Participation on Women's Health: Evidence from a National Longitudinal Study." *Journal of Occupational Medicine,* vol. 30 (1989), pp. 977–83.

Whitebook, Marcy, Carollee Howes, and Deborah Phillips. *Who Cares? Child Care Teachers and the Quality of Care in America: Final Report of the National Child Care Staffing Study.* Oakland, Cal.: Child Care Employee Project, 1989.

Whitebook, Marcy, Deborah Phillips, and Carollee Howes. *National Child Care Staffing Study Revisited: Four Years in the Life of Center-Based Child Care.* Oakland, Cal.: Child Care Employee Project, 1993.

Raising Children: Unmarried Older Mothers

Baruch, Grace, Rosalind Barnett, and Caryl Rivers. *Lifeprints.* New York: McGraw-Hill, 1983.

Baydar, Nazli, and Jeanne Brooks-Gunn, "Effects of Maternal Employment and Child-Care Arrangements on Preschoolers' Cognitive and Behavioral Outcomes: Evidence from Children of the National Longitudinal Survey of Youth." *Developmental Psychology*, vol. 27, no. 6 (1991), pp. 932–45.

Belsky, Jay, and Russell A. Isabella. "Marital and Parent-Child Relationships in Family of Origin and Marital Change Following the Birth of a Baby: A Retrospective Analysis." *Child Development*, vol. 56 (1985), pp. 342–49.

Belsky, Jay, and John Kelly. *Transition to Parenthood: How a First Child Changes a Marriage*. New York: Delacorte Press, 1994.

Berman, Phyllis W., and Frank A. Pedersen, eds. *Men's Transition to Parenthood: Longitudinal Studies of Early Family Experience*. Hillsdale, N.J.: Lawrence Erlbaum Associates, 1987.

Cherlin, Andrew J. "The Changing American Family and Public Policy." In *The Changing American Family and Public Policy*. Andrew J. Cherlin, ed. Washington, D.C.: The Urban Institute Press, 1988.

Chira, Susan. "New Realities Fight Old Images of Mother." *The New York Times*, Oct. 4, 1992.

Demo, David H., and Alan C. Acock. "Family Diversity and the Division of Domestic Labor: How Much Have Things Really Changed?" *Family Relations*, vol. 42, July 1993, pp. 323–31.

Gottfried, Adele Eskeles, and Allen W. Gottfried, eds. *Maternal Employment and Children's Development: Longitudinal Research*. New York: Plenum Press, 1988.

Mattes, Jane, ed. *Single Mothers by Choice Newsletter*, 1983–96.

Perry-Jenkins, Maureen. "Social Context as a Moderator of Work-Family Relationships: The Case of Working-Class, Two-Parent and Single-Parent Families." Paper presented at National Council on Family Relations Annual Conference, 1992.

Rubenstein, Carin. "The Baby Bomb: Research Reveals the Astonishingly Stressful Social and Emotional Consequences of Parenthood." *Good Health Magazine*, *The New York Times*, Oct. 8, 1989.

Schor, Juliet. "Gender and Working Time: Male Models of Employment." Paper presented at Henry A. Murray Research Center, Radcliffe College, Nov. 9, 1993.

Where's Daddy? Unmarried Adolescent Mothers

Austin, Bobby William, ed. *What a Piece of Work Is Man! A Discussion of Issues Affecting African-American Men and Boys*. W. K. Kellogg Foundation, May 1992.

Blankenhorn, David. "Fatherless America." Speech delivered at the Center of the American Experiment, Minneapolis, Jan. 13, 1993.

Children's Defense Fund. "Adolescent and Young Adult Fathers: Problems and Solutions." Washington, D.C.: Children's Defense Fund Adolescent Pregnancy Prevention Clearinghouse, May 1988.

———. "Declining Earnings of Young Men: Their Relation to Poverty, Teen

Pregnancy, and Family Formation." Washington, D.C.: Children's Defense Fund Adolescent Pregnancy Prevention Clearinghouse, May 1987.

Coleman, James S. "Families and Schools." *Educational Researcher,* Aug.–Sept. 1987, pp. 32–38.

Crockenberg, Susan, Karlen Lyons-Ruth, and Susan Dickstein. "The Family Context of Infant Mental Health: II. Infant Development in Multiple Family Relationships." In *Handbook of Infant Mental Health,* Charles H. Zeanah, ed. New York: Guilford Press, 1993.

Crockett, Lisa J., David J. Eggebeen, and Alan J. Hawkins. "Father's Presence and Young Children's Behavioral and Cognitive Adjustment." *Journal of Family Issues,* vol. 14, no. 3 (1993), pp. 355–77.

Edin, Kathryn. "Single Mothers and Child Support: The Possibilities and Limits of Child Support Policy." *Children and Youth Services Review,* vol. 17, nos. 1/2 (1995), pp. 203–30.

Educational Testing Service. "America's Smallest School: The Family." Princeton, N.J.: Educational Testing Service, 1992.

Furstenberg, Frank F., Jr. "Daddies and Fathers: Men Who Do for Their Children and Men Who Don't." Paper prepared for Manpower Demonstration Research Corporation, New York City, July 1992.

———, J. Brooks-Gunn, and S. Philip Morgan. *Adolescent Mothers in Later Life.* New York: Cambridge University Press, 1987.

———, and K. M. Harris. "When Fathers Matter and Why Fathers Matter: The Impact of Paternal Involvement on the Offspring of Adolescent Mothers." In *Young Unwed Fathers,* R. Lerman and T. Ooms, eds. Philadelphia: Temple University Press, 1993.

———, Judith A. Levine, and Jeanne Brooks-Gunn. "The Children of Teenage Mothers: Patterns of Early Childbearing in Two Generations." *Family Planning Perspectives,* vol. 22, no. 2 (1990), pp. 54–61.

———, S. Philip Morgan, and Paul D. Allison. "Paternal Participation and Children's Well-being After Marital Dissolution." *American Sociological Review,* vol. 52 (1987), pp. 695–701.

———, Kay E. Sherwood, and Mercer L. Sullivan. *Caring and Paying: What Fathers and Mothers Say About Child Support.* New York: Manpower Demonstration Research Corporation, July 1992.

Levine, James A. "Involving Fathers in Head Start: A Framework for Public Policy and Program Development." *Families in Society,* Jan. 1993, pp. 4–19.

King, Valarie. "Nonresident Father Involvement and Child Well-Being: Can Dads Make a Difference?" *Journal of Family Issues,* vol. 15, no. 1 (1994), pp. 78–95.

Lamb, Michael E. "Paternal Influences on Child Development." Paper presented at "Changing Fatherhood" conference, Tilburg, the Netherlands, May 1994.

Marsiglio, William. "Contemporary Scholarship on Fatherhood: Culture, Identity, and Conduct." *Journal of Family Issues,* vol. 14, no. 4 (1993), pp. 484–509.

McCord, Joan. "Family Relationships, Juvenile Delinquency, and Adult Criminality." *Criminology*, vol. 29 (Aug. 1991), pp. 397–417.

———. "A Longitudinal View of the Relationships Between Paternal Absence and Crime." In *Abnormal Offenders, Delinquency and the Criminal Justice System*, J. Gunn and D. P. Farrington, eds. Chichester, England: John Wiley & Sons, 1982.

———. "Long-term Perspective on Parental Absence." In *Straight and Deviant Pathways from Childhood to Adulthood*, Lee Robbins and Michael Rutter, eds. Cambridge, England: Cambridge University Press, 1990.

Mott, Frank L. *Absent Fathers and Child Development: Emotional and Cognitive Effects at Ages Five to Nine*. Report for the National Institute of Child Health and Human Development. Columbus, Oh.: Ohio State University, Center for Human Resource Research, March 1993.

———. "When Is a Father Really Gone?: Paternal Child Contact in Father Absent Homes." *Demography*, vol. 27, no. 4 (1990), pp. 499–517.

Parke, Ross D. "Fathers and Families." In *Handbook of Parenting*, vol. 3: *Status and Social Conditions of Parenting*, M. Bornstein, ed. Hillsdale, N.J.: Lawrence Erlbaum & Associates, 1995.

Sampson, Robert J., and John H. Laub, "Urban Poverty and the Family Context of Delinquency: A New Look at Structure and Process in a Classic Study." *Child Development*, vol. 65 (1994), pp. 523–40.

Smollar, Jacqueline, and Theodora Ooms. *Young Unwed Fathers: Research Review, Policy Dilemmas and Options*. Washington, D.C.: U.S. Department of Health and Human Services, Oct. 1987.

Sullivan, Mercer L. *The Male Role in Teenage Pregnancy and Parenting: New Directions for Public Policy*. New York: Vera Institute of Justice, 1990.

Sum, Andrew, and Jay Ostrower. "Fathers, Child Support and Welfare Reform: The Missing Link." Boston: Pioneer Institute, Aug. 1994.

Wattenberg, E., M. Resnick, and R. Brewer. *A Study of Paternity Decisions of Young, Unmarried Parents*. Minneapolis: Center for Urban and Regional Affairs, University of Minnesota, 1991.

Where's Daddy? Unmarried Older Mothers

Center for Law and Social Policy. "A CLASP Report on Welfare Reform Developments." *CLASP Update*, Sept. 12, 1994, pp. 2–14.

Demo, David H., and Alan C. Acock. "Family Structure and Adolescent Behavior." Paper submitted at the annual meeting of the American Sociological Association, Aug. 1992.

Goodman, Ellen. "The Flip Side to Unwed Motherhood—An Unhappy Marriage." *The Boston Globe*, Dec. 9, 1993.

McLanahan, Sara, and Karen Booth. "Mother-Only Families: Problems, Prospects, and Politics." *Journal of Marriage and Family*, vol. 51 (Aug. 1989), pp. 557–80.

Mattes, Jane. "The SMC 2000 Study—Who Are We? Report #2." *Single Mothers by Choice Newsletter*, March 1994.

Mechaneck, Ruth, Elizabeth Klein, and Judith Kuppersmith. "Single Mothers by Choice: A Family Alternative." In *Women, Power and Therapy: Issues for Women*, Marjorie, Braude, ed. New York: Haworth Press, 1988.

Meet the Press. NBC-TV News, Feb. 13, 1994.

Murray, Charles. "The Coming White Underclass." *The Wall Street Journal*, Oct. 29, 1993.

Murray, David W. "Poor Suffering Bastards: An Anthropologist Looks at Illegitimacy." *Policy Review*, spring 1994, pp. 9–15.

Parke, Ross D., and Peter N. Stearns. "Fathers and Child Rearing." In *Children in Time and Place: Developmental and Historical Insights*, G. Elder, J. Modell, and R. Parke, eds. New York: Cambridge University Press, 1993.

Phares, Vicky. "Where's Poppa? The Relative Lack of Attention to the Role of Fathers in Child and Adolescent Psychopathology." *American Psychologist*, vol. 47, no. 5 (1992), pp. 656–64.

Pollitt, Katha. "Motherhood Without Marriage." *Glamour*, Oct. 1993.

This Week with David Brinkley. ABC-TV News, Nov. 28, 1993.

Unmarried Mothers: Who We Are and Where We're Headed

Bruce, Judith, Cynthia B. Lloyd, and Ann Leonard. Families in Focus: *New Perspectives on Mothers, Fathers, and Children*. New York: Population Council, 1995.

Carnegie Council on Adolescent Development. *Great Transitions: Preparing Adolescents for a New Century*. New York: Carnegie Corporation of New York, 1995.

———. *A Matter of Time: Risk and Opportunity in the Nonschool Hours*. New York: Carnegie Corporation of New York, 1992.

———. *What Young Adolescents Want and Need from Out-of-School Programs: A Focus Group Report*. Washington, D.C.: Carnegie Council on Adolescent Development, Jan. 1992.

Dodson, Lisa. "We Could Be Your Daughters: Girls, Sexuality and Pregnancy in Low-Income America." Cambridge, Mass.: Radcliffe Public Policy Institute, Radcliffe College, 1996.

Duff, Christina. "More Than Friends: The Tie That Binds Is Glittering Anew." *The Wall Street Journal*, April 3, 1996.

Furstenberg, Frank F., Jr., and K. M. Harris. "When Fathers Matter/Why Fathers Matter: The Impact of Paternal Involvement on the Offspring of Adolescent Mothers." In *Young Unwed Fathers*, R. Lerman and T. Ooms, eds. Philadelphia: Temple University Press, 1993.

Alan Guttmacher Institute. *Sex and America's Teenagers*. New York: Alan Guttmacher Institute, 1994.

Hamburg, Beatrix A. *Life Skills Training: Preventive Interventions for Young Adolescents. Report of the Life Skills Training Working Group*. Washington, D.C.: Carnegie Council on Adolescent Development, 1990.

Hamburg, David, and Rudy Takanishi. "Preparing for Life: The Critical Transition of Adolescence." *American Psychologist*, vol. 44, no. 5 (1989), pp. 825–27.

Gallagher, Maggie. "Why Murphy Brown Is Winning." *The Wall Street Journal*, June 3, 1996.

Maynard, Rebecca. "Teenage Childbearing and Welfare Reform: Lessons from a Decade of Demonstration and Evaluation Research." *Children and Youth Service Review*, vol. 17, nos. 1/2 (1995), pp. 309–32.

McLanahan, Sara S. "Parent Absence or Poverty—Which Matters More?" In *Consequences of Growing Up Poor*, Greg Duncan and Jeanne Brooks-Gunn, eds. New York: Russell Sage Foundation Press, in press.

Moore, Kristin A., and Barbara W. Sugland. "Next Steps and Best Bets: Approaches to Preventing Adolescent Childbearing." Prepared for Manpower Demonstration Research Corporation, New York City, Jan. 1996.

Moore, Kristin A., Brent C. Miller, Barbara W. Sugland, et al. "Beginning Too Soon: Adolescent Sexual Behavior, Pregnancy, and Parenthood." Washington, D.C.: Child Trends, 1995.

Murray, Charles. Testimony before the Subcommittee on Human Resources, Congressional Committee on Ways and Means, July 29, 1994.

National Center for Health Statistics. "Births and Deaths: United States, 1995." *Monthly Vital Statistics Report*, vol. 45, no. 3, supplement 2. Washington, D.C.: U.S. Public Health Service, Oct. 1996.

Nicholson, Heather Johnston, et al. *Gender Issues in Youth Development Programs*. Washington, D.C.: Carnegie Council on Adolescent Development, Feb. 1992.

Osofsky, Joy D., Della M. Hahn, and Claire Peebles. "Adolescent Parenthood: Risks and Opportunities for Mothers and Infants." In *Handbook of Infant Mental Health*, Charles H. Zeanah, ed. New York: Guilford Press, 1993.

Osofsky, Joy D., Howard J. Osofsky, and Martha Ourieff Diamond. "The Transition to Parenthood: Special Tasks and Risk Factors for Adolescent Parents." In *The Transition to Parenthood: Current Theory and Research*, Gerald Y. Michaels and Wendy A. Goldberg, eds. New York: Cambridge University Press, 1988.

Presser, H. "The Social and Demographic Consequences of Teenage Childbearing for Urban Women: Final Report to NICHD." Washington, D.C.: National Technical Information Service, 1980.

Steinberg, Laurence. *Beyond the Classroom: Why School Reform Has Failed and What Parents Need to Do*. New York: Simon & Schuster, 1996.

Tierney, Joseph P., and Jean Baldwin Grossman. *Making a Difference: An Impact Study of Big Brothers/Big Sisters*. Philadelphia: Public/Private Ventures, Nov. 1995.

Yoshikawa, Hirokazu. "Long-Term Effects of Early Childhood Programs on Social Outcomes and Delinquency." In *Long-Term Outcomes of Early Childhood Programs: The Future of Children*, vol. 5, no. 3 (winter 1995), pp. 51–75.

Wilson, James Q. "The Family Values Debate." *Commentary*, April 1993, pp. 24–3.

Index

Abolition of Marriage, The (Gallagher), 420
abortion:
    community attitudes toward, 95, 96
    legalization of, 48
    of unmarried adolescents, 44
    U.S. vs. European rates of, 97
    young men's views on, 79
Acock, Alan C., 262, 263
Adams, Gina, 64
"Adolescent and Young Adult Fathers,"
    (Children's Defense Fund) 309
adolescents:
    adult discomfort with sexuality of, 94–95, 97,
      419
    adult support in development of, 45, 47,
      74–75, 98–99, 101, 418, 428, 431–32
    boyfriends as father figures for, 86–87,
      336–39
    community efforts toward pregnancy
      prevention for, 94–101, 424, 429–30
    contraceptive use resisted by, 36
    developmental vulnerability of, 427–30
    hope and motivation lacked by, 43–46, 47,
      66–72, 73–74
    low self-esteem in, 66–67
    role models for, 45, 47, 79
    sexual activity of, 35–36
adoption, 154–61
    of children born out of wedlock, 25, 38, 368
    of children with special needs, 156, 159
    costs of, 156, 159, 239
    cultural stigmatization of, 157
    decision process for, 155–56, 160
    evaluation process for, 114–15
    expenses incurred in, 105
    international, 156, 159, 161, 236
    interruption of, 103

    maternal bond in, 161
    by older unmarried women, 103, 105,
      114–15, 124, 154–61, 236
    open records on, 142, 154, 368–69
    as redemptive option for pregnant white girls,
      51–52
    single status or age as obstacle to, 124, 156
    teen mothers' resistance to, 38
Adoption Triangle, The (Baran and Pannor), 142
adultery, donor insemination as, 134–35
adulthood, pregnancy as means of transition to,
    75–76, 306–7
advertisements, sexuality in, 94, 418
African Americans:
    as cultural models, 335, 337
    discrimination in views on sexuality of,
      51–52
    educated women as role models for, 79
    employment and wage inequalities of, 28, 29,
      33, 310, 331
    feelings of racist victimization in, 79–80, 331
    grandmothers as primary caretakers for, 191
    high-school graduation rates for, 77
    matriarchal family models for, 27, 313–16,
      333–34
    media portrayals of, 311
    motherhood vs. professional goals for, 78–79,
      331–32
    nonmarital births of, 27–29, 331, 393
    northern migration of, 28
    older unmarried mothers among, 117
    paternal participation of, 301
    single-parent families among, 25
aggressive behavior:
    early childhood developmental influences on,
      183, 184
    father-absence linked to, 295, 296

aggressive behavior (*cont.*)
    four factors of influential parental behavior
        in, 297–99
AIDS, 63, 131–32
Albelda, Randy, 30
Alliance for Young Families, 170–71, 173
ambition, adolescent loss of, 43–46, 206
American Enterprise Institute, 393
American Society of Reproductive Medicine,
    135
"America's Smallest School," 300
Andrea (author's Little Sister), 431–32
Angelou, Maya, 224–25
Anna (counselor for adolescent mothers),
    34–47, 63–64, 86, 101, 199–202, 218
anonymous-donor insemination, 129–37
    children's feelings about, 129–30, 134,
        136–37, 141–42, 143, 340–41, 344–47,
        354, 358, 361–62, 363–65, 370
    contact procedures for children born of,
        136–37, 140, 141, 142–43, 370–71
    decision process for, 129–32, 139, 144, 155,
        354, 363–65
    donor profiles available on, 131–32, 136–37,
        140, 143–44, 341, 346, 364, 370
    genetic characteristics and, 129–30, 136, 346,
        347
    legal aspects of, 134–36, 144, 151
    medical history access for, 131, 136
    screening procedures employed in, 136
    siblings connected by, 137, 345–46
Apfel, Nancy, 174, 192, 193, 202, 203, 218–19,
    223, 224
attachment, emotional, 183–84, 249, 298

baby boom population, childlessness among,
    117
baby hunger, 112–13
Baran, Annette, 141–42, 143
Bartholet, Elizabeth, 157–61
Baylor College of Medicine, 183
Belsky, Jay, 261
Berlin, Gordon, 310
Beyond Motherhood (Safer), 123, 417
Beyond the Classroom (Steinberg), 428
Big Sisters/Big Brothers, 348, 430–32
biological clock, 9, 105
birth certificate, father's signature on, 59,
    371
birth control pills, 36, 90
birthrates:
    for European vs. U.S. teens, 97
    for older unmarried women, 117

racial factors and, 27, 29, 117, 393
for unmarried teens, 47, 48, 413
for U.S. unmarried women, ii, 25, 47, 48,
    410–15
blacks, *see* African Americans
Black Teenage Mothers (Williams), 50–51
Blankenhorn, David, 296
blue-collar employment, decline in, 26, 28
Bombardieri, Merle, 110–13, 114, 433
Boston Globe, 85, 400
Boston Medical Center, Teen & Tot Adolescent
    Center at, 76
brain development, early environmental
    influences on, 182–83, 188
Brandeis University, Family and Children's
    Policy Center at, 51
Brazelton, T. Berry, 176
Brinkley, David, 394, 396
Bronfenbrenner, Urie, 298
Brown, Sarah, 418, 430
Bush, George, 120

California, University of, 249, 262, 414
California Cryobank, 131, 143–44
Callaway, Rebecca, 22
careers, women's personal lives vs., 117–18,
    125–26, 133, 331–32, 335–36
Carnegie Council on Adolescent Development,
    46, 74–75, 418–19, 427, 430
Carnegie Task Force on Meeting the Needs of
    Young Children, 182, 184, 185
Carrera, Michael, 98–101
Annie E. Casey Foundation, 49
Catholicism, donor insemination prohibited by,
    134
CBS News, 122
Census Bureau, U.S.:
    one-person households recorded by, 24,
        397
    on single-parent family incomes, 29
Center for Human Resource Research, 301
cheerleaders, Texas school's response to
    pregnancies of, 95–96
Chicago, University of, 77, 300
Chicago Tribune, 183
child care:
    attachment development and, 249
    cost of, 30, 207, 239, 245, 246, 252
    from family day-care providers, 245–46
    family help with, 38, 39, 190–92
    illness and, 281–82
    informal arrangements vs. center-based
        facilities for, 169–70, 176

low wages for, 176
within marriage, 130, 260–61, 329–30, 335, 336, 400–401
older mothers' arrangements for, 238, 245–48, 275
quality considerations for, 175–76, 248, 250
in schools of teen parents, 85, 162, 163–64, 166, 170
state welfare assistance with, 166–67, 168, 185
support networks for, 281–83
teen mothers' achievements aided by access to, 166–73, 177
in workplace, 251
younger fathers' participation in, 36, 59, 93, 165, 210–13, 214–15, 217–18, 290, 291–92, 301, 307–9, 311–12, 315, 316–17, 318–19, 322, 336, 338

child development:
absent fathers and, 292–93, 295–99, 333, 350–54, 358–59, 422–24
in children of teen mothers, 179–89, 425–27
day-care quality linked to, 175–77, 248, 250
in earliest years, 31, 182–87, 426–27
at elementary-school age, 31, 333–35
emotional attachment in, 183–84, 249, 298
for firstborn children before birth of siblings, 173–74
parental education level and, 184, 185–87
play styles and, 352
reading incorporated in, 184, 185–86
research on unmarried motherhood and, 31–33, 240–41
same-sex role models in, 295, 333–35, 348–50
self-development opportunities in, 272–73
socioeconomic impact on, 84, 423–25
working mothers and, 248–50, 268–69

childlessness:
career advantages of, 125–26
education level and, 117–18
of elderly women, 118
feminine identity undercut by, 122–24

children:
after-school care for, 23
community safety and, 22, 24, 225, 233
developmental consequences of unmarried motherhood for, 31–33, 173–89, 240–41, 292–93, 295–99, 333

financial responsibility for, 59, 404–5
physical abuse of, 78
in poverty, 30, 310, 395
sexual molestation of, 54–55, 61, 180, 230–32, 292
welfare payments for, 30, 409
of working parents, 23–24, 248–51

Children's Aid Society, 99
Children's Defense Fund, 25, 46, 309
Child Trends, Inc., 426
China, People's Republic of, adoptions from, 156, 236
Chira, Susan, 269, 271
civil rights movement, 27, 28
Clinton, William Jefferson (Bill), 100, 394
Coleman, James, 300

college education:
childlessness and, 117–18
costs of, 234, 239, 242
for younger unmarried mothers, 38, 40, 178–79, 224–28, 232–35, 326, 331

commercial culture, sexuality promoted in, 94, 418
Commonwealth Club of California, 119
community safety, 22, 24
condoms, 36
male opposition to, 63, 66
for protection against sexually transmitted disease, 43
school distribution of, 85
Congress, U.S., on pregnancy or parenthood of students, 95n
Connecticut, University of, 351
Conover, J., 153
conservatives, social criticism from, 393–99
Constitution, U.S., 135

contraceptives:
adolescent access to, 85, 94, 97–98, 99, 165
disease prevention with, 43
education on, 35, 43, 98
European vs. U.S. access to, 94, 97–98
family-planning counseling and, 34–36
by injection, 43
misuse of, 90
personal responsibility for, 42, 63
school distribution of, 85
teen indifference toward use of, 36, 42, 44, 56–57, 62–63
time-release implants for (Norplant), 36
types of, 36
young men's attitudes toward, 42, 63, 66
see also specific contraceptives

control:
in marital relationships, 50, 55, 58, 60–61, 336–38, 402, 419–20
pregnancy as assertion of, 61, 91–93, 419
relinquishing of, 69
sexual abuse as lack of, 61
traditional male image of, 334
coparenting, 137–38, 384
Cornell University, 298
Crime and Justice, vol. 7 (Tonry and Morris, eds.), 297n
Crime in the Making (Laub and Sampson), 297–98
criminal behavior, fatherlessness associated with, 296
Curtis, Jessica, 247–48, 258

Dash, Leon, 46
Dating Violence Intervention Project, 61
daughters:
fathers' absence experienced by, 86–88, 141, 215, 217–18, 293, 294
firstborn, 173
parents' relationship as model for, 295
Deadly Consequences (Prothrow-Stith), 240
delinquency, family-process factors for, 297–99
Demo, David H., 262, 263
Depo-Provera, 43
depression:
early brain development and, 183
in teen mothers, 181, 206, 207–8, 214
diaphragms, 36
discipline, parental:
consistent styles of, 223, 229, 298
fatherhood and, 221–22
harshness of, 182, 213
limits provided by, 407–8
physical punishment as, 184, 187–89, 215–17, 408
diseases, sexually transmitted, 35, 36, 43, 136
see also specific diseases
divorce:
absent fathers after, 130, 141, 347
children's reactions to, 241–42
escalation of, 25, 117, 420–21
in 1950's, 22
unmarried motherhood vs., 49, 241–42, 420–21
Do I Have a Daddy?, 339–40
domestic service jobs, 28
Double-Dip Feelings, 362
drug use, 305, 306, 325

Duke Journal of Gender Law & Policy, 157
Dunlevy Milbank Center, 100

economic issues:
abortion choices influenced by, 44
adolescent sense of future tied to, 46
age for motherhood influenced by, 82–84
in backgrounds of teen mothers, 44
decrease in marriage linked to, 49–50, 83–84, 117
of income levels for single-parent families, 29–31, 242–44
racial differences in, 28, 29, 33, 310, 331
in stigmatization vs. acceptance of unmarried mothers, 84–85
for two-income families, 23
for unmarried teen mothers, 39–40, 309–10
Edelman, Marian Wright, 46, 121
education:
in alternative schools, 53, 55–56
childless women and, 117–18
at college level, 38, 40, 178–79, 224–28, 232–35, 239, 242, 326, 331
for fatherless children, 299–301, 333
for high school degree, 38, 39, 77; *see also* high school
income vs., 38, 39
mental retardation risk linked to mother's level of, 182
personal attention in, 56, 70
savings for, 239, 242
on sexual issues, 35, 43, 70, 72, 85, 97, 98, 99, 101, 164, 179
teen motherhood linked to dropouts from, 34, 46
women's gains in, 117
Educational Testing Service, 300
elderly, childlessness and, 118
employment:
for both parents, 23
educational limitations on, 38, 39
family obligations accommodated in, 23, 239, 249, 250–51
internship programs for, 178–79
in manufacturing sector, 26, 28
psychological benefits of, 249
racial inequality in, 28
welfare reforms geared toward, 250
young men's loss of opportunity for, 49
endometriosis, 146
Eshleman, Susan, 388
Etzioni, Amitai, 421

Europe, sexuality and reproductive policies in, 94, 97–98

families:
    alternative forms of, ix, 347
    child care help provided by, 38, 39, 190–224
    of elderly women, 118
    fathers' role in, 295–97, 351–52, 415, 420
    five contemporary trends for, 415
    lack of shared time in, 23–24
    late-twentieth-century changes in, 20–27
    older mothers aided by, 126–28, 266–68
    as self-reliant units, 280
    size of, 22
    support provided to teen mothers by, 38, 39, 63–64, 83, 90, 163–64, 167–68, 190–224
    television portrayals of, 16, 23, 54, 89, 269
    workplace accommodations to, 23
Families and Work Institute, 176
"Families in Focus" (Bruce, Lloyd, and Leonard), 415
Family and Children's Policy Center, 51
Family Bonds (Bartholet), 157–58
family day care, 176, 245–46
Family Life Education and Adolescent Sexuality Program, 99–100
family planning:
    teen counseling on, 34–36
    see also contraceptives; sex education
Family Research Council, 29
family values, ix, 396, 397
Fatherhood Project, 316, 317
Fatherless America (Blankenhorn), 296
fathers, absent:
    anonymous sperm donation and, 130, 135–36, 137, 140–41, 340–41, 344–47, 354, 358, 361–62, 363–65, 370–71
    answers to children's queries on, 291–95, 339–42, 354, 356–62
    child-development issues and, 292–93, 295–99, 333, 350–54, 358–59, 422–24
    in childhoods of unmarried parents, 86–88, 141, 215, 217–18, 293, 294, 296, 303–4, 306, 307, 312, 313–14, 346, 369, 370
    children's yearnings for, 285, 286–88, 326, 362–64, 369–70, 372, 403, 421
    counseling on, 403
    cultural criticism of, 296, 299–300, 387–99
    after divorce, 130, 141, 347
    generational history of, 303–4
    lack of research on, 351–54
    in prison, 217, 310, 322, 323
    quality of relationship and, 302–3

    racial differences in, 301
    relations renewed with, 288–92, 307
    societal consequences of, 296–301
    support payments enforced on, 305–6, 308, 310–11, 324, 326, 404–5
    surrogate figures for, 284–89, 292–93, 294–95, 301, 313–14, 327, 329–30, 332, 333, 335–36, 348–49, 354, 378, 407, 421
"Fathers, Child Support and Welfare Reform" (Sum and Ostrower), 309
fathers, young, 303–22
    absent fathers in childhoods of, 303–4, 306, 307, 312, 313–14
    child-care participation by, 36, 59, 93, 165, 210–13, 214–15, 217–18, 290, 291–92, 301, 307–9, 311–12, 315, 316–17, 318–19, 322, 336, 338
    decline of income opportunities for, 49–50, 304, 305, 309, 310, 331
    early deaths of, 310
    education of, 305, 309
    financial support provided by, 42, 58–59, 295, 301, 304, 305–6, 308, 310–11, 316, 320, 326, 420
    gender mistrust and, 320–22
    as marriage prospects, 53, 59–60, 83–84, 166, 286, 309, 323, 324–25, 331, 332, 420
    mothers' criteria for parental involvement of, 79–80, 165–66, 210–13, 214, 217–18, 288–92, 294, 301, 303–4, 314–15, 317, 318–20, 321–30, 334, 337–38, 422
    remedial programs for, 304, 316–17, 318, 320
    as role models for children, 79–80, 309, 332
    traditional sex-role expectations of, 50, 290, 316, 324
    welfare-system disincentive for participation from, 43, 305, 308–9, 310–11
feminine identity, motherhood as confirmation of, 122–24, 417
Feminine Mystique, The (Friedan), 10, 122
feminism, 338
fertility treatments:
    administration of, 104, 132
    age limitations for, 158
    cost of, 104, 155, 158, 160
    effectiveness of, 132
    through in vitro fertilization, 158
    marital status required for, 158
    medical insurance coverage of, 103–4, 158
    motivation for, 159–60
    surgical methods of, 157
Fitzwater, Marlin, 120
Fleming, Anne Taylor, 258–59

food stamps, 90
Fourteenth Amendment, 135
Franklin, Benjamin, 49
Frazier, E. Franklin, 27
Friedan, Betty, 10, 122
Furstenberg, Frank, Jr., 302, 320–21, 322,
    424–25

Gallagher, Maggie, 420
gender mistrust, 320–21
general equivalency diploma (GED), 42, 46,
    55–56, 305
General Relief, 166–67, 168
Geronimus, Arline T., 82–84
Gingrich, Newt, 395
Glamour, 121–22
GnRH, 104
gonorrhea, 36
Goodman, Ellen, 400
Good Mother, The (Miller), 270–71
Girl Scouts, 430
grandchildren, 118
grandmothers, 190–203, 218–22
Growing Up with a Single Parent (McLanahan
    and Sandefur), 32, 302
Alan Guttmacher Institute, 97–98

Hacker, Andrew, 29
Hamburg, Beatrix A., 427–28
Harvard Law School, 157, 159
Head Start, 176, 317
health:
    economic status connected to, 82–83
    of infants, 182
Heart Conditions (Lewis), 266
Hempstead, Texas, students barred from
    cheerleading squad in, 95–96
high school:
    derogatory attitudes toward teen mothers in,
        177–79
    dropout-rate influences for, 296–97
    general equivalency diploma for, 42, 46,
        55–56, 305
    on-site child-care facilities at, 85, 162,
        163–64, 166, 170, 175
    race-related completion rates for teen
        mothers in, 77
    sex education in, 85
    for younger unmarried mothers, 38, 39,
        162–65, 166–71, 177–79
HIV virus, 136, 139
Hochschild, Arlie, 262, 263
Hoffman, Lois, 248

home ownership, 21–22
hope, adolescent loss of, 43–46, 47, 67–72,
    73–74
Horowitz, Michael J., 395–96
Hotz, V. Joseph, 77
household labor, 251–55, 259, 260, 262–63,
    337, 338
housing:
    subsidies for, 171
    for teenage mothers and children, 34, 43,
        191, 209, 211–12
Hughes, Langston, 68
Hunter College, 98, 100
hypermasculinity, 295

illegitimacy:
    anonymous-donor insemination as basis for,
        135
    as pejorative terminology, 387–99
Illinois, University of, 249
income:
    racial disparities in, 28, 29, 33
    societal distribution of, 97
    for women vs. men, 28–29, 50
In Country (Mason), 84
infant development:
    brain stimulation required for, 182–83
    maternal attachment as central to, 184
Institute for American Values, 296
Institute for Social Science Research, 122
internship programs, 178–79
interview subjects:
    Alicia, 53–54
    Angela, 243–45, 265–66
    Belinda, 109
    Bethany, 267–68, 339–50, 354, 357, 378
    Carol, 155–56, 159, 236–40, 242, 243,
        245–47
    Carolyn, 359–60, 362
    Christina, 259–60, 263–65
    Daniella, 198–99
    Debbie, 34–38, 40–45, 46, 47, 174
    Diana, 107, 108, 109
    Jacqueline, 86–87
    Janice, 114–16, 124
    Jessie, 102, 103, 106–7
    Joan, 137–41, 142, 144
    Kerry, 125–33, 137, 138, 250–58, 266
    Laura, 388–92, 396, 397–98, 399, 401–8
    Lavina, 194–97, 322–28
    Marsha, 123–24, 270–74, 363–65
    Michelle, 45
    Molly, 154, 375–76

Morena, 224–35, 284–95, 301, 304, 313, 322
Myieka, 54–61, 185–90, 191, 294
Naomi, 77–81, 84, 329–38, 365
Oscar, 304–6, 307, 308, 311–13, 315
Paula, 144–50, 151, 160, 275–79, 281–83, 378–87
Rachel, 365–75, 378
Sarah, 162–70, 171, 172, 174, 177–81, 182, 185, 190, 219–22, 299, 328–29
Shanika, 65–74, 75, 76, 209–18, 294, 321
Sharon, 107–8, 109
Sid, 307–9, 310, 311, 312, 313–14, 315
Susan, 87–94, 204–9, 318–20, 372
Victoria, 105
Vince, 314, 315–16
in vitro fertilization (IVF), 158
"Involving Fathers in Head Start" (Levine), 317

Jefferson Medical College, 133
Job Corps, 81
Johns Hopkins University, 81
Johnson, Lyndon B., 27
Jones, Beverly, 65, 67

King, Martin Luther, Jr., 28
known donors, 115, 128–29, 137–39
    legal concerns for, 150–54, 353–54, 378–87
    parenting relationship of, 144–46
Kohlenberg, Tesi, 76
Kopetski, Mike, 395–96
Kotulak, Ronald, 183

Labor, U.S. Department of, 23
Laub, John, 297–98
Lawrence T. Paquin School, 74
Leadbeater, Bonnie, 75–76, 420
lesbian mothers, 138, 347
Lethal Secrets (Baran and Pannor), 142
Levine, James, 316–17
Lewis, Sara, 266
life expectancy, racial differences in, 83
Lifeprints, 249
Life Without Father (Popenoe), 399
Loeber, Rolf, 297n
loneliness, of childlessness vs. single parenthood, 12, 109–10, 265–66
Ludtke, Betty, 22
Ludtke, Leslie, 21, 22
Ludtke, Mark, 22

McCord, Joan, 297
McLanahan, Sara S., 32, 86, 296–97, 302, 423
manufacturing sector, employment decline in, 26, 28
marriage:
    adolescent attitudes toward, 49, 50, 53–54, 64, 309
    age for, 49, 424
    child-care responsibilities in, 130, 260–61, 329–30, 335, 336, 400–401
    control concerns for, 50, 55, 58, 60–61, 336–38, 419–20
    economic factors and decrease in, 49–50, 83–84, 117
    emotional demands of, 258–59, 337
    female self-reliance and, 121–22, 335–36, 400–401, 420
    financial motivation for, 53–54
    greater numbers of births without, 47–52, 117, 399
    household labor division in, 262–63, 264, 337, 338
    instability of, 54, 59, 60, 117, 420–21, 424–25
    pregnant teens' rejection of, 38, 53–61, 78, 166, 332, 419–20
    race-related views on, 78, 331
    reassessment of, 400–401
    traditional sex-role expectations within, 50, 261, 262–63, 335–36
    welfare as disincentive for, 305, 310–11
masculine identity, development of, 295, 333–35, 348–50
Mason, Bobbie Ann, 84
Massachusetts, University of, 30
Massachusetts, welfare program reductions in, 166–67
maternity homes, 51–52
maternity leave, 250–51, 277
Mattes, Jane, 355, 357, 360–62, 365
Maynard, Rebecca, 429
Mechaneck, Ruth, 354
Medicaid, 171, 173, 424
Meet the Press, 394
menstruation, earlier onset of, 49
mental illness, early environmental stress as factor in, 183
mental retardation, mother's educational level as risk factor for, 182
Michigan, University of, 82, 248
Miller, Sue, 270
miscarriage, 132
Moffitt, Robert A., 81

Moore, Kristin, 426
Morris, Norval, 297*n*
motherhood:
    biological drive toward, 105
    career commitment vs., 125–26, 133, 268–69,
        282, 283, 331–32
    in current labor market, 23
    feminine identity linked to, 122–24, 417
    full-time, 22, 24, 275–79, 282, 283
    health factors and, 82–83
    ideal model vs. realistic goals for, 268–74
    older unmarried women's desires for, 103,
        104–6, 110, 112–14, 120, 416
    socioeconomic factors in timing of, 82–85
    traditional views on professional life vs.,
        117–18, 248
    see also unmarried mothers
"Motherhood without Marriage" (Pollitt), 400
Mott, Frank, 301–2
Moynihan, Daniel Patrick, 27–28, 331, 393,
    395, 409–14, 415, 422
Mulroney, Brian, 119–20
Murphy Brown, 118–20, 242, 393, 394, 397,
    419, 420
Murray, Charles, 393–95, 396–97, 399, 410
Murray, David W., 398–99
Musick, Judith S., 74, 75, 86, 87, 417

Nachtigall, Robert, 104–5
Nation, 400
National Adoption Information Clearinghouse,
    159
National Campaign to Prevent Teen Pregnancy,
    418, 430
National Center for Health Statistics, 29*n*,
    117
National Institute of Child Health and Human
    Development (NICHD), 248–49
National Longitudinal Survey of Youth, 77
National Organization for Women, 96
"Negro Family, The" (Moynihan), 27–28
New York, programs for adolescent pregnancy
    prevention in, 98–100
New York Times, 85, 96, 269, 271, 417
Norplant, 36
Northeastern University, 309
Nurturing Program, 197

Ohio State University, Center for Human
    Resource Research at, 301
old age, childlessness in, 118
orphanages, 393, 395
Osofsky, Joy D., 425

out-of-wedlock births:
    adoption placement from, 25, 38, 368
    conservative criticism of, 393–99
    maternal ages for, 25–26
    recent escalation of, 25, 393, 410–15, 422
    Supreme Court ruling on, 135
ovulation, medical stimulation of, 103, 104,
    132

Pannor, Reuben, 142, 143
parental rights, 76
parenting:
    adolescent exposure to responsibility of,
        80–81
    behavior problems influenced by four aspects
        of, 297–99
    chronic unresponsiveness in, 182, 183–84,
        213
    disciplinary styles in, 182, 184, 187–89, 213,
        215–17, 221–22, 229, 297, 407–8
    marital relationship affected by, 260–61
    openness in, 227–28, 230, 232, 235
    professional lives vs. personal responsibilities
        of, 78–79, 227, 228, 232–35, 247–48,
        268–69, 275–79, 281–82, 283, 331–32
    reading incorporated in, 184, 185–86
    realistic goals for, 268–74
    sex education in, 70, 72, 164
    time constraints in, 23–24, 246, 251–55,
        332
    two-generational arrangements in, 192–224
Parke, Ross D., 352
paternity, legalization of, 59, 308, 310, 371
Pennsylvania, University of, 302, 429
Pennsylvania State University, 261
People magazine, 263
Pergonal, 104, 132
Perry, Bruce, 183
Perry-Jenkins, Maureen, 249
Perry Preschool, 172, 426–27
Phares, Vicki, 351–52
physical punishment, 184, 187–89, 215–17
Pierson, Martha, 183
Planned Parenthood (New York), 96
Pleck, Joseph, 262–63
Pollitt, Katha, 121–22, 400
"Poor Suffering Bastards" (Murray), 398–99
Popenoe, David, 399
Population Council, 415
poverty:
    blacks blamed for, 52
    among children of unmarried mothers, 30,
        310, 395, 423–24

defined, 44n
health risks of, 82–83
ill effects of father-absence vs., 423
younger childbearing age linked to, 82–84, 85
pregnancy:
adult identity achieved through, 74–76, 81,
306–7
by artificial insemination, 115–16, 128,
131–32, 133
fertility treatments for, 103–4, 132, 155, 158,
160
mood swings related to, 92
policies for prevention of, in adolescents,
94–101, 318, 427, 429–30
positive attention received through, 61–62
racial differences in social attitudes toward,
51–52
school policies on, 95–96
prenatal care, 31
public services for teens in need of, 40
preschool development, 31, 182–87, 317,
425–27
Prothrow-Stith, Deborah, 240
punishment:
mutual determination of, 222
for out-of-wedlock births, 394–95
physical, 184, 187–89, 215–17

Quayle, J. Danforth (Dan), 119–20, 121, 393,
394, 397, 419, 420

racial differences:
in age for optimum maternal health, 83
in behavior of absent fathers, 301
on career vs. motherhood, 78–79
economic, 28, 29, 33, 310, 331
in family structure, 27, 301, 313–16, 333–34
in life expectancy, 83
in numbers of older unmarried mothers, 117
personal response to stress of, 79–80
in proportion of nonmarital childbearing, 48,
81–82, 393
in redemptive potential ascribed to unwed
pregnant teens, 51–52
in timing of motherhood, 82
Radcliffe College, Public Policy Institute at,
418
Raspberry, William, 394
reading to young children, 184, 185–86
religion, teen pregnancy and, 97
"Report to Congress on Out-of-Wedlock
Childbearing," 81
Republican party, 120, 166, 395, 397

responsibility:
adulthood defined by, 75–76
financial, 163
parental, 232, 267–68, 319–20
retardation, child's, and mother's inability to
finish high school, 182
Rivers, Caryl, 249
romantic relationships:
control issues in, 91–93, 336–38, 402
incompatible views on childbearing within,
6–9, 10, 11–12, 15, 108–9
parenthood goals and, 108–9, 146, 214–15,
321–22, 326, 342–44, 401–2
physical abuse within, 80, 92, 212–13, 214,
215, 321, 325
sexual pressures within, 86–87, 92, 419
Roper Organization, 117
Rothman, Cappy, 144
rural communities, unmarried adolescent
parents in, 84, 85
Russert, Tim, 394
Russia, children adopted from, 156
Rutgers University, 399

Safer, Jeanne, 123, 417
safety:
of child care, 175
community sense of, 22, 24, 225, 233
Sampson, Robert J., 297–99
Sandefur, Gary, 32, 302
Sanger, Alexander, 96–97, 101
Sanger, Margaret, 97
school:
alternative programs for teen parents in, 53,
55–56, 220
community policies on pregnancy in, 95–96
condom distribution in, 85
federal laws on discrimination against
pregnant girls in, 95, 96
private vs. public, 397
sex education in, 85, 98, 179
teen mothers as dropouts from, 34, 46, 55,
68–69, 70–71, 185, 218
see also education; high school
Second Shift, The (Hochschild), 262
Seitz, Victoria, 174, 192, 193, 202, 203, 218–19,
223, 224
self-esteem, development of, 98, 99, 220
self-reliance, American ethic of, 280
sex education:
abstinence advocated in, 85, 99
in adolescent development programs, 101
on birth control, 35, 43, 98

sex education (*cont.*)
  on emotional issues, 94
  nonjudgmental model for, 97
  from parents, 70, 72, 164
  in school systems, 85, 98, 179
sexual abuse, 54–55, 61, 188, 230–32, 288
sexual activity:
  abstinence from, 36, 85, 99
  of adolescents from low-income backgrounds,
    44
  age for onset of, 44
  coercion of, 62
  to continue relationship, 86–87
  contraception and, 36, 42, 43, 44, 56–57,
    62–63, 85, 90, 94, 97–98, 99, 165
  counseling services for adolescents on, 35–37
  diseases transmitted by, 35, 36, 43, 136
  emotional intimacy sought through, 72–73
  European vs. U.S. discussions of, 94
  marketing strategies and, 94, 418
  parental role models and, 295
  pregnancy due to ignorance about, 38
  race-related stigmatization of, 51–52
  reproductive efforts separated from, 109
  societal tolerance broadened on, 49, 117,
    135
Shalala, Donna, 100
siblings:
  from anonymous sperm donors, 139, 345–46
  for children of older unmarried women, 248,
    255–57
  spacing of births for, 173–74
Single Mothers by Choice, 111, 137, 242, 247,
    258, 353, 355, 356–57, 360, 376–78,
    387–88
Single Mothers by Choice (Mattes), 355
"Single Mothers by Choice" (Mechaneck,
    Klein, and Kuppersmith), 353–54, 356
single parents:
  adoption rate increased for, 159
  children's resentment toward, 87
  from divorce vs. nonmarital relationships,
    25–26, 33, 241–42
  dual roles undertaken by, 287–88, 313–14,
    333–34
  income levels for, 29–31, 242–44
  percentage of, 25
  societal assumptions about, 270–72, 299–300,
    387–99
  unshared responsibility for, 267–68
slavery, 28
Solinger, Rickie, 51, 52
Solomon, 150

sons, paternal relationships needed by, 295,
    329–30, 348–50
Sousa, Carol, 61–62
Sperm Bank of California, 140, 143
sperm banks, 3–4, 8, 15, 131, 140, 143–44
sperm donation:
  anonymous providers of, 16–17, 129–37,
    139–44, 151
  development of, 133–34
  insemination procedures for, 115–16, 128,
    131–32, 133
  from known fathers, 115, 128–29, 137–39,
    144–46, 353–54, 378–87
  legal considerations for, 11, 106, 129,
    134–36, 144, 150–54, 378–82
  romantic relationships during process of, 108
  secrecy maintained on, 133, 134, 136–37,
    356–58
sponges, contraceptive, 36
"Starting Points" (Carnegie), 182
Steinberg, Laurence, 428
Steinem, Gloria, 261
stepfathers, sexual molestation by, 54–55, 188
Stern, Gabriella, 170, 171
Sterns, Peter N., 352
Stith, Rosetta, 74
Stouthamer-Loeber, Magda, 297n
stress hormones, 183
"suitable home" laws, 52
Sullivan, Mercer L., 316
Sum, Andrew, 309
Supreme Court, U.S., on equal protection for
    out-of-wedlock births, 135

Teenage Parent Welfare Demonstration, 429
Teen & Tot Adolescent Center, 76
television:
  children's exposure to, 24
  images of motherhood on, 16, 269
  introduction of, 22–23
  as mainstay of child care, 24, 176
  male violence shown on, 334
  marital stability depicted on, 54
  older unmarried mother on, 118–20, 121, 242
  portrayals of family life on, 23, 89, 269, 292,
    311
Temple University, 249, 297, 428
This Week with David Brinkley, 394
three-job marriage, 23
Tilly, Chris, 30
Time magazine, x, 4, 10, 45
Todd, Briley, 151–53
Todd, Francine, 152–53

Tonry, Michael, 297n
Tremblay, Richard, 184
Two Nations (Hacker), 29

Uniform Parentage Act (UPA), 135–36
unmarried mothers:
    additional out-of-wedlock births to, 36, 37,
        40–43, 52, 54, 173–74, 187, 248, 255–57
    ages of, 25–26
    author's personal decision as, ix, xii, 3–19,
        112–13, 432–34
    blame vs. shame attached to, 51–52
    divorced mothers vs., 49, 241–42
    dual roles for, 287–88, 313–14, 333–34
    income levels of, 29–31
    less prenatal care obtained by, 31
    punitive governmental policies toward, 52,
        387, 394–96, 409–10
    racial/ethnic backgrounds of, 26, 27–29, 393
    in research on child development, 31–33,
        240–41
    social stigmatization of, 49, 51, 118, 270–72,
        299–300, 387–99
    U.S. birthrates for, ii, 25, 47, 48, 410–15, 422
unmarried mothers, adolescent:
    absent fathers in backgrounds of, 86–88, 215,
        293
    adult identity achieved by, 74–76, 81, 306–7,
        417
    boyfriends of, 36, 42, 53, 66, 72–74, 79–80,
        86–87, 91–93, 164, 165–66, 210–13, 214,
        217, 284–87, 288–89, 321–26
    childhood sexual abuse of, 54–55, 61, 188
    counseling services for, 34–47
    day-care programs used by, 162–63, 166–73,
        175–77
    educational limitations for, 38, 46, 71
    emotional motivations for pregnancies of, 35,
        36, 45, 46, 53, 61–62, 64, 172, 220–21,
        416–17
    employment for, 165, 226
    in Europe vs. U.S., 97–98
    family backgrounds of, 26, 44, 45, 53, 54–55,
        65, 68–69, 77–78, 86–88, 163, 188
    family support systems for, 38, 39, 63–64, 83,
        90, 163–64, 167–68, 190–224
    on fathers' participation, 79–80, 165–66,
        210–13, 214, 217–18, 288–92, 294, 295,
        301, 303–4, 314–15, 317, 318–20, 321–30,
        334, 337–38; *see also* fathers, young
    financial difficulties of, 39–40, 46, 56, 90,
        165, 207, 226–27
    future planning by, 45, 56, 71–72, 207

    generational history of, 55, 218, 421
    government benefits tied to school
        completion and housing for, 170, 191–92
    higher education difficulties for, 38, 39,
        178–79, 212–13, 224–28, 232–35, 326, 331
    in high school, 38, 39, 162–65, 166–71,
        177–79
    high school graduation rates vs. racial
        backgrounds of, 77
    hopelessness of, 66–72, 73–74, 206, 207–8,
        214
    housing facilities designed for, 34, 43, 192,
        209, 211–12
    lack of foresight in, 39–41
    low-income backgrounds of, 43–44, 71
    mainstream stigmatization vs. low-income
        acceptance of, 84–85
    marriage rejected by, 38, 53–61, 78, 89–90,
        332, 419–20
    numbers of, 26, 47–48
    on older mothers, 78–79
    parental rejection of, 85, 212
    parenting skills of, 168–69, 179–89, 192–235,
        327–28, 425–26
    paternal surrogates for children of, 284–89,
        292–93, 294–95, 330, 332, 333, 335–36
    peer pressure and, 35, 417
    peer respect for, 85–86, 90, 420
    political activism of, 167
    pregnancy as escape from adolescent status
        for, 74–76, 306–7, 417–18
    prenatal services for, 40
    as primary caregivers, 162–66, 168–69,
        202–3
    punitive government policies toward, 52, 81
    racial differences among, 48, 51–52, 81–82
    recreational opportunities sacrificed by, 163
    role models for, 34, 39–40, 163, 224–25, 417
    in rural communities, 85
    as school dropouts, 34, 46, 55, 68–69, 70–71,
        185, 218
    school-system accommodations for, 85, 162,
        163–64, 166, 170, 220
    social life limited for, 163, 187
    societal views on redemptive potential of,
        51–52
    stigmatization vs. acceptance for, 84–86
    successive children born to, 36, 37, 40–43,
        52, 54, 173–74, 187
    teachers' and school administration's
        negative attitude toward, 177–79
    on welfare, 30, 34, 38, 56, 90, 166–68, 170,
        191–92, 205, 208, 226, 323, 327

unmarried mothers, older:
  absence of fathers addressed by, 339–77, 421
  adjustments undergone by, 237–38
  adoptions by, 103, 105, 142, 154–61, 236
  anonymous sperm donations used by, 106,
    129–37, 140–44, 151, 155, 340–41,
    363–65
  on benefits vs. disadvantages of single status,
    254, 258–68, 279
  child-care arrangements of, 238, 245–48, 275
  contrast with childhood experiences of,
    140–41, 248, 421
  coparenting arrangements with, 137–38
  counseling for, 110–13, 114
  criticism encountered by, 14–15, 18–19, 148,
    149–50, 239–40, 388–92, 403–4
  decision-making processes for, 3–19, 110–16,
    124–33, 137, 146–47, 363–65, 416, 422,
    432–34
  divorced mothers vs., 241–42
  emotional motivations for, 12, 112–14, 138,
    160–61, 416
  family support systems for, 126–28, 266–68
  fathers' relationships with, 105, 129–30,
    144–46, 353–54, 365–74, 378–87, 401–8
  fatigue of, 236, 237, 264, 277, 278–79, 342,
    343
  fertility problems of, 103–4, 157–58, 159–60
  financial circumstances for, 30–31, 106, 147,
    238–39, 242–44, 248, 255–56, 260, 404–5
  group meetings on, 102–10, 272, 360–62,
    376–77
  household help for, 251–55, 259, 260
  known sperm donors and, 106, 115, 128–29,
    137–39, 144–46, 150–54, 353–54, 378–87
  lack of research material on, 240–41, 353,
    423
  legal issues for, 106, 150–54, 378, 379–82
  lesbians as, 138
  media discussions of, 118–22
  Murphy Brown as model of, 118–20, 242,
    393, 394, 397, 419, 420
  numbers of, 26
  personal time for, 253, 255, 265, 271, 272,
    273
  political controversy on, 118–20
  romantic involvements of, 105–9, 256, 257,
    259–60, 264–65, 270, 342–44, 354,
    374–77, 384–87
  second children for, 248, 255–57
  support networks for, 17, 18–19, 249, 263–64,
    274, 279–83, 348–49, 378, 419
  time constraints on, 246–47, 251–55, 343
  working lives of, 237, 247–48, 275, 276–77,
    281–82
  younger women's attitude toward, 78–79
UPA (Uniform Parentage Act), 135–36

vaginal inserts, 36
Ventura, Stephanie J., 29n
Veterans Administration, 22
violence:
  contemporary fears of, 24
  early childhood development of tendencies
    toward, 183, 184
  father-absence and, 296
  socioeconomic factors and, 240
  on television, 334

wages:
  of child-care providers, 176
  garnishment of, 305–6, 308, 326, 405
  sexual disparities in, 28–29, 50
  for younger males, 49, 305, 309–10
Wake Up Little Susie (Solinger), 51
Wall Street Journal, 170, 393
Washington, University of, 61
Washington Post, 46
"We Could Be Your Daughters" (Dodson), 418
Weinraub, Marsha, 249
welfare system:
  absurdities of, 167–68
  blacks blamed for increase in, 52
  day-care vouchers curtailed by, 166–67, 185
  demeaning treatment from caseworkers in,
    60–61, 233
  as disincentive for paternal support, 43, 305,
    308–9, 310–11
  educational advancement enabled by, 331
  employment transitions from, 250
  in Massachusetts, 166–67, 168
  1996 federal reforms of, ix, 170, 191–92, 306,
    318, 409
  nonmarital birthrate rise and, 81, 97, 318
  opposition to cuts proposed for, 167
  public opposition to, 47
  punitive efforts of, 52, 81, 409
  recipients' desire for independence from, 56,
    71, 208, 226, 233, 323, 327
  wage garnishment and, 305–6, 308, 326
  white women vs. black women in, 81
  for young unmarried mothers, 30, 34, 38, 56,
    90, 166–68, 170, 191–92, 205, 208, 226,
    323
"Where's Poppa?" (Phares), 351–52
Williams, Constance Willard, 51

Wilson, James Q., 414–15
women's movement, 10, 261, 338
workforce:
    black women vs. white women in, 28
    grandmothers in, 191
    mothers in, 237, 248–50, 268–69, 275–77,
        281–83
    young men in, 49–50, 304, 305, 309

Xytex, 136, 137

Yale University, 75, 173–74, 176, 192
Yoshikawa, Hirokazu, 427
Young, Poor and Pregnant (Musick), 74

Zigler, Edward, 176